Vietnam and America

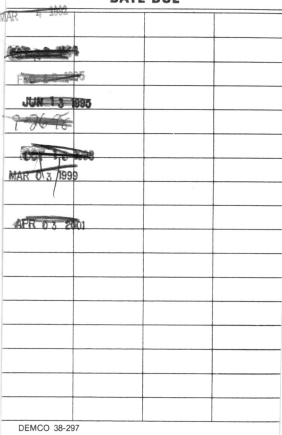

Vietnam and America

DATE DUE

MAR 4 1992			
FEB 1995			
JUN 13 1995			
1 26 96			
OCT 15 1998			
MAR 03 1999			
APR 03 2001			

DEMCO 38-297

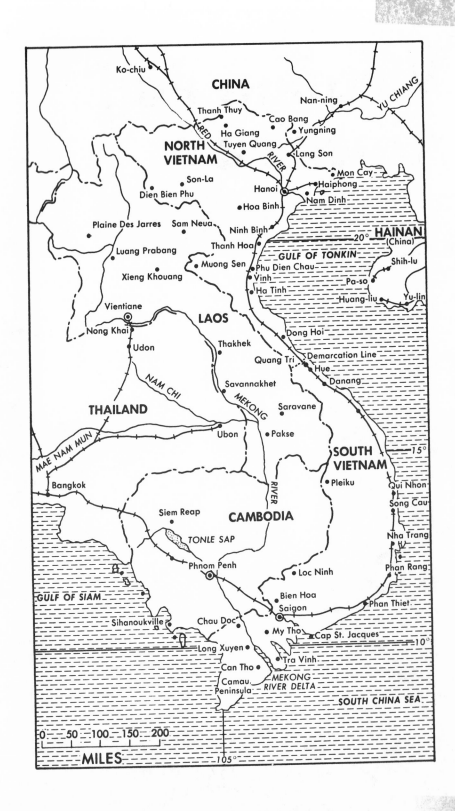

Vietnam and America:
A DOCUMENTED HISTORY

By
Marvin E. Gettleman,
Jane Franklin,
Marilyn Young,
and H. Bruce Franklin

Grove Press
New York

Published by Grove Press
a division of Wheatland Corporation
841 Broadway
New York, N.Y. 10003

First Grove Press Edition 1985
First Evergreen Edition 1985

Library of Congress Cataloging-in-Publication Data
Main entry under title:

Vietnam and America.

  Bibliography: p.
  Includes index.
  1. Vietnamese Conflict, 1961–1975—Addresses,
essays, lectures. 2. Vietnam—History—20th century—
Addresses, essays, lectures. I. Gettleman, Marvin E.
DS557.7.V5614 1985 959.704′3 84-48110
ISBN 0-394-54134-0
ISBN 0-8021-3097-6 (pbk.)

Printed in the United States of America
This book is printed on acid-free paper.

10 9 8 7 6 5 4 3 2

Dedicated to our children (and to all children):

Daniel E. Gettleman

Todd A. Gettleman

Eva Gettleman-Braiman

Rebecca Gettleman-Braiman

Michael Schrecker

Daniel Schrecker

Karen Franklin

Gretchen Franklin

Robert Morgan Franklin

Lauren Young

Michael Jacob Young

Contents

General Introduction

If I recall correctly, when France gave up Indochina as a colony, the leading nations of the world met in Geneva with regard to helping those colonies become independent nations. And since North and South Vietnam had been, previous to colonization, two separate countries, provisions were made that these two countries could by a vote of all their people together, decide whether they wanted to be one country or not.

And there wasn't anything <u>surreptitious</u> about it, that when Ho Chi Minh refused to participate in such an election—and there was provision that people of both countries could cross the border and live in the other country if they wanted to. And when they began leaving by the thousands and thousands from North Vietnam to live in South Vietnam, Ho Chi Minh closed the border and again violated that part of the agreement.

And openly, our country sent military advisers there to help a country which had been a colony have such things as a national security force, an army, you might say, or a military to defend itself. And they were doing this, if I recall correctly, also in civilian clothes, no weapons, until they began being blown up where they lived and walking down the street by people riding by on bicycles and throwing pipe bombs at them. And then they were permitted to carry sidearms or wear uniforms. But it was totally a program until John F. Kennedy—when these attacks and forays became so great that John F. Kennedy authorized the sending in of a division of Marines. And that was the first move toward combat troops in Vietnam.*

—President Ronald Reagan, February 18, 1982

In 1965, as US Marines first went ashore to join the 21,000 US military "advisers" already in Vietnam, it seemed to many Americans that the US government was in the process of making a terrible "mistake." A step-by-step escalation ap-

---

**Public Papers of the Presidents of the United States: Ronald Reagan, 1982*, Vol. I (Washington, D.C.: US Government Printing Office, 1983), pp. 184–185.

peared to be taking us ever deeper into the quagmire of a nasty war in some remote corner of southeast Asia.

The tiny handful of Americans familiar with the major features of the history of the region, particularly Vietnam and the rest of Indochina, sensed that the mistake was probably coming from ignorance. Perhaps the policy makers in Washington, and certainly the great mass of Americans, were unaware of the history that had led our nation into a hopeless and potentially devastating confrontation in Vietnam. What seemed to be needed was education. Then, either the politicians would understand the errors of their ways or the American people would bring them to their senses.

This was the impulse that led to the teach-in movement of early 1965, along with a flood of publications intended to educate America about Vietnam. The four editors of this book all participated in this educational enterprise. One of them, Marvin Gettleman, produced what was to become a basic text for those involved in the growing national debate, *Vietnam: History, Documents, and Opinions on a Major World Crisis* (New York: Fawcett, 1965), a collection of primary and secondary documents weaving a history of Vietnam and America's deepening war. Together with an enlarged edition (New York: Mentor, 1970), this book became not only the all-time best seller on Vietnam (over 600,000 copies) but also part of the very reality it set out to study. For the movement against the war, organized first as a spontaneous educational project, soon developed into an integral part of the history of the war.

That early impulse to educate an ignorant government came to seem more and more naïve as it became ever clearer that the successive administrations in Washington knew the truth all along and were consciously deceiving the American people. To some, this seemed an extreme position, for in those relatively innocent days, many Americans could not believe that the government would systematically lie. But then, in 1971, came the unauthorized release of *The Pentagon Papers*, a top-secret multivolume history prepared by the government itself. All the claims of the antiwar movement turned out to be true, including the willful deception of the people by the government, all proven beyond doubt by the government's own collection of primary and secondary documents. Ironically, the Gettleman volume and much of the splendid scholarship performed by amateurs and professionals during that 1965–1971 period now seemed a bit superfluous. The truth was out. The lies were exposed. Everybody agreed we should find the fastest way out of the war—or so it seemed. All Americans, even the President himself, seemed united on one thing, as Richard Nixon had put it when accepting his 1968 nomination: "We need a policy to prevent more Vietnams."

"No more Vietnams" became perhaps the closest we had to a national consensus, though it meant quite different things to different people. To some it meant that the United States should stop interfering in other nations' right to self-determination. To the Pentagon and the White House, it seemed to mean that no Vietnam should exist at all, as Indochina was reduced to a devastated wasteland during the years of America's retreat, perhaps to teach the lesson that no other nation should ever again defy America's will. "No more Vietnams" also came to stand for the desire to expunge Vietnam from our memory. To mention Vietnam was to call up horrors, shame, guilt, rage, and a bitterly divided America, and to evoke nightmares, ghosts, skeletons, bodies of Vietnamese and Americans buried or mutilated.

But by the late 1970s, that national consensus of "No more Vietnams" was becoming a major obstacle for the US government, which was stepping up its intervention in Latin America, Africa, Asia, and the Middle East, preparing to reinstitute draft registration, and initiating the most colossal military buildup in US history. Since the old official history of Vietnam and America had been replaced by a truer and far less convenient history, it was necessary to rewrite history once again. Hence, a new body of writings emerged (known by the collective term "revisionism") which sought to return to the myths that had been dispelled by the knowledge we had gained at such a terrifying price.

Gone was the monumental wartime scholarship that had traced the long, complex history of Vietnam's struggle for independence. The story now began not with Vietnam's history of resistance to Chinese, Japanese, and French colonialism, but with US concern about the victory of communism in China. Wiped out was the truth about the Geneva agreements, which had unconditionally recognized the unity and independence of Vietnam, and about the subversion of those agreements by a puppet regime placed in Saigon by the United States. In its place was that old concoction, long since discredited, of an invasion of the brave little nation of "South Vietnam" by the communist aggressors from "North Vietnam." The diplomatic history of the war was now entirely rewritten, as if the *Pentagon Papers* had never appeared. Gone also was the true military history of the war, with its humiliating defeat of the US colossus, to be replaced by a notion—alarmingly similar to the Nazi explanation of Germany's defeat in World War I—that the generals had really been winning the war, only to be stabbed in the back by politicians, journalists, pacifists, and pampered college students anxious to avoid the draft. And what the United States did to Vietnam was now reversed, with Vietnam becoming the perpetrator of atrocities and war crimes against the United States.

Simultaneously, the main themes of this "revisionist" history now poured forth in the form of lavishly financed, popular entertainment, such as the movie *The Deer Hunter* (designated by Hollywood the "Best Picture" of 1978), which systematically reversed the images that had been engraved on our minds by the most familiar TV and newspaper pictures of the war. Soon the new president for the early 1980s could speak of Vietnam as a "noble cause," another Hollywood production using for its plot that ludicrously false history prefacing this Introduction.

This new version of the history of Vietnam and America has become a necessity for today's policy makers. For only an America ignorant and innocent of Vietnam can again freely move against the self determination of other nations. Only an America persuaded that Vietnam was a "noble cause" can take pride in invading small Caribbean islands. And only an America that has erased the history of the Vietnam war can protect death squads that ritually mutilate and rape their victims, try to preserve right-wing dictatorships with Marine "peacekeepers," military "advisers," and air-naval bombardments of villages, create "third-force" military assaults on popular socialist governments, and squander the future of America to build a military juggernaut whose use would end the future of the human species.

To us, it once again seems vital to have available a true documentary history, one that includes what we knew by 1970 and what we have learned since about that nearly apocalyptic struggle of Vietnam and America.

Marvin Gettleman
Jane Franklin
Marilyn Young
H. Bruce Franklin

April, 1985

Part I

BACKGROUND TO REVOLUTION

Editors' Introduction

When William Graham Sumner published his classic *Folkways* in 1906, he coined the term "ethnocentrism." He defined it as the tendency of every group or nation to nourish its own vanity, boast its own superiority, exalt its own divinities, and look with contempt on outsiders.[1] A modern form of ethnocentrism is to deny the relevance, or even the existence, of the historical experience of peoples with which we become involved. This tendency is particularly acute in the United States, the unique breeding ground of what C. Vann Woodward has called "the American legend of success and victory, a legend that is not shared by any other people of the civilized world." Woodward goes on to say:

This unique good fortune has isolated America, I think rather dangerously, from the common experience of the rest of mankind, all the great peoples of which have without exception known the bitter taste of defeat and humiliation. It has fostered the tacit conviction that American ideals, values, and principles inevitably prevail in the end. . . . [this] assumption exposes us to the temptation of believing that we are somehow immune from the forces of history.[2]

Vietnam's history is ignored only at considerable risk, since the key to its conflict with the United States is to be found in a historical past marked by subjugation and struggle for independence. Incorporated by the conquering Han dynasty into the vast Chinese empire in about 100 B.C., Vietnam was a part of China for the next thousand years. During this period, as the historical essay by Roy Jumper and Marjorie Normand (Reading 1) explains, Chinese culture penetrated deeply. Only

---

1. William Graham Sumner, *Folkways: A Study of the Sociological Importance of Usages, Manners, Customs, Mores and Morals* (1906, reprinted New York: 1959), p. 13.
2. C. Vann Woodward, "The Irony of Southern History," in *The Burden of Southern History* (1960, reprinted New York: 1961), pp. 168–169.

a small group of clans in the Red River delta preserved elements of the Viet language, and taking advantage of China's military weakness in the tenth century, this group won Vietnam's independence. For the next 800 years the Viet empire pushed southward, displacing some groups altogether, and absorbing others until, by the early nineteenth century, it had obtained its present shape—an elongated "S" made up of two great river deltas, the Mekong and the Red River, joined by a strip of coast. In the course of this history, the Vietnamese fought the Chinese no less than six times: defending themselves against the Song in 1075, repelling the Mongols three times in the thirteenth century, expelling the Ming in the fifteenth and the Qing in the eighteenth century.

Unified, independent and at peace by the early nineteenth century, Vietnam under the Nguyen dynasty (which established an effective centralized imperial system by 1802) was nevertheless unable to withstand the pressure of French efforts to detach the southern provinces as an outright colony. Cochin China, as the six southern provinces were called, became French territory; by 1885, northern and central Vietnam had fallen as well, to be administered as nominal protectorates until 1945 when Ho Chi Minh declared Vietnam independent and unified once more.

Vietnamese resistance to the French was fierce; indeed, the French could not even make the hollow claim that the country was wholly "pacified" until 1913. In the long run, the most powerful organized resistance came from those who were able to combine a broad nationalist appeal with the desire and ability to mobilize the majority of the population against French rule. Ho Chi Minh, founder of the Indochinese Communist Party, integrated passionate nationalism with the skills and knowledge he had gained in a lifetime of revolutionary agitation—in France and China as well as Vietnam.[3]

At Versailles in 1919, Ho Chi Minh (then using the pseudonym, Nguyen Ai Quoc, or Nguyen The Patriot) appealed directly to Woodrow Wilson in the name of Wilson's own principles of self-determination. The letter (Reading 3) asked not for immediate independence but for the extension of the rights of citizenship, the heritage of the French revolution, to the Vietnamese. The failure of this appeal, as well as the impact of the Russian Revolution on colonial peoples throughout Asia, turned Ho (much as it had Mao Zedong in China) from a vague commitment to nationalism and liberalism to a study of Marxism-Leninism and a precise commitment to Communist revolution.

---

3. See Reading 4 for Ho Chi Minh's own account of his political development. See also Jean Lacouture, *Ho Chi Minh* (New York: Vintage Books, 1968) for the only full-length biography in English. David Marr's *Vietnamese Tradition on Trial, 1920–1945* (Berkeley: University of California Press, 1981) puts Ho's career in the context of other resistance leaders and provides a most useful analysis of his particular strengths.

1. Vietnam: The Historical Background*

By Roy Jumper and Marjorie Weiner Normand

In this necessarily brief summary, Jumper and Normand provide an outline of Vietnamese history which underlines the duration of the struggle for independence and unity. In the twentieth century, the early leadership role played by the Indochinese Communist Party helps to explain why, despite an extensive search, the United States was never able to discover an effective "third force" which might embody an anti-Communist nationalist alternative to the Communists.

Vietnam stands unique as the only country in Southeast Asia subjected to pervasive and continuous Chinese influence and domination for over a thousand years. The Vietnamese, their origins and early history obscure, began to figure in ancient Chinese annals during the third century B.C. The first verified date of importance in Vietnamese history is the founding of the kingdom of Nam-Viet, in 208 B.C. Composed of parts of present-day southern China together with three provinces in northern Vietnam, Nam-Viet during the Han dynasty was an autonomous kingdom under a vague Chinese suzerainty.[1] In 111 B.C. it was annexed by China, and for the next millennium, until A.D. 939, it was governed as a Chinese province, Giao Chi.[2]

Vietnamese history is that of a people more than of a geographic area, for present-day Vietnam is far more extensive than it was under Chinese rule, when the Vietnamese were centered on the Red River delta and the northeastern coastal plain. They pushed south slowly, their progress shaped by the geographical configuration of the country. What is known today as Vietnam occupies the eastern seaboard of a peninsula curving into the South China Sea at the southeastern tip of Asia. Vietnam is shaped like the letter S. In the north is the intensively cultivated and highly productive Red River delta; these flatlands give way to a long undulating coast with small fertile plains interspersed by rocky prominences jutting out to the sea; and farther south the thin coastal strip widens and eventually slopes into the rich alluvial soil of the Mekong delta, the farthest limit of Vietnamese expansion. Inland, the mountains of the north merge into the Annamite chain which runs parallel to the coast and descends into a series of plateaus in the west inhabited by primitive mountain tribes.

---

*Roy Jumper, who worked with the Michigan State University Advisory Group in Vietnam (1962–1963), is currently at the School of Public and Environmental Affairs, University of Indiana. Marjorie Weiner Normand wrote *We the Vietnamese, Voices from Vietnam* with François Sully (New York: Praeger, 1971). The selection is from "Vietnam," in George McTurnan Kahin, ed., *Government and Politics in Southeast Asia* (2d ed., Ithaca, N.Y.: Cornell University Press, 1964), pp. 375–390.

1. D.G.E. Hall, *A History of South-East Asia* (London: Macmillan, 1960), p. 170.

2. Vietnam was also known by the Chinese as An Nam, or "pacified South." The name Viet Nam, preferred by Vietnamese, was officially adopted in 1802 by Emperor Gia Long.

Traditional Vietnam

The era before 939 was marked by the gradual imposition of Chinese economic, social, and political institutions. Chinese governors brought in their political and economic organization, instituted a mandarin-type bureaucracy, and introduced Confucian ethics and the Chinese writing system. It is unclear, however, to what extent Chinese culture and institutions, channeled to the upper levels of society, actually modified the political condition of the peasantry.[3]

Frequent attempts to overthrow Chinese rule culminated in a victory in 939, when the Vietnamese were able to capitalize on the anarchy prevalent in China following the fall of the T'ang dynasty to throw off direct Chinese domination. For the next 500 years, although nominally united under a centralized kingship, the country was in fact almost constantly rent by dynastic struggles and the wars of rival princely families. Successful dynasties had a threefold task: to maintain their authority against internal competitors, to protect the Red River delta against Chinese invasion, and to provide land for an expanding population by pushing southward.

The issue with China was finally settled in 1427 when the great warrior Le Loi recaptured Hanoi from Chinese forces which had held it for some twenty years, proclaimed himself emperor, and established the Le dynasty. From this time until the Tay Son Rebellion in the 1770s, the Le emperors held nominal sway over Vietnam. Strife continued among the great mandarin houses, however, and rivalries eventually coalesced into two dominant factions: the Trinh in the north and the Nguyen in the south. Despite their predominant power, the Trinh never succeeded in conquering the Nguyen, nor did they dare usurp the throne, for fear of Chinese intervention. The victory in 939 did not bring a decisive break with the past; until the time of the French conquest, Vietnam remained a tributary state of China, sending triennial payments of ivory, precious stuff, and gold as symbolic tokens of submission, in return for the seal of investiture through which Peking confirmed the legitimate succession.[4] Even Le Loi hastily sent the requisite tribute to procure the Chinese emperor's acquiescence to his accession, forestall any direct intervention, and ensure the concomitant guarantee of support from China in times of military crisis.

If the tributary tie with China was not found incompatible with real independence, neither was the widespread acceptance of Chinese cultural and political borrowings. Perhaps the most important aspects of Chinese civilization adopted by the Vietnamese were the political and social organizations represented by the mandarinate; the examination system; and the moral precepts embodied in Confucianism. Absolute authority in principle emanated from the emperor, who held the

---

3. On the Chinese imprint see Léonard Aurouseau, "La première conquête chinoise des pays annamites: Origine du peuple annamite," *Bulletin de l'Ecole Française d' Extrême-Orient*, XXIII (1932), 137–264.

4. Tran Trong Kim, *Viet Nam Su Luoc* ("Brief History of Vietnam"; Hanoi: Tan Viet, 1951), p. 410.

"mandate of heaven" as the representative of divine power on earth, similar to the celestial sovereigns of China. Below the emperor, an elaborate central administration functioned, modeled on that of China but substantially modified by local Vietnamese conditions. The real basis for power during these war-torn times was military might rather than legalized imperial authority. The court in fact was isolated from its people and largely confined to ritual; it did not constitute an effective channel of communication or control.[5]

Officials staffing the administrative service—the mandarinate—were divided into two branches, military and civil, each subdivided into nine grades. They were recruited by a complicated system of competitive examinations based on Confucian scholarship. To become a mandarin, the candidate spent many years in preparation for the examinations which would determine his degree of knowledge and resultant official rank. Study centered on rhetoric, ancient Vietnamese and Chinese history, poetry, and ethics, and the ability to write poetry and draft government regulations. Candidates worked themselves up through a series of examinations beginning at provincial and regional levels, success in which procured entry into the teaching field and the lower levels of rural administration. Those who succeeded at the national or the court examinations normally entered directly into the corps of mandarins.

In its pure form the mandarinate system meant that the country's ruling class was identical with its educated minority. The ideal of advancement according to ability was not always realized, however. Although in theory even the poorest peasant competed equally with the highest noble, in practice only the sons of great and wealthy families could devote their time exclusively to study in order to attain the necessary scholarly background.[6]

The Chinese Confucian ideal on which the mandarinate was based represented a single hierarchy of values that the mandarins had a vested interest in maintaining. What Hsiao-t'ung Fei says of traditional China is also applicable to traditional Vietnam: the mandarins "monopolized authority based on wisdom of the past. . . . Their main task was the perpetuation of established norms in order to set up a guide for conventional behavior."[7] The values inherent in Confucianism and manifest in the mandarin system gave rise to few impulses for social change. This static world view failed to cope with the kinds of dynamic problems generated by later outside events; however, it served to provide an internal order which helped compensate for the harsh social and economic conditions produced by almost constant

5. The court was composed of all high officials, including high dignitaries and mandarins above the rank of bureau chief (Roy Jumper and Nguyen Thi Hue, *Notes on the Political and Administrative History of Viet Nam, 1802–1962* [Saigon: Michigan State University, Viet Nam Advisory Group, 1962], p. 29).

6. The historians Tran Van Giap, De Lanessan, and Dumarest emphasized the hereditary character of administration (cited in Jumper and Hue, p. 68). On the examination system see Louis Cury, *La Société annamite: Les lettrés, les mandarins, le peuple* (Paris: Jouve, 1910), and Robert de la Susse, "Les concours littéraires en Annam," *Revue Indochinoise*, XIX (1913), 139–158.

7. Hsiao-t'ung Fei, *China's Gentry* (Chicago: University of Chicago Press, 1953), p. 74.

warfare. Confucian principles emphasized the personal virtues of loyalty, morality, and obedience and the social importance of hierarchy, status, and order.

Life in Vietnam was very much rural-oriented. Even in the eighteenth century there were few urban centers. The basic administrative and social unit was the village, which in the north formed a nearly autonomous unit, fulfilling political, economic, social, and religious needs. As the Vietnamese moved southward, the villages they established played a less important role because of their rootless, even frontier, qualities. In both cases, since the great majority of the population was involved in rice cultivation, the village was the primary unit for facilitating rice production. On a national scale, the improvement and expansion of agriculture and the maintenance of an elaborate system of dikes constituted the major responsibilities of the central government.[8]

During this time, Vietnamese efforts were also directed toward removing the two obstacles to their territorial expansion southward: the kingdom of Champa along the coastal plains of central Vietnam and, to the southwest beyond Champa, the powerful Khmer empire. Champa was eliminated as a major rival after a series of wars culminating in a decisive battle in 1471 which the Vietnamese won. They subsequently annexed the Cham kingdom, destroying forever its unity and military strength. Today, little remains of Champa except for a few Indic ruins and a small, fast-disappearing minority of Cham in villages along the southern coast, centered around Phan Rang.

Under the Nguyen lords, who established a rival principality south of the Gianh River near the present site of Hue, the march south was continued, this time at the expense of the Khmers. The Vietnamese met with little formal resistance and followed up their successful forays with settlements. They easily moved into Khmer territory in the rich Mekong delta, which presented vast reaches of relatively unpopulated land ideally suited for rice cultivation. By the mid-eighteenth century, the Vietnamese had reached the Gulf of Siam, the farthest limits of their conquest.

The last phase of Vietnamese territorial expansion coincided with the beginning of regular European contact. From the seventeenth to the nineteenth century four European nations—England, France, the Netherlands, and Portugal—competed for commercial and religious privileges in Vietnam. Although by the beginning of the eighteenth century European trade with Vietnam had declined, Western missionary activity, particularly by the French, continued despite the opposition of the mandarinate, which viewed Christianity as a threat to the ordered social structure that maintained the ruling class in its dominant position. During both the seventeenth and eighteenth centuries, periods of intense persecution alternated with edicts of toleration in the domains of the Trinh in the north and those of the Nguyen in the south.[9]

---

8. In return, the central government required the village to pay its taxes, provide military recruits, and maintain internal order.

9. On the eve of the French intervention the Christian community was estimated to have numbered 300,000, despite recurrent persecution. Two basic studies on this subject are Tran Minh Tiet, *Histoire des persécutions au Vietnam* (Paris: Imp. Notre Dame de la Trinité, 1955), and John R. Shortland,

The relative equilibrium established by the rival houses was disrupted by an uprising known as the Tay Son revolt, led by three brothers.[10] They succeeded in putting the Nguyen ruling house to flight, then defeated the Trinh armies and a Chinese invading force, and brought substantial unity to Vietnam. Their victory proved ephemeral, however. A Nguyen prince, Nguyen Anh, began the slow and arduous task of reconquering his territory. He first regained Saigon and the southern regions, moved up toward the center, reconquering Hue, invaded the north and captured Hanoi. His military victories were abetted by Monsignor Pigneau de Behaine, bishop of Adran, who had tried to enlist official support from the French government[11] and, this failing, procured the aid of French volunteers from Pondicherry. They trained Nguyen Anh's army, equipped his navy, and directed the construction of fortifications. On June 1, 1802, more than twenty-five years after the Tay Sons raised the standard of revolt, Nguyen Anh proclaimed himself emperor of Vietnam at Hue and took the name Gia Long.[12]

Gia Long ruled from 1802 to 1820, and many of the early years were devoted to military activity, to the difficult task of pacifying and rebuilding the empire after decades of a shattering civil war. His personal qualities of leadership, courage, and intelligence were offset by less fortunate aspects of his rule; his government was in effect an oppressive, military despotism. Gia Long was no innovator. He conserved the traditional administrative framework and reinstituted the competitive examinations. While continuing the always heavy burden of taxes and the use of forced labor without recompense (*corvée*) for constructing the government's numerous public works, he is also credited with attempting to alleviate his people's ·distress by redistributing ricelands, revising and unifying the code of law, standardizing weights and measures, and reforming land registration (*cadastre*).[13]

The Persecutions of Annam: A History of Christianity in Cochinchina and Tongking (London: Burns and Oates, 1875).

10. The brothers were Nguyen Van Hue, who established himself at Hanoi and was proclaimed Emperor Quang Trung; Nguyen Van Nhac, who ruled at Hue; and Nguyen Van Lu, who was located in the extreme south.

11. Pigneau de Behaine journeyed to France in 1787, accompanied by the four-year-old heir apparent of Nguyen Anh, Prince Canh. He concluded a treaty of alliance with France in the name of Nguyen Anh but discovered in Pondicherry that French promises of aid were not forthcoming.

12. He sought and was granted formal investiture by the Chinese in 1803 in return for tribute sent every two years and homage performed every four years (Hall, p. 371).

13. Pierre Huard and Maurice Durand, *Connaissance du Viet-Nam* (Paris: Imprimerie Nationale, 1954), pp. 34–35. Several accounts in English by foreign visitors emphasize the oppressive and brutal nature of government in traditional Vietnam. Officials constantly thrashed people with bamboo rods for the slightest offense. Nobody other than an official enjoyed any rights or personal freedom. See John White, *History of a Voyage to the China Sea* (Boston: Wells and Lilly, 1823); John Crawfurd, *Journal of an Embassy from the Governor General of India to the Courts of Siam and Cochinchina* (2d ed.; London: Colburn and Bentley, 1830); George Finlayson, *The Mission to Siam and Hué, the Capital of Cochinchina in the years 1821–2* (London: John Murray, 1826). In an earlier work Samuel Baron describes "the most material passages of trade, government and customs of the country, and vice and virtue of the people, at least so far as will content and satisfy a moderate mind" (*A Description of the Kingdom of Tonqueen* [n.p., 1685]).

His successor, the Emperor Minh Mang, ruled from 1820 to 1841. Nurtured, like his father, on a military heritage, Minh Mang undertook to extend a uniform administrative system throughout his empire and to create a strongly centralized regime. He was well educated and particularly devoted to Chinese literature and law and Confucian traditions. This attachment to Confucian ethics spurred him to oppose the spread of Christianity, a religion which preached against the Confucian concept of an absolute and divine monarchy. An imperial edict issued in 1833 declared the profession of Christianity a crime punishable by death, and in the following years French missionaries were hounded out of the country, imprisoned, or executed. Persecution was intensified after a revolt in Lower Cochinchina was reputedly supported by Vietnamese Christians, and a French missionary, Father Marchand, was found among the rebel captives.[14] Before his death, Minh Mang appears to have reconsidered this policy of persecution in the fear of antagonizing France. The next emperor, Thieu Tri (1841–1847), pursued an anti-Christian policy with even more vigor, however, leaving the Emperor Tu Duc (1848–1883) to cope with the consequent breakdown of relations with France and its unhappy results.

The reign of the first two Nguyen emperors, and especially that of Minh Mang, is sometimes referred to nostalgically as a "golden age" of Vietnamese history,[15] and it is imperative to look behind the façade of regulated hierarchical authority for a realistic appraisal of the power structure. There was, in fact, a weak kingship system, bolstered not only by the authority of the civil mandarinate but also by the might of the army. Under Gia Long, generally insecure conditions prevailed in many rural areas, and he exercised only nominal control over a large part of the countryside. Even his successors failed to impose law and order in all parts of their realm. Furthermore, the emperor shared real power with the governors-general of the several regions, although in principle his authority extended directly into the province and district down to the canton and village. Nor was the relationship between the emperor and high mandarins always clearly defined. The emperor's councilors were chosen from among the top mandarins, who in practice often held several high positions at once, making it difficult for them competently to fulfill all their functions. Rivalries among mandarins were notorious and especially vicious during the reign of Minh Mang.[16] The situation was exacerbated by the personal remoteness of the emperor, sheltered behind the high walls of the imperial capital at Hue and largely deprived of contact with and knowledge of the state of the peasantry in rural areas. Imperial isolation was encouraged by the mandarins, who sought to enhance their personal power by confining the court largely to ritualistic functions and ceremonies.

The policy of the Nguyen emperors toward the West, especially on the accession of Tu Duc, represented an attempt to maintain the old order by closing off the

---

14. Jules Silvestre, "L'insurrection de Gia Dinh," *Revue Indochinoise*, XXIV (1915), 1–37.

15. See Marcel Gaultier, *Gia Long* (Saigon: Ardin, 1933) and *Minh Mang* (Paris: Larose, 1935), and also Charles B. Maybon, "Nguyen Anh, Empereur et fondateur de dynastie: Gia Long (1802–1820)," *Revue Historique Coloniale* (Paris), 1919, pp. 47–126.

16. Tran Trong Kim, p. 50.

country to foreign influences, both religious and commercial. Maltreatment of the missionaries, however, provided the French with a pretext for intervening in local affairs, and during the 1840s French naval vessels stormed into Vietnamese ports to demand—and obtain—the release of imprisoned missionaries. Matters came to a head when Tu Duc decided to isolate Vietnam completely and stamp out all Christian communities.[17] Following the death of French and Spanish missionaries, a joint Franco-Spanish task force invaded Tourane, and in February 1859 they turned south and took Saigon. The French moved inland to capture the three provinces adjacent to Saigon and by a treaty signed with Tu Duc in 1862 confirmed this conquest. French occupation of Cochinchina was completed in 1867 when Admiral de la Grandière occupied the three western provinces on the grounds that anti-French rebels were using the provinces still under Vietnamese control as a base of operations and refuge.

The French next turned their attention to the north, where the Emperor Tu Duc exercised very little control. The conquest of Hanoi by a small French force in 1873 was soon thereafter disavowed by the French government. Tu Duc's prestige was so impaired by his defeat, however, that he was unable to extend government authority in Tonkin and appealed to the Chinese emperor, under the terms of vassalage, to re-establish order.[18] In response to the movement of Chinese troops into the north, the French sent a squadron to Haiphong, and, in 1883, a force of some 600 men again attacked and took the citadel of Hanoi. By the terms of the treaty signed on August 25, 1883, the court at Hue formally recognized the French protectorate over Tonkin and Annam—Tu Duc having previously granted France sovereignty over Cochinchina—but guerrilla warfare raged on in several parts of the country. Vietnamese independence had come to an end, but Vietnamese resistance to French rule, in both the north and the south, continued into the twentieth century.[19]

The French Impact

The pattern of French colonial rule had a major impact on the course of Vietnamese history: it introduced economic, political, and social changes which dislocated the traditional mode of life and produced a poorly integrated society in which a small, urban-oriented Westernized elite was largely alienated from the bulk of the village-based population. It also inspired a violent nationalist response

---

17. Hall, pp. 558–559.

18. Hall maintains that Tu Duc was playing the Chinese against the French by emphasizing his vassalage to the former despite French admonitions, in the hope that they would get embroiled in a dispute which would sap the strength of both (pp. 570–571). A Franco-Chinese treaty signed May 11, 1884, formally recognized the validity of treaties between France and Vietnam.

19. On the other hand, much of Vietnam was immediately pacified, and thus French rule brought peace and security for the first time to an important part of the population. [The most detailed account of the French economic impact is Martin Murray's *The Development of Capitalism in Colonial Indochina (1870–1940)* (Berkeley: University of California Press, 1980).—eds.]

to the displacement of the traditional system of government by French colonial power, a response characterized by innumerable attempts to overthrow French rule, led first by the traditional elite and then by new leaders born during the period of foreign subjugation.

By terms of the treaty of 1884 defining the limits of French authority in Vietnam, Tonkin was to be administered indirectly by French *résidents* operating alongside the existing hierarchy of mandarins, while Annam was also to retain the emperor and court. Technically, only Cochinchina ranked as a colony and was placed under direct French control. Annam and Tonkin, together with Laos and Cambodia, were classed as protectorates and joined with Cochinchina in the Indochinese Union in 1887. The distinction between direct and indirect rule, however, constitutes one of the great myths of Colonial administration; its effect was legal rather than practical, since in fact French authority throughout Indochina was absolute.[20]

The pattern of French colonial administration in Indochina was hierarchical, "government from the top down rather than from the bottom up."[21] The Indochinese Union was administered by a Governor-General directly responsible to the Ministry of Colonies in Paris. French rule was characterized by a succession of vacillating policies emanating from Paris, accompanied by a rapid turnover of high officials and frequent administrative reorganization. Much of the difficulty was attributable to Paris, which lacked firsthand knowledge of Vietnamese affairs yet was unable to refrain from constant meddling through administrative directives or by appointing new governors-general who were often selected for political reasons and not on the basis of experience in colonial administration. Between 1892 and 1930, Indochina had twenty-three governors-general in addition to an even greater number of colonial ministers. Theoretically the Governor-General disposed of great power, but since he was rarely a professional colonial administrator, his authority was often effectively blocked by career colonial officials.

The Governor-General's scope of authority was further circumscribed by the concentration of power in the hands of French regional and provincial officials. Cochinchina, Tonkin, and Annam were each administered separately and only tenuously linked in the Indochinese Union. Cochinchina was ruled directly by a governor assisted by two assemblies.[22] At the provincial level it was administered by French chiefs of province assisted by a provincial council which voted the provincial budget. In Tonkin, French power was increased gradually, all of it concentrated eventually in the hands of the French *Résident*.[23] In Annam, the emperor

---

20. Hall, p. 644.

21. Rupert Emerson, *Representative Government in Southeast Asia* (New York: Institute of Pacific Relations, 1955), p. 171.

22. They were the Private Council, of an advisory character, and the Colonial Council, which voted the budget.

23. The French had first established the office of viceroy *(kinh luoc)*, held by a Vietnamese mandarin who, as official representative of the emperor, would serve as a liaison with the French *Résident Supérieur* in Tonkin. The multiple powers of this official were transferred to the French *Résident* in 1897, thus ending even the pretext of a traditional system of regional supervision.

was retained as a symbolic monarchy at Hue, and the French even intervened at this level, exiling recalcitrant emperors.[24] In short, while a façade of Vietnamese control was permitted in Annam and Tonkin, French authority permeated all levels of the central administrative hierarchy in all three regions, though the form differed. In Cochinchina especially, it even penetrated to the district and village level. There, the civil system of separation of judicial and administrative powers served to strip the canton chiefs and village elders of their police and judicial powers, which were given to French policemen and judges.

Another policy which facilitated the penetration of French control was the widespread use of French personnel at local administrative levels, in positions which, in other colonies in Southeast Asia, were usually filled by indigenous officials. Virginia Thompson wrote of the plethora of French *fonctionnaires* whose salaries devoured the colonial budget: they were too numerous for what they accomplished and far too few to do what was necessary.[25] Vietnamese mandarins, especially in Cochinchina and Tonkin, lost all initiative and responsibility and filled only secondary positions. The debasement of their authority, plus the substitution of Western education for Confucian culture based on traditional morality, contributed to the increased venality and corruption of those mandarins who cooperated with the French, thus compromising them hopelessly in the eyes of the local population.

French colonial policy as it evolved under Governor-General Paul Doumer (1897–1902) and subsequent administrations was largely shaped by the concept of Indochina as a profitable economic enterprise to be exploited for the benefit of the mother country. The economy was dominated by a combination of private French investors and the Bank of Indochina, which developed into the real political and financial nerve center of all Indochina. Established to provide the colony with monetary exchange and to encourage economic development by extending credit, the Bank of Indochina became the instrument for channeling metropolitan capital into the colony and directing its investment at highly profitable rates. French interests permeated all sectors of the economy but exercised almost exclusive control over mineral extraction, the rubber industry, and manufacturing. The Chinese community controlled the rice trade and was active in retailing, while Vietnamese economic ambitions were generally confined to landowning, where profits were derived from high rents and usurious rates of interest on money advanced to tenant farmers.

The economic impact of French rule did not change the preponderantly agrarian nature of the Vietnamese economy, and by 1940 the peasantry still constituted 85 to 90 per cent of the total population. The structure of landownership, however, was considerably altered. In Tonkin and Annam the pattern had been fairly well fixed in advance of the French so that, despite the economic changes that took

---

24. Imperial authority was further diminished by depriving the Co Mat, the traditional Secret Council of the emperor, of executive powers and transforming it into the principal Vietnamese advisory body to the French administration.

25. Virginia Thompson, *French Indochina* (London: George Allen & Unwin, 1937), p. 86.

place, a large proportion of proprietors still cultivated their own lands. But because of population pressures, holdings were fragmented and provided little more than subsistence for the majority of the population.[26] In contrast to Tonkin and Annam, land was abundant in Cochinchina, and vast projects of reclamation added considerably to the available acreage. This land was concentrated in large estates devoted to rice production and owned by both Vietnamese and French landlords or in French-owned rubber plantations. The growth of the rubber industry further modified the economic organization of Cochinchina by creating a labor shortage met by transplanting thousands of Tonkinese workers to the south where they lived and worked under conditions approximating peonage.

Although a higher proportion of peasants rented land from absentee landlords in Cochinchina than in Tonkin and Annam, the lot of the peasant was miserable in all three regions. High taxation was a contributing factor in forcing owners to sell or mortgage their property, and usurious interest rates produced a vicious system of rural indebtedness.[27] Another abuse causing great misery in the countryside resulted from the establishment of governmental monopolies on the purchase and distribution of alcohol, opium, and salt, thus depriving many villages of their secondary means of livelihood. In general, then, French economic achievements were not shared by the rural population, which was little affected by the extensive program of public works and road building.

The French colonial system also acted to destroy the village as a social and economic unit producing social security for the poor. French-trained Vietnamese officials were given authority formerly exercised by the village notables, who thereby lost prestige and with it much of their tradition-based authority over the villagers. With the breakdown in local authority, much village communal land was lost to speculation by notables and mandarins, and following upon the disruption of this traditional form of social insurance came an increase in pauperism and vagrancy. The growth of urban centers and a cash economy also contributed to the destruction of communal life, as did the French emphasis on individual as against communal responsibility. The village persisted as the primary locus of rural life, but it lost much of its cohesiveness and autonomy.

Colonial rule did not completely restructure Vietnamese society, which remained essentially peasant-oriented, though it did upset the social setting at many points. The most injurious social measure in Cochinchina was the introduction of a French legal code administered by French judges. Most judges were ignorant of Vietnamese customs and language and relied on Vietnamese interpreters, who were often open to bribery and corruption. The traditional mode of life was further modified by the process of urbanization; this gave rise to a rootless indigenous

---

26. In Tonkin 62 per cent of the peasantry eventually owned less than .9 acre and 30 per cent less than .4 acre. Conditions in Annam were only slightly better (Ellen J. Hammer, *The Struggle for Indochina* [Stanford: Stanford University Press, 1954], p. 65).

27. Also contributing to rural poverty were the occasional crop failures and very large expenditures upon marriages, funerals, dead ancestors, and the celebration of festivals such as the New Year.

proletariat and absorbed the attention of many of the wealthy landowners who had hitherto played an important role in village society.

Finally, the introduction of French education did much to reshape the class structure. Guided in the early days of French rule by the ideals of assimilation[28]— with the goal of turning Indochina into a cultural carbon copy of the mother country—the colonial regime reformed the Vietnamese schools and substituted French-type education for traditional moral teachings and the French language and *quoc ngu* (the romanized transcription of Vietnamese) for Chinese characters. Both the reformed Vietnamese schools and the new French schools emphasized quality rather than quantity, and the system, wholly inadequate to fulfill the Vietnamese demand for learning, produced a talented though small Vietnamese leadership group.[29]

Lucian Pye comments that the Vietnamese proved the most gifted of all Southeast Asians in assimilating Western culture and adapting to Western standards and they alone, of the peoples of the region, have successfully followed careers in Europe.[30] This elite education served to create a disgruntled educated class aspiring to the high political and administrative posts closed to them by the colonial regime. Unemployed or underpaid in secondary governmental positions, the disillusioned elite formed the nucleus around which patriotic anti-French activity would coalesce at the earliest opportunity. Within the elite it is important to distinguish the members who attended French schools from those trained in the reformed Vietnamese schools. Those educated in the French schools tended to become non-Communist nationalists, while those who made up the Communist leadership[31] attended either the reformed Vietnamese schools or none at all.

---

28. Initially, there was a great debate between those who advocated "assimilation" and those who favored a policy of "association" based upon respect for indigenous institutions.

29. On the eve of the French intervention, the traditional system of education, patterned on that of ancient China, included at the village level an estimated 20,000 one-teacher private schools supplemented by state-supported provincial and district classes. At the summit of the system was the National College (Quoc Tu Giam) for royal princes and mandarins. During French rule there were only 14 secondary schools in all Vietnam, including several excellent French *lycées* which they still operate. A single university at Hanoi was founded in 1917 but was subsequently closed on several occasions because of student political agitation. After 1903, when the knowledge of French became a prerequisite for all administrative employment in Vietnam, most of the elite families struggled to send at least one son to France for university instruction.

30. "This is a reflection," Pye says, "not only of French policy but also of the fact that the Vietnamese are the products of a sophisticated traditional civilization that placed high value on intellectual attainment and the disciplining of the mind" (Lucian W. Pye, "The Politics of Southeast Asia," in G. A. Almond and J. S. Coleman, eds., *Politics of the Developing Areas* [Princeton: Princeton University Press, 1960], p.95).

31. Hardly any leaders or members of the Workers' Party were educated in French schools. Two things most leaders of Communist North Vietnam have in common are periods of training in China during the 1920s under the auspices of the Revolutionary Youth League and of imprisonment by the French in the early 1930s. [Two books by David Marr have transformed our understanding of the development of Vietnamese nationalism: *Vietnamese Anticolonialism, 1885–1925* (Berkeley: Univer-

The Growth of Nationalism

The roots of Vietnamese national unity extend back to the period of Chinese domination, and the Vietnamese struggle for independence has an equally long historical tradition. Armed opposition to French rule, led by high-ranking mandarins and members of the imperial family continued until 1916; the objectives were to oust the hated foreigner and restore the former dynastic order. During the decade before the First World War, both the leadership and the purpose of the Vietnamese resistance began to change. French economic and cultural penetration, and especially the French educational system, gave rise to a small group of Western-oriented intellectuals convinced of the need to modernize and industrialize their country and to broaden the primarily political anti-French struggle to include goals of social and economic change.

During the 1920s, several attempts were made by Vietnamese scholars and nationalists to achieve moderate reforms through cooperation with the colonial regime. When their programs were flatly rejected, they turned once again to violent methods and to clandestine organizations. Many underground nationalist societies were Marxist-oriented, although the dominant nationalist organization in the twenties, the Viet Nam Quoc Dan Dang (VNQDD—Vietnamese Nationalist Party), was not. Its aim was the revolutionary overthrow of French rule and the establishment of a republican government along the lines of the Chinese Kuomintang, which served as its organizational model. The VNQDD led an uprising which began on the night of February 9, 1930, when the Vietnamese garrison at Yen Bay on the Chinese border rose in revolt. This was expected to foment a general revolution, but French authorities had been alerted and they easily quelled the disturbances. The VNQDD was destroyed as an effective organization for nearly fifteen years, reappearing under Chinese auspices during the Second World War.

The disappearance of the VNQDD from the political scene greatly facilitated the rise of Vietnamese communism to a position of dominance. The fusion of three competing Communist groups into a united Indochinese Communist Party (ICP)[32] was arranged in 1930 by the Comintern representative in Southeast Asia, Nguyen Ai Quoc,[33] who gave the fledgling organization clearly defined relations with the

---

sity of California Press, 1971) and *Vietnamese Tradition On Trial, 1920–1945* (Berkeley: University of California Press, 1981). For the situation in the 1930s, see Ngo Vinh Long's *Before the Revolution* (Cambridge, MA: M.I.T. Press, 1973).—eds.]

32. I. Milton Sacks, "Marxism in Viet Nam," in Frank N. Trager, ed., *Marxism in Southeast Asia* (Stanford: Stanford University Press, 1959), pp.115–124.

33. Nguyen Ai Quoc (Nguyen the Patriot) was the pseudonym used by Nguyen Tat Thanh, better known as Ho Chi Minh. Born in 1890, he left Vietnam in 1911 as a cabin boy on a merchant vessel and was known to be in Paris at the time of the Versailles conference. He became active in the French Socialist Party and attended its congress in 1920, voting with the majority which split off and formed the French Communist Party. In 1923 he was sent to Moscow as the French Communist Party delegate to the Peasant International (Krestintern). He remained there for more than a year to study communism and attend the Fifth Congress of the Communist International (Comintern) in 1924. He then accompanied Mikhail Borodin, the senior Soviet advisor to the Kuomintang, to Canton, where he ostensibly worked as a translator, a cover for his task of organizing an Indochinese Communist movement. In

international Communist apparatus.[34] Soon after its inception, the ICP sought to rival the VNQDD uprising by organizing mass peasant demonstrations to dramatize the widespread agrarian misery then prevalent as a result of successive crop failures. These were followed by a series of strikes in plantations and factories and culminated in peasant revolts and the creation of "soviets" in the two provinces of Ha Tinh and Nghe An.[35] French retribution was swift and brutal. By 1932 an estimated 10,000 political prisoners languished in jail, and many Communist leaders were executed. The organization of the ICP was further disrupted, and its ties to the Comintern severed, by the arrest of Nguyen Ai Quoc in 1931 in Hong Kong.

Unlike the VNQDD, the ICP was weakened but not decimated by French repression. By 1933 the party was again operative. It soon regained pre-eminence in the revolutionary movement, although it shared this leadership in Cochinchina with several Trotskyist groups. During the late 1930s ICP adherence to the Popular Front, its rationale deriving from European politics, cost the party a sizable portion of its support. By 1938, with the fall of the Popular Front in France, the ICP was driven underground and many of its militants were arrested. The eve of the Second World War found the leadership of the ICP forced to reorganize in exile in southern China. However, by its activities and organizational skill, the ICP had come to dominate the revolutionary scene in Vietnam and had laid the foundation for its subsequent claims to historic leadership of the Vietnamese nationalist movement.

1925 he created the Association of Revolutionary Youth, a precursor of the ICP (Sacks, *op. cit.*, pp.108–111; Donald Lancaster, *The Emancipation of French Indochina* [London: Oxford University Press, 1961], pp.79–83; Bernard B. Fall, *The Two Viet-Nams* [New York: Praeger, 1963], pp.81–103).

34. At the time of its formation, the ICP had a membership of 211 Vietnamese Communists in all, according to an official source (*Thirty Years of Struggle of the Party* [Hanoi: Foreign Languages Publishing House, 1960], p.24). One year later, ICP membership had reputedly grown to about 1,500, augmented by some 100,000 peasants affiliated in peasant organizations (Hammer, *op. cit.*, p. 82).

35. These "soviets" apparently distributed communal land to peasants and took over local administration (Le Thanh Khoi, *Le Viet-Nam* [Paris: Editions de Minuit, 1955], p. 445). For an official Communist evaluation of the strength and weakness of ICP policy during this period, including criticisms of the party "line," see *Thirty Years of Struggle*, pp. 31–37. [On this vital moment in Vietnamese revolutionary history see Marr, *Vietnamese Tradition on Trial*, pp. 378 ff. See also Milton E. Osborne, "Continuity and Motivation in Vietnamese Revolution: New Light from the 1930s," *Pacific Affairs* 47, 1 (Spring 1974), pp. 37–55.—eds.]

2. Royal Edict on Resistance (1885)*

By Emperor Ham Nghi

Ham Nghi, twelve years old when he assumed the throne in 1884, signed the Patenotre treaty which, until 1946, governed relations between France and Vietnam. In 1885, in conjunction with high officials determined to resist the French conquest, the King issued his proclamation calling for all groups in society to resist in accordance with their station and means. The royalist movement he called forth, the Can Vuong, was able to survive even after Ham Nghi himself was captured and exiled to Algeria in 1888.

My virtue is as gossamer; now that I am confronted with these changes, I am unable to take the lead. The capital has been lost. The Imperial carriage has departed. I am responsible for all this, and I feel an infinite shame. However, since we are still bound by moral obligations, none of you—mandarins, ministers, literati, high or low—shall abandon me. Those with intelligence shall contribute ideas; those with strength shall lend their force. The rich shall give money to buy military supplies. The peasants and villagers shall not refuse hardship or evade danger. It is right that this should be so.

To uphold the weak, to support the faltering, to confront difficulties and reduce danger, none shall spare their efforts. Perhaps with Heaven's assistance, we shall be able to turn chaos into order, danger into peace, and finally retrieve our entire territory. Under these circumstances, the fate of the nation must be the fate of the people. Together we shall work out our destiny and together we shall rest. Is this not the best solution?

On the contrary, should you fear death more than you feel loyalty to your King, should your domestic worries override your concern for the affairs of state, should officials flee danger on every occasion and soldiers desert their ranks to hide; again, should the people withhold righteous assistance to the State in this time of danger, and scholars shun prominent positions for obscurity, would they not then be superfluous in this world? You might wear robes and headdresses, but your attitude would be that of animals. Who can accept such behavior?

The court has always had its tradition of generous rewards and heavy penalties. Act to avoid remorse in the future.

End of the edict.

---

*Translated by Truong Buu Lam, from his book *Patterns of Vietnamese Response to Foreign Intervention: 1885–1900* (New Haven: Yale University Southeast Asia Studies Monograph Series No. 11, 1967), pp. 116–119 for complete text and notes. Compare with Ho Chi Minh's call founding the Viet Minh, Reading 7.

3. First Appeal to the United States (June 1919)*

By Ho Chi Minh

In this polite appeal to the principles of Wilsonian self-determination, Ho Chi Minh avoids insisting on immediate independence for Vietnam. Instead, he claims legal and political rights for which France presumably stands. At the same time, Ho is careful to hold full independence as the ultimate goal, albeit confined here to a subordinate clause ("while waiting for the principle of national self-determination to pass from ideal to reality . . ."). This would not be the last time Ho Chi Minh tried to convince Western democracies to live up to what they said (Reading 11).

A. Letter of Nguyen Ai Quoc to the American Secretary of State

Paris, 18 June, 1919

To his Excellency, the Secretary of State of the Republic of the United States, Delegate to the Peace Conference[1]

Excellency,

We take the liberty of submitting to you the accompanying memorandum setting forth the claims of the Annamite people on the occasion of the Allied victory.

We count on your great kindness to honor our appeal by your support whenever the opportunity arises.

We beg your Excellency graciously to accept the expression of our profound respect.

> For the Group of
> Annamite Patriots
>
> [signed] NGUYEN AI QUOC[2]
> 56, rue Monsieur le Prince—Paris

B. Revendications du Peuple Annamite [Claims of the Annamite People]

Since the victory of the Allies, all the subject peoples are frantic with hope at the prospect of an era of right and justice which should begin for them by virtue of the formal and solemn engagements, made before the whole world by the various powers of the *entente*[3] in the struggle of civilization against barbarism.

---

*Translations of the French originals in the National Archives, Washington, D.C.

1. The U.S. Secretary of State at the time was Robert Lansing.—eds.

2. Ho Chi Minh's pseudonym at the time.

3. The *entente*, or Allied powers during World War I, included France, England, and after 1917, the United States.—eds.

While waiting for the principle of national self-determination to pass from ideal to reality through the effective recognition of the sacred right of all peoples to decide their own destiny, the inhabitants of the ancient Empire of Annam, at the present time French Indochina, present to the noble Governments of the *entente* in general and in particular to the honorable French Government the following humble claims:

(1) General amnesty for all the native people who have been condemned for political activity.

(2) Reform of Indochinese justice by granting to the native population the same judicial guarantees as the Europeans have, and the total suppression of the special courts which are the instruments of terrorization and oppression against the most responsible elements of the Annamite people.

(3) Freedom of press and speech.

(4) Freedom of association and assembly.

(5) Freedom to emigrate and to travel abroad.

(6) Freedom of education, and creation in every province of technical and professional schools for the native population.

(7) Replacement of the regime of arbitrary decrees by a regime of law.

4. *"The Path Which Led Me to Leninism"* *(1960)**

By Ho Chi Minh

Ho Chi Minh's path to revolution mirrors that of many Asian nationalists of his generation. In much the same way, Professor Li Dazhou, stunned by the very fact of the Bolshevik Revolution, called on his Chinese students to join him in studying Marxism and Leninism and, a few years later, founded the Chinese Communist Party.[1] So too, Li and the early members of the Chinese party would move from an impassioned embrace of the Russian Revolution to an effort to spell out its meanings from their specific situation. In this autobiographical fragment, Ho describes, in a somewhat bemused fashion, his own faltering steps towards Leninism.

After World War I, I made my living in Paris, now as a retoucher at a photographer's, now as a painter of "Chinese antiquities" (made in France!). I would

---

*Written in April 1960 for inclusion in the Soviet Review *Problems of the East* on the occasion of the ninetieth anniversary of Lenin's birthday, in Ho Chi Minh, *Selected Works* (4 vols.; Hanoi: Foreign Languages Publishing House, 1960–1962) IV, pp. 448–450.

1. See Jacques Guillermaz, *A History of the Chinese Communist Party, 1921–1949* (New York: Random House, 1972), Chap. I.

distribute leaflets denouncing the crimes committed by the French colonialists in Vietnam.

At that time, I supported the October Revolution only instinctively, not yet grasping all its historic importance. I loved and admired Lenin because he was a great patriot who liberated his compatriots; until then, I had read none of his books.

The reason for my joining the French Socialist Party was that these "ladies and gentlemen"—as I called my comrades at that moment—had shown their sympathy toward me, toward the struggle of the oppressed peoples. But I understood neither what was a party, a trade-union, nor what was Socialism nor Communism.

Heated discussions were then taking place in the branches of the Socialist Party, about the question whether the Socialist Party should remain in the Second International, should a Second-and-a-half International be founded or should the Socialist Party join Lenin's Third International? I attended the meetings regularly, twice or three times a week and attentively listened to the discussion. First, I could not understand thoroughly. Why were the discussions so heated? Either with the Second, Second-and-a-half or Third International, the revolution could be waged. What was the use of arguing then? As for the First International, what had become of it?

What I wanted most to know—and this precisely was not debated in the meetings—was: Which International sides with the peoples of colonial countries?

I raised the question—the most important in my opinion—in a meeting. Some comrades answered: It is the Third, not the Second International. And a comrade gave me Lenin's "Thesis on the National and Colonial Questions" published by *l'Humanité* to read.

There were political terms difficult to understand in this thesis. But by dint of reading it again and again, finally I could grasp the main part of it. What emotion, enthusiasm, clear-sightedness, and confidence it instilled in me! I was overjoyed to tears. Though sitting alone in my room, I shouted aloud as if addressing large crowds: "Dear martyrs, compatriots! This is what we need, this is what we need, this is the path to our liberation!"

After that, I had entire confidence in Lenin, in the Third International.

Formerly, during the meetings of the Party branch, I had only listened to the discussion; I had a vague belief that all were logical, and could not differentiate as to who were right and who were wrong. But from then on, I also plunged into the debates and discussed with fervor. Though I was still lacking French words to express all my thoughts, I smashed the allegations attacking Lenin and the Third International with no less vigor. My only argument was: "If you do not condemn colonialism, if you do not side with colonial people, what kind of revolution are you waging?"

Not only did I take part in the meetings of my own Party branch, but I also went to other Party branches to lay down "my position." Now I must tell again that Comrades Marcel Cachin, Vaillant Couturier, Monmousséau, and many others helped me to broaden my knowledge. Finally, at the Tours Congress, I voted with them for our joining the Third International.

At first, patriotism, not yet Communism, led me to have confidence in Lenin, in the Third International. Step by step, along the struggle, by studying Marxism-Leninism parallel with participation in practical activities, I gradually came upon the fact that only Socialism and Communism can liberate the oppressed nations and the working people throughout the world from slavery.

There is a legend, in our country as well as in China, on the miraculous "Book of the Wise." When facing great difficulties, one opens it and finds a way out. Leninism is not only a miraculous "Book of the Wise," a compass for us Vietnamese revolutionaries and people; it is also the radiant sun illuminating our path to final victory, to Socialism and Communism.

5. Founding of the Communist Party of Indochina (1930)*

By Ho Chi Minh

As a Comintern agent during the 1920s (see Reading 3), Ho Chi Minh was able to organize young Vietnamese studying in China into a Vietnam Young Revolutionary Comrades' League, and within this Youth League, a Communist Youth Group was formed. By 1930, strains in the League threatened to destroy the organization altogether. Instead, at an important conference chaired by Ho, a single Communist party was founded in February 1930. In the reading below, the clear echoes of Ham Nghi's call to resist the French (Reading 2) can be heard, as well as the theory and practice of more recent revolutionary efforts.

Workers, peasants, soldiers, youth, and pupils! Oppressed and exploited compatriots!

Sisters and brothers! Comrades!

Imperialist contradictions were the cause of the 1914–1918 World War. After this horrible slaughter, the world was divided into two camps: one is the revolutionary camp including the oppressed colonies and the exploited working class throughout the world. The vanguard force of this camp is the Soviet Union. The other is the counter-revolutionary camp of international capitalism and imperialism whose general staff is the League of Nations.

During this World War, various nations suffered untold losses in property and

---

*This program (dated February 18, 1930) was drafted by Comintern representative Nguyen Ai Quoc (Ho Chi Minh), and adopted at a conference of Communists from Tonkin, Annam, and Cochin China held in Hong Kong. It appears in Ho Chi Minh, *Selected Works* (4 vols., Hanoi: Foreign Languages Publishing House, 1960–1962), II, pp. 145–148.

human lives. The French imperialists were the hardest hit. Therefore, in order to restore the capitalist forces in France, the French imperialists have resorted to every underhand scheme to intensify their capitalist exploitation in Indochina. They set up new factories to exploit the workers with low wages. They plundered the peasants' land to establish plantations and drive them to utter poverty. They levied many heavy taxes. They imposed public loans upon our people. In short, they reduced us to wretchedness. They increased their military forces, firstly to strangle the Vietnamese revolution; secondly to prepare for a new imperialist war in the Pacific aimed at capturing new colonies; thirdly to suppress the Chinese revolution; fourthly to attack the Soviet Union because the latter helps the revolution of the oppressed nations and the exploited working class. World War Two will break out. When it breaks the French imperialists will certainly drive our people to a more horrible slaughter. If we give them a free hand to prepare for this war, suppress the Chinese revolution, and attack the Soviet Union, if we give them a free hand to stifle the Vietnamese revolution, it is tantamount to giving them a free hand to wipe our race off the earth and drown our nation in the Pacific.

However, the French imperialists' barbarous oppression and ruthless exploitation have awakened our compatriots, who have all realized that revolution is the only road to life; without it they will die out piecemeal. This is the only reason why the Vietnamese revolutionary movement has grown ever stronger with each passing day: the workers refuse to work, the peasants demand land, the pupils strike, the traders boycott. Everywhere the masses have risen to oppose the French imperialists.

The Vietnamese revolution has made the French imperialists tremble with fear. On the one hand, they utilize the feudalists and comprador bourgeois in our country to oppress and exploit our people. On the other, they terrorize, arrest, jail, deport, and kill a great number of Vietnamese revolutionaries. If the French imperialists think that they can suppress the Vietnamese revolution by means of terrorist acts, they are utterly mistaken. Firstly, it is because the Vietnamese revolution is not isolated but enjoys the assistance of the world proletarian class in general and of the French working class in particular. Secondly, while the French imperialists are frenziedly carrying out terrorist acts, the Vietnamese Communists, formerly working separately, have now united into a single party, the Communist Party of Indochina, to lead our entire people in their revolution.

Workers, peasants, soldiers, youth, pupils!

Oppressed and exploited compatriots!

The Communist Party of Indochina is founded. It is the party of the working class. It will help the proletarian class lead the revolution in order to struggle for all the oppressed and exploited people. From now on we must join the Party, help it and follow it in order to implement the following slogans:

1. To overthrow French imperialism, feudalism, and the reactionary Vietnamese capitalist class.

2. To make Indochina completely independent.

3. To establish a worker-peasant and soldier government.

4. To confiscate the banks and other enterprises belonging to the imperialists and put them under the control of the worker-peasant and soldier government.

5. To confiscate all of the plantations and property belonging to the imperialists and the Vietnamese reactionary capitalist class and distribute them to poor peasants.

6. To implement the eight hour working day.

7. To abolish public loans and poll tax. To waive unjust taxes hitting the poor people.

8. To bring back all freedom to the masses.

9. To carry out universal education.

10. To implement equality between man and woman.

NGUYEN AI QUOC

Part II

WAR AND
INDEPENDENCE

Editors' Introduction

On July 4, 1964, Dean Rusk delivered an address at Independence Hall, Philadelphia, on "the Universal Appeal of the Declaration of Independence."[1] There was only one mention of Vietnam in Rusk's talk, a brief reference to the "gangster war . . . of terror and aggression" the Communists were "waging against the people of . . . South Vietnam."[2] He missed an opportunity to comment on the irony of the fact that the very Communists he was referring to chose to begin their modern national history with the words: "All men are created equal. . . ."[3]

This restatement of the principles of Jeffersonian democracy appeared in Ho Chi Minh's September 1945 declaration of independence of the newly created Democratic Republic of Vietnam (DRV). This first Asian socialist state (not until four years later would Mao Zedong's forces come to power and establish the People's Republic of China) was at the outset a fragile entity. Originating in the final days of World War II, after Japanese forces in Indochina had turned on their former allies, the "Vichy French"[4] colonialists, the DRV was ignored by the victorious allies meeting at Potsdam, who arranged for the Japanese to surrender to the British in the south and the Nationalist Chinese in the north, without any reference to what was actually happening in Vietnam itself.

Yet the history of the war years necessarily shaped events in ways the Allies had not foreseen and could not control. In 1941 the Indochinese Communist Party formally disbanded in favor of a new organizational form—a league for Vietnam-

---

1. US *Department of State Bulletin*, 51 (July 20, 1964), pp. 74–78.

2. Ibid., p. 75.

3. DRV Declaration of Independence, see Reading 9.

4. Vichy was the resort town in eastern France which became the capital of the pro-Nazi government established to rule those parts of France not occupied by Germany after the French surrender in 1940. An anti-Nazi government-in-exile headed by Charles de Gaulle functioned in London during the war. The leaders of both the "Free French" and Vichy were determined to retain European control over their former empire.

ese independence (Viet Minh) whose broad coalition of politics and nationalist appeal won increasing numbers of adherents to its ranks (Reading 7).

Acting boldly to seize independence in the last months of the war, the leadership of the Viet Minh hoped to actualize the Allies' wartime promises assuring colonial peoples of Allied support for self-determination. Instead, with the active aid of both the United States and Great Britain, the French began their drive to reconquer Vietnam (Readings 8, 9, and 10).

Until sufficient French troops could be transported to Vietnam, the British (in charge of Vietnam south of the 16th parallel) re-armed the Japanese, using them to help keep "order."[5] In the streets of Saigon, Robert Trumbull reported, the French Foreign Legion, its ranks full of German former prisoners of war "swaggered drunkenly . . . singing the Horst Wessel song." A preview of the decades to come, "Vietnamese patriots were being arrested and tortured by the French security police, whose favorite method of interrogation involved the use of electrodes attached to the genitals."[6] And then, in due course, came the French troops. Harold Isaacs watched them land:

. . . thousands every week, first in French transports and then in a long succession of American ships, flying the American flag and manned by American crews. They came ashore in their American uniforms, with their American lendlease weapons, tanks, trucks, jeeps. They marched past cheering crowds of relieved French civilians and moved out almost immediately to the flat ricelands of the peninsula to restore French order.[7]

Although most accounts date the Franco-Vietnamese war from 1946 to its official end in Geneva in 1954, the war in effect began in the south in 1945; 1946 marks not its beginning but its spread northward. Explaining their policy to themselves and the world, the French insisted that their effort transcended a simple colonial reconquest and that it was a war France fought on behalf of the entire noncommunist ("free") world. In the words of General Jean de Lattre de Tassigny, the war "no longer concerns France except to the extent of her promises to Vietnam and the part she has to play in the defense of the free world. Not since the Crusades has France undertaken such disinterested action. This war is the war of Vietnam for Vietnam."[8] And so, of course, it was, though not exactly as de Lattre intended.

In 1949, partly in response to American pressure, the French granted a simulacrum of independence to a unified Vietnamese government under Bao Dai, a figurehead whom the French had first installed as Emperor in 1933. The Eisenhower administration quickly recognized this artifact as the legitimate government of the country.

Meanwhile, the Vietnamese were developing the strategy and tactics of a rev-

---

5. See Joseph Buttinger, *Vietnam, A Dragon Embattled*, vol. 1 (New York: Praeger, 1967), pp. 335, 336 and p. 625, fn 51.

6. Ibid., p. 631.

7. Ibid., p. 630.

8. Ibid., p. 669.

olutionary people's war. Dismissed by Kennedy administration advisers like Roger Hilsman as "Communist fantasies,"[9] they nevertheless operated with great efficiency. Here we include selections from the military writings of General Vo Nguyen Giap, the architect of the Vietnamese victory at Dien Bien Phu. A little more than twenty years later, a younger protégé of Giap, Van Tien Dung, led his troops to a comparable victory over the American-backed forces of a successor to Bao Dai's regime (Reading 68).

6. A Succession of Enemies: Japan and France versus Vietnam, 1940–1954*

By Roy Jumper and Marjorie Weiner Normand

In this continuation of their historical essay (Reading 1), Jumper and Normand describe the confused situation in Vietnam during the Second World War, when it was subject to two, rather than one, colonial overlords. The narrative then describes the early postwar years, when it was clear that France would reject all Vietnamese efforts to secure autonomy. For the French the question remained how little could be granted within the context of an on-going French Union. For the Vietnamese the question was reversed: What concessions might be made to France within the context of an independent, unified, sovereign Vietnam. By 1954, the issue seemed to have been resolved in Vietnam's victory.

The Second World War

The fall of France left the colonial regime in Indochina to fend for itself in the face of Japanese menaces. After a series of ultimatums, negotiations, and even a brief but bloody clash between French and Japanese troops, the pro-Vichy colonial administration capitulated to Japanese demands. The form of Japanese occupation in Indochina was unique in Southeast Asia: Japan recognized French sovereignty and left local administration and security functions in French hands; in return, Indochinese military facilities and economic resources were placed at Japan's disposal. The tenuous balance between French and Japanese authority was maintained until March 9, 1945, when the Japanese military command occupied Indochina by force. Unhampered by loyalty to French colonial rule, the Emperor Bao Dai,

---

*From "Vietnam," in George McTurnan Kahin, ed., *Government and Politics of Southeast Asia*, 2d ed. (Ithaca, NY: Cornell University Press, 1964), pp. 391–399. Footnotes renumbered.

9. See Roger Hilsman's foreword to the American edition of Vo Nguyen Giap's *People's War, People's Army* (subtitled "The Viet Cong Insurrection Manual for Underdeveloped Countries" by its American publisher) (New York: Bantam Books, 1967).

prompted by the Japanese, proclaimed Vietnam's independence and secured from Japan the nominal unification of all three regions of Vietnam. Despite its pretensions to power, however, the imperial government found its authority in the countryside nonexistent as local administration was passing into other Vietnamese hands.[1]

During the early years of the war, many Vietnamese revolutionary organizations and individuals regrouped in southern China. ICP leaders held an important meeting of the Central Committee in May 1941 and launched the Vietnam Independence League (Viet Nam Doc Lap Dong Minh Hoi), better known as the Viet Minh. Its purpose was to serve as a coordinating organization for both individuals and affiliated groups, and its program stressed a national liberation policy uniting all major strata of society.[2] Communist demands for agrarian reform and class struggle were subordinated to the common goal of national independence. During the period between 1943 and the Japanese coup of 1945 the Viet Minh concentrated its efforts on two goals: to expand its organization by developing mass support and to build up its armed strength.[3] Immediately following the Japanese surrender on August 13, 1945, a national congress of the Viet Minh approved a policy of insurrection, adopted a ten-point program, and elected a National Liberation Committee headed by Ho Chi Minh, which was tantamount to a provisional government.[4] Viet Minh partisans took over in Hanoi, and on August 26 Bao Dai abdicated in favor of the provisional government of the Democratic Republic of Vietnam (DRV). The ex-emperor was immediately appointed Supreme Political Adviser to the new regime and provided it with an important symbol of legitimacy and continuity. On September 2, an estimated half a million people gathered in Hanoi to hear Ho Chi Minh read a Declaration of Independence and proclaim the birth of the Democratic Republic of Vietnam.

The Aftermath: France versus the Viet Minh

In the chaotic days following the Japanese surrender, the Viet Minh hoped to establish an independent, functioning national government and present the Allies

---

1. Philippe Devillers, *Histoire du Viet-Nam de 1940 à 1952* (Paris: Editions du Seuil, 1952), pp. 129–131.

2. I. Milton Sacks, "Marxism in Vietnam," in Frank N. Trager, ed., *Marxism in Southeast Asia* (Stanford: Stanford Univ. Press, 1959), p. 146.

3. Vo Nguyen Giap, commander in chief of the Vietnam People's Army, gives December 22, 1944, as the date of formation of the Liberation Army in Cao Bang province. It consisted of 34 men, poorly armed. It grew to number about 1,000 before the Japanese coup and increased to 5,000 at the time of the Japanese surrender (Vo Nguyen Giap, *Ten Years of Fighting and Building of the Vietnamese People's Army* [Hanoi: Foreign Languages Publishing House, 1955], pp. 11–12).

4. Earlier the Viet Minh formed National Liberation Committees which were "pregovernmental" in character; that is, they combined administrative, political, and military duties (*Breaking Our Chains* [Hanoi: Foreign Languages Publishing House, 1960], pp. 7–17). The main points in the program were to seize power, gain independence for the Democratic Republic of Vietnam, develop the army, abolish inequitable taxes, promulgate democratic rights, redistribute communal lands, and maintain good relations with the Allies. No mention was made of land reform (*ibid.*, pp. 68–70).

with a *fait accompli*. In north and central Vietnam the Viet Minh moved into a power vacuum with the aid of Bao Dai's abdication. In the south, however, factionalism among competing nationalist groups prevented their agreement on a common policy toward the Allies, and especially toward France. With great difficulty the Viet Minh managed to bring the various groups together in an uneasy united front, the Provisional Executive Committee of the South, but its ascendancy within the committee was marginal.[5] The fatal blow to Viet Minh ambitions in the south, however, resulted not so much from the fragmentation of the nationalist movement there as from arrangements made at the Potsdam Conference in the summer of 1945. The conference stipulated that Chinese troops would reoccupy Vietnam north of the 16th parallel and British forces would take over in the south. General Douglas Gracey, the British commander, arrived in Saigon on September 12, 1945. Despite orders to confine his activities to disarming the Japanese, Gracey permitted French prisoners of war to secure arms and stood aside while they executed a coup, taking over governmental authority from the Committee of the South in Saigon.[6] The French military commander, General Leclerc, arrived shortly thereafter and proceeded to "pacify" the countryside. The French takeover was officially completed with the arrival of Admiral Thierry d'Argenlieu as High Commissioner and the subsequent withdrawal of British troops in January 1946.

The Chinese troops who arrived in the north under the command of General Lu Han in early September 1945 created different but equally difficult problems for the Viet Minh. With them came the Dong Minh Hoi (the Vietnam Revolutionary League—Cach Menh Dong Minh Hoi), a Kuomintang-sponsored nationalist coalition, and the VNQDD. Operating under an umbrella of Chinese protection, these organizations demanded inclusion in Ho Chi Minh's government in positions of leadership. The ICP was officially dissolved on November 11, 1945, as a political concession, and was replaced with an Association of Marxist Studies. To give the government some semblance of legality and to improve its relations with the victorious Allies, the Viet Minh organized national elections in January 1946. Even before the elections were held, the Viet Minh allotted the VNQDD and Dong Minh Hoi 50 seats and 20 seats respectively in the new National Assembly.[7] A new coalition government emerged including representatives of both opposition parties, but the government continued to be guided by the Viet Minh and President Ho Chi Minh.

The presence of these Kuomintang-supported nationalists in the government was turned into a political asset by the Viet Minh, who emphasized the former's share in the responsibility for an unpopular agreement signed with France on

---

5. Initially the committee was comprised of 9 members, of whom 6 were Communists. It was thereafter reconstituted with 9 nationalists to 4 Communists (Devillers, p. 156).

6. For several days afterward, terror reigned in Saigon, as first the French settlers and then the Vietnamese reacted with violence.

7. Sacks, p. 159. An official source, in reporting the election results, gives them a total of 48 seats, as follows: 22 to the Dong Minh Hoi and 26 to the VNQDD (Viet-Nam Delegation in France, Information Service, *The Democratic Republic of Viet-Nam* [Paris: Imprimerie Centrale Commerciale, 1948], p. 13).

March 6, 1946. By terms of this agreement France recognized the Democratic Republic of Vietnam as a "free state, having its own government, parliament, army and treasury, belonging to the Indochinese Federation and to the French Union."[8] France also agreed to sponsor a referendum to determine whether Tonkin, Annam, and Cochinchina should be united and gradually to withdraw French troops from Vietnam. The DRV in turn promised not to oppose the arrival of French troops sent to relieve the Chinese occupation.

The March 6 accord provided both sides with a breathing spell but was considered definitive by neither. The provision to allow French troops unimpeded access to the north provoked considerable public outcry, and it took the combined eloquence of DRV Commander in Chief Vo Nguyen Giap and Ho Chi Minh to secure approval for this risky compromise.[9] The Viet Minh used the time gained in signing the accord to consolidate its hold on the government, eliminate its more extremist opponents, and press for further negotiations.[10] Subsequent conferences proved fruitless, however; both at Dalat in the latter part of April 1946 and at Fontainebleau in early July, negotiators on both sides found it impossible to reach an understanding. Two basic issues—what constituted a "free state" within the French Union and the status of Cochinchina—proved insurmountable obstacles to an agreement.[11]

Following the failure to salvage more than a *modus vivendi* from the Fontainebleau conference, the situation in the north rapidly deteriorated. On November 22,

---

8. Text in Allan B. Cole, ed., *Conflict in Indo-China and International Repercussions: A Documentary History, 1945–1955* (Ithaca, NY: Cornell University Press, 1956), pp. 40–41. [Reading 12 presents the text of this agreement (by a different translator).—eds.]

9. In fact, the situation was so tenuous that the Viet Minh insisted on keeping negotiations secret until other nationalist parties could be implicated in the settlement. (Donald Lancaster, *The Emancipation of French Indochina* [London: Oxford University Press, 1961], p. 145). For a summary of the public speeches of Ho and Giap explaining the necessity for accepting limitations on Vietnam's independence in view of unfavorable international circumstances, see Devillers, pp. 228–231.

10. During the short-lived reign of the Committee of the South and even after the French coup, the Viet Minh, under the direction of the veteran Communist Tran Van Giau, had been busy strengthening its hold by eliminating its opponents, principally the Trotskyists, many of whom were arrested, assassinated, or otherwise removed from the scene. Giau also alienated the Cao Dai and the Hoa Hao. In the north, the Viet Minh bided its time until the Chinese withdrawal. Then, with French assistance, Vo Nguyen Giap proceeded to crush the anti-French VNQDD and the Dong Minh Hoi (Lancaster, pp. 136–139, 166–167).

11. It has been suggested that during the course of negotiations, Viet Minh leaders became disillusioned by the French Communists' unwillingness to champion the cause of Vietnamese independence and jeopardize their popularity with the French electorate. At that time the French Communists, anxious to preserve *tripartisme* and remain in the government, probably counseled moderation to the Vietnamese on the assumption that the forthcoming election in France would put a Communist-led government into power (Lancaster, p. 162). Gordon Wright reinforces this viewpoint with the observation that after the 1946 election the Communists openly opposed French national sentiment for the first time since liberation by refusing to vote special credits to finance France's military action in Vietnam (Gordon Wright, *The Reshaping of French Democracy* [New York: Reynal & Hitchcock, 1948], pp. 249–250).

1946, fighting broke out in the port city of Haiphong, and the following day the French bombarded the Vietnamese quarter of the city. On December 19, after French military authorities ordered the disarming of the Viet Minh militia (Tu Ve), the Vietnamese attacked French positions in Hanoi and were driven out after bitter fighting. The war had begun. And the outbreak of hostilities succeeded in accomplishing for the Viet Minh what it had been unable to achieve on its own—the rallying of Vietnamese of all political beliefs to the Viet Minh banner in the struggle against French colonial rule.[12]

Loss of an Empire

The war was fought on both sides with extreme violence and cruelty. It raged the length and breadth of the country for almost eight years and produced severe suffering among the rural population. Initially victorious French troops cleared the major cities and towns of DRV forces, which withdrew into the mountain strongholds of northern Vietnam and inaccessible swamplands in the south. There, General Giap regrouped his men and braced for a protracted, three-stage guerrilla war in accordance with Mao Tse-tung's guiding principle, that of a "nation-wide, total and long-term" resistance.[13] While the Vietnam People's Army (VPA) was making extensive preparations for waging a political-military "people's war"[14] dependent for its success on winning popular support and securing a peasant base for its operations,[15] French military strategists clung to classic concepts of warfare based on conventional tactics and necessitating the maintenance of heavily fortified positions and extensive supply lines. French control thus centered on urban areas and lines of communication, and a military stalemate was produced. The international situation turned favorable to the DRV with the arrival of the Chinese Communist army on the Vietnamese border in December 1949. This facilitated the flow of

---

12. Whether or not a more flexible French policy at this time could have caused a permanent rift between the Vietnamese independence movement and international communism is an interesting—but unanswerable—question. However, the element of nationalism and the component of non-Communist nationalists in the Viet Minh was of much more importance in this early period than it is now fashionable to suggest.

13. Hoang Quoc Viet, *Brief Review of the Viet-Nam Situation* (Viet-Nam Information Service, Nov. 1951), p. 8. It has been pointed out that DRV military operations differed in the north and south. Only in northern Vietnam was the Vietnam People's Army equipped to enter stage three by the end of the war. The situation in the south lagged militarily and politically, and some of the pertinent guerrilla concepts, including that of a protracted war, are still operative there. See George K. Tanham, *Communist Revolutionary Warfare: The Vietminh in Indochina* (New York: Praeger, 1961), p. 15 and *passim*.

14. For an elaboration of Giap's views on guerrilla warfare in general and the unique aspects of the Vietnamese war, see Vo Nguyen Giap, *People's War, People's Army* (New York: Praeger, 1962). [See also Readings 15, 30, 68.—eds.]

15. The peasants were expected to provide food, shelter, intelligence, transport, and hiding places. This principle of Mao's is called "security of the rear" (Tanham, p. 23).

military aid to the VPA and eventually produced the proper conditions for launching a general counteroffensive.

Their failure to win by force of arms alone led French authorities to attempt a political counter to DRV leadership of the independence movement: they proposed to establish a nationalist government under ex-Emperor Bao Dai. The French government eventually agreed to Bao Dai's moderate demands for authority over internal affairs and, in the Elysée Agreements of March 1949, sanctioned the unification of Vietnam and its entry into the French Union as an Associated State. Bao Dai returned to Vietnam in April 1949 as "head of state" of a unified Vietnam. His regime took over many administrative services from French authorities and assumed a number of symbolic functions of government. But little real transfer of power was effected, nor could it be so long as France retained control over foreign relations and defense.[16] Caught between French intransigence and Vietnamese aspirations, Bao Dai found himself without either political prestige or authority, his position dependent upon French military might. For the vast majority of Vietnamese, the issue still remained colonialism versus nationalism.

Before 1950 DRV energies were absorbed in the basic issue of survival; its efforts were directed primarily toward building up its armed forces and securing bases of support in peasant villages.[17] To attract peasant loyalty without alienating the landlords, the government moved cautiously in the area of agrarian reform. It made an effort to satisfy peasant land hunger by redistributing lands belonging to "French colonialists and Vietnamese traitors"[18] but affirmed its respect for the institution of private property and its desire to rally all sectors of the population, under the slogan of "independence and unity," in the common cause of ending French colonial rule. To facilitate the spread of its political propaganda, the DRV initiated an intensive anti-illiteracy program; social and economic reforms were emphasized; and adherence to communism or belief in the class struggle were specifically disavowed.[19]

The DRV shifted its political strategy in 1940–1950. Although the framework of a national front government was maintained, the DRV openly acknowledged its

---

16. Furthermore, French nationals were guaranteed their privileged legal status and economic interests; fiscal policy continued in French hands with the piaster tied to the franc; and the French military command controlled the Vietnamese army.

17. Sacks, pp. 162–164.

18. General agrarian legislation was passed in July 1949. The new law attacked the major problems of excessive land rents and usury rates by reducing rents a flat 25 per cent, regulating money-lending, and guaranteeing certain rights of tenure to the tenant farmer. [For a more recent account, see William J. Duiker, *The Communist Road to Power in Vietnam* (Boulder, Colo.: Westview Press, 1981).—eds.]

19. Ho Chi Minh stated: "We do not advocate class struggle for an obvious reason. All the classes of Viet-Nam have been bled white beyond recovery by the French imperialists. . . . The yellow five-corner star (of Viet-Nam) . . . symbolized the solidarity of the five classes of the people, namely the intellectuals, the farmers, the workers, the traders and the soldiers. . . . Nearly all the present members of the government are intellectuals" (*Bulletin of the Viet-Nam American Friendship Association*, published by Vietnam News Service [New York, July 21,1947] p. 5).

Communist ties, both internally and internationally. Diplomatic relations were established with Communist China and the Soviet Union in January 1950, and the ICP was reconstituted as the Vietnam Workers' Party (Lao Dong Dang) on March 3, 1951, its leadership of the DRV publicly affirmed. In 1953 a Communist-type agrarian reform program was begun in earnest, as the first step toward transforming the North Vietnamese economy along socialist lines.

The United States accorded diplomatic recognition to the Bao Dai government on February 7, 1950, and increased its already substantial financial commitment to the French military effort in Vietnam. The deteriorating French military position, however, led to France's acceptance of the possibility of arriving at a negotiated settlement with the DRV, and an international conference to discuss both Indochina and Korea was convoked. Meanwhile, General Giap attacked the heavily fortified French position at Dien Bien Phu, in the northwestern mountains near the border of Laos. Despite a heroic defense by French Union forces, Viet Minh strategy and arms proved superior, and the world watched a colonial power defeated on the field of battle. The French government, citing the massive Chinese equipment, especially heavy artillery, brought into play at Dien Bien Phu, appealed for direct United States military intervention in the form of an air strike. The American government refused this request when Britain urged that a peaceful solution be sought at the Great Powers meeting at Geneva.

On May 8, 1954, the Indochina phase of the Geneva Conference opened,[20] only one day after the fall of Dien Bien Phu. French desires to end "la sale guerre," as the inconclusive and demoralizing war in Indochina had been dubbed, was reflected in the investiture of Pierre Mendès-France as Premier of France on June 17, 1954. He dramatically promised to reach an honorable settlement at Geneva by July 20 or resign.

Mendès-France met his deadline, and a cease-fire accord was signed in the early morning of July 21. It provided for the provisional partition of Vietnam at the 17th parallel;[21] staged withdrawal of all troops to their respective zones, to be completed within 300 days; military equipment to enter Vietnam on a replacement basis only and troops on a rotation basis only, with introduction of new military personnel or war material from the outside expressly forbidden; free movement of civilians between the two zones until the end of the 300-day troop evacuation period; and the establishment of an International Armistice Control Commission[22] to supervise the execution of the provisions. A 13-point Final Declaration, agreed

---

20. It was attended by the United States, the United Kingdom, France, the Associated States of Vietnam, Cambodia, and Laos, the Union of Soviet Socialist Republics, the Chinese People's Republic, and the Democratic Republic of Vietnam.

21. According to Raymond Aron there existed a secret agreement between Mendès-France and Molotov whereby Russia would force the DRV to agree to generous armistice terms in return for France's rejection of the European Defense Community (Lancaster, pp. 336–337).

22. The Armistice Commission was made up of representatives of Canada, Poland, and India, with India serving as chairman. For details see *Further Documents Relating to the Discussion of Indochina at the Geneva Conference*, Misc. no. 20 (London: H.M. Stationery Office, June 1954).

to by a roll call of all members of the conference with the exception of the United
States and the State of Vietnam, made general arrangements for national North-
South elections to unify Vietnam, to be held in July 1956, preceded by consulta-
tions beginning one year previously, between the "competent representative au-
thorities of the two zones."[23] July 1956 passed without national elections, and
Vietnam remained split between the two separate and competing political entities,
the Communist-run Democratic Republic in the North and the American-supported
Republic of Vietnam in the South.

7. Founding of the Doc-Lap Dong Minh Hoi (June 1941)*

By Ho Chi Minh

*In the northern village of Pac Bo, Cao Bang province, on the Sino-Vietnamese
border, the Viet Minh was founded and with it the beginnings of a territorial base
and an armed force. As one historian has put it, the Viet Minh united what "proved
to be an unstoppable combination of Vietnamese nationalism and communism."* [1]
*Here, as in his famous "Letter from Abroad," written a few weeks after this found-
ing document, Ho appealed to the "common cause" of the entire Vietnamese
people and called forth centuries of heroes to join in the struggle: "The sacred
call of the fatherland is resounding in our ears, the ardent blood of our heroic
predecessors is seething in our hearts. The fighting spirit of the people is mounting
before our eyes." It is important to add that this was not to be a national victory*

---

23. In a unilateral declaration the United States took note of partition arrangements and pledged
"to seek to achieve unity through free elections supervised by the United Nations to insure that they
are conducted fairly." The declaration further provided that the United States "would view any renewal
of the aggression . . . as seriously threatening international peace and security" (Cole, ed., p. 175).
The State of Vietnam refused to agree even verbally to the partition provision and reserved the right
to "safeguard the national interests of the Vietnamese people." See *New York Times*, July 21, 1954,
dispatch by Thomas J. Hamilton. See also Bernard B. Fall, "The Cease Fire in Indochina—An Appraisal, II," *Far Eastern Survey*, XXIII (Oct. 1954), 153. According to a report by Tillman Durdin,
"A number of members of the Viet Minh delegation have openly declared Chinese and Molotov
pressure forced them to accept less than they rightfully should have obtained" (*New York Times*, July
25, 1954). [Durdin was one of a group of journalists close to the Saigon Military Mission (SMM) in
its early post-Geneva years. See Reading 19.—eds.]

*Revolutionary League for the Independence of Vietnam (Viet Minh). The selection is from a
letter dated June 6, 1941, of Nguyen Ai Quoc (Ho Chi Minh), in Ho Chi Minh, *Selected Works* (4
Vols., Hanoi: Foreign Languages Publishing House, 1960–1962), II, 151–154.

1. James Pinckney Harrison, *The Endless War: Fifty Years of Struggle in Vietnam* (New York:
The Free Press, 1982), p. 83.

alone, but a revolutionary one, too: "the Vietnamese revolution will certainly triumph. The world revolution will certainly triumph." [2] *The Viet Minh itself, in Ho's conception, was to be an umbrella organization representing all classes of Vietnamese society.* [3]

Elders! Prominent personalities! Intellectuals, peasants, workers, traders, and soldiers! Dear compatriots!

Since the French were defeated by the Germans, their forces have been completely disintegrated. However, with regard to our people, they continue to plunder us pitilessly, suck all our blood, and carry out a barbarous policy of all-out terrorism and massacre. Concerning their foreign policy, they bow their heads and kneel down, shamelessly cutting our land for Siam;[4] without a single word of protest, they heartlessly offer our interests to Japan. As a result, our people suffer under a double yoke: they serve not only as buffaloes and horses to the French invaders but also as slaves to the Japanese plunderers. Alas! What sin have our people committed to be doomed to such a wretched plight!

Now, the opportunity has come for our liberation. France itself is unable to dominate our country. As to the Japanese, on the one hand they are bogged in China, on the other, they are hamstrung by the British and American forces, and certainly cannot use all their forces to contend with us. If our entire people are united and single-minded, we are certainly able to smash the picked French and Japanese armies.

Some hundreds of years ago, when our country was endangered by the Mongolian invasion, our elders under the Tran dynasty rose up indignantly and called on their sons and daughters throughout the country to rise as one in order to kill the enemy. Finally they saved their people from danger, and their good name will be carried into posterity for all time. The elders and prominent personalities of our country should follow the example set by our forefathers in the glorious task of national salvation.

Rich people, soldiers, workers, peasants, intellectuals, employees, traders, youth, and women who warmly love your country! At present time national liberation is the most important problem. Let us unite together! As one mind and strength we shall overthrow the Japanese and French and their jackals in order to save people from the situation between boiling water and burning heat.

Dear compatriots!

---

2. Ho Chi Minh, *Selected Writings* (Hanoi, 1977), pp. 44–46.

3. See David Marr, *Vietnamese Tradition on Trial, 1920–1945* (Berkeley: University of California Press, 1981), pp. 400–412 for a discussion of the many elements of Vietnamese tradition and Marxist-Leninist practice that went into the theory and functioning of the Viet Minh.

4. Taking advantage of the French defeat in Europe, Siam [Thailand] raised ancient claims to French territory in Indochina, backing up these claims with military moves that the French could halt only with the aid of a Japanese fleet. By negotiations carried out through 1941 France was obliged to cede considerable territory to Siam. See Donald Lancaster, *The Emancipation of French Indochina* (London: Oxford University Press, 1961), pp. 94–95.—eds.

National Salvation is the common cause to the whole of our people. Every Vietnamese must take part in it. He who has money will contribute his money, he who has strength will contribute his strength, he who has talent will contribute his talent. I pledge to use all my modest abilities to follow you, and am ready for the last sacrifice.

Revolutionary fighters!

The hour has struck! Raise aloft the insurrectionary banner and guide the people throughout the country to overthrow the Japanese and French! The sacred call of the fatherland is resounding in your ears; the blood of our heroic predecessors who sacrificed their lives is stirring in your hearts! The fighting spirit of the people is displayed everywhere before you! Let us rise up quickly! Compatriots throughout the country, rise up quickly! United with each other, unify your action to overthrow the Japanese and the French. Victory to Vietnam's Revolution!

Victory to the World's Revolution!

8. *Imperial Abdication (August 1945)**

By Bao Dai

Bao Dai's abdication was his first and last act of genuine nationalism. Raised in France, he was brought back to Vietnam by the French in 1933 as Emperor. Promising reform and "modernization," Bao Dai tried to gather conservative nationalists around his throne. Ngo Dinh Diem was approached and briefly lent his name to the regime but soon left. Rather than reform, repression intensified in this period. After the Japanese coup de force in March 1945, Bao Dai was once again a willing servant, accepting "independence" from the Japanese, and declaring Vietnam unified and free at last of French colonial control. After his abdication in August 1945, Ho Chi Minh appointed him, as part of a broad government of national reconciliation, to be Supreme Political Adviser. By accepting this appointment, Bao Dai made it difficult for the French to use him as an anti-Communist rallying point. But not for long. As fighting intensified between the Democratic Republic of Vietnam and France, Bao Dai found life on the French side of the lines far more attractive than continued service with the Republic. By 1949, he was ready once more to lend himself to colonial schemes, this time as "head of state" under the Élysée Agreements of March 1949.

The happiness of the people of Vietnam!
The Independence of Vietnam!

La République [Hanoi], Issue no. 1 (October 1, 1945), translated in Harold R. Isaacs, ed., *New Cycle in Asia: Selected Documents on Major International Development in the Far East, 1943–1947* (New York: Macmillan, 1947), pp. 161–162.

To achieve these ends, we have declared ourself ready for any sacrifice and we desire that our sacrifice be useful to the people.

Considering that the unity of all our compatriots is at this time our country's need, we recalled to our people on August 22: "In this decisive hour of our national history, union means life and division means death."

In view of the powerful democratic spirit growing in the north of our kingdom, we feared that conflict between north and south would be inevitable if we were to wait for a National Congress to decide us, and we know that this conflict, if it occurred, would plunge our people into suffering and would play the game of the invaders.

We cannot but have a certain feeling of melancholy upon thinking of our glorious ancestors who fought without respite for 400 years to aggrandize our country from Thuan Hoa to Hatien.

Despite this, and strong in our convictions, we have decided to abdicate and we transfer power to the Democratic Republican Government.

Upon leaving our throne, we have only three wishes to express:

1. We request that the new Government take care of the dynastic temples and royal tombs.

2. We request the new Government to deal fraternally with all the parties and groups which have fought for the independence of our country even though they have not closely followed the popular movement; to do this in order to give them the opportunity to participate in the reconstruction of the country and to demonstrate that the new regime is built upon the absolute union of the entire population.

3. We invite all parties and groups, all classes of society, as well as the royal family, to solidarize in unreserved support of the democratic government with a view to consolidating the national independence.

As for us, during twenty years' reign we have known much bitterness. Henceforth, we shall be happy to be a free citizen in an independent country. We shall allow no one to abuse our name or the name of the royal family in order to sow dissent among our compatriots.

Long live the independence of Vietnam!

Long live our Democratic Republic!

9. Vietnam Declaration of Independence (September 2, 1945)*

Throughout the period of Japanese occupation, the Viet Minh had been organizing for eventual armed uprising and independence. Formation of youth groups, wom-

---

*From Ho Chi Minh, *Selected Works* (4 vols; Hanoi: Foreign Languages Publishing House, 1960–1962), III, pp. 17–21.

en's and peasants' associations, a literacy campaign, and self-defense training, had all been part of the Viet Minh effort during the war years. These activities continued after the Japanese seized power in March 1945, until the moment was considered ripe for a general insurrection. In August 1945 the Japanese surrendered unconditionally; in the same month the Vietnamese August Revolution began. It was, David Marr writes, "in the first instance a giant, spontaneous outpouring of emotion, and secondarily a well-organized Leninist seizure of power." [1] *By September, a functioning government, calling itself the Democratic Republic of Vietnam, was a reality, well established before the arrangements made for Vietnam by the powers at Potsdam could begin.*

Archimedes Patti, an American OSS agent who was in Vietnam at the time, expressed surprise when he was read a draft text of the declaration of independence Ho Chi Minh had prepared. Hearing the words of the American declaration quoted, he "turned to Ho in amazement and asked if he really intended to use it in his declaration. I don't know why it nettled me—perhaps a feeling of proprietary right, or something equally inane. . . . Ho sat back in his chair, his palms together with fingertips touching his lips ever so lightly, as though meditating. Then with a gentle smile he asked softly, 'Should I not use it?'" On the first Sunday in September, before a vast crowd in Hanoi's Ba Dinh square, Ho Chi Minh began to read the declaration. After the opening lines he paused, looked out at the crowd and asked: "'Do you hear me distinctly, fellow countrymen?' The crowd roared back: 'YES!'" [2]

"A ll men are created equal. They are endowed by their Creator with certain inalienable rights; among these are Life, Liberty, and the pursuit of Happiness."

This immortal statement was made in the Declaration of Independence of the United States of America in 1776. In a broader sense, this means: All the peoples on the earth are equal from birth, all the peoples have a right to live, to be happy and free.

The Declaration of the French Revolution made in 1791 on the Rights of Man and the Citizen also states: "All men are born free and with equal rights, and must always remain free and have equal rights."

Those are undeniable truths.

Nevertheless, for more than eighty years, the French imperialists, abusing the standard of Liberty, Equality, and Fraternity, have violated our Fatherland and oppressed our fellow-citizens. They have acted contrary to the ideals of humanity and justice.

---

1. David Marr, *Vietnamese Tradition on Trial* (Berkeley: University of California Press, 1981), p. 408.
2. Archimedes L. A. Patti, *Why Vietnam? Prelude to America's Albatross* (Berkeley: University of California Press, 1980), pp. 223, 250.

In the field of politics, they have deprived our people of every democratic liberty.

They have enforced inhuman laws; they have set up three distinct political regimes in the North, the Center and the South of Vietnam in order to wreck our national unity and prevent our people from being united.

They have built more prisons than schools. They have mercilessly slain our patriots; they have drowned our uprisings in rivers of blood.

They have fettered public opinion; they have practised obscurantism against our people.

To weaken our race they have forced us to use opium and alcohol.

In the field of economics, they have fleeced us to the backbone, impoverished our people, and devastated our land.

They have robbed us of our rice fields, our mines, our forests, and our raw materials. They have monopolized the issuing of bank-notes and the export trade.

They have invented numerous unjustifiable taxes and reduced our people, especially our peasantry, to a state of extreme poverty.

They have hampered the prospering of our national bourgeoisie; they have mercilessly exploited our workers.

In the autumn of 1940, when the Japanese Fascists violated Indochina's territory to establish new bases in their fight against the Allies, the French imperialists went down on their bended knees and handed over our country to them.

Thus, from that date, our people were subjected to the double yoke of the French and the Japanese. Their sufferings and miseries increased. The result was that from the end of last year to the beginning of this year, from Quang Tri province to the North of Vietnam, more than two million of our fellow-citizens died from starvation. On March 9, the French troops were disarmed by the Japanese. The French colonialists either fled or surrendered showing that not only were they incapable of "protecting" us, but that, in the span of five years, they had twice sold our country to the Japanese.

On several occasions before March 9, the Vietminh League urged the French to ally themselves with it against the Japanese. Instead of agreeing to this proposal, the French colonialists so intensified their terrorist activities against the Vietminh members that before fleeing they massacred a great number of our political prisoners detained at Yen Bay and Caobang.

Notwithstanding all this, our fellow-citizens have always manifested toward the French a tolerant and humane attitude. Even after the Japanese putsch of March 1945, the Vietminh League helped many Frenchmen to cross the frontier, rescued some of them from Japanese jails, and protected French lives and property.

From the autumn of 1940, our country had in fact ceased to be a French colony and had become a Japanese possession.

After the Japanese had surrendered to the Allies, our whole people rose to regain our national sovereignty and to found the Democratic Republic of Vietnam.

The truth is that we have wrested our independence from the Japanese and not from the French.

The French have fled, the Japanese have capitulated, Emperor Bao Dai has abdicated. Our people have broken the chains which for nearly a century have fettered them and have won independence for the Fatherland. Our people at the same time have overthrown the monarchic regime that has reigned supreme for dozens of centuries. In its place has been established the present Democratic Republic.

For these reasons, we, members of the Provisional Government, representing the whole Vietnamese people, declare that from now on we break off all relations of a colonial character with France; we repeal all the international obligation that France has so far subscribed to on behalf of Vietnam and we abolish all the special rights the French have unlawfully acquired in our Fatherland.

The whole Vietnamese people, animated by a common purpose, are determined to fight to the bitter end against any attempt by the French colonialists to reconquer their country.

We are convinced that the Allied nations which at Tehran and San Francisco have acknowledged the principles of self-determination and equality of nations, will not refuse to acknowledge the independence of Vietnam.

A people who have courageously opposed French domination for more than eight years, a people who have fought side by side with the Allies against the Fascists during these last years, such a people must be free and independent.

For these reasons, we, members of the Provisional Government of the Democratic Republic of Vietnam, solemnly declare to the world that Vietnam has the right to be a free and independent country—and in fact is so already. The entire Vietnamese people are determined to mobilize all their physical and mental strength, to sacrifice their lives and property in order to safeguard their independence and liberty.

10. The French Return: Two State Department Views (April 1945)*

In Southeast Asia as elsewhere in the world, the postwar disposition of disputed territory was of constant concern to the Allies. For De Gaulle, leader of the anti-Vichy Free French forces, participation in the "liberation" of Indochina from Japanese control was crucial if France was to reclaim its colonial empire after the war; the British were less devoted to Gaullist ambition than they were to the prin-

---

*A. Excerpt from memorandum for the President, Division of European Affairs, April 20, 1945, in *U.S.-Vietnam Relations 1945–1967: The Pentagon Papers* (Washington, D. C.: GPO), Bk. 8, V.B. 2, pp. 7–8. Hereafter *The Pentagon Papers* (GPO ed.). B. Excerpt from memorandum for the President, Far Eastern Division, April 21, 1945. Ibid., pp. 13–15.

ciple of continued colonial control as such; and the United States, anxious to create a world in what historian William Appleman Williams calls its "anticolonial imperialist" image, sought to constrain the French. As President Roosevelt wrote to Secretary of State Cordell Hull in January 1944, Indochina should be administered by an international trusteeship: "France has had the country . . . for nearly one hundred years, and the people are worse off than they were at the beginning. . . . The people of Indochina are entitled to something better than that."[1]

By March 1945, Roosevelt's position had softened. In the face of British and French resistance, he now spoke only of limiting French control rather than establishing an international trusteeship. Moreover, the State Department, in both its Far Eastern and European Divisions, was more concerned with the postwar strength of France than with that country's sorry record of colonial exploitation. To be sure, some aspects of former French control would have to be modified—its policy of "commercial exclusiveness," for example. The problem, as one State Department memo made abundantly clear, was this: "It is to the interest of the United States to dissociate itself in every feasible way from the imperialism of the European powers in the Far East."[2] The issue, of course, lay in how the word "feasible" would be interpreted.

Some indication of what was and was not feasible is given in the two readings below, one a memorandum on Indochina policy from the European division of the State Department, the other a rival memorandum from the Far Eastern division. Both were responding to an urgent State-War-Navy Coordinating Committee request for policy clarification. The revisions by the Far Eastern division (in the direction of pressuring the French to make reforms) so deeply disturbed Assistant Secretary of State James C. Dunn that he left an angry message for Acting Secretary of State Joseph Grew arguing that no memorandum be sent to the President rather than sending the one drafted by the Far Eastern division. The United States might, if it chose, use its influence to urge France to improve conditions in Indochina. But now was the time "for us to cooperate wholeheartedly with France." In a conversation with French Foreign Minister Georges Bidault, Dunn remarked, "the latter stressed his fears for western civilization as a result of the dominance of Russia in Europe."[3] The message ends in this apparent non sequitur. But its internal logic—the link between support for French colonialism and the defense of "western civilization"—became commonplace in the Truman years.

Given this background it is not surprising that Truman, at Potsdam in August, agreed to a plan of military operations that divided Indochina at the 16th parallel,

---

1. President Franklin D. Roosevelt to Secretary of State Cordell Hull, January 24, 1944. In *The Pentagon Papers* (GPO edition), Bk. 1, V.B. 1, p. A–14.

2. Draft memorandum by G. H. Blakeslee, Far Eastern Division, Department of State, April 1945. In Gareth Porter, ed., *Vietnam: A History in Documents* (New York: New American Library, 1981), p. 15.

3. James C. Dunn to Joseph Grew, April 23, 1945, *The Pentagon Papers* (GPO edition), Bk. 8, V.B. 2, p. 18.

giving the British control over the south and the Chinese, under Chiang Kai-shek, control over the north. It was clear at the time that this division would facilitate the return, at least in the south, of French troops. In September 1945, British General Douglas D. Gracey released French prisoners of war, re-armed Japanese troops and then ordered these and other units under his command to seize power from the Viet Minh government, which had been established earlier in the month. There was no protest from the United States.[4]

A. The European Desk Perspective

General de Gaulle and his Government have made it abundantly clear that they expect a proposed Indo-Chinese federation to function within the framework of the "French Union." There is consequently not the slightest possibility at the present time or in the foreseeable future that France will volunteer to place Indo-China under an international trusteeship, or will consent to any program of international accountability which is not applied to the colonial possessions of other powers. If an effort were made to exert pressure on the French Government, such action would have to be taken by the United States alone for France could rely upon the support of other colonial powers, notably Great Britain and the Netherlands. Such action would likewise run counter to the established American policy of aiding France to regain her strength in order that she may be better fitted to share responsibility in maintaining the peace of Europe and the world.

Recommendations

In the light of the above considerations, the following recommendations, which have been communicated to the War and Navy Departments, are submitted for your approval.

1. The Government of the United States should neither oppose the restoration of Indo-China to France, with or without a program of international accountability, nor take any action toward French overseas possessions which it is not prepared to take or suggest with regard to the colonial possessions of our other Allies.

2. The Government of the United States should continue to exert its influence with the French in the direction of having them effect a liberalization of their past policy of limited opportunities for native participation in government and administration, as well as a liberalization of restrictive French economic policies formerly pursued in Indo-China.

3. The French Provisional Government should be informed confidentially that, owing to the need of concentrating all our resources in the Pacific on operations already planned, large-scale military operations aimed directly at the liberation of Indo-China cannot be contemplated at this time.

---

4. On this period see Archimedes Patti, *Why Vietnam? Prelude to America's Albatross* (Berkeley: University of California Press, 1980), Chap. 32. See also Reading 12.

4. French offers of military and naval assistance in the Pacific should be considered on their merits as bearing upon the objective of defeating Japan, as in the case of British and Dutch proposals. The fact that acceptance of a specific proposal might serve to strengthen French claims for the restoration of Indo-China to France should not be regarded as grounds for rejection. On the contrary, acceptance of French proposals for military assistance in the defeat of Japan should be regarded as desirable in principle, subject always to military requirements in the theater of operations.

5. While avoiding specific commitments with regard to the amount of character of any assistance which the United States may give to the French resistance forces in Indo-China, this Government should continue to afford all possible assistance provided it does not interfere with the requirements of other planned operations.

6. In addition to the aid which we are able to bring from the China theater of operations to the French forces resisting the Japanese in Indo-China, the United States should oppose no obstacle to the implementation of proposals looking toward the despatch of assistance to those forces from the southeast Asia theater of operations, provided such assistance does not constitute a diversion of resources which the Combined Chiefs of Staff consider are needed elsewhere.

B. The Far Eastern Desk Perspective

[Paragraphs omitted.—eds.]

4. It is established American policy to aid France to regain her strength in order that she may be better fitted to share responsibility in maintaining the peace of Europe—where her chief interests lie—and of the world. However, in pursuing this policy, the United States must not jeopardize its own increasingly important interests in Southeast Asia.

5. The United States Government has publicly taken the position that it recognizes the sovereign jurisdiction of France over French possessions overseas when those possessions are resisting the enemy, and has expressed the hope that it will see the reestablishment of the integrity of French territory.

6. Until the last few weeks the French administration of Indochina has collaborated with the Japanese in marked distinction to the administrations of colonial areas belonging to our other Allies.

7. President Roosevelt recognized the future increasing importance to the United States of Southeast Asia. He saw the necessity of aiding the 150,000,000 people there to achieve improved social, economic and political standards.

He realized that dynamic forces leading toward self-government are growing in Asia; that the United States—as a great democracy—cannot and must not try to retard this development but rather act in harmony with it; and that social, economic or political instability in the area may threaten the peace and stability of the Far East and indeed the world.

8. As his solution of this problem, as it relates to Indochina, President Roosevelt long favored placing Indochina under a trusteeship. However, on April 3,

1945, the Secretary of State with the approval of the President issued a statement relative to the plans approved at Yalta which would indicate that Indochina could come under the trusteeship structure only by voluntary action of the French. It is abundantly clear that there is no possibility at the present time or in the foreseeable future that France will volunteer to place Indochina under trusteeship, or consent to any program of international accountability which is not applied to the colonial possessions of other powers. If an effort were made to exert pressure on the French Government, such action would have to be taken by the United States alone for France could rely upon the support of other colonial powers, notably Great Britain and the Netherlands.

9. The prewar French administration in Indochina was the least satisfactory colonial administration in Asia, both as regards the development and interest of the native peoples and as regards economic relations with other countries. Among the Annamites there is increasing opposition to French rule. The Chinese are giving active support to the independence movement. France will probably encounter serious difficulty in reimposing French control in Indochina.

10. If really liberal policies towards Indochina are not adopted by the French—policies which recognize the paramount interest of the native peoples and guarantee within the foreseeable future a genuine opportunity for true, autonomous self-government—there will be substantial bloodshed and unrest for many years, threatening the economic and social progress and the peace and stability of Southeast Asia.

11. On several occasions in the past few years, French authorities have issued policy statements on the future of Indochina. These show a growing trend toward greater autonomy for the French administration of Indochina, but even the recent statement of March 24 is vague and, when examined with care, indicates little intention of permitting genuine self-rule for the Indochinese. The change in French attitude towards Indochina is believed to have been occasioned by clearer realization of the the the anti-French sentiment among the Annamites and a belief that American approval ot French restoration can be won only by a liberalization of its policies towards Indochina.

12. China is exercised at the economic stranglehold which France formerly exercised through control of the Yunan Railroad and the port of Haiphong, and is particularly perturbed at the danger to its southwest flank first made visible by the surrender of Indochina to the Japanese.

13. It is stated American policy that the cession of territory by Indochina to Thailand in 1941 is not recognized and that this territory must be returned to Indochina. This territory, however, had in earlier years been wrested by the French from Thailand and its inhabitants are culturally akin to the Thai. Similarly, parts of Laos are Thai in character. Whatever the legalistic background may be, the entire border region between Indochina and Thailand will be a source of potential conflict unless a fair and appropriate frontier is determined by an impartial international commission. The Thai Government will accept any frontier so determined.

14. It will be an American victory over Japan which will make possible the liberation of Indochina. We are fighting to assure peace and stability in the Far East and will, in fact, bear the major responsibility for its maintenance after the war. Encouragement of and assistance to the peoples of Southeast Asia in developing autonomous, democratic self-rule in close, willing association with major Western powers would not only be in harmony with political trends in that area, but would appear to be the one practical solution which will assure peace and stability in the Far East. If this policy is not followed, the millions who live in that area may well embrace ideologies contrary to our own—or ultimately develop a pan-Asiatic movement against the Western world. It is not unreasonable, therefore, for the United States to insist that the French give adequate assurance as to the implementing of policies in Indochina which we consider essential to assure peace and stability in the Far East.

11. Vietnam's Second Appeal to the United States: Cable to President Harry S. Truman (October 17, 1945)*

By Ho Chi Minh

Part of an unsuccessful campaign to get Western leaders to recognize the legitimacy of Vietnamese national aspirations in the immediate postwar period, this telegram from Ho Chi Minh to US President Harry S. Truman went unanswered. It was in that sense a replay of Ho's similarly unavailing attempt to get in touch with the administration of a previous Democratic president, Woodrow Wilson, a quarter century earlier (Reading 3). The communication to President Harry Truman presented here became generally known after the release of a mass of hitherto secret material on the US war against Vietnam, material that became known as The Pentagon Papers.[1]

Ho Chi Minh summarizes much recent history in this cable: the role of the pro-Nazi Vichy French government in permitting Japanese occupation of Indochina; the support given to the Allied cause by the Viet Minh, who mounted guerrilla actions against the Japanese and received some vague promises of American support for Vietnamese independence after the war; the evident aim of the anti-Vichy French government to restore French hegemony over the former Indochinese em-

---

The Pentagon Papers (GPO ed.), I, pp. 73–74.

1. See the discussion of *The Pentagon Papers*, including the three available editions, in Appendix B.

pire. Whatever validity these historical arguments had, they were insufficient to prevent an American-backed return of these former colonies to France and its inevitable consequence—yet another Vietnamese struggle for the independence they claimed in the August Revolution of 1945.

Establishment of [a United Nations] Advisory Commission for the Far East is heartily welcomed by Vietnamese people in principle. Taking into consideration primo the strategical and economical importance of Vietnam secundo the earnest desire which Vietnam deeply feels and has unanimously manifested to cooperate with the other democracies in the establishment and consolidation of world peace and prosperity we wish to call the attention of the Allied nations on the following points:

First absence of Vietnam and presence of France in the Advisory Commission leads to the conclusion that France is to represent the Vietnamese people at the Commission stop. Such representation is groundless either *de jure* or *de facto*. *De jure* no alliance exists any more between France and Vietnam. Baodai abolished treaties of 1884 and 1863. Baodai voluntarily abdicated to hand over government to Democratic Republican Government [Reading 3—eds.]. Provisional Government rectorated [sic] abolishment of treaties of 1884 and 1863. *De facto* since March ninth France having handed over governing rule to Japan has broken all administrative links with Vietnam, since August 18, 1945, Provisional Government has been a *de facto* independent government in every respect, recent incidents in Saigon instigated by the French roused unanimous disapproval leading to fight for independence.[2]

Second France is not entitled because she had ignominiously sold Indo China to Japan and betrayed the Allies. Third Vietnam is qualified by Atlantic Charter and subsequent peace agreement and by her goodwill and her unflinching stand for democracy to be represented at the Advisory Commission. We are convinced that Vietnam at Commission will be able to bring effective contribution to solution of pending problems in Far East whereas her absence would bring forth unstability [sic] and temporary character to solutions otherwise reached. Therefore we express earnest request to take part in Advisory Commission for Far East. We should be very grateful to your excellency and Premier Attlee Premier Stalin Generalisimo Tchang Kai Shek for the conveyance of our desiderata to the United Nations.

---

2. For the outbreak of Franco-Vietnam conflict, see the Introduction to Part II.—eds.

12. Franco-Vietnamese Agreement on the Independence of Vietnam (March 1946)*

By the spring of 1946, Ho Chi Minh had successfully negotiated with the French to eliminate the troubling presence of Chinese Nationalist troops, whose propensity to loot and rape had increased the suffering of a population still struggling against famine. With their withdrawal, the Vietnamese had also eliminated the possibility of a Chinese-sponsored "nationalist" regime. Now there remained only the French. A compromise agreement reached on March 6 allowed for the return of French troops, agreed to Vietnamese status as a "free" rather than independent state, and bound the French to a referendum on the status of southern Vietnam. For the Vietnamese, the choice was stark. "We agreed to allow 15,000 French troops to enter the North for a specific period of time in order to boot out 180,000 brutal soldiers of Chiang Kai-shek," Vo Nguyen Giap argued. "It is better to sniff French dung for a while," Ho Chi Minh urged his more uncompromising comrades, "than eat China's all our lives."[1]

The agreement was broken almost at once by the French, whose military command in the south simply announced the formation of a separate Republic of Cochin China. Nevertheless, Ho Chi Minh continued to negotiate in France, returning to Vietnam in October with a modus vivendi *which promised political freedom to Vietnamese in the south and worked out details for the establishment of mixed Franco-Vietnamese commissions to supervise foreign trade and customs. It was a dispute over who constituted legitimate authority in Haiphong Harbor that led to the all-out French attack on the city in November 1946, and the renewal of Vietnam's armed struggle for independence.*

In December, Ho Chi Minh appealed to the country as he had in 1941—"those who have rifles will use their rifles: those who have swords will use their swords. . . ." He had worked hard to avoid war: "We are not unaware of what is in store for us. France disposes of terrifying weapons. The struggle will be atrocious." Nevertheless, "the Vietnamese people are willing to endure everything rather than give up their freedom."[2]

1. The French Government recognizes the Republic of Vietnam as a free state, having its Government, its Parliament, its army, and its finances, and forming part of the Indochinese Federation and the French Union.

Bulletin Hebdomadaire, Ministère de la France d'Outremer, no. 67 (March 18, 1946), translated in Harold R. Isaacs, *New Cycle in Asia: Selected Documents on Major International Developments in the Far East, 1943–1947* (New York, 1947), p. 169.

1. Quoted in James Pinckney Harrison, *The Endless War, Fifty Years of Struggle in Vietnam* (New York: The Free Press, 1982), p. 109.

2. Ibid., p. 114. In general, Harrison's account of the 1945–1946 negotiations is excellent, pp. 105–114.

With regard to the unification of the three Ky (Nam Ky, or Cochin China, Trung Ky, or Annam, Bac Ky, or Tonkin), the French Government undertakes to follow the decisions of the people consulted by referendum.

2. The Government of Vietnam declares itself ready to receive the French army in friendly fashion when, in accord with international agreements, it relieves the Chinese troops. An annex attached to the present Preliminary Convention will fix the terms under which the operation of relief will take place.

3. The stipulations formulated above shall enter into effect immediately upon exchange of signatures. Each of the contracting parties shall take necessary steps to end hostilities, to maintain troops in their respective positions, and to create an atmosphere favorable for the immediate opening of friendly and frank negotiations. These negotiations shall deal particularly with the diplomatic relations between Vietnam and foreign states, the future status of Indochina, and economic and cultural interests. Hanoi, Saigon, and Paris may be indicated as the locales of the negotiations. Signed: [Jean] Sainteny, Ho Chi Minh, Vu Huong Khanh.[3]

13. Sponsoring French Colonialism: The State Department Decision (May 1950)*

By Secretary of State Dean Acheson

American military aid to the French began as early as January 1946, and by May 1947, recognition of French sovereignty in Indochina was national policy.[1] When the Chinese Communists proclaimed the establishment of a People's Republic of China in October 1949, US policy moved swiftly to full-scale material support of the French war against the Viet Minh. In the following Reading, Secretary of State Acheson firmly tied American national interests to the victory of French colonialism. By the end of the French war, the United States was paying 80 percent of its cost.

The [French] Foreign Minister and I have just had an exchange of views on the situation in Indochina and are in general agreement both as to the urgency of

---

3. Sainteny was a French intelligence officer who served as French Commissioner to Vietnam in 1945–1946. Vu Huong Khanh was an official in the VNQDD (see Reading 1 for an account of this nationalist, anti-Communist organization).—eds.

*Statement of Secretary of State Dean Acheson at Ministerial Level meeting in Paris (May 8, 1950), *Department of State Bulletin*, XXII (May 22, 1950), p. 821.

1. Archimedes Patti, *Why Vietnam? Prelude to America's Albatross* (Berkeley: University of California Press, 1980), pp. 380, 386.

the situation in that area and as to the necessity for remedial action. We have noted the fact that the problem of meeting the threat to.the security of Vietnam, Cambodia, and Laos which now enjoy independence within the French Union is primarily the responsibility of France and the Governments and peoples of Indochina. The United States recognizes that the solution of the Indochina problem depends both upon the restoration of security and upon the development of genuine nationalism and that United States assistance can and should contribute to these major objectives.

The United States Government, convinced that neither national independence nor democratic evolution exists in any area dominated by Soviet imperialism, considers the situation to be such as to warrant its according economic aid and military equipment to the Associated States of Indochina and to France in order to assist them in restoring stability and permitting these states to pursue their peaceful and democratic development.

14. Taking Up the White Man's Burden: Two American Views (1954)*

By John Foster Dulles and Richard M. Nixon

As French defeat in Indochina became more certain, the necessity for the United States to pick up the anti-communist torch where France dropped it was explained to the public by leading government officials such as Secretary of State Dulles and Vice-President Nixon. The selections below describe the US tactic of seeking peace through war, and freedom through the dispatch of troops to old colonial battlefields. Nixon offers, as well, a succinct description of one possible set of falling dominoes which a Viet Minh victory would initiate. In this version of the game, the main enemy target of the Communists is Japan, an enemy during World War II but now deemed a major force for stability in Asia.

To provide a legal framework for what had already been determined to be a necessary on-going policy of harassment against North Vietnam and sustenance for a non-communist government in the south, in August 1954, the National Security Council recommended the negotiation of a collective security treaty for Southeast Asia. Such a treaty would, the NSC memorandum pointed out, "provide . . . a legal basis to the President to order an attack on Communist China in the event it commits armed aggression which endangers the peace, safety and vital interests of the United States," allow for American assistance to be offered to a

---

*A. Speech to The Overseas Press Club, New York City (March 29, 1954), in *Department of State Bulletin*, XXX (April 12, 1954), pp. 539–540. B. *New York Times*, April 17, 1954.

"legitimate local government which requires assistance to defeat local Communist subversion or rebellion not constituting armed attack," and allow the United States "freedom to use nuclear weapons" if necessary.[1] *One month later, the Southeast Asia Treaty Organization (SEATO) was established, pledging the governments of Australia, France, New Zealand, Pakistan, the Philippines, Thailand, Great Britain, and the United States to come to each others' aid and, of more immediate importance, to the aid of Cambodia, Laos "and the free territory under the jurisdiction of the State of Vietnam," none of which was a signatory.*[2] *The legal framework and the public rationale for full American intervention in Vietnam were now in place.*

A. Opposition to the Spread of Communism by Whatever Means: Secretary of State John Foster Dulles

. . . If the Communist forces won uncontested control over Indochina or any substantial part thereof, they would surely resume the same pattern of aggression against other free peoples in the area.

The propagandists of Red China and Russia make it apparent that the purpose is to dominate all of Southeast Asia. . . .

The United States has shown in many ways its sympathy for the gallant struggle being waged in Indochina by French forces and those of the Associated States.[3] Congress has enabled us to provide material aid to the established governments and their peoples. Also, our diplomacy has sought to deter Communist China from open aggression in that area.

President Eisenhower, in his address of April 16, 1953, explained that a Korean armistice would be a fraud if it merely released aggressive armies for attack elsewhere. I said last September that if Red China sent its own army into Indochina, that would result in grave consequences which might not be confined to Indochina.

Recent statements have been designed to impress upon potential aggressors that aggression might lead to action at places and by means of free-world choosing, so that aggression would cost more than it could gain.

The Chinese Communists have, in fact, avoided the direct use of their own Red Armies in open aggression against Indochina. They have, however, largely stepped up their support of the aggression in that area. Indeed, they promote that aggression by all means short of open invasion.

Under all the circumstances it seems desirable to clarify further the United States position.

---

1. NSC 5492/2 (August 20, 1954), in Gareth Porter, ed., *Vietnam: A History in Documents* (New York: New American Library, 1981), pp. 164–166.

2. For text of the treaty see *Background Information Relating to Southeast Asia and Vietnam* (revised June 16, 1965), Report of the US Senate Committee on Foreign Relations (89th Congress, 1st session) (Washington, D.C.: 1965), pp. 62–66.

3. The reference is to the struggle against the Viet Minh.—eds.

Under the conditions of today, the imposition on Southeast Asia of the political system of Communist Russia and its Chinese Communist ally, by whatever means, must be a grave threat to the whole free community. The United States feels that that possibility should not be passively accepted but should be met by united action. This might involve serious risks. But these risks are far less than those that will face us a few years from now if we dare not be resolute today.

The free nations want peace. However, peace is not had merely by wanting it. Peace has to be worked for and planned for. Sometimes it is necessary to take risks to win peace just as it is necessary in war to take risks to win victory. The chances for peace are usually bettered by letting a potential aggressor know in advance where his aggression could lead him.

I hope that these statements which I make here tonight will serve the cause of peace. . . .

B. Fear of Impending French Defeat: Vice-President Richard M. Nixon

. . . What is to be done [about the war in Indochina]? For one, the problem is not one of materials and wasn't four months ago. More men are needed and the question is where to get them. They will not come from France, for France is tired of the war, as we were tired of Korea. Therefore, additional man power must come from Vietnam, Cambodia, and Laos, particularly Vietnam. The French, however, while slow in training the native soldiers, resent the idea that the United States or others should send men to do the job.

More difficult is the job of spirit. Encouragement must be given to fight and resist. Some say if the French got out, the Vietnamese will fight with more spirit, because they would be fighting for their independence.

But the Vietnamese lack the ability to conduct a war by themselves or govern themselves. If the French withdrew, Indochina would become Communist-dominated within a month.

The United States as a leader of the free world cannot afford further retreat in Asia. It is hoped the United States will not have to send troops there, but if this government cannot avoid it, the Administration must face up to the situation and dispatch forces.

Therefore, the United States must go to Geneva and take a positive stand for united action by the free world. Otherwise it will have to take on the problem alone and try to sell it to the others.

French pressure will be exerted at the conference (beginning April 26) for negotiation and the end of the fighting. The British will take a similar position, because of mounting Labor Party pressure and defections in the Conservative ranks. The British do not want to antagonize Red China, which they have recognized.

This country is the only nation politically strong enough at home to take a position that will save Asia.

Negotiations with the Communists to divide the territory would result in Communist domination of a vital new area. Communist intransigence in Korea perhaps will teach the French and the British the futility of negotiation and bring them over to the plan of "united action" proposed by Secretary of State Dulles [i.e., the SEATO treaty—eds.]. . . .

It should be emphasized that if Indochina went Communist, Red pressures would increase on Malaya, Thailand, and Indonesia and other Asian nations. The main target of the Communists in Indochina, as it was in Korea, is Japan. Conquest of areas so vital to Japan's economy would reduce Japan to an economic satellite of the Soviet Union. . . .

15. Vietnamese Victory: Dien Bien Phu, 1954*

By Vo Nguyen Giap

In the wake of the French defeat in Indochina came a post-factum "battle of the books" in France, during which time various participants delivered their explanations and justifications. Few were more prolific than General Henri Navarre, Commander of French forces in Indochina and initiator of the "Navarre Plan," under which the French fortified the village of Dien Bien Phu, near the Laotian border, and invited the Vietnamese to attack. In his Agonie de l'Indochine *(Paris, 1956), Navarre explained how Dien Bien Phu was to be a trap for his Vietnamese counterpart, General Vo Nguyen Giap. Anticipating the defensive tone of recent US military men, who have tried to explain not why they lost in Vietnam, but why they weren't allowed to win, Navarre complained about the "defeatism and treason" on the home front that hampered French forces in Indochina.[1] But another former French army officer in Indochina put the shortcomings of French commanders into a clearer perspective. In his* Battle of Dienbienphu, *Jules Roy wrote:*

To command in Indochina meant possessing luxurious villas, cars and women, entertaining and intriguing. War was accompanied by a circus of officers, tents, refrigerators, staffs and organizations designed to enable these staffs to move about, sit down, eat and sleep in comfort. How many divisional brigade and regimental commanders knew how to suffer with their men, lead the same life they did, and move about on foot, invisible, silent and formidable as the enemy who surrounded them? How many a battalion commander of the Foreign Legion got a coolie to follow him into action, carrying a cask of wine to warm his guts? In spite of the tons of bombs dropped on the Viet lines of communication, the

---

*Excerpts from Vo Nguyen Giap, *People's War: People's Army* (Hanoi: Foreign Languages Publishing House, 1961), *passim.*

1. Henri Navarre, *Le temps des Vérités* (Paris: Plon, 1979), pp. 280–282.

road by which the People's Army received its munitions was never cut, and it was not Chinese aid which defeated General Navarre, but Peugeot bicycles, with loads of four or five hundred pounds, pushed along by men who never ate their fill and who slept on nylon sheets spread on the ground. General Navarre was not defeated by the enemy's resources, but by his intelligence and his will to win.[2]

Some indication of this will and determination is given in this Reading. Vo Nguyen Giap, former history professor, was Defense Minister of the Democratic Republic of Vietnam.

The Resistance War: A People's War

Following the success of the Revolution, the Party clearly realised the danger of aggression from the French colonialists. Even in the Declaration of Independence [Reading 9—eds.] and the Oath of Independence, the Party called for a heightening of vigilance, and mobilised the people to be prepared to defend the Fatherland.

The French colonialists' aggressive war broke out in Saigon when people's power had not yet been consolidated and great difficulties in all fields lay ahead of us. Never had our country borne the yoke of so many foreign armies. The Japanese had capitulated but were still in possession of their arms. The Chiang Kai-shek army which landed in the North, did its best . . . to overthrow people's power. In the South, British forces occupied the country up to the 16th parallel and tried to help the French colonialists expand their aggressive war. . . .

The signing of the Preliminary Convention on March 6, 1946 [Reading 12—eds.] between the French and our forces was the result of this correct policy and strategy. Due to the concession granted by us, part of the French army could land at certain localities in north Viet Nam to relieve the Chiang troops. On the French Government's side, it recognised that the Democratic Republic of Viet Nam was a free country within the framework of the French Union, having its own government, army, parliament, finance, etc. . . .

With the Preliminary Convention, we had carried out the policy of "making peace to go forward." Immediately after the signing of the convention, there was a time when illusions of peace partly influenced our vigilance towards the colonialists' reactionary schemes. . . .

At the beginning, owing to the fact that there were progressive elements in the French government and due to tactical necessity, we named as our enemy French reactionary colonialists. But later, especially from 1947 on, the French government definitely became reactionary, the aggressors were unmistakably the French imperialists who were the enemy of our entire people and were invading our country. In this situation, the national factor was of utmost importance. To fight French

---

2. Jules Roy, *The Battle of Dienbienphu*, translated by Robert Baldick (New York: Harper & Row, 1965), p. 305.

imperialism, it was necessary to unite the whole nation, all revolutionary classes, patriotic elements, to strengthen and widen the National United Front. Our Party obtained great success in its policy of uniting the people. The slogan: "Unity, unity and broad unity—success, success and great success," put forth by President Ho Chi Minh, became a great reality. The anti-imperialist National United Front in our country was a model of the broadest national front in a colonial country.

The revolution for national liberation under the leadership of the Communist Party never deviated from the democratic revolution. The anti-imperialist task always went side by side with the anti-feudal task, although the former was the more urgent; Viet Nam was a backward agricultural country and the great majority of the population were peasants. While the working class is the class leading the revolution, the peasantry is the main force of the revolution, full of anti-imperialist and anti-feudal spirit. Moreover, in waging the Resistance War, we relied on the countryside to build our bases to launch guerrilla warfare in order to encircle the enemy in the towns and eventually arrive at liberating the towns. Therefore, it was of particular importance to pay due attention to the peasant question and the anti-feudal question to step up the long Resistance War to victory. . . .

In 1952–1953, our Party decided to mobilise the masses for a drastic reduction of land rent and to carry out land reform, implementing the slogan "land to the tiller." Hence, the resistance spirit of millions of peasants was strongly roused, the peasant-worker alliance strengthened, the National United Front made firmer, the administration and army consolidated and resistance activities intensified. There were errors in land reform but they were, in the main, committed after the restoration of peace and thus did not have any effect on the Resistance War. It should be added that not only was land reform carried out in the North, but in south Viet Nam, land was also distributed to the peasants after 1951. The carrying out of land reform during the Resistance War was an accurate policy of a creative character of our Party.

Looking back, on the whole, our Party stuck to the national democratic revolution line throughout the Resistance War. Thanks to this, we succeeded in mobilizing our people *to launch the people's war*, using the enormous strength of the people to vanquish the aggressors. . . .

Under the Party's leadership, the people's administration played an important part in the mobilisation of manpower and wealth for the Resistance. "All for the front, all for victory" was the slogan for our nation and it showed the determination of our people to concentrate all their forces to fight to the bitter end to overthrow the French imperialists and their henchmen, liberate the country and wrest back independence and land. This was the slogan of the people's war. . . .

Enemy Strategy: Party Strategy

Launching the Resistance War, our Party accurately assessed the strong and weak points of the enemy and ours and clearly saw the balance of forces and the enemy strategic schemes in order to define our strategic principle.

The *enemy*, an imperialist power much weakened after World War Two, was still strong as compared with us. Moreover, he possessed a seasoned professional army equipped with up-to-date arms, well supplied and experienced in aggressive wars. His weak point lay in the unjust character of his war. As a result, he was internally divided, not supported by the people of his own country and did not enjoy the sympathy of world opinion. His army was strong at the beginning but its fighting spirit was deteriorating. French imperialism had other weak points and difficulties, namely: limited manpower and wealth, their dirty war was strongly condemned by their countrymen, etc.

On *our side*, our country was originally a colonial and semi-feudal country whose independence was newly won back. Thus, our forces in all fields were not yet consolidated, our economy was a backward agrarian one, our army untried guerrilla troops with few and obsolete arms, our supplies insufficient and our cadres lacking experience. Our strong point lay in the just nature of our Resistance War. Hence, we succeeded in uniting our entire people. Our people and troops were always imbued with the spirit of sacrificing themselves in fighting the enemy, and enjoyed the sympathy and support of people throughout the world.

These were the main features of the two sides in the last Resistance War. They clearly pointed out that the enemy's strong points were our weak ones and our strong points were his weak ones, but the enemy's strong points were temporary ones while ours were basic ones.

Owing to the above-mentioned characteristics, *the enemy's strategic principle was to attack swiftly and win swiftly*. The more the war was protracted the lesser would be his strong points, and their weak points would grow weaker. This strategic principle was in contradiction with the French imperialists' limited forces which had grown much weaker after World War Two. Consequently, in their schemes of invading our country, they were compelled to combine their plan of attacking swiftly and win swiftly with that of invading step-by-step, and even of negotiating with us in their time-serving policy to muster additional forces. Despite the difficulties and obstacles caused by their weak points, whenever they had the possibility, they would immediately carry out their plan of attacking swiftly and winning swiftly, hoping to end the war by a quick victory. . . .

Realising clearly the enemy's strong and weak points and ours, to cope with the enemy's strategic scheme, *our party set forth the guiding principle of a long-term Resistance War*. Facing an enemy who temporarily had the upper hand, our people was not able to strike swiftly and win swiftly but needed time to overcome its shortcomings and increase the enemy's weak points. Time was needed to mobilise, organise and foster the forces of Resistance, to wear out the enemy forces, gradually reverse the balance of forces, turning our weakness into strength and concurrently availing ourselves of the changes in the international situation[3] which

---

3. Giap refers here to the anti-colonial tendencies in the late 1940s and early 1950s, as well as to the defeat of Chiang Kai-shek's regime by the Communists on the mainland of China.—eds.

was growing more and more advantageous to our Resistance, eventually to triumph over the enemy.

The general law of a long revolutionary war is usually to go through three stages: defensive, equilibrium and offensive. Fundamentally, in the main directions, our Resistance War also followed this general law. Of course, the reality on the battlefields unfolded in a more lively and more complicated manner. Implementing the guiding principle of a long war, after a period of fighting to wear out and check the enemy troops, we carried out a strategic withdrawal from the cities to the countryside in order to preserve our forces and defend our rural bases. . . . From 1950 onwards, campaigns of local counter-offensives were successively opened and we won the intiative on the northern battlefront. The Dien Bien Phu campaign in early 1954 was a big counter-offensive which ended the Resistance War with a great victory. . . .

Guerrilla War: Only the First Stage

To bring the Resistance War to victory, it was not enough to have a correct strategic guiding principle but an appropriate *guiding principle of fighting* was also necessary in order successfully to carry out that strategic guiding principle. In general, our Resistance War *was a guerrilla war moving gradually to regular war, from guerrilla warfare to mobile warfare combined with partial entrenched camp warfare*. Basically, we had grasped that general law; hence we were successful. However, we did not thoroughly grasp it from the beginning but only after a whole process of being tested and tempered in the practice of war.

In the Resistance War, *guerrilla warfare* played an extremely important role. Guerrilla warfare is the form of fighting of the masses of people, of the people of a weak and badly equipped country who stand up against an aggressive army which possesses better equipment and technique. This is the way of fighting the revolutionary war which relies on the heroic spirit to triumph over modern weapons, avoiding the enemy when he is the stronger and attacking him when he is the weaker, now scattering, now regrouping one's forces, now wearing out, now exterminating the enemy, determined to fight him everywhere, so that wherever the enemy goes he would be submerged in a sea of armed people who hit back at him, thus undermining his spirit and exhausting his forces. In addition to the units which have to be scattered in order to wear out the enemy, it is necessary to regroup big armed forces in favourable conditions in order to achieve supremacy in attack at a given point and at a given time to annihilate the enemy. Successes in many small fights added together gradually wear out the enemy manpower while little by little fostering our forces. The main goal of the fighting must be destruction of enemy manpower, and ours should not be exhausted from trying to keep or occupy land, thus creating final conditions to wipe out the whole enemy forces and liberate our country.

Guerrilla warfare was obviously a form of fighting in full keeping with the characteristics of our Resistance War. . . .

From the strategic point of view, guerrilla warfare, causing many difficulties and losses to the enemy, wears him out. To annihilate big enemy manpower and liberate land, guerrilla warfare has to move gradually to *mobile warfare*. As our Resistance War was a long revolutionary war, therefore guerrilla warfare not only could but had to move to mobile warfare. Through guerrilla activities, our troops were gradually formed, fighting first with small units then with bigger ones, moving from scattered fighting to more concentrated fighting. Guerrilla warfare gradually developed to mobile warfare—a form of fighting in which principles of regular warfare gradually appear and increasingly develop but still bear a guerrilla character. Mobile warfare is the fighting way of concentrated troops, of the regular army in which relatively big forces are regrouped and operating on a relatively vast battlefield, attacking the enemy where he is relatively exposed with a view to annihilating enemy manpower, advancing very deeply then withdrawing very swiftly, possessing to the extreme, dynamism, initiative, mobility and rapidity of decision in face of new situations. As the Resistance War went on, the strategic role of mobile warfare became more important with every passing day. Its task was to annihilate a bigger and bigger number of the enemy forces in order to develop our own, while the task of guerrilla warfare was to wear out and destroy the enemy's reserves. Therefore, mobile warfare had to go side by side with annihilating warfare. Only by annihilating the enemy's manpower, could we smash the enemy's big offensives, safeguard our bases and our rear-line, move to win the initiative in the operation, wipe out more and more important enemy manpower, liberating larger and larger localities one after the other and eventually arrive at destroying the whole enemy armed forces and liberating our whole country.

Implementing the guiding principle of moving gradually from guerrilla warfare to mobile warfare, from the outset, there was in our guerrilla troops, besides one part operating separately, another with concentrated activity, and this was the first seeds of mobile warfare. In 1947, with the plan of independent companies operating separately and concentrated battalions, we began to move to more concentrated fighting, then to mobile warfare. In 1948, we made relatively great ambuscades and surprise attacks with one or several battalions. In 1949, we launched small campaigns not only in the North but also on other battlefronts. From 1950, we began to launch campaigns on an ever larger scale enabling mobile warfare to play the main part on the northern battlefield, while entrenched camp warfare was on the upgrade. This fact was clearly manifest in the great Dien Bien Phu campaign.

We used to say: guerrilla war must multiply. To keep itself in life and develop, guerrilla warfare has necessarily to develop into mobile warfare. This is a general law. In the concrete conditions of our Resistance War, there could not be mobile warfare without guerrilla warfare. But if guerrilla warfare did not move to mobile warfare, not only the strategic task of annihilating the enemy manpower could not be carried out but even guerrilla activities could not be maintained and extended. To say that it is necessary to develop guerrilla warfare into mobile warfare does not mean brushing aside guerrilla warfare, but that in the widely extended guerrilla activities, the units of the regular army gradually grew up and were able to wage mobile warfare and side by side with that main force there must always be numerous guerrilla troops and guerrilla activities.

Once mobile warfare appeared on the battlefront of guerrilla war, there must be close and correct co-ordination between these forms of fighting to be able to step up the Resistance War, wear out and annihilate bigger enemy forces and win ever greater victories. This is another general law in the conduct of the war. On the one hand, guerrilla warfare had to be extended to make full use of the new favourable conditions brought about by mobile warfare, in order to co-ordinate with mobile warfare to wear out and annihilate a great number of enemy manpower and through these successes continue to step up mobile warfare. On the other hand, mobile warfare had to be accelerated to annihilate big enemy manpower, and concurrently create new favourable conditions for a further extension of guerrilla warfare. In the course of the development of mobile warfare, owing to the enemy's situation and ours on the battlefields, entrenched camp warfare gradually came into being. Entrenched camp warfare which became part and parcel of the mobile warfare, kept developing and occupied a more and more important position.

The conduct of the war must maintain a correct ratio between the fighting forms. At the beginning, we had to stick to guerrilla warfare and extend it. Passing to a new stage, as mobile warfare made its appearance, we had to hold firm the co-ordination between the two forms, the chief one being guerrilla warfare; mobile warfare was of lesser importance but was on the upgrade. Then came a new and higher stage, mobile warfare moved to the main position, at first, only on one battlefield—local counter-offensive came into being—then on an ever wider scope. During this time, guerrilla warfare extended but, contrary to mobile warfare, it moved back from the main position to a lesser but still important one, first on a given battlefront then on an ever-wider scope. . . .

The strategy of long-term war and the guiding principle of fighting from guerrilla war gradually moving to regular war with the forms of guerrilla warfare, mobile warfare including entrenched camp warfare, were very successful experiences of our national liberation war. These were the strategy and tactics of the people's war, the art of military conduct of the people's war, of the revolutionary war in a small and backward agricultural country under the leadership of our Party. . . .

Equipment, Training, Leadership and Popular Action

To organise an army, the *question of equipment* must be solved because arms and equipment are the material basis of the combativeness of the army. Without arms it is of no use to speak of organising an army and of waging armed struggle. In the first stage of the building of the army, owing to our backward national economy, with almost no industry, and with the army's rear in mountain and rural areas only, the equipping of our army encountered many difficulties. The Party pointed out to the army that it had to look for its equipment on the front line, to capture the enemy weapons to arm itself and shoot at the enemy with his guns. We scored great success in implementing this principle. The great part of our regular army and guerrilla units were armed with weapons captured on the battlefronts. The French Expeditionary Corps practically became carriers engaged in supplying our army with U.S.-type arms. On the other hand, our Party guided the workers in the spirit of self-reliance, and found means to manufacture a part of the arms and munitions for the army. In circumstances of extreme hardship and privation, the workers in the arms-factories raised to new heights the heroic and creative spirit of the Vietnamese working class, overcoming very great material and technical difficulties in order to turn scrap-iron into weapons for our troops to exterminate the enemy.

In these circumstances, our Party educated the army to develop the fine nature of a revolutionary army to increase the political supremacy in order to make good our weakness in equipment. Hence our army succeeded, with inferior arms, in defeating the enemy who was many times stronger in weapons. It has become an extremely fine tradition of our army—to vanquish modern weapons with an heroic spirit. However, because of our inferior weapons, in the Resistance War our army and people had to fight in extremely hard and difficult circumstances, to make great sacrifices and shed much blood. We must always realise that inferiority in arms and equipment is a big weakness that must be overcome at all costs. . . .

During the process of its formation and development, the people's armed forces not only include a regular and local armies but also a big self-defence force. Immediately after the Party had set the task of preparing for an armed uprising, on the basis of the intensified political movement of the masses, there appeared the multiformed semi-armed and armed organisations, aimed at gradually shifting the masses' political struggle to the armed struggle. These were the organisational forms of self-defence units, of fighting self-defence units, then of guerrilla teams in the underground armed bases. . . . [Space limitations prevent presentation of Giap's analysis of the early stages of the Franco-Vietnamese war. By its eighth year, 1953, this war was going badly for the French, and a change in leadership and strategy seemed called for. General Henri Navarre was brought in.—eds.]

The Navarre Plan and the Vietnamese Response

Since the frontier campaign,[4] our army had scored successive victories in many campaigns and kept the intiative on all battlefronts in north Viet Nam. After the liberation of Hoa Binh, the guerrilla bases in the Red River delta were extended, and vast areas in the North-West were won back one after the other. The enemy found themselves in a daily more dangerous situation, and were driven on to the defensive. The Franco-American imperialists saw that to save the situation they had to bring in reinforcements, re-shuffle generals and map out a new plan. At that time, the war in Korea had just come to an end. The U. S. imperialists were more

---

4. This campaign took place along the Vietnamese-Chinese border in 1950.—eds.

and more involved in plotting to protract and extend the war in Indochina. It was
in these circumstances that they worked out the "Navarre plan"—a plan to continue and extend the war—which had been carefully studied and prepared in Paris
and Washington.

In a word, *the "Navarre plan" was a large-scale strategic plan aimed at wiping out the greater part of our main forces within eighteen months, and occupying
our whole territory, in order to turn Viet Nam permanently into a colony and
military base of the American and French imperialists.*

In accordance with this plan, in the first stage, fairly strong mobile forces
would be regrouped in the Red River delta to attack and wear out our main forces,
at the same time occupying Dien Bien Phu with a view to turning the temporarily
occupied area in the North-West into a strong springboard. . . .

In Autumn 1953, General Navarre launched this Machiavellian strategic plan.
With the slogans "always keep the initiative" and "always on the offensive," the
High Command of the French Expeditionary Corps concentrated in the Red River
delta 44 mobile battalions, launched fierce mopping-up operations in its rear, attacked Ninh Binh, Nho Quan, threatened Thanh Hoa, parachuted troops on Lang
Son and threatened Phu Tho. At the same time, they armed local bandits to sow
confusion in the North-West. Then, on January 20, 1954, Navarre dropped parachute troops to occupy Dien Bien Phu. His plan was to reoccupy Na San, consolidate Lai Chau and extend the occupied zone in the North-West.

About November, after wiping out a part of the enemy's forces on the Ninh
Binh battlefront, our army opened the Winter-Spring campaign to smash the "Navarre plan" of the American and French imperialists.

In December 1953, our troops marched on the North-West, annihilated an important part of the enemy's manpower, liberated Lai Chau and encircled Dien Bien
Phu.

Also in December, the Pathet Lao forces and the Viet Nam People's Volunteers
launched an offensive in Middle Laos, wiped out important enemy forces, liberated
Thakhek, and reached the Mekong river.

In January 1954, in the Fifth zone, our troops launched an offensive on the
Western Highlands, annihilated considerable enemy manpower, liberated the town
of Kontum, and came into contact with the newly liberated Bolovene Highlands,
in Lower Laos.

Also in January of that year, the Pathet Lao forces and the Viet Nam People's
Volunteers launched an offensive in Upper Laos, swept away important enemy
forces, liberated the Nam Hu basin and threatened Luang Prabang.

Throughout this period, in the areas behind the enemy lines in north Viet Nam,
in Binh Thi Thien, as well as in the southernmost part of Trung Bo and in Nam
Bo, guerrilla warfare was greatly intensified.[5]

---

5. Binh Thi Thien refers to the three provinces of Central Vietnam: Quang Binh, Quang Tri and
Thua Thien. Trung Bo is the Central administrative division of Vietnam, Nam Bo being the southern
division.—eds.

In the second week of March, thinking that the period of offensive of our troops was at an end, the enemy regrouped a part of his forces to resume the "Atlanta" campaign in the South of Trung Bo and occupy Quy Nhon on March 12.

On the next day, March 13, our troops *launched the big offensive against the Dien Bien Phu entrenched camp*.

Our troops fought on the Dien Bien Phu battlefield for 55 days and nights until the complete destruction of the entrenched camp on May 7, 1954. . . .

The war unleashed by the Franco-American imperialists was an unjust war of aggression. This colonial war had no other aim than to occupy and dominate our country. The aggressive nature and object of the war forced the enemy to scatter his forces to occupy the invaded localities. The carrying out of the war was for the French Expeditionary Corps a continuous process of dispersal of forces. The enemy divisions were split into regiments, then into battalions, companies and platoons, to be stationed at thousands of points and posts on the various battlefronts of the Indochina theatre of operations. The enemy found himself face to face with a contradiction: Without scattering his forces it was impossible for him to occupy the invaded territory; in scattering his forces, he put himself in difficulties. His scattered units would fall easy prey to our troops, his mobile forces would be more and more reduced and the shortage of troops would be all the more acute. On the other hand if he concentrated his forces to move from the defensive position and cope with us with more initiative, the occupation forces would be weakened and it would be difficult for him to hold the invaded territory. Now, if the enemy gives up occupied territory, the very aim of the war of re-conquest is defeated. . . .

Dien Bien Phu being the keystone of the Navarre plan, we considered that it should be wiped out if the Franco-American imperialist plot of protracting and expanding the war was to be smashed. However, the importance of Dien Bien Phu could not be regarded as a decisive factor in our decision to attack it. In the relation of forces at that time, could we destroy the fortified entrenched camp of Dien Bien Phu? Could we be certain of victory in attacking it? Our decision had to depend on this consideration alone.

Dien Bien Phu was a very strongly fortified entrenched camp. But on the other hand, it was set up in a mountainous region, on ground which was advantageous to us, and decidedly disadvantageous to the enemy. Dien Bien Phu was, moreover, a completely isolated position, far away from all the enemy's bases. The only means of supplying Dien Bien Phu was by air. These circumstances could easily deprive the enemy of all initiative and force him on to the defensive if attacked.

On our side, we had picked units of the regular army which we could concentrate to achieve supremacy in power. We could overcome all difficulties in solving the necessary tactical problems; we had, in addition, an immense rear, and the problem of supplying the front with food and ammunition, though very difficult, was not insoluble. Thus we had conditions for retaining the initiative in the operations.

It was on the basis of the analysis of the enemy's and our own strong and weak points that we solved the question as to whether we should attack Dien Bien Phu or not. *We decided to wipe out at all costs the whole enemy force at Dien Bien Phu*, after having created favourable conditions for this battle by launching numerous offensives on various battlefields and by intensifying preparations on the Dien Bien Phu battlefield. This important decision was a new proof of the dynamism, initiative, mobility and rapidity of decision in face of new situations displayed in the conduct of the war by the Party's Central Committee. Our plan foresaw the launching of many offensives on the points where the enemy was relatively weak, availing ourselves of all opportunities to wipe out enemy's manpower in mobile warfare. But whenever it was possible and success was certain, we were resolved not to let slip an opportunity to launch powerful attacks on strong points to annihilate the more concentrated enemy forces. Our decision to make the assault on the Dien Bien Phu fortified camp clearly marked a new step forward in the development of the Winter-Spring campaign, in the annals of our army's battles and in the history of our people's resistance war. . . .

The French and American military authorities believed that the fortified entrenched camp of Dien Bien Phu was impregnable. They were certain that an offensive against Dien Bien Phu would be suicidal, that failure was inevitable. Therefore, during the first weeks of the campaign, the French High Command firmly believed that there was little possibility of an offensive against Dien Bien Phu by our army. Until the last minute, the offensive launched by our men was unexpected by the enemy.

General Navarre had over-estimated the Dien Bien Phu defences. He believed that we would be unable to crush even one centre of resistance. Because, unlike the simple strong-posts at Na San or Hoa Binh, these were centres of resistance forming a much more complex and strongly fortified defence system.

The destruction of the fortified entrenched camp as a whole was, to Navarre's mind, still less feasible. In his opinion, his artillery and air forces were powerful enough to wipe out all forces coming from outside before these could be deployed in the valley and approach the fortifications. He was not in the least worried about our artillery which he thought weak and not transportable to the approaches of Dien Bien Phu. Nor was he anxious about his own supplies, because both airfields, surrounded by the defence sectors, could not be in danger. Never did it enter his head that the whole fortified camp could be annihilated by our troops.

The enemy's estimates were obviously wishful thinking but they were not totally without foundation. In fact, the Dien Bien Phu fortified entrenched camp had many strong points which had given our army new problems of tactics to solve before we could annihilate the enemy. . . .

The fortified entrenched camp had quite powerful artillery fire, tank and air forces. This was another strong point of the enemy, a very great difficulty of ours, especially since we had only very limited artillery fire and no mechanised or air forces. *We overcame this difficulty by digging a whole network of trenches that encircled and strangled the entrenched camp,* thus creating conditions for our men to deploy and move under enemy fire. Our fighters dug hundreds of kilometres of trenches. These wonderful trenches enabled our forces to deploy and move in open country under the rain of enemy napalm bombs and artillery shells. But to reduce the effect of enemy fire was not enough, *we still had to strengthen our own fire-power*. Our troops cut through mountains and hacked away jungles to build roads and haul our artillery pieces to the approaches of Dien Bien Phu. Where roads could not be built, artillery pieces were moved by nothing but the sweat and muscle of our soldiers. Our artillery was set up in strongly fortified firing positions, to the great surprise of the enemy. Our light artillery played a great part in the Dien Bien Phu battle.

While neutralising the enemy's strong points, we had to make the most of his weak points. His greatest weakness *lay in his supply*, which depended entirely on his air forces. Our tactics were from the very beginning to use our artillery-fire to destroy the air-strips, and our anti-aircraft guns to cope with the activities of enemy planes. Later, with the development of the waves of attacks, everything was brought into play to hinder enemy supply and gradually stop it altogether.

These are a few of the problems of tactics we solved in the Dien Bien Phu campaign. They were solved on the basis of our analysis of the enemy's strong and weak points, combining technique with the heroism and hard-working and fighting spirit of a People's Army. . . .

On our side, the army and people actively prepared the offensive, carrying out the orders of the Party's Central Committee and the Government; the army and people mustered all their strength to guarantee the success of the Winter-Spring campaign, to which Dien Bien Phu was the key. Our troops succeeded in liberating the surrounding regions, isolating Dien Bien Phu, obliging the enemy to scatter forces and thus reduce their possibilities of sending reinforcements to the battle-field. We made motor roads, cleared the tracks to haul up artillery pieces, built casemates for the artillery, prepared the ground for the offensive and encirclement; in short, transformed the relief of the battlefield terrain with a view to solving the tactical problems. We overcame very great difficulties. We called upon our local compatriots to supply food, to set up supply lines hundreds of kilometres long from Thanh Hoa or Phu Tho to the North-West, crossing very dangerous areas and very high hills. We used every means to carry food and ammunition to the front. Our troops and voluntary workers ceaselessly went to the front and actively partic-ipated in the preparations under the bombs and bullets of enemy aircraft.

In the first week of March, the preparations were completed: the artillery had solid casemates, the operational bases were established, food and ammunition were available in sufficient quantity. After having been educated in the aim and significance of the campaign, all officers and soldiers were filled with a very high determination to annihilate the enemy. . . .

[As the encirclement drew tighter the] enemy was driven into a square kilo-metre, entirely exposed to our fire. There was no fortified height to protect them. The problem of supply became very grave. Their situation was critical: the last hour of the entrenched camp had come.

In the afternoon of May 7th, from the East and West, we launched a massive combined attack upon the headquarters at Muong Thanh. At several posts, the enemy hoisted the white flag and surrendered. At 5.30 P.M. we seized the head-quarters: General de Castries and his staff were captured.

The remaining forces at Dien Bien Phu surrendered. The prisoners of war were well treated by our troops.

The "Determined to fight and to win" banner of our army fluttered high in the valley of Dien Bien Phu. On this very night, we attacked the South sub-sector. The whole garrison of more than 2,000 men was captured.

The historic Dien Bien Phu campaign ended in our complete victory. Our troops had fought with an unprecedented heroism for 55 days and 55 nights.

During this time, our troops were very active in all theatres of operations in co-ordination with the main front. . . .

Such are the broad outlines of the military situation in Winter 1953 and Spring 1954.

On all fronts, we put out of action 112,000 enemy troops and brought down or destroyed on the ground 177 planes.

At Dien Bien Phu, we put out of action 16,200 enemy troops, including the whole staff of the entrenched camp, one general, 16 colonels, 1,749 officers and warrant-officers, brought down or destroyed 62 planes of all types, seized all the enemy's armaments, ammunition and equipment, and more than 30,000 para-chutes.

These great victories of the Viet Nam People's Army and people as a whole at Dien Bien Phu and on the other fronts had smashed to pieces the "Navarre plan," and impeded the attempts of the Franco-American imperialists to prolong and extend the war. These great victories liberated the North of Viet Nam, contributed to the success of the Geneva Conference and the restoration of peace in Indo-China on the basis of respect of the sovereignty, independence, national unity and territorial integrity of Viet Nam and of the two friendly countries, Cambodia and Laos.

Part III

GENEVA: THE PEACE SUBVERTED

Editors' Introduction

Events in Indochina during the administration of President Dwight D. Eisenhower were an intense embarrassment to the US government. Having won the 1952 presidential election in part on the charge that the outgoing Democrats had "lost China," the Republicans were determined to prevent any other Asian countries' "going Communist." American policy had long been based on supporting the French, but the military gains of the resistance forces were rapidly invalidating US assumptions of eventual French victory. Perhaps even more disturbing was the popularity of the Communist insurgents. Reporting on this to the Defense Department in early 1954, the US Joint Chiefs of Staff ascribed the Communists' advantage to their "superior capability in the field of propaganda" and their ability to "pervert" the issue in Vietnam into "a choice between national independence and French Colonial rule. . . ."

> While it is obviously impossible to make a dependable forecast as to the outcome of a free election, current intelligence leads the Joint Chiefs of Staff to a belief that a settlement based on free elections would be attended by almost certain loss of the Associated States of Indochina to Communist control.[1]

Eisenhower made this point more bluntly in his memoirs:

> I have never talked or corresponded with a person knowledgeable in Indochinese affairs who did not agree that had elections been held at the time of the fighting, possibly 80 per cent of the population would have voted for the Communist Ho Chi Minh as their leader rather than Chief of State Bao Dai.[2]

---

1. JCS Memorandum, March 12, 1954, in *The Pentagon Papers* (Gravel edition), vol. 1, p. 448.
2. Dwight D. Eisenhower, *Mandate for Change* (Garden City, N.Y.: Doubleday, 1963), p. 372.

The conclusion seemed inescapable: put somebody in charge in Vietnam who would undercut the popular support enjoyed by the Communists.

The person chosen for this awesome responsibility of turning back the tide of Communist victory in Asia was Ngo Dinh Diem. The readings in this section provide a variety of perspectives on the enigmatic Diem. A former official in the French colonial administration of Vietnam, Diem later broke with the French and traveled widely, attracting the attention of a number of influential Americans, such as Massachusetts Senator John F. Kennedy and Roman Catholic Cardinal Francis Spellman of New York. In Reading 24, journalist Robert Scheer provides a provocative account of Diem's American backing. One of his early supporters, Michigan State University Professor Wesley Fishel, offers an adulatory analysis of Diem's alleged "Democratic One-Man Rule" in Reading 22, while Colonel Edward Lansdale in Reading 19 narrates American military efforts to create and maintain Diem's government in its early days.

Readings 16 through 18 give the official text of the Geneva Accords and other key documents from the 1954 period. From this point on, every US administration was to claim that these Accords had divided Vietnam into two nations, "North Vietnam" and "South Vietnam," separated at the 17th parallel of latitude. In fact, these Accords emphatically state that the 17th parallel was to be merely a "provisional military demarcation line" to separate the French armed forces from those of the Democratic Republic of Vietnam, and this line "should not in any way be interpreted as constituting a political or territorial boundary" (Reading 16, Articles 1 and 2; Reading 17, Clause 6). The other key factor contributing to the collapse of the Geneva peace agreement was Ngo Dinh Diem's refusal, backed by the United States, to hold the election scheduled for 1956 to reunify the country, as specified by the 1954 Accords (Reading 21). This refusal doomed the Geneva settlement and made another round of conflict inevitable.

16. The Geneva Cease-Fire (July 20, 1954)*

This document and the Final Declaration of the Geneva Conference (Reading 17) are among the most important of the Vietnam war. The Vietnam cease-fire agreement (there were similar agreements for Laos and Cambodia[1]) was signed, appropriately enough, by only the combatants, the people who had been fighting in Indochina for nearly a decade. One side strove to retain French hegemony; the

---

*Excerpted from *Further Documents Relating to the Discussion of Indochina at the Geneva Conference* (Miscellaneous no. 20 [1954], Command Paper, 9239). London: Great Britain Parliamentary Sessional Papers, XXXI (1953–1954), pp. 27–38.

1. For the texts of the cease-fire agreements relating to Laos and Cambodia, see Marvin E. Gettleman et al., eds., *Conflict in Indochina* (New York: Random House/Vintage, 1970), Readings 7, 8.

other side sought to liberate their country from foreign domination. Careful study of these texts yields interesting results: first, that there is no mention of a country called either "South Vietnam" or "North Vietnam"; there are mentioned only the Democratic Republic of Vietnam and the French State of Vietnam, nominally headed by the playboy emperor, Bao Dai. Naturally, the Bao Dai regime did not sign the cease-fire clauses in the Accords; what few armed forces it had were fighting for the French side against their fellow-Vietnamese. Yet later, the State of Vietnam, and its successor entity, the Republic of Vietnam, when backed by the Americans, refused to honor the Geneva Accords on the grounds that the Bao Dai regime was not a legal party to them (Readings 18, 21). Out of that refusal would spring two more decades of fighting.

PROVISIONAL MILITARY DEMARCATION LINE AND DEMILITARIZED ZONE

Article 1

A provisional military demarcation line shall be fixed, on either side of which the forces of the two parties shall be regrouped after their withdrawal, the forces of the People's Army of Vietnam [P.A.V., or Vietminh, forces—eds.] to the north of the line and the forces of the French Union to the south. [The line ran roughly along the 17th parallel.—eds.] . . .

It is also agreed that a demilitarized zone shall be established on either side of the demarcation line, to a width of not more than 5 kms. from it, to act as a buffer zone and avoid any incidents which might result in the resumption of hostilities.

Article 2

The period within which the movement of all forces of either party into its regrouping zone on either side of the provisional military demarcation line shall be completed shall not exceed three hundred (300) days from the date of the present Agreement's entry into force. . . .

[Administrative details are omitted.—eds.]

Article 5

To avoid any incidents which might result in the resumption of hostilities, all military forces, supplies, and equipment shall be withdrawn from the demilitarized zone within twenty-five (25) days of the present Agreement's entry into force.

Article 6

No person, military or civilian, shall be permitted to cross the provisional military demarcation line unless specifically authorized to do so by the Joint Commission.[2]

---

2. This refers to a Joint DRV-French Commission for supervising the details of the cease-fire. The Joint Commission must be distinguished from the International Commission for Supervision and Control (see Reading 17) and from the co-chairmen (the USSR and Great Britain) of the Geneva Conference.—eds.

Article 7

No person, military or civilian, shall be permitted to enter the demilitarized zone except persons concerned with the conduct of civil administration and relief and persons specifically authorized to enter by the Joint Commission.

Article 8

Civil administration and relief in the demilitarized zone on either side of the provisional military demarcation line shall be the responsibility of the Commanders-in-Chief of the two parties in their respective zones. The number of persons, military or civilian, from each side who are permitted to enter the demilitarized zone for the conduct of civil administration and relief shall be determined by the respective Commanders, but in no case shall the total number authorized by either side exceed at any one time a figure to be determined by the . . . Joint Commission. The number of civil police and the arms to be carried by them shall be determined by the Joint Commission. No one else shall carry arms unless specifically authorized to do so by the Joint Commission.

Article 9

Nothing contained in this chapter shall be construed as limiting the complete freedom of movement—into, out of, or within the demilitarized zone—of the Joint Commission, its joint groups, the International Commission to be set up as indicated below, its inspection teams and any other persons, supplies, or equipment specifically authorized to enter the demilitarized zone by the Joint Commission. Freedom of movement shall be permitted across the territory under the military control of either side over any road or waterway which has to be taken between points within the demilitarized zone when such points are not connected by roads or waterways lying completely within the demilitarized zone.

PRINCIPLES AND PROCEDURE
GOVERNING IMPLEMENTATION OF
THE PRESENT AGREEMENT

Article 10

The Commanders of the Forces on each side, on the one side the Commander-in-Chief of the French Union forces in Indochina and on the other side the Commander-in-Chief of the People's Army of Vietnam, shall order and enforce the complete cessation of all hostilities in Vietnam by all armed forces under their control, including all units and personnel of the ground, naval, and air forces.

Article 11

In accordance with the principle of a simultaneous cease-fire throughout Indochina, the cessation of hostilities shall be simultaneous throughout all parts of Vietnam, in all areas of hostilities and for all the forces of the two parties. . . .

[Section on precise timing of the cease-fire is omitted.—eds.]

From such time as the cease-fire becomes effective in North Vietnam, both parties undertake not to engage in any large-scale offensive action in any part of the Indochinese theater of operations and not to commit the air forces based on North Vietnam outside that sector. The two parties also undertake to inform each other of their plans for movement from one regrouping zone to another within twenty-five (25) days of the present Agreement's entry into force. . . .

[Military details are omitted.—eds.]

Article 14

Political and administrative measures in the two regrouping zones, on either side of the provisional military demarcation line:

(a) Pending the general elections which will bring about the unification of Vietnam, the conduct of civil administration in each regrouping zone shall be in the hands of the party whose forces are to be regrouped there in virtue of the present Agreement.

(b) Any territory controlled by one party which is transferred to the other party by the regrouping plan shall continue to be administered by the former party until such date as all the troops who are to be transferred have completely left that territory so as to free the zone assigned to the party in question. From then on, such territory shall be regarded as transferred to the other party, who shall assume responsibility for it.

Steps shall be taken to ensure that there is no break in the transfer of responsibilities. For this purpose, adequate notice shall be given by the withdrawing party to the other party, which shall make the necessary arrangements, in particular by sending administrative and police detachments to prepare for the assumption of administrative responsibility. . . . The transfer shall be effected in successive stages for the various territorial sectors.

The transfer of the civil administration of Hanoi and Haiphong to the authorities of the Democratic Republic of Vietnam shall be completed within the respective time-limits laid down in Article 15 for military movements.

(c) Each party undertakes to refrain from any reprisals or discrimination against persons or organizations on account of their activities during the hostilities and to guarantee their democratic liberties.

(d) From the date of entry into force of the present Agreement until the movement of troops is completed, any civilians residing in a district controlled by one party who wish to go and live in the zone assigned to the other party shall be permitted and helped to do so by the authorities in that district.

Article 15

The disengagement of the combatants, and the withdrawals and transfers of military forces, equipment, and supplies shall take place in accordance with the following principles:

(a) The withdrawals and transfers of the military forces, equipment, and supplies of the two parties shall be completed within three hundred (300) days, as laid down in Article 2 of the present Agreement;

(b) Within either territory successive withdrawal shall be made by sectors, portions of sectors, or provinces. Transfers from one regrouping zone to another shall be made in successive monthly installments proportionate to the number of troops to be transferred;

(c) The two parties shall undertake to carry out all troop withdrawals and transfers in accordance with the aims of the present Agreement, shall permit no hostile act, and shall take no step whatsoever which might hamper such withdrawals and transfers. They shall assist one another as far as this is possible;

(d) The two parties shall permit no destruction or sabotage of any public property and no injury to the life and property of the civil population. They shall permit no interference in local civil administration;

(e) The Joint Commission and the International Commission shall ensure that steps are taken to safeguard the forces in the course of withdrawal and transfer. . . .

BAN ON THE INTRODUCTION OF FRESH
TROOPS, MILITARY PERSONNEL, ARMS,
AND MUNITIONS, MILITARY BASES

Article 16

With effect from the date of entry into force of the present Agreement, the introduction into Vietnam of any troop reinforcements and additional military personnel is prohibited.

It is understood, however, that the rotation of units and groups of personnel, the arrival in Vietnam of individual personnel on a temporary duty basis, and the return to Vietnam of the individual personnel after short periods of leave or temporary duty outside Vietnam shall be permitted under the conditions laid down below:

(a) Rotation of units (defined in paragraph *(c)* of this Article) and groups of personnel shall not be permitted for French Union troops stationed north of the provisional military demarcation line laid down in Article 1 of the present Agreement during the withdrawal period provided for in Article 2.

However, under the heading of individual personnel not more than fifty (50) men, including officers, shall during any one month be permitted to enter that part of the country north of the provisional military demarcation line on a temporary duty basis or to return there after short periods of leave or temporary duty outside Vietnam.

(b) "Rotation" is defined as the replacement of units or groups of personnel by other units of the same echelon or by personnel who are arriving in Vietnam territory to do their overseas service there.

(c) The units rotated shall never be larger than a battalion—or the corresponding echelon for air and naval forces.

(d) Rotation shall be conducted on a man-for-man basis, provided, however, that in any one quarter neither party shall introduce more than fifteen thousand

five hundred (15,500) members of its armed forces into Vietnam under the rotation policy.

(e) Rotation units (defined in paragraph *(c)* of this Article) and groups of personnel, and the individual personnel mentioned in this Article, shall enter and leave Vietnam only through the [designated] entry points. . . .

(f) Each party shall notify the Joint Commission and the International Commission at least two days in advance of any arrivals or departures of units, groups of personnel, and individual personnel in or from Vietnam. Reports on the arrivals or departures of units, groups of personnel, and individual personnel in or from Vietnam shall be submitted daily to the Joint Commission and the International Commission.

All the above-mentioned notifications and reports shall indicate the places and dates of arrival or departure and the number of persons arriving or departing.

(g) The International Commission, through its Inspection Teams, shall supervise and inspect the rotation of units and groups of personnel and the arrival and departure of individual personnel as authorized above at the [designated] points of entry. . . .

Article 17

(a) With effect from the date of entry into force of any present Agreement, the introduction into Vietnam of any reinforcements in the form of all types of arms, munitions and other war material, such as combat aircraft, naval craft, pieces of ordnance, jet engines and jet weapons, and armored vehicles, is prohibited.

(b) It is understood, however, that war material, arms, and munitions which have been destroyed, damaged, worn out, or used up after the cessation of hostilities may be replaced on the basis of piece-for-piece of the same type and with similar characteristics. Such replacements of war material, arms, and ammunitions shall not be permitted for French Union troops stationed north of the provisional military demarcation line laid down in Article 1 of the present Agreement, during the withdrawal period provided for in Article 2. . . .

[Details on designated entry points are omitted.—eds.]

(d) Apart from the replacements permitted within the limits laid down in paragraph *(b)* of this Article, the introduction of war material, arms, and munitions of all types in the form of unassembled parts for subsequent assembly is prohibited.

(e) Each party shall notify the Joint Commission and the International Commission at least two days in advance of any arrivals or departures which may take place of war material, arms, and munitions of all types.

In order to justify the requests for the introduction into Vietnam of arms, munitions, and other war material (as defined in paragraph *(a)* of this Article) for replacement purposes, a report concerning each incoming shipment shall be submitted to the Joint Commission and the International Commission. Such reports shall indicate the use made of the items so replaced.

(f) The International Commission, through its Inspection Teams, shall supervise and inspect the replacements permitted in the circumstances laid down in this Article.

Article 18

With effect from the date of entry into force of the present Agreement, the establishment of new military bases is prohibited throughout Vietnam territory.

Article 19

With effect from the date of entry into force of the present Agreement, no military base under the control of a foreign State may be established in the re-grouping zone of either party; the two parties shall ensure that the zones assigned to them do not adhere to any military alliance and are not used for the resumption of hostilities or to further an aggressive policy. . . .

[Technical details are omitted.—eds.]

PRISONERS OF WAR
AND CIVILIAN INTERNEES

Article 21

The liberation and repatriation of all prisoners of war and civilian internees detained by each of the two parties at the coming into force of the present Agreement shall be carried out under the following conditions:

(*a*) All prisoners of war and civilian internees of Vietnam, French, and other nationalities captured since the beginning of hostilities in Vietnam during military operations or in any other circumstances of war and in any part of the territory of Vietnam shall be liberated within a period of thirty (30) days after the date when the cease-fire becomes effective in each theater.

(*b*) The term "civilian internees" is understood to mean all persons who, having in any way contributed to the political and armed struggle between the two parties, have been arrested for that reason and have been kept in detention by either party during the period of hostilities.

(*c*) All prisoners of war and civilian internees held by either party shall be surrendered to the appropriate authorities of the other party, who shall give them all possible assistance in proceeding to their country of origin, place of habitual residence, or the zone of their choice.

MISCELLANEOUS

Article 22

The Commanders of the Forces of the two parties shall ensure that persons under their respective commands who violate any of the provisions of the present Agreement are suitably punished. . . .

[Details about recovery of deceased military personnel are omitted.—eds.]

Article 24

The present Agreement shall apply to all the armed forces of either party. The armed forces of each party shall respect the demilitarized zone and the territory under the military control of the other party, and shall commit no act and undertake no operation against the other party and shall not engage in blockade of any kind in Vietnam.

For the purposes of the present Article, the word "territory" includes territorial waters and air space. . . .

[Operational details are omitted.—eds.]

Article 27

The signatories of the present Agreement and their successors in their functions shall be responsible for ensuring the observance and enforcement of the terms and provisions thereof. The Commanders of the Forces of the two parties shall, within their respective commands, take all steps and make all arrangements necessary to ensure full compliance with all the provisions of the present Agreement by all elements and military personnel under their command. . . .

[Further operational details are omitted.—eds.]

Done in Geneva at 2400 hours on the 20th of July, 1954, in French and in Vietnamese, both texts being equally authentic.

For the Commander-in-Chief
of the French Union Forces
in Indochina:

    [Henri] DELTIEL
    Brigadier-General

For the Commander-in-Chief of the
People's Army of Vietnam:

    TA QUANG BUU,
    Vice-Minister of National
    Defense of the Democratic
    Republic of Vietnam

17. Final Declaration of the Geneva Conference (July 21, 1954)*

The participants in the 1954 Geneva Conference on Indochina were: the Kingdom of Cambodia, the Democratic Republic of Vietnam (DRV), France, the Kingdom of Laos, the People's Republic of China, the State of Vietnam, the Union of Soviet Socialist Republics, the United Kingdom (Great Britain), and the United States. Although this final Declaration of the Geneva Conference expressed the official consensus of these participants, there were ominous sounds of opposition. A month

---

Further Documents Relating to the Discussion of Indochina at the Geneva Conference (Miscellaneous no. 20 [1954], Command Paper, 9239). London: Great Britain Parliamentary Sessional Papers, xxxi (1953–1954), pp. 9–11.

earlier, US delegate Walter Bedell Smith had telegraphed to Washington his "con-
tempt" for any plan by which the DRV would gain control over the Red River delta
in the north. And Secretary of State Dulles was at the same time still considering
US armed intervention.[1] *At the Conference, both the State of Vietnam (which con-*
tested sovereignty with the DRV) and the United States expressed reservations (see
Reading 18). Later, backed by the United States, the State of Vietnam blocked
implementation of key clauses 6 and 7, thus dooming the entire Geneva settlement.

1. The Conference takes note of the agreements ending hostilities in Cambodia,
Laos, and Vietnam and organizing international control and the supervision of the
execution of the provisions of these agreements.

2. The Conference expresses satisfaction at the end of hostilities in Cambodia,
Laos, and Vietnam; the Conference expresses its conviction that the execution of
the provisions set out in the present declaration and in the agreements of the cessation of hostilities will permit Cambodia, Laos, and Vietnam henceforth to play
their part, in full independence and sovereignty, in the peaceful community of
nations.

3. The Conference takes note of the declarations made by the Governments of
Cambodia and Laos of their intention to adopt measures permitting all citizens to
take their place in the national community, in particular by participating in the next
general elections, which, in conformity with the constitution of each of these countries, shall take place in the course of the year 1955, by secret ballot and in conditions of respect for fundamental freedoms.

4. The Conference takes note of the clauses in the agreement on the cessation
of hostilities in Vietnam prohibiting the introduction into Vietnam of foreign troops
and military personnel as well as of all kinds of arms and munitions. The Conference also takes note of the declarations made by the Governments of Cambodia
and Laos of their resolution not to request foreign aid, whether in war material, in
personnel, or in instructors except for the purpose of the effective defense of their
territory and, in the case of Laos, to the extent defined by the agreements of the
cessation of hostilities in Laos.

5. The Conference takes note of the clauses in the agreement on the cessation
of hostilities in Vietnam to the effect that no military base under the control of a
foreign State may be established in the regrouping zones of the two parties, the
latter having the obligation to see that the zones allotted to them shall not constitute
part of any military alliance and shall not be utilized for the resumption of hostilities or in the service of an aggressive policy. The Conference also takes note of the
declarations of the Governments of Cambodia and Laos to the effect that they will
not join in any agreement with other States if this agreement includes the obligation to participate in a military alliance not in conformity with the principles of the

---

1. John Foster Dulles telegram, June 14, 1954, and Walter Bedell Smith telegram, June 17, 1954,
in *The Pentagon Papers* (GPO edition).

Charter of the United Nations or, in the case of Laos, with the principles of the agreement on the cessation of hostilities in Laos or, so long as their security is not threatened, the obligation to establish bases on Cambodian or Laotian territory for the military forces of foreign powers.

6. The Conference recognizes that the essential purpose of the agreement relating to Vietnam is to settle military questions with a view to ending hostilities and that the military demarcation line is provisional and should not in any way be interpreted as constituting a political or territorial boundary. The Conference expresses its conviction that the execution of the provisions set out in the present declaration and in the agreement on the cessation of hostilities creates the necessary basis for the achievement in the near future of a political settlement in Vietnam.

7. The Conference declares that, so far as Vietnam is concerned, the settlement of political problems, effected on the basis of respect for the principles of independence, unity, and territorial integrity, shall permit the Vietnamese people to enjoy the fundamental freedoms, guaranteed by democratic institutions established as a result of free general elections by secret ballot. In order to ensure that sufficient progress in the restoration of peace has been made, and that all the necessary conditions obtain for free expression of the national will, general elections shall be held in July 1956 under the supervision of an international commission composed of representatives of the Member States of the International Supervisory Commission, referred to in the agreement on the cessation of hostilities. Consultations will be held on this subject between the competent representative authorities of the two zones from July 20, 1955, onward.

8. The provisions of the agreements on the cessation of hostilities intended to ensure the protection of individuals and of property must be most strictly applied and must, in particular, allow everyone in Vietnam to decide freely in which zone he wishes to live.

9. The competent representative authorities of the North and South zones of Vietnam, as well as the authorities of Laos and Cambodia, must not permit any individual or collective reprisals against persons who had collaborated in any way with one of the parties during the war, or against members of such persons' families.

10. The Conference takes note of the declaration of the Government of the French Republic to the effect that it is ready to withdraw its troops from the territory of Cambodia, Laos, and Vietnam, at the request of the Governments concerned and within periods which shall be fixed by agreement between the parties except in the cases where, by agreement between the two parties, a certain number of French troops shall remain at specified points and for a specified time.

11. The Conference takes note of the declaration of the French Government to the effect that for the settlement of all the problems connected with the re-establishment and consolidation of peace in Cambodia, Laos, and Vietnam, the French Government will proceed from the principle of respect for the independence and sovereignty, unity and territorial integrity of Cambodia, Laos, and Vietnam.

12. In their relations with Cambodia, Laos, and Vietnam, each member of the Geneva Conference undertakes to respect the sovereignty, the independence, the unity, and the territorial integrity of the above-mentioned States, and to refrain from any interference in their internal affairs.

13. The members of the Conference agree to consult one another on any question which may be referred to them by the International Supervisory Commission, in order to study such measures as may prove necessary to ensure that the agreements on the cessation of hostilities in Cambodia, Laos, and Vietnam are respected.

18. Close of the Geneva Conference (July 21, 1954)*

Anthony Eden, British Foreign Minister, chaired the final session of the Geneva Conference. There was evident haste to conclude. The Conference had been in session for over three months. The few discordant notes struck at this final session foretold future problems. Historical territorial disputes between the Vietnamese and Cambodians surfaced briefly. But far more ominous was the effort of the delegation from the State of Vietnam to dissociate itself from the political settlement outlined at Geneva. According to this government an "'agreement' with such an adversary [as the DRV] could only be a fool's bargain."[1] US representative Walter Bedell Smith either echoed or was an original source of this negativism. Smith significantly qualified the US pledge to abide by the Geneva Agreements by indicating that his government would defer to the State of Vietnam should it refuse to join with the DRV in a united Vietnam, as envisioned at Geneva. The refusal soon followed (Reading 21).

The Chairman (Mr. Eden): As I think my colleagues are aware, agreement has now been reached on certain documents. It is proposed that this Conference should take note of these agreements. I accordingly propose to begin by reading out a list of the subjects covered by the documents, which I understand every delegation has in front of them.

First, agreement on the cessation of hostilities in Vietnam; second, agreement on the cessation of hostilities in Laos; third, agreement on the cessation of hostili-

---

Further Documents Relating to the Discussion of Indochina at the Geneva Conference (Miscellaneous no. 20 [1954], Command Paper, 9239). London: Great Britain Parliamentary Sessional Papers, xxxi (1953–1954), pp. 5–9.

1. Embassy of State of Vietnam, Washington, D. C. *Vietminh Violations of the Geneva Armistice Agreement* (Washington, D. C. [1955]), p.1.

ties in Cambodia. I would draw particular attention to the fact that these three agreements now incorporate the texts which were negotiated separately concerning the supervision of the Armistice in the three countries by the International Commission and the joint committees.

I should also like to draw the attention of all delegations to a point of some importance in connexion with the Armistice Agreements and the related maps and documents on supervision. It has been agreed among the parties to each of these Agreements that none of them shall be made public for the present, pending further agreement among the parties. The reason for this, I must explain to my colleagues, is that these Armistice terms come into force at different dates. And it is desired that they should not be made public until they have come into force.

The further documents to which I must draw attention, which are in your possession, are: fourth, declaration by the Government of Laos on elections; fifth, declaration by the Government of Cambodia on elections and integration of all citizens into the national community; sixth, declaration by the Government of Laos on the military status of the country; seventh, declaration by the Government of Cambodia on the military status of the country; eighth, declaration by the Government of the French Republic on the withdrawal of troops from the three countries of Indochina.

Finally, gentlemen, there is the Draft Declaration by the conference, which takes note of all these documents. I think all my colleagues have copies of this Draft Declaration before them. I will ask my colleagues in turn to express themselves upon this Declaration.

M. Mendès-France (France): Mr. Chairman, the French Delegation approves the terms of the Declaration.

Mr. Phoui Sananikone (Laos): The Delegation of Laos has no observations to make on this text.

Mr. Chou En-lai (People's Republic of China): We agree.

The Chairman: On behalf of Her Majesty's government in the United Kingdom, I associate myself with the final Declaration of this Conference.

M. Molotov (U.S.S.R.): The Soviet Delegation agrees.

Mr. Tep Phan (Cambodia): The Delegation of Cambodia wishes to state that, among the documents just listed, one is missing. This is a Cambodian Declaration which we have already circulated to all delegations. Its purport is as follows: Paragraphs 7, 11, and 12 of the final Declaration stipulate respect for the territorial integrity of Vietnam. The Cambodian Delegation asks the Conference to consider that this provision does not imply the abandonment of such legitimate rights and interests as Cambodia might assert with regard to certain regions of South Vietnam. . . .

In support of this Declaration, the Cambodian Delegation communicates to all members of this Conference a note of Cambodian lands in South Vietnam.

The Chairman: If this Declaration has not inscribed on the agenda on the list of documents I have read out, it is because it has only at this instant reached me. I do not think it is any part of the task of this Conference to deal with any past controversies in respect of the frontiers between Cambodia and Vietnam.

Mr. Pham Van Dong (Democratic Republic of Vietnam): Mr. Chairman, I agree completely with the words pronounced by you. In the name of the Government of the Democratic Republic of Vietnam we make the most express reservations regarding the statement made by the Delegation of Cambodia just now. I do this in the interests of good relations and undersanding between our two countries.

The Chairman: I think the Conference can take note of the statements of the Delegation of Cambodia just circulated and of the statement of the Representative of the Democratic Republic of Vietnam.

I will continue calling upon countries to speak on the subject of the Declaration. I call upon the United States of America.

Mr. Bedell Smith (United States): Mr. Chairman, Fellow Delegates, as I stated to my colleagues during our meeting on July 18, my Government is not prepared to join in a Declaration by the Conference such as is submitted. However, the United States makes this unilateral declaration of its position in these matters:

The Government of the United States being resolved to devote its efforts to the strengthening of peace in accordance with the principles of the United Nations

Takes Note of the Agreements concluded at Geneva on July 20 and 21, 1954, between *(a)* the Franco-Laotian Command and the Command of the People's Army of Vietnam; *(b)* the Royal Khmer Army Command and the People's Army of Vietnam; *(c)* the Franco-Vietnamese Command and the Command of the People's Army of Vietnam, and of paragraphs 1 to 12 of the Declaration presented to the Geneva Conference on July 21, 1954.

The Government of the United States of America

Declares with regard to the aforesaid Agreements and paragraphs that (i) it will refrain from the threat or the use of force to disturb them in accordance with Article 2 (Section 4) of the Charter of the United Nations dealing with the obligation of Members to refrain in their international relations from the threat or use of force and (ii) it would view any renewal of the aggression in violation of the aforesaid Agreements with grave concern and as seriously threatening international peace and security.

In connection with the statement in the Declaration concerning free election in Vietnam, my Government wishes to make clear its position which it has expressed in a Declaration made in Washington on June 29, 1954, as follows:

"In the case of nations now divided against their will, we shall continue to see to achieve unity through free elections, supervised by the United Nations to ensur that they are conducted fairly."[2]

---

2. From Eisenhower-Churchill joint "Potomac Declaration."—eds.

With respect to the statement made by the Representative of the State of Vietnam, the United States reiterates its traditional position that peoples are entitled to determine their own future and that it will not join in an arrangement which would hinder this. Nothing in its declaration just made is intended to or does indicate any departure from this traditional position.

We share the hope that the agreement will permit Cambodia, Laos, and Vietnam to play their part, in full independence and sovereignty, in the peaceful community of nations, and will enable the peoples of that area to determine their own future.

The Chairman: The Conference will, I think, wish to take note of the statement of the Representative of the United States of America.

Mr. Tran Van Do (State of Vietnam): Mr. Chairman, as regards the final Declaration of the Conference, the Vietnamese Delegation requests the Conference to incorporate in this Declaration after Article 10, the following text:

The Conference takes note of the Declaration of the Government of the State of Vietnam undertaking: to make and support every effort to re-establish a real and lasting peace in Vietnam; not to use force to resist the procedures for carrying the cease-fire into effect, in spite of the objections and reservations that the State of Vietnam has expressed, especially in its final statement.

The Chairman: I shall be glad to hear any views that my colleagues may wish to express. But as I understand the position, the final Declaration has already been drafted and this additional paragraph has only just now been received; indeed, it has been amended since I received the text a few minutes ago. In all the circumstances, I suggest that the best course we can take is that the Conference should take note of the Declaration of the State of Vietnam in this respect. If any of my colleagues has a contrary view, perhaps they would be good enough to say so. (None.) If none of my colleagues wishes to make any other observations, may I pass to certain other points which have to be settled before this Conference can conclude its labours?

The first is that, if it is agreeable to our colleagues, it is suggested that the two Chairmen should at the conclusion of this meeting address telegrams to the Governments of India, Poland, and Canada to ask them if they will undertake the duties of supervision which the Conference has invited them to discharge. Is that agreeable? (Agreed.) Thank you.

The last is perhaps the least agreeable chapter of all our work. Certain costs arise from the decisions which the Conference has taken. It is suggested that it should be left here to your Chairmen as their parting gift to try to put before you some proposal in respect of those costs. I only wish to add in this connexion that, as this conference is peculiar in not having any Secretariat in the usual sense of the term, the two Chairmen with considerable reluctance are prepared to undertake this highly invidious task. The costs to which I refer are not our own but those of the International Commission.

Does any delegate wish to make any further observation? (None.)

Gentlemen, perhaps I may say a final word as your Chairman for this day. We have now come to the end of our work. For a number of reasons it has been prolonged and intricate. The co-operation which all delegates have given to your two Chairmen has enabled us to overcome many procedural difficulties. Without that co-operation, we could not have succeeded in our task. The Agreements concluded today could not, in the nature of things, give complete satisfaction to everyone. But they have made it possible to stop a war which has lasted for eight years and brought suffering and hardship to millions of people. They have also, we hope, reduced international tension at a point of instant danger to world peace. These results are surely worth our many weeks of toil. In order to bring about a cease-fire, we have drawn up a series of agreements. They are the best that our hands could devise. All will now depend upon the spirit in which those agreements are observed and carried out.

Gentlemen, before we leave this hospitable town of Geneva, I'm sure you would wish your Chairmen to give a message of gratitude to the United Nations and its able staff who have housed and helped us in our work.

And lastly let me express our cordial thanks to the Swiss Government and to the people and authorities of Geneva who have done so much to make our stay here pleasant as well as of service to the cause of peace.

Mr. Bedell Smith (U.S.A.): If I presume to speak for my fellow delegates, it is because I know that they all feel as I do. I hope that they join me in expressing our thanks to the two Chairmen of this Conference. Their patience, their tireless efforts, and their goodwill have done a great deal to make this settlement possible. We owe them our sincere thanks.

Mr. Molotov (U.S.S.R.): Mr. Chairman, as one of the Chairmen at the Geneva Conference, I would like to reply to the remarks just made by Mr. Bedell Smith, who spoke highly of the work done by the Chairmen. Naturally I must stress the outstanding services and the outstanding role played by our Chairman of today, Mr. Eden, whose role in the Geneva Conference cannot be exaggerated. And I would also like to reply and thank Mr. Bedell Smith for his warm words of today.

The Chairman: Has any other delegate anything they want to say?

Mr. Tran Van Do (State of Vietnam): Mr. Chairman, I expressed the view of the Delegation of the State of Vietnam in my statement and I would have this Conference take note of it in its final act.

The Chairman: As I think I explained, we cannot now amend our final act, which is the statement of the Conference as a whole, but the Declaration of the Representative of the State of Vietnam will be taken note of.

Any other observations? (None.)

I would like to be allowed to add my thanks for what General Bedell Smith has said and also to thank M. Molotov for his words. Both are undeserved, but even if things are not true, if they are nice things it's pleasant to hear them said.

But I do want to close this Conference with this one sentence: I'm quite sure that each one of us here hopes that the work which we have done will help to strengthen the forces working for peace.

19. Cold War Combat: Tactics After Geneva*

By CIA Operative Edward G. Lansdale

While for many people the Vietnam War was a tragic, bitter conflict, others in the service of the US government were keen to put into practice the arcane skills of covert combat, disinformation, sabotage, assassination, "psywar" (psychological warfare), and the like. US Army Colonel Edward G. Lansdale was the most prominent example of this type; he was the model for "Pyle" in Graham Greene's The Quiet American *and for "Col. Hillandale" in William J. Lederer and Eugene Burdick's* The Ugly American. *A former advertising executive who had helped suppress a Communist-led guerrilla movement in the Philippines (and, as this Reading shows, maintained close ties to Filipino anti-Communist groups), Lansdale gloried in being a "flamboyant and imaginative operator whose schemes ranged from the macabre to the bizarre."* [1]

The documents presented here give the flavor of this early, almost romantic stage of US involvement in Vietnam. The first, describing the operations of Lansdale and his team in 1954–1955, is a report of the Saigon Military Mission headed by Colonel Lansdale. The second, apparently from July, 1961, is a memorandum from Brigadier General Lansdale, who had by this time become "Pentagon expert on guerrilla warfare," to General Maxwell D. Taylor, President Kennedy's military adviser, on "Resources for Unconventional Warfare" in Southeast Asia. Copies were sent to Secretary of Defense Robert S. McNamara, Deputy Secretary of Defense Roswell Gilpatric, Secretary of State Dean Rusk, CIA Director Allen Dulles, and Deputy CIA Director, General C. P. Cabell. Most of the activities described below were precisely forbidden by the terms of the Geneva Accords.

---

*A. Condensed from "Lansdale Team's Report on Covert Saigon Mission in 1954 and 1955," *The Pentagon Papers* (Gravel edition), vol. 1, pp. 573–583. B. Condensed from a memorandum from Edward G. Lansdale to Maxwell D. Taylor, *The Pentagon Papers* (Gravel edition), vol. 2, pp. 643–649.

1. George C. Herring, *America's Longest War: The United States and Vietnam, 1950–75* (New York: John Wiley & Sons, 1979), p. 50. For more about Lansdale's crucial role in the Diem regime, see Readings 20 and 24.

A. Report from Saigon Military Mission (1954–55)

I. Foreword

. . . This is the condensed account of one year in the operations of a "cold war" combat team, written by the team itself in the field, little by little in moments taken as the members could. The team is known as the Saigon Military Mission. The field is Vietnam. There are other teams in the field, American, French, British, Chinese, Vietnamese, Vietminh, and others. Each has its own story to tell. This is ours.

The Saigon Military Mission entered Vietnam on 1 June 1954 when its Chief arrived. However, this is the story of a team, and it wasn't until August 1954 that sufficient members arrived to constitute a team. So, this is mainly an account of the team's first year, from August 1954 to August 1955.

It was often a frustrating and perplexing year, up close. The Geneva Agreements signed on 21 July 1954 imposed restrictive rules upon all official Americans, including the Saigon Military Mission. An active and intelligent enemy made full use of legal rights to screen his activities in establishing his stay-behind organizations south of the 17th Parallel and in obtaining quick security north of that Parallel. The nation's economy and communications system were crippled by eight years of open war. The government, including its Army and other security forces, was in a painful transition from colonial to self rule, making it a year of hot-tempered incidents. Internal problems arose quickly to points where armed conflict was sought as the only solution. The enemy was frequently forgotten in the heavy atmosphere of suspicion, hatred, and jealousy.

The Saigon Military Mission received some blows from allies and the enemy in this atmosphere, as we worked to help stabilize the government and to beat the Geneva time-table of Communist takeover in the north. However, we did beat the time-table. The government did become stabilized. The Free Vietnamese are now becoming unified and learning how to cope with the Communist enemy. We are thankful that we had a chance to help in this work in a critical area of the world, to be positive and constructive in a year of doubt.

II. Mission

The Saigon Military Mission (SMM) was born in a Washington policy meeting early in 1954, when Dien Bien Phu was still holding out against the encircling Vietminh. The SMM was to enter into Vietnam quietly and assist the Vietnamese, rather than the French, in unconventional warfare. The French were to be kept as friendly allies in the process, as far as possible.

The broad mission for the team was to undertake paramilitary operations against the enemy and to wage political-psychological warfare. Later, after Geneva, the mission was modified to prepare the means for undertaking paramilitary operations in Communist areas rather than to wage unconventional warfare. . . .

III. Highlights of the Year

a. Early Days

The Saigon Military Mission (SMM) started on 1 June 1954, when its Chief, Colonel Edward G. Lansdale, USAF, arrived in Saigon with a small box of files and clothes and a borrowed typewriter, courtesy of an SA–16 flight set up for him by the 13th Air Force at Clark AFB. Lt.-General John O'Daniel and Embassy Charge Rob McClintock had arranged for his appointment as Assistant Air Attache, since it was improper for U.S. officers at MAAG at that time to have advisory conferences with Vietnamese officers. Ambassador Heath had concurred already. . . . Secret communications with Washington were provided through the Saigon station of CIA.

There was deepening gloom in Vietnam. Dien Bien Phu had fallen. The French were capitulating to the Vietminh at Geneva. The first night in Saigon, Vietminh saboteurs blew up large ammunition dumps at the airport, rocking Saigon throughout the night. General O'Daniel and Charge McClintock agreed that it was time to start taking positive action. O'Daniel paved the way for a quick first-hand survey of the situation throughout the country. McClintock paved the way for contacts with Vietnamese political leaders. Our Chief's reputation from the Philippines had preceded him. Hundreds of Vietnamese acquaintanceships were made quickly.

Working in close cooperation with George Hellyer, USIS Chief, a new psychological warfare campaign was devised for the Vietnamese Army and for the government in Hanoi. Shortly after, a refresher course in combat psywar was constructed and Vietnamese Army personnel were rushed through it. . . . Rumor campaigns were added to the tactics and tried out in Hanoi. It was almost too late.

The first rumor campaign was to be a carefully planted story of a Chinese Communist regiment in Tonkin taking reprisals against a Vietminh village whose girls the Chinese had raped, recalling Chinese Nationalist troop behavior in 1945 and confirming Vietnamese fears of Chinese occupation under Vietminh rule; the story was planted by soldiers of the Vietnamese Armed Psywar company in Hanoi dressed in civilian clothes. The troops received their instructions silently, dressed in civilian clothes, went on the mission, and failed to return. They had deserted to the Vietminh. Weeks later, Tonkinese told an excited story of the misbehavior of the Chinese Divisions in Vietminh territory. Investigated, it turned out to be the old rumor campaign, with Vietnamese embellishments.

There was political chaos. Prince Buu Loc no longer headed the government. Government ministries all but closed. . . .

On 1 July, Major Lucien Conein arrived, as the second member of the team. He is a paramilitary specialist, well-known to the French for his help with French-operated maquis in Tonkin against the Japanese in 1945, the one American guerrilla fighter who had not been a member of the Patti Mission. He was assigned to MAAG for cover purposes. . . .

Ngo Dinh Diem arrived on 7 July, and within hours was in despair as the French forces withdrew from the Catholic provinces of Phat Diem and Nam Dinh in Tonkin. Catholic militia streamed north to Hanoi and Haiphong, their hearts filled with anger at French abandonment. . . . The Tonkinese had hopes of American friendship and listened to the advice given them. . . . Tonkin's government changed as despair grew. On 21 July, the Geneva Agreement was signed. Tonkin was given to the Communists. Anti-Communists turned to SMM for help in establishing a resistance movement. . . .

Diem himself had reached a nadir of frustration, as his country disintegrated after the conference of foreigners. With the approval of Ambassador Heath and General O'Daniel, our Chief drew up a plan of overall governmental action and presented it to Diem, with Hellyer as interpreter. It called for fast constructive action and dynamic leadership. Although the plan was not adopted, it laid the foundation for a friendship which has lasted.

Oscar Arellano visited Saigon again. Major Charles T. R. Bohanan, a former team-mate in Philippine days, was in town. At an SMM conference with these two, "Operation Brotherhood" was born: volunteer medical teams of Free Asians to aid the Free Vietnamese who have few doctors of their own. Washington responded warmly to the idea. President Diem was visited; he issued an appeal to the Free World for help. The Junior Chamber International adopted the idea. SMM would monitor the operation quietly in the background.

President Diem had organized a Committee of Cabinet Ministers to handle the problem of refugees from the Communist North. The Committee system was a failure. . . . [Col. Lansdale] suggested to Ambassador Heath that he call a U.S. meeting to plan a single Vietnamese agency, under a Commissioner of Refugees to be appointed by President Diem, to run the Vietnamese refugee program and to provide a channel through which help could be given by the U.S., France, and other free nations. The meeting was called and the plan adopted, with MAAG under General O'Daniel in the coordinating role. Diem adopted the plan. The French pitched in enthusiastically to help. CAT asked SMM for help in obtaining a French contact for the refugee airlift, and got it. In return, CAT provided SMM with the means for secret air travel between the North and Saigon. . . .

b. August 1954

An agreement had been reached that the personnel ceiling of U.S. military personnel with MAAG would be frozen at the number present in Vietnam on the date of the cease-fire, under the terms of the Geneva Agreement. In south Vietnam this deadline was to be 11 August. It meant that SMM might have only two members present, unless action were taken. General O'Daniel agreed to the addition of ten SMM men under MAAG cover, plus any others in the Defense pipeline who arrived before the deadline. . . .

Meetings were held to assess the new members' abilities. None had had political-psychological warfare experience. Most were experienced in paramilitary and clandestine intelligence operations. Plans were made quickly, for time was running out in the north; already the Vietminh had started taking over secret control of Hanoi and other areas of Tonkin still held by French forces.

Major Conein was given responsibility for developing a paramilitary organization in the north, to be in position when the Vietminh took over. . . . [His] . . . team was moved north immediately as part of the MAAG staff working on the refugee problem. The team had headquarters in Hanoi, with a branch in Haiphong. Among cover duties, this team supervised the refugee flow for the Hanoi airlift organized by the French. . . .

A second paramilitary team was formed to explore possibilities of organizing resistance against the Vietminh from bases in the south. . . .

Actually, support for an effort such as SMM is a major operation in itself, running the gamut from the usual administrative and personnel functions to the intricate business of clandestine air, maritime, and land supply of paramilitary materiel. In effect, they became our official smugglers as well as paymasters, housing officers, transportation officers, warehousemen, file clerks, and mess officers. . . .

c. September 1954

Highly-placed officials from Washington visited Saigon and, in private conversations, indicated that current estimates led to the conclusion that Vietnam probably would have to be written off as a loss. We admitted that prospects were gloomy, but were positive that there was still a fighting chance. . . .

[At this time SMM became aware of] a plot by the Army Chief of Staff, General Hinh, to overthrow the government. Hinh had hinted at such a plot to his American friends, using a silver cigarette box given him by Egypt's Naguib to carry the hint. SMM became thoroughly involved in the tense controversy which followed, due to our Chief's closeness to both President Diem and General Hinh. He had met the latter in the Philippines in 1952, was a friend of both Hinh's wife and favorite mistress. (The mistress was a pupil in a small English class conducted for mistresses of important personages, at their request. . . .)

While various U.S. officials . . . participated in U.S. attempts to heal the split between the President and his Army, Ambassador Heath asked us to make a major effort to end the controversy. This effort strained relations with Diem and never was successful, but did dampen Army enthusiasm for the plot. At one moment, when there was likelihood of an attack by armored vehicles on the Presidential Palace, SMM told Hinh bluntly that U.S. support most probably would stop in such an event. At the same time a group from the Presidential Guards asked for tactical advice on how to stop armored vehicles with the only weapons available to the Guards: carbines, rifles, and hand grenades. The advice, on tank traps and destruction with improvised weapons, must have sounded grim. The following morning, when the attack was to take place, we visited the Palace; not a guard was left on the grounds; President Diem was alone upstairs, calmly getting his work done.

As a result of the Hinh trouble, Diem started looking around for troops upon whom he could count. Some Tonkinese militia, refugees from the north, were assembled in Saigon close to the Palace. But they were insufficient for what he needed. Diem made an agreement with General Trinh Minh The, leader of some 3,000 Cao Dai dissidents in the vicinity of Tayninh, to give General The some needed financial support; The was to give armed support to the government if necessary and to provide a safe haven for the government if it had to flee. The's guerrillas, known as the Lien Minh, were strongly nationalist and were still fighting the Vietminh and the French. At Ambassador Heath's request, the U.S. secretly furnished Diem with funds for The, through the SMM. Shortly afterwards, an invitation came from The to visit him. Ambassador Heath approved the visit. . . .

The northern SMM team under Conein had organized a paramilitary group, (which we will disguise by the Vietnamese name of Binh) through the Northern Dai Viets, a political party with loyalties to Bao Dai. The group was to be trained and supported by the U.S. as patriotic Vietnamese, to come eventually under government control when the government was ready for such activities. Thirteen Binhs were quietly exfiltrated through the port of Haiphong, under the direction of Lt Andrews, and taken on the first stage of the journey to their training area by a U.S. Navy ship. This was the first of a series of helpful actions by Task Force 98, commanded by Admiral Sabin.

Another paramilitary group for Tonkin operations was being developed in Saigon through General Nguyen Van Vy. In September this group started shaping up fast, and the project was given to Major Allen. (We will give this group the Vietnamese name of Hao). . . .

Towards the end of the month, it was learned that the largest printing establishment in the north intended to remain in Hanoi and do business with the Vietminh. An attempt was made by SMM to destroy the modern presses, but Vietminh security agents already had moved into the plant and frustrated the attempt. This operation was under a Vietnamese patriot whom we shall call Trieu; his case officer was Capt Arundel. Earlier in the month they had engineered a black psywar strike in Hanoi: leaflets signed by the Vietminh instructing Tonkinese on how to behave for the Vietminh takeover of the Hanoi region in early October, including items about property, money reform, and a three-day holiday of workers upon takeover. The day following the distribution of these leaflets, refugee registration tripled. Two days later Vietminh currency was worth half the value prior to the leaflets. The Vietminh took to the radio to denounce the leaflets; the leaflets were so authentic in appearance that even most of the rank and file Vietminh were sure that the radio denunciations were a French trick.

The Hanoi psywar strike had other consequences. Binh had enlisted a high police official of Hanoi as part of his team, to effect the release from jail of any team members if arrested. The official at the last moment decided to assist in the leaflet distribution personally. Police officers spotted him, chased his vehicle through the empty Hanoi streets of early morning, finally opened fire on him and caught him. He was the only member of the group caught. He was held in prison as a Vietminh agent.

d. *October 1954*

Hanoi was evacuated on 9 October. The northern SMM team left with the last French troops, disturbed by what they had seen of the grim efficiency of the Vietminh in their takeover, the contrast between the silent march of the victorious Vietminh troops in their tennis shoes and the clanking armor of the well-equipped French whose western tactics and equipment had failed against the Communist military-political-economic campaign.

The northern team had spent the last days of Hanoi in contaminating the oil supply of the bus company for a gradual wreckage of engines in the buses, in taking the first actions for delayed sabotage of the railroad (which required teamwork with a CIA special technical team in Japan who performed their part brilliantly), and in writing detailed notes of potential targets for future paramilitary operations (U.S. adherence to the Geneva Agreement prevented SMM from carrying out the active sabotage it desired to do against the power plant, water faciliies, harbor, and bridge). The team had a bad moment when contaminating the oil. They had to work quickly at night, in an enclosed storage room. Fumes from the contaminant came close to knocking them out. Dizzy and weak-kneed, they masked their faces with handkerchiefs and completed the job.

Meanwhile, Polish and Russian ships had arrived in the south to transport southern Vietminh to Tonkin under the Geneva Agreement. This offered the opportunity for another black psywar strike. A leaflet was developed by Binh with the help of Capt Arundel, attributed to the Vietminh Resistance Committee. Among other items, it reassured the Vietminh they would be kept safe below decks from imperialist air and submarine attacks, and requested that warm clothing be brought; the warm clothing item would be coupled with a verbal rumor campaign that Vietminh were being sent into China as railroad laborers.

SMM had been busily developing G–5 of the Vietnamese Army for such psywar efforts. Under Arundel's direction, the First Armed Propaganda Company printed the leaflets and distributed them, by soldiers in civilian clothes who penetrated into southern Vietminh zones on foot. (Distribution in Camau was made while columnist Joseph Alsop was on his visit there which led to his sensational, gloomy articles[2] later . . .).

Contention between Diem and Hinh had become murderous. . . . Finally, we learned that Hinh was close to action; he had selected 26 October as the morning for an attack on the Presidential Palace. Hinh was counting heavily on Lt-Col Lan's special forces and on Captain Giai who was running Hinh's secret headquarters at Hinh's home. We invited these two officers to visit the Philippines, on the pretext that we were making an official trip, could take them along and open the way for them to see some inner workings of the fight against Filipino Communists which they probably would never see otherwise. Hinh reluctantly turned down his own invitation; he had had a memorable time of it on his last visit to Manila in 1952. Lt-Col Lan was a French agent and the temptation to see behind-the-scenes was too much. He and Giai accompanied SMM officers on the MAAG C–47 which

---

2. Among these articles was "Viet Minh Gaining Support by Deceit," *Time* 65 (January 5, 1955).—eds.

General O'Daniel instantly made available for the operation. 26 October was spent in the Philippines. The attack on the palace didn't come off.

e. November 1954

General Lawton Collins arrived as Ambassador on 8 November. . . .

Collins, in his first press conference, made it plain that the U.S. was supporting President Diem. The new Ambassador applied pressure on General Hinh and on 29 November Hinh left for Paris. His other key conspirators followed.

Part of the SMM team became involved in staff work to back up the energetic campaign to save Vietnam which Collins pushed forward. Some SMM members were scattered around the Pacific, accompanying Vietnamese for secret training, obtaining and shipping supplies to be smuggled into north Vietnam and hidden there. In the Philippines, more support was being constructed to help SMM, in expediting the flow of supplies, and in creating Freedom Company, a non-profit Philippines corporation backed by President Magsaysay, which would supply Filipinos experienced in fighting the Communist Huks to help in Vietnam (or elsewhere). . . .

On 23 November, twenty-one selected Vietnamese agents and two cooks of our Hao paramilitary group were put aboard a Navy ship in the Saigon River, in daylight. They appeared as coolies, joined the coolie and refugee throng moving on and off ship, and disappeared one by one. It was brilliantly planned and executed, agents being picked up from unobtrusive assembly points throughout the metropolis. Lt Andrews made the plans and carried out the movement under the supervision of Major Allen. The ship took the Hao agents, in compartmented groups, to an overseas point, the first stage in a movement to a secret training area.

f. December 1954

. . . discussions between the U.S., Vietnamese and French had reached a point where it appeared that a military training mission using U.S. officers was in the immediate offing. General O'Daniel had a U.S.-French planning group working on the problem, under Col Rosson. One paper they were developing was a plan for pacification of Vietminh and dissident areas; this paper was passed to SMM for its assistance with the drafting. SMM wrote much of the paper, changing the concept from the old rigid police controls of all areas to some of our concepts of winning over the population and instituting a classification of areas by the amount of trouble in each, the amount of control required, and fixing responsibilities between civil and military authorities. With a few changes, this was issued by President Diem on 31 December as the National Security Action (Pacification) Directive. . . .

There was still much disquiet in Vietnam, particularly among anti-Communist political groups who were not included in the government. SMM officers were contacted by a number of such groups who felt that they "would have to commit suicide in 1956" (the 1956 plebiscite promised in the 1954 Geneva agreement), when the Vietminh would surely take over against so weak a government. One group of farmers and militia in the south was talked out of migrating to Madagascar by SMM and staying on their farms. A number of these groups asked SMM for help in training personnel for eventual guerrilla warfare if the Vietminh won. Persons such as the then Minister of Defense and Trinh Minh The were among those loyal to the government who also requested such help. It was decided that a more basic guerrilla training program might be undertaken for such groups than was available at the secret training site to which we had sent the Binh and Hao groups. Plans were made with Major Bohanan and Mr. John C. Wachtel in the Philippines for a solution of this problem; the United States backed the development, through them, of a small Freedom Company training camp in a hidden valley on the Clark AFB reservation.

Till and Peg Durdin of the N.Y. Times, Hank Lieberman of the N.Y. Times, Homer Bigart of the N.Y. Herald-Tribune, John Mecklin of Life-Time, and John Roderick of Associated Press, have been warm friends of SMM and worked hard to penetrate the fabric of French propaganda and give the U.S. an objective account of events in Vietnam. The group met with us at times to analyze objectives and motives of propaganda known to them, meeting at their own request as U.S. citizens. These mature and responsible news correspondents performed a valuable service for their country. . . .

g. January 1955

The Vietminh long ago had adopted the Chinese Communist thought that the people are the water and the army is the fish. Vietminh relations with the mass of the population during the fighting had been exemplary, with a few exceptions; in contrast, the Vietnamese National Army had been like too many Asian armies, adept at cowing a population into feeding them, providing them with girls. SMM had been working on this problem from the beginning. Since the National Army was the only unit of government with a strong organization throughout the country and with good communications, it was the key to stabilizing the situation quickly on a nation-wide basis. If Army and people could be brought together into a team, the first strong weapon against Communism could be forged.

The Vietminh were aware of this. We later learned that months before the signing of the Geneva Agreement they had been planning for action in the post-Geneva period; the National Army was to be the primary target for subversion efforts, it was given top priority by the Central Committee for operations against its enemy, and about 100 superior cadres were retrained for the operations and placed in the [words illegible] organization for the work, which commenced even before the agreement was signed. We didn't know it at the time, but this was SMM's major opponent, in a secret struggle for the National Army. . . .

General O'Daniel was anticipating the culmination of long negotiations to permit U.S. training of the Vietnamese Armed Forces, against some resistance on the part of French groups. In January, negotiations were proceeding so well that General O'Daniel informally organized a combined U.S.-French training mission which eventually became known as the Training Relations & Instruction Mission

(TRIM) under his command, but under the overall command of the top French commander, General Paul Ely.

The French had asked for top command of half the divisions in the TRIM staff. Their first priority was for command of the division supervising National Security Action by the Vietnamese, which could be developed into a continuation of strong French control of key elements of both Army and population. In conferences with Ambassador Collins and General O'Daniel, it was decided to transfer Colonel Lansdale from the Ambassador's staff to TRIM, to head the National Security division. Colonel Lansdale requested authority to coordinate all U.S. civil and military efforts in this National Security work. On 11 January, Ambassador Collins announced the change to the country team, and gave him authority to coordinate this work among all U.S. agencies in Vietnam. . . .

President Diem had continued requesting SMM help with the guard battalion for the Presidential Palace. We made arrangements with President Magsaysay in the Philippines and borrowed his senior aide and military advisor, Col Napoleon Valeriano, who had a fine combat record against the Communist Huks and also had reorganized the Presidential Guard Battalion for Magsaysay. Valeriano, with three junior officers, arrived in January and went to work on Diem's guard battalion. Later, selected Vietnamese officers were trained with the Presidential Guards in Manila. An efficient unit gradually emerged. Diem was warmly grateful for this help by Filipinos who also continually taught our concept of loyalty and freedom.

The patriot we've named Trieu Dinh had been working on an almanac for popular sale, particularly in the northern cities and towns we could still reach. Noted Vietnamese astrologers were hired to write predictions about coming disasters to certain Vietminh leaders and undertakings, and to predict unity in the south. The work was carried out under the direction of Lt Phillips, based on our concept of the use of astrology for psywar in Southeast Asia. Copies of the almanac were shipped by air to Haiphong and then smuggled into Vietminh territory.

Dinh also had produced a Thomas Paine type series of essays on Vietnamese patriotism against the Communist Vietminh, under the guidance of Capt. Arundel. These essays were circulated among influential groups in Vietnam, earned front-page editorials in the leading daily newspaper in Saigon. Circulation increased with the publication of these essays. The publisher is known to SMM as The Dragon Lady and is a fine Vietnamese girl who has been the mistress of an anti-American French civilian. Despite anti-American remarks by her boy friend, we had helped her keep her paper from being closed by the government . . . and she found it profitable to heed our advice on the editorial content of her paper.

Arms and equipment for the Binh paramilitary team were being cached in the north in areas still free from the Vietminh. Personnel movements were covered by the flow of refugees. Haiphong was reminiscent of our own pioneer days as it was swamped with people whom it couldn't shelter. Living space and food were at a premium, nervous tension grew. It was a wild time for our northern team.

First supplies for the Hao paramilitary group started to arrive in Saigon. These shipments and the earlier ones for the Binh group were part of an efficient and effective air smuggling effort by the 581st [word illegible] Wing, U.S. Air Force, to support SMM, with help by CIA and Air Force personnel in both Okinawa and the Philippines. SMM officers frequently did coolie labor in manhandling tons of cargo, at times working throughout the night. . . . All . . . officers pitched in to help, as part of our "blood, sweat and tears.". . .

By 31 January, all operational equipment of the Binh paramilitary group had been trans-shipped to Haiphong from Saigon, mostly with the help of CAT, and the northern SMM team had it cached in operational sites. Security measures were tightened at the Haiphong airport and plans for bringing in the Hao equipment were changed from the air route to sea. . . .

. . . Major Conein had briefed the members of the Binh paramilitary team and started them infiltrating into the north as individuals. The infiltration was carried out in careful stages over a 30 day period, a successful operation. The Binhs became normal citizens, carrying out every day civil pursuits, on the surface.

We had smuggled into Vietnam about eight and a half tons of supplies for the Hao paramilitary group. They included fourteen agent radios, 300 carbines, 90,000 rounds of carbine ammunition, 50 pistols, 10,000 rounds of pistol ammunition, and 300 pounds of explosives. Two and a half tons were delivered to the Hao agents in Tonkin, while the remainder was cached along the Red River by SMM, with the help of the Navy. . . .

j. April 1955

. . . the Hao paramilitary team had finished its training at the secret training site and been flown by the Air Force to a holding site in the Philippines, where Major Allen and his officers briefed the paramilitary team. In mid-April, they were taken by the Navy to Haiphong, where they were gradually slipped ashore. Meanwhile, arms and other equipment including explosives were being flown into Saigon via our smuggling route, being readied for shipment north by the Navy task force handling refugees. The White team office gradually became an imposing munitions depot. Nightly shootings and bombings in restless Saigon caused us to give them dispersed storage behind thick walls as far as this one big house would permit. SMM personnel guarded the house night and day, for it also contained our major files other than the working file at our Command Post. All files were fixed for instant destruction, automatic weapons and hand grenades distributed to all personnel. It was a strange scene for new personnel just arriving. . . .

Haiphong was taken over by the Vietminh on 16 May. Our Binh and northern Hao teams were in place, completely equipped. It had taken a tremendous amount of hard work to beat the Geneva deadline, to locate, select, exfiltrate, train, infiltrate, equip the men of these two teams and have them in place, ready for actions required against the enemy. It would be a hard task to do openly, but this had to be kept secret from the Vietminh, the International Commission with its suspicious French and Poles and Indians, and even friendly Vietnamese. Movement of personnel and supplies had had to be over thousands of miles. . . .

B. Memorandum from Lansdale (1961)

South Vietnam

1. Vietnamese

a. First Observation Group

This is a Special Forces type of unit, with the mission of operating in denied (enemy) areas. It currently has some limited operations in North Vietnam and some shallow penetrations into Laos. Most of the unit has been committed to operations against Viet Cong guerrillas in South Vietnam. . . .

The Group and its activities are highly classified by the Government of Vietnam. Only a select few senior RVNMAF officers have access to it. Operations require the approval of President Diem, on much the same approval basis as certain U.S. special operations. The unit is separate from normal RVNAF command channels.

The Group was organized in February, 1956, with the initial mission of preparing stay-behind organizations in South Vietnam just below the 17th Parallel, for guerrilla warfare in the event of an overt invasion by North Vietnamese forces. It was given combat missions against Viet Cong guerrillas in South Vietnam last year, when these Communist guerrillas increased their activities. The plan is to relieve the Group from these combat assignments, to ready its full strength for denied area missions, as RVNAF force increases permit relief. It is currently being organized into twenty teams of 15 men each, with two RS–1 radios per team, for future operations. . . .

2. U.S.

a. Defense

1). There are approximately 6 officers and 6 enlisted men from the 1st Special Group on Okinawa currently attached to the MAAG to assist with Ranger-type training.

2). There are three 4-man intelligence training teams present—Combat Intelligence, Counter-Intelligence, Photo-Interpretation and Foreign Operations Intelligence (clandestine collection) in addition to eight officers and two enlisted intelligence advisors on the MAAG staff.

3). There are two Psychological Warfare staff officers on the MAAG staff and a 4-man Civil Affairs mobile training team (3 officers—1 enlisted man) advising the G–5 staff of the Vietnamese Army in the psy/ops-civic action fields.

b. CIA

1). There are 9 CIA officers working with the First Observation Group in addition to one MAAG advisor.

2). CIA also has five officers working with the Vietnamese Military Intelligence Service and one officer working with the covert [one word illegible] of the Army Psychological Warfare Directorate. . . .

[We are omitting Lansdale's description of unconventional-warfare resources in Thailand.—eds.]

Laos

1. Lao

a. Commandos

According to CINCPAC, there are two special commando companies in the Lao Armed Forces (FAL), with a total strength of 256. These commandos have received Special Forces training.

b. Meo Guerrillas

About 9,000 Meo tribesmen have been equipped for guerrilla operations, which they are now conducting with considerable effectiveness in Communist-dominated territory in Laos. They have been organized into Auto-Defense Choc units of the FAL, of varying sizes. Estimates on how many more of these splendid fighting men could be recruited vary, but a realistic figure would be about 4,000 more, although the total manpower pool is larger.

Political leadership of the Meos is in the hands of Touby Lyfoung, who now operates mostly out of Vientiane. The military leader is Lt-Col Vang Pao, who is the field commander. Command control of Meo operations is exercised by the Chief CIA Vientiane with the advice of Chief MAAG Laos. The same CIA para-military and U.S. military teamwork is in existence for advisory activities (9 CIA operations officers, 9 LTAG/Army Special Forces personnel, in addition to the 99 Thai PARU under CIA control) and aerial resupply.

As Meo villages are over-run by Communist forces and as men leave food-raising duties to serve as guerrillas, a problem is growing over the care and feeding of non-combat Meos. CIA has given some rice and clothing to relieve this problem. Consideration needs to be given to organized relief, a mission of an ICA nature, to the handling of Meo refugees and their rehabilitation.

c. National Directorate of Coordination

This is the Intelligence arm of the RLG. Its operations are mainly in the Vientiane area at present. It has an armed unit consisting of two battalions and is under the command of Lt-Col Siho, a FAL officer. In addition to intelligence operations this force has a capability for sabotage, kidnapping, commando-type raids, etc.

d. There is also a local veteran's organization and a grass-roots political organization in Laos, both of which are subject to CIA direction and control and are capable of carrying out propaganda, sabotage and harassment operations. Both are located (in varying degrees of strength and reliability) throughout Laos. . . .

Others

1. Asian

a. Eastern Construction Company (Filipinos)

This is a private, Filipino-run public service organization, similar to an employment agency, with an almost untapped potential for unconventional warfare (which was its original mission). It now furnishes about 500 trained, experienced Filipino technicians to the Governments of Vietnam and Laos, under the auspices of MAAGs (MAP) and USOMs (CIA activities). Most of these Filipinos are currently augmenting U.S. military logistics programs with the Vietnamese Army and Lao Army. They instruct local military personnel in ordnance, quartermaster, etc., maintenance, storage, and supply procedures. MAAG Chiefs in both Vietnam and Laos have rated this service as highly effective. CIA has influence and some continuing interest with individuals.

The head of Eastern Construction is "Frisco" Johnny San Juan, former National Commander, Philippines Veterans Legion, and former close staff assistant to President Magsaysay of the Philippines (serving as Presidential Complaints and Action Commissioner directly under the President). Its cadre are mostly either former guerrillas against the Japanese in WWII or former Philippine Army personnel. Most of the cadre had extensive combat experience against the Communist Huk guerrillas in the Philippines. This cadre can be expanded into a wide range of counter-Communist activities, having sufficient stature in the Philippines to be able to draw on a very large segment of its trained, experienced, and well-motivated manpower pool.

Eastern Construction was started in 1954 as Freedom Company of the Philippines, a non-profit organization, with President Magsaysay as its honorary president. Its charter stated plainly that it was "to serve the cause of freedom." It actually was a mechanism to permit the deployment of Filipino personnel in other Asian countries, for unconventional operations, under cover of a public service organization having a contract with the host government. Philippine Armed Forces and government personnel were "sheep-dipped" and served abroad. Its personnel helped write the Constitution of the Republic of Vietnam, trained Vietnam's Presidential Guard Battalion, and were instrumental in founding and organizing the Vietnamese Veterans Legion.

When U.S. personnel instrumental in the organization and operational use of Freedom Company departed from the Asian area, direct U.S. support of the organization (on a clandestine basis) was largely terminated. The Filipino leaders in it then decided to carry on its mission privately, as a commercial undertaking. They changed the name to Eastern Construction Company. The organization survived some months of very hard times financially. Its leaders remain as a highly-motivated, experienced, anti-Communist "hard core."

b. Operation Brotherhood (Filipino)

There is another private Filipino public-service organization, capable of considerable expansion in socio-economic-medical operations to support counter-guerrilla actions. It is now operating teams in Laos, under ICA auspices. It has a measure of CIA control.

Operation Brotherhood (OB) was started in 1954 by the International Jaycees, under the inspiration and guidance of Oscar Arellano, a Filipino architect who was Vice President for Asia of the International Jaycees. The concept was to provide medical service to refugees and provincial farmers in South Vietnam, as part of the 1955 pacification and refugee program. Initially Filipino teams, later other Asian and European teams, served in OB in Vietnam. Their work was closely coordinated with Vietnamese Army operations which cleaned up Vietminh stay-behinds and started stabilizing rural areas. . . .

c. The Security Training Center (STC)

This is a counter-subversion, counter-guerrilla and psychological warfare school overtly operated by the Philippine Government and covertly sponsored by the U.S. Government through CIA as the instrument of the Country Team. It is located at Fort McKinley on the outskirts of Manila. Its stated mission is: "To counter the forces of subversion in Southeast Asia through more adequate training of security personnel, greater cooperation, better understanding and maximum initiative among the countries of the area." . . .

The training capability of the STC includes a staff of approximately 12 instructors in the subjects of unconventional and counter-guerrilla warfare. . . .

d. CAT. Civil Air Transport (Chinese Nationalist)

CAT is a commercial air line engaged in scheduled and non-scheduled air operations throughout the Far East, with headquarters and large maintenance facilities located in Taiwan. CAT, a CIA proprietary, provides air logistical support under commercial cover to most CIA and other U.S. Government agencies' requirements. CAT supports covert and clandestine air operations by providing trained and experienced personnel, procurement of supplies and equipment through overt commercial channels, and the maintenance of a fairly large inventory of transport and other type aircraft under both Chinat and U.S. registry.

CAT has demonstrated its capability on numerous occasions to meet all types of contingency or long-term covert air requirements in support of U.S. objectives. During the past ten years, it has had some notable achievements, including support of the Chinese Nationalist withdrawal from the mainland, air drop support to the French at Dien Bien Phu, complete logistical and tactical air support for the Indonesian operation, air lifts of refugees from North Vietnam, more than 200 overflights of Mainland China and Tibet, and extensive air support in Laos during the current crisis. . . .

2. U.S.

b. CIA

1). Okinawa—Support Base

Okinawa Station is in itself a paramilitaray support asset and, in critical situations calling for extensive support of UW activity in the Far East, could be devoted in its entirety to this mission. Located at Camp Chinen, it comprises a self-contained base under Army cover with facilities of all types necessary to the storage, testing, packaging, procurement and delivery of supplies—ranging from weapons and explosives to medical and clothing. Because of its being a controlled area, it can accommodate admirably the holding of black bodies in singletons or small groups, as well as small groups of trainees. . . .

4). Saipan Training Station

CIA maintains a field training station on the island of Saipan located approximately 160 miles northeast of Guam in the Marianas Islands. The installation is under Navy cover and is known as the Naval Technical Training Unit. The primary mission of the Saipan Training Station is to provide physical facilities and competent instructor personnel to fulfill a variety of training requirements including intelligence tradecraft, communications, counter-intelligence and psychological warfare techniques. Training is performed in support of CIA activities throughout the Far East area.

In addition to the facilities described above, CIA maintains a small ship of approximately 500 tons' displacement and 140 feet in length. This vessel is used presently to provide surface transportation between Guam and Saipan. It has an American Captain and First Mate and a Philippine crew, and is operated under the cover of a commercial corporation with home offices in Baltimore, Maryland. Both the ship and the corporation have a potentially wider paramilitary application both in the Far East area and elsewhere.

20. Heroin and Politics in Saigon*

By Alfred W. McCoy

France may have lost the war, but French influence remained strong. The United States had yet to establish primacy in any part of Vietnam. In the following selection, Alfred McCoy describes the intricate interweaving of politics and underworld activities in Saigon. Originally, the Binh Xuyen were river pirates, who first appeared in Saigon in the early 1920s. Flourishing on their organization of the opium trade, prostitution, and extortion, they represented, by the 1940s, a significant political force whose allegiance was sought by the Viet Minh, among others.

*Alfred W. McCoy, *The Politics of Heroin in Southeast Asia*, with Cathleen B. Read and Leonard P. Adams II (New York: Harper & Row, 1972), pp. 120–125. Prof. Alfred W. McCoy currently teaches at the University of New South Wales in Australia. He is the editor of an important collection of essays, *Southeast Asia under Japanese Occupation* (New Haven: Yale University Southeast Asian Studies, 1980), co-editor with Nina Adams of *Laos: War and Revolution* (New York: Harper & Row, 1970) and co-editor with Edilberto De Jesus of *Philippine Social History: Global Trade and Local Transformations* (Honolulu: University of Hawaii Press, 1982).

For a time the Binh Xuyen participated in a nationalist coalition with the Viet Minh, only to break away over an issue of discipline.

If Diem was to truly rule in Saigon the power of the Binh Xuyen had to be broken. To break them would mean, as well, to break the continuing influence and control of the French secret police. The CIA enthusiastically welcomed this task. And just as the French secret police had used the opium trade to fund counterinsurgency in their war against the Viet Minh, so the CIA, in their struggle against the National Liberation Front, soon embraced the drug traffic as well. Saigon governments selected and supported by the United States, from Diem through Ky and Thieu, were deeply engaged in a trade that fed the heroin habits of Americans at home and abroad.

N go Dinh Diem was a political unknown who had acceded to the premiership largely because Washington was convinced that his strong anti-Communist, anti-French beliefs best suited American interests. But the immediate problem for Diem and the Americans was control of Saigon. If Diem were to be of any use to the Americans in blocking the unification of Vietnam, he would have to wrest control of the streets from the Binh Xuyen. For whoever controlled the streets controlled Saigon, and whoever controlled Saigon held the key to Vietnam's rice-rich Mekong Delta.

While the French and American governments politely disavowed any self-interest and tried to make even their most partisan suggestions seem a pragmatic response to the changing situation in Saigon, both gave their intelligence agencies a free hand to see if Saigon's reality could be molded in their favor. Behind the smiles on the diplomatic front, Colonel Lansdale,[1] of the CIA, and the French 2eme Bureau, particularly Captain Savani, engaged in a savage clandestine battle for Saigon.

In the movie version of Graham Greene's novel on this period, *The Quiet American*, Colonel Lansdale was played by the World War II combat hero, Audie Murphy. Murphy's previous roles as the typical American hero in dozens of black hat-white hat westerns enabled him accurately to project the evangelistic anti-Communism so characteristic of Lansdale. What Murphy did not portray was Lansdale's mastery of the CIA's repertoire of "dirty tricks" to achieve limited political ends. When Lansdale arrived in Saigon in May 1954 he was fresh from engineering President Ramon Magsaysay's successful counterinsurgency campaign against the Philippine Communist Party. As the prophet of a new counterinsurgency doctrine and representative of a wealthy government, Lansdale was a formidable opponent.

In seeking to depose Bay Vien,[2] Colonel Lansdale was not just challenging the 2eme Bureau, he was taking on Saigon's Corsican community—Corsican business-

---

1. For more on Lansdale, see Readings 19 and 24.—eds.
2. Elected head of the Binh Xuyen in February 1946. For more on his career, see McCoy, *Politics of Heroin*, p. 115.—eds.

men, Corsican colonists, and the Corsican underworld. From the late nineteenth century onward, Corsicans had dominated the Indochina civil service.[3] At the end of World War II, Corsican resistance fighters, some of them gangsters, had joined the regular army and come to Indochina with the Expeditionary Corps. Many remained in Saigon after their enlistment to go into legitimate business or to reap profits from the black market and smuggling that flourished under wartime conditions. Those with strong underworld connections in Marseille were able to engage in currency smuggling between the two ports. The Marseille gangster Barthélemy Guerini worked closely with contacts in Indochina to smuggle Swiss gold to Asia immediately after World War II.[4] Moreover, Corsican gangsters close to Corsican officers in Saigon's 2eme Bureau purchased surplus opium and shipped it to Marseille, where it made a small contribution to the city's growing heroin industry.[5]

The unchallenged leader of Saigon's Corsican underworld was the eminently respectable Mathieu Franchini. Owner of the exclusive Continental Palace Hotel, Franchini made a fortune playing the piaster-gold circuit between Saigon and Marseille during the First Indochina War.[6] He became the Binh Xuyen's investment counselor and managed a good deal of their opium and gambling profits. When Bay Vien's fortune reached monumental proportions, Franchini sent him to Paris where "new found Corsican friends gave him good advice about investing his surplus millions.[7] And according to reliable Vietnamese sources, it was Franchini who controlled most of Saigon's opium exports to Marseille. Neither he nor his associates could view with equanimity the prospect of an American takeover.

Many people within the 2eme Bureau had worked as much as eight years building up sect armies like the Binh Xuyen; many Corsicans outside the military had businesses, positions, rackets, and power that would be threatened by a decline in French influence. While they certainly did not share Premier Mendès-France's ideas of cooperation with the Viet Minh, they were even more hostile to the idea of turning things over to the Americans.

When Lansdale arrived in Saigon in May 1954 he faced the task of building an alternative to the mosaic of religious armies and criminal gangs that had ruled South Vietnam in the latter years of the war. Ngo Dinh Diem's appointment as premier in July gave Lansdale the lever he needed. Handpicked by the Americans, Diem was strongly anti-French and uncompromisingly anti-Communist. However,

---

3. Pierre Brocheux, "L'Economie et la Société dans L'Ouest de la Cochinchine pendant la Période coloniale (1890–1940)" (Ph.D. thesis, University of Paris, 1969), p.298.

4. Eugène Saccomano, *Bandits à Marseille* (Paris: Julliard, 1968), p. 44.

5. In 1958 a U.S. narcotics agent told a Senate subcommittee, "When French Indochina existed, there were quantities of opium that were shipped to the labs . . . around Marseille, France, to the Corsican underworld there, and then transshipped to the United States" (U.S. Congress, Senate Select Committee on Improper Activities in the Labor Management Field, *Hearings*, 85th Cong., 2nd sess., 1959, p. 1225, cited in *Earth*, March 1972, pp. 93–94).

6. Lucien Bodard, *L'Humiliation* (Paris: Gallimard, 1965), pp. 80–81.

7. Lucien Bodard, *The Quicksand War: Prelude to Vietnam* (Boston: Little, Brown and Co., 1967), pp. 121, 124.

he had spent most of the last decade in exile and had few political supporters and almost no armed forces. Premier in name only, Diem controlled only the few blocks of downtown Saigon surrounding the presidential palace. The French and their clients—ARVN, the Binh Xuyen, and the armed religious sects, Cao Dai and Hoa Hao—could easily mount an anti-Diem coup if he threatened their interests. Lansdale proceeded to fragment his opposition's solid front and to build Diem an effective military apparatus. French control over the army was broken and Col. Duong Van Minh ("Big Minh"), an American sympathizer, was recruited to lead the attacks on the Binh Xuyen. By manipulating payments to the armed religious sects, Lansdale was able to neutralize most of them, leaving the Binh Xuyen as the only French pawn. The Binh Xuyen financed themselves largely from their vice rackets, and their loyalty could not be manipulated through financial pressures. But, deserted by ARVN and the religious sects, the Binh Xuyen were soon crushed.

Lansdale's victory did not come easily. Soon after he arrived he began sizing up his opponent's financial and military strength. Knowing something of the opium trade's importance as a source of income for French clandestine services, he now began to look more closely at Operation X[8] with the help of a respected Cholon Chinese banker. But the banker was abruptly murdered and Lansdale dropped the inquiry. There was reason to believe that the banker had gotten too close to the Corsicans involved, and they killed him to prevent the information from getting any further.[9]

An attempted anti-Diem coup in late 1954 led to Lansdale's replacing the palace guard. After the Embassy approved secret funding (later estimated at $2 million), Lansdale convinced a Cao Dai dissident named Trinh Minh Thé to offer his *maquis* near the Cambodian border as a refuge in case Diem was ever forced to flee Saigon.[10] When the impending crisis between the French and the Americans threatened Diem's security in the capital, Thé moved his forces into the city as a permanent security force in February 1955 and paraded 2,500 of his barefoot soldiers through downtown Saigon to demonstrate his loyalty to the premier.[11] The 2eme Bureau was outraged at Lansdale's support for Thé. Practicing what Lansdale jocularly referred to as the "unorthodox doctrine of zapping a commander,"[12] Thé had murdered French General Chanson in 1951 and had further incensed the French when he blew up a car in 1953 in downtown Saigon, killing a number of

---

8. The clandestine opium trade conducted by the French secret service which financed counterinsurgency efforts in Vietnam under the French and, in a different form, the United States. See McCoy, *Politics of Heroin*, pp. 92 f.—eds.

9. Interview with Gen. Edward G. Lansdale, Alexandria, Virginia, June 17, 1971.

10. Bernard B. Fall, *The Two Vietnams* (New York: Frederick A. Praeger, 1967), pp. 245–246; The New York Times, *The Pentagon Papers* (New York: Quadrangle Books, 1971), p. 60. Hereafter *The Pentagon Papers* (NY Times edition).

11. Edward G. Lansdale, *Subject: The Cao Dai*, memo to Ambassador Bunker and members, U.S. Mission council (May 1968), p. 14.

12. Ibid., p. 2.

passersby. 2ᵉᵐᵉ Bureau officers personally visited Lansdale to warn him that they would kill Thé, and they "usually added the pious hope that I would be standing next to him when he was gunned down."[13]

On February 11, 1955, the French army abdicated its financial controls and training responsibilities for ARVN to the United States, losing not only the ARVN but control of the Hoa Hao and Cao Dai religious sects as well. Approximately 20,000 of them had served as supplementary forces to the French and Vietnamese army,[14] and had been paid directly by the 2ᵉᵐᵉ Bureau. Now, with their stipends cut and their numbers reduced, they were to be integrated into ARVN, where they would be controlled by Diem and his American advisers.

Lansdale was given $8.6 million to pay back salaries and "bonuses" to sect commanders who cooperated in "integrating" into the ARVN.[15] Needless to say, this aroused enormous hostility on the part of the French. When Lansdale met with General Gambiez of the French army to discuss the sect problem, the tensions were obvious:

We sat at a small table in his office. . . . A huge Alsatian dog crouched under it. Gambiez informed me that at one word from him, the dog would attack me, being a trained killer. I asked Gambiez to please note that my hands were in my pockets as I sat at the table; I had a small .25 automatic pointing at his stomach which would tickle him fatally. Gambiez called off his dog and I put my hands on the table. We found we could work together.[16]

By February the 2ᵉᵐᵉ Bureau realized that they were gradually losing to Lansdale's team, so they tried to discredit him as an irresponsible adventurer in the eyes of his own government by convening an unprecedented secret agents' tribunal. But the session was unsuccessful, and the 2ᵉᵐᵉ Bureau officers were humiliated; their animosity toward Lansdale no doubt intensified.[17]

But the French were not yet defeated, and late in February they mounted a successful counteroffensive. When Diem refused to meet the sects' demands for financial support and integration into ARVN, the French seized the opportunity and brought all the sect leaders together in Tay Ninh on February 22, where they formed the United Front and agreed to work for Diem's overthrow. Money was to be provided by the Binh Xuyen. When a month of fruitless negotiations failed to wring any concessions from Diem, the United Front sent a five-day ultimatum to

13. Ibid., p. 11.

14. Lt. Col. Grimaldi, Inspecteur des Forces Supplétives, Inspection des Forces Supplétives du Sud Vietnam, *Notions de Case sur les Forces Supplétives du Sud Vietnam* (S.P.50.295, May 15, 1954), p. 24.

15. Fall, *The Two Vietnams*, pp. 245–246.

16. Lansdale, memo to Ambassador Bunker *et al.*, May 1968, pp. 15–16.

17. Interview with Gen. Edward G. Lansdale, Alexandria, Virginia, June 17, 1971; Edward G. Lansdale, *In the Midst of Wars* (New York: Harper & Row, 1972), pp. 221–224.

Diem demanding economic and political reforms.[18] Suddenly the lethargic quadrille of political intrigue was over and the time for confrontation was at hand.

Lansdale was now working feverishly to break up the United Front and was meeting with Diem regularly.[19] With the help of the CIA station chief, Lansdale put together a special team to tackle the Binh Xuyen, the financial linchpin of the United Front. Lansdale recruited a former Saigon police chief named Mai Huu Xuan, who had formed the Military Security Service (MSS) with two hundred to three hundred of his best detectives when the Binh Xuyen took over the police force in 1954. Embittered by four years of losing to the Binh Xuyen, the MSS began a year-long battle with the Binh Xuyen's action committees. Many of these covert cells had been eliminated by April 1955, a factor that Xuan feels was critical in the Binh Xuyen's defeat.[20] Another of Lansdale's recruits was Col. Duong Van Minh, the ARVN commander for Saigon-Cholon. Lansdale made ample discretionary funds available to Minh, whom he incorporated in his plans to assault the Binh Xuyen.[21]

The fighting began on March 28 when a pro-Diem paratroop company attacked the Binh Xuyen-occupied police headquarters. The Binh Xuyen counterattacked the following night and began with a mortar attack on the presidential palace at midnight. When French tanks rolled into the city several hours later to impose a cease-fire agreed to by the United States, Lansdale protested bitterly to Ambassador Collins, "explaining that only the Binh Xuyen would gain by a cease fire."[22]

For almost a month French tanks and troops kept the Binh Xuyen and ARVN apart. Then on April 27 Ambassador Collins met with Secretary of State Dulles in Washington and told him that Diem's obstinancy was the reason for the violent confrontation in Saigon. Dismayed, Dulles cabled Saigon that the U.S. was no longer supporting Diem.[23] A few hours after this telegram arrived, Diem's troops attacked Binh Xuyen units, and drove them out of downtown Saigon into neighboring Cholon. Elated by Diem's easy victory, Dulles cabled Saigon his full support for Diem. The Embassy burned his earlier telegram.[24]

During the fighting of April 28 Lansdale remained in constant communication with the presidential palace, while his rival, Captain Savani, moved into the Binh Xuyen headquarters at the Y Bridge in Cholon, where he took command of the bandit battalions and assigned his officers to accompany Binh Xuyen troops in the house-to-house fighting.[25] The Binh Xuyen radio offered a reward to anyone who

---

18. Lansdale, *In the Midst of Wars*, pp. 245–247; *Pentagon Papers* (Gravel edition), vol. I, p. 230.

19. *The Pentagon Papers* (NY Times edition), p. 21.

20. Interview with Gen. Mai Huu Xuan, Saigon, Vietnam, July 19, 1971.

21. Lansdale, *In the Midst of Wars*, p. 270.

22. *The Pentagon Papers* (Gravel edition), vol. 1, p. 231.

23. Ibid., p. 233.

24. *The Pentagon Papers* (NY Times edition), p. 22.

25. Interview with Lt. Col. Lucien Conein, McLean, Virginia, June 18, 1971. [For more on the role of Conein, see Reading 19.—eds.]

could bring Lansdale to their headquarters where, Bay Vien promised, his stomach would be cut open and his entrails stuffed with mud.[26]

On May 2 the fighting resumed as ARVN units penetrated Cholon, leveling whole city blocks and pushing the Binh Xuyen steadily backward. Softened by years of corruption, the Binh Xuyen bandits were no longer the tough guerrillas of a decade before. Within a week most of them had retreated back into the depths of the Rung Sat Swamp.

Although the war between Diem and Bay Vien was over, the struggle between Lansdale and the Corsicans was not quite finished. True to the Corsican tradition, the defeated French launched a vendetta against the entire American community. As Lansdale describes it:

A group of soreheads among the French in Saigon undertook a spiteful terror campaign against American residents. Grenades were tossed at night into the yards of houses where Americans lived. American owned automobiles were blown up or booby-trapped. French security officials blandly informed nervous American officials that the terrorist activity was the work of the Viet Minh.[27]

A sniper put a bullet through Lansdale's car window as he was driving through Saigon, a Frenchman who resembled him was machine-gunned to death in front of Lansdale's house by a passing car. When Lansdale was finally able to determine who the ringleaders were (many of them were intelligence officers), grenades started going off in front of their houses in the evening.[28]

During his May 8–11, 1955, meeting with French Premier Edgar Faure in Paris, Dulles asserted his continuing support for Diem, and both agreed that France and the United States would pursue independent policies in Indochina. The partnership was over; France would leave, and the United States would remain in Vietnam in order to back Diem.[29]

21. Elections and Reunification Denied (1955)*

Few issues pose the problem of what is a war for "national liberation" more clearly than the question of national unity. The Viet Minh had been the historic

---

*Embassy of [the Republic of] Vietnam, Washington, D.C., Press and Information Service, Vol. I, No. 18 (July 22, 1955) and No. 20 (August 19, 1955).

26. Lansdale, memo to Ambassador Bunker *et al.*, May 1968, p. 17.

27. Lansdale, *In the Midst of Wars*, pp. 316–317.

28. Ibid., p. 318.

29. *The Pentagon Papers* (Gravel edition), vol. 1, pp. 238–239.

champion of such unity against the French colonialists' efforts to separate south-
ern Vietnam from the rest of the country.[1] *The Geneva Accords of 1954 provided*
clear procedures for reunifying Vietnam at the close of the bloody Franco-Viet-
namese conflict: temporary military disengagement into two zones, consultative
conferences between representatives of the armed forces in each zone in 1955, and
elections to reunify the country in 1956. In July 1955, the government of the Dem-
ocratic Republic of Vietnam formally proposed "the holding on schedule" of the
meeting of "competent authorities of the North and the South."

Our compatriots from the South to the North, irrespective of classes, creeds and political affiliations have deeply at heart the reunification of the country, and are looking forward
to the early convening of the consultative conference and to its good outcome. All the
countries responsible for the guarantee of the implementation of the Geneva Agreements
and in general all the peace-loving countries in the world are anxious to see that the consultative conference will be held and yield good results and that the reunification of our
country will be achieved.[2]

This Reading presents President Ngo Dinh Diem's rejection of the appeal by the
DRV leadership to participate in the consultative conferences, and the attempt to
shift the onus of responsibility for this non-participation onto the Communists.

The National Government has emphasized time and time again the price it has
paid for the defense of the unity of the country and of true democracy. We did
not sign the Geneva Agreements. We are not bound in any way by these Agreements, signed against the will of the Vietnamese people. Our policy is a policy of
peace, but nothing will lead us astray from our goal: the unity of our country—a
unity in freedom and not in slavery.

Serving the cause of our nation more than ever, we will struggle for the reunification of our homeland. We do not reject the principle of free elections as peaceful and democratic means to achieve that unity. Although elections constitute one
of the bases of true democracy, they will be meaningful only on the condition that
they are absolutely free.

Faced now with a regime of oppression as practiced by the Vietminh, we remain skeptical concerning the possibility of fulfilling the conditions of free elections in the North. We shall not miss any opportunity which would permit the
unification of our homeland in freedom, but it is out of the question for us to
consider any proposal from the Vietminh if proof is not given that they put the
superior interests of the national community above those of Communism, if they
do not cease violating their obligations as they have done by preventing our coun-

---

1. Philippe Devillers and Jean Lacouture, *End of a War: Indochina, 1954* (New York: Frederick
A. Praeger, 1969), pp. 7–15.

2. Pham Van Dong and Ho Chi Minh to Bao Dai and Ngo Dinh Diem, July 19, 1955. In Gareth
Porter, ed., *Vietnam: A History in Documents* (New York: New American Library, 1979), p. 178.

trymen of the North from going South or by recently attacking, together with the Communist Pathet Lao, the friendly state of Laos.

The mission falls to us, the Nationalists, to accomplish the reunification of our country in conditions that are most democratic and most effective to guarantee our independence. The free world is with us. Of this we are certain. I am confident that I am a faithful interpreter of our state of mind when I affirm solemnly our will to resist Communism.

To those who live above the 17th Parallel, I ask them to have confidence. With the agreement and the backing of the free world, the National Government will bring you independence in freedom.

*   *   *

In a radio broadcast of last July 16, the Government of the State of Vietnam clearly defined its position regarding the problem of territorial reunification.

The Government does not consider itself bound in any way by the Geneva Agreements which it did not sign. It affirms once again that, placing the interests of the nation as its first consideration, it is determined, in any circumstances, to reach the obvious goal of its policy—the unity of the country in peace and freedom.

The Vietminh authorities sent a letter dated July 19 to the Government in which they asked for a pre-election consultation conference, thus, for propaganda purposes, seeking to give credence to the false idea that they would be defenders of territorial unity.

It is recalled that last year at Geneva, the Vietminh claimed a viable economic zone while recommending the partition. At the same time, the delegation of the State of Vietnam proposed an armistice, even though provisional, without partitioning Vietnam in order to safeguard the sacred right of the Vietnamese people to territorial unity, national independence, and freedom. Through the voice of its delegation, the Government affirmed that it hoped to fulfill the aspirations of the Vietnamese people by every means at its disposal resulting from the independence and sovereignty solemnly recognized by France toward the State of Vietnam which is the only legal State.[3]

The policy of the Government remains unchanged toward the partitioning of the country accomplished against its will. Serving the cause of true democracy, the Government is anxious that all Vietnamese throughout the entire country may live without fear and that they be totally free from all dictatorship and oppression. The Government considers the principle of essentially free elections a democratic and

---

3. We are unable to give any full treatment to questions of international law in this book, but Bao Dai's abdication in 1945 and the Franco-Vietnamese treaty of 1946 (Readings 8, 12), not to speak of the DRV's victory in the resistance war of 1946–1954, would seem to establish a strong claim for the Hanoi regime to be the legal state in Vietnam. See Richard A. Falk et al., eds., *Vietnam and International Law* (Flanders, NJ: O'Hare Books, 1967).—eds.

peaceful institution, but believes that conditions of freedom of life and of voting must be assured beforehand. From this point of view, nothing constructive will be done as long as the Communist regime of the North does not permit each Vietnamese citizen to enjoy democratic freedoms and the basic fundamental rights of man.

22. "Vietnam's Democratic One-Man Rule"*

By Wesley R. Fishel

Educated at the University of Chicago and having taught at Michigan State University, Wesley Fishel pursued an unconventional academic career. He served as adviser to President Ngo Dinh Diem, as chief adviser to the Michigan State University Vietnam Project, and as Chairman of the Diemist lobby in the United States, the American Friends of Vietnam (for discussion of this organization, and Fishel's role in it, see Reading 24). Given these political and institutional connections, it is not surprising that Fishel would write the paean of praise to Ngo Dinh Diem presented here. But some years later, after the Ngo dynasty's policies had generated intense opposition in southern Vietnam, and after the US government withdrew its support and permitted Diem and his brother, Ngo Dinh Nhu, to be assassinated (Readings 33 and 34), Fishel had occasion to re-evaluate the Vietnamese leader he had so enthusiastically supported in the 1950s.

By 1964 he found Ngo Dinh Diem's philosophy to be nothing less than "peasant-based revolutionary fascism."[1] There are serious problems with even this newer interpretation of Diem. Ngo Dinh Diem's base of support was never in the southern Vietnam peasantry, which turned sharply against him in the mid- and late-1950s. Nor could it be said that he espoused any genuinely "revolutionary" goals. The efforts of academics like Professor Fishel were important in providing respectable cover for an energetic public relations campaign in the United States. But in the long run, no cosmetic retouching could make up for Diem's growing unpopularity with the people of Vietnam.

"When I use a word," Humpty Dumpty said, in rather a scornful tone, "it means just what I choose it to mean, neither more nor less."

"The question is," said Alice, "whether you *can* make words mean so many different things."

"The question is," said Humpty Dumpty, "which is to be master, that's all."

---

*From *The New Leader* [New York] 42 (November 2, 1959), pp. 10–13.

1. Wesley R. Fishel, "Vietnam: Is Victory Possible?", Foreign Policy Association, *Headline Series*, No. 163 (February, 1964), p. 16.

Every age has its shibboleths, every people its fetishes and phobias. The color words which express our fears and hopes, our likes and dislikes, constitute a semantic corset in which we bind ourselves as we march bravely along in a world populated by scientific goblins, technological sprites, and ideological angels and demons.

Our angels today are "democrats" and "anti-Communists"; our demons are "dictators" and "Communists." These creatures come in many shapes, varied sizes and diverse forms. And when we stop every now and then to think about our "friends" and our "foes" we feel more than a little confused. For we are living in a world that has suddenly changed and expanded. The family of nations is no longer a comfortably small club of European "Powers," more or less Christian in character (with Japan holding "alternate membership"). No, now it includes all sorts of heathens—many of them brown, still others black, and most of them non-Christian!

In tropical West Africa, out of the loins of the British Commonwealth, is born a "constitutional" "democratic" state named Ghana. And before the ink is dry on its birth certificate, its elected leader is imprisoning his opponents and castigating his country's constitution in a most disconcerting manner. And on the ruins of the Dutch empire in the farthermost Indies, an elected President who talks a good game of Jefferson has created what sounds like a contradiction in terms: a "guided democracy."

If things seem a bit confusing to us, it is because we are truly prisoners of our political vernacular. Even as our cultures haven't managed to keep pace with developments in technology, our languages have failed to stay abreast of political change. Recently, one articulate observer shrugged his verbal shoulders in annoyance over the inadequacies of the English language. He recognized the emotional trap involved in the word "dictatorship," and he explained that when he talked about the political systems of Asia he was referring to "Hamiltonian rather than Jeffersonian principles." At the same time, he concluded, let's be "more blunt and use the word dictatorship, in spite of its associations." The essential point, as he sees it, is "whose dictators" are going to rule Asia. But is this a valid conclusion? Are we faced only with a choice between—to use the horrible term once more—dictators of different complexions? Let us examine here his prime example: Vietnam.

For ninety years Vietnam was a colony of France, kept subjugated by force. By their occupation of French Indochina from 1940 to 1945, the Japanese ended for all time the legend of white invincibility. After V-J Day, the attempted restoration of full French control over Vietnam was never successful. And after the disaster at Dienbienphu in 1954, the French regime of Pierre Mendès-France "simplified" France's costly involvement in the peninsula: he turned over the northern half of Vietnam to the Communist Vietminh—and gave them a promissory note on the southern half, collectable after elections which presumably would take place two years later.

As we now know—much to our satisfaction and to the confusion of our enemies—things just didn't work out the way the negotiators at Geneva in July 1954 thought they would. And the principal reason for this surprising development has been the leadership given the free remnant of Vietnam since 1954 by Ngo Dinh Diem.

Is Ngo Dinh Diem a "dictator" or a "democrat"? As one examines the structure of the Republic of Vietnam and the behavior of President Ngo, he learns that (a) Ngo Dinh Diem has all the authority and all the power one needs to operate a dictatorship, but (b) he isn't operating one! Here is a leader who speaks the language of democracy, who holds the powers of a dictator, and who governs a Republic in accordance with the terms of a Constitution. The Constitution was written at his request by a National Assembly which he caused to be elected by the people of the Republic.

Ngo Dinh Diem did not *have* to do this. His authority and power at that moment were so absolute that he could have ruled for many years as a dictator, had he chosen to do so. But he chose instead the path of limited government, out of a long-standing and unshakable belief, which he had enunciated publicly time and again even before he came to power, that the keys to the restoration of Vietnam's stature were "the independence of the nation and the liberty of the people."

He came to power on July 7, 1954, having been selected by the Emperor Bao Dai—a lifelong political opponent—and with French approval, to be the "fall guy" when the terms of the Geneva accords would be announced. For it was a foregone conclusion as early as the first week in May 1954 that France was going to have to give up Indochina, unless it was willing to take its chances on a further expansion and extension of a war which had already cost it fantastic treasure in both lives and material wealth. France was not willing. The new French Premier, Mendès-France, set himself a time limit for the settlement of the Indochina problem. And he understood that the settlement would offer France, at best, a period of grace before the end.

Ngo took office as Prime Minister with "full powers, civil and military." This extraordinary grant of authority was his price for accepting the task of attempting the impossible: holding his country together in the face of a devastating flood of Communist military victories. Within three weeks, his country was cut in two and he was left with an incredible set of problems to resolve. True, the shooting war apparently was ended, at least for the time being. But under the provisions of the Geneva agreements, he had to repatriate his military forces from the now-Communist north and resettle whatever civilians might choose to move from the north to his zone of Vietnam. His representatives at Geneva had refused to sign the accords; nevertheless, his Government was regarded by its French sponsors and many other powers as responsible under them.

During the next 300 days (the time allotted for free movement between the two zones), Ngo's Government, aided by the U.S. and France, received and temporarily resettled—without a single untoward incident or an epidemic of disease—some

850,000 refugees from the Communist zone. And today virtually all these people are self-supporting citizens, truly a record to remember when one thinks of the tragedy that has marked similar refugee movements elsewhere in the world.

But this was not all. The new Prime Minister learned quickly enough that his "full powers, civil and military," existed principally on paper. He could not control the police: They were the *property*—bought and paid for—of the Binh Xuyen, a gang of thugs and racketeers who also had a well-trained and well-equipped army, and who controlled gambling, narcotics, and prostitution in the capital city of Saigon. The National Army was commanded by an opportunistic Chief of Staff, General Nguyen Van Hinh, who held a commission simultaneously as a major in the French Air Force, and who thought he could make a better Prime Minister than Ngo Dinh Diem.

Vast sections of real estate in South Vietnam were ruled in feudal fashion by leaders of the Cao Dai and Hoa Hao religious sects, which also maintained their own armies (subsidized by the French) and set a high price on their cooperation with the new Prime Minister. The Communists, after partition, withdrew their main fighting forces to the north, but left behind several thousand cadres, who were instructed to await "the day" when their leaders would move back in and take over. And the French, who regarded Ngo as anti-French, not only expected him to fall momentarily; they even made occasional unofficial efforts to assist him out of office.

Finally there were the bureaucrats. France had never permitted the Vietnamese to run their own government and administration, notwithstanding many highly publicized promises to that effect. Vietnamese cabinet ministers before Ngo's time were surrounded by French "advisors"; Duong-tan-Tai, a former Minister of Finance in one of the earlier "independent" cabinets of Bao Dai, likes to tell how the next nearest Vietnamese in his administrative hierarchy was some four levels below him. So Ngo inherited a civil service which had had virtually no experience in decision-making positions.

Ngo managed to survive. He ousted the Chief of Staff without a fight, drove the Binh Xuyen armies from the capital in a series of bloody encounters, won over or vanquished the military forces of the Cao Dai and the Hoa Hao, resettled the refugees, and reduced the Communist capability in South Vietnam from that of mounting a coup against him to one of sheer nuisance activity.

Naturally, this all required strong leadership and considerable political flexibility and manipulative skill. Nevertheless, it was rather difficult for our journalists on the scene (or on the rewrite desks back in New York) and for our political commentators to make up their minds about him. During his first 300 days Ngo was described variously as: weak, strong, monklike or ascetic, friendly, stern, inefficient, honest, corrupt, anti-French, anti-American, America's puppet, sectarian (a reference to the fact that he is a Roman Catholic), Cardinal Spellman's choice, indecisive, strong-minded, slow-acting, decisive, clumsy, skillful, conservative, liberal, and heaven only knows what else.

As a matter of fact, the only thing on which thoughtful pundits agreed during

Ngo's first year in office was that his administration would fold at any moment; its failure was inevitable. And yet Ngo is with us today, and his regime now is assuredly one of the most stable and honest on the periphery of Asia. He has made highly acclaimed state visits to Washington, Manila, New Delhi, Rangoon, and Bangkok, and his Government is recognized by forty-five members of the United Nations. Surely here is an unusual man—and a frequently misunderstood one.

He is a devout Roman Catholic, holding the reins of government in a state whose people are largely Taoist and Buddhist in their religious and philosophical outlook. Perhaps 10 per cent of the population is Catholic, but the Vietnamese are notable for their spirit of religious toleration. It is worth observing that although President Ngo destroyed the political and military power of the two native religions of Vietnam, Cao Dai and Hoa Hao, they reportedly have gained thousands of new adherents in the past three years. And yet, during the critical days of 1954–1955, rumors of impending religious warfare circulated through the diplomatic colony in Saigon. What was not generally recognized was that most of these rumors originated with Europeans, or with ax-grinding Vietnamese who understood that religious issues are often extremely important in European and American politics.

Indeed, this is the heart of our problem. We see Asian situations through Western eyes and in terms of Western traditions and Western situations. We persist in attempting to apply our standards, 1959-style, to peoples and situations where they have little or no direct relevance. That our Asian friends and enemies understand this habit of ours is clear, as witness the burbling praise of American democratic thought and institutions that issued from the lips of President Achmed Sukarno of Indonesia during his state visit to the United States three years ago; and compare those words with his later remarks (and acts) after his return to his own country.

In Vietnam, as in the other new states of Asia that have burst forth like popping corn in the years since World War II, independence could not have been achieved and cannot be maintained, under prevailing world conditions, without strong leadership. And strong leadership implies the possession of great power. As Sebastian Chamfort remarked to Marmontel, who was deploring the excesses of the French Revolution: "Do you suppose, then, that revolutions are made with rose water?"

As one travels through these newly born countries, he comes to realize that from the standpoint of the history of thought, the peoples of Southeast Asia are not, generally speaking, sufficiently sophisticated to understand what we mean by democracy and how they can exercise and protect their own political rights. And even though the leaders of the new states are making efforts to increase their peoples' understanding of democratic concepts, their consciousness will be many years in awakening. With literacy rates that range from a low of perhaps 10 per cent to a high of possibly 50 per cent, the peoples of Southeast Asia should not be expected to understand, let alone embrace, the difficult articles of our democratic faith and practice. Furthermore, we often forget that our principles, stemming from Judaic-Christian-Hellenic traditions, are a far cry from "The Way" of Taoism or the orderly, correct society preached by Confucius.

This is not to say that the stirring principles of the Declaration of Independence do not exercise a magnetic attraction on many Asians. It is rather to caution that the articulate few in Southeast Asia who understand, accept, and even preach the gospel of democracy are still *the few*. The unlettered majority, while they too may find the sound of the words appealing, are far more interested in the more immediate and tangible issues of securing and guarding their independence, increasing their standard of living, and developing their countries. That individual human rights may often be neglected or sacrificed in this period of national infancy should not be surprising. We may find much consolation, however, in the fact that many of the new leaders in Southeast Asia are thinking and planning in terms of enlarged areas of freedom for individual citizens, when such developments will be possible without endangering "the independence of the nation and the liberty of the people."

We do ourselves and our Asian neighbors a distinct disservice when we insist on stretching them or shrinking them to fit our particular semantic bed. Implicit in this Procrustean semantics is the assumption of the superiority of our ideas and our ways of doing things. Not only is this in itself a rather undemocratic (or, at least, unegalitarian) assumption, but it brands us as ideologically blind and inflexible. We are unlikely to win many friends or campaigns in Asia if we continue to proceed from this snobbish base.

Ngo Dinh Diem, for example, rejects both absolute individualism and absolute state power. Whether or not we agree with his interpretation of history and his view of the ends of government, they are at the very least worthy of consideration. Transmitting to the National Assembly his ideas on what the then-projected Constitution of the Republic should contain, he wrote:

> We affirm that the sole legitimate end and object of the State is to protect the fundamental rights of the human person to existence and to the free development of his intellectual, moral, and spiritual life.
>
> We affirm that democracy is neither material happiness nor the supremacy of numbers. Democracy is essentially a permanent effort to find the right political means for assuring to all citizens the right of free development and of maximum initiative, responsibility and spiritual life. . . .
>
> Citizens are born free and equal before the law. The State should assure them equal conditions for the exercise of their rights and the accomplishment of their duties. It owes aid and protection to the family so that harmonious family life can develop. Citizens have the right to a secure and peaceful life, to justly remunerated work, to sufficient individual property to assure a dignified and free life, to democratic freedoms, and to the full development of their personalities.
>
> They have the duty of developing the national heritage for the Common Good and for universal peace, of safe-guarding freedom and democracy, of defending the Nation and the Republic against all those who seek to destroy the foundation of the common life and the Constitution.

This Asian leader, who in four years' time has steered his little country from the edge of chaos to peace, stability, and a gradually increasing tempo of development, understands well the problems involved in establishing and maintaining a "democratic" state. He is a man of few illusions. He has studied the writings of Western theorists, and he has observed the tendency toward the development of the "welfare state" in the Western democracies. He has also witnessed the failure of parliamentary institutions in many of those countries. And so, in inaugurating the first session of the National Assembly (March 15, 1956), he said:

The most urgent task before us is to organize political power in such a fashion as to make it manifest and appropriate for giving shape to long-range general policy, and at the same time preserving the fundamental rights of the Nation and of the individual human personality. . . . [We must balance] the requirements of ever-unifying power against the growing pressures of life.

For a country as exposed as ours is from within and without, the possibilities of realizing the democratic ideal are of necessity limited. But we would betray the people were we incapable of responding to their ardent desire for a government of true freedom.

The living and unconquerable faith which sustained us through the last two years of heavy trials, the watchful intelligence which kept us from giving in to despair and as a consequence turning to fascism, these must also furnish us with the resourcefulness and concentration to foster the growth of the permanent orientation of free men toward a democratic structure suited to the conditions and possibilities of the moment, but built out of a genuine respect for the dignity of the individual, from an ideal conception of community life where the common good takes precedence over the good of the individual, from a pluralism which does not represent either social conservatism or a collection of anarchical contradictions.

No one who has known Ngo Dinh Diem well can fail to be impressed by his determination to keep his country alive and bring increasing benefits, happiness, and freedoms to his countrymen. That he is criticized is sure. But then, as Disraeli said, "the depository of power is always unpopular." It may seem paradoxical to some that out of strong governmental power may come individual freedom. But considering the context in which Vietnam exists, can one think of a more dependable method of assuring it?

We ought also to remember that while we put great store in "government by law," the Confucian ideal of "government by virtue" has for 2,500 years been a guiding principle in those Asian lands which felt the influence of Chinese political thought. Ngo was brought up in this tradition. His speeches and his writings reflect his debt to it. He would agree with Confucius that government by virtue, by moral influence, and by personal example is of paramount importance. At the same time, he was educated by the West and spent more than three years in the U.S. (1950–1953), examining what we had to offer. Perhaps we can learn from this man who is endeavoring to create an acceptable synthesis of East and West in Vietnam.

There is little percentage in continuing to try to force these (or any other) Asians into categories of our own making, which reflect only our own experience and wisdom. One of these days our political theorists will come up with a new vocabulary which will enable us to describe more satisfactorily the new orders in Asia. Until then, we should do well to attempt to understand what is taking place in these countries, and to remember that politics is not geometry and that arbitrary definitions do not render its conclusions indisputable.

23. A Flawed Commitment: US Endorsement, with Conditions, of Ngo Dinh Diem (1954)*

By President Dwight D. Eisenhower

Serving as president during most of the decade of the 1950s, Eisenhower will long be remembered for delivering a "farewell address" to the American people in 1961 which warned of the "almost overpowering influence" of "an immense military establishment and a large arms industry."

In the councils of government we must guard against the acquisition of unwarranted influence . . . by [this] military-industrial complex. The potential for the disastrous rise of misplaced power exists and will persist.[1]

Nevertheless, it was the Eisenhower administration that not only deepened US involvement in the French war in Vietnam, but actually created the regime of Ngo Dinh Diem after the French were defeated.

In the letter to Ngo Dinh Diem reprinted here, Eisenhower promised military aid in what proved to be the illusory hope that the Diem regime would undertake "needed reforms." Eisenhower and his successors over time (Reading 27) became painfully aware of Ngo Dinh Diem's unwillingness or inability to create a satisfactory government. For nearly a decade the American military-industrial complex, augmented by influential figures in the academic, religious, and political sectors, aligned US policy with this narrowly-based, repressive regime. It was only when

---

Department of State Bulletin, xxxi (November 15, 1954), pp. 735–736.

1. *Public Papers of the President: Dwight D. Eisenhower* (Washington, D.C.: U.S. Government Printing Office, 1961), pp. 1045–1050. On the Eisenhower presidency, see Blanche Wiesen Cook, *The Declassified Eisenhower: A Divided Legacy of Peace and Political Warfare* (Garden City, New York: Doubleday & Co., 1981). Cf. Paul A. C. Koistinen, *The Military-Industrial Complex: A Historical Perspective* (New York: Praeger Publishers, 1980).

a popular, revolutionary opposition emerged, and the Ngo Dinh Diem dynasty encountered widespread resistance (Readings 28, 29), that he and his entourage became dispensable (Reading 34).

[October 23, 1954]

Dear Mr. President:

I have been following with great interest the course of developments in Vietnam, particularly since the conclusion of the conference at Geneva. The implications of the agreement concerning Vietnam have caused grave concern regarding the future of a country temporarily divided by an artificial military grouping, weakened by a long and exhausting war, and faced with enemies without and by their subversive collaborators within.

Your recent request for aid to assist in the formidable project of the movement of several hundred thousand loyal Vietnamese citizens away from areas which are passing under a *de facto* rule and political ideology which they abhor, are being fulfilled. I am glad that the United States is able to assist in this humanitarian effort.

We have been exploring ways and means to permit our aid to Vietnam to be more effective and to make a greater contribution to the welfare and stability of the Government of Vietnam. I am, accordingly, instructing the American Ambassador to Vietnam [Donald R. Heath] to examine with you in your capacity as Chief of Government, how an intelligent program of American aid given directly to your Government can serve to assist Vietnam in its present hour of trial, provided that your Government is prepared to give assurances as to the standards of performance it would be able to maintain in the event such aid were supplied.

The purpose of this offer is to assist the Government of Vietnam in developing and maintaining a strong, viable state, capable of resisting attempted subversion or aggression through military means. The Government of the United States expects that this aid will be met by performance on the part of the Government of Vietnam in undertaking needed reforms. It hopes that such aid, combined with your own continuing efforts, will contribute effectively toward an independent Vietnam endowed with a strong Government. Such a Government would, I hope, be so responsive to the nationalist aspirations of its people, so enlightened in purpose and effective in performance, that it will be respected both at home and abroad and discourage any who might wish to impose a foreign ideology on your free people.

Sincerely,
Dwight D. Eisenhower

24. Genesis of United States Support for the Regime of Ngo Dinh Diem*

By Robert Scheer

As Robert Scheer shows in this Reading, some groups have privileged access to the machinery of foreign policy and to the mechanisms of mass persuasion to sustain particular policies. The coalition that formed in the early 1950s to support the regime of Ngo Dinh Diem in Vietnam is the subject of this penetrating piece, based upon interviews and public documents, and anticipating many of the revelations which would later appear in The Pentagon Papers.

A former editor of Ramparts *magazine, Robert Scheer is the co-author with Maurice Zeitlin of* Cuba: Tragedy in Our Hemisphere *(New York: Grove Press, 1963) and* With Enough Shovels *(New York: Vintage Books, 1983).*

Years of Preparation

[Ngo Dinh] Diem had been destined, by family position and training, for service in the Mandarite, the feudal administrative apparatus that had always governed Vietnam and that the French bent to their own purposes. He belonged to that group of officials who believed in the traditional Vietnamese monarchy and the Mandarin hierarchy that served it. They hoped for eventual independence, but sought the moderate path of reform from within the French colonial hierarchy.

At the time Diem had been part of the French colonial government, other nationalists, including Communists, Trotskyites, and pro-Kuomintang groups, had chosen the path of violent opposition to the French. In the early 1930's the Indochinese Communists, led by Ho Chi Minh, had played the most prominent role in this movement and the "terror" unleashed by the French broke against them. Ho was arrested in Hong Kong and the situation inside Vietnam was disastrous to his cause. As Ellen Hammer described it in *The Struggle for Indochina*,

> The French Legion terrorized north and central Annam. The prisons were filled and thousands were killed. The year 1931 was a time of terror in which perished not only many Communists, but Nationalists and liberals, and many others, innocent victims of French action.

In September of 1933, at the age of 33, Diem abandoned the possibilities of reform from within and left the French administration to go into retirement. But he did not, and never was to, take up active opposition to the French. His decision was determined by a style of political life that he had retained from his Mandarin

---

*From *How the United States Got Involved in Vietnam* (Report to the Center for the Study of Democratic Institutions [Santa Barbara, California], 1965), pp. 13–16, 20–38.

background. Diem believed in intercession by Providence and his politics were marked by an extreme fatalism. He felt that if one upheld one's personal integrity, remained dedicated, and issued a clear and courageous call to the powers of this world, it would be answered. He had first addressed his call to the French. When that failed, he turned to the Japanese when they occupied Vietnam in 1940. After the war, he tried again with the French, and when that showed little promise, he turned to the Americans.

This last turn came in 1950 when Diem, who was then in Japan, encountered Wesley Fishel, a young assistant professor of political science at the University of California at Los Angeles. [See Reading 22—eds.] In an interview with this author Fishel said that he later persuaded Diem to travel to the United States to plead his case and convinced Michigan State University, to which Fishel had moved, to sponsor the trip. Diem was to spend a considerable part of the next three years in the United States. His brother, Bishop Can, was an important contact with the American Catholic Church, and Diem lived for some time in the Maryknoll Seminaries in New Jersey and New York State. The latter school was under the jurisdiction of Cardinal Spellman, and Diem soon developed a close relationship with this important American Catholic. The Cardinal became one of Diem's most influential backers in the United States and there is no doubt that this support was crucial, for among other things, it certified Diem as an important anti-Communist—no small matter during the McCarthy period.

Diem was thus launched upon a career as a lobbyist, which was perhaps the most successful role in his political life. He managed to enlist in his cause not only the sympathy of Spellman but also that of liberal and sophisticated political figures who were ordinarily at odds with the conservative prelate.

Supreme Court Justice William O. Douglas was one of the first of this group to champion Diem, in his book *North from Malaya*, published in 1952. Douglas had traveled in Vietnam and was convinced that the French could not win against the popular support of the Communist-led Viet Minh. This posed a dilemma for Douglas, which he thought was resolved when he met Diem in Washington upon his return from Vietnam. Diem represented the third force Douglas believed the United States could back: "Ngo Dinh Diem is revered by the Vietnamese because he is honest and independent and stood firm against the French influence." At the same time Douglas admitted that "there is little doubt that in a popularity contest Ho Chi Minh would still lead the field."

Douglas told this author that he arranged a breakfast meeting at which he introduced Diem to Senators Mike Mansfield and John F. Kennedy. Mansfield was to become the Senate's leading authority on Vietnam and as Majority Leader was an important architect of the Kennedy Administration's Vietnam policy some seven years later. During this earlier period, 1951–54, Mansfield and Kennedy became arch-critics of the French role in Vietnam and proponents of an independent nationalist alternative. To them, Diem appeared as that alternative.

In a widely quoted speech delivered in the Senate on April 6, 1954, just prior to the negotiations at Geneva, Senator Kennedy offered a pointed critique of the

Eisenhower Vietnam policy. He feared the Republicans might permit a negotiated peace leading to a compromise government in which Ho Chi Minh would be represented. He opposed Ho's participation in the governing of Vietnam, while conceding Ho's popular support: "It should be apparent that the popularity and prevalence of Ho Chi Minh and his following throughout Indochina would cause either partition or a coalition Government to result in eventual domination by the Communists." Kennedy recommended that we force the French to grant independence to Vietnam, form an independent government that excluded the Viet Minh, support that Government's army, and "whenever necessary . . . [make] some commitment of our manpower." It was a strong attack on French colonialism, as Kennedy was also to make in the case of Algeria, but it made no gesture toward self-determination for the Vietnamese. The future President's concern was "for the security of the free world, and for the values and institutions which are held dear in France and throughout the non-Communist world, as well as in the United States.". . .

The U.S. "Adopts" Diem

The installation of Diem as the Premier of Vietnam helped focus U.S. policy in Southeast Asia. Diem was committed to the re-making of Vietnamese society according to a not always lucid, but always anti-Communist and anti-French, model that required for its enactment the concentration of total power in the hands of a small and trusted group. According to Bernard Fall, in *The Two Vietnams*, Diem, unlike some of his advisers, never had any doubts about the necessity for tight central control to divert the nationalist revolution from Communist objectives. Ho and Giap, the Communist leaders of the Viet Minh, were heroes of the resistance to the French. Diem understood that changing the course of their revolution required the liquidation of the Viet Minh and the "re-education" of the majority of the population that supported the movement. It was a formidable task for a regime that had arisen late in the day and by grace of a foreign power.

Diem in his first year in office moved to consolidate his control by crushing all sources of opposition—the religious sects and nationalist but anti-Diem politicians, along with the cadres left behind by the Viet Minh. These came to be called the Viet Cong. It was soon clear that Diem would refuse to provide for the popular mandate called for in the Geneva agreements. Each step to that end required American support and conflicted with the interests of the French, who wanted to limit Diem's power, keep the situation fluid, and maintain whatever influence they could.

Eisenhower was sympathetic to the French position, as his later writings make clear. He recognized not only Ho's popularity but the high cost of any effort to crush his movement. He resisted grandiose schemes for building up Diem's regime as a western-style alternative to the Viet Minh, and the man he chose as his Special Ambassador to Vietnam, General Lawton Collins, shared these sentiments. But the Eisenhower Administration was particularly vulnerable to political pressure, and it was during this unsettled period that Diem's pre-Geneva lobbying began to bear fruit.

One of the first voices raised publicly on behalf of a "hard line" of all-out support for Diem was that of Cardinal Spellman. In a speech before the American Legion Convention on August 31, 1954, he was quoted by *The New York Times*:

If Geneva and what was agreed upon there means anything at all, it means . . . Taps for the buried hopes of freedom in southeast Asia! Taps for the newly betrayed millions of Indochinese who must now learn the awful facts of slavery from their eager Communist masters! Now the devilish techniques of brainwashing, forced confessions and rigged trials have a new locale for their exercise.

Spellman emphasized the essential theses of the cold war containment policy: ". . . Communism has a world plan and it has been following a carefully set-up time table for the achievement of that plan . . ." ". . . the infamies and agonies inflicted upon the hapless victims of Red Russia's bestial tyranny. . . ." A show of strength was required, ". . . else we shall risk bartering our liberties for lunacies, betraying the sacred trust of our forefathers, becoming serfs and slaves to Red rulers' godless goons." The danger lay in the illusion of peace with the Communists:

"Americans must not be lulled into sleep by indifference nor be beguiled by the prospect of peaceful coexistence with Communists. How can there be peaceful coexistence between two parties if one of them is continually clawing at the throat of the other . . .? Do you peacefully coexist with men who thus would train the youth of their godless, Red world . . .?"

The Cardinal demonstrated his support of Diem by going to Vietnam to deliver personally the first check for Catholic Relief Services funds spent in Vietnam. Others of Diem's early supporters followed suit. Wesley Fishel, the Michigan State University professor who had originally induced Diem to come to the United States, turned up in Vietnam as one of his chief advisers, with residence in the presidential palace. Another American inhabitant of the palace was Wolf Ladejinsky, a New Dealer who had stayed on in the Department of Agriculture only to be fired under pressure from Senator Joseph McCarthy for alleged (but never proved) radical connections. Ladejinsky had worked on the Japanese land reform program, and Diem hired him to work on land problems in Vietnam—proof to many American liberals of Diem's commitment to serious social reform.

Another visitor to Diem was Leo Cherne, who had helped to found the Research Institute of America, one of the first of the management-research firms designed to help American corporations cope with the expanding government of the post–1930's. It also supplied its 30,000 business clients with general political information. Cherne was also president of the International Rescue Committee, an organization aimed at helping refugees from communism.

Cherne went to Vietnam in September of 1954 and spent two and a half weeks there, becoming very interested in Diem's potentialities as a democratic, nationalist alternative to the Communists. In a cable he sent back to the subscribers to his Research Institute he reported:

> . . . have been talking intimately with American officials here, including Ambassador Heath. Conferred at length yesterday with Vietnam Premier Ngo Dinh Diem . . . success of effort to hold Vietnam from Communists depends on whether all non-Communist Vietnamese can unite for struggle. U.S. embassy, strongly supporting Diem, views him as key to the whole situation. Political and financial instability . . . unless Vietnamese Government can organize important forces and U.S. continues pouring in substantial help and money. . . . If free elections held today all agree privately Communists would win . . . situation not hopeless . . . future depends on organizing all resources to resettle refugees, sustain new bankrupt government, give people something to fight for and unite them to resist Communism. . . . West can't afford to lose from now on.

Upon returning to the United States, Cherne sent his second-in-command in the International Rescue Committee, Joseph Buttinger, to set up an office in Vietnam. At this time Buttinger was involved in Socialist politics as an editor of *Dissent* magazine; during the mid-Thirties, under the name of Gustave Richter, he had been the leader of the underground Social Democratic Party in Austria. This had been a bitter experience. His one accomplishment, as he writes about it in his memoirs, *In the Twilight of Socialism*, had been to stop the growth of the Communists.

A year after this book was published, a C.I.A. agent named Edward Lansdale [see Reading 20—eds.] introduced Buttinger to the men around Ngo Dinh Diem, and after some three months in Vietnam Buttinger believed Diem to be the answer to the Communist revolution. As Buttinger remarked to this author, "He was strong and shrewd and determined to stay in power and would stay in power."

During the late fall of 1954, while Buttinger was in Vietnam, a serious split was developing among Americans concerned with Vietnam. As Cherne's telegram indicated, U.S. missions in Saigon were strongly backing Diem. For example, an abrupt halt was called to the revolt of General Hinh, the head of the Vietnamese army and an officer in the French army as well. When General Collins arrived in mid-November of 1954, as Eisenhower's Special Ambassador, he made it clear that the United States would not pay the army if Diem was overthrown. In a matter of days Hinh was sent out of the country and dismissed as head of the army.

However, from the very beginning Diem displayed that tendency toward autocracy and family rule for which the mass media of the United States would belatedly condemn his administration eight years later. In early 1955, when he moved to crush the religious sects, whose military forces rivaled his power, some influential Americans began to side with the French against him. The most important of these was General Collins, and his view was shared by other American observers. Among them was the newspaper columnist Joseph Alsop, who contended that

Diem's base of support was too narrow to rival that of the Viet Minh. (Both men were later to renew their support of Diem after he·defeated the sects.)

At this juncture, when it looked as if the United States might dispose of Diem, his reservoir of support, his "lobby," proved decisive. In the ensuing struggle the curious alliance of Lansdale, the C.I.A. agent, Buttinger, the ex-Austrian Socialist, and Cardinal Spellman won the day.

On the official level, Lansdale convinced his Director, Allen Dulles, of Diem's efficiency, and the latter convinced his brother, who, as Secretary of State, talked with the President. The recent book on the C.I.A., *The Invisible Government*, by David Wise and Thomas B. Ross, places the total responsibility for swinging U.S. support to Diem at this stage on Lansdale, but the private political pressures were important. Buttinger returned from Vietnam excited about Diem but fearful that the United States was not totally committed to him. He turned to the group around the International Rescue Committee, one of the most useful of them being the public relations counsel for the organization, Harold Oram. Oram knew the head of the Catholic Relief Services in Washington and that gentleman introduced Buttinger to Cardinal Spellman. The Cardinal was still an enthusiastic believer in Diem, and Buttinger alerted him to the impending crises in Diem's fortunes.

Spellman sent Buttinger back to Washington to meet with Joseph P. Kennedy and finally, according to Buttinger in an interview with this author, these two powerful men, in a long-distance telephone conversation, decided to whom Buttinger should tell his story. In Washington, Kennedy introduced him to Senator Mike Mansfield and to Kenneth Young of the State Department. John F. Kennedy was in California at the time but Buttinger had a long conversation with his adminstrative assistant.

Meanwhile, Cardinal Spellman had arranged meetings with the editorial board of the New York *Herald Tribune*, the chief editors of *Life* and *Time*, and several editors of *The New York Times*. On January 29, 1955, two days after Buttinger's visit to the *Times*, that paper carried an editorial which closely paralleled Buttinger's arguments on Diem's behalf. Buttinger also elaborated his position in *The Reporter* of January 27, 1955, and *The New Republic* of February 28, 1955.

From the Spring of 1955 on, the U.S. commitment to Diem was complete. This meant that the United States would ignore any French protestations and the Geneva Accords—including the provisions calling for reunification through free elections, which, as even Diem's most ardent supporters conceded, would bring the Communist-oriented Viet Minh to power. A Cardinal, a C.I.A. agent, and an ex-Austrian Socialist seemed to have carried the day against the instincts of a General turned President.

The Flight to Freedom

One provision of the Geneva Accords, it will be remembered, had specified that during a 300-day period following the signing of the Accords "any civilians . . . who wish to go and live in the zone assigned to the other party shall be

permitted and helped to do so. . . ."[Reading 16, Articles 2, 14, and 15.—eds.]
This led to a great flow of refugees between the Spring of 1954 and the Spring of
1955. The bulk of the movement was from the Viet Minh area in the North to the
South and eventually involved close to a million people. (According to Bernard
Fall, only about 150,000 refugees went North to the Viet Minh.)

These statistics were interpreted in the United States as a repudiation of Viet
Minh rule by the Vietnamese people—a mass flight to freedom. But the interpretation ignored two facts: 1) the number of people going North was held to a small
total by order of the Viet Minh, which wanted its sympathizers to remain in the
South to prepare for the elections; 2) the bulk of those going South fell into two
groups—dependents of the colonial native army (200,000) and Catholics
(679,000).

The Catholics were a by-product of the French rule, members of a minority
religion who had been brought by Portuguese and French missionaries into a pre-
dominantly Buddhist population. The Catholic communities in the North had enjoyed a protected status under the French and they had raised militia units that
fought beside the French against the Viet Minh. With the collapse of the French,
these communities feared reprisals, or at least grave restrictions on their activities,
under the new Viet Minh rule.

One American who did much to blur the distinction between the Catholic minority and the rest of the population in the North was Tom Dooley, a young Navy
doctor turned writer, whose book *Deliver Us From Evil* had a great impact on the
American public. Dooley had gone to Vietnam as part of the U.S. Navy's program
of aid in transporting the refugees to the South. He witnessed the great suffering
of an uprooted people. As a Catholic, he was particularly impressed with their
religious opposition to communism and the fact that they fled with the physical
symbols of that religion in hand:

> . . . recognizing us as friends and not as foes, they hoisted, on a broken spar, their own
> drenched flag; a flag they had hidden for years . . . their symbol, their emblem, their
> heraldry . . . a yellow and gold flag displaying the Pope's tiara and the keys of Saint Peter.

Working among the Catholic refugees, Dooley took no account of the fact that 90
per cent of the Vietnamese population would be indifferent to the yellow and gold
flag, even in the unlikely event that they understood its symbolism.

To Dooley, even aside from the religious aspect, these people were on the side
of the "free world" in opposition to the total evil of communism: ". . . how, outside
expanding Russia, do you go about being an Imperialist nowadays?" "Ho Chi
Minh has been a Moscow trained puppet from the start." "The Godless cruelties of
Communism. . . ." "The Communist bosses would. . . ." "The poisons of Communist hatred. . . ."

The Viet Minh was indicted:

They preached hatred against the institutions, traditions and customs of colonial Vietnam. Everything "feudal" or "reactionary" was to be destroyed . . . their Christian catechisms were burned and they were burned and they were told that religion is only an opiate.

Dooley combined his anti-communism with a strenuous belief in an American-style economic system as the basis of any country's prosperity and freedom:

. . . we continually explained to thousands of refugees, as individuals and in groups, that only in a country which permits companies to grow large could such fabulous charity be found. . . . These companies [that sent drugs] . . . responded with the enthusiasm of great corporations in a great country.

With this ideological background, it becomes easier to understand Dooley's rather extensive rewriting of history. No act attributed to the Communists was dismissed as unbelievable or as requiring factual substantiation. All of them fitted the "devil theory" and were passed on to the millions who read his book, heard his lectures, and saw the film based on *Deliver Us from Evil*.

Dooley's account of the American effort begins not with the $2.6 billion spent in support of the French between 1950–54, but rather with the mission to aid the refugees. "We had come late to Vietnam, but we had come. And we brought not bombs and guns, but help and love."

The 17th parallel that divided the refugees from the free world was "the rim of Hell" with "the demons of Communism stalking outside and now holding the upper half of the country in their strangling grip." Those who fought the "devils" were, by definition, heroes:

The Vietnam governor of our small area was a patriot by the name of Nguyen Luat. He had been educated in France and chose to return to his own nation of Vietnam. . . . During the war he had fought with the French as an officer.

This "patriot" thus fought on the side of the colonialists against the majority of his countrymen.[1]

It is unfair to treat Dooley's book as history, although it may have served as such for many of its readers. Its significance was to provide a vocabulary of Communist horror that found its way into the speeches of Presidents and was, for many ordinary Americans, their only significant emotional encounter with communism in Asia. According to Dooley, Ho Chi Minh had begun his war against the French in December, 1946, "by disembowelling more than 1,000 native women in Hanoi" who were associated with the French. There had been rumors about this, but no

---

1. A number of the military men the United States later supported in Vietnam after Diem's passing had also fought on the French side, including Nguyen Cao Ky and Nguyen Van Thieu.—eds.

factual evidence is provided in any of the standard accounts of that period. An authoritative refutation is supplied by the French writer, Paul Mus:

> I am today in a position to state and to prove that four-fifths of the stories or reports of awful atrocities inflicted by the Vietnamese on our compatriots in Hanoi, December 19, 1946, are either made up or in error.

Dooley lent highly emotional support to the goals of American foreign policy in Vietnam, but he sharply criticized inefficiency in execution. America proved receptive to this type of criticism and Dooley became a folk hero. In 1960 the Gallup Poll found him to be one of the ten most admired Americans.

Dooley believed in his work and his writing, and was deeply moved, as he said, when President Diem gave him the highest award of his land. It attests to his innocence that he did not know that the choice for the award had been inspired by the C.I.A.'s man in Vietnam, Colonel Edward Lansdale.

On January 25, 1955, *Look* carried an impressive photostory of the flight of the refugees. The article was by Leo Cherne and it combined a poignant description of the plight of the refugees with a political message. The sub-heading stated the theme: "Battered and shunted about by war, they are too weary to resist the Reds without us." The United States had a responsibility to become involved further in Vietnam because the South is "still free but will fall under Red control if Communists win elections set for July of 1956." And this was the likely event, said Cherne, for "if elections were held today, the overwhelming majority of Vietnamese would vote Communist." But if the South Vietnamese might be indifferent to the Communist menace, others were not:

> Asians are convinced that U.S. prestige and influence in Asia cannot survive another defeat. Europe wants to see whether the Communists will be stopped here or will grow into an irresistible force. . . .

Cherne stated the U.S. predicament: "No more than 18 months remain for us to complete the job of winning over the Vietnamese before they vote. What can we do?"

The answer was for the United States to "mobilize democratic leadership," which could be found among the Catholic refugees. The International Rescue Committee was helping to do this by ferreting out the educated men among the refugees and funneling them into the government administration.

It was later to be charged by many in the United States that Diem's regime floundered on his pro-Catholic prejudice. But the heavy use of Catholic refugees as administrators was natural, because they were certified opponents of the Viet Minh who also were educated. As Cherne said of the Catholic refugees, "There is an army of 400,000 Vietnamese ready and anxious to convince their countrymen that they must choose freedom." By embracing the refugees, Diem helped maintain his administration in power, but he also planted seeds for the anti-Catholic demonstrations that led to the fall of his government in 1963.

There is no doubt that the movement and resettlement of 900,000 refugees from North to South Vietnam was the most successful program of the Diem administration. It was also the first immediate result of massive American aid, which laid out about $89 for each refugee (in a country with an $85 per year per capita income). The U.S. Seventh Fleet joined the French Navy to move the refugees, and private agencies (Catholic Relief Services, International Rescue Committee, Red Cross, Junior Chamber of Commerce, Michigan State University, etc.) poured in to assist the large numbers of French and American government personnel in Saigon.

Once the refugees had been transported, the paramount task was to see to their permanent well-being by integrating them into the economy. The South was underpopulated and this facilitated the provision of land to the refugees. Usually, the refugees had moved as whole villages, with their hierarchies and leadership generally intact. During the first two years of the program, most of these were supported by a U.S. relief program of dollar aid and surplus agricultural food distributed by the Catholic Relief Services. In his book, *The Two Vietnams*, Bernard Fall concluded, "Obviously most of these refugees were then still living from handouts rather than from the fruits of their labor." A good portion of the land cleared for them was in the Cai San project, where 90,000 were settled in an area formerly sparsely populated. This was the showplace for government tours by visitors to Vietnam. The land was cleared by 100 tractors ordered by the United States Operations Mission, which also brought in technicians and representatives of the tractor firms from the United States to train native operators. The United States supplied the seed for the newly turned fields and the materials for schools and houses.

This was an effective crash program of *American* aid; it had little to do with the ability of the Diem government to develop the economy as a whole. In fact, the refugee program had a negative impact on the Vietnamese not so favored. An essentially "welfare" movement tailored to the needs of a minority group by a minority leader was bound to grate on the non-Catholic majority. The religious problem in Vietnam had some of its roots in this program. In the final analysis, the refugees were *not* integrated into South Vietnamese society.

Diem's "Lobby": The American Friends of Vietnam

The "flight to freedom" of the refugees provided an important public relations basis for continued U.S. involvement in Vietnam and was used as such by those Americans concerned about Diem's future. The U.S. government had helped Diem over the hurdles posed by the rival sects, the opposition elements, the Viet Minh, and the "non-elections." But if Diem as Chief of State, an office he assumed on October 26, 1955, was to continue to hold off the Viet Minh, he would have to develop a governmental structure, provide political stability, and carry out a program of economic development. All of this would require massive American aid, both economic and technical. The flight of the refugees and the wide publicity given to it in the United States made the American public receptive.

At this point, the various individuals committed to the development of Vietnam as a showcase of democracy began to draw together as an unofficial "Vietnam lobby." The founding of the American Friends of Vietnam in the fall of 1955 provided the "lobby" with a formal organization. This group led the fight on Diem's behalf during the next six years.

The announced purpose of the American Friends of Vietnam was "to extend more broadly a mutual understanding of Vietnamese and American history, cultural customs, and democratic institutions." In actuality, it was concerned with the political objective of committing the United States to a massive aid program on Diem's behalf. In pursuit of that policy, the organization cited the alleged success of the program to date in creating an "economic and political miracle" in Vietnam.

The Friends was primarily an organization of the liberal center. Its founding members as listed on its letterhead included Senators Kennedy and Neuberger, Max Lerner, Arthur Schlesinger, Jr., Representatives Edna Kelly and Emmanuel Celler, with the Socialist Norman Thomas and the "right wing" Governor J. Bracken Lee. This provided an attractive political balance. Power in the organization resided in a fourteen-member executive committee, some of whose members were also on the board of directors of the International Rescue Committee, including Leo Cherne and Joseph Buttinger. Cardinal Spellman and the Church's program in Vietnam were represented on the board by Monsignor Harnett, head of the Catholic Relief Services.

Two members of the executive committee, Norbert Muhlen and Sol Sanders, were on the staff of *The New Leader*, and the political philosophy of that magazine, militant anti-communism plus sympathy for government-inspired social reform, best summarizes the philosophy of most of the executive committee members. Another member of the executive committee was Elliot Newcomb, who was later to become the treasurer of the organization. Newcomb and Harold Oram, who had introduced Joseph Buttinger to the Catholic officials, were partners in a public relations firm, Newcomb-Oram, which two months before the formation of the American Friends of Vietnam had signed a contract with Diem's government to handle its public relations in the United States. Newcomb subsequently left the firm, but Oram continued to be registered with the Justice Department as a foreign agent acting for the Diem government until June 30, 1961. The Diem government paid the Oram firm a $3,000 monthly fee plus expenses, with a third of it earmarked for a full-time campaign director. This position was held from 1956 to the end of the contract in 1961 by Gilbert Jonas, who had been executive secretary of the American Friends of Vietnam and later became its secretary and assistant treasurer.

Up to this point Vietnam had not been a popular subject for American scholarship or journalism. There were few "experts" on the area in the universities or the press. The vastly expanded American role in the period following the Geneva

Accords produced a great demand for knowledge about the country. As a result, those who were most intimately involved in the American program there generally blossomed as the chief sources of information and opinion. This was natural, but most of them were committed protagonists and their writing soon became propaganda for the cause. This was particularly true of university participation. The one group of social scientists most informed about the area was pulled in to work on a U.S.-sponsored program that came to typify American political involvement in Vietnam. This was the group sent out by Michigan State University.

The Michigan State University Project

In 1955, '56, '57, even '58 President Ngo Dinh Diem and his entire government had a fantastically complete, and almost naive, confidence in Americans, per se.

Especially "on the in" in those days was the Michigan State University Group, paid by the U.S. Government under a contract to "advise" the Vietnamese Government in a number of fields of activity. Among their "advisory" duties was the formation of what is now referred to by "foreign adventurers" and the foreign press as "the secret police of Mr. Ngo Dinh Nhu."

The M.S.U. group proceeded with "training" for several years. The head of the M.S.U. group was considered the most "in" man among the foreigners and many considered him more "in" than the President's own ministers.

The M.S.U. group enjoyed an extraordinary power based on this confidence. Not only did they "train" but they also "controlled" in large measure the now famous "secret police."

The most "in" man of 1955 referred to in this 1963 editorial from *The Times of Vietnam*, a Diem-controlled paper, was Wesley Fishel, the young professor who had persuaded Diem to come to the United States to line up American support for his cause. Fishel first went to work for the Diem government in 1954 as an "advisor on government reorganization." He was also a member of the personal staff of Special Ambassador Collins, and, in Fishel's words to this author, "I was the only contact that he [Collins] had with Diem that was at all effective for many months. . . . After two years I surfaced—to use a C.I.A. term—to become head of the M.S.U. program."

In addition to Fishel's and Diem's interest the decision to formally associate Michigan State involved higher policy considerations. The National Security Council in the spring of 1955 had decided on continuing all-out U.S. support for Diem. No less a personage than Vice-President Nixon called John Hannah, the President of Michigan State, to elicit his support. Hannah was told, according to Fishel, that Vietnam had been declared top priority and that it was in the national interest for his university to become involved. Officially, the project would be part of the International Cooperation Administration program of assistance to underdeveloped countries. It was in fact the largest operation and would involve 54 professors and 200 Vietnamese assistants. It was also to fill a special need.

The Geneva Accords had prohibited increases in the strength of either side through the introduction of "all types of arms" or build-ups in troop strength. The presence of the International Control Commission (made up of nationals of Canada, Poland, and India) offered the prospect of unfavorable publicity to the United States if its Military Assistance Advisory Group, United States Operations Mission, or C.I.A. agents operated openly. The Michigan group would serve as "cover."

Diem, as a minority figure in his own country, required a strengthened police power. The Diem government had reason to expect an attack from segments of the armed forces hostile to it or from police units under the control of the bandit Binh Xuyen sect. It was for this reason, according to Fishel, that Art Brandstatter, head of the Michigan State University School of Police Administration and ex-Colonel of M.P.s, began training Diem's Palace Guard. As part of this training program, described in M.S.U. monthly reports, the Palace Guard was supplied with guns and ammunition the Michigan State professors obtained from the U.S.-M.A.A.G.

Bao Dai, when he had been Chief of State, had placed the national police and security services under the control of the Binh Xuyen, and they were hostile to the Diem government. By April of 1955, Diem could call upon army troops whose loyalties had been ensured by Ambassador Collins' statement that the United States would only meet the payroll of an army committed to the Diem government. These were employed to crush the Binh Xuyen. The Michigan State professors decided to concentrate their energies on the reconstitution of the police apparatus. Their monthly report for July, 1955, stated:

It has been generally agreed and the Ambassador has specifically asked that we concentrate almost exclusively on the police and field administration projects until the elections of next July. . . . It is now felt by the MSU team that in order to be in accord with U.S. policy locally it is necessary to engage almost exclusively in immediate impact programs until after the elections in July, 1956 and that the immediate impact programs in our program are the field administration and the police projects.

By November, 1955, the professors were able to state in their monthly report:

During the month of October we received a notice of Washington's approval of the recommended expanded police program submitted August 29th. We started immediately to implement this program. Conferences were held at USOM on October 10th and the Embassy on October 23rd and 24th, trying to coordinate Internal Security operations in Vietnam, in which our government has an interest.

With Washington's sanction, the professors reorganized the old French-sponsored Sureté into a new "Vietnamese Bureau of Investigation," which was modeled upon the FBI but would "also be responsible for the many other enforcement duties that are peculiar to this part of the world, such as information and postal control, etc." The police force was turned into a paramilitary unit, trained in particular to deal with uprisings on the part of the citizenry. Once Saigon was secured, it became essential to pacify the countryside, and so the Civil Guard, a rural-based militia of 40,000 men, was organized. The immigration authorities were trained to fingerprint the Chinese population, which was distrusted by the Diem government, and all agencies of government were trained in maintaining security dossiers. The monthly records of the project list a wide variety of guns, ammunition, vehicles, grenades, handcuffs, and tear-gas equipment that the Michigan State team passed on from "official U.S. agencies" to their Vietnamese protégés. From 1955 to 1960, the Michigan team had the major responsibility for training, equipping, and financing the police apparatus for Diem's state.

The M.S.U. team, of course, had other responsibilities for building a governmental structure. The professors worked on the constitution, redesigned parts of the bureaucracy, developed a school of public administration and the beginnings of a civil service. In their attempts to gear the government to a solution of the serious social problems confronting it, the M.S.U. project published many studies. They were couched in the jargon of public administration and were aimed at increasing the efficiency of Diem's operations. These documents never mentioned the facts of the dictatorship under which the Diem family consistently stood in the way of the reforms suggested. The M.S.U. team constructed a beautiful paper government that never was translated into reality.

The failure of the M.S.U. project may have resulted in part from that "in-ness" to which *The Times of Vietnam* referred. President Hannah was an important Republican figure and had been an Assistant Secretary of Defense. Interviews with some members of the project revealed that involvement in a high priority government program gave them a heady feeling of glamour and prestige. As one member frankly states, "I saw the job in Vietnam primarily from the standpoint of my own career development. I had taught public administration and I saw this as a job with experience, with an entrée back into the academic world."

The project favored a technical approach to social problems. This "scientific style" provided a justification for academics functioning in a strange land as controlled agents of their government and permitted them to perform tasks that would otherwise have run contrary to the personal ethics of many of them. The interviews this author had with various members of the M.S.U. team revealed a strong sensitivity to the titles, positions, awards, and other attentions of the institutions with which they had contact. Later, their attitudes were to range from the rather cynical view of one project head who stated: "Knock it out of your head that 99 per cent of university guys are educators—they are all operators," to those who became tormented by the moral implications of their work in Vietnam. In this category was one economist who thought that the academic program of the Diem government was an almost total failure and concluded that the peasants might have been better off with the other side. But although he was to write about Vietnam, he did not express such thoughts, and his reasons for not doing so were described as follows:

If you are an ordinary person you will be listened to insofar as it sounds right. Otherwise you're considered a deviant. Only if you have high status will a deviant be listened to. . . . I suppose people would most likely figure that I was a crackpot who lacks good judgment—not cashiered for this but always a question mark—wouldn't say you're subversive—but would influence their judgment about my judgment.

If they were reticent while in Vietnam, some of the professors became highly prolific on paper after their return to the United States at the end of their tours of duty. Much of our public expertise on Vietnam has come from alumni of the M.S.U. project; they are the authors of many of the articles about Vietnam not only in scholarly journals but in the mass media. In this writing, they have concerned themselves with many social and political problems facing Vietnam, but nowhere have they engaged in a critical analysis of the M.S.U. project itself. They had played a vital role in building the governmental apparatus for the Diem administration, but much of their work was irrelevant and self-defeating, and many of them came to feel that a good part of it was, in an old-fashioned sense, immoral.

[Further excerpts from Robert Scheer's pathbreaking study, *How the United States Got Involved in Vietnam*, are included in Reading 25.—eds.]

Part IV

THE REVOLUTION AGAINST DIEM

Editors' Introduction

Instead of the peace, unity, and independence promised by the 1954 Geneva Accords, the years after the French defeat brought a new era of suffering, repression, and war for the people of Vietnam. A land devastated by successive waves of foreign invasion was now—in direct violation of those Accords—cut into two pieces, severing the economic arteries vital to each.

The northern zone, deprived of its traditional rice supply from the Mekong Delta in the south, launched a desperate land reform program that generated popular resistance and harsh repression. By the fall of 1956, the costly mistakes had been acknowledged and a "rectification campaign" then initiated a milder approach to rural reconstruction. By 1957, agricultural production was double what it had been in 1955.[1]

In the southern zone, the continued enlargement of areas under the control of Ngo Dinh Diem was touted in the United States as an exemplary exercise in US-assisted "nation-building" (Reading 22). But while Diem's American backers were hailing the "miracle" of his "democratic one-man rule," in reality his power—which never extended very deeply into the countryside—tottered precariously on a narrow base, maintained only by a persistent extension of state terror (Readings 19–21).

Washington was well aware that Diem was a dubious choice. As Secretary of State John Foster Dulles secretly explained to his French counterpart in 1955, the United States could simply not find "a better man" to carry out its designs.[2] Therefore, as Dulles summarized in his cabled report, the following was to be US policy for the foreseeable future:

---

1. Le Chau, *Le Viet Nam socialiste: une économie de transition* (Paris: F. Maspero, 1966); Gérard Chaliand, *Les Paysans du nord-vietnam et la guerre* (Paris: F. Maspero, 1968); Eric R. Wolf, *Peasant Wars of the Twentieth Century* (New York: Harper & Row, 1969), Chap. 4; George Kahin and John W. Lewis, *The United States in Vietnam*, revised edition (New York: Dell, 1969).

2. Dulles cable to US State Department, May 8, 1955, in *The Pentagon Papers* (GPO ed.), vol. 10, pp. 962–963.

Diem is only means US sees to save South Vietnam and counteract revolution. US sees no one else who can. Whatever US view has been in past, today US must support Diem wholeheartedly.[3]

Dulles went on to acknowledge candidly that "in US view present revolution is not yet dominated or influenced by Communists to any appreciable degree." He admitted Diem's "weaknesses," but lamented: "There was no practical way of getting rid of him."

The French responded that "Diem is not only incapable but mad." They predicted that "one way or another, he will bring on a Viet Minh victory." But they had to admit that they had no better puppet to offer.

Those 1955 worries of the French and American policy makers were well founded: Every foreign power to intervene in Vietnam eventually attempted to install some group of Vietnamese figures to prevent a Communist victory. But each of these efforts to energize or create a "third force" proved less substantial than the previous ones. Any such scheme was probably doomed from the time of the August Revolution of 1945.

If Diem were ever to become the actual leader of the southern half of the "Republic of Vietnam" (which claimed to be the government of all Vietnam), he would have to broaden his base to include more than the Catholic minority among an overwhelmingly non-Christian people. Yet instead, he concentrated ever more power in his own Catholic family and their immediate supporters.

Meanwhile, the US program for economic development in the south, as Robert Scheer shows in Reading 25, was generating more problems. The much-touted land reform (planned by US officials such as Roy L. Prosterman, some of whom would fashion similar programs for El Salvador decades later)[4] actually required peasants to pay for lands they already considered theirs because of the previous land reform carried out by the Viet Minh. Much of the land "redistribution" consisted of taking land away from southerners and giving it to Catholic refugees from the North.[5]

Diem's intensifying repression (Reading 26) in the countryside led inevitably to spontaneous resistance and rebellion. As tens of thousands of fighters against French colonialism, including many former Viet Minh cadres, were rounded up to be executed or imprisoned, the old anticolonial infrastructure was forced to reorganize and fight back if it was to survive. This was the death knell of the Diem regime, whose own survival depended almost entirely on maintaining a monopoly of violence. As Noam Chomsky has succinctly summed up the whole process:

---

3. Ibid. Subsequent quotations are from the same source.

4. On the land reform in El Salvador, and its links with earlier policies in Vietnam, see Marvin Gettleman, Patrick Lacefield, Louis Menashe, David Mermelstein, and Ronald Radosh, eds., *El Salvador: Central America in the New Cold War* (New York: Grove Press, 1981), Readings 23–28.

5. *Pentagon Papers* (Gravel edition), pp. 254–255.

It reached the point where by 1959 the Vietminh leadership—the communist party leadership—was being decimated. Cadres were being murdered extensively. Finally in May of 1959 there was an authorization to use violence in self-defense, after years of murder, with thousands of people killed in this campaign organized by the United States. As soon as [the Vietminh] began to use violence in self-defense, the whole Saigon government apparatus fell apart at once because it was an apparatus based on nothing but a monopoly of violence. And once it lost that monopoly of violence it was finished. And that's what led the United States to move in. There were no North Vietnamese around.[6]

Reading 28 presents an autobiographical memoir of Nguyen Thi Dinh, one of the rural insurgents threatened in this campaign of terror.

Though unable to create a genuinely independent regime in South Vietnam, Ngo Dinh Diem retained sufficient independence of Washington's wishes to invoke considerable displeasure, despite the public position that the Vietnamese leader was a thoroughly reliable ally and paragon of virtue (Reading 27). To the intense frustration of a series of US ambassadors in Saigon, Diem resolutely rejected American advice that he initiate needed reforms and broaden the base of his regime—which was, even by the early 1960s, still limited to his family and Catholic refugees from the north. In the summer of 1963, Diem veered in two seemingly opposite directions, either one sufficient to fatally alienate him from Washington: He put out feelers to the DRV authorities in Hanoi about a possible settlement that would exclude the United States[7] and he and his brother, secret police head Ngo Dinh Nhu, unleashed the ferocious attack on the Buddhist church described in Reading 33.

Diem's fate was sealed when the American embassy in Saigon established contact with a group of Saigon generals anxious to be rid of him. Reading 34 shows how easily they had their way.

25. Behind the Miracle of South Vietnam*

By Robert Scheer

The "political miracle" of the Ngo Dinh Diem regime touted by US policy makers beginning in the late 1950s was little more than a vast public relations campaign on the part of the US government designed to sell to the US people the image of

---

*From *How the United States Got Involved in Vietnam* (Report to the Center for the Study of Democratic Institutions [Santa Barbara, California], 1965), pp. 38–66.

6. "The Lessons of the Vietnam War—an Interview with Noam Chomsky," *Indochina Newsletter* 18 (November–December, 1982), p. 3.

7. On the contact with the north, see George C. Herring, *America's Longest War: The United States and Vietnam, 1950–1975* (New York: John Wiley & Sons, 1979), p. 94.

Diem as a miraculous savior of Vietnam: staunch anti-communist, defender of the (primarily Roman Catholic) faith, and champion of capitalist values. In this Reading, Scheer deftly describes how the realities of life in South Vietnam under the Diem regime—government corruption, inefficiency, authoritarianism, and bloody anti-subversion campaigns, along with the attendant failure of the US-designed and US-funded land reform and aid programs—pricked holes in Diem's overblown image that even the US press could not ignore. When the public relations bubble burst in 1959, Diem seized upon a new approach to securing US support in the face of increasing widespread opposition at home: allegations of major aggressive attacks upon the South by the North.

The "Miracle's" Public Relations Base

In 1957, after three years in power, [Ngo Dinh] Diem traveled to the United States for an official visit. By then he had crushed the rival power of religious sects and opposition politicians and had won the commitment of the United States to finance his regime and supply it with a large force of Americans to implement the aid program.

It was during this trip that the celebration of the "Miracle of Vietnam" began in earnest. Diem was "handled" by the Oram public relations firm and the American Friends of Vietnam [Reading 24—eds.]. He received the red-carpet treatment in official circles and in the press. He was flown in on President Eisenhower's personal plane, the "Columbine," and the President met him at the airport. According to the account in *The New York Times* of May 9, 1957,

In salvaging South Vietnam from the disorder that threatened its existence after partition in 1955 and by establishing democratic forms, President Diem has carved a deep niche in official esteem in Washington.

This was evident in the character of the welcome. During the last four years, President Eisenhower has met only one other foreign leader, King Saud of Saudi Arabia, on arrival.

Diem addressed a joint session of Congress and then journeyed to New York City. He breakfasted with Cardinal Spellman and, as *The New York Times* of May 13, 1957, reported, he occupied a place of honor at St. Patrick's Cathedral, where Bishop Flannery sermonized: "The entire world acclaimed him when this God-fearing anti-Communist and courageous statesman saved Vietnam." Mayor Wagner, in welcoming Diem to the city, described him as a man "to whom freedom is the very breath of life itself," "a man history may yet adjudge as one of the great figures of the Twentieth Century," and defined the government he headed as a "political miracle."

The social highlight of Diem's trip came at a dinner in New York, jointly sponsored by the American Friends of Vietnam and the International Rescue Committee, at which Henry R. Luce presided. Angier Biddle Duke presented Diem with the Richard E. Byrd Award for "inspired leadership in the cause of the free world." President Eisenhower sent a message commemorating the Award, which stated: "In the tradition of a great explorer, Byrd, the Premier of Vietnam [by] his inspiring leadership in the cause of the free world is opening up vast areas for the peaceful progress of mankind." Perhaps the most candid comment of the whole trip was the one made by Diem himself in accepting the award: "Your aid enables us to hold this crucial spot and to hold it at less expense to you and at less danger to the world than you could have done it yourself."

During his stay in the United States, many of the speeches that Diem delivered were written for him by Joseph Buttinger. *The New York Times* of May 12, 1957, noted in an editorial, entitled "Diem on Democracy," that he "has added a strongly spiritual, rather than political note in his definition" of democracy and that

this could have been expected from a man of deep religious heart. It is also not surprising that a firm concept of human rights should come from a man of erudition. . . . With such a declaration, we believe, Thomas Jefferson would have no quarrel. . . . This is straight talk from a courageous man. It is welcome here and it should be heard in some other quarters. There is no "neutralism" on human rights, and this is the basis for President Diem's stand.

Life in the May 13, 1957, issue was more reserved in its celebration of Diem's democratic spirit than the *Times*. In a layout entitled "The Tough Miracle Man of Vietnam," the magazine adhered to the "miracle" line, but admitted that it was accompanied by some toughness:

Behind a facade of photographs, flags and slogans there is a grim structure of decrees, "re-education centers," secret police. Presidential "Ordinance No. 6" signed and issued by Diem in January, 1956, provides that "individuals considered dangerous to national defense and common security may be confined on executive order" in a "concentration camp." . . . Only known or suspected Communists who have threatened or violated public security since July, 1954 are supposed to be arrested and "re-educated" under these decrees. But many non-Communists have also been detained. . . . The whole machinery of security has been used to discourage active opposition of any kind from any source.

Nevertheless, *Life* expressed enthusiasm:

Ngo Dinh Diem is respected in Vietnam today for the miracles he has wrought. . . . To a world daunted by the idea that circumstances are bigger than men, one man with a purpose is demonstrating what he calls "the power of the human personality."

Diem had "miraculously" overcome one apparently insurmountable obstacle after another. His most significant "hurdle," according to *Life*, "was the famous Geneva election":

. . . He knew that it was not a question of who could win the projected plebiscite: it was a question of who the people would expect to win, and all too many of them would have hedged by voting on the assumption that the Vietminh might win. *Diem saved his people from this agonizing prospect* simply by refusing to permit the plebiscite and thereby he avoided national suicide. [italics added]

As time went on, the descriptions of Diem's "miracle" became more sophisticated and the "miracle" itself more encompassing. The Americans most actively involved in Diem's program came to be the most important propagandists for it in American journals; *viz,* Wolf Ladejinsky, writing in the December 24, 1959, issue of *The Reporter*:

When, on the anniversary of Vietnam's independence, I asked Pres. Ngo about his role in it, he replied that he was but an instrument of the invisible hand of the Lord. Whether he led the country single-handed or in close cooperation with divine Providence, there is much about his five years in office that is almost incredible.

Ladejinsky recognized that democracy was less than perfect under Diem—"He believes in democracy, but he is compelled to ration it"—but such restrictions were necessary to provide political stability and economic improvement in the face of the Communist menace:

The overwhelming majority of the people in South Vietnam are not affected by the regime's authoritarianism. They have probably never enjoyed greater freedom in the conduct of their life and work or benefited in a greater variety of ways. Impatience with the government on the part of those intellectuals who want power for the asking doesn't extend to the peasantry.

This account of the peasants' desires was offered as authoritative, since the author was employed by the Diem government from the beginning as chief foreign adviser on agrarian problems. It served to provide a justification for the Diem regime more acceptable to *The Reporter's* liberal readers than the image provided by *Life* of Diem's saving "his people" from the "agonizing prospect" of elections. . . .

The important questions became what sort of revolution Diem was making and why it required the stringency that his regime was exerting. These questions had been hinted at . . . in an article [Wesley] Fishel wrote for the Autumn, 1959, *Yale Review*, in which he predicted the political future with notable inaccuracy:

On October 26, 1959, South Vietnam will celebrate its fourth anniversary as the Republic of Vietnam. The anticipated elections of 1956 have never been held, and the Communist capability in Vietnam, south of the 17th Parallel, has been reduced to one of sheer nuisance activity. . . . It is one Asian area where Communism has been rolled back, and rolled back without war.

The major accomplishment of the Diem regime, then, was that it had stopped the Communists from controlling all of Vietnam; and an apparatus of force was required for that purpose. Fishel thought the task to have been completed: "There is little likelihood of a revolution against the regime," he wrote in the *Yale Review* article. And in *The New Leader* article [see Reading 22—eds.]: "His [Diem's] regime now is assuredly one of the most stable and honest on the periphery of Asia."

In still another area, Fishel's predictions were refuted by subsequent events. He noted that some observers of Vietnam had pointed to Diem's Catholicism and feared that this would cause political and social friction, but Fishel felt this to be an irrelevant projection of Western views: "Religious issues are often important in European and American politics," but not in Vietnam.

In November, 1959, the American Friends of Vietnam sponsored a conference devoted to the theme of South Vietnam's progress. Fishel reported: "I can testify that there has been measurable progress toward responsibility and freedom," and Wolf Ladejinsky added, in *News From Vietnam*, November, 1959:

In his efforts to deal with rural problems, President Diem and his government have not resorted to force, setting up class against class, or to any of the methods used by the Communists to impose their brand of agrarianism. Social peace has been maintained throughout.

None of this suggests that the press of the United States would not have hailed the Vietnam "miracle" without the efforts of the lobby. There was the usual tendency to follow the official line and believe the best of the man whom *Time* in its November 21, 1960, issue described as "doughty little Diem" and whom it had chosen as "the father of his country . . . without him the whole nation would have fallen to the communist Viet Minh." In *Newsweek* for June 29, 1959, Ernest K. Lindley was convinced that South Vietnam "has had more striking progress in more ways than any other nation I have visited so far" and that Diem was "one of the ablest free Asian leaders."

The lobby's main effort was to provide an ideological framework to explain away the uncomfortable facts that occasionally found their way into the mass media as "a necessary reaction to the Communist menace" confronting Diem. The "miracle" thesis formulated by the lobby was accepted by most of the mass media during the first five years of Diem's regime. It was generally accepted that aid to Vietnam had produced a success story: the Diem government had turned back the threat of communism by initiating vast programs of economic and political reform and greatly improving the lives of the people. American aid and advice had helped to develop a "nationalist alternative" to the Viet Minh and the country was making rapid strides toward political stability and economic independence.

Between 1954 and 1958 Diem's government did attain a degree of stable rule over parts of South Vietnam. But it is clear now that it was not evolving toward a free society. Indeed, the essential condition of its stability was the absence of political freedom. From the very beginning the Diem regime showed no reluctance to utilize political terror to strengthen and maintain its rule. During this period the United States set out to ensure the loyalty of the army to Diem, as the Michigan State professors had done in the course of training the secret police and the Palace Guard. Colonel Lansdale of the C.I.A. also was concerned with winning over the peasants and toward that end organized Civic Action teams which roamed the countryside with megaphones and film projectors extolling the virtues of the Diem regime. The M.S.U. group later took over this project, but it was able to report only limited success. It was difficult to recruit members for the teams and they were forced to rely heavily on refugees from the North loyal to Diem. As John D. Montgomery reported in his book, *The Politics of Foreign Aid*,

. . . The villagers who were the project's beneficiaries sometimes resented the visiting teams because they were staffed with refugees from the north—strangers who spoke a different dialect and practiced a different religion. Almost all refugees from the Communist regime in North Viet-Nam were Roman Catholics, and the government's costly program for them, together with the policy of using such strong anti-Communists as Civic Action leaders, stimulated much envy and resentment.

The Diem government's contribution to the idea of civic action was to unleash a reign of terror upon the countryside. There were massive anti-Communist renunciation campaigns [see Reading 28—eds.]. Thousands of people suspected of sympathizing with the Viet Minh were sent to re-education centers. Those thought to be active Viet Cong agents were jailed or shot. Prizes were offered for turning in one's parents or relatives, and detailed statistics were compiled on the number who confessed and were re-educated.

Article 14c of the Geneva Accords had protected the rights of those sympathetic to the belligerents in the war, but the Diem government did not permit the International Control Commission to investigate charges of violation of these provisions. It was the view of the Commission that because of the obstruction of the Diem government, "The Commission is therefore no longer able to supervise the implementation of this article by the Government of the Republic of South Vietnam."

The Accords embodied concepts ostensibly cherished by the "free world," and it was these provisions the Diem government refused to uphold. For example, the Sixth Interim Report of the International Control Commission reported that the Viet Minh offered "to have complete freedom of movement between the two zones" making an "iron" or "bamboo" curtain impossible, but the forces in the South rejected this. During the summer of 1955, demonstrations in Saigon against the Geneva Accords had resulted in the burning of the hotel that housed the Control Commission.

The Viet Minh, on the other hand, was more respectful of the Accords because they were counting on the Commission's carrying out the elections. The Sixth Interim Report of the unanimous finding of the Commission stated: ". . . the degree of co-operation given by the two parties has not been the same. While the Commission has experienced difficulties in North Vietnam, the major part of its difficulties has arisen in South Vietnam."

These reports indicate that the apparent political stability of the Diem regime in those first five years was due primarily to the Viet Minh willingness to withhold pressure in view of its virtually certain victory at the polls under the Geneva Accords. This is conceded in the account of that period offered in the U.S. State Department's White Paper of October, 1961:

> It was the Communists' calculation that nationwide elections scheduled in the accords for 1956 would turn all Viet-Nam over to them. . . . The primary focus of the Communists' activity during the post-Geneva period was on political action . . . the refusal [to hold elections] came as a sharp disappointment to Hanoi, whose political program for two years had been aimed at precisely that goal. The failure of 1956 was a severe blow to the morale of the Viet Cong organization in the South. . . . The period of 1956–58 was one of rebuilding and reorganization for the Viet Cong.

By 1959, the Viet Minh had finally written off the possibility of elections and turned to military means. Thus ended the illusory stability of the Diem regime.

The Land Reform Program

The division in South Vietnam between the Catholic refugees and the rest of the population was widened by the agrarian reform program on behalf of the refugees, but it was upon the success of this program that the hope of an economic "miracle" for the country depended. To the refugees arriving as strangers from the North, the agrarian program was a boon. It settled them on abandoned land and provided a subsistence living and necessary seed and implements until they could be self-sufficient. Although there was some chafing at the insistence of the Diem government on retaining ownership of the lands, the program represented an obvious net gain for the refugees.

There was nothing comparable for the indigenous population. Although the Viet Minh had always taxed the peasants to support the war against the French, it had provided them with tangible benefits in return. Its coming led to the disappearance of the landlords, and the peasants were urged to seize the land they had tilled for others. But peasant support for the Viet Minh was based on a good deal more than a mere accounting of immediate interests.

Joseph Alsop was one of the few Westerners to tour rural South Vietnam while it was still occupied by the Viet Minh. In an article for *The New Yorker* (June 25, 1955) he recounted:

> I would like to be able to report—I had hoped to be able to report—that on that long, slow canal trip to Vinh Binh (Mekong Delta) I saw all the signs of misery and oppression that have made my visits to East Germany like nightmare journeys to 1984. But it was not so.

At first it was difficult for me, as it is for any Westerner, to conceive of a Communist government's genuinely "serving the people." I could hardly imagine a Communist government that was also a popular government and almost a democratic government. But this is just the sort of government the palm-hut state actually was while the struggle with the French continued. The Vietminh could not possibly have carried on the resistance for one year, let alone nine years, without the people's strong, united support.

Diem had few illusions about the loyalty of the rural populace and was content with a program of pacification rather than of winning support. His American advisers, however, recognized the inherent weakness of such a state of affairs. They felt that some positive support for the Diem government had to be added to that given by refugees if communism in South Vietnam was to be contained. An axiom of American foreign policy is that an exploited and impoverished peasantry provides fertile soil for communism, as in China; therefore, intelligent land reform, preserving private property and simultaneously creating a new middle class of farmers, is a necessity for "free world" objectives. In President Eisenhower's note to Diem soon after he became Premier, he called for "indispensable reforms," which implied agrarian reform. But the Diem government, Robert Scigliano wrote in *South Vietnam: Nation Under Stress*, only began to work in earnest on this program after Eisenhower's appointee, Ambassador Collins, "reportedly stipulated effective agrarian reform as a condition of the increased American aid which President Diem was seeking."

By 1959, the resulting land reform was being acclaimed in the United States as the single most important achievement of the Diem administration. Its provisions, on paper, were suited to the goal of creating a rural middle class. Contracts were designed between landlord and tenant to fix maximum rents and guaranteed a period of tenure for at least five years. A later ordinance specified that all holdings in rice land exceeding 100 hectares (about 247 acres) would be purchased by the government from the landlords. Ten per cent of the purchase price was to be paid in cash and the balance in non-transferable government bonds bearing 3 per cent interest and redeemable in twelve years. The purchased land was then to be resold to the tenants at the same price, to be paid by them to the government.

The huge rubber plantations (mostly French-owned) were left intact under a provision excluding all crops but rice. This was because of their efficiency; unlike many of the larger rice operations they had continued even under the Viet Minh. In addition, rubber provided an important source of foreign exchange.

United States counterpart funds paid the salaries of the 700 administrative personnel working on the agrarian reform program. The cost of the land transfer program was estimated at $68.6 million, but only $6.4. million was required in the first stage. The U.S. government, hesitant about allocating money for the "expropriation" of private property, provided $4,000,414 for "administrative" expenses. It did, however, provide for a $3,000,000 increase in "highway maintenance" funds which was then transferred by the Vietnamese government to land purchase. These outlays and the 80 per cent of South Vietnamese budget supplied by U.S. funds meant that the operation was totally dependent upon U.S. sponsorship.

The tenants ended up paying a higher rate than the amount specified by the law, but this, according to Wolf Ladejinsky, represented an improvement over the pre-war rate. In fact, in "Agrarian Reform in Vietnam," published in *Problems in Freedom*, edited by Wesley Fishel, Ladejinsky went even further: "Perhaps the real significance of these measures is that they represent the first breach in the traditional view of landlordism as the basis of wealth, political power and social prestige." The U.S. State Department asserted that the very success of the program inspired the renewal of Communist aggression.

There is no doubt that the land reform program was related to the renewal of guerrilla warfare—an irony since American insistence on the program was based on a belief that such policies would forestall support for the guerrillas rather than inspire it. But the policy, whatever its merits on paper, was a stop-gap measure after the fact. The rule of the Viet Minh in the South preceding Geneva had meant the flight of the landlord and the seizure of land by the tenant. This made the later Diem land reform act seem like a measure that took from the peasants rather than gave to them. This point is admitted by the two Americans most enthusiastic about and most intimately involved in the land reform program, J. Price Gittinger and Wolf Ladejinsky. In *Far Eastern Survey*, January and February, 1960, Gittinger wrote:

As implementation began in early 1955, an interesting paradox in landlord and tenant attitudes emerged. Much of Free Viet-Nam had either recently been recovered from Communist control, or Viet-Minh forces still retained paramount influence. In these areas, particularly those in south Viet-Nam, landlords had sometimes not collected rent for as long as eight years. Therefore, landlords looked upon the contract program as a means to assure them a rental of at least 25 percent of the crop. On the other hand tenants in these areas resisted the program, since they had been paying no rent at all.

In "Agrarian Reform in Vietnam" in the Fishel book, Ladejinsky wrote:

Many a tenant had not paid rent in years, and thus even the admittedly low rent of 15 to 25 percent appeared to be an imposition. Others whose occupation of land had been sanctioned by the Communists believed that their ownership had already been confirmed, and that signing a contract now would invalidate their claim to ownership.

The most politically effective response on the part of the government would have been to legalize take-overs that had occurred under the Communists. But this solution would have struck at the basic respect for property underlying the type of rural middle-class society that the United States and the Diem government were attempting to create. John Montgomery in *The Politics of Foreign Aid* described the Vietnamese government as "not wishing to disturb the strong landowning classes." The program reaffirmed the sacredness of property and at the same time enhanced the landlords' financial position. According to Montgomery,

It was true that the landlords opposed the low rentals, but it was equally true that their experiences in the past decade had had a sobering effect. They were interested in selling their land.

The receipt of 10 per cent in cash and the rest in bonds redeemable in twelve years from a government underwritten by the United States was an appealing reward for land that had been written off as lost.

In its actual operation, land reform legitimized the return of the landlord to the countryside he had fled, to collect rents he had ceased to collect, and to receive money for land he had long abandoned. This is the link between the land reform program and the increase in guerrilla warfare. Observers Scigliano, Montgomery, Ladejinsky, and many journalists agreed that peasant dissatisfaction with land reform was a breeding ground for the growth of Communist power in South Vietnam.

The U.S. Aid Program

From 1955 to 1962, the U.S. supplied the Vietnamese with more than $2 billion in aid. Of this amount, $1.4 billion was intended for economic assistance. According to the "miracle" thesis Vietnam was the brightest spot in the foreign aid program: in other countries such aid might be wasted on corrupt and reactionary leaders, but in Vietnam it was being used to start the country on the path toward economic development. It had, to use Leo Cherne's phrase, left the "entire economy reinvigorated by Ngo's skillful, tenacious and vigorous government." The introduction of more than $2 billion into a country with an annual gross national product of $1.2 billion could hardly fail to be invigorating, but permanent economic development is a more elusive goal.

The bulk of the aid was in the form of counterpart funds to pay for the excess of imports over exports. In 1958 South Vietnam imported $232 million worth of goods and exported only $55 million. U.S. dollars paid for 85 per cent of the imports. In 1959 the United States paid for 75 per cent of the imports; in 1960, for 84 per cent. If the United States had not supplied this dollar aid, the goods could only have been imported by drawing on the gold and foreign exchange reserves of the South Vietnamese government or by increasing exports. The economy never developed sufficiently to permit the latter; and since total gold and foreign exchange reserves of the Vietnamese government in 1958 amounted to $159 million, drawing on this could only have been possible for one year. Thanks to the largesse of the American aid program, these reserves were increased by $57 million between 1958 and 1960.

The U.S. aid program permitted the South Vietnamese to consume an amount of foreign goods (15 to 20 per cent of the GNP) in excess of what its economy could afford. Since these goods were imported by private dealers in response to private demand, a false prosperity resulted, particularly in Saigon, which did not reflect the state of the economy as a whole. But, as John Montgomery writes, an important element of the program was ". . . to find a political instrument for generating support for the Diem regime. A plentiful supply of consumer goods would provide the middle class (army officers, civil servants and small professional people) with goods they wanted and could afford to buy."

But army officers, civil servants, and the small professionals who serviced their needs were only in a position to buy goods because of other aspects of the U.S. aid program. Saigon importers paid in South Vietnamese piasters for goods originally bought with U.S. dollars. These piasters were then turned over to the South Vietnamese government to pay for its army and civil service. A high rate of imports was encouraged by U.S. acceptance of a very low official exchange rate of 35/1 (as compared with 75/1 free market), which meant that the importer was actually obtaining goods at half their real cost. On the basis of available evidence, provided by the Michigan State economists and other experts, it is apparent that at least three-fourths of American aid was used for the importation of either consumer goods or raw materials for the production of consumer goods.

The aid program was intended to provide an atmosphere of prosperity and to insure political support for the Diem administration. But it was also considered necessary in order to build a military apparatus in South Vietnam capable of containing the Communists, and the bulk of economic aid thus was channelled to pay the army and support the government. In Vietnam, as elsewhere, most of what is called "economic aid" in the U.S. foreign aid program is actually "defense support." As the Mansfield Senate Subcommittee pointed out in 1960,

The subcommittee was impressed by the apparently far greater degree of effectiveness in the administration of the military, as contrasted with non-military aid programs in Vietnam. A number of reasons seem to underlie the difference. Certainly the former has been, from the outset, the tail that wags the dog. The military aid program has had first and predominant call on aid funds. In fact the non-military programs were developed largely in response to that call and continue to operate primarily on that basis. By far the greatest part of the so-called economic aid in Vietnam takes the form of defense support and, hence, has been channeled indirectly into the military aid program.

Aside from paying the total cost of the South Vietnamese army, the United States paid for most other expenditures of the South Vietnamese government. Official estimates of the percentage of South Vietnam's budget borne by U.S. aid vary from 60 to 75 per cent. Even this underestimates the real dependence on U.S. aid: the bulk of the taxes collected by the South Vietnamese government were from imports. This permitted the South Vietnamese government to impose a high rate of taxation without halting imports because the United States accepted the cut-rate 35/1 exchange.

The inability of the Diem government to collect taxes except from U.S.-subsidized imports reflected its administrative weakness and lack of contact with the population. One M.S.U. economist made the observation upon his return that

. . . Vietnam today still remains the prototype of a dependent economy, its levels of national income as dependent on outside forces as was the case when the country was a French colony. After six years of large-scale American aid, Vietnam is becoming a permanent mendicant. Certainly, if aid were eliminated tomorrow, there would be an unpaid army and unfed civilians. American aid has built a castle on sand.

Aside from the preoccupation with military security, the U.S. aid program was handicapped by its commitment to private enterprise. It favored the subsidized import program to preserve the private sector and aid its expansion. The Diem government recognized that unplanned private investment would not be sufficient and it therefore attempted to develop a system of planning and government investment. But the United States would not allow its aid to be used in support of this program. John Montgomery noted in *The Politics of Foreign Aid*:

. . . The United States permitted capital equipment to be imported under the program only for privately owned and operated enterprises, while for its part the Vietnamese government, unwilling to permit any basic industries to be controlled by French or Chinese, demanded the right to a majority of stock in all important enterprises.

Only 20 per cent of American economic aid was assigned to specific social and economic projects, and much of this was for military support programs with, at best, indirect development value, e.g., the highway program (40 per cent of project aid). The rate of investment was far below that required to keep up with the 3 per cent annual growth in population. The fact that foreign reserves increased as much as they did testifies to the government's laxity in matters of economic development. To quote another Michigan State economist: "The economic solution to the problem of economic growth in Vietnam is relatively simple; the real problems, the serious problems, lie in the area of administration and politics."

South Vietnam, with a minute capital investment, one quarter of the working class of its largest city unemployed, and most of the rural population working a four-month year, devoured incredible amounts of American aid to provide consumer goods for its privileged and government classes.

The "Miracle" Collapses

In 1959 the "miracle" bubble of Vietnam burst; it had been nothing more than a miracle of public relations. In the spring of that year the correspondent for the *Wall Street Journal* (April 2, 1959) took an accounting of the miracle and concluded: ". . . the accomplishment, so far, rests on American aid. Without that aid there would be no Vietnam!" In July of 1959, Albert M. Colegrove, a veteran

Scripps-Howard reporter, went to Vietnam and came back with the "dirt" on the traditionally vulnerable foreign program. When reported to the two and one-half million readers of the newspaper chain, it created a stir. Colegrove was primarily concerned with "waste" in the program—unnecessary freezers for Americans, excessive allowances, graft—and was outraged that military vehicles were unaccounted for and that Americans lived in villas with an excessive number of servants.

Colegrove was summoned to Washington for a hearing before the Mansfield Subcommittee, accompanied by his publisher. Colegrove in no way disputed the basis of the American program; he agreed that we were needed there to protect the freedom of the Vietnamese against the Communist intruders. The closest he came to criticism of the purposes was when he said:

> After several years we keep talking about the courageous government and I'll grant you that they are courageous. But it is four or five long years since the crises there. . . . After several years of American aid and alleged guidance, Vietnam still has the same problem as bad as ever.

After a battery of questions, some of which challenged his mental competence and his patriotism, Colegrove tried to get back into the mainstream:

> I do not think there is any doubt but what the main mission . . . has been accomplished. It is just the cost which I question. . . . I think that the present government of Vietnam is—well, I think it is a miracle that it exists; that it has overcome almost unbelievable obstacles; that we can be thankful that President Diem moved into that situation when he did.

The next major critical note in the dialogue was struck by William J. Lederer and Eugene Burdick in *The Ugly American*: Uncle Sam was too bureaucratic and tended to get involved in grandiose projects of economic development that never reached the people. The solution proposed by the authors was to let more "average, common-sense" Americans loose to impart their know-how to the natives. But the real problem in Vietnam was the opposite—the U.S. had *not* invested in serious programs of economic development—and the strangest thing about the novel is that it wholly ignored the military nature of the foreign aid program.

The Ugly American is pure American homespun. In it, there are no serious political revolutions, but only misunderstandings caused by stuffed shirts and bureaucrats who get in the way of the good guys who are out to destroy evil. It is comic-book politics and its central hero is a Steve Canyon type named Col. Hillandale. Yet this gross over-simplification of foreign policy was accepted as serious social criticism, as proof of the healthiness of a democratic society. Millions of people, including President Eisenhower, accepted what was in essence an irrelevant critique. For Col. Hillandale was said to have been patterned after the real life Col. Lansdale, who had been one of the men most responsible for getting the

United States involved in Vietnam. The model for the hero of *The Ugly American* had helped shape the very program the book derided.

The tarnishing of Diem's "image" in the United States was accompanied by signs of serious disintegration in Vietnam itself. Diem was aware of what this sort of discontent might mean in estranging the United States. He knew that his government could not survive if the massive aid program were cut off. And he concluded he would have to base his appeal on the issue of anti-communism. This emphasis had been made clear when Diem and Chiang Kai-shek, exchanging visits, chose the occasion of Diem's visit to Formosa, on January 29, 1960, to issue the following joint statement, as reported in *The New York Times* of January 30:

. . . It is the earnest hope of the two Chiefs of State that the temporary lull existing in the European scene will not lure the Free World off its guard, particularly in the Far East and Southeast Asia, where threat of aggression persists as long as the Chinese mainland remains under the yoke of International Communism. The aid received by the free Asian countries on the periphery of or in the path of aggression from the Communist bloc should therefore not be reduced, but should be further strengthened so as to enable them to meet effectively both the overt and covert Communist action.

Earlier, the Diem regime had played down the Communist threat. Its boast was that it had restored security to the countryside. But now, with the "Communist danger" the basis for assuring continued American aid, the "secure" countryside suddenly was overrun with "Communist terrorists."

This shift in the official line created some confusion. In June of 1959, for example, Senator Mansfield at a Senate committee meeting had quoted the statement of Major General Myers, formerly Deputy Chief of the U.S. Mission in Vietnam, that the Viet Cong in the South were ". . . gradually nibbled away until they ceased to be a major menace to the government. In fact, estimates at the time of my departure indicated that there was a very limited number of hostile individuals under arms in the country. Two territorial regiments, reinforced occasionally by one or two regular army regiments, were able to cope with their depredations."

This statement had been made on April 17, 1959, and U.S. Ambassador Durbrow attested to its accuracy as late as June, 1959. It was soon to be contradicted by reports such as the one in *The New York Times* of October 31, 1959: "A top-level Vietnamese source said today that the two-week-long campaign [in the southernmost province] had resulted in the killing of about 300 Communists and the capture of 400. He said an additional 700 had surrendered and an undetermined number had been wounded."

In an attempt to explain such discrepancies, Diem's officials, during 1960, began to expound the theory of continual Communist aggression from the North. It was said that Communist agents from the North terrorized the villagers into joining their cause and that whole companies of well-armed invaders were arriving in the South, having traveled over the "Ho Chi Minh Trail." This was to become the basis, during the Kennedy Administration, for greater U.S. involvement in

Vietnam, and for bombing raids across the border under President Johnson. But there is little evidence from the critical period 1959–60 to support such a contention.

Observations that ran counter to the official line were provided by a RAND Corporation researcher, George K. Tanham, who traveled in South Vietnam during 1960 in an effort to evaluate the guerrilla fighting that had developed. In his 1961 book, *Communist Revolutionary Warfare*, he reported:

The so-called Ho Chi Minh trail is no more than a series of paths that run north and south through the mountains and are not suitable for large arms shipments. . . . To judge by equipment and arms that have been captured from the Communists, they have been fighting largely with home-made weapons and with such material of French and American make as they have been able to steal or capture.

Tanham concluded his book with the following paragraph:

However, the crucial fact today is that the Communists are arousing the people to fight and work for them. It is easy but wrong to attribute their success solely to terrorist methods. They are systematically creating the "sea" that Mao thought essential for military success and eventual political control. Diem has been unable to win popular support either on a nationalist basis or with personal loyalty as a motivating force. Until his government has the active and continuing support of the Vietnamese masses and the troops, all the economic and military aid in the world, though it may delay it, will not halt the Communist advance.

An account of this period was also provided by Philippe Devillers, a French writer on Vietnamese history, in an article in the *China Quarterly* for January– March, 1962. Devillers argued that the Communists in the South entered the fight against Diem reluctantly, not on orders from Hanoi or Peking but in response to the terror campaign that Diem had conducted against former members of the Viet Minh in the countryside from the time he first assumed power in 1954. "The insurrection," Devillers wrote, "existed before the Communists decided to take part, and they were simply forced to join in. And even among the Communists the initiative did not originate in Hanoi, but from the grassroots, where the people were literally driven to take up arms in self-defense.". . .

At the end of April, 1960, eighteen Vietnamese nobles, including a number of former ministers, petitioned Diem to liberalize his regime. According to *The New York Times* of April 29, "The petition said continual arrests had filled prisons to overflowing and asserted that a swollen Government bureaucracy was corrupt and inefficient." The petitioners were conservative men, well-known for their strong anti-communism and past ties with the French administration. It was striking that they felt called upon to warn Diem publicly that his policies would soon give rise to "soaring waves of hatred and resentment of a terribly suffering people standing up to break the chains that restrain them."

Then on November 21, 1960, Diem's worst crisis in this period came when his elite paratroopers rose in revolt. Thousands of civilians joined with them and marched on Diem's palace, but in the end, after 400 lay dead, Diem remained in power. This event broke through the complacency of the American press. *Newsweek* for November 21, 1960, warned: "The revolt has been crushed, but it remained a grim signal to Diem of the extent of opposition to his authoritarian regime." *Life* for November 28, 1960, reported: "Diem was in more trouble than ever. He was once a national hero. Now, thanks to his increasingly high-handed policies his best units could no longer be relied on. . . ." *Time* for November 21, 1960, quoted a paratrooper captain who had joined the "revolt": "All Diem has done in six years in office is indulge in nepotism. He has generals who don't even command a company. He lives in an ivory tower surrounded by his family. . . ." And *Time* added: "Pleading the Communist threat, Diem has ruled with rigged elections, a muzzled press, and political re-education camps that now hold 30,000. His prosperous key advisers are four brothers and a pretty sister-in-law."

These events, which occurred during the last months of the Eisenhower Administration, began to build pressure for a reevaluation of U.S. policy. There were indications of increasing disenchantment in Washington with the attempt to create a showcase of American aid in Vietnam. What is more, key members of the "Vietnam lobby" were also becoming disillusioned with Diem. Joseph Buttinger had gone to work with Vietnam exiles in the United States preparing for Diem's overthrow. As early as February, 1960, Leo Cherne had gone to Vietnam at the behest of many leaders of the American Friends of Vietnam to ask Diem to change his ways. The Michigan State University project ended in 1961, and Wesley Fishel, its innovator, was no longer on close terms with Diem.

The Kennedy Policies

John F. Kennedy took office in January, 1961. Vietnam had been one of his early concerns and it occupied a high place among the international problems he now had to confront.

As a result of the book on the C.I.A., *The Invisible Government*, many Americans are aware of the role played by the C.I.A. and its chief agent in Vietnam, Edward Lansdale, in involving the United States in Vietnam at the time of the Geneva settlement in 1954. It seems to have gone unnoticed, however, that Lansdale played an equally important role during the first year of the Kennedy Administration in committing the United States to a far deeper involvement in that country. In January of 1961 Lansdale, by then a Major General, was sent to Vietnam by Secretary of Defense Gates to prepare an over-all study of the situation. He reported that the situation was near total collapse and that if the policies of the Diem government and its advisers continued to be pursued the country would soon be lost. However, if Lansdale's recommendations were followed, the situation could be saved. The report caused a stir in the Kennedy Administration. The President called Lansdale to congratulate him and to suggest that a portion of the report be published in the *Saturday Evening Post* (as it was in the May 20, 1961 issue)

In May, 1961, Kennedy asked Secretary of Defense Roswell Gilpatric to set up a special task force under General Lansdale to begin shaping the new policies of the United States toward Vietnam. The group hammered out a basic agreement after about three weeks of strenuous argument [see Reading 19B—eds.]. There were varied views as to the extent and nature of the new U.S. commitment. According to General Lansdale, in an interview with the author, the discussion became emotionally charged, and comments such as "People are getting killed out there," or "You're a traitor," or "You want to kill a lot of Vietnamese?" were typical.But for all of this intensity of opinion it does not seem that anyone suggested, as had the French and General Eisenhower some years before, that the root of the problem may have lain in the popular support of the Viet Cong. It was not that the men on the committee gainsayed Ho's popularity. On the contrary, their major criticism of the effort in Vietnam concerned the inability of the Diem government to arouse popular support through social reform. But they looked upon this as a factor that was negotiable.

It had always been Lansdale's belief that the Communists were "outselling" us, and that through proper social programs, combined with an imaginative propaganda program, the United States could outsell *them*. As he noted as recently as October, 1964, in an article in *Foreign Affairs*, "The Vietnamese need a cause and we have not supplied it."

The political member of the committee was Sterling Cottrel, a State Department career officer, who was to head the task force after its initial three weeks under Lansdale, when the Pentagon turned over the prerogatives of leadership to the State Department. Cottrel was sympathetic to the "hard" position. He had recently returned from serving as Admiral Felt's political officer in the Pacific fleet. He held that the United States must continue to support Diem despite his failings: "I argued that this was an Oriental dictator and you couldn't change the spots on the tiger. . . ."

Cottrel was particularly irked at those who said that the war could not be won if Diem continued to rule, including such members of the old Vietnam lobby as Fishel and Buttinger. Like other hard-headed professionals, Cottrel did not consider Diem that important.What the professionals were concerned about was an extension of U.S. influence and the better use of U.S. expertise and equipment. As Cottrel stated in a conversation with this writer,

> Others wanted to have Diem delegate authority—a lot of our Michigan State people who had been out there had said this was an administrative nightmare—Fishel was for letting Diem rot at the end of '61—we started getting this noise, this yak, when we first started supporting Diem—they said it wouldn't work because of Diem—so I argued, hell—the provincial chiefs have to be friends of Diem but let us work with provincial chiefs whom Diem trusts—we can bypass hierarchy, ministers, ship stuff right to the provincial chiefs—get the show on the road—we wrapped the stuff up and sent it to the provinces—we were able to bypass Diem.

One indication that the style of operation had changed was the transfer of the Government of Vietnam's public relations account from the Oram group to the much larger advertising firm of Kastor, Hilton, Chesley, Clifford and Atherton in May of 1961. It became a much more costly account involving about $200,000 a year. This proved to be a strictly commercial operation devoid of the political doubts and confusions of the earlier group.

The task force also decided to increase the number of U.S. advisers and to change the nature of their duties. The first group of 100, trained in the Army's Special Forces program, went to Vietnam in May of 1961. It was also decided to increase the size of the Vietnamese Army from 150,000 to 250,000 (in violation of the Geneva Accords limit of 150,000) and to concentrate its training on counter-insurgency. A similar program was intended for the civil guard. There was also some planning for social reforms to mobilize peasant support. This was a variation of the "New Villages" concept that had been used by the British in Malaya, and the expert on that project, Robert Thompson, was induced to go to Vietnam.

When the task force felt the need of academic advice in July of 1961, it did not turn to the old group of professors who had helped create the "miracle" and were now disenchanted with it, but rather to an outsider, Eugene Staley, of the Stanford Research Institute. Cottrel described the process of selection:

> . . . We agreed to send out the best economist we could collect to look at their economy to assess how the resources could best be utilized to this end. I had a list of economists and when we decided on Staley I went to Bowles [Chester Bowles, then Under-Secretary of State] and asked him if he would call Staley on the President's behalf—easier for Bowles to put on pressure than the President. Before Staley went out I took him to the White House to meet the President—then he sailed off and came back with the report—then we started pushing the stuff out, the hardware.

It seems to have been Staley's job to report on the economic feasibility as well as the costs of the program. His inch-thick and still secret report reinforced the suggestions of the task force. According to a "leak," *Time* for August 4, 1961, stated: "Overall, the report would commit the U.S. to the most detailed program of economic and social reform that the U.S. has ever undertaken." It called for an immediate increase of 20,000 in the armed forces, guerrilla training, and approved the idea of strategic hamlets or "New Villages" as economically feasible units. *Time* reported further:

> Diem completed 27 agrovilles last year [see Reading 28—eds.], but reaped nothing but antagonism when overzealous Diem men yanked peasants away from their fields just at harvest time, put them to work at forced labor to build the new agrovilles. To compound the peasants' anger, it frequently turned out there wasn't enough room for them in the agrovilles that they had been forced to build. But Staley concluded that the basic idea was good, hopes the U.S. will finance the construction of at least another 100 in the next twelve months.

Time may have given too much credit to Staley for his sponsorship of the strategic hamlet program. His report was concerned with the technical economic aspects of the program, such as the cost of barbed wire. Cottrel recalls that the President was enthusiastic about the strategic hamlet idea, having always believed that one should learn from the experience of other countries—in this case the British in Malaya. Lansdale, on the other hand, opposed them. When asked about them by this writer, Lansdale replied:

I don't believe in police measures—genocide, transmigration of villages, curfews, use of force—must allow the development of governments of some popular will—you don't put the people you're fighting for in a cage of some sort—I don't believe in that—if these folks would voluntarily want to go in a strategic hamlet, and there have been some—go to people and explain the benefits—this certainly wasn't the case in Vietnam, they were told to do things and moved around, the penalties for not doing were severe—areas outside strategic hamlets were combat areas—I think this was deep distrust of the people.

The strategic hamlet program was incorporated into the overall operations and grew to be the major vehicle for whatever social reforms the United States had in mind for isolating the guerrillas from the people.

Later, in October, 1961, an omnibus task force—the Taylor Mission—went to Vietnam and directed the earlier segments of the program into two main channels. U.S. military equipment and expertise would be used in a counter-insurgency program that would be made more efficient than before by by-passing the Diem bureaucracy with thousands of American advisers working with combat units. The second part of the program was a recognition that the Viet Cong was fighting a guerrilla war that depended upon peasant sympathy. The peasants therefore had to be separated from the guerrillas through "clear and hold" operations. This involved clearing out the guerrillas and moving the peasants into fortified hamlets, surrounded by barbed wire or bamboo spears, and guarded by local troops.

This program departed from Lansdale's idea of winning the peasants over first and then arming them. It assumed the indifference or hostility of the peasants, but attributed it to Viet Cong "terror" or Diem's policies. It was reasoned that if the peasants were given the security of the strategic hamlets, though initially it might be against their will, they would eventually come to support the Diem government. In the meantime, the Viet Cong would have lost its source of men and food.

In October, 1961, the Administration offered justification of an increased participation in Vietnam in the White Paper entitled "A Threat to the Peace; North Vietnam's Effort to Conquer South Vietnam." [For more about this 1961 White Paper, see Reading 37—eds.] To quote Dean Rusk's introduction, the Paper set out to expose "the determined and ruthless campaign, propaganda, infiltration, and subversion by the Communist regime in North Vietnam to destroy the Republic of Vietnam. . . ." The permanent division of the territory into two independent countries was accepted as a fact, despite the Geneva Accords, as was the refusal of elections.

The White Paper conceded that the bulk of the Viet Cong guerrillas were South Vietnamese peasants living in their native villages and supporting themselves by tilling their native soil, but this is explained by reference to Viet Cong terrorism:

Undoubtedly there are some volunteers. But the record shows that many young Vietnamese are dragooned into service with the Viet Cong. Some are kidnapped; others are
threatened; still others join to prevent their families from being harried.

A statement by Under-Secretary George Ball amplified this thesis:

The guerrillas whom the Vietnamese Army is fighting are under distinct handicaps. In
many cases they are poorly trained and equipped and not motivated by deep convictions.
Rather they are merely unsophisticated villagers or peasants who have been conscripted by
terror or treachery. In such case they are likely to have had only rudimentary training in
weapons handling and tactics. Their equipment may be makeshift, often just what they can
capture or fabricate themselves. . . . Only the leaders and the hardcore have a strong ideological commitment. The rank and file are their puppets . . . those whom they have
bought, coerced, or intimidated.

It is difficult for government officials of any persuasion to recognize good in an
enemy, but this attitude left only an awkward explanation for the successful course
of the Viet Cong fight. The United States seemed to be arguing that coercion alone
could intimidate peasants into fighting fanatically with fabricated weapons against
vastly superior forces. Yet the Diem government had been attempting to intimidate
them for six years without any success at all in enlisting their support.

The source of the Viet Cong's weapons did make the State Department uncomfortable, as the White Paper indicated:

The weapons of the Viet Cong are largely French, or U.S. made, or handmade on
primitive forges in the jungles. . . . The Communists have avoided any large-scale introduction of Soviet-bloc arms into South Vietnam for this would be too clear evidence of
their direct involvement.

If the arms were largely captured ones, and the guerrillas mostly native recruits, what was being infiltrated? The evidence of the White Paper shows that
several thousand trained and dedicated Communists who had gone South with the
Viet Minh in 1954 had gone back to the North for training and were now being
smuggled back into the South. The State Department did not answer the Viet Minh
argument that these men had no other option since the West had blocked peaceful
means of change by election left open by the Geneva Accords. Nor did it address
itself to the implicit question of how these thousands were able to succeed against
the better armed 300,000 troops of the government.

26. The Legal Underpinnings of Government Terror in South Vietnam: Law 10/59*

It would be an understatement to point out that the regime of Ngo Dinh Diem lacked legitimacy. Representing little in the indigenous society of southern Vietnam, unable to escape the onus of rejecting the reunification of the country (Reading 21), and opposed by former resistance fighters who enjoyed all the glory and prestige of having defeated French imperialism in Vietnam, the regime fell back on sheer anti-communism for its attempt to establish legitimate order in the region. Law 10/59, promulgated on May 6, 1959, was a centerpiece of the "Anti-Communist Denunciation Campaign" of the mid- and late-1950s. Tens of thousands of suspects were arrested and many were executed, as Reading 28 reveals. While anticommunism might have pleased the American backers of Ngo Dinh Diem, and was certainly a congenial doctrine for a Roman Catholic Mandarin like Diem, it backfired in southern Vietnam. As the US government scholars who prepared The Pentagon Papers *admitted, the anti-Communist campaign rendered "the central government . . . visible—and resented—at the village level as it had never been before in Vietnam."[1] Out of that resentment would soon spring the National Liberation Front of South Vietnam (Reading 29).*

A. Law 10/59

Article 1

Sentence of death, and confiscation of the whole or part of his property, with loss of rank in the case of army men, will be imposed on whoever commits or attempts to commit one of the following crimes with the aim of sabotage, or of infringing upon the security of the State, or injuring the lives or property of the people:

1. Deliberate murder, food poisoning, or kidnapping;

2. Destruction, or total or partial damaging of one of the following categories of objects by means of explosives, fire, or any other means:

(a) Dwelling-houses, whether inhabited or not, churches, pagodas, temples, warehouses, workshops, farms and all outbuildings belonging to private persons;

(b) Public buildings, residences, offices, workshops, depots, and, in a more general way, all constructions of any kind belonging to the State, and any other

---

*A. Abridged from Pham Van Bach, *et al.* [Members of the Juridical Studies Section of the National Scientific Research Board of the Democratic Republic of Vietnam], *Fascist Terror in South Vietnam: Law 10/59* (Hanoi, 1961), pp. 71–77. B. Excerpts from Saigon newspaper *Cach Manh Quoc Gia*, various issues from August 25 to September 2, 1959, in *Fascist Terror in South Vietnam: Law 10/59* (Hanoi, 1961), pp. 78–81.

1. *The Pentagon Papers* (Gravel edition), vol. 1, p. 312.

property, movable or immovable, belonging to, or controlled by the State, or which is under the system of concession, or of public management;

(c) All air, land, and water means of transport, all kinds of vehicles;

(d) Mines, with machines and equipment;

(e) Weapons, military material and equipment, posts, buildings, offices, depots, workshops, and constructions of any kind relating to defense or police forces;

(f) Crops, draft animals and farm implements, forests of any kind;

(g) Installations for telecommunications, postal service, broadcasting, the production and distribution of electricity and water, as well as all buildings, constructions, instruments used in connection with the above;

(h) Dikes, dams, roads, railways, airfields, seaports, bridges, channels, or works relating to them;

(i) Waterways, large or small, and canals.

Article 2

Sentence of hard labor for life, and confiscation of the whole or part of his property, with loss of rank in the case of army men, will be imposed upon whoever commits or attempts to commit one of the following crimes with the aim of sabotage, or of infringing upon the security of the State, or of injuring the lives or property of the people:

1. Robbery, either armed or committed by two or more persons;

2. Interruption of land or water traffic by terrorist acts, threats to use arms, or any other means;

3. Threats of assassination, of arson of houses and crops, or of kidnapping, either direct or indirect;

4. Hindrance to the holding of a market on the usual day;

5. Any act of destruction or sabotage not mentioned in the above provisions.

Article 3

Whoever belongs to an organization designed to help to prepare or to perpetrate crimes enumerated in Articles 1 and 2, or takes pledges to do so, will be subject to the sentences provided for in the said articles.

Article 4

Offenders, accomplices, and instigators of the crimes coming within the competence of the special military courts, as provided for in the second part of the present law, will not benefit from extenuating circumstances.

Article 5

Any person charged with a crime falling within the competence of the special military courts who is the first person to give information to the Government or the military, administrative, or judicial authorities before such a crime is committed or attempted, and while no legal proceedings have yet opened, or, in case of legal proceedings having already been opened, helps to arrest the authors or accomplices, will not be subject to the sentence provided for and will be able to enter a plea of extenuating circumstances.

However, the accused who enjoys non-application of sentence may be subject to forced residence, or prohibition from remaining in certain specified areas, for a period to be determined by the court.

Article 6

Three special military courts are set up and based in Saigon, Ban Me Thuot, and Hué.

The jurisdiction of the Saigon special military court extends over the southern province, that of Ban Me Thuot special military court over the province of the central High Plateaus, that of the Hué special military court over the provinces of the central plains.

As the need arises, other special military courts may be set up by decree, which will also determine their respective jurisdictions vis-à-vis the courts already existing. . . .

Article 7

Each special military court will consist of:

—A field or general officer graduated in law: president;

—The mayor of the town, or the chief of the province in which the court is sitting or a representative: counsellor;

—A field or general officer: counsellor.

The president or counsellors of the court will be appointed by decree of the Minister for Defense for the Assistant Secretary of State for Defense for a term of six months. In case of a lack of field officers, company officers will be chosen where possible.

If need be, substitutes may also be immediately appointed according to the above procedure. . . .

[Details of the administrative structure of the special military courts are omitted here.—eds.]

Article 15

The accused has the right to have his case conducted by counsel. In case he has none, the public prosecutor or the president of the court shall appoint counsel for him.

Article 16

The decisions of the special military court are not subject to appeal, and no appeal is allowed to the High Court. . . .

Article 18

Sentence of death will only be acted upon after the appeal for mercy has been rejected.

Article 19

If need be, the methods of application of the present law will be determined by decree.

Article 20

All legal provisions which are contrary to the present law are hereby repealed.

The present law will be published in the Official Journal of the Republic of Vietnam.

Saigon, May 6, 1959   NGO DINH DIEM

B. Application of the Law

It is necessary to review all the organizations of the Vietcong or other organizations set up by them, and proceed with a classification of persons belonging to the following organizations:

The Vietcong founded the "Vietminh League," the "Democratic Party," and the organizations of the youth, women, peasants and workers "for national salvation," etc. In the Nam Phan[2] they made use of the Vanguard Youth Organization to their own benefit.

In 1946, the Vietcong founded the "Lien Viet Front," the Socialist Party, the General Confederation of Labor (member of the World Trade Unions of the Communist International), and innumerable organs of the civil and military power such as the administrative committees, the people's councils, the liberation army, the relieving troops,[3] etc.

During the war period, from 1946 to 1954, the Vietcong established many other organizations under the various signboards, "for national salvation," "for the Resistance," "for the revolution," "for peace," such as the "Administrative and Resistance Committees," the "Committee for the Defense of Peace," the "Cultural Association for National Salvation," the "Association of Resistant Catholics," the "Association of Buddhists for National Salvation," the "Association of the Fighters' Mothers," and such military and paramilitary formations as "the People's Army," the "Guerrilla fighters," the "Self-Defense Corps," the "Shock Youth," the "White-haired Fighters," the "Death Volunteers," etc.

With regard to persons belonging to the above-mentioned organizations founded by the Vietcong before 1945, the Government will verify, differentiate, and adopt the following attitude:

All members, cadres, and leaders of the Indochinese Communist Party and the Vietnam Workers' Party (i.e. the Vietcong) cannot be considered as former Resistance members. The reason is that they have not pursued the fulfillment of the

---

2. Cochin China, or Nam Bo.—eds.

3. They were the Vietnamese unit which relieved Chiang Kai-shek's troops, along with the units of the French Expeditionary Corps, in accordance with the March 6, 1946, Preliminary Agreement. (Reading 12).—eds.

objectives of the Resistance, as has been said previously. On the contrary, they pursued Communist objectives, and sought to turn Vietnam into a colony and the Vietnamese into the slaves of Red imperialism. They are Communists, traitors, and agents of Russia and China.

It is impossible to admit the arguments advanced by a number of Communist Party members for their defense, saying that they have adhered to this party for the purpose of an ideological resistance. This is precisely the argument most often used by the Vietcong to conceal the other schemes of the Communist Party and to monopolize the title of Resistance member for them. . . .

With regard to families having their members re-grouped to the North and those entertaining relations with the cadres and members of the Communist Party and the Workers' Party, the government and the people will compel them to cut off any political relations with the latter (that is to say to abstain from supplying them with food, money, medicine, and daily necessities, from giving them information and from sustaining the Vietcong, etc.) and, on the basis of the personal activity of each of them, will determine who is a Resistance member and a patriot, who is a Vietcong saboteur. . . .

Those who adhere to the illegal organizations secretly left behind in South Vietnam by the Vietcong or set up by them after the signing of the Geneva Agreements are, without exception, elements who deliberately help the Vietcong and work for the interests of foreign Communist imperialists, Russian or Chinese, carrying out activities of subversion, espionage, and betrayal. They are not Resistance members and patriots. The illegal and treacherous organizations secretly left behind or created by the Vietcong in the Southern zone after the conclusion of the Geneva Agreements are: the "Workers' Party," the "Fatherland Front," the "Peace Movement," the "Liberation Front," the "Labor Youth," the "Religious Sects League," the "Religious Sects Alliance," and the various armed formations of the Vietcong.

—To severely punish the Vietcong who profit by the title of former Resistance members to carry out sabotage.

27. Washington's Man in Saigon: American Commitment to South Vietnam (1961)*

By Vice-President Lyndon B. Johnson, President Ngo Dinh Diem, and President John F. Kennedy

When John F. Kennedy defeated the Republican contender, Richard Nixon, in the presidential election of 1960, he inherited, and then deepened and extended, an

Department of State Bulletins, XXXVI (June 19, 1961), pp. 956–957; XXXVII (January 1, 1962), pp. 13–14.

*ambiguous commitment to an anti-communist regime in South Vietnam. The back-
ing given to the regime of Ngo Dinh Diem had supposedly been conditional on
that government's undertaking what President Dwight D. Eisenhower in 1954
called "needed reforms" (Reading 23). Seven years later, as the letter presented
here shows, the emphasis placed on internal reform had been overshadowed by
global cold war considerations. In the view of President Kennedy and many of his
advisers, "South Vietnam would become a test case of America's determination to
uphold its commitments in a menacing world and of its capacity to meet the new
challenges posed by guerrilla warfare in the emerging nations."* [1]

*Seeing the situation as a conflict with "Communism" to be won by militarily
defeating "guerrilla warfare" consistently deflected attention from the problems of
the southern Vietnamese countryside where the war would be won or lost. As
Reading 28 shows, the insurgents who were fighting against Diem and his American supporters never allowed their attention to be so diverted.*

A. Joint Declaration by U.S. Vice-President Johnson and Ngo Dinh Diem (May 13, 1961)

[Saigon]

. . . The United States . . . is conscious of the determination, energy, and
sacrifices which the Vietnamese people, under the dedicated leadership of President Ngo Dinh Diem, have brought to the defense of freedom in their land.

The United States is also conscious of its responsibility and duty, in its own
self-interest as well as in the interest of other free peoples, to assist a brave country
in the defense of its liberties against unprovoked subversion and Communist terror.
It has no other motive than the defense of freedom.

The United States recognizes that the President of the Republic of Vietnam,
Ngo Dinh Diem, who was recently reelected to office by an overwhelming majority
of his countrymen despite bitter Communist opposition, is in the vanguard of those
leaders who stand for freedom on the periphery of the Communist empire in Asia.

Free Vietnam cannot alone withstand the pressure which this Communist empire is exerting against it. Under these circumstances—the need of free Vietnam
for increased and accelerated emergency assistance and the will and determination
of the United States to provide such assistance to those willing to fight for their
liberties—it is natural that a large measure of agreement on the means to accomplish the joint purpose was found in high-level conversations between the two
Governments.

Both Governments recognize that under the circumstances of guerrilla warfare
now existing in free Vietnam, it is necessary to give high priority to the restoration

---

1. George C. Herring, making good use of *The Pentagon Papers*, accurately captures the perspective of the Kennedy crisis managers (*America's Longest War: The United States and Vietnam,
1950–75* [New York: John Wiley & Sons, 1979], p.75).

of a sense of security to the people of free Vietnam. This priority, however, in no way diminishes the necessity, in policies and programs of both Governments, to pursue vigorously appropriate measures in other fields to achieve a prosperous and happy society. . . .

B. President Diem to President Kennedy

December 7, 1961

Dear Mr. President:
Since its birth, more than six years ago, the Republic of Vietnam has enjoyed the close friendship and cooperation of the United States of America.

Like the United States, the Republic of Vietnam has always been devoted to the preservation of peace. My people know only too well the sorrows of war. We have honored the 1954 Geneva Agreements even though they resulted in the partition of our country and the enslavement of more than half of our people by Communist tyranny. We have never considered the reunification of our nation by force. On the contrary, we have publicly pledged that we will not violate the demarcation line and the demilitarized zone set up by the Agreements. We have always been prepared and have on many occasions stated our willingness to reunify Vietnam on the basis of democratic and truly free elections.

The record of the Communist authorities in the northern part of our country is quite otherwise. They not only consented to the division of Vietnam, but were eager for it. They pledged themselves to observe the Geneva Agreements and during the seven years since have never ceased to violate them. They call for free elections but are ignorant of the very meaning of the words. They talk of "peaceful reunification" and wage war against us.

From the beginning, the Communists resorted to terror in their efforts to subvert our people, destroy our government, and impose a Communist regime upon us. They have attacked defenseless teachers, closed schools, killed members of our anti-malarial program, and looted hospitals. This is coldly calculated to destroy our government's humanitarian efforts to serve our people.

We have long sought to check the Communist attack from the North on our people by appeals to the International Control Commission. Over the years, we have repeatedly published to the world the evidence of the Communist plot to overthrow our government and seize control of all of Vietnam by illegal intrusions from outside our country. . . .

. . . the Vietnamese nation now faces what is perhaps the gravest crisis in its long history. For more than 2,000 years my people have lived and built, fought and died in this land. We have not always been free. Indeed, much of our history and many of its proudest moments have arisen from conquest by foreign powers and our struggle against great odds to regain or defend our precious independence. But it is not only our freedom which is at stake today, it is our national identity. For, if we lose this war, our people will be swallowed by the Communist bloc, all our proud heritage will be blotted out by the "Socialist society" and Vietnam will leave the pages of history. We will lose our national soul.

Mr. President, my people and I are mindful of the great assistance which the United States has given us. Your help has not been lightly received, for the Vietnamese are proud people, and we are determined to do our part in the defense of the free world. It is clear to all of us that the defeat of the Vietcong demands the total mobilization of our government and our people, and you may be sure that we will devote all of our resources of money, minds, and men to this great task.

But Vietnam is not a great power and the forces of international Communism now arrayed against us are more than we can meet with the resources at hand. We must have further assistance from the United States if we are to win the war now being waged against us.

We can certainly assure mankind that our action is purely defensive. Much as we regret the subjugation of more than half of our people in North Vietnam we have no intention, and indeed no means, to free them by use of force.

I have said that Vietnam is at war. War means many things, but most of all it means the death of brave people for a cause they believe in. Vietnam has suffered many wars, and through the centuries we have always had patriots and heroes who were willing to shed their blood for Vietnam. We will keep faith with them.

When Communism has long ebbed away into the past, my people will still be here, a free united nation growing from the deep roots of our Vietnamese heritage. They will remember your help in our time of need. This struggle will then be a part of our common history. And your help, your friendship, and the strong bonds between our two peoples will be a part of Vietnam, then as now.

C. President Kennedy to President Diem

December 14, 1961

Dear Mr. President:

I have received your recent letter in which you described so cogently the dangerous condition caused by North Vietnam's efforts to take over your country. The situation in your embattled country is well known to me and to the American people. We have been deeply disturbed by the assault on your country. Our indignation has mounted as the deliberate savagery of the Communist program of assassination, kidnapping, and wanton violence became clear.

Your letter underlines what our own information has convincingly shown—that the campaign of force and terror now being waged against your people and your Government is supported and directed from the outside by the authorities at Hanoi. They have thus violated the provisions of the Geneva Accords designed to ensure peace in Vietnam and to which they bound themselves in 1954.

At that time, the United States, although not a party to the Accords, declared that it "would view any renewal of the aggression in violation of the Agreements with grave concern and as seriously threatening international peace and security." We continue to maintain that view.

In accordance with that declaration, and in response to your request, we are prepared to help the Republic of Vietnam to protect its people and to preserve its independence. We shall promptly increase our assistance to your defense effort as well as help relieve the destruction of the floods which you describe. I have already given the orders to get these programs underway.

The United States, like the Republic of Vietnam, remains devoted to the cause of peace and our primary purpose is to help your people maintain their independence. If the Communist authorities in North Vietnam will stop their campaign to destroy the Republic of Vietnam, the measures we are taking to assist your defense efforts will no longer be necessary. We shall seek to persuade the Communists to give up their attempts of force and subversion. In any case, we are confident that the Vietnamese people will preserve their independence and gain the peace and prosperity for which they have sought so hard and so long.

28. "No Other Road to Take": Origin of the National Liberation Front in Ben Tre*

By Mrs. Nguyen Thi Dinh

The standard US government rationale for intervention in Vietnam, developed at length in the "White Paper" of 1965, was that the struggle erupted over North Vietnam's attempt to conquer the independent nation in South Vietnam. A central tenet of this argument draws on chronology: In its directives of 1959 and early 1960, the Lao Dong Party (Communist Party) in Hanoi called for intensified struggle in the South. The National Liberation Front of South Vietnam was formed in December 1960 (Reading 29). To American spokesmen the idea that there might be any measure of independence among the revolutionaries of South Vietnam was heresy, and in retrospect it now appears clear that important stategical and especially logistical guidance came from the North. The resistance memoir reprinted here from a translation of the Vietnamese original illustrates the coordination of insurgency in two eras.

During the early stages of the resistance war against the French, a Viet Minh activist traveled to Hanoi to obtain military supplies. Ho Chi Minh told her that a shipment of weapons would be sent south.

However, our country is poor; when you young brothers and sisters go back you must fight the French well and seize their weapons to use. Then you'll have a large reserve . . . to draw on.[1]

---

*Excerpts from *Khong Con Duong Nao Khac* [*No Other Road to Take*], by Mrs. Nguyen Thi Dinh (Hanoi: Nha Xuat Ban Phu Nu, 1968), translated by Mai Elliott, pp. 49–77, passim.
1. *Khong Con Duong Nao Khac*, p. 38.

After the defeat of the French, former Viet Minh fighters in the South were subject to an intense repression that is all too vividly reflected in this reading. Hounded and harassed by the Diem regime, southern insurgents managed nevertheless to mount a wide variety of oppositional activities, as Mrs. Nguyen Thi Dinh's account of the late 1950s shows. Clearly, the southern insurgency was no isolated, purely spontaneous local activity. It followed a period of unified national activity against the French imperialists, and displayed many elements of continuity with the earlier struggle. Yet, if it were not in the perceived interest of the dedicated southern cadres to struggle against Ngo Dinh Diem and his American backers, it would be hard to explain the dedication and heroism of these Vietnamese.

This autobiographical memoir of the developing revolutionary struggle in the Southern Vietnamese province of Ben Tre was written in November 1965 by the former chairperson of the South Vietnam Liberation Women's Association and Deputy Commander of the National Liberation Front Armed Forces.

It was . . . in this period [1958] that I received the news that my nephew Di, a cadre in Giong Trom district during the 9-year Resistance and the son of my brother, had recently been captured and murdered by the enemy. One day, at dusk, I stopped by my house in Hoa Thanh hamlet to find out more about Di's death and to check the situation. It was already dark but my mother had not stopped working and was still arduously digging up the earth. When she heard me calling her, she threw the pickaxe at the foot of an orange tree and said in a sad and angry tone of voice:

—I toil hard but in this kind of situation who knows whether I'll stay alive to enjoy the fruits of my labor.

She sighed with worry and asked me:

—Youngest one, you're back because you heard about Di, didn't you? You too, you must be careful.

Saying this, she covered her face and sobbed loudly. I felt choked with emotion.

That night, a niece of mine told me in detail about Di's glorious death. After peace returned, reactionaries who had taken up the priestly garb built a chapel in Luong Hoa village as a branch of the Ba Chau and Roman Church. On the day the chapel was inaugurated, Ngo—the parish priest—invited the villagers to attend. [During the ceremony] he stood up and made propaganda in front of the faithful, distorting the truth. He said that the Lord had brought peace and then praised "President Ngo" as the No. 1 patriotic resistant.

Di was there that day. During the nine years of Resistance, Di was the Chairman of the Village Resistance Administrative Committee and the Secretary of the Village Party Committee. He had braved a lot of hardships to work for the people so they all loved and trusted him. Di let the priest finish and then stood up to point out the truth which contradicted everything the priest had said. Peace was restored only because the people of the entire country had fought for nine years. Only the Government of the Democratic Republic of Vietnam headed by Mr. Ho Chi Minh led the national resistance against the French and brought it to victory. As for Ngo Dinh Diem, he was living in America in those years, getting fat on good food. He was not even in Vietnam, so how could he have been in the Resistance? The people were very pleased with what Di said and applauded loudly. The Priest had to shut up and no longer dared to tell lies.

From then on, Di withdrew into clandestine operations. But in April 1958 he was surrounded and captured by the enemy in Xom Cui. They locked him up in Luong Quoi and tortured him violently. They questioned him:

—Why didn't you regroup [to the North]? Why did you stay behind to sabotage the peace? Who else stayed behind with you?

Di accused them in return:

—I'm a former member of the Resistance. I fought the French to win peace and independence, I haven't committed any crimes. It's you who follow the Americans, it's you who have sold out the South to them, [and it's you] who have killed and harmed patriotic people. It's you who are sabotaging the Geneva Accords.

Other than that he did not say anything else. Seeing that they had failed to break this young but heroic cadre with torture, the enemy took him and locked him up in the Province Security Police office. Here, Di continued to heroically denounce Ngo Dinh Diem as a henchman of the American imperialists who had sabotaged the Geneva Accords. When he heard the news of Di's arrest, Ngo—the parish priest—plotted with the province chief to liquidate this cadre of the resistance. One night, they brought a jeep to the prison door and dragged Di away. All the brothers in jail knew they were taking Di away to liquidate him, so they struggled to keep him back. Di also put up a fierce fight and refused to go, but being bare handed in such a situation what could he and the other prisoners do against a bloodthirsty gang with weapons in their hands. So they dragged Di to the car, drove him to Cau Van bridge on the Luong Hoa road and shot him there in order to dampen our struggle movement. When they heard the shots, the villagers lit torches and poured out. The enemy panicked and fled. Di was not dead then. He calmly comforted his family and the people surrounding him:

—Please, mother, friends, do not weep, and listen to me. They're very inhumane and cruel. They tortured me and tried to force me to give them information on the basic level organizations. But they did not get anywhere so they took me away to kill me in order to frighten you and make you afraid to oppose them. Don't be afraid, our revolution will certainly win. Take me to the province town so I can struggle and expose their crimes.

So, in the middle of the night, the people carried Di to the Luong Hoa post and then to the province town. All along the way Di condemned the enemy and appealed to the people to struggle with determination. Oblivious to the unrestrained and painful blows of the enraged enemy, Di continued to curse them without letup until he could talk no more.

The situation everywhere became more gloomy. Right in my native village at this time, the Diem clique established a Council of Notables and set up Phan, a notorious tyrant, as Chairman. They built two large posts at both ends of the village. Their henchmen—from the militiamen to the secret and regular police—came from landlord families and were a bunch of crooks and tyrants. They aggressively searched each house, weapons in hand, and demanded that the people deliver paddy to the landlords. If they suspected someone of being a Viet Cong, they arrested and murdered him without flinching, as they had murdered my nephew.

All of Ben Tre province lived in this oppressive and suffocating atmosphere. Many patriotic people were rounded up, taken away and liquidated. We immediately thought that in order to survive we would have to consolidate and expand our ranks for the struggle, otherwise if we let the masses remain quiet, dispersed and unorganized, we would all perish. . . .

I quickly relayed the news [of widespread repression] to every area so that our organizations could immediately expose the crime of the enemy, incite profound hatred among the masses against the enemy, and so that they would continue to nurture and expand the reliable grassroot bases of the revolution. At the same time the higher levels also issued a similar directive and reminded us to absolutely withdraw into clandestine action, live in secret hideouts, travel and operate entirely at night.

I left that evening, disguised as a nun, in the company of a novice of the pagoda who was about 15 years old. The two of us walked for a long time and finally at 3 o'clock in the morning arrived at another basic level organization to meet comrade Tung, a district cadre. From then on, comrade Tung and I resolutely contacted people and set up grassroot bases. During those extremely difficult years filled with hardships, like all the other comrades, I had to hide and sleep in the bushes, but the people did their best to protect and help us. One night, comrade Tung and I were sleeping in a garden in Phu An Hoa village. It was already 10 o'clock but the barking of dogs in the settlement was getting fiercer and fiercer—starting first far away and then spreading closer and closer—and then we heard the scream of a woman. A while later, a person came and informed us that Mrs. Nam, our liaison agent, who was operating overtly under legal cover, had been arrested. The enemy tortured her brutally and asked her where we were but she adamantly said she did not know. They beat her till they broke both of her legs, but still could not break the iron will of a human being who had discarded her own life to protect the revolution. I haven't heard any news about her and do not know whether she is still alive or dead.

Also, while in this area, comrade Tung and I once made a trip from Phu An Hoa village to Phuoc Thanh village, near the An Hoa canal, to reach the house of a woman who was a sympathizer. Not daring to walk on the road for fear of running into the enemy, we waded in the irrigation ditches running along the orchards. The night was as black as ink, and it was raining in a drizzle, but we kept having to climb out of one ditch into another, and our legs became rubbery with fatigue. Once, I bumped my head against a coconut tree that had fallen across the ditch and a huge bump swelled on top of my head. Once in a while I pitched forward and fell into the ditch, my chest hitting the embankment, and I became numb with pain. Tung had to lead me by the hand part of the way, as though he was guiding a blind woman. We picked our way through the darkness and walked from 7:00 P.M. till 3:00 A.M. when we finally reached the house of a hard-core sympathizer. His family consisted of himself, his wife and their two children. Thanh, the girl, was 13 years old, and Cong, the boy, was 5 years old. After we finished eating, it was already daylight. Comrade Tung went to stay with another family. Mr. and Mrs. Tu left to work in the fields, leaving Thanh to watch the house. I was exhausted and overslept. At around 10:00 A.M., dogs started to bark from afar and then the barking spread closer. Thanh ran out to take a look and then ran back, her face ashen with fear, and said in a panic:

—Soldiers are coming, Miss Nam!

I quickly calmed her down:

—Nothing will happen, keep calm. I'll go down into the secret hideout, close the cover after me.

As I talked, I lifted the cover and jumped down. Water in the hole sloshed and overflowed. It was a dangerous situation, but there was nothing better I could do. Thanh who was quick witted poured the pot full of cooked bran for feeding the pigs over the shelter cover. The pot broke, the bran splattered everywhere and covered the opening of the shelter. She slapped Cong's face and said:

—You broke the pot of bran, when mother comes back she'll beat you to death, you'll see!

Poor Cong did not understand anything and the painful blow made him wail. Right at that moment, dozens of soldiers entered and saw Cong crying and the pot of bran broken to pieces. Thanh nodded in greeting and then continued to scold her brother. The soldiers stood around, asked a few questions and then left. I heaved a sigh of relief and greatly admired Thanh's brilliant idea. After the soldiers had gone a long time, I got out of the shelter, took both children in my arms and told them softly:

—You two saved my life.

The day I left, Thanh did not want to let me go. She wept pitifully and kept asking me to take her along.

At this time, the enemy was hunting down and arresting cadres relentlessly. One after another, five of the leading district cadres were arrested. The higher levels sent comrade Sau Quan to replace Thanh Ha. The situation was very gloomy. The hounds—security policemen and informers—were poking around everywhere. At night, the villages were deserted and dead quiet since every family was forbidden to go out and had to stay indoors. When cadres came back to visit, the villagers wept bitterly and said:

—The revolution must do something, otherwise if things go on like this you brothers and sisters will all be arrested and murdered.

In this period, it was extremely difficult for us to find a place to stay. Our old hideouts had been discovered, and though we had set up new ones we did not dare to go there either. Having no other alternative, comrade Sau Quan and I discussed withdrawing to Luong Phu village, in Gion Trom district, an area which the enemy had not paid much attention to. However, our grassroot bases there were still very sparse. We stayed in the house of one of my sisters, right next to the Luong Phu post and across from the Luong Hoa post. A few days later we moved in with a new sympathizer, a very kind old lady who took care of a pagoda. But a few days after we got there the hounds picked up our scent. One day, brother Sau Quan and I were staying in the private quarters of this lady when up to a platoon of security policemen suddenly appeared, surrounded the pagoda and burst inside the house to search. Thanks to a secret shelter underneath the Buddhist altar we escaped death. Not finding us in the pagoda, the enemy searched and interrogated the houses next door. Sau Quan and I had to quickly find a way to get out of the area. It was the middle of the day. Taking advantage of a moment when the enemy let down their guard, Sau Quan crawled into the garden and then climbed and hid at the top of a coconut tree. Unfortunately I could not climb, so I hastily put on some Buddhist nun's garments, disguised myself as a novice and, in the company of a 13-year-old novice, sneaked to a sampan and took the risk of rowing away in search of another grassroot base. In the end, I took the risk of returning to Hoa Thanh hamlet, Luong Hoa village where I was born. This was where I had operated when I first started to work for the revolution. Here I would be close to my family. I was confident that the people would protect me, even though this area—and in particular my family and relatives—were under tight enemy surveillance. After ten years, when they suddenly saw me return in this extremely tense situation many villagers were so scared that they went white with fear. But just a couple of days later I succeeded in persuading five or six families to accommodate us—these were all families of very poor peasants.

I was moved by [these] noble sentiments toward the revolution. Although Diem had issued the 10/59 decree [see Reading 26—eds.] which stipulated that if a "Viet Cong" cadre was found in any house, the owner would be thrown in jail and his property confiscated, the people were not afraid. On the contrary, they continued to love and protect the cadres as before. However, to guard against anything unexpected which might happen, I adamantly asked them to let me go and sleep outside near the secret hideout. As the night advanced, the wind became chilly and I felt numb with cold. I was sitting all hunched up near the shelter when suddenly I heard dogs barking loudly. I noticed that my heart started to beat wildly because in that period the barking of dogs at night signalled that soldiers were searching for our people. Suddenly I saw crisscrossing beams of flashlights and heard shouts and thudding sounds of beating coming from Tu's house. I knew the enemy was on our trail and hastily climbed into the bunker. Unfortunately the rain had clogged the air vent with mud. Sitting in the bunker for a while I began to feel dizzy and almost passed out. I had to climb out and crawl to the sugarcane field where I covered myself with leaves. I spent all that day lying in the sugarcane field. I was soaking wet but did not dare go back to the house because our liaison agent had not come to contact me. Besides, it was impossible to leave at this point. I lay there, reviewing in my mind each and every grassroot base. More than half of the hardcore sympathizers had been uncovered. Our survival depended on whether or not we could expand the number of sympathizers. We had often told each other that unless we held on to the people we could not maintain the movement. This was the most critical problem. I thought of going to the house of a very good relative of mine in order to contact the people and recruit a number of sympathizers. However, I recalled the recent story of comrade Chien going to the house of one of his relatives, and this put me on guard.

One time, comrade Chien, who was in charge of Thanh Phu district, was travelling in the company of another comrade. When they were close to his house, they found themselves caught in an enemy operation. Chien escaped, but the other comrade was killed. The enemy searched his wallet and found pictures of both himself and Chien, which they posted at the communal house and claimed they had killed two "Viet Cong." Chien hid in the ricefields until nightfall and then picked his way through the darkness to the house of his aunt. Chien knocked on the door and announced himself, but his aunt started to shout:

—I don't have any relatives! Go away!

Chien knew she was afraid it was an enemy agent pretending to be her relative in order to test her. However, if he lingered there and the hamlet chief found out, he would be in danger. So he turned around and left, feeling sad and angry at the enemy who had driven even relatives to suspect one another.

It was dark again. I was deep in thought trying to find some ways to consolidate and expand the movement when I heard footsteps approaching the secret hideout and someone calling softly:

—Ba, my child, it's me, mother. I've brought you something to eat.

I ran toward her, and before I could comfort her and shore up her spirit, she said:

—They've arrested Tu, but I'm not worried because you and the others are alright. Even if that scoundrel Diem arrests and kills me, I won't abandon you.

Her words warmed my heart. I forgot the cold and clasped her hands tightly:

—You're right, mother. No matter what the Diem gang does they won't be able to stamp out the revolution. One of these days they will have to answer for their crimes in front of the people.

Suddenly I thought of the folk poem I had memorized long ago:

"The people's hearts are like sunflowers
Hundreds of thousands of them all turn toward the sun.
Even if everything in nature changes
They pledge to remain steadfast and loyal to the revolution."

During those dark and gloomy years in the South, the American-Diem gang did their best to suppress and kill patriotic people. They did not hesitate to use any schemes, no matter how savage [to achieve their aims] and created untold suffering and miseries for the women.

I still remember comrade Bien, a company cadre who asked me before he regrouped to the North to take care of Chin, his wife, a good sympathizer in the village. Chin was still young, only about 20 years old, and had a tanned complexion. She was not beautiful but was very charming. She was childless and lived by herself. When we met for the first time she said:

—Bien loves me a lot and so even if our separation lasts for 100 years I'll wait for him.

I guided her into becoming a very reliable supporter.

Nhi, the daughter of a landlord, lived in the same village. She had small beady eyes which were constantly darting flirtatious glances at the men. She was also married to a military cadre who had regrouped to the North. Half in jest, half seriously, she once asked Chin:

—How long do you think you can wait for your husband?

As people say, "children take after their parents." After the Diem gang came into power, they set up Nhi's father—a landlord—as the hamlet chief. During the "ly khai" (renunciation of communism) campaign[2] the Americans and Diem forced the women whose husbands had regrouped to the North to announce that they had rejected their husbands and severed their allegiance to the "Viet Cong." They even invented a ceremony during which those who had made the renunciation were "accepted into the fold." Prompted by her father, Nhi volunteered to come forward and declare that she had severed her allegiance to the "Viet Cong" represented by her husband, to marry a puppet lieutenant with a mouth filled with gold teeth. The two of them went to the city to have clothes made. When she came back, Nhi was wearing a transparent and skintight nylon blouse and bouffant hairdo which looked like an owl's nest. Nhi went to see Chin and poured honeyed words into her ears:

—My girl, life's not very long. If we don't live it up we'll miss a lot of things and we'll grow old before we know it.

Chin was kind to the buddha but not to the devil. She insulted her to her face:

—Only you can entertain such thoughts. I haven't lost my conscience and cannot betray my husband's love, as you've done.

Nhi accepted defeat because she could not make Chin change her mind. Next came the turn of a policeman wearing a dangling Colt pistol who came to court Chin and persuade her to become his concubine. Chin refused. He then changed his tune and gave her two choices:

—You either follow the nationalists or support the communists, you must choose one of these two roads.

Chin replied:

—What does the love between a wife and husband have anything to do with the nationalists, why should I make the choice?

He tried to trap her:

---

2. This was a campaign launched by Diem to force former members of the Resistance to renounce their allegiance to the Viet Minh. The penalty for refusing to go along was imprisonment, torture, and sometimes execution. For a very vivid and informative description of this campaign see Nguyen Duc Thuan, *Bat Khuat* (Indomitable) (Hanoi: Thanh Nien, 1967). The author was tortured and thrown into the tiger cage at Con Son for refusing to renounce his allegiance.—*Trans.*

—If you want to go to the North to rejoin your husband, I'll ask the nationalists to let you go.

Chin answered cleverly:

—It's up to the nationalists. Which woman doesn't want to rejoin her husband?

He grimaced:

—Don't you know that the French boat which carried the regroupees capsized and sank in the open seas and everyone aboard drowned? Why waste time waiting?

—I'll decide what to do when I know for certain my husband's dead.

He became threatening:

—Let me tell you, the nationalists are about to march to the North and sweep away all the communists. There's no doubt about that. You watch out!

Poor Chin, she was entirely on her own so how could she cope with this band of tigers craving for human flesh? I thought of transferring her to another area, but one night the policeman came and arrested her right in her house. She struggled and scratched his face but he did not let go. He raped her and then stabbed her to death. However, even in death she was not left in peace. This brute slashed open her belly, cut out her gall bladder which he presented to the authorities [to support his] claim that he had killed a Viet Cong in order to obtain a reward from that harridan Le Xuan.[3]

Besides Miss Chin, the wife of comrade Muoi Van was also most faithful. It was his wife's death which plunged me deep in thought. Mrs. Muoi was a Southerner, simple, good hearted and straightforward like thousands of other women. During the nine years of Resistance, her husband was away on mission for long stretches of time, dropping in to see his family once in a while when he had the chance and then going off again. On her own, she worked hard to support her children and contribute to the resistance. All her children, the boys as well as the girls, later left to work for the revolution. After peace returned, Muoi and his children stayed behind with the people and did not regroup to the North. The enemy knew this and tracked them down relentlessly. Unable to find them, they came and arrested Mrs. Muoi. They asked her:

—Where is your husband at this moment?

She maintained she did not know, though they beat her and tortured her brutally. Before dying, she pointed to her chest and screamed in their faces:

—My husband and my children are lodged deep in my heart. If you wretches want to find them, you'll have to cut out my heart and look inside.

The heroic sacrifice of Mrs. Muoi expressed the indomitable fighting spirit of thousands of women in the South. I used the examples of Mrs. Muoi and Chin to educate the other women. While I was mobilizing their spirits and deepening their hatred [of Saigon authorities], [among the women] was Hanh, a girl from Thanh Phu district who was then about 23–24 years old. She was beautiful but did not want to get married. Whenever anyone asked her about this, she simply said:

---

3. Madame Ngo Dinh Nhu's maiden name.—*Trans.*

—I must take part in the resistance first.

Once when she met me she said with determination:

—If I find myself in the same situation as sisters Muoi and Chin, I'm sure I can do as well as they did.

Later, Hanh was captured by the enemy while she was operating in the district. Seeing that Hanh was beautiful they tried to entice her with every means at their disposal, but she did not change her mind. The famished wolves then resorted to brutal acts. They stripped her naked, tied her up, and employed all their savage tricks. They even rubbed hot pepper into her vagina, but failed to break this heroic girl. Several of them broke beer bottles, thrust the necks into her, pulled out the bloody things, raised them up and laughed. They tortured her for a long time without success, so they took her to see Tuc, a traitor who had surrendered to the enemy, and had him try to persuade her. The moment she saw this scoundrel, she spat in his face and cursed him:

—You wretched traitor and surrenderer *(dau hang)*.

Tuc bowed his head and did not dare to look her in the eyes. The enemy tortured Hanh violently and tenaciously for six continuous months. Hanh was reduced to a skeleton covered with skin. She lay immobile, paralyzed, and could only move her fingers and talk in whispers. However, she did not stop cursing Diem and the Americans. . . .

At the end of 1959, I was busily engaged in my work when I was urgently called to help provide guidance for dealing with the enemy's plot of setting up an agroville in Thanh Thoi village, Mo Cay district. The villagers were angry and up-in-arms because they had been ordered by Diem and the Americans to tear down their houses and move within a month. An entire area of fertile ricefields, luxuriant fruit trees and densely populated settlements—from the Rach Bam arroyo to the Cau Cong bridge, over 10 kilometers in length—had to be completely evacuated for the establishment of an agroville. The enemy's plot was to assemble all families with relatives who had regrouped to the North and those of the cadres who had left to work for the revolution, and patriotic people, in this hell on earth.

Diem and the Americans had chosen Thanh Thoi village as a testing ground to develop the experience which they would then apply all over the South. When they met us, the villagers said:

—If we're going to die, we're going to die right here, we're not going anywhere.

We were very happy to hear the people say this because only by relying on the unity and determination of the entire population could we foil the cruel scheme of the enemy. As anticipated, a month passed without any villagers obeying the order to dismantle their houses, although the enemy exerted intense pressure and blatantly resorted to force. Two companies under the command of Ba Huong were brought in and these then coordinated with two battalions from the 7th division to blanket all neighboring villages. Every day, they set fire to houses, cut down trees and crushed lush ricefields with tractors. The brutes poured toward the house of sister Tu. Her husband had been killed in action fighting for the Resistance. After the Dien Bien Phu victory the revolution gave her 3 *công* of land to farm and support her five young children. After peace returned, she painstakingly built an embankment to grow tangerines, clod of earth by clod of earth. The tangerines were beginning to ripen when the soldiers came to cut them down. Watching them destroy what she had constructed with sweat and tears, she shouted in anger:

—Heavens above, what kind of government is this that can be so cruel?

Her children rushed in and tried to prevent the soldiers from cutting down the trees, but the soldiers were unmoved for they could not care less whether the people starved and died.

All the young people were conscripted to do forced labor, and anyone who resisted was arrested and jailed. Under the burning sun, about 5,000 villagers—young and old, men and women—were gathered and forced to destroy hundreds of acres of lush rice plants already bearing young grains bursting with milky sap. The soldiers took measurements and as soon as they finished measuring the people would have to start digging. The villagers huddled together in one spot and refused to dig. A couple of old people came forward and protested:

—The government said it is concerned about the life of the people but haven't done anything to prove it. Now it is forcing us to tear down our houses, destroy and burn our properties, dig up the graves of our ancestors, and perform exhausting corvée tasks.[4] How are the people going to survive?

Ba Huong—a fellow notorious for his brutality—seeing that the people were protesting and refusing to work, picked up his whip, ran over menacingly and lashed wildly at the villagers:

—You mother . . . how dare you resist the orders of the government? Where are the soldiers? Shoot immediately anyone who refuses to work.

Many people in this area had died from hunger, diseases, and the abuses of the soldiers. [For example, once] the soldiers entered the house of Miss Ch., pinned her to the ground, and took turns raping her until she passed out. [Another time] they entered An Loc hamlet in broad daylight and raped a 12-year-old girl who died from the profuse bleeding. Any villager who objected was accused of being a Viet Cong. Phu—a local brute—once led Ba Huong's band into the village where they shot two 12-year-old boys herding buffaloes, cut off the heads and carried them back to the agroville to claim they had eliminated two dangerous Viet Cong reconnaissance agents.

Motivated and guided by the cadres, the people from Thanh Thoi village and Mo Cay district joined forces with the villagers conscripted to perform corvée—forming a group about 1,000 strong who moved forward en masse to present their demands to Ba Huong:

—We oppose forced labor!

—We demand compensation for damaged property and lost income!

—We demand that we be allowed to return to our old homes to farm and earn our living.

---

4. Forced labor without recompense.—eds.

Huong roared:

—Did you listen to the urgings of the Viet Cong and come here to struggle?

Mrs. Bay stepped forward and said:

—Look, my husband and myself along with our nine children depend entirely on the income from our five *công* of fruit grove to live, now you've forced us to cut all the trees down. Then you forced my husband to do corvée work. You don't give him any rice to eat and beat him violently besides. Let me ask you, how is our family going to survive?

Huong lunged and kicked her in the stomach, and she fell rolling on the ground. He lashed her with his whip and cursed her:

—She's the leader, let me beat her one hundred lashes till she dies.

Then he ordered the soldiers to assault the people. The villagers screamed and protested violently, and rushed in to rescue Mrs. Bay who had become unconscious, her body all black and blue from beating. A little later she revived, looked at the people and said:

—Don't worry, I'm still alive. Just carry me to the district town to struggle and expose this gang.

As Tet drew near the Americans and Diem intensifed their pressure to have the agroville completed. They even brought in conscripted laborers from all six provinces of Central Nam Bo to work on the agroville. Every day, more than 10,000 people lived at the site in extremely crowded conditions. The flames of hatred smoldered in the hearts of the people, ready to erupt at the right opportunity. One day, Ba Huong ordered the buildings spruced up to welcome Diem who was coming to inspect the agroville. The villagers went looking for the cadres to relay the news and to solicit their opinion. On the appointed day, the soldiers beat the drums, making a dreadful din, searched each house and forced the people to hang out flags and don new clothes to welcome "President Diem." That day, I stayed close by to keep track of the situation. Following the cadres' instructions faithfully, the village notables—formally dressed, petitions hidden in the sleeves of their robes—stood in the front row. The villagers called out to each other to go and welcome the president, and with everyone bustling about, the atmosphere was very different from the one prevailing normally. The security police and militia were overjoyed, convinced they would be rewarded for their work this time around.

That morning, wherever Diem went, telephones rang to announce his movement. He went to Mo Cay, Thom, and then arrived in Thanh Thoi. The moment his car came to a stop the villagers—defying the thick ring of security and regular police—took off the outer layer of clothing and appeared in ragged and filthy clothes. They wrapped their heads in mourning bands and rushed onto the road, moaning and weeping as though they were at a funeral. It was complete chaos. The policemen blew their whistles, tried to hold the people back with their rifle butts, and fired madly into the air, but could not prevent the ring of people from closing around Ngo Dinh Diem's car. The notables handed their petitions directly to Diem, while the people handed theirs to the soldiers and reporters. Seizing this opportunity, many women and children clung to Diem and the officers by hanging on to their jackets, weeping pitifully and demanding the release of their husbands and parents. Ngo Dinh Diem, greatly embarrassed, stood up to make a few promises and then fled from the scene. After this defeat, at the orders of the Americans and Diem, their lackeys took revenge on the people and launched a fierce wave of repression in Mo Cay district and all over Ben Tre province. . . .

The time finally came when the ardent aspiration of our people and cadres was at last satisfied. I received a letter from the higher levels instructing me to attend a conference to hear a new and extremely important resolution. While helping me prepare [for the trip], the comrades in the Ben Tre leadership committee told me over and over again:

—Do your best to get there. No matter what the difficulties are, try by all means to bring back the new policy and transmit it to us, will you?

I understood the anxiety of the comrades and, aware of how eagerly they awaited the news, my enthusiasm and agitation intensified as I departed. On this trip there were two things which made me enthusiastic and eager: meeting the higher echelons to inform them of the aspirations of the masses, and finding out whether their policy conformed to the wishes of the people.

When I reached the conference site the first man I met was Bay Ruong. He asked me about the conditions in my locality and helped me gain a better understanding of the overall situation. We waited for almost a month before Sau Duong finally returned from a meeting with the higher levels. When I met Sau Duong, Hai Dien and Ba Bon and saw that they were alright I felt very happy. Sau Duong had lost a lot of weight and looked very pale. These brothers had had to live out in the bushes and it was inevitable that they fell prey to diseases and became emaciated. Sau Duong was always in a cheerful mood and every time I ran into him he told me countless stories about enthusiastic and burning struggles. He presided over the conference. Since peace was restored six years ago this was the first time that I attended such an important meeting. Sau Duong gave a report on the current situation and the policy adopted by the higher levels. The moment he mentioned this policy I felt an immense joy and happiness. It clearly called for the mobilization of the people all over the South to carry out political struggle in conjunction with military action. The moment they heard military action mentioned the conference burst out in stormy applause. The higher levels had followed exactly the aspirations of the lower levels in an extraordinary manner. Seeing that the comrades were too enthusiastic about military action, Sau Duong had to remind them over and over again:

—Comrades, please remember that political struggle is the main policy, armed action only supplements it and is aimed at mobilizing the peasants to rise up and destroy the enemy's suffocating control in order to become masters of the countryside, of their villages and hamlets.

When we discussed the favorable and unfavorable factors involved, I felt uneasy about the fact that we did not possess any weapons, and without weapons how were we going to combine [political action] with armed struggle? I boldly asked:

—Unless you give us some weapons we won't be able to combine [political struggle] with armed action.

Sau Duong burst out laughing:

—Go back and tell the enemy to hand over their weapons for you to use. To tell the truth, even if we had weapons here you wouldn't be able to carry them back with you.

I answered stubbornly:

—Never mind, just give me the weapons and I'll find a way to take them back with me.

The day before I left, Sau Duong came to see me and asked:

—As far as the policy to combine [political action] with armed struggle is concerned, do you think the cadres and people will go along with it?

I replied firmly:

—They'll be terribly pleased! Everyone has been waiting just for this.

—You're being subjective and ascribing your own inclination to others!

I was positive:

—I'm only afraid that once Ben Tre turns to military action we won't be able to restrain them.

He asked:

—What are your plans of action when you go back there?

The memory of the tumultuous days of the August 1945 Revolution suddenly came back to me. I told the comrades about my wish and dream: we would have to carry out a concerted uprising in order to achieve certain success. After I left the conference site, I had just gone a short distance when I ran into an enemy mop-up operation. I was stranded in the ricefields for a whole week. Each night I waded in the water and covered about 10 kilometers without any food in my stomach. Every time I set foot in the ricefields, leeches came swarming all around. I felt very anxious, as though I was sitting on fire, afraid that the comrades from the other provinces would reach their destinations first and carry out the uprising without our province joining in, so that when our turn came the enemy would have taken their precautions.

I reached Tra Vinh exactly on 30 December 1959 and tried to contact the province leadership committee but they had moved elsewhere. The local infrastructure did not know where they had gone because the comrade in charge of the province liaison station had been arrested. I was worried and wondered who else had been captured. Recently, the enemy had jailed and killed four or five comrades in the province leadership committee. . . . [After I located the Committee] they immediately asked:

—What's the new policy?

I could not hide my enthusiasm:

—It's great!

But when I asked them about the province leadership committee, none of them knew where it was. Comrade Hai Thuy had been staying in this area to keep track of the task of proselytizing enemy troops. Ba Dao had been away on mission for a week and had not had any contact with the committee. I was mad with worry. There was no better solution, so I told them about the new resolution and asked for their opinion. I said:

—If we wait till we find the whole province leadership committee we will lose the opportunity. We represent only a minority of the committee here because only comrade Hai Thuy and I are members of the province leadership committee, so we can't take it upon ourselves to act right away. However, will we dare to take action and bear responsibility [toward the committee]?

When they heard me say this, the comrades sat silent and deep in thought. Normally when uprising and armed struggle were mentioned they would be full of ardor. During the discussion, most of the comrades were enthusiastic about the fact that the higher levels had allowed [political action] to be combined with armed struggle, but they wondered how the uprising could be carried out when we had no weapons. Once the uprising occurred and the enemy struck back, what would we rely on to defend ourselves? If we rose up but failed to hold our grounds, the enemy would terrorize us and an additional number of comrades operating clandestinely would be uncovered. What would we do then?

In the end, we unanimously decided to emulate the experience of the 9-year resistance and of the August revolution which were brought to success by people who were barehanded. At present, there were many more factors in our favor [than during the resistance]: the masses understood the revolution and had acquired a definite level of consciousness, and their hatred of the enemy was very deep and intense. The ranks of the cadres were still thin, but they were firm and determined to destroy the enemy. The ranks of the enemy were rent with dissension and a number of them had links with the revolution. We were supported by a strong and reconstructed socialist North. I told the comrades:

—The main thing is for us to have confidence in the masses and to stay close to them to carry out the struggle. If we do this we'll achieve success.

In the political field, we planned to set up a hard-core force which would operate openly under legal cover to mobilize the people over a wide area. We should lose no time in recruiting good people into revolutionary organizations so as to expand our military and political forces quickly and strongly in order to create conditions for continuous attacks and to achieve continuous success. We would make preparations to win over the soldiers' families and mobilize and motivate them—once the uprising started—to go into the posts and appeal to their husbands or sons to turn around and join the revolution. The most serious difficulty confronting us at this juncture was the shortage of cadres at a time when there were so many tasks to attend to. So, we decided to recall all the *dieu lang*[5] cadres and to mobilize all the cadres in the province and district agencies and send them to the villages and hamlets to directly motivate the people. Finally before parting we unanimously adopted the following slogans: (a) the attacks should be relentless,

---

5. Cadres who had been sent to operate underground in a local area.—*Trans.*

(b) once the movement was set in motion, it should be developed to its utmost capacity, without constraints, and (c) once the storm and wind started to blow, the boats should boldly hoist their sails and glide over the waves. (The intention here was to counteract hesitation and reluctance to boldly move forward.)

When it came to the division of labor, the comrades assigned me the task of keeping track of the overall movement. Comrades Thuy and Ba Dao were put in charge of military affairs, while Sau Huan and Ba Cau returned to Minh Tan and Mo Cay to propagate the policy and then go down to the villages to directly lead the movement. Each of them would be in charge of from one to three villages.

During this period informers were everywhere keeping an eye on things, so we only indoctrinated a number of hard-core sympathizers and grassroot bases, usually referred to as the "steadfast and loyal masses" (*quan chung chi cot*), about our policy, but we did not tell them when the uprising would occur. In addition, we stimulated the hatred of the people and motivated them to wait for the day of action. Though we maintained absolute secrecy, the preparations among the people were very energetic and spirited. Boys and girls gathered in groups of three or five to practice martial arts. Forges worked day and night turning out machetes. In some areas people moved the forges into the forest to work. The carpenters produced [dummy] rifles, while the people were busy getting drums and wooden blocks ready.

The work was proceeding at a furious pace when we were struck by dreadful news which hit like a thunderbolt. It was January 14th. While I was in Binh Khanh village to check the situation and contribute my ideas to the leadership there, someone came and told me that Bay Tranh had been captured by the soldiers. . . .

Comrade Tranh was arrested because he had tried to contact his wife who was not active in the revolution and lived in Ba Tri. They had been married a long time and had a few children. During his illness he occasionally sent news to his wife and asked her to come and visit him. This time, he asked an acquaintance to take a letter to her, in which he pretended to be a merchant arranging a meeting with her for a business transaction. The enemy in Ba Tri got hold of the letter and arrested her. They tortured her for a long time and in the end, unable to bear it any longer, she confessed that the letter was from her husband. They forced her to take them to the meeting place so they could capture Bay Tranh. She struggled with herself for a long time and finally came to the naive conclusion that the designated site was probably just the place where she could contact him and not the place where he was living. She had no choice but to take the enemy there, hoping that he would run away when he found out that she was under arrest and would not wait for her. But contrary to her expectations she guided the enemy to capture her husband. They searched him and found a grenade he had procured for the day of the concerted uprising.

The . . . uprising was scheduled to take place in two days' time. If Bay Tranh . . . confessed, the enemy would be on guard and we would run into a lot of difficulties. At that time, comrade Hai Thuy who was stationed in the area further north was making preparations to destroy the post in Dinh Thuy village which was the locality slated to rise up first. The situation was extremely critical. I wanted to go and see comrade Hai Thuy immediately to discuss a plan to deal with all eventualities, but to go from Binh Khanh to Dinh Thuy I would have to pass by many dangerous enemy posts. I had to take the risk of making the trip in the company of Mrs. Hai, a very reliable sympathizer. She was about sixty years old. The two of us ferried a sampan, pretending to be traders, going through Mo Cay district town and then past the Dinh Thuy post to meet comrade Hai Thuy on January 16th. When she got home, Mrs. Hai was arrested by the enemy who tortured her savagely, but she maintained her spirit as Bay Tranh had done and refused to divulge anything. This was why the enemy was unable to find out anything.

During those last couple of days [before the uprising] Hai Thuy and I felt very nervous and anxious. Each day seemed to pass by so slowly. On the morning of January 17th, the atmosphere everywhere was busy and festive. Comrade Hai Thuy said:

—If nothing happens this morning, we should go ahead.

I agreed because I was afraid that the longer we delayed the more likely our plan would be discovered. Hai Thuy kept me in Dinh Thuy to reinforce the leadership of the test site and to keep track of the overall situation.

January 17th, 1960, was a day full of hope and worry for the patriotic people in Ben Tre province. I waited for the attack on the canton [division] militia unit, composed of two squads stationed in Dinh Thuy village, to occur. The comrades had decided to attack while the militiamen were sleeping and off their guards. At the appointed time, a hard-core youth who knew the militia commander entered in a panic to look for him concerning an urgent matter. This fellow was still awake while his troops were sound asleep. Our forces, disguised as ordinary merchants, lay in ambush around the communal house. Being suspicious by nature, the commander pulled out his Sten pistol and came to the door of the communal house. His arms akimbo, he tilted his bearded chin and asked haughtily:

—What's the matter?

Our comrade obsequiously bent down to whisper in his ear, as though to transmit something important, then suddenly raised his arm and hit him hard on the nape of the neck. He collapsed right away. Our forces poured in and called on the troops to surrender. A number of them bolted and fled in disorder, while the rest surrendered. We captured enough weapons to equip about a squad of men. The Dinh Thuy post was only about one kilometer from here. Hai Thuy was afraid that the soldiers belonging to the unit of the canton [division] militia commander would go and warn the post which would then take precautions, so he ordered the immediate capture of the post at 3:00 P.M. There were sympathizers among the soldiers in this post, and before the news [of the attack on the militia unit] reached the post, our infiltrators rose up and burned it down. The flames billowed high in the sky. The brothers brought back about ten additional rifles.

We let a number of soldiers flee to Mo Cay district town to report that Viet Cong troops had come to take Dinh Thuy post and were on their way to Mo Cay in large numbers. As we had suspected, the enemy in Mo Cay just fired a few artillery rounds and stayed put in their post, not daring to send out reinforcements. Our first attack was successful and we had seized a large number of weapons. We were greatly encouraged and were even more determined to smash the viselike grip of the enemy. I discussed with comrade Hai Thuy about sending two rifles each to Thanh Phu and Minh Tan districts to use as "capital" and relaying the news of victory in Mo Cay to the comrades so they could emulate us. The rest of the weapons were handed over to Hai Thuy and Ba Dao to replace the wooden rifles.

The forces encircling the posts had been ordered to burn down any posts they captured. The people immediately tore up the flags, and burned down the plaques bearing their house numbers and their family registers.[6] On the roads, the villagers cut down trees to erect barriers and block the movement of the enemy. On both banks of the river where communication trenches and barbed wire crisscrossed in a tangled maze, boats stopped to listen to our propaganda. All the posts were surrounded by the people who made appeals to the soldiers through bullhorns. Once in a while, "a heavy gun" exploded (actually bamboo sections filled with acetylene). It was a night of terrifying thunder and lightning striking the enemy on the heads. Attacked by surprise, they were scared out of their wits and stayed put in the posts. Occasionally explosive charges exploded, sounding like mortars or grenade launchers. The people who had the most difficult task tonight were the units in charge of eliminating tyrannical local officials and agents—the core of the machinery of control in the hamlets and villages. Each member had to disguise himself with mask and change his clothing in order to prevent the enemy from recognizing him. Only a few comrades appeared publicly to mobilize the people and act as their representatives to condemn this group [e.g., the officials and agents]. At 5:00 A.M., we sent for the comrade in charge of the elimination of tyrants in the closest village to review the results. Carrying a machete, he came to report:

—Everything's been done. The local officials and agents all lost their customary arrogance and became humble. When we rushed in and shouted to them, only one reactionary fled, the rest surrendered right away. They were all shaking and trembling. . . .

As the situation evolved successfully, the leadership of the committee of the Concerted Uprising right that night drafted a military order which was then posted everywhere in the areas under the temporary control of the enemy to heighten the prestige of the revolution. The contents of the military order included the following points:

—All soldiers, no matter how serious their crimes were, if they repented and rejoined the ranks of the people with their weapons, would be forgiven.

—Village and hamlet officials, heads of inter-family groups, security policemen and informers who resigned and surrendered to the people would be forgiven by the people.

---

6. These were administrative devices used by the government of Ngo Dinh Diem to ensure better control of the population.—*Trans.*

—Landlords who had relied on the power of the enemy to seize the land of the peasants and increase their rents should return what they had taken to the peasants. . . .

In the night of the 18th and in the early morning of the 19th of January, the villagers held a rally to display the strength and ardor of the people. The villagers felt very satisfied, especially when the policemen, tyrants, officials, spies and landlords with blood debts were led out to be executed.

About ten days later the enemy began to recover their wits. Mo Cay district town and a number of posts were still intact. The enemy finally realized that we had risen up with bare hands and that no 502nd Battalion, no South Vietnam or North Vietnam Liberation Forces had come to our assistance. But by the time they discovered this it had become too late. Their government apparatus in the countryside and their frightening grip over the villages and hamlets had been broken. They immediately sent a large column to push into Binh Khanh and Phuoc Hiep villages, but each time they came they suffered some losses.

On 22 February 1960 they sent a company from Mo Cay to attack Phuoc Hiep. We set up an ambush with over a platoon of men and destroyed one of their platoons, seized two submachine guns, two semiautomatic rifles and ten Mas rifles. They were determined to deploy all their strength and retaliate against us. Around February 24th, they focused their attack on Phuoc Hiep, Binh Khanh and Dinh Thuy, the three villages that had risen up with great force during the concerted uprising in Mo Cay district. They assembled about 13,000 soldiers who pushed their way in from Saigon, Tra Vinh and Ben Tre province town. Their propaganda said that they would annihilate us and restore order. Seeing the large enemy force, the villagers became worried and demoralized. We were also caught in the enemy encirclement, but our policy specified that the cadres should not abandon the people and should stay at all costs to resist the sweep operation, maintain the movement and prevent it from collapsing. Comrades Hai Thuy and Ba Dao were in charge of keeping track of the enemy's movements, selecting the weakest of their columns and waiting till nightfall to destroy it to break the back of the operation. The soldiers angrily searched everywhere without finding our forces. Meanwhile, wherever they went they were wounded by the "sky horse" rifles (*ngua troi*). At 5:00 P.M. on the 25th, comrade Thuy led an attack on a company size column and after 15 minutes of fighting destroyed about two platoons. In their fright and confusion the enemy shot each other, killing an additional number. Taking advantage of the darkness, we withdrew safely, losing only one comrade who was killed by a stray bullet.

The "sky horse" rifle appeared for the first time in this battle. This was an invention by a guerrilla who devised it from the principle of explosives, used in producing land mines. The barrel of the rifle consisted of a long steel pipe. The rifle had legs like a mortar and was detonated when a wire was pulled as in the case of mines. The charge consisted of explosives mixed with steel pellets and glass shards dipped in urine and snake poison. The firing range was 10 meters, and anyone who was hit—even if it was just a scratch on the skin—would die right away. The masses spread the rumor that this was a new weapon, and whenever they heard the "sky horse" mentioned, the enemy soldiers fled in disorder.

While the enemy was concentrating their forces to surround us, the leadership committee had each area spread the news that we were about to attack Mo Cay district town and Ben Tre province town. At the same time we had the people prepare sampans and get ready to supply rice to large units. As expected, the enemy heard the news the next day. They gave up the operation, and withdrew their forces in a panic to defend these towns. In this operation, seeing that our losses had been insignificant while the enemy lost over one hundred men, the people felt very encouraged. The women capitalized on this situation to work on the soldiers, and a large number of them deserted. Small children picked up and delivered to us thousands of cartridges belonging to the enemy. However, the reactionary enemy left behind a force to occupy Phuoc Hiep in the hope of intimidating the people and of gradually encroaching on our territory and then taking it back. Most of these troops were Catholics and they were extremely brutal and reactionary. Within ten days, they arrested twenty youths, liquidated them and buried them around the post. They conscripted the villagers to do forced labor, building the road from Phuoc Hiep to Binh Khanh, and terrorized the people in an extremely brutal manner.

The villagers' ardor declined noticeably. The comrades in the village pleaded with us to send armed units down to destroy the post. We also wanted to destroy this gang badly and relieve our anger, but our armed forces were still weak. So we discussed ways to put a stop to the enemy's killing while still maintaining the initiative and the legal status of the masses. Everyone unanimously agreed that we should organize immediately a large group of women who would push their way into Mo Cay district town to denounce the crimes of the soldiers in Phuoc Hiep.

The first time, over 5,000 women—including old women, young girls and children—from the villages of Phuoc Hiep, Binh Khanh, Dinh Thuy, Da Phuoc Hoi, An Dinh and Thanh Thoi, formed a huge force, wearing mourning bands and ragged clothes and carrying their children, and surged into Mo Cay district town. They demanded an end to terrorism and compensation for the deaths caused by the soldiers, and punishment of the brutes in Phuoc Hiep village. The district chief was scared out of his mind and shouted to the soldiers to shut the gates tightly and not to allow anyone to enter. The people stayed in front of the district headquarters, defecating and urinating on the spot, and refused to go home. Among the women was an 18-year-old girl who had been blind since childhood but was very enthusiastic about struggling against the enemy. A policeman teased her:

—This blind girl can't see anything, and what does she feel she can accomplish by joining the struggle?

She retorted right away:

—I'm blind but I know enough to follow the path of light, and this is much better than you people who can see but are following a blind road.

The policeman did not know what to say. The women praised her:

—She's blind but she's enlightened.

The girl was also a good singer. During the struggle she sang guerrilla songs which left the soldiers reflective and less arrogant. The tug of war lasted for five days and five nights, and each day the group was reinforced with more women coming to lend a hand, and the struggle became more inflamed. In the end, the district chief had to open the gate and come out to accept the demands of the people, agreeing to withdraw all the soldiers from Phuoc Hiep village. At the height of the "concerted uprising" in Ben Tre province, the successful struggle of the women in Mo Cay district on March 15th, 1960 initiated a new form of struggle by the masses which proved to be very effective. The Americans and Diem were very afraid of this powerful force [constituted by women] and gave it a special name: the long-haired troops. . . .

At the beginning of April 1960, we held a meeting to make a preliminary review of the success of the concerted uprising in the districts of Cu Lao Minh island and to draw experiences for timely contribution to the uprising which was scheduled to take place all over Ben Tre province. Our experiences were very rich but our level of understanding was low so we failed to bring out the best experiences of the masses. Later, the higher levels reviewed our experiences and deduced the policy of attacking the enemy on "two legs"(*hai chan*) and with "three prongs" (*ba mui giap cong*).[7] I was very pleased with this policy and proceeded to apply it to mobilize the movement and spread it to every area. . . .

The people of Ben Tre province who had endured untold miseries during the past six years could now laugh, sing and live. A new spirit was burning all over the countryside. The political forces held animated discussions about the struggle. Carpenters and blacksmiths raced to produce knives and machetes to kill the enemy. The workshops improved the sky-horse rifles, making them more lethal, and produced a batch of new weapons called "mut nhet" (primed rifles). At this time, the armed forces of the province were over one company in strength and each district had from one to two squads. Each village had from one to three rifles, but the majority of these were French muskets. Young girls stayed up many nights to sew "Main Force" green uniforms for the troops. An information office was set up in each hamlet in Giong Trom, Mo Cay and Chau Thanh districts. On each side of the road, slogans were drawn on tree trunks and caught everyone's eyes. On some days people from the province town came by the hundred to visit the liberated areas.

After the gigantic foray of a 15,000 strong political force into Ben Tre province town, the Ben Tre Province Committee of the National Front for the Liberation of South Vietnam was officially presented to the people. The creation of the Front was of vital significance for its aim was to consolidate the people's right to be masters of the countryside. While the high point of the concerted uprising was rising like a tidal wave sweeping everything in its path, the people became more insistent in their demand that the revolution set up an official organization to represent the strength, unity and fighting force of the people, which would continue to lead the people to advance forward toward new successes in the resistance to

---

7. The "two legs" are military action and political action. The three prongs are: *chinh tri* (political action), *quan su* (military action) and *binh van* (proselytizing enemy soldiers).—*Trans.*

save the country and oppose the American imperialist invaders and their henchmen—Ngo Dinh Diem and the gang of traitors. This was why the "National Front
for the Liberation of South Vietnam"—the sole organization leading the resistance
by the entire population of the South—was timely created and presented to the
people on December 20th, 1960 [see Reading 29—eds.].

Aware of this spirit, we made urgent preparations in order to present the Ben
Tre Province Liberation Front Committee to the people on December 26th, 1960,
that is to say six days after the birth of the National Front for the Liberation of
South Vietnam. We decided to make it a big occasion by convoking a conference
which would be attended by representatives of every population strata in order to
set up the Province Liberation Front Committee, and organizing a ceremony for
about 10,000 people representing the countryside, the urban areas, all the religious
groups and the families of soldiers. We selected My Chanh, located less than five
kilometers from Ba Tri district town, as the site for the presentation ceremony. The
population here was large and the village was located in a favorable strategic terrain and had a big market, the Ben Bao market.

At dusk on the 26th, the rally began. We had electric lights and microphones
which had been sent by workers in the province town as their contribution to the
rally. Seeing the flag being hoisted which brightened up a whole section of the sky,
we all felt very moved. So much blood shed by the comrades and people had dyed
this glorious and eternal flag.

The Liberation Front Committee comprised 15 people who represented every
social strata, religious group and political party. The committee solemnly appeared
in front of the people and each member gave a speech. Mr. Ngoi, the representative
of the Cao Dai Thien Tien sect, Mr. Ho Hao Nghia, representing university and
high school students, Mr. Ngoi, representing the national bourgeoisie, Mrs. Muoi
Quoi, representing the women, brother Ba, representing the peasants—they all
condemned the crimes of the enemy and expressed their gratitude toward and their
confidence in the revolution, and pledged to unite and fight to the end to overthrow
the Americans and Diem.

I had the honor of representing the People's Revolutionary Party[8] and the
Front, and on their behalf I made promises and pledges, and called on the people
to propel the fight strongly forward. When I stepped down from the podium, many
women embraced me and inquired after me with great concern. An old lady
grasped my hand and wept:

—I'm Bich's aunt.[9] Heavens, if he were still alive today he would be so happy
seeing this scene.

Heavens! We embraced each other in happiness and sorrow. I was very moved
and told her:

—Besides Bich, both my parents have been killed. I don't have anyone left,

---

8. This is the Southern branch of the Lao Dong (Workers) Party.—*Trans.*

9. Bich was Mrs. Nguyen Thi Dinh's husband, a Viet Minh cadre who was arrested by the French
and killed in 1943. *Khong Con Duong Nao Khac*, pp. 28–35.—eds.

but there are so many other mothers and fathers who love me even more than their own children.

Talking about Bich in this place where he was born, I thought that this ceremony, by evoking an old memory, had taken on an added significance for me. I felt greatly cheered and asked my husband's aunt:

—If the enemy comes tomorrow and asks what you're doing here tonight, what will you say?

She replied without hesitating:

—What do you think I'll say? I'll say that the Front was born, that liberation troops and people attended in great numbers, in the tens of thousands. I wasn't afraid of them before, so why should I be afraid of them now that our forces are as strong as this?

I looked at the large popular force and felt overjoyed. The armed units had expanded rapidly. Ben Tre province now had close to a battalion of adequately armed troops. This was a real battalion, not a "fake" one. As for the strong and large "long-haired" force, I did not even know how many battalions of them there were. From now on, on the road of resisting the Americans and their lackeys, our people would stand firm on the two powerful legs of military and political strength to fight and achieve victory. There was no other road to take.

In the face of this enormous and imposing force of people, I felt very small, but I was full of self-confidence, like a small tree standing in a vast and ancient forest. In struggling against the enemy, I had come to fully realize that we had to have the strength of the whole forest in order to be able to stay the force of the strong winds and storms. As I thought about the protection and support of the people, about the enormous efforts that the revolution had expanded in educating and nurturing me, about the countless comrades and beloved people—some of whom I had mentioned but whose names I could never exhaustively enumerate— I felt more intimately bound, more so than ever before, to the road I had taken and had pledged to follow until my last days. This was the road for which I would sacrifice everything for the future of the revolution and for the interests of the masses. For me there was no other road to take.

After the ceremony broke up, I walked among the troops, carrying my knapsack. A few shots echoed from an enemy post nearby. A fighter joked:

—Hey, they're firing to salute the birth of the Front!

Another one immediately brushed his remark aside:

—Saluting like that isn't adequate. One of these days we'll have to go to the post and force them to kneel down to greet the Front and to surrender!

Everyone burst out laughing. We made our way leisurely on the large road, talking noisily as we walked under the sky of liberation full of stars and cooled by a strong breeze. And from all four directions of the island I could hear the rifle shots of the guerrillas encircling and destroying the posts, as though urging everyone to quickly rush forward and eliminate the Americans and Diem to liberate the South, so that the people of the whole country could soon be reunited under the spring sky of our native land full of the sweet fragrance of the milk fruit.

29. Founding Program of the National Liberation Front of South Vietnam*

During the Vietnam war, information about the insurgents whom the US govern-ment called the enemy was not easy to come by. For most American readers, the only accessible accounts were those written by people either in the direct employ of the US government (including the CIA[1]) or on leave from government service to publish interpretations which generally coincided with official Washington views. Preeminent among this group of "court scholars" is the former US Information Agency official, Douglas Pike, whose 1966 book Viet Cong *attempted to prove that the program of the National Liberation Front (NLF) was a pipe dream; that the social changes carried out in liberated zones were "more apparent than real"; that NLF administrative techniques were "more manipulated than participa-tional," as its cadres were unable to overcome the crippling localism and parochialism of the Vietnamese villagers.[2] In a later work, Pike predicted that the Vietnamese revolutionaries would reluctantly concede failure in the South and rec-oncile themselves to an indefinitely divided country.[3]*

It would be an exaggeration to argue that the United States was beaten in Vietnam because it relied on such flawed interpretations, but the absence of reli-able data about Asia had much to do with the events of a generation earlier that go by the name "McCarthyism."[4] Far wider than the anti-communist inquisition presided over by Wisconsin Senator Joseph McCarthy, the attack on radicalism during the late 1940s and 1950s decimated the corps of American Asia specialists, and reenforced an anti-intellectual bias against scholarship that might be sympa-thetic to the revolutionary side.[5]

Thus, the book by one of the few Western journalists actually to travel in Na-tional Liberation Front zones in South Vietnam, Wilfred G. Burchett's Vietnam: Inside Story of the Guerrilla War *(New York: International Publishers, 1965), was*

---

*Liberation Radio/South Vietnam (February 13–14, 1961), Foreign Broadcast Information Ser-vice Daily Reports.

1. See the article by CIA agent George Carver, "The Faceless Viet Cong," *Foreign Affairs* (April, 1966). For Carver's CIA affiliation, see Frank Snepp, *Decent Interval* (New York: Random House, 1977), p. 237. (Snepp also worked for the CIA.)

2. Douglas Pike, *Viet Cong: The Organization and Techniques of the National Liberation Front of South Vietnam* (Cambridge: MIT Press, 1966), p. 382.

3. Pike, *War, Peace and the Viet Cong* (Cambridge: MIT Press, 1969), Chap. 5.

4. McCarthyism still awaits a convincing overall study. Until that time, David Caute's ency-clopedic *The Great Fear: The Anti-Communist Purge Under Truman and Eisenhower* (New York: Simon & Schuster, 1978) is serviceable. Ellen Schrecker's forthcoming *Academic McCarthyism* (New York: Oxford University Press, 1985) will clarify much about the intellectual purges of the McCarthy era.

5. For an insightful account, see Ross Y. Koen, *The China Lobby in American Politics*, edited with an introduction by Richard C. Kagan (New York: Harper & Row, 1974; first published—and suppressed—1960).

either ignored or dismissed as "pro-communist." McCarthyism, the pathological intolerance of radicalism, thus sentenced Americans to interpretations, like those of Douglas Pike, that supported the previously set assumptions of Washington policy makers.

Here, in their own words, is what the people in the National Liberation Front thought they were and what they were fighting for.

I. *Overthrow the camouflaged colonial regime of the American imperialists and the dictatorial power of Ngo Dinh Diem, servant of the Americans, and institute a government of national democratic union.*

The present South Vietnamese regime is a camouflaged colonial regime dominated by the Yankees, and the South Vietnamese Government is a servile government, implementing faithfully all the policies of the American imperialists. Therefore, this regime must be overthrown and a government of national and democratic union put in its place composed of representatives of all social classes, of all nationalities, of the various political parties, of all religions; patriotic, eminent citizens must take over for the people the control of economic, political, social, and cultural interests and thus bring about independence, democracy, well-being, peace, neutrality, and efforts toward the peaceful unification of the country.

II. *Institute a largely liberal and democratic regime.*

1. Abolish the present constitution of the dictatorial powers of Ngo Dinh Diem, servant of the Americans. Elect a new National Assembly through universal suffrage. 2. Implement essential democratic liberties: freedom of opinion, of press, of assembly, of movement, of trade-unionism; freedom of religion without any discrimination; and the right of all patriotic organizations of whatever political tendency to carry on normal activities. 3. Proclaim a general amnesty for all political prisoners and the dissolution of concentration camps of all sorts; abolish fascist law 10/59 [see Reading 26—eds.] and all the other antidemocratic laws; authorize the return to the country of all persons persecuted by the American-Diem regime who are now refugees abroad. 4. Interdict all illegal arrests and detentions; prohibit torture; and punish all the Diem bullies who have not repented and who have committed crimes against the people.

III. *Establish an independent and sovereign economy, and improve the living conditions of the people.*

1. Suppress the monopolies imposed by American imperialists and their servants; establish an independent and sovereign economy and finances in accordance with the national interests; confiscate to the profit of the nation the properties of the American imperialists and their servants. 2. Support the national bourgeoisie in the reconstruction and development of crafts and industry; provide active protection for national products through the suppression of production taxes and the limitation or prohibition of imports that the national economy is capable of producing: reduce customs fees on raw materials and machines. 3. Revitalize agriculture; modernize production, fishing, and cattle raising; help the farmers in putting

to the plow unused land and in developing production; protect the crops and guarantee their disposal. 4. Encourage and reinforce economic relations between the city and country, the plain and the mountain regions; develop commercial exchanges with foreign countries, regardless of their political regime, on the basis of equality and mutual interests. 5. Institute a just and rational system of taxation; eliminate harassing penalties. 6. Implement the labor code; prohibition of discharges, of penalties, of ill-treatment of wage earners; improvement of the living conditions of workers and civil servants; imposition of wage scales and protective measures for young apprentices. 7. Organize social welfare: find work for jobless persons; assume the support and protection of orphans, old people, invalids; come to the help of the victims of the Americans and Diemists; organize help for areas hit by bad crops, fires, or natural calamities. 8. Come to help of displaced persons desiring to return to their native areas and to those who wish to remain permanently in the South; improve their working and living conditions. 9. Prohibit expulsions, spoliation, and compulsory concentration of the population; guarantee job security for the urban and rural working populations.

IV. *Reduce land rent; implement agrarian reform with the aim of providing land to the tillers.*

1. Reduce land rent; guarantee to the farmers the right to till the soil; guarantee the property right of accession to fallow lands to those who have cultivated them; guarantee property rights to those farmers who have already received land. 2. Dissolve "prosperity zones," and put an end to recruitment for the camps that are called "agricultural development centers." Allow those compatriots who already have been forced into "prosperity zones" and "agricultural development centers" to return freely to their own lands. 3. Confiscate the land owned by American imperialists and their servants, and distribute it to poor peasants without any land or with insufficient land; redistribute the communal lands on a just and rational basis. 4. By negotiation and on the basis of fair prices, repurchase for distribution to landless peasants or peasants with insufficient land those surplus lands that the owners of large estates will be made to relinquish if their domain exceeds a certain limit, to be determined in accordance with regional particularities. The farmers who benefit from such land distribution will not be compelled to make any payment or to submit to any other conditions.

V. *Develop a national and democratic culture and education.*

1. Combat all forms of culture and education enslaved to Yankee fashions; develop a culture and education that is national, progressive, and at the service of the Fatherland and people. 2. Liquidate illiteracy; increase the number of schools in the fields of general education as well as in those of technical and professional education, in advanced study as well as in other fields; adopt Vietnamese as the vernacular language; reduce the expenses of education and exempt from payment students who are without means; resume the examination system. 3. Promote science and technology and the national letters and arts; encourage and support the

intellectuals and artists so as to permit them to develop their talents in the service of national reconstruction. 4. Watch over public health; develop sports and physical education.

VI. *Create a national army devoted to the defense of the Fatherland and the people.*

1. Establish a national army devoted to the defense of the Fatherland and the people; abolish the system of American military advisers. 2. Abolish the draft system; improve the living conditions of the simple soldiers and guarantee their political rights; put an end to ill-treatment of the military; pay particular attention to the dependents of soldiers without means. 3. Reward officers and soldiers having participated in the struggle against the domination by the Americans and their servants; adopt a policy of clemency toward the former collaborators of the Americans and Diemists guilty of crimes against the people but who have finally repented and are ready to serve the people. 4. Abolish all foreign military bases established on the territory of Vietnam.

VII. *Guarantee equality between the various minorities and between the two sexes; protect the legitimate interests of foreign citizens established in Vietnam and of Vietnamese citizens residing abroad.*

1. Implement the right to autonomy of the national minorities: found autonomous zones in the areas with minority population, those zones to be an integral part of the Vietnamese nation. Guarantee equality between the various nationalities: each nationality has the right to use and develop its language and writing system, to maintain or to modify freely its *mores* and customs; abolish the policy of the Americans and Diemists of racial discrimination and forced assimilation. Create conditions permitting the national minorities to reach the general level of progress of the population: development of their economy and culture; formation of cadres of minority nationalities. 2. Establish equality between the two sexes; women shall have equal rights with men from all viewpoints (political, economic, cultural, social, etc.). 3. Protect the legitimate interests of foreign citizens established in Vietnam. 4. Defend and take care of the interests of Vietnamese citizens residing abroad.

VIII. *Promote a foreign policy of peace and neutrality.*

1. Cancel all unequal treaties that infringe upon the sovereignty of the people and that were concluded with other countries by the servants of the Americans. 2. Establish diplomatic relations with all countries, regardless of their political regime, in accordance with the principles of peaceful coexistence adopted at the Bandung Conference. 3. Develop close solidarity with peace-loving nations and neutral countries; develop free relations with the nations of Southeast Asia, in particular with Cambodia and Laos. 4. Stay out of any military bloc; refuse any military alliance with another country. 5. Accept economic aid from any country willing to help us without attaching any conditions to such help.

IX. *Re-establish normal relations between the two zones, and prepare for the peaceful reunification of the country.*

The peaceful reunification of the country constitutes the dearest desire of all our compatriots throughout the country. The National Liberation Front of South Vietnam advocates the peaceful reunification by stages on the basis of negotiations and through the seeking of ways and means in conformity with the interests of the Vietnamese nation. While awaiting this reunification, the governments of the two zones will, on the basis of negotiations, promise to banish all separatist and war-mongering propaganda and not to use force to settle differences between the zones. Commercial and cultural exchanges between the two zones will be implemented; the inhabitants of the two zones will be free to move about throughout the country as their family and business interests indicate. The freedom of postal exchanges will be guaranteed.

X. *Struggle against all aggressive war; actively defend universal peace.*

1. Struggle against all aggressive war and against all forms of imperialist domination; support the national emancipation movements of the various peoples. 2. Banish all war-mongering propaganda; demand general disarmament and the prohibition of nuclear weapons; and advocate the utilization of atomic energy for peaceful purposes. 3. Support all movements of struggle for peace, democracy, and social progress throughout the world; contribute actively to the defense of peace in South-east Asia and in the world.

30. "The Political and Military Line of Our Party"*

By General Vo Nguyen Giap

Neither the French nor the US military leaders truly comprehended the nature of the war they were fighting in Vietnam. This was despite the fact that Vo Nguyen Giap, the military theoretician of their adversaries, had repeatedly explained in print, for over three decades, the theory and practice of "people's war" in Vietnam.

The most persistent misunderstanding on the part of the US and French military strategists confused people's war with guerrilla war. Both the French and US repeated the deadly mistake of thinking that whenever their opponent shifted to conventional warfare, with large well-equipped units fighting to seize and hold

---

*From *Vietnamese Studies*, Number 7 (Hanoi, 1965), pp. 123–152. Originally published in *Nhan Dan*, December 22, 1964.

terrain, this somehow signalled the failure of people's war, which these foreign strategists equated with guerrilla war. Thus, the French generals thought that they had led General Giap into a fatal trap at Dien Bien Phu, just as General Westmoreland, 14 years later, thought that he had tricked Giap into positional warfare around Khe Sanh, and then mistook the Tet Offensive for either a "diversion" or a "last desperate effort," in either event a sign that people's war had "failed" (Readings 52 and 53).

In fact, the theory of people's war postulates three ·major stages—guerrilla war, mobile war, positional war—gradually unfolding as the people's political and military strength grows. The appearance of large well-equipped units engaging in conventional offensives does not indicate that guerrilla war has failed, but just the opposite: It has succeeded enough to launch the next stage. This theory was formulated by Mao Zedong (see, for example, "The Three Stages of a Protracted War" and "Mobile Warfare, Guerrilla Warfare, and Positional Warfare" in On Protracted War *[1938]), and the military history of the Chinese revolution followed the same general lines of development as the military history of the Vietnamese revolution. Both histories began with ragged little bands of guerrillas, such as the thirty-four men Giap led to liquidate two French garrisons in 1944, and ended with the irresistible lightning advance of a large modern army, such as the final Chinese offensive of 1949 and the final Vietnamese offensive of 1975.*

Why did the US military leaders make precisely the same errors as their French predecessors? After all, General Westmoreland asserts that he studied both the French defeat and the writings of General Giap. One problem is that those fighting against people's war justified their own behavior with beliefs contradictory to the basic premises of Giap's theory. For the essence of the theory of people's war is that it is a just *struggle of the* people *against foreign and domestic oppression and exploitation. So to comprehend the theory and intensity of the war being waged against them, the French and US leaders would somehow have had to assume this vision of their own cause as* unjust. *Thus it is no surprise that they dismissed the theory's essential* content *as mere communist propaganda, while focusing exclusively on the military* forms *of the struggle. In doing so, they fulfilled their own role in the theory, defending the property rights of landlords and capitalists, foreign economic interests, and hated puppet rulers, all with the most devastating weapons they could use. As a result they drove more and more of the peasants and workers into supporting the people's war.*

Nor could they comprehend an opponent such as Vo Nguyen Giap, whose own life embodies his people's struggle against oppression. For him, the word "oppression" is not propaganda or some empty abstraction. Dismissed from school in his early teens for supporting Vietnamese national independence, Giap was imprisoned in 1930 at the age of 18 for leading a demonstration in Hue in support of peasants' rights. In 1941, the pro-Nazi French authorities outlawed the Communist Party and arrested Giap's young wife and her sister. They guillotined his sister-in-law, and put his wife and their infant in prison, where both died.

Armed Struggle Is the Prolongation of Political Struggle

The military line of our party derives from and always follows its political line; it endeavors to achieve the political aims of the revolution through armed struggle or political struggle combined with armed struggle. Our revolution must go through the stage of national people's democratic revolution and advance toward the socialist revolution, bypassing the stage of capitalist development. Our military line is based on the line of a thoroughly national people's democratic revolution; it is the *line of the people's revolutionary war*, the war of a people made up mainly of peasants, which is aimed at overthrowing imperialism and feudalism, reconquering independence for the nation and giving land back to the tillers. It is the line of thorough war of national liberation, a just war to counter the unjust war of aggression waged by the enemy.

The two revolutionary tasks, the national and the democratic, are closely linked with each other. That is why, in order to give a strong impulse to the people's revolutionary war and bring it to a victorious conclusion, it is indispensable to mobilize and organize the entire people, particularly to mobilize and organize the large mass of peasants under the leadership of the working class, and to solve a whole series of questions relating to the democratic revolution, especially the agrarian question.

To wage a revolutionary war thoroughly victoriously, it is indispensable to strengthen the leadership of the vanguard Party of the working class. It is this leadership which has created all the conditions and provided all the guarantees to insure the transition from the national people's democratic revolution to the socialist revolution through a continuous revolutionary process. On this road, the people's armed forces, which are in fact those of the laboring people—workers and peasants—are constantly directed and educated by the Party. . . .

On the other hand, our country was a colonial and semifeudal country with a territory which was not very vast, a population which was not very large, and an economy which was essentially agrarian and backward. Our enemies—Japanese fascists or French colonialists—were much stronger than we materially, having a developed capitalist economy and powerful regular armies. At present in the South, United States imperialism, served by its lackeys, is also an economically and militarily strong enemy.

In these conditions, our military line is that followed by *a small nation struggling against a much stronger enemy*. This strategy has been successful in solving, creatively and adequately, a fundamental problem: relying on our absolute political superiority, on the righteousness of our cause, and on our people's unity in struggle, it is possible *to use what is weak to fight what is strong, to defeat the most modern weapons with a revolutionary spirit*. Consequently, a small nation is quite capable of defeating the professional army of the imperialist aggressors. . . .

On the one hand, our people's revolutionary struggle in the present period applies the precious experience of fraternal countries in revolutionary struggle; on the other hand, it continues and develops to a high degree our people's *traditions of indomitable struggle against foreign aggression* and the spirit of resolute and heroic struggle of our peasants' uprisings in the past. Marxism-Leninism never disowns the history and the great constituent virtues of a nation; on the contrary, it raises these virtues to new heights in the new historical conditions. During the many thousand years of their history, our people repeatedly rose up to struggle heroically against foreign aggression and reconquer national independence. In those armed struggles, our people made creative contributions to military art; they relied on justice and humanity to defeat a powerful enemy, used what was weak to fight what was strong, won victories with forces of small size in large-scale wars; sometimes they attracted the enemy far into our own territory to annihilate them; sometimes they temporarily withdrew troops from the capital, seeking favorable occasions and places gradually to drive the enemy to defeat and liberate the country; sometimes they built up revolutionary armed forces in regions of mountains and forests, creating bases for a protracted struggle until the enemy was completely defeated; sometimes they mobilized the peasants' combative spirit, created a large and mighty army, and wiped out the enemy's main forces by unexpected and bold maneuvers. . . .

From Revolutionary Violence to the Uprising of the Entire People and the People's War

People's war is the basic conception in our Party's military line; it constantly affirms the revolutionary character, the just character, of people's war, the decisive role of the masses, the leading role of our Party. It is the expression of our Party's class viewpoint, of its reliance on the masses.

Our Party's conception of people's war is a new *development of the conception of revolutionary violence* in the revolutionary context of our country.

The Marxist-Leninist doctrine on class struggle and the dictatorship of the proletariat affirms the role of violence in revolution, makes a distinction between unjust, counter-revolutionary violence and just, revolutionary violence, between the violence of the exploiting classes and that of the masses. . . .

Our nationwide resistance war,[1] which was a people's war, was a new development; it was a *true revolutionary war, a war by the entire people, a total war*. A revolutionary war, because it was carried out on the basis of the mobilization and organization of the masses, with the aim of achieving a national democratic revolution. A war by the entire people, because it was a war in which a whole nation struggled in unity, each citizen becoming a combatant, a war in which our Party's correct revolutionary line succeeded in grouping all patriotic strata of the population in a broad front based on a strong worker-peasant alliance, and mobilizing them for the struggle. A total war, because armed struggle was frequently combined with political struggle, because at the same time as we engaged in a

---

1. The war against French colonialism.—eds.

military struggle, we carried out reduction of land rent, land reform, political struggle in urban centers and enemy-occupied areas, and struggle in the economic and cultural fields.

It should be stressed that during the resistance, we used *armed struggle as an essential form of struggle*, with the countryside as a base. The enemy we faced was the expeditionary corps of French colonialism, an old-type colonialism. It was only through armed struggle that it was possible, in such circumstances, to decimate and annihilate the enemy, and win victory for the resistance.

In the South of our country, in the conditions of struggle against neo-colonialism and the "special war" of United States imperialism, historical conditions present some aspects which are similar to those of the resistance against French colonialism, but others which are peculiar to the liberation war in South Vietnam. Our people in the South enjoy a clear political superiority over the enemy; they also have traditions of and experience in political struggle and armed struggle and are animated with ardent patriotism and high revolutionary spirit; the enemy are strong materially and technically, but the social bases of the reactionary forces in the service of the United States imperialists being extremely weak, they are in a state of complete political isolation, and their political weakness is irremediable. Because of our country's temporary partition, a phase has appeared of acute political struggle against the war unilaterally started by the enemy, developing afterward into political struggle combined with armed struggle. The war of liberation now being waged by our countrymen in the South is *a revolutionary war, a war by the entire people, a total war* using simultaneously the two forms of struggle, *regarding both as fundamental and decisive*. Armed struggle has developed on the basis of political struggle brought to a higher level; these two forms of struggle develop simultaneously in a vigorous manner and stimulate each other. Armed struggle which becomes more and more vigorous does not make political struggle decrease in intensity but, on the contrary, gives it a stronger impulse; together they pursue the aim of annihilating and dislocating enemy armed forces, striking vigorously where the enemy is basically weak, on the political ground. . . .

From the Revolutionary People to the Revolutionary Armed Forces

The Marxist-Leninist doctrine holds that revolutionary struggle in general and armed struggle in particular must be the work of the masses who, once they are conscious of the political aims of the revolution, are ready to be organized and resolute in rising up to fight, so that they become capable of defeating the most wicked enemy. As Lenin said, "The masses who shed their blood on the battlefield are the factor which brings victory in a war."

In order to carry out a people's war, the entire people must be mobilized and armed. Our Party's fundamental concept in this matter is that of the *people's armed forces*. This concept is indicative of the revolutionary character, the popular and class character of the armed forces; it is indicative of the Party's absolute leadership of the armed forces.

Because armed struggle is the continuation of political struggle, no powerful armed forces could be built without the people's mighty political strength. Looking back at our people's long and arduous revolutionary struggle, we can clearly see that the years of bitter political struggle after our Party was founded, to enlighten and organize the masses, to build the worker-peasant alliance, to create a People's United Front, to affirm the leading role of the Party, were the years of preparation of forces for the subsequent armed struggle. . . . The political force of the masses, of the people, is the strongest possible base on which to develop the armed forces. . . .

In recent years, our countrymen in the South at first also relied basically on their political force when they heroically rose up to fight against a wicked enemy. Their innumerable heroic deeds are further proof that the source of strength of the armed forces in a revolutionary war is the strength of the united struggle of the entire people; that once patriotism and revolutionary ideas have penetrated deep into the people, they become an invincible force. . . .

Born of the people, the people's armed forces can grow in strength only thanks to their unreserved support and by continuously learning from their revolutionary spirit and rich experience in revolutionary struggle. To consolidate and continuously develop blood relations with the people, our armed forces have not only to fight, but also to work and produce, remaining always close to the political movement of the masses.

The people's armed forces are the revolutionary armed forces of the laboring people, of the workers and peasants; they fight to defend the interests of the people, the class, and the nation. These armed forces must be placed under the leadership of the vanguard party if they are to have a revolutionary character and an increasingly high combative spirit. That the armed forces should have a revolutionary character, a class character, is the essential point in our Party's theory on the building of the armed forces. . . .

In order to carry out a people's war, the armed forces must have adequate forms of organization comprising *main-force troops, regional troops, militia,* and *self-defense units.* The main-force troops are mobile units which may be used in fighting in any part of the country. Regional troops are the mainstay of armed struggle in a region. Militia and self-defense groups are extensive semiarmed forces of the laboring people who, while continuing their production work, are the main instrument of the people's power at the base.

The practice of revolutionary armed struggle by our people has proved that the three above-mentioned forms of organization of the armed forces are wholly adequate for the tasks of promoting a people's war, for mobilizing and arming the entire people for the war. We have to look back at our people's struggle through successive periods to grasp fully the importance and strategic role of those three categories of armed forces. If we had not organized secret self-defense units during the preinsurrection period, the powerful armed forces such as we had later on would never have come into being; if during the resistance we had not organized an extensive network of self-defense groups and strong regional units, guerrilla warfare could not have developed to a high degree, and still less could we have built a powerful main force. On the other hand, if we had not had a large mobile main force when the armed struggle was at a victorious stage, there would have been no great battles to annihilate enemy forces, no victorious campaigns, and the glorious Dien Bien Phu battle would not have taken place. Today in the South of our country, in the main the armed forces are developing according to the same laws as those discussed above. The extensive semiarmed organizations efficaciously supported the movement of the masses in the countryside, when the people were rising up to free themselves from the enemy's grip, undertake partial uprisings at the base, and promote guerrilla warfare. It was while these political and armed struggles were raging that the three categories of armed forces were formed and developed. The South Vietnam Liberation Army has been growing rapidly and unceasingly. We can say that the above three forms of organization have extremely close, organic relations, which ensure an inexhaustible source of strength from the masses of the people for the people's armed forces, and make it possible for them not only to carry out their task of annihilating enemy forces but also to protect our political and economic bases and preserve the potential of the liberation war.

Our country has no vast territory, no large population; numerically, our armed forces cannot compare with those of large countries. For this very reason, to defend our country efficaciously, to defeat an enemy who is stronger than we materially and technically, we have to apply those three forms of armed forces strictly. Extensively and strongly organized militia and self-defense groups, strong regional troops, powerful and highly mobile main-force troops: that is a sine qua non condition for developing our fighting power and raising our national defense capacity to a high degree, even in the present conditions, when our People's Army is being built into a modern regular army.

From Correct Revolutionary Strategy and Tactics to Military Art in a People's War

To insure the success of a revolutionary war, it is necessary to have both correct strategy and correct tactics, which constitute the *military art of the people's war*. . . .

Our military art is that of a small nation, whose armed force is still weak in equipment and technique but which rises up to fight against an enemy who is materially much stronger. This is a military art, whose characteristic is to *defeat material force with moral force, defeat what is strong with what is weak, defeat what is modern with what is primitive, defeat the modern armies of the aggressive imperialists with the people's patriotism and determination to carry out a thorough revolution.*

Our military art has successfully solved a number of questions relating to strategy, operations, and tactics, with a view to defeating a strong enemy; it has correctly determined *the relations between man and weapons, politics and technique,* regarding the human factor, the political factor, as the decisive factor, while considering weapons and technique also important. Now that the people's armed forces have the possibility of having better equipment, of being strengthened materially and technically, our military art is still firmly maintaining the above guiding principles, combining politics and technique on the basis that politics and fighting spirit are the essential factor, which enhances to the highest degree the fighting power of the armed forces. . . .

The people's war generally takes place in conditions when our side enjoys absolute political superiority over an enemy materially stronger than we are. Considering the revolutionary character of the war and the balance of concrete forces, our military art has determined the following strategic orientation: *to promote a war by the entire people, a total and protracted war.* We have to wage a long war in which our political superiority will prevail, and we can gradually increase our strength, pass from a position of weakness to a position of strength, change the balance of forces between us and the enemy, and ensure victory for our side. . . .

According to our military theory, in order to ensure victory for the people's war when we are stronger than the enemy politically and the enemy is stronger than we materially, it is necessary to promote an extensive *guerrilla war* which will develop gradually into a *regular war* combined with a guerrilla war. Regular war and guerrilla war are closely combined, stimulate each other, deplete and annihilate enemy forces, and bring final victory. Looking back at our people's armed struggle through successive periods, we can fully realize the strategic role of guerrilla war combined with regular war. Without the guerrilla war in the early days, there would have been no August general uprising, no victorious regular war during the resistance. Today on the South Vietnam battlefields, guerrilla war in the form of partial uprisings in the countryside has attained an extremely important strategic role and is developing to an increasingly high degree. On the other hand, if guerrilla war had not been combined with regular war, our people could not have won a decisive victory in the previous sacred resistance war. Guerrilla war and regular war are indispensable forms of war in a people's war, but this does not mean that in all circumstances a people's war must necessarily begin as a guerrilla war, and develop afterward into a regular war. Should the enemy now launch an aggressive war against the North of our country, on account of the concrete conditions on our side and theirs, regular war and guerrilla war would be waged simultaneously.

In all wars, the activities of the armed forces are either offensive or defensive. A revolutionary war also uses both these forms but regards offensive activities as the most essential. As a result of concrete practice of revolutionary armed struggle, our military art has created original forms of struggle: *guerrilla warfare, mobile warfare,* and *positional warfare.* All these forms, in offensive and defensive operations, can raise to the highest degree the determination of the people's armed forces to wipe out the enemy, to defeat what is strong with what is weak, that is, their determination to carry out a thorough revolution. . . .

From Political Bases Among the Masses to a Popular National Defense

A strongly organized rear is always a factor of success because it is a source of political and moral stimulation and mobilization to the front, a source of supply of manpower, materials, and money for the war. As the war grows in scale, the role of the rear becomes increasingly important.

We attach the greatest importance to the role of the rear in a war. As soon as the question of armed struggle was posed, another question was also posed—that of having places where our people's armed forces could be hidden, trained, supplied, strengthened, and could rest. While revolutionary struggle was developing, we created a rear where there had been none, developed it, beginning with political bases among the masses, and now have a relatively complete system of popular national defense. We can say that in the early days when our Party made the decision to prepare for an armed struggle, we did not have a single inch of free territory; at that time, the only rear we had was our secret political bases, and the complete loyalty of the people who had become conscious of their revolutionary cause. It was from these secret political bases that our Party—our first guerrilla units were then concentrating on armed propaganda, political activities being regarded as more important than military activities—endeavored to build up secret bases for the armed struggle, and gradually came to wage partial guerrilla war and to create a free zone. Afterward, during the precious long resistance war, we had vast free zones as a strongly organized rear for the armed struggle, besides the guerrilla bases and guerrilla zones in the enemy's rear. Our rear, which was increasingly strengthened in every aspect, was the starting point from which our concentrated main-force units launched offensive operations on battlegrounds favorable to us; this rear made it possible to prepare and supply efficaciously the armed forces, in increasingly great counteroffensive campaigns. In the enemy-occupied areas, the rear was at first places where the politically conscious people hid cadres and guerrilla fighters in underground caches, sometimes for several months at a time; these places developed into guerrilla bases and guerrilla zones. In the liberation war now waged by our countrymen in the South, as a result of the political struggle of the masses combined with vigorous and extensive guerrilla warfare, liberated zones have come into being and are expanding, playing an increasingly important role in bringing about victory.

Looking back at our people's armed struggle through successive periods, we can fully grasp the strategic significance of the rear in relation to the war and draw this conclusion: from the viewpoint of the people's war, *the building-up and consolidation of the rear must be carried out in every aspect*; the political, economic, and military aspects are equally important, but most important is the political factor, the "people" factor. That is why in the last war, with the support of the people, we succeeded in building up relatively safe bases, not only in inaccessible mountainous regions, but also in the midst of the vast, open delta region, crisscrossed with rivers and studded with enemy posts.

At present, the liberated North, engaged in successful socialist construction, is our vast and strong rear; it is the base for the entire Vietnamese people's struggle for their revolutionary cause.

31. US National Security Memorandum: Policy-Planning for Counterinsurgency, 1962*
By McGeorge Bundy

Counterinsurgency was one of the less savory aspects of John F. Kennedy's vision of a revived America in the 1960s. The idea was simple: Study the classic texts on revolutionary warfare, distill the lessons imbedded in them, train American "Special Forces" in the necessary arcane skills, and send them into the jungles and rice paddies of Southeast Asia to defeat the revolutionaries and win the hearts and minds of the natives. This is the vision[1] that underlies the bureaucratic summary presented here of a global counterinsurgency program. McGeorge Bundy, brought from Harvard to serve as National Security Advisor in the White House, was an enthusiastic advocate of counterinsurgency; when counterinsurgency eventually failed in Vietnam, Bundy became at least as enthusiastic an advocate of bombing to defeat the insurgents.[2] He is now a professor of history at New York University.

June 19, 1962

TO: The Secretary of State
      The Secretary of Defense
      The Attorney General
      The Director of Central Intelligence
      The Director, United States Information Agency

SUBJECT:
Development of U.S. and Indigenous Police, Paramilitary and Military Resources

The President has approved the following statement and proposed assignments of responsibilities to various agencies as recommended by the Special Group (Counterinsurgency):

The study of U.S. and indigenous paramilitary resources . . . reflects gratifying progress in the development of an adequate U.S. capability to support both the training and active operations of indigenous paramilitary forces. Certain deficiencies, however, were clearly revealed. The deficiencies, to which all efforts and shortcomings to date are related, should be the basis upon which internal defense requirements are established for each country to be assisted.

---

*From *The Pentagon Papers* (Gravel edition), vol. 2, pp. 681–684.

1. For an analysis of the illusions of counterinsurgency, see I.F. Stone, *In a Time of Torment* (New York: Random House, 1967), Part VIII.

2. For Bundy's advocacy of stepped-up air war, see *The Pentagon Papers* (Gravel edition), vol. 3, pp. 687–691.

1. Country Internal Defense Plans

With one or two exceptions, there exist no outline plans to unify and orchestrate U.S. internal defense programs and activities in friendly countries facing a threat of subversive insurgency, or which provide strategic guidance for assisting such countries to maintain internal security. The Department of State has prepared a list identifying the countries facing a threat of subversive insurgency and will direct the formulation of outline plans for internal defense (Country Internal Defense Plans) by the Country Team in each such country which encompass the total U.S.-supported internal defense field. *These plans will include the military, police, intelligence and psychological measures comprising a well rounded internal defense plan and will be consistent with the military, economic, political and social measures constituting the overall country plan.* . . . the Special Group will keep these country internal defense plans under periodic review, and insure prompt resolution of interdepartmental problems arising in connection with their implementation.

2. Improvement of Personnel Programs of Agencies Concerned with Unconventional Warfare

A study will be made by the Armed Forces and appropriate civil agencies concerned with unconventional warfare activities of how to improve their personnel programs. Particular attention will be directed to the following:

(a) Personnel programming for officers and men, including establishment of career programs which protect the special skills and professional qualifications of personnel assigned to unconventional warfare duties.

(b) Ability to perform efficiently in foreign areas in conditions of stress and danger for prolonged periods.

(c) Moral factors such as family housing, tours of duty, hardship allowances, hazardous duty pay, special recognition such as rewards.

3. Orientation of Personnel

As part of the current effort to train more personnel in the problems confronting underdeveloped societies, both civil and military agencies of the Government will assign, where feasible and subject to the availability of funds and personnel, middle-grade and senior officers to temporary duty for orientation purposes in selecting countries experiencing internal security problems.

4. Deployment of Counterinsurgency Personnel

In order to insure a timely deployment of qualified counterinsurgency specialists to impending crisis areas, CIA and AID will take action to insure that adequate qualified personnel with paramilitary skills are available. Periodic reports of progress to achieve this objective will be submitted to the Special Group (Counterinsurgency) by CIA and AID.

5. Support of Covert Paramilitary Operations

More Special Forces personnel will be assigned to support CIA covert paramilitary operations where acute insurgency situations exist. The Department of Defense has taken steps to expedite these assignments. In addition the Department of Defense will increase its capability to fund, support, and conduct wholly or partly overt paramilitary operations under the criteria of NSAM 57 which distinguishes responsibilities of the Department of Defense and CIA:

> Where such an operation is to be wholly covert or disavowable, it may be assigned to CIA, provided that it is within the normal capabilities of the agency. Any large paramilitary operation wholly or partly covert which requires significant numbers of militarily trained personnel, amounts of military equipment which exceed normal CIA-controlled stocks and/or military experience of a kind and level peculiar to the Armed Services is properly the primary responsibility of the Department of Defense with the CIA in a supporting role.

This cooperation will be intensified and the President will be given periodic reports on the progress of these efforts.

6. Increased Use of Third Country Personnel

The Department of Defense, in collaboration with the Department of State and the Central Intelligence Agency, will undertake a study to determine on a selective basis the feasibility of the concept of the increased use of third-country personnel in paramilitary operations. Particular attention will be given to the following:

(a) The whole range of this concept from the current limited use of Thai and Filipino technicians in Laos to the creation of simply equipped regional forces for use in remote jungle, hill and desert country. Such forces would be composed of foreign volunteers supported and controlled by the U.S.

(b) The feasibility of using third-country military or paramilitary forces to operate under their own or other national auspices in crisis areas.

7. Exploitation of Minorities

In view of the success which has resulted from CIA/US Army Special Forces efforts with tribal groups in Southeast Asia, continuing efforts will be made to determine the most feasible method of achieving similar results in other critical areas. On a selective basis, CIA and the Department of Defense will make studies of specific groups where there is reason to believe there exists an exploitable minority paramilitary capability.

8. Improvement of Indigenous Intelligence Organizations

Recent experience shows that most underdeveloped countries need more efficient intelligence coordination and dissemination systems to counter subversive insurgency. Therefore, the CIA will expand its present training and support efforts to achieve needed improvements in indigenous intelligence organizations and that other U.S. agencies contribute to this CIA coordinated program.

9. Research and Development for Counterinsurgency

The Department of Defense and the Central Intelligence Agency will carry in their research and development programs a special section devoted to the requirements of counterinsurgency. The Special Group (Counterinsurgency) will follow up on this action and receive reports from time to time with regard to progress in developing modern equipment suitable to meet the requirements of counterinsurgency.

32. The Rise and Fall of "Counterinsurgency": 1961–1964*

By David G. Marr

What counterinsurgency meant in practice is dramatized in this autobiographical account by David Marr, a US Marine Corps intelligence officer during the war, and now one of the leading historians of Vietnamese history. In his considerations of Vietnamese nationalism and the development of the Vietnamese revolution, Marr reveals the flaws at the heart of the counterinsurgency "analysis." [1]

John F. Kennedy came to the White House in early 1961 on only the slimmest of pluralities. Yet he had taken the measure of the public, beyond party affiliations, and judged it to be deeply troubled by the Sputnik diplomacy of the Soviet Union and painfully eager for reassertion of the American Dream throughout the world. The myth of a monolithic international Communist conspiracy directed against a pristine Free World continued to energize millions.

Ngo Dinh Diem was Vietnamese anticommunism incarnate. He had helped repress the Indochinese Communist party in the 1930s. His elder brother had been killed by the Viet-Minh in 1945. With American assistance he had mounted a massive propaganda campaign in 1954 to persuade the Catholic minority of north

---

The Pentagon Papers (Gravel edition), vol. 5, pp. 202–210.

1. David G. Marr, *Vietnamese Anticolonialism, 1885–1925* (Berkeley: University of California Press, 1971); *Vietnamese Tradition on Trial, 1920–1945* (Berkeley: University of California Press, 1981). For a more fully developed analysis of US military strategy, see Marr's essay, "The Technological Imperative in U.S. War Strategy in Vietnam," Mary Kaldor and Asbjorn Edie, *The World Military Order* (New York: Macmillan, 1979), pp. 17–48.

and north-central Vietnam that the Holy Virgin Mary was leaving for Saigon, and that those who failed to follow her would be ruthlessly exterminated by the victorious Viet-Minh. Then, from 1956 onward, he had himself proceeded to kill or incarcerate tens of thousands of South Vietnamese as suspected Communists.

Three confrontations preoccupied President Kennedy during his first year in office: Cuba, Berlin and Laos. In Cuba, the Bay of Pigs fiasco gave the entire Kennedy Administration a touchy inferiority complex, which often led it to be more combative elsewhere. Berlin, however, could not be settled on American terms without risk of nuclear holocaust. And Laos was a tormented, confusing mudhole. The United States, it was said by mid–1961, would be lucky to stave off complete Communist victory in Laos with some sort of internationally sanctioned neutralist coalition, no matter how shaky.

This sort of thinking led the Kennedy Administration to fix its eyes more and more on South Vietnam. There, despite massive increments of U.S. military and economic assistance, Ngo Dinh Diem was again facing millions of South Vietnamese who openly denied the legitimacy of his regime. Whatever the realities of the situation, Diem clearly regarded the new National Liberation Front, founded in December 1960, as a mere appendage thrust at him by his real Communist enemies—Nikita Khrushchev, Mao Tse-tung, and Ho Chi Minh. He was very upset by evident U.S. unwillingness to attack forcefully in Laos, and he badgered every American he met with quotations from Khrushchev's January 1961 speech on Soviet support for wars of national liberation.

Diem need not have bothered. Cold War warriors like Rostow, Rusk, Taylor, Lansdale and McNamara were all on the same wavelength. As the Laos negotiations dragged on through the summer and fall of 1961, the Kennedy Administration made deadly serious plans to "draw the line" in South Vietnam. Similarly to China in the late 1940s, the United States would try to do the impossible—"save" a country from its own people.[2] Inevitably this was phrased in terms of preventing a Communist sweep of not only South Vietnam, but of all mainland Southeast Asia and perhaps the entire western Pacific.[3]

The great hope of the Kennedy Administration in Vietnam was counterinsurgency. As with most theories, this quickly came to mean different things to different people. Nevertheless, as counterinsurgency was in fact applied in South Vietnam, it bore striking resemblances to nineteenth-century French techniques going by the title of "pacification," or for that matter, earlier tactics used by Vietnamese monarchs to suppress peasant rebellions.[4]

---

2. The "saving" metaphor crops up repeatedly in documents of the period. In *The Pentagon Papers*, Gravel ed., see for example: Gen. Lansdale, II:38; Vice-President Johnson, II:59; and Rusk/McNamara, II:111.

3. Vice-President Johnson presents perhaps the most fearful picture. Gravel ed., II:57.

4. The fact that even today American policymakers adhere to the term "pacification," and that their Saigon counterparts still employ the old feudal Vietnamese equivalent, *binh-dinh*, is testimony to how little they know, or care, about Vietnamese history and popular historical memories.

From the very beginning, counterinsurgency in Vietnam emphasized military considerations over political ones, enforcement of "physical security" over more subtle questions of social change or psychological loyalties. In short, it was blatant counterrevolution over revolution, although few Americans involved at the time seemed prepared to acknowledge this.

As a young U.S. Marine Corps intelligence officer I learned these things slowly, more or less from the ground floor working upward. Sent to the Monterey Army Language School in 1961 to study Vietnamese, for example, I soon discovered that almost all of the vocabulary was military and, worse yet, Vietnamese instructors were being forced to coin entirely new words to conform with a set of technical English terms prescribed for all thirty-four languages taught at the school. Not surprisingly, when tried out in Vietnam such words received nothing but blank stares, and were promptly forgotten.

More seriously, as the only Vietnamese-speaking American among 550 marines making up the first marine helicopter squadron sent to Vietnam by President Kennedy, I was surprised to discover that my immediate superiors were only interested in classical combat intelligence, not the "new" counterinsurgency variables taught by Thompson, Trager, Lansdale, Fall, or Valeriano. My colonel simply wanted to know if "the enemy" was located in village "A" or village "B," whether he had weapons larger than 30 caliber that would force us to fly above 1,500 feet,[5] and what the weather was going to be like tomorrow. The colonel cared not a wink about the political "infrastructure," the relationship of the "insurgents" to the local population, or the social program and essential motivations of the NLF.

In August 1962 we had a key role in one of the first division-size search-and-destroy operations conducted by the Saigon army. Code-named "Binh Tay" (Pacify the West), the objective was to break up several elite NLF battalions and to scare the local populace into submission with a massive display of helicopters, fighter-bombers, armored personnel carriers and gunboats. As might have been predicted, however, the NLF saw what was happening several days in advance and quickly moved into inaccessible mangrove forests or broke into small teams, hid their weapons, and blended with the villagers for the duration of the operation. Once the aircraft, armored vehicles and trucks left the area—leaving behind smoking villages, plowed-up rice fields, and several hundred dead citizens—the NLF battalions resumed their operations with more success and public support than before. A report that I filed up the U.S. Marine chain-of-command, strongly critical of this approach to counterinsurgency, received no attention whatsoever.[6]

While my superior officers on the one hand thus showed no interest in the political subtleties of the conflict, on the other hand they did many things of a

---

5. Back in these "good old days" of U.S. intervention, the NLF had very few 50 caliber machine guns, seized from ARVN. 20 millimeter antiaircraft guns were nonexistent, not to mention larger-caliber weapons and missiles.

6. A glowing if brief account of Operation Binh Tay is contained in *Time* magazine, August 31, 1962.

political nature that played right into the hands of the NLF. For example, helicopters were sent almost every day to several fortified Catholic communities in the area, laden with a shopping list ranging from barbed wire to beer. These were militantly anti-Communist refugees from the North, in a surrounding sea of antagonized Buddhists, Hoa Hao and ethnic Cambodians, and their only reliable means of supply were our U.S. helicopters. In another incident, taking place after our squadron had been switched with a U.S. Army Squadron and sent to Da-Nang, reckless marine drivers ran over several innocent Vietnamese pedestrians. The marine colonel in command alienated not only the local townspeople, but also the Vietnamese police investigators by deciding unilaterally to spirit the offenders out of the country, on the grounds that a court case would "damage their military careers." Another colonel flew in a piano and a stereo set for his favorite Vietnamese girl friend, and provided her family with the lucrative fresh vegetable and garbage contracts for the marine base. Yet when the mayor of Da-Nang proposed that rampant prostitution be handled by concentrating it in one large, inspected whorehouse for Americans, the colonels all protested that the merest whiff in U.S. Capitol corridors of such an arrangement would cost them their careers. While in retrospect each of these incidents may appear minor, particularly when compared with American-perpetrated outrages after 1965, it is important to see how things really got started, and why many ordinary Vietnamese had reason to hate the United States long before the first combat battalions set foot on their soil.

Reassigned to the U.S. Pacific command headquarters in Hawaii in mid–1963, it was a revelation for me to discover that not only the colonels, but also generals and admirals were fundamentally bored by the political complexities of Vietnam. After the overthrow of Ngo Dinh Diem, in November 1963, I thought it particularly important to try to brief them on all the changes taking place, on each of the new faces showing up. Soon my feelings were hurt, however, when they cut my regular political analysis in half, a mere five minutes out of a one-hour briefing. Whenever they had no choice but to mention the name of a Vietnamese personality, they would resort to nicknames such as "Big" and "Little" Minh, the "Dragon Lady" (Madame Nhu), and "Colonel Yankee."[7]

Later in a major marine training exercise on Molokai Island, I tried to incorporate some rudimentary political elements into a rather standard intelligence scenario. But the commander of the attacking blue forces, the "good guys" of the operation, simply ignored those aspects and marched his forces from one ridgeline to the next in classic Korean War fashion. Back at headquarters in Honolulu, I got into an intense argument with my intelligence contemporaries over which had to come first in counterinsurgency, physical security of the populace against "guer-

---

7. The latter refers to Colonel Nguyen Van Y, head of Saigon's "Central Intelligence Organization"—an apparatus originally forced on Diem by the United States to try to unify intelligence processing and interpretation. Surprisingly, the "Yankee" nickname even crops up in a 1961 cable from Ambassador Durbrow. Gravel ed., II:28.

rilla terrorism," or fundamental political and social changes that would make the government legitimate and security a more manageable problem.

When I left the Marine Corps in June 1964 it was already obvious that enforcement of physical security—convenient rhetoric for violent repression—had become the overwhelming theme in counterinsurgency. At the time it seemed to me a clear case of stupidity, due to our lack of knowledge of the particular historical situation in Vietnam, and perhaps too our more general insensitivity toward the problems of nonwhite peoples in the world. Since then I have come to the realization that neither knowledge nor more sensitivity would have changed U.S. policy much, assuming that our overall strategic objective of defeating communism in Vietnam remained the same.

Grim anticommunism, aimed at combating a supposedly grim, monolithic communism, made any serious, high-level consideration of the history, culture and political dynamics of Vietnam essentially irrelevant. If the *real* enemies were in Moscow and Peking, and the local people were mere pawns in a giant power play, then what did it matter that local Communists had led the mass victorious anticolonial struggle in Vietnam, or that the NLF was more popular than the Saigon regime? To a certain extent, American policymakers knew, or at least sensed, that they were working from a position of real political weakness in South Vietnam. Yet they went ahead anyway, and developed all sorts of financial, military and technocratic gimmicks to try to compensate. When it was perceived, in late 1964 or early 1965, that all these measures had failed, it became necessary to take more drastic steps that had been implicit all along: bombing the North and throwing in U.S. combat troops. Meanwhile, many of the practices developed in the 1961–1964 period continued, but with a ruthlessness that made a mockery of any political program put forth by either the U.S. or Saigon. The original Eisenhower phrase, "winning hearts and minds," had been reduced in the field to an acronym—WHAM—and ironically this brought out the true content of counterinsurgency.

The complete ascendancy of repressive military tactics and thinking during the counterinsurgency phase had many other implications. First of all, it almost always led to sublime overconfidence. General Lansdale, who had helped establish Diem and might have known how frail the system really was, wrote policy papers for President Kennedy in early 1961 that exuded optimism and recommended simply a little more muscle for the Saigon army (ARVN) and some minor bureaucratic reshuffling (Gravel edition, II: 23–27, 52–53). Since NLF strength was usually viewed in terms of a certain number of soldiers and weapons, not as a mass revolutionary movement, it is hardly surprising that U.S. military contingency planners consistently underestimated the number of troops and amounts of money needed to defeat the enemy.[8]

Paradoxically, each new increment of American military technology in Viet-

---

8. See for example the 1961 JCS estimates whereby 40,000 U.S. troops would be sufficient to "clean up" the Viet-Cong, or 205,000 to handle the situation if both the DRV *and* China entered the conflict too. Gravel ed., II: 108–109.

nam represented an unwitting admission of counterinsurgency failure, and indeed further served to nail the lid on the coffin. Our glistening helicopter squadrons, such sources of pride and expectation among the generals, were a prime example. "The sky is a highway without roadblocks," rhapsodized Senator Henry Jackson in 1963 after careful briefings from his Pentagon cronies. "The helicopter," he continued, "frees the government forces from dependence on the poor road system and the canals which are the usual arteries of communication."[9] However, such mobility bore a very serious, if hidden price tag. Since about 80 percent of the people of Vietnam happened to live along those "usual arteries," and since the helicopter could never hope to tie in all or most of the villages on a day-to-day basis, increased air travel tended inevitably to draw the Saigon regime ever further away from the humdrum realities of creating political and social credibility at the local level. As the American crews and ARVN soldiers floated blithely across the monsoon clouds, swooping down occasionally to wreak destruction or supply an isolated blockhouse, the NLF went ahead patiently to expand its organization along the roads and canals, gradually surrounding the district and provincial towns. When it finally became evident to U.S. military planners that helicopters were not stopping the enemy, it was natural they would miss or ignore the real reasons and choose instead to escalate the technology with fighter-bombers, gunships, and— eventually—B–52s, that penultimate weapon of mass indiscriminate terror.

But generals were not the only ones subject to grave miscalculation. Dean Rusk and Robert McNamara thought that a combination of Vietnamese draft reform, stepped up mobilization and streamlining of the ARVN command structure would be enough to turn the tide.[10] Sir Robert Thompson proposed to combine "clear and hold" operations with the most stringent police measures, out of which grew the ambitious and abortive strategic hamlet program (Gravel ed., II: 139–140).[11] Even Roger Hilsman, who perhaps spoke up more often than most on the NLF as a political rather than military threat, still accepted the argument that physical security was an essential prerequisite to his pet "civic action" programs (Gravel ed., II: 142).

Behind such security fixations lay several *a priori* judgments on the Vietnamese people and Vietnamese society. It was usually assumed, for example, that the Vietnamese peasants worried only about where their next bowl of rice was coming from. They had little interest in affairs beyond their home village. Their ideal was to be "left alone." Unlike more advanced Westerners, it was said, Vietnamese peasants found little meaning or value in political ideology, except perhaps some archaic Confucian maxims. Those accepting Communist ideology had been duped or coerced, or perhaps attracted by promises of bigger rice bowls. In short, with neither the desire nor capability for profound national identifications, the peasants

---

9. Senator Henry Jackson, "A Key to Victory in Vietnam," *Army*, March 1963, p.62.

10. "Memorandum for the President," November 11, 1961. Gravel ed., II:115.

11. II:139–140. Thompson's subordinate, Denis Duncanson, has written the most comprehensive defense of these repressive tactics, in *Government and Revolution in Vietnam* (Oxford, 1968).

were mere "reeds in the wind," and would lean whichever way the guns were pointed. It thus followed that the outside elite with the best techniques of organized violence would inevitably triumph. From physical security all else flowed.

Needless to say, the French colonials had harbored such patronizing, racist ideas about the Vietnamese peasantry long before American counterinsurgency specialists picked them up. At Dien Bien Phu and scores of lesser-known battlefields, the French paid with their lives for their prejudices, simply refusing to believe that hundreds of thousands of Vietnamese peasants would fight and die, willingly, for a cause beyond themselves. American specialists like Lansdale, Trager and Pike never got this message, or if they did, they blanked it out in favor of a neater, less disturbing Communist/anti-Communist dynamic.[12]

In somewhat similar fashion, *all* Vietnamese, including the educated elites, were expected by American policymakers to respond in fairly obvious fashion to U.S. applications of pleasure or pain. From Walt Rostow in Washington, with his programs of graduated terror against Hanoi, to U.S. privates in the field, tossing chewing gum to scurrying Vietnamese children, Pavlovian carrot-and-stick reasoning held complete sway.[13] Once in a while even the canine aspect of Pavlov's model peeked through, as when Rostow recommended that we tell Moscow to "use its influence with Ho Chi Minh to call his dogs off, mind his business, and feed his people."[14]

When Vietnamese failed to salivate on schedule, the inevitable U.S. reaction was to escalate the increments of pleasure and pain. Sometimes our own Saigon clients were the least predictable, as in August 1963 when Diem and his brother Nhu ignored intense American pressures and proceeded to raid the Buddhist pagodas.[15] In the end, Diem and Nhu became so angry and cynical about American attitudes and activities that they put out vague feelers to Ho Chi Minh and the NLF. This was a deadly mistake on their part, however, since we only valued them for their militant antipathy to the Communists. The United States ended up having the old dogs killed and picking some new ones to work on.

The entire relationship between U.S. master and Vietnamese client deserves

---

12. Douglas Pike, *Viet-Cong, the Organization and Techniques of the National Liberation Front of South Vietnam* (MIT Press, 1966). Edward G. Lansdale, *In the Midst of Wars* (Harper and Row, 1972).

13. In the period 1961–1964, see especially the famous Staley Report, where the overall objective is to "surpass the critical threshold of the enemy resistance" (Gravel ed., II:63). The authors of the Pentagon Papers are no less guilty of such reasoning, as when on the basis of 1961–1967 experiences they conclude that there is a need for more "stick" and less "carrot" with the Saigon regime (Gravel ed., II:415). In late 1962 I traveled from village to village with U.S. Special Forces "civic action" teams and watched them gain public attention by passing out thousands of pieces of hard candy to children. The candy had been donated in big tins by an American manufacturer.

14. See also the authors of the Pentagon Papers using such images, as when they state that the United States forced General Nguyen Chanh Thi to get "back on his leash before it was too late" (Gravel ed., II:99).

15. The authors of the Pentagon Papers label this an "impudent" slap in the face to the United States. Gravel ed., II:203.

some exploration here, since it was an integral part of each counterinsurgency scheme in the period 1961–1964, and since the basic arrangement existing today really solidified by no later than June 1965. American military and government personnel, particularly those with extensive field experience in Vietnam, have often vehemently denied the whole master-client relationship, citing numerous factual examples where South Vietnamese "counterparts" ignored or even rejected their "advice." On the other hand, most critics of U.S. involvement have developed an image whereby an all-powerful American puppeteer simply pulled the strings on an otherwise inert Saigon puppet. And certain events can be cited to buttress this position too—for example, the overthrow of Diem, the dumping of General Duong Van Minh three months later, and the strong anticoup protection given Nguyen Cao Ky and Nguyen Van Thieu after mid–1965.

However, neither position is completely accurate. First of all, the U.S.-Saigon relationship changed perceptibly over time. In 1954–1956 the U.S. was very deeply involved in selecting Diem, pushing him ahead of all French candidates, and then giving him the necessary money, guns and political protection to crush each opposition element, one by one. During the next four years, nevertheless, the United States stepped back from day-to-day management and allowed Diem to handle matters in more or less his own way, confident of course that his staunch anticommunism was the best servant of our interests.

But by late 1961 Diem's position, and that of the entire Saigon regime, was clearly eroding away. President Kennedy reacted by sending in not only the armed U.S. helicopter squadrons, mentioned previously, but also modern prop-jet transports, logistical support groups, and numerous overt and covert intelligence teams. Equally significant was the shift in missions for U.S. advisory elements already in place. From late 1961 onward, there was to be "U.S. participation in the direction and control of GVN military operations," and on the civilian side U.S. personnel were briefed for "insertion into the Governmental machinery of South Viet-Nam."[16] Although it was to be several years before such arrangements were put in writing with the Saigon regime, in fact a parallel U.S. hierarchy had been established and came to assume progressively more power as the political and military situation continued to deteriorate inside South Vietnam.

An interesting case of how the system developed and operated is in intelligence and counterintelligence. By 1961 American officials could see that the South Vietnamese regime was not getting reliable information at village and district levels. And since there was a jumble of separate intelligence agencies, sometimes conflicting with each other, what little information the regime did acquire was not being handled properly. In Quang Tri province, for example, I found that while the seven district chiefs passed their data and captured NLF suspects to the Secret Police (Cong An), the latter refused to let the military Sector Commander's S–2 (intelligence officer) see any of it or interrogate prisoners. The Secret Police also kept a tight hold over their personality files, which were heavy on former Viet-Minh

---

16. "Memorandum for the President," November 11, 1961. Gravel ed., II:114.

activists. However—and this is the important part—the Secret Police *did* grudg-
ingly allow the American provincial adviser the access that they denied to the
Sector Commander, so that the American served increasingly as an informed intermediary.

Meanwhile, the regular ARVN units in Quang Tri were out of both of these
channels entirely, sending their scant information back to First Division headquarters in Hue. This problem was "solved" by having the U.S. advisers assigned to
these regular army echelons exchange data with the U.S. provincial adviser. Not
surprisingly, the latter individual became increasingly powerful in Quang Tri, especially since he also had a special "slush-fund" to pay off his own agents and to
parcel out to his "counterpart" on an achievement basis.

Beyond the three networks mentioned above, there was also a Vietnamese
"DMZ Security" group, which sent intelligence directly to the Presidential Palace
in Saigon. And there was an apparatus called SMIAT (Special Military Intelligence
Advisory Team), completely controlled by Americans, which was trying to build
a major clandestine agent net across the border into Laos and North Vietnam. All
five elements, however, relied heavily on a relatively small number of paid informants, often the same people who had lived well off the French in a similar capacity.

That admittedly cursory analysis I made of the intelligence situation in all of
central Vietnam in 1962–1963 led me to some unsettling conclusions about the
various Vietnamese involved, and, beyond that, their apparent alienation from the
bulk of the populace.[17] From the Pentagon Papers it is evident that Americans at
much higher levels in both Saigon and Washington saw essentially the same things,
in other bureaus and ministries as well as intelligence. Yet their responses were
always technocratic, half-baked, as if they were trying to avoid probing too far for
fear the whole house of cards might come tumbling down.

In intelligence, for example again, they moved on the one hand to pressure
Diem to reorganize and consolidate the Vietnamese "intelligence community," although he still saw solid anticoup benefits in keeping it divided. On the other hand,
the United States steadily expanded its own autonomous network in Vietnam, as a
bypass mechanism and a powerful means of manipulation. After the army's overthrow of Diem, U.S. knowledge of the thoughts and activities of Saigon's top
leadership increased considerably, since the military was the one group we had
infiltrated early, had plenty of files on, and could easily surround with "advisers"
on a day-to-day basis. As might be expected, nevertheless, such developments
tended to startle, to antagonize, many Vietnamese officers (usually under the rank
of colonel) who had been shielded from the true master-client relationship during
the Diem period. Some of them withdrew from the army in disgust. Others stayed
on, but showed their displeasure at American manipulation so much that they were
given "bad marks" and confined to paper-pushing jobs in supply, transportation,

---

17. In all fairness I should state here that I had not yet come to question the right of the United
States to be in Vietnam, only the seemingly shoddy way we were doing things. It wasn't until early
1966 that I concluded we had no business there at all.

engineering and the like.[18] There were always other officers to take their places, however, men who *knew* they were servants of the Americans, and, for one reason or another, were ready to make a good thing of it.

Thus it was that, not only in intelligence, but in all other sensitive fields, a crew of sycophants, money-grubbers, and psychopaths moved to the fore. Essentially serving as power-brokers, they found endless ways both to oppress their fellow countrymen and to delude their American masters. General Nguyen Khanh was the epitome of this new "leadership." For twelve months after derailing General Minh in January 1964, he held center stage in Saigon, posturing, shifting ground, bluffing Ambassador Taylor, trying to neutralize his younger rivals, preaching militant anticolonialism for public consumption while working feverishly behind the scenes for ever-deeper U.S. involvement. By early 1965 the United States was "in" as never before, but General Khanh had incurred the wrath of Ambassador Taylor to such a degree that he must have known his days were numbered.[19] Unlike the Diem/Lodge situation, however, General Khanh had taken the necessary personal precautions. Today he lives a comfortable émigré existence in Paris.

General Khanh also demonstrates in many ways why these cynical, corrupt people were clients or servants of the United States, but not really "puppets." For example, Khanh played upon deep American fears of a "neutralist solution" to discredit the Duong Van Minh leadership group and gain support for his coup.[20] Once in power, Khanh kept stalling on his commitments to the United States to mobilize the army and populace against the "Viet Cong threat," perhaps knowing it was futile. Instead, he pushed constantly for U.S. bombing of the North, U.S. ground troops in the South, and a commitment to him as dictator-president of the country. Ironically, the more the United States committed itself to Vietnam, the less reason there was for Khanh or any of his successors to think about "internal reform," much less social revolution.[21]

---

18. During this period American "advisers" regularly sent in evaluations of their counterparts. These were combined with meticulous reports from supervisory personnel at bases in the United States where almost all South Vietnamese officers underwent training, and with gossip from paid agents, to make up an ever-expanding U.S. intelligence personality file. If a Vietnamese officer was listed as "friendly," "cooperative," "eager to learn," "competent in English," he had a bright future. However, if he was "reserved," "suspicious," "reluctant to accept advice," he was in for trouble.

19. A serious student of this whole master-client symbiosis could begin with the relationship between Taylor and Khanh over time. Taylor was outfoxed so often that it became something of a joke in top Saigon circles. But when Taylor came to realize this, of course he had the last word.

20. There is far more evidence than is presented in the Pentagon Papers to indicate that the United States was very worried about President de Gaulle's neutralization proposals and the effects they might be having on the Saigon regime. David Marr, "Background on Coup in South Vietnam, 30 Jan. 1964," unpublished manuscript. David Marr, "The Political Crisis in Viet-Nam: 1963–1964," also unpublished. General Khanh, in a recent interview, has claimed that his American adviser, Colonel Jasper Wilson, helped him take over. Pacific News Service press release, February 1972.

21. The Pentagon Papers demonstrate that whereas U.S. policymakers occasionally perceived this dilemma, they had no real answers to it. Gravel ed., II:96, 202–203, 280–281, 309, 330–332, 336, 345.

Without question, it was the very *weakness* of the combined U.S.-Saigon position that gave Khanh, Ky, Thieu, Khiem, and all the others a significant degree of leverage with their masters. Once these men were convinced that U.S. power and prestige was irrevocably committed, they could let the energetic, grim-faced Americans worry about holding off the Communists, while they spent most of their time trying to consolidate personal and clique power and privilege. Whenever the Americans protested about the Vietnamese not "carrying their share of the burden," they could make some more promises and reshuffle a few commanders or ministers. If this wasn't enough, they might strike a pained anticolonialist posture and hint at negotiations with the enemy (both Khanh and Ky did this)—although this was always a risky last resort.

The United States could and did respond to these tactics several times by dumping one man or one clique. But the overall situation was always so tenuous that we could never risk throwing out the entire crew. Since our clients understood this fully as well as we did, they eventually made tacit arrangements among themselves to slow down the political attrition, "divide up the territory," and share the spoils. Being highly ambitious men, this has not always worked.[22] Nevertheless, the continuity since June 1965, when General Ky took over as premier, has been striking. And it is likely to continue for as long as the United States remains committed to killing Vietnamese in order to save them. But not a day longer.

33. The Buddhist Crisis of 1963: The View from Washington*

From *The Pentagon Papers*

Although Buddhism was the dominant religion of Vietnam, it coexisted, sometimes uneasily, with other creeds.[1] The leaders of Roman Catholicism, a foreign import, took on the task of eradicating "heathen error." However, French colonial rule in practice was relatively tolerant of indigenous belief systems; the French were mainly interested in the economic exploitation of their Indochinese colonies.[2] But

---

22. One of the best examples is the continuing cutthroat competition at the highest levels for control of the illicit drug traffic. See Alfred McCoy, *The Politics of Heroin in Southeast Asia*, Harper and Row, 1972. [See Reading 20 for an excerpt from this book.—eds.]

*From *The Pentagon Papers* (Gravel edition), II, pp. 225–228, 232–236.

1. David Marr, *Vietnamese Anticolonialism, 1885–1925* (Berkeley, University of California Press, 1971) pp. 20–21; Nguyen Khac Vien, *Tradition and Revolution in Vietnam* (Berkeley: Indochina Resource Center, 1974), pp. 27–29.

2. John F. Cady, *The Roots of French Imperialism in Eastern Asia* (Ithaca: Cornell University Press, 1954), pp. 294–295.

when, after the Geneva Conference of 1954, a Vietnamese Roman Catholic assumed leadership in Saigon, he had few local constituents other than the Vietnamese Catholics, many of whom came south under the regroupment procedures in the Geneva Accords (Readings 16, 24). Perhaps such a regime was bound to be rejected by the Buddhist majority, but available documentation suggests that Ngo Dinh Diem's government initiated the clashes. Perhaps even more revealing is the fact that the Buddhist crisis took US authorities by surprise. This was yet another instance of American self-deception, stemming from the US practice of creating in countries like Vietnam a facade of having trusty and affable allies ruling over contented populations. Events of the summer and fall of 1963 were to puncture such illusions.

The Crisis Erupts

The incident in Hue on May 8, 1963, that precipitated what came to be called the Buddhist crisis, and that started the chain of events that ultimately led to the overthrow of the Diem regime and the murder of the Ngo brothers, happened both inadvertently and unexpectedly. No one then foresaw that it would generate a national opposition movement capable of rallying virtually all non-communist dissidence in South Vietnam. More importantly, no one then appreciated the degree of alienation of Vietnam's people from their government, nor the extent of the political decay within the regime, a regime no longer capable of coping with popular discontent.

The religious origins of the incident are traceable to the massive flight of Catholic refugees from North Vietnam after the French defeat in 1954. An estimated one million Catholics fled the North and resettled in the South. Diem, animated, no doubt, by religious as well as humanitarian sympathy, and with an eye to recruiting political support from his coreligionists, accorded these Catholic refugees preferential treatment in land redistribution, relief and assistance, commercial and export-import licenses, government employment, and other GVN largess. Because Diem could rely on their loyalty, they came to fill almost all important civilian and military positions. As an institution, the Catholic Church enjoyed a special legal status. The Catholic primate, Ngo Dinh Thuc, was Diem's brother and advisor. But prior to 1962, there had been no outright discrimination against Buddhists. However, among South Vietnam's 3–4 million practicing Buddhists and the 80% of the population who were nominal Buddhists, the regime's favoritism, authoritarianism, and discrimination created a smoldering resentment.

In April 1963, the government ordered provincial officials to enforce a long-standing but generally ignored ban on the public display of religious flags. The order came just after the officially encouraged celebrations in Hue commemorating the 25th anniversary of the ordination of Ngo Dinh Thuc, the Archbishop of Hue, during which Papal flags had been prominently flown. The order also came, as it happened, just prior to Buddha's birthday (May 8)—a major Buddhist festival. Hue, an old provincial capital of Vietnam, was the only real center of Buddhist learning and scholarship in Vietnam and its university had long been a center of left-wing dissidence. Not surprisingly, then, the Buddhists in Hue defiantly flew their flags in spite of the order and, when the local administration appeared to have backed down on the ban, were emboldened to hold a previously scheduled mass meeting on May 8 to commemorate Buddha's birthday. Seeing the demonstration as a challenge to family prestige (Hue was also the capital of the political fief of another Diem brother, Ngo Dinh Can) and to government authority, local officials tried to disperse the crowds. When preliminary efforts produced no results, the Catholic deputy province chief ordered his troops to fire. In the ensuing melee, nine persons were killed, including some children, and fourteen were injured. Armored vehicles allegedly crushed some of the victims. The Diem government subsequently put out a story that a Viet Cong agent had thrown a grenade into the crowd and that the victims had been crushed in a stampede. It steadfastly refused to admit responsibility even when neutral observers produced films showing government troops firing on the crowd.

Diem's mandarin character would not permit him to handle this crisis with the kind of flexibility and finesse it required. He was incapable of publicly acknowledging responsibility for the tragedy and seeking to conciliate the angry Buddhists. He was convinced that such a public loss of face would undermine his authority to rule, oblivious to the fact that no modern ruler can long ignore massive popular disaffection whatever his own personal virtues may be. So the government clung tenaciously to its version of what had occurred.

The following day in Hue over 10,000 people demonstrated in protest of the killings. It was the first of the long series of protest activities with which the Buddhists were to pressure the regime in the next four months. The Buddhists rapidly organized themselves, and on May 10, a manifesto of the Buddhist clergy was transmitted to the government demanding freedom to fly their flag, legal equality with the Catholic Church, an end of arrests and freedom to practice their beliefs, and indemnification of the victims of the May 8th incident with punishment for its perpetrators. These five demands were officially presented to President Diem on May 15, and the Buddhists held their first press conference after the meeting. Publicized hunger strikes and meetings continued throughout May, but Diem continued to drag his feet on placating the dissenters or settling issues. On May 30, about 350 Buddhist monks demonstrated in front of the National Assembly in Saigon, and a 48-hour hunger strike was announced. On June 3, a demonstration in Hue was broken up with tear gas and several people were burned, prompting charges that the troops had used mustard gas. On June 4, the government announced the appointment of an interministerial committee headed by Vice President Tho to resolve the religious issue, but by this time such gestures were probably too late. Large portions of the urban population had rallied to the Buddhist protest, recognizing in it the beginnings of genuine political opposition to Diem. On June 8, Mme. Nhu exacerbated the problem by announcing that the Buddhists were infiltrated by communists.

Throughout the early days of the crisis, the U.S. press had closely covered the events and brought them to the attention of the world. On June 11, the press was tipped off to be at a downtown intersection at noon. Expecting another protest demonstration, they were horrified to witness the first burning suicide by a Buddhist monk. Thich Quang Duc's fiery death shocked the world and electrified South Vietnam.

Negotiations had been taking place between Vice President Tho's committee and the Buddhists since June 5, with considerable acrimonious public questioning of good faith by both sides. After the suicide, the U.S. intensified its already considerable pressure on the government to mollify the Buddhists, and to bring the deteriorating political situation under control. Finally, on June 16, a joint GVN-Buddhist communique was released outlining the elements of a settlement, but affixing no responsibility for the May 8 incident. Violent suppression by the GVN of rioting the next day, however, abrogated the spirit of the agreement. The Nhus, for their part, immediately undertook to sabotage the agreement by secretly calling on the GVN-sponsored youth organizations to denounce it. By late June, it was apparent that the agreement was not meant as a genuine gesture of conciliation by Diem, but was only an effort to appease the U.S. and paper over a steadily widening fissure in internal politics.

The evident lack of faith on the part of the government in the June 16 agreement discredited the conciliatory policy of moderation that the older Buddhist leadership had followed until that time. In late June, leadership of the Buddhist movement passed to a younger, more radical set of monks, with more far-reaching political objectives. They made intelligent and skillful political use of a rising tide of popular support. Carefully planned mass meetings and demonstrations were accompanied with an aggressive press campaign of opposition to the regime. Seizing on the importance of American news media, they cultivated U.S. newsmen, tipped them off to demonstrations and rallies, and carefully timed their activities to get maximum press coverage. Not surprisingly, the Ngo family reacted with ever more severe suppression to the Buddhist activists, and with acrimonious criticism and even threats to the American newsmen. . . .

Within the regime, Nhu and his wife were severely criticizing Diem for caving in under Buddhist pressure. Mme. Nhu publicly ridiculed the Buddhist suicide as a "barbecue," accused the Buddhist leaders of being infiltrated with communists, and construed the protest movement as Viet Cong inspired. Both Nhu and his wife worked publicly and privately to undermine Diem's feeble efforts at compromise with the Buddhists, and rumors that Nhu was considering a coup against his brother began to circulate in July.

A U.S. Special National Intelligence Estimate on July 10 concluded with the perceptive prediction that if the Diem regime did nothing to implement the June 16 agreement and to appease the Buddhists, the likelihood of a summer of demonstrations was great, with the strong possibility of a non-communist coup attempt. By mid-August, a week before Nhu launched general raids on Buddhist pagodas in Saigon and elsewhere, the CIA had begun to note malaise in the bureaucracy and the army:

Since the Buddhist dispute with the Diem government erupted on 8 May, there have been a series of reports indicating not only intensified plotting and grumbling among Diem's traditional non-Communist critics, but renewed restiveness and growing disaffection in official civilian and military circles over Diem's handling of the dispute.

This estimate went on to detail numerous rumors of coup plots in existence since at least late June. But Nhu, in a bold move designed to frighten coup plotters, and to throw them off guard, had called in the senior generals on July 11, reprimanded them for not having taken action to squelch revolt, and questioned their loyalty to the regime. Nhu's move seemed to have temporarily set back all plans for an overthrow. CIA also reported rumors that Nhu himself was planning a "false coup" to draw out and then crush the Buddhists.

In August, Buddhist militancy reached new intensity; monks burned themselves to death on the 5th, 15th, and 18th. The taut political atmosphere in Saigon in mid-August should have suggested to U.S. observers that a showdown was on the way. When the showdown came, however, in the August 21 raids on the pagodas, the U.S. mission was apparently caught almost completely off guard. . . .

The Pagoda Raids and Repercussions

Shortly after midnight on August 21, six days after [Ambassador Frederick] Nolting's frustrated departure, Nhu, shattering any remaining illusions about the GVN's conciliatory approach to the Buddhists, and betraying Diem's parting pledge to Nolting, staged a general assault on Buddhist pagodas. In Saigon, Hue, and other coastal cities, the regime's private shock troops—the U.S.-trained Special Forces—and the combat police invaded the pagodas and arrested hundreds of Buddhist monks, effectively destroying an American policy and marking the beginning of the end of the Diem regime.

On August 18, ten senior generals had met and decided that they would ask Diem for a declaration of martial law to permit them to return Buddhist monks from outside Saigon to their own provinces and pagodas, hopefully reducing tensions in the capital. Among those in attendance at the meeting were General Ton That Dinh, military governor of Saigon and commander of III Corps surrounding it, and General Huynh Van Cao, IV Corps commander, both of whom owed their positions to their loyalty to the regime. Either or both of them probably reported the outcome of this meeting to Diem and Nhu.

In any case, Nhu had decided to eliminate the Buddhist opposition, and to confront the U.S. with a fait accompli on [new U.S. Ambassador Henry Cabot] Lodge's arrival; he assumed the U.S. would protestingly acquiesce, as it always had in the past. On the afternoon of the 20th, Nhu met with a small group of generals, including Don, Khiem, and Dinh who presented the martial law proposal to Diem. At a meeting later that evening, Diem acquiesced in the generals' plan and at midnight the decree was published under the signature of General Don, Chief of the Joint General Staff. Meanwhile, unbeknown to the generals, Nhu had already alerted Colonel Tung's Special Forces and the combat police. Once the facade of martial law was in place, so the army would be blamed for the raids, Nhu gave the word and the crackdown began. To further implicate the army, some of the combat police wore paratroop uniforms. Pagodas were ransacked in all the major South Vietnamese cities, and over 1400 Buddhists, primarily monks, were arrested. In the raid on Xa Loi pagoda in Saigon about thirty monks were wounded or injured, and several were subsequently listed as missing; exact casualties were never established. Diem had approved the martial law decree without consulting his cabinet, but it was never established whether he knew of and approved Nhu's plans for the pagoda raids. Significantly, he never subsequently sought to dissociate himself from Nhu or the raids. . . .

In planning the raids, Nhu had been extremely careful not to have word leak to the U.S. mission (although the Buddhists and the U.S. press corps had been tipped off by their own informants). On the morning after the attack, Richardson, the CIA chief and the senior American civilian in Saigon, emphatically denied to [*New York Times* reporter David] Halberstam any foreknowledge of the plan. To further isolate the U.S. from an accurate assessment during the operations, Nhu had the telephone lines to the Embassy and the homes of all senior U.S. personnel cut shortly after the raids got under way. His efforts had the desired effect. It was several days before the U.S. mission in Saigon and officials in Washington could piece together what happened. In Washington, Harriman and Michael Forrestal, a member of McGeorge Bundy's staff at the White House, drafted a stiff public statement that was released by the State Department at 9:30 the following morning. It deplored the raids as "a direct violation by the Vietnamese Government of assurances that it was pursuing a policy of reconciliation with the Buddhists." But the first U.S. intelligence reports, based on information from Nhu, accepted army responsibility for the raids, and treated their coincidence with the martial law decree as, in effect, a military coup. In an August 21 memorandum for the Secretary of Defense, the Director of DIA, General Carroll, wrote, "Although the military moves are based on an alleged presidential proclamation, the military leaders have, in effect, assumed full control."

When the raids occurred, Lodge, Nolting, and Roger Hilsman, the Assistant Secretary of State for the Far East, had been conferring in Honolulu. Lodge was immediately instructed to proceed to Saigon. After a brief stop in Tokyo, Lodge touched down in Saigon at 9:30 P.M. on August 22, in an atmosphere charged with tension and official U.S. confusion. Awaiting him was a cable from Hilsman asking for a clarification of the situation. Had the military taken over and retained Diem as a figurehead; had Diem strengthened his own position by calling in the military; or were the Nhus really calling the shots? Within twenty-four hours, Lodge had sent a preliminary reply: there had been no coup, but there seemed also to be no diminution in the roles of the Nhus, although the power roles within the regime were unclear.

That same day, the first military feelers had been put out from the Vietnamese generals to determine what the U.S. reaction would be to a military coup. General

Don, the commander of the armed forces under the martial law decree, had a long, rambling conversation with a CAS officer. He first outlined the true role the army had played in the events of August 20–21 and then inquired why the U.S. had blamed the army for the raids on the pagodas:

General Don has heard personally that the military is being blamed by Vietnamese public for the attack on the pagodas. He said that the US Govt is at fault for this misconception because VOA announced that the military took action against the pagodas. Don queried why VOA did not admit that Colonel Tung's Special Forces and the Police carried out the action. Don believes this would help the military at this point. Don stated that the USA should now make its position known.

In a conversation the same day with Rufus Phillips of USOM, General Kim, deputy to General Don, bitterly attacked Nhu, charging him with responsibility for the raids, and deploring his dominant role in the government. He said that unless the popular impression that the army was responsible for the raids were corrected, the army would be handicapped in its fight against the VC. He stated that a firm U.S. stand for the removal of the Nhus would unify the army and permit it to act against them. These two direct and obviously reinforcing requests for U.S. support for military action aimed at Nhu's ouster marked the formal beginning of the U.S. involvement in the protracted plotting against the Diem regime. Two senior civilians in the government, Diem's chef de cabinet, Vo Van Hai, and Secretary of State, Nguyen Dinh Thuan, were simultaneously telling U.S. contacts that Nhu's elimination from the government was vital and that the U.S. should take a strong stand against him.

On August 24, Lodge cabled his appraisal of the situation to Washington, based on these conversations. "Nhu," he reported, "probably with full support of Diem, had a large hand in planning of action against Buddhists, if he did not fully mastermind it. His influence has also been significantly increased." Nhu had simply taken advantage of the concern of certain generals, possibly not fully informing the regular army of the planned action. Nonetheless, none of the important Saigon area troop commanders (Don, Dinh, and Tung) were presently disaffected with the regime. Furthermore, absence of clear-cut military leadership and troop strength in Saigon for a move against the Nhus would make U.S. support of such an action a "shot in the dark."

For the State Department, the problem of clarifying the public record about the raids and affixing responsibility for them had become acute by August 24. The press reports emanating from Saigon had from the outset blamed Nhu for the raids, but VOA, with a large audience in Vietnam, continued to report the official U.S. position that the army was culpable. The accumulating evidence against Nhu and the likelihood of severe damage to army morale if VOA did not broadcast a clarification seemed to call for retractions.

The second issue for Washington was Nhu. The generals had asked, in effect, for a green light to move against him, but Lodge had cautioned against it. Hilsman reports that as he, Harriman, Forrestal, and Ball deliberated over the drafting of a reply on that Saturday morning, the statement of Thuan to Phillips that "under no circumstance should the United States acquiesce in what the Nhus had done," was given great weight. Admiral Felt telephoned Washington from CINCPAC to support a strong U.S. stand against the Nhus. The unanswered question, of course, was whether the Nhus could be removed without also sacrificing Diem, and if not, whether the resulting political instability would not have an even more detrimental effect on the war effort than maintaining Diem.

The August 24 cable of instructions to Lodge resulting from these deliberations outlined an important, and subsequently controversial, new policy approach for the U.S. in South Vietnam. Its opening paragraphs crisply set forth the new American view:

It is now clear that whether military proposed martial law or whether Nhu tricked them into it, Nhu took advantage of its imposition to smash pagodas with police and Tung's Special Forces loyal to him thus placing onus on military in eyes of world and Vietnamese people. Also clear that Nhu has maneuvered himself into commanding position.

US Government cannot tolerate situation in which power lies in Nhu's hands. Diem must be given chance to rid himself of Nhu and his coterie and replace them with best military and political personalities available.

If, in spite of all your efforts, Diem remains obdurate and refuses, then we must face the possibility that Diem himself cannot be preserved.

Lodge was instructed to tell the GVN the U.S. could not accept the actions against the Buddhists and that prompt dramatic steps to redress the situation must be taken. The key military leaders were to be privately informed that,

. . . US would find it impossible to continue support GVN militarily and economically unless above steps are taken immediately which we recognize requires removal of Nhus from the scene. We wish give Diem reasonable opportunity to remove Nhus, but if he remains obdurate, then we are prepared to accept the obvious implication that we can no longer support Diem. You may also tell appropriate military commanders we will give them direct support in any interim period of breakdown central government mechanism.

Finally, the message recognized the need to publicly exonerate the army from the raids and asked Lodge to approve a VOA broadcast to that effect. Lodge was requested, as well, to survey urgently for alternative leadership.

Clearance of the draft message was complicated by the coincident week-end absence from Washington of most of the top level members of the Administration. The President was in Hyannis Port; Rusk was in New York; and McNamara and McCone were away on vacation. Both the President and the Secretary of State were reached, however, and approved the draft. Deputy Secretary of Defense Roswell Gilpatric approved for Defense, and General Taylor for the JCS. Schlesinger, in his account of the incident, suggests that the cable was hasty and ill-considered, and that the President immediately began to back away from it.

Lodge replied the following day endorsing the strong position but proposing to forego a futile approach to Diem and to state our position instead only to the generals, thus throwing all our weight behind a coup. The cable stated:

> Believe that chances of Diem's meeting our demands are virtually nil. At the same time, by making them we give Nhu chance to forestall or block action by military. Risk, we believe, is not worth taking, with Nhu in control combat forces Saigon. Therefore, propose we go straight to Generals with our demands, without informing Diem. Would tell them we prepared have Diem without Nhus but it is in effect up to them whether to keep him.

Hilsman asserts that the cable also reflected Lodge's view that since our disapproval of GVN action was well known, it was not fitting for the U.S. to go to Diem, it was Diem who should come to us.

In a separate CAS cable the same day, Richardson, the CIA Chief of Station in Saigon, reported that at a meeting with Lodge and Harkins it had been agreed that Diem would not remove Nhu and that therefore, assuming State's cable of instructions on 24 August represented Washington's basic policy, the consensus was that contact should be immediately made with generals such as Minh and Khanh to assess the degree of unity and determination of senior officers. Minh was considered the best possible interim leader, with Vice President Tho as the most attractive candidate for President among the civilians. The cable concluded with the view that a junta would probably operate behind the scenes in the event of a successful coup, and that the U.S. should leave the specific tactics of a coup up to the generals. There is a hiatus in the available cable traffic at this point, but Hilsman indicates that Washington decided on Sunday, August 25, to defer a direct approach to Diem until more was known about the situation.

In Lodge's reply, he had also apparently approved the proposed VOA broadcast to exonerate the army. Hilsman briefed the press on the basis of a previously approved draft statement on August 25. The statement expressed strong U.S. disapproval of the raids, which were attributed to Nhu. In reporting the story, the press speculated that such a strong statement probably indicated that measures such as aid suspension were being considered. VOA had been instructed to broadcast only the substances of the U.S. statement as provided in the press guidance and nothing more. The instructions somehow got mislaid; and on Monday morning, August 26, just several hours before Lodge was to present his credentials to Diem, VOA broadcast in full a UPI story which flatly asserted that "the US may sharply reduce its aid to Vietnam unless President Diem gets rid of secret police officials responsible for the attacks." Lodge was understandably upset, and sent a testy cable rhetorically inquiring whether he really was in charge of tactics as he had been given to understand. Rusk sent a personal cable of apology to Lodge, and VOA promptly broadcast a denial of U.S. intent to cut aid, but the initial damage had been done.

The Vietnamese reaction to the attack on the pagodas during this time had been dramatic. In the United States, Mme. Nhu's father and mother, respectively the

Vietnamese Ambassador to the U.S. and the Vietnamese observer at the UN, had both resigned, making bitter public statements denouncing the raids. In South Vietnam, the Foreign Minister, Vo Van Mau, had resigned and shaved his head like a Buddhist monk in protest. On August 23, students at the faculties of medicine and pharmacy at the University of Saigon turned out to stage mass demonstrations on behalf of the Buddhists. The GVN reacted in the only way it seemed to know, with massive arrests. But the demonstrations continued, and when the university was closed, the protest was taken up by high school and junior high school students. These were dramatic evidences indeed of the degree of disaffection with the regime, since most of these students were from the middle class families that formed the bureaucracy and the army leadership. Students in Vietnam had no substantial record of political activism as was the case with their counterparts in other parts of Asia, like Korea. Furthermore, some of the Buddhist leadership had survived the raids and gone underground and were soon passing out leaflets on the streets again. On the day of the raids, two monks had taken refuge in the USOM building next door to Xa Loi pagoda. The following day, three others, including the militant young leader Thich Tri Quang, took refuge in the U.S. Embassy, where they were warmly received by Lodge and remained until the successful November coup.

34. Diem Must Go: The US Saigon Embassy Orchestrates a Coup d'Etat (1963)*

Documenting the events of the summer and fall of 1963 leading to the overthrow and assassination of Ngo Dinh Diem, the following selection is from the heavy cable traffic that passed between the US Embassy in Saigon and Washington, D.C. Rarely do outsiders get such a glimpse of foreign policy in the making. In this particular episode the Americans ruefully regret their lack of control over the situation in Vietnam. Unable to get Diem to mend his ways, a divided US command in Saigon reluctantly gave a group of plotting Vietnamese generals a green light to proceed. Even while Diem was talking on the telephone with US Ambassador Henry Cabot Lodge, the conspiring generals had seized strategic points in and around Saigon. They then forced the hated security forces of Ngo Dinh Nhu to surrender and hunted down Diem and Nhu, who had fled the Presidential palace. Despite US promises of safe conduct, the Ngo brothers were murdered by southern Vietnamese army officers. When the word reached Washington, President Kennedy "leaped to his feet and rushed from the room with a look of shock and dismay on his face. . . ."[1] In three weeks Kennedy himself would be a victim of assassination.

---

*From *The Pentagon Papers* (*NY Times* edition), pp. 194–232.

1. General Maxwell Taylor's recollections, quoted in George C. Herring, *America's Longest War: The United States and Vietnam, 1950–1975* (New York: John Wiley & Sons, 1979), p. 107.

A. Buddhist Crisis Alienates U.S. State Department

Cablegram from the State Department to Ambassador Henry Cabot Lodge in Saigon, Aug. 24, 1963

It is now clear that whether military proposed martial law or whether Nhu tricked them into it, Nhu took advantage of its imposition to smash pagodas with police and . . . Special Forces loyal to him, thus placing onus on military in eyes of world and Vietnamese people. Also clear that Nhu has maneuvered himself into commanding position.

U.S. Government cannot tolerate situation in which power lies in Nhu's hands. Diem must be given chance to rid himself of Nhu and his coterie and replace them with best military and political personalities available.

If, in spite of all your efforts, Diem remains obdurate and refuses, then we must face the possibility that Diem himself cannot be preserved.

We now believe immediate action must be taken to prevent Nhu from consolidating his position further. Therefore, unless you in consultation with [General Paul D.] Harkins [U.S. military commander in Vietnam] perceive overriding objections you are authorized to proceed along following lines:

(1) First we must press on appropriate levels of GVN following line:

(a) USG cannot accept actions against Buddhists taken by Nhu and his collaborators under cover martial law.

(b) Prompt dramatic actions redress situation must be taken including repeal of decree 10 [see Reading 26.—eds.], release of arrested monks, nuns, etc.

(2) We must at same time also tell key military leaders that U.S. would find it impossible to continue support GVN militarily and economically unless above steps are taken immediately which we recognize requires removal of Nhus from the scene. We wish give Diem reasonable opportunity to remove Nhus, but if he remains obdurate, then we are prepared to accept the obvious implication that we can no longer support Diem. You may also tell appropriate military commanders we will give them direct support in any interim period of breakdown central government mechanism.

(3) We recognize the necessity of removing taint on military for pagoda raids and placing blame squarely on Nhu. You are authorized to have such statements made in Saigon as you consider desirable to achieve this objective. We are prepared to take same line here and to have Voice of America make statement along lines contained in next numbered telegram whenever you give the word, preferably as soon as possible.

Concurrently, with above, Ambassador and country team should urgently examine all possible alternative leadership and make detailed plans as to how we might bring about Diem's replacement if this should become necessary.

Assume you will consult with General Harkins re any precautions necessary protect American personnel during crisis period.

You will understand that we cannot from Washington give you detailed instructions as to how this operation should proceed, but you will also know we will back you to the hilt on actions you take to achieve our objectives.

Needless to say we have held knowledge of this telegram to minimum essential people and assume you will take similar precautions to prevent premature leaks.

B. Ambassador Lodge's Pessimism

Cablegram from Ambassador Lodge to Secretary of State Dean Rusk and Assistant Secretary of State Roger Hilsman, Aug. 25, 1963

Believe that chances of Diem's meeting our demands are virtually nil. At same time, by making them we give Nhu chance to forestall or block action by military. Risk, we believe, is not worth taking, with Nhu in control combat forces Saigon.

Therefore, propose we go straight to Generals with our demands, without informing Diem. Would tell them we prepared have Diem without Nhus but it is in effect up to them whether to keep him. Would also insist generals take steps to release Buddhist leaders and carry out June 16 agreement.

Request immediate modification instructions. However, do not propose move until we are satisfied with E and E plans. Harkins concurs. I present credentials President Diem tomorrow 11 A.M.[2]

C. Plotting for the Coup Begins

Cablegram from Ambassador Lodge to Secretary Rusk, Aug. 29, 1963

We are launched on a course from which there is no respectable turning back: the overthrow of the Diem government. There is no turning back in part because U.S. prestige is already publicly committed to this end in large measure and will become more so as the facts leak out. In a more fundamental sense, there is no turning back because there is no possibility, in my view, that the war can be won under a Diem administration, still less that Diem or any member of the family can govern the country in a way to gain the support of the people who count, i.e., the educated class in and out of government service, civil and military—not to mention the American people. In the last few months (and especially days) they have in fact positively alienated these people to an incalculable degree. So that I am personally in full agreement with the policy which I was instructed to carry out by last Sunday's telegram.

2. The chance of bringing off a Generals' coup depends on them to some extent; but it depends at least as much on us.

3. We should proceed to make all-out effort to get Generals to move promptly. To do so we should have authority to do following:

(a) That Gen. Harkins repeat to Generals personally message previously transmitted by CAS officers. This should establish their authenticity. Gen. Harkins should have order on this.

(b) If nevertheless Generals insist on public statement that U.S. aid to VN through Diem regime has been stopped, we would agree, on express understanding

---

2. Ambassador Lodge was replacing Frederick E. Nolting at this very moment.—eds.

that Generals will have started at same time. (We would seek persuade Generals that it would be better to hold this card for use in event of stalemate. We hope it will not be necessary to do this at all.)

(c) VNese Generals doubt that we have the will power, courage, and determination to see this thing through. They are haunted by the idea that we will run out on them even though we have told them pursuant to instructions, that the game had started. [Point 4 not published—eds.]

5. We must press on for many reasons. Some of these are:

(a) Explosiveness of the present situation which may well lead to riots and violence if issue of discontent with regime is not met. Out of this could come a pro-Communist or at best a neutralist set of politicians.

(b) The fact that war cannot be won with the present regime.

(c) Our own reputation for steadfastness and our unwillingness to stultify ourselves.

(d) If proposed action is suspended, I believe a body blow will be dealt to respect for us by VNese Generals. Also, all those who expect U.S. to straighten out this situation will feel let down. Our help to the regime in past years inescapably gives a responsibility which we cannot avoid.

6. I realize that this course involves a very substantial risk of losing VN. It also involves some additional risk to American lives. I would never propose it if I felt there was a reasonable chance of holding VN with Diem.

[Point 7 unavailable.]

8. . . . Gen. Harkins thinks I should ask Diem to get rid of the Nhus before starting the Generals' action. But I believe that such a step has no chance of getting the desired result and would have the very serious effect of being regarded by the Generals as a sign of American indecision and delay. I believe this is a risk which we should not run. The Generals distrust us too much already. Another point is that Diem would certainly ask for time to consider such a far-reaching request. This would give the ball to Nhu. . . .

D. Washington's 11th Hour Program to Get Ngo Dinh Diem to Reform His Regime

Cablegram from White House to Ambassador Lodge, Sept. 17, 1963. The Pentagon study says this message followed a meeting of the National Security Council but adds, "There is no evidence on the degree of consensus of the principals in this decision."

1. Highest level meeting today has approved broad outline of an action proposals program designed to obtain from GVN, if possible, reforms and changes in personnel necessary to maintain support of Vietnamese and US opinion in war against Viet Cong. This cable reports this program and our thinking for your comment before final decision. Your comment requested soonest.

2. We see no good opportunity for action to remove present government in immediate future; therefore, as your most recent messages suggest, we must for

the present apply such pressures as are available to secure whatever modest improvements on the scene may be possible. We think it likely that such improvements can make a difference, at least in the short run. Such a course, moreover, is consistent with more drastic effort as and when means become available, and we will be in touch on other channels on this problem.

3. We share view . . . that best available reinforcement to your bargaining position in this interim period is clear evidence that all U.S. assistance is granted only on your say-so. Separate telegram discusses details of this problem, but in this message we specifically authorize you to apply any controls you think helpful for this purpose. You are authorized to delay any delivery of supplies or transfer of funds by any agency until you are satisfied that delivery is in U.S. interest, bearing in mind that it is not our current policy to cut off aid entirely. In other words, we share your view that it will be helpful for GVN to understand that your personal approval is a necessary part of all U.S. assistance. We think it may be particularly desirable for you to use this authority in limiting or rerouting any and all forms of assistance and support which now go to or through Nhu or individuals like Tung who are associated with him. This authorization specifically includes aid actions currently held in abeyance and you are authorized to set those in train or hold them up further in your discretion. We leave entirely in your hands decisions on degree of privacy or publicity you wish to give to this process.

4. Subject to your comment and amendment our own list of possible helpful action by government runs as follows in approximate order of importance:

A. Clear the air—Diem should get everyone back to work and get them to focus on winning the war. He should be broadminded and compassionate in his attitude toward those who have, for understandable reasons, found it difficult under recent circumstances fully to support him. A real spirit of reconciliation could work wonders on the people he leads; a punitive, harsh or autocratic attitude could only lead to further resistance.

B. Buddhists and students—Let them out and leave them unmolested. This more than anything else would demonstrate the return of a better day and the refocusing on the main job at hand, the war.

C. Press—The press should be allowed full latitude of expression. Diem will be criticized, but leniency and cooperation with the domestic and foreign press at this time would bring praise for his leadership in due course. While tendentious reporting is irritating, suppression of news leads to much more serious trouble.

D. Secret and combat police—Confine its role to operations against the VC and abandon operations against non-Communist opposition groups thereby indicating clearly that a period of reconciliation and political stability has returned.

E. Cabinet changes to inject new untainted blood, remove targets of popular discontent.

F. Elections—These should be held, should be free, and should be widely observed.

G. Assembly—Assembly should be convoked soon after the elections. The Government should submit its policies to it and should receive its confidence. An assembly resolution would be most useful for external image purposes.

H. Party—Can Lao party should not be covert or semi-covert but a broad association of supporters engaged in a common, winning cause. This could perhaps be best accomplished by

I. Repeal or suitable amendment Decree 10.

J. Rehabilitation by ARVN of pagodas.

K. Establishment of Ministry of Religious Affairs.

L. Liberation of passport issuances and currency restrictions enabling all to leave who wish to.

M. Acceptance of Buddhist Inquiry Mission from World Federation to report true facts of situation to world.

5. You may wish to add or subtract from the above list, but need to set psychological tone and image is paramount. Diem has taken positive actions in past of greater or less scope than those listed, but they have had little practical political effect since they were carried out in such a way as to make them hollow or, even if real, unbelievable (e.g., martial law already nominally lifted, Assembly elections scheduled, and puppet bonzes established).

6. Specific "reforms" are apt to have little impact without dramatic, symbolic move which convinces Vietnamese that reforms are real. As practical matter we share your views that this can best be achieved by some visible reduction in influence of Nhus, who are symbol to disaffected of all that they dislike in GVN. This we think would require Nhus' departure from Saigon and preferably Vietnam at least for extended vacation. We recognize the strong possibility that these and other pressures may not produce this result, but we are convinced that it is necessary to try.

7. In Washington, in this phase, we would plan to maintain a posture of disapproval of recent GVN actions, but we would not expect to make public our specific request of Diem. Your comment on public aspects of this phase is particularly needed.

8. We note your reluctance to continue dialogue with Diem until you have more to say, but we continue to believe that discussions with him are at a minimum an important source of intelligence and may conceivably be a means of exerting some persuasive effect even in his present state of mind. If you believe that full control of U.S. assistance provides you with means of resuming dialogue, we hope you will do so. We ourselves can see much virtue in effort to reason even with an unreasonable man when he is on a collision course. We repeat, however, that this is a matter for your judgment.

9. Meanwhile, there is increasing concern here with strictly military aspects of the problem, both in terms of actual progress of operations and of need to make effective case with Congress for continued prosecution of the effort. To meet these needs, President has decided to send Secretary of Defense and General Taylor to Vietnam, arriving early next week. It will be emphasized here that it is a military mission and that all political decisions are being handled through you as President's Senior Representative.

10. We repeat that political program outlined above awaits your comment be-

fore final decision. President particularly emphasizes that it is fully open to your criticism and amendment. It is obviously an interim plan and further decisions may become necessary very soon.

E. The Ngos Can't Change

Cablegram from Ambassador Lodge to State Department "for President only," *Sept. 19, 1963.*

1. Agree that no good opportunity for action to remove present government in immediate future is apparent and that we should, therefore, do whatever we can as an interim measure pending such an eventuality.

2. Virtually all the topics under paragraph 4, letters A to M, have been taken up with Diem and Nhu at one time another, most of them by me personally. They think that most of them would either involve destroying the political structure on which they rest or loss of face or both. We, therefore, could *not* realistically hope for more than lip service. Frankly, I see no opportunity at all for substantive changes. . . .

3. There are signs that Diem-Nhu are somewhat bothered by my silence. According to one well placed source, they are guessing and off-balance and "desperately anxious" to know what U.S. posture is to be. They may be preparing some kind of a public relations package, possibly to be opened after the elections. I believe that for me to press Diem on things which are *not* in the cards and to repeat what we have said several times already would be a little shrill and would make us look weak, particularly in view of my talk with Nhu last night at a dinner where I had a golden opportunity to make [your] main points. . . .

4. Also, I doubt that a public relations package will meet needs of situation which seems particularly grave to me, notably in the light of General Big Minh's opinion[3] expressed very privately yesterday that the Viet Cong are steadily gaining strength; have more of the population on their side than has the GVN; that arrests are continuing and that the prisons are full; that more and more students are going over to the Viet Cong; that there is great graft and corruption in the Vietnamese administration of our aid; and that the "Heart of the Army is *not* in the war.". . .

5. As regards your paragraph 3 on withholding of aid, I still hope that I may be informed of methods, as requested . . . September 11, which will enable us to apply sanctions in a way which will really affect Diem and Nhu without precipitating an economic collapse and without impeding the war effort. We are studying this here and have not yet found a solution. If a way to do this were to be found,

---

3. Vietnamese General Duong Van Minh, who helped carry out the coup against Diem, was rewarded afterward by a position on the ruling Military Council. But Minh's government was overthrown in another military coup in January of 1964 (the second in what was to be a series). Minh made another brief reappearance as President of the government in Saigon in April 1975 and surrendered to the DRV armed forces marching into Saigon. See also Reading 68.—eds.

it would be one of the greatest discoveries since the enactment of the Marshall Plan in 1947 because, so far as I know, the U.S. had never yet been able to control any of the very unsatisfactory governments through which we have had to work in our many very successful attempts to make these countries strong enough to stand alone.

6. I also believe that whatever sanctions we may discover should be directly tied to a promising coup d'etat and should *not* be applied without such a coup being in prospect. In this connection, I believe that we should pursue contact with Big Minh and urge him along if he looks like acting. I particularly think that the idea of supporting a Vietnamese Army independent of the government should be energetically studied.

7. I will, of course, give instructions that programs which one [sic] can be effectively held up should be held up and not released without my approval provided that this can be done without serious harmful effect to the people and to the war effort. Technical assistance and (omission) support to communications support programs may be one way. This would be a fly-speck in the present situation and would have *no* immediate effect, but I hope that U.S. (omission) may get Vietnamese officials into the habit of asking me to release items which are held up and that, over a long period of time, it might create opportunities for us to get little things done.

8. But it is not even within the realm of possibility that such a technique could lead them to do anything which causes loss of face or weakening of their political organization. In fact, to threaten them with suppression of aid might well defeat our purposes and might make a bad situation very much worse.

9. There should in any event be no publicity whatever about this procedure. If it is possible (omission) a program, I intend to (omission).

10. As regards . . . "dramatic symbolic moves," I really do not think they could understand this even if Thao wanted to; although I have talked about it to Diem, and to Nhu last night. . . . They have scant comprehension of what it is to appeal to public opinion as they have really no interest in any other opinion than their own. I have repeatedly brought up the question of Nhu's departure and have stressed that if he would just stay away until after Christmas, it might help get the Appropriation Bill through. This seems like a small thing to us but to them it seems tremendous as they are quite sure that the Army would take over if he even stepped out of the country.

11. . . . . I have, of course, no objection to seeing Diem at any time that it would be helpful. But I would rather let him sweat for awhile and not go to see him unless I have something really new to bring up. I would much prefer to wait until I find some part of the AID program to hold up in which he is interested and then have him ask me to come and see him. For example, last night's dinner which I suspect Nhu of stimulating is infinitely better than for me to take the initiative for an appointment and to call at the office. Perhaps my silence had something to do with it.

F. Divergent American Views: Harkins vs. Lodge

Excerpts from Cablegrams from General Paul Harkins to General Maxwell Taylor, Oct. 30, 1963

The Ambassador and I are certainly in touch with each other but whether the communications between us are effective is something else. I will say Cabot's methods of operations are entirely different from Amb Nolting's as far as reporting in the [word illegible] is concerned. . . .

There is a basic difference apparently between the Ambassador's thinking and mine on the interpretation of the guidance contained in CAP 63560 dated 6 October and the additional thoughts, I repeat, thoughts expressed in CAS Washington 74228 dated 9 October. I interpret CAP 63560 as our basic guidance and that CAS 74228 being additional thoughts did not change the basic guidance in that no initiative should now be taken to give any active covert encouragement to a coup. The Ambassador feels that 74228 does change 63560 and that a change of government is desired and feels . . . that the only way to bring about such a change is by a coup.

I'm not opposed to a change in government, no indeed, but I'm inclined to feel that at this time the change should be in methods of governing rather than complete change of personnel. I have seen no batting order proposed by any of the coup groups. I think we should take a hard look at any proposed list before we make any decisions. In my contacts here I have seen no one with the strength of character of Diem, at least in fighting Communists. Certainly there are no Generals qualified to take over in my opinion.

I am not a Diem man per se. I certainly see the faults in his character. I am here to back 14 million SVN people in their fight against communism and it just happens that Diem is their leader at this time. Most of the Generals I have talked to agree they can go along with Diem, all say it's the Nhu family they are opposed to.

Perhaps the pressures we have begun to apply will cause Diem and Nhu to change their ways. This apparently not evident as yet. I'm sure the pressures we have begun to apply if continued will affect the war effort. To date they have not. I am watching this closely and will report when I think they have.

I do not agree with the Ambassador's assessment . . . that we are just holding our own. The GVN is a way ahead in the I, II and parts of the III Corps and making progress in the Delta. Nothing has happened in October to change the assessment you and Secretary McNamara made after your visit here.

I would suggest we not try to change horses too quickly. That we continue to take persuasive actions that will make the horses change their course and methods of action. That we win the military effort as quickly as possible, then let them make any and all the changes they want.

After all, rightly or wrongly, we have backed Diem for eight long hard years. To me it seems incongruous now to get him down, kick him around and get rid of him. The U.S. has been his mother superior and father confessor since he's been in office and he has leaned on us heavily.

Leaders of other under-developed countries will take a dim view of our assistance if they too were led to believe the same fate lies in store for them.

. . . I am unable to concur in statement that quote one cannot drive as much around the country as one could two years ago end of quote. I believe it will be some time before, if we ever do, experience mass surrenders of the VC. I am unable to concur in statement that VC is quote in fact, reckoned at a higher figure than it was two years ago end quote. I have not observed the signs that hatred of the government has tended to diminish the Army's vigor, enthusiasm and enterprise. I find it difficult to believe the few rumors one hears regarding Generals being paid off with money and flashy cars. Most cars I see in use by Generals are same they have been using for past two years and few if any qualify as flashy to my mind. I do not concur with the evaluation of the 14 October report of the Delta Subcommittee of the Committee on Province Rehabilitation which states that the VC are gaining. . . .

G. The Go-Ahead Signal

Cablegram from McGeorge Bundy to Ambassador Lodge, Oct. 30, 1963.

. . . This paragraph contains our present standing instructions for U.S. posture in the event of a coup.

a. U.S. authorities will reject appeals for direct intervention from either side, and U.S.-controlled aircraft and other resources will not be committed between the battle lines or in support of either side, without authorization from Washington.

b. In event of indecisive contest, U.S. authorities may in their discretion agree to perform any acts agreeable to both sides, such as removal of key personalities or relay of information. In such actions, however, U.S. authorities will strenuously avoid appearance of pressure on either side. It is not in the interest of USG to be or appear to be either instrument of existing government or instrument of coup.

c. In the event of imminent or actual failure of coup, U.S. authorities may afford asylum in their discretion to those to whom there is any express or implied obligation of this sort. We believe however that in such a case it would be in our interest and probably in interest of those seeking asylum that they seek protection of other Embassies in addition to our own. This point should be made strongly if need arises.

d. But once a coup under responsible leadership has begun, and within these restrictions, it is in the interest of the U.S. Government that it should succeed. . . .

H. Last Words with Ngo Dinh Diem

Excerpt from cablegram from Ambassador Lodge to State Department, Nov. 1, 1963. President Diem telephoned Ambassador Lodge at 4:30 P.M. (Saigon time) and the following conversation ensued:

DIEM: Some units have made a rebellion and I want to know what is the attitude of the U.S.?

LODGE: I do not feel well enough informed to be able to tell you. I have heard the shooting, but am not acquainted with all the facts. Also it is 4:30 A.M. in Washington and the U.S. Government cannot possibly have a view.

DIEM: But you must have some general ideas. After all, I am a Chief of State. I have tried to do my duty. I want to do now what duty and good sense require. I believe in duty above all.

LODGE: You have certainly done your duty. As I told you only this morning, I admire your courage and your great contributions to your country. No one can take away from you the credit for all you have done. Now I am worried about your physical safety. I have a report that those in charge of the current activity offer you and your brother safe conduct out of the country if you resign. Had you heard this?

DIEM: No. (And then after a pause) You have my telephone number.

LODGE: Yes. If I can do anything for your physical safety, please call me.

DIEM: I am trying to re-establish order.

[Diem and his brother were murdered shortly after this conversation.—eds.]

I. Reaffirmation of "Established U.S. Policy" After Assassinations

Excerpts from National Security Action Memorandum 273,[4] Nov. 26, 1963, four days after the assassination of President Kennedy, as provided in the body of the Pentagon study. The paragraph in italics is a summary made by the authors of The Pentagon Papers, *not a direct quotation from NSAM 273.*

The President expects that all senior officers of the government will move energetically to insure the full unity of support for established U.S. policy in South Vietnam. Both in Washington and in the field, it is essential that the government be unified. It is of particular importance that express or implied criticism of officers of other branches be assiduously avoided in all contacts with the Vietnamese government and with the press. . . .

We should concentrate our efforts, and insofar as possible we should persuade the government of South Vietnam to concentrate its effort, on the critical situation in the Mekong Delta. This concentration should include not only military but political, economic, social, educational and informational effort. We should seek to turn the tide not only of battle but of belief, and we should seek to increase not only the controlled hamlets but the productivity of this area, especially where the proceeds can be held for the advantage of anti-Communist forces. . . .[5]

It is a major interest of the United States government that the present provisional government of South Vietnam should be assisted in consolidating itself in holding and developing increased public support.

---

4. For further reference to NSAM 273, see Reading 35.—eds.

5. This particular paragraph in *The Pentagon Papers* (*NY Times* edition) has typographical errors; so we are using the paragraph as quoted in the Gravel edition, vol. 3, p. 18.—eds.

. . . *And in conclusion, plans were requested for clandestine operations by the GVN against the North and also for operations up to 50 kilometers into Laos; and, as a justification for such measures, State was directed to develop a strong, documented case to demonstrate to the world the degree to which the Viet Cong is controlled, sustained and supplied from Hanoi, through Laos and other channels.* . . ."

Part V

THE AMERICANIZATION OF THE WAR

Editors' Introduction

The assassination of Ngo Dinh Diem on November 2, 1963 marked the end of the myth of an independent democratic South Vietnam. From now on the US government, which had conspired with Vietnamese generals in its pay to overthrow Diem, its own chosen ruler of South Vietnam, had to operate through a succession of military dictators, all linked directly to the Pentagon's military command structure.

These generals were not, however, mere obedient puppets; they seemed to be endlessly plotting among themselves for personal power. In one twenty-month period following Diem's death, ten different governments grabbed power in Saigon. Coup followed coup with such disturbing consequences that finally US Ambassador Maxwell Taylor called together some of the leading plotters, such as Generals Ky and Thieu, to scold them in no uncertain terms: "Do you all understand English? . . . I told you clearly . . . we Americans were tired of coups. . . . Now you have made a real mess" (*Pentagon Papers*, Vol. 2, p. 346).

These generals owed their power to the vast sums of US military aid that had overwhelmed Saigon's civilian political structure and turned the armed forces into a giant with no indigenous social base, constantly being inflated through its pipeline from Washington. Most of these top officers had served in the French colonial forces fighting against the Viet-Minh-led movement for national independence and most were natives of North Vietnam, an especially embarrassing fact for Washington, which was trying to convince the world that Vietnamese living north of the 17th parallel were "foreigners" to South Vietnam.

Since a government ruled by these generals had no realistic chance of winning a broad popular base of support in the South, Washington was forced to choose between disengagement from these Saigon regimes or an increasingly direct, ever-growing US military intervention. The choice was made and executed in a series of steps from late November 1963 through March 1965. The American war had begun.

On November 22, 1963, three weeks after the assassination of President Diem, President John F. Kennedy was assassinated. On November 26, Lyndon Johnson, four days after his inauguration as President, issued NSAM 273, initiating a plan for covert military attacks on North Vietnam, with "estimates of such factors as: a. Resulting damage to NVN; b. The plausibility of denial; c. Possible NVN retaliation," as well as covert military operations within Laos (Reading 35). These operations were, of course, "covert" and "secret" mainly to the American people; they were not hidden from, but aimed directly at, the government in Hanoi.

The secret plan to Americanize the war was to proceed in this order: covert attacks against the Democratic Republic of Vietnam (DRV), financed and organized by the United States but executed by mercenaries and Saigon forces; appointment of a new US commander to prepare for the enlargement of bases and an eventual influx of large numbers of US combat troops; overt US attacks on the North as "retaliation" for any military response it made against the covert attacks; a gradual shift from "retaliatory" attacks to sustained US air attacks on the North; deployment of US troops, first to defend the US air bases, then to gain control of the countryside. Part of this secret plan to escalate and widen the war was to obtain from Congress a resolution granting military *carte blanche*. Thus armed, the Pentagon strategists believed they could deploy the ground forces, ships, and air power deemed necessary to "win."

Central to the new strategy was what the Pentagon historians called "an elaborate program of covert military operations against the state of North Vietnam," begun on February 1, 1964, under the code name "Operation Plan 34A" (Oplan 34A). Simultaneously, plans were drawn up for a "retaliatory" bombing of North Vietnam should the DRV defend itself against any of the US military units supporting the attacks. And a resolution was prepared for submission to Congress at the opportune moment. In June, General William Westmoreland was placed in command of the 16,000 US military "advisers" on Vietnamese soil (see Reading 52 for Westmoreland's preeminent role in the Americanization of the war).

Meanwhile, the South Vietnamese generals began to jump the gun on the new strategy. Instead of merely claiming to be defending against "aggression from the North," they now openly proclaimed the aim of "bringing the war to the North," and "marching North to liberate and reunify Vietnam." Thus, on July 19, 1964, General Khanh, then Premier, urged a rally of 100,000 people in Saigon to prepare for "liberating their native land," as government cheerleaders urged the crowd to echo his shouts of *"Bac thien!"* (To the North!). The same day, in a news conference reported in *The New York Times*, July 23, 1964, Nguyen Cao Ky, commander of South Vietnam's air force, proclaimed that "combat teams had been sent on sabotage missions inside Communist North Vietnam and that Vietnamese pilots were being trained for possible larger-scale attacks." Ky also announced that "teams have entered North Vietnam by air, sea, and land," and that such "clandestine missions had been dispatched at intervals for at least three years."

On August 2, Oplan 34A raids were conducted against the coastal defenses of North Vietnam. The US destroyer *Maddox* opened fire on three North Vietnamese

PT boats in the vicinity. On August 4, the *Maddox* and another destroyer reported that they were under attack—an attack which most likely never occurred (Reading 36). Within hours, air raids against the DRV were launched from US carriers while President Johnson explained on national TV that these raids were in retaliation for unprovoked attacks. Three days later, Congress passed the Gulf of Tonkin Resolution, the document prepared months earlier, giving the President unlimited authorization to conduct war in Southeast Asia (Reading 36).

Meanwhile, President Johnson was running as the antiwar candidate against Barry Goldwater in the first presidential election featuring Vietnam as a major issue. The President constantly reiterated his promise not to send US military forces to fight in Vietnam:

"We don't want our American boys to do the fighting for Asian boys." (September 25)

"We are not going north and we are not going south; we are going to try to get them to save their own freedom with their own men." (September 28)

"We are not about to send American boys nine or ten thousand miles away from home to do what Asian boys ought to be doing themselves." (October 21)

Johnson won in an overwhelming landslide, interpreted by many as the first tabulation of the American people's feelings about participating in the war in Vietnam.

On January 20, 1965, Lyndon Johnson was inaugurated as the elected President. On February 8, North Vietnam was subjected to "retaliatory" air raids (Operation Flaming Dart). On February 13, "the President decides to inaugurate ROLLING THUNDER sustained bombing of the North" (*Pentagon Papers*, Gravel edition, Vol. 3, p. 276). On February 27, the State Department issued its "White Paper" (Reading 37) claiming "aggression" from North Vietnam. On February 28, Washington and Saigon jointly announced that they would soon begin continuous air attacks on North Vietnam (Operation Rolling Thunder).

The systematic air war against North Vietnam began on March 2, and continued, with some interruptions, for almost eight years. The first openly acknowledged US ground combat units—two Marine battalions—landed at Da Nang on March 8, ostensibly to defend that base being used in the air war. The Vietnam War was about to become thoroughly Americanized.

35. The Blueprint for an Americanized War*

From *The Pentagon Papers*

The following selections from The Pentagon Papers *document the secret plans to Americanize the war. The Pentagon historians trace the origin of the covert action*

---

*From *The Pentagon Papers* (Gravel edition), vol. 3, pp. 141, 149–151, 182–183, 510–512.

program back to May 1963, when the Joint Chiefs of Staff directed the formulation of a plan for "non-attributable" military attacks on North Vietnam to be carried out "with US military materiel, training and advisory assistance."

The documents show the plan being activated by President Johnson's NSAM 273[1] of November 26, 1963 and the December formulation of Oplan 34A, with its secret attacks on the DRV, along with plans for air raids. The March 18, 1964 memorandum from the Joint Chiefs of Staff refers to the then current covert military actions, discusses the planning of "Time-phased US and GVN deployments, pre-positioning and augmentation required to implement envisaged operations," as well as the completion of "target lists," and then lays out future escalation "in the following order: border control actions, retaliatory actions, and graduated overt military pressures."

In a memorandum dated March 20, 1964, President Johnson discusses the plans with Ambassador Henry Cabot Lodge, whom he instructs to undertake a mission "precisely for the purpose of knocking down the idea of neutralization wherever it rears its ugly head, and on this point I think that nothing is more important than to stop neutralist talk wherever we can by whatever means we can."

The May 19, 1964 document from the Joint Chiefs of Staff reveals that Oplan 34A operations have been going on for at least three months. Future plans, "at rate commensurate with growing operational capacities of MACV and GVN forces," include sabotage, "NASTY PT" strikes (discussed in Reading 36), and air strikes by General Ky's US-equipped Saigon air force.

The final selection presents the immediate background of the Gulf of Tonkin "incidents."

The Plan for a Secret War

26 Nov 1963

In a review of discussions of Vietnam policy held at Honolulu, 20 November 63, newly installed President Johnson directs (among other measures) that "planning should include different levels of possible increased activity, and in each instance there should be estimates of such factors as:

    a. Resulting damage to NVN;

    b. The plausibility of denial;

    c. Possible NVN retaliation;

    d. Other international reaction."

The directive also called for a plan, to be submitted for approval, for military operations "up to a line up to 50 km. inside Laos, together with political plans for minimizing the international hazards of such an enterprise." (NSAM 273)

15 Dec. 1963

In response to JCS request of 26 Nov 63, MACV and CAS, Saigon forward a

---

1. For further reference to NSAM 273, see Reading 34, section I.

joint plan of combined GVN/USG operations against NVN. Designated OPLAN 34A, the proposal providing "a spectrum of capabilities of RVNAF to execute against NVN" that would "convince the DRV leadership that they should cease to support insurgent activities in the RVN and Laos." It contained 72 actions, many of which were covert and only 16 of which were considered "punitive or attritional." In forwarding letter, CINCPAC urges that Category IV actions, largely air attacks, "appear to have the highest probability of success." (CINCPAC letter to JCS, 19 Dec 63)

Initiation of Covert Operations, February–June 1964

On 1 February 1964, the United States embarked on a new course of action in pursuance of its long-standing policy of attempting to bolster the security of Southeast Asia. On that date, under direction of the American military establishment, an elaborate program of covert military operations against the state of North Vietnam was set in motion. There were precedents: a variety of covert activities had been sponsored by the American CIA since 1961. Intelligence agents, resupplied by air, had been dispatched into North Vietnam; resistance and sabotage teams had been recruited inside the country; and propaganda leaflets had been dispensed from "civilian mercenary" aircraft. But the program that began in February 1964 was different, and its impact on future U.S. policy in Southeast Asia was far-reaching.

1. Covert Action Program: Scope and Character

The covert action program beginning in February 1964 was different, first of all, because it was a *program*. Designed to extend over a period of 12 months, it was divided into three phases distinguished by the character and intensity of their respective operations. The first phase (February through May) called for intelligence collection through U–2 and communications intelligence missions and psychological operations involving leaflet drops, propaganda kit deliveries, and radio broadcasts. It also provided for about "20 destructive undertakings, all within . . . early prospective [GVN] capabilities . . . [and] designed to result in substantial destruction, economic loss and harassment." The second and third phases involved the same categories of action, but of increased tempo and magnitude, and with the destructive operations extending to "targets identified with North Vietnam's economic and industrial well-being." Once started, the program was intended to inflict on North Vietnam increasing levels of punishment for its aggressive policies.

The 1964 program was different also because it was placed under control of an operational U.S. military command. Though the program was designed to be carried out by GVN or third country personnel, plans were developed by COMUSMACV and the GVN jointly and given interagency clearance in Washington through a special office under the JCS. CINCPAC and the appropriate CIA station furnished the necessary training and equipment support and COMUSMACV exercised operational control. Since subsequent phases of the covert program were to be based on a continuous evaluation of actions already taken, operation reports were submitted periodically through JCS staff channels for review by various Washington agencies.

Normally such routine staffing arrangements tend to encourage expectations of continued program actions. Moreover, they foreshadow bureaucratic pressures for taking stronger measures should previous ones fail to produce desired results. In the case of the covert operations program, these tendencies were reinforced through the evocation of a GVN policy commitment and the involvement of GVN officials in its implementation.

2. *Origins and Development: Presidential Support and Approval*

The covert program was spawned in May of 1963, when the JCS directed CINCPAC to prepare a plan for GVN "hit and run" operations against NVN. These operations were to be "non-attributable" and carried out "with U.S. military materiel, training and advisory assistance." Approved by the JCS on 9 September as CINCPAC OPLAN 34–63, the plan was discussed during the Vietnam policy conference at Honolulu, 20 November 1963. Here a decision was made to develop a combined COMUSMACV-CAS, Saigon plan for a 12-month program of covert operations. Instructions forwarded by the JCS on 26 November specifically requested provision for: "(1) harassment; (2) diversion; (3) political pressure; (4) capture of prisoners; (5) physical destruction; (6) acquisition of intelligence; (7) generation of intelligence; and (8) diversion of DRV resources." Further, that the plan provide for "selected actions of graduated scope and intensity to include commando type coastal raids." To this guidance was added that given by President Johnson to the effect that "planning should include . . . estimates of such factors as: (1) resulting damage to NVN; (2) the plausibility of denial; (3) possible NVN retaliation; and (4) other international reaction." The MACV-CAS plan, designated OPLAN 34A, and providing for "a spectrum of capabilities for RVNAF to execute against NVN," was forwarded by CINCPAC on 19 December 1963.

The idea of putting direct pressure on North Vietnam met prompt receptivity on the part of President Johnson. According to then Assistant Secretary of State, Roger Hilsman, it was just a few days before the military-CIA submission that State Department Counselor Walt Rostow passed to the President "a well-reasoned case for a gradual escalation."

Major General F. T. Unger of the Joint Chiefs of Staff to CINCPAC, March 18, 1964

Refs:
  a. JCS 5375;
  b. OPLAN 34A;
  c. OPLAN 33;
  d. OPLAN 99;
  e. JCS 2343/326–6

Subj: Planning Actions, Viet Nam

1. As a result of approval of recommendations in paragraph 12, section VII, reference a, planning for military actions in support of RVN has been identified in the following categories:

a. Border control actions
b. Retaliatory actions
c. Graduated overt military pressures.

In light of the above, planning for current and future military actions in support of the RVN must be aligned with the appropriate categories. It is appreciated that elements of several of these actions are contained in several extant plans (refs b, c, and d); however, these must now be drawn together in a cohesive plan or plans to permit sequential implementation as may be desired by higher authority within categories above. JCS views on operations in para c above are contained in ref e.

2. The product of the new planning should include:

a. Mission and objectives

b. Time-phased US and GVN deployments, pre-positioning and augmentation required to implement envisaged operations, as well as to deter enemy reaction, within the time parameters of para 12, Section VII, ref a. (Time parameters are now under review and may be changed.)

c. Complete target lists together with desired damage criteria as well as impact on enemy capability; or specific objective area.

d. Actions to be taken in event of enemy escalation.

e. US support required for unilateral RVNAF operations.

f. Reconnaissance operations and planning.

3. Planning should be in such detail as to permit review of individual actions or small increments in progressing through operations outlined above. As a matter of urgency, it is requested that planning be undertaken in the following order: border control actions, retaliatory actions, and graduated overt military pressures, and that elements of planning be forwarded to the JCS as completed. Request ASAP your schedule for completion of planning actions.

President Johnson to Ambassador Lodge, March 20, 1964

1. We have studied your 1776 and I am asking State to have Bill Bundy make sure that you get out latest planning documents on ways of applying pressure and power against the North. I understand that some of this was discussed with you by McNamara mission in Saigon, but as plans are refined it would be helpful to have your detailed comments. As we agreed in our previous messages to each other, judgment is reserved for the present on overt military action in view of the consensus from Saigon conversations of McNamara mission with General Khanh and you on judgment that movement against the North at the present would be premature. We have share (sic) General Khanh's judgment that the immediate and essential task is to strengthen the southern base. For this reason our planning for action against the North is on a contingency basis at present, and immediate problem in this area is to develop the strongest possible military and political base for possible later action. There is additional international reason for avoiding immediate overt action in that we expect a showdown between the Chinese and Soviet Communist parties soon and action against the North will be more practicable after than before a showdown. But if at any time you feel that more immediate action is urgent, I

count on you to let me know specifically the reasons for such action, together with your recommendations for its size and shape.

2. On dealing with deGaulle, I continue to think it may be valuable for you to go to Paris after Bohlen has made his first try. (State is sending you draft instruction to Bohlen, which I have not yet reviewed, for your comment.) It ought to be possible to explain in Saigon that your mission is precisely for the purpose of knocking down the idea of neutralization wherever it rears its ugly head, and on this point I think that nothing is more important than to stop neutralist talk wherever we can by whatever means we can. I have made this point myself to Mansfield and Lippmann and I expect to use every public opportunity to restate our position firmly. You may want to convey our concern on this point to General Khanh and get his ideas on the best possible joint program to stop such talk in Saigon, in Washington, and in Paris. I imagine that you have kept General Khanh abreast of our efforts in Paris. After we see the results of the Bohlen approach you might wish to sound him out on Paris visit by you.

"North Vietnam Operations": Summary of Joint Chiefs Memo, May 19, 1964

JCS appraised "achievements and limitations" of first 3 months of 34A operations: Overall objective cited as "to help convince NVN leadership that it is in its own self-interest to desist from its aggressive policies." "Ancillary objectives": (1) to gain more info (2) intensify current psychological war and resistance operations to weaken Hanoi's control of the population of NVN and commit regime to costly counter-measures.

Past three months indicate "slow beginning." "There are, however, indications that attempts at infiltration and continuing psychological activities, together with widespread press and radio speculation over the extension of the war, have had an effect /?/ on the DRV. Its reaction tends to substantiate the premise that Hanoi is expending substantial resources in defensive war."

JCS conclude: (1) GVN's general lack of program direction caused by 30 January coup; (2) program begun before special material and personnel required were assembled; (3) overflights of Laos essential to it for operational reasons; (4) bad weather and insufficient intelligence have hampered operations; (5) "potential of the program remains high."

JCS advocate continuing for Phase II period (Jan thru Sep) "at rate commensurate with growing operational capacities of MACV and GVN forces." (Electronic intelligence; sabotage teams; C–123 airlift; NASTY PT craft; all cited as new and invaluable resources available to program.) VNAF air strikes recommended.

Prelude to the Gulf of Tonkin "Incidents"

[Several paragraphs missing]

The next DE SOTO Patrol did not occur until 31 July, on which the *U.S.S. Maddox* was restricted to a track not closer than 8 n.m.[2] off the North Vietnamese

---

2. Nautical miles—eds.

mainland. Its primary mission, assigned on 17 July, was "to determine DRV coastal activity along the full extent of the patrol track." Other specific intelligence requirements were assigned as follows:

(a) location and identification of all radar transmitters, and estimate of range capabilities; (b) navigational and hydro information along the routes traversed and particular navigational lights characteristics, landmarks, buoys, currents and tidal information, river mouths and channel accessibility, (c) monitoring a junk force with density of surface traffic pattern, (d) sampling electronic environment radars and navigation aids, (e) photography of opportunities in support of above. . . .

Separate coastal patrol operations were being conducted by South Vietnamese naval forces. These were designed to uncover and interdict efforts to smuggle personnel and supplies into the South in support of the VC insurgency. This operation had first been organized with U.S. assistance in December 1961; to support it a fleet of motorized junks was built, partially financed with U.S. military assistance funds. During 1964 these vessels operated almost continually in attempts to intercept communist seaborne logistical operations. As Secretary McNamara told Senate committees:

In the first seven months of this year [1964], they have searched 149,000 junks, some 570,000 people. This is a tremendous operation endeavoring to close the seacoasts of over 900 miles. In the process of that action, as the junk patrol has increased in strength they [sic] have moved farther and farther north endeavoring to find the source of the infiltration.

In addition to these acknowledged activities, the GVN was also conducting a number of operations against North Vietnam to which it did not publicly admit. Covert operations were carried out by South Vietnamese or hired personnel and supported by U.S. training and logistical efforts. Outlined within OPLAN 34A, these operations had been underway theoretically since February but had experienced what the JCS called a "slow beginning." Despite an ultimate objective of helping "convince the North Vietnamese leadership that it is in its own self-interest to desist from its aggressive policies," few operations designed to harass the enemy were carried out successfully during the February–May period. Nevertheless, citing DRV reactions tending "to substantiate the premise that Hanoi is expending substantial resources in defensive measures," the JCS concluded that the potential of the OPLAN 34A program remained high and urged its continuation through Phase II (June–September). [Several paragraphs missing]

36. The Gulf of Tonkin "Incidents" and Resolution*

On August 2 and 4, 1964, certain "incidents" took place in the Gulf of Tonkin, just off the coast of North Vietnam. Within hours of the second incident, President Johnson was explaining in a television address to the American people that US ships had been attacked without provocation on the high seas by North Vietnam, and that waves of US airplanes were already commencing a massive "retaliation" on port and defense facilities along the North Vietnamese coast.

On August 7, Congress—by a vote of 416–0 in the House and 88–2 in the Senate—handed the President his Gulf of Tonkin Resolution, the closest approximation to a Declaration of War passed during all the years of US combat in Vietnam. The only opposing votes were cast by Senators Ernest Gruening (Alaska) and Wayne Morse (Oregon). The resolution denounced the alleged attacks on US ships as "part of a deliberate and systematic campaign of aggression" by North Vietnam and ceded to the President the right "to take all necessary steps" in Southeast Asia, "including the use of armed force."

The Gulf of Tonkin incidents mark the first admitted participation of the United States as a belligerent fighting against the Democratic Republic of Vietnam. The Gulf of Tonkin Resolution essentially abrogated the constitutional power of Congress to declare war.

What actually took place in the Gulf of Tonkin? Most histories of the war still refer to "attacks" by North Vietnamese PT boats on US destroyers. Yet, this is not the conclusion reached in any serious studies of the subject. Several extremely well researched books—such as Joseph C. Goulden, Truth Is the First Casualty: The Gulf of Tonkin Affair—Illusion and Reality *(1969); Eugene G. Windchy,* Tonkin Gulf *(1971); and Anthony Austin,* The President's War: The Story of the Tonkin Gulf Resolution and How the Nation Was Trapped in Vietnam *(1971)—have independently demonstrated beyond a reasonable doubt that the August 2nd incident could best be described as an attack by the US destroyer* Maddox *on North Vietnamese patrol boats, and that the August 4th incident was in all likelihood a phantom battle between two US destroyers and an imaginary enemy. These analyses have proven that the official US chronology of events, such as the documents reprinted below, is blatantly false.*

To understand what did happen, one must place the Gulf of Tonkin incidents in the context of the U.S. officials' planned Americanization of the war (see the Introduction and Reading 35). One basic military goal of Oplan 34A was to probe and weaken the coastal defenses of North Vietnam, possibly for an eventual invasion. Commando raids on coastal radar and patrol boat facilities were designed not

---

*A. Collected in 1964. B. From *Department of State Bulletin* 51 (August 24, 1964). C. From *The Pentagon Papers* (Gravel ed.), vol. 3, pp. 553–556.

*only to disable North Vietnamese defenses but also to disclose their capabilities
and limitations. Therefore, coordinated with Oplan 34A raids were espionage
probes by US planes and ships whose highly sophisticated electronic monitoring
equipment painted a detailed picture of the North Vietnamese radar activated to
defend against the attacking forces. The ships participating in this espionage activity were designated "De Soto" patrol vessels.*

*The first alleged attack on a US ship took place on August 2 and involved the
destroyer USS Maddox, a De Soto patrol vessel conducting an espionage mission
within the twelve-mile territorial waters limit claimed by the DRV. Contrary to
Washington denials at the time, the Maddox was actually operating in close coordination with especially brazen Oplan 34A raids being conducted in the immediate
vicinity. The Maddox's alleged ignorance of these raids is belied by the fact that
the destroyer, which carried a Vietnamese-speaking intelligence team, was actively
monitoring both radar and radio channels of the DRV.*

*In the early morning hours of July 31, US gunboats attacked the North Viet-
namese coastal islands of Hon Me and Hon Ngu. Nominally under the command
of the Saigon government, these gunboats were actually part of Oplan 34A and
were under US command (see Reading 35). They were furnished and equipped by
the United States, and all the combat personnel—a mixture of European and
Chinese Nationalist mercenaries and members of the South Vietnamese military—
were paid by the United States.*

*On August 1, the Maddox reconnoitered close to both islands that had just
been attacked, coming, by official US admission, within at least 13 miles of Hon
Ngu and four to six miles of Hon Me. On August 2, the Maddox returned to the
vicinity of Hon Me, from which three North Vietnamese patrol boats put out in the
direction of the destroyer, which then turned and headed away from the coast.
When the three tracking boats got within a range of 5.8 miles (10,000 yards), the
Maddox opened fire on them. These first shots were officially described as "warning shots," though no such thing applies to the vessels of war and though later
testimony from the Maddox's gun boss stated unequivocally that his orders were
"shoot to kill." When the PT boats got within 6,000 yards—about as close as the
destroyer had been to their base on Hon Me—the Maddox opened up with all guns
that could be brought to bear.*

*The three boats continued their approach, eventually launching at least one
torpedo and firing machine guns at the Maddox and at US planes sent to attack
them. The only damage ever claimed by the United States (for either August 2 or
4) was a single bullet hole in the Maddox. One or more of the PT boats may have
been badly damaged or destroyed.*

*On August 3, the Maddox, joined by another destroyer, the USS Turner Joy,
resumed its De Soto electronic espionage, returning once again to the vicinity of
Hon Me and then proceeding north, according to the plan of the Pacific forces
commander, Admiral Sharp, to draw North Vietnamese patrol boats "away from
area of 34-A ops." These raids resumed that night with attacks on two additional
coastal defenses of the DRV.*

On the dark and somewhat stormy night of August 4, about 65 miles off the coast of the DRV, the Turner Joy opened full fire on an unidentified radar blip, assumed to be a North Vietnamese PT boat, at a range of almost six miles. Then the captain of the Maddox, mistaking his own sonar's pings off his own rudder for enemy torpedoes, commenced a series of wild evasive maneuvers that produced more and more sonar pings off the rapidly gyrating rudder, interpreted as more and still more torpedoes. For hours, the Maddox and the Turner Joy engaged in a ferocious battle with a phantom enemy that was never visible to the US planes combing the area and illuminating it with flares. Blips would appear and disappear on radar, in patterns commonly associated with meteorological disturbances characteristic of the Gulf of Tonkin. Some of these were interpreted as enemy boats sunk, though an extensive search of the area in daylight was never to reveal a single piece of flotsam or oil slick. The only definite target upon which the Maddox trained its guns that night turned out to be the Turner Joy, which was saved from destruction when the main gun director of the Maddox refused to execute the direct order to fire. No damage was inflicted on either US vessel or any US plane.

Each of the independently researched book-length investigations has come to the same conclusion. As Anthony Austin put it, "One is compelled to agree with Fulbright when he says, 'The fact is there was no attack at all.'" It was Senator Fulbright who, trusting the Administration's version of this dubious incident, had led the Senate to pass that fateful Gulf of Tonkin Resolution, upon which the US government was now to rely for legal authority to wage war in every corner of Vietnam.

The last items in this Reading, documents from The Pentagon Papers, outline the next steps in the planned Americanization of the war.

A. Official Accounts

Defense Department Press Release, August 2, 1964

The following was released by CINCPAC at 1015 EDT today:

While on routine patrol in international waters at 020808 GCT (1608 local time), the U.S. destroyer MADDOX underwent an unprovoked attack by three PT-type boats in latitude 19–40 North; longitude 106–34 East; in the Tonkin Gulf.

The attacking boats launched three torpedoes and used 37 millimeter gunfire. The MADDOX answered with five-inch gunfire. Shortly thereafter four F–8 (Crusader) aircraft from the USS TICONDEROGA joined in the defense of MADDOX, using ZUNI rockets and 20 millimeter strafing attacks. The PT boats were driven off, with one seen to be badly damaged and not moving and the other two damaged and retreating slowly.

No casualties or damage were sustained by MADDOX or the aircraft.

Defense Department Press Release. August 3, 1964

The following is a chronology of the incident concerning the USS MADDOX (DD–731) on August 2, 1964:

(All times are Eastern Daylight Time)

11:00 P.M., August 1:

MADDOX reported observing an estimated 75 junks near her assigned patrol area off the North Viet Nam coast. She reported changing her course in order to avoid the junk concentration and indicated that there was no evidence of any hostility.

1:30 A.M., August 2:

MADDOX reported that three torpedo boats were on a southerly course heading toward the ship at extreme range (over 10 miles). The MADDOX at this point was about 30 miles from the coast.

3:40 A.M., August 2:

MADDOX reported she was being approached by the high speed (estimated 45 to 50 knots) craft whose apparent intention was to conduct a torpedo attack and that she intended to open fire in self-defense if necessary.

4:08 A.M., August 2:

MADDOX reported she was being attacked by the three PT craft. She opened fire with her five-inch battery after three warning shots failed to slow down the attackers.

4:08 A.M., August 2:

The PT's continued their closing maneuvers and two of the PT's closed to 5000 yards, each firing one torpedo. The MADDOX changed course in an evasive move and the two torpedoes passed close aboard on the starboard side (100 to 200 yards).

USS TICONDEROGA (CVA–14) advised she was sending four already airborne F–8E's (CRUSADERS) with rockets and 20 mm. ammunition to provide air cover for MADDOX. The pilots were instructed not to fire unless MADDOX or the aircraft were fired upon.

4:21 A.M., August 2:

The third PT moved up to the beam of the MADDOX and received a direct hit by a five-inch round, and at the same time dropped a torpedo into the water which was not seen to run. Machine gun fire from the PT's was directed at the MADDOX. However, there was no damage or injury to personnel. The MADDOX continued in a southerly direction to join with the C. TURNER JOY (DD–951) as TICONDEROGA aircraft commenced attacking the PT's. ZUNI rocket runs and 20 mm strafing attacks were directed against two of the PT's and they were damaged. The third PT remained dead in the water after the direct hit by the MADDOX. At 4:29 A.M., the aircraft broke off the engagement and escorted the MADDOX towards South Viet Nam waters.

The C. TURNER JOY has joined with the MADDOX and they are continuing patrols in the area in international waters. Aircraft from the TICONDEROGA are providing protective coverage.

B. The Gulf of Tonkin Resolution, August 7, 1964

To Promote the Maintenance of International Peace and Security in Southeast Asia

Whereas naval units of the Communist regime in Vietnam, in violation of the principles of the Charter of the United Nations and of international law, have deliberately and repeatedly attacked United States naval vessels lawfully present in international waters, and have thereby created a serious threat to international peace; and

Whereas these attacks are part of a deliberate and systematic campaign of aggression that the Communist regime in North Vietnam has been waging against its neighbors and the nations joined with them in the collective defense of their freedom; and

Whereas the United States is assisting the peoples of southeast Asia to protect their freedom and has no territorial, military or political ambitions in that area, but desires only that these peoples should be left in peace to work out their own destinies in their own way: Now, therefore, be it

Resolved by the Senate and House of Representatives of the United States of America in Congress assembled.

That the Congress approves and supports the determination of the President as Commander in Chief, to take all necessary measures to repel any armed attack against the forces of the United States and to prevent further aggression.

SEC.2. The United States regards as vital to its national interest and to world peace the maintenance of international peace and security in southeast Asia. Consonant with the Constitution of the United States and the Charter of the United Nations and in accordance with its obligations under the Southeast Asia Collective Defense Treaty, the United States is, therefore, prepared, as the President determines, to take all necessary steps, including the use of armed force, to assist any member or protocol state of the Southeast Asia Collective Defense Treaty requesting assistance in defense of its freedom.

SEC.3. This resolution shall expire when the President shall determine that the peace and security of the area is reasonably assured by international conditions created by action of the United Nations or otherwise, except that it may be terminated earlier by concurrent resolution of the Congress.[1]

C. The Secret Americanization Continues

Memorandum From the Joint Chiefs of Staff Office of the Special Assistant for Counterinsurgency and Special Activities August 27, 1964

For Mr. William Bundy; Mr. J. T. McNaughton
Subject: OPLAN 34A—September Schedule
Reference: MACSOG Message 8616 DTG 240855Z August

1.On June 24, 1970, the Senate voted 81–10 to repeal this resolution.—eds.

1. Attached hereto is COMUSMACV's proposed schedule of 34A actions for September.

2. All of the actions listed have either been specifically approved previously or are similar to such approved actions. For example, Action (3) (d) was specifically approved by consideration of JCSM–426–64 dated 19 May 1964, while Action (3) (b) is similar to a previously approved action against a security post.

3. The method of attack has been changed in some instances from destruction by infiltration of demolition teams to the concept of standoff bombardment from PTF's. These actions are so indicated in the attachment.

Rollen H. Anthis
Major General, USAF

Attachment

The proposed September 34A actions are as follows:

(1) Intelligence Collection Actions

(a) 1–30 September—Ariel photography to update selected targets along with pre- and post-strike coverage of approved actions.

(b) 1–30 September—Two junk capture missions; remove captives for 36–48 hours interrogation; booby trap junk with antidisturbance devices and release; captives returned after interrogation; timing depends upon sea conditions and current intelligence.

(2) *Psychological Operations*

(a) 1–30 September—In conjunction with approved overflights and maritime operations, delivery of propaganda leaflets, gift kits, and deception devices simulating resupply of phantom teams.

(b) 1–30 September—Approximately 200 letters of various propaganda themes sent through third country mail channels to North Vietnam.

(c) 1–30 September—Black Radio daily 30-minute programs repeated once, purports to be voice of dissident elements in North Vietnam.

(d) 1–30 September—White Radio broadcast of eight-and-one-half hours daily, propaganda "Voice of Freedom."

(3) *Maritime Operations*

(a) 1–30 September—Demolition of Route 1 bridge by infiltrated team accompanied by fire support teams, place short-delay charges against spans and caissons, place antipersonnel mines on road approaches. (This bridge previously hit but now repaired).

(b) 1–30 September—Bombard Cape Mui Dao observation post with 81 MM mortars and 40 MM guns from two PTFs.

(c) 1–30 September—Demolition of another Route 1 bridge (see map), concept same as (3) (a) above.

(d) 1–30 September—Bombard Sam Son radar, same as (3) (b).

(e) 1–30 September—Bombard Tiger Island barracks, same as (3) (b).

(f) 1–30 September—Bombard Hon Ngu Island, same as (3) (b).

(g) 1–30 September—Bombard Hon Matt Island, same as (3) (b) and run concurrently with (3) (f).

(h) 1–30 September—Destruction of section of Hanoi-Vinh railroad by infiltrated demolition team supported by two VN marine squads, by rubber boats from PTFs, place short-delay charges and anti-personnel mines around area.

(i) 1–30 September—Bombard Hon Me Island in conjunction with (3) (a) above, concept same as (3) (b).

(j) 1–30 September—Bombard Cape Falaise gun positions in conjunction with (3) (h) above, concept same as (3) (b).

(k) 1–30 September—Bombard Cape Mui Ron in conjunction with junk capture mission, concept same as (3) (b).

(4) *Airborne Operations*—Light-of-moon period 16–28 September

(a) Four missions for resupply of in-place teams.

(b) Four missions for reinforcement of in-place teams.

(c) Four missions to airdrop new psyops/sabotage teams depending upon development of drop zone and target information. These are low-key propaganda and intelligence gathering teams with a capability for small-scale sabotage on order after locating suitable targets.

(5) Dates for actual launch of maritime and airborne operations are contingent upon the intelligence situation and weather conditions.

Memorandum from Secretary of Defense Robert S. McNamara to the Chairman, Joint Chiefs of Staff, August 31, 1964

Subject: JCSM–729–64: Target Study—North Vietnam

1. I have examined with great interest and satisfaction your recent analysis of the 94 targets in North Vietnam. The detail and precision with which you have described and defined the targets, the attack objectives, and the weapons and sorties required to accomplish those objectives testify to the care with which you have undertaken your task and the weeks of effort which you have devoted to it. Earlier versions of your target studies have already proved to be of great value in connection with the recent reprisals against North Vietnam.

2. Would there be sufficient stocks of ordnance and POL in the theater to carry out OPLAN 32, Phase IV, *after* carrying out the largest pattern of attack shown in your memorandum (paragraph 8d)?

3. I should like to receive, within the next several weeks, your views concerning the economic and military effect upon North Vietnam of the patterns of attack contemplated. To put the matter more precisely, assume that attacks 8b, c and d were carried out and that the attacks resulted in the damage levels described in your target studies. In these circumstances, what would be your estimate:

(a) Of the effects upon the capabilities of North Vietnam

i. to support and assist the PL and VC.

ii. to escalate through the use of DRV forces against SVN and Laos.

(b) Of the effects upon the economy of North Vietnam (in terms of such factors as internal transportation, imports and exports, industrial production and food production and distribution) within the short run (say three months) and in the long-run (say five years).

4. If the destruction of the 94 targets were not to succeed in its objective of destroying the DRV will and capability, what courses of action would you recommend? Would you recommend further attack on the 94 targets or the addition of more targets? What preparations would be necessary (e.g., target analysis, logistics) in order to carry out such attacks?

37. Rationale for Escalation: The US Government "White Paper" of 1965*

Now that US forces were fully engaged, some official rationalization of the war was necessary. In 1965 a "White Paper" laying out the government case for intervention was released. An official history of the war as of 1965, the facts and arguments presented in these excerpts from the White Paper were refuted by I. F. Stone (Reading 38).[1]

Introduction

South Vietnam is fighting for its life against a brutal campaign of terror and armed attack inspired, directed, supplied, and controlled by the Communist regime in Hanoi. This flagrant aggression has been going on for years, but recently the pace has quickened and the threat has now become active.

The war in Vietnam is a new kind of war, a fact as yet poorly understood in most parts of the world. Much of the confusion that prevails in the thinking of many people, and even many governments, stems from this basic misunderstanding. For in Vietnam a totally new brand of aggression has been loosed against an independent people who want to make their own way in peace and freedom.

---

*From *Aggression From the North: The Record of North Vietnam's Campaign to Conquer South Vietnam* [U.S. Department of State Publication 7839; Far Eastern Series 130] (Washington, D.C., [February] 1965).

1. In 1981 a White Paper on the situation in El Salvador was released. Entitled "Communist Interference in El Salvador," the report was a rationale for the Reagan administration's deepening involvement in what many observers saw as "another Vietnam." As in the 1965 document, the 1981 White Paper played down indigenous factors in the insurgency and instead portrayed it as a "textbook case" of outside aggression. This time journalists such as Robert Kaiser of the *Washington Post* and Jonathan Kwitny of the *Wall Street Journal*, as well as scholars such as James Petras, performed the function I. F. Stone had for Vietnam. Upon close examination, the 1981 paper was shown to be deeply flawed in data and reasoning. It revealed, as did the 1965 White Paper, an obsessive tendency to discover outside, conspiratorial forces to explain what could be much more economically accounted for by indigenous factors. See: *Communist Interference in El Salvador*, US Department of State, Special Report No. 80 (February 23, 1981) reprinted in Marvin E. Gettleman, Patrick Lacefield, Louis Menashe, David Mermelstein, Ronald Radosh, eds., *El Salvador: Central American in the New Cold War* (New York: Grove Press, 1981), Readings 35, 36, 37.

Vietnam is *not* another Greece, where indigenous guerrilla forces used friendly neighboring territory as a sanctuary.

Vietnam is *not* another Malaya, where Communist guerrillas were, for the most part, physically distinguishable from the peaceful majority they sought to control.

Vietnam is *not* another Philippines, where Communist guerrillas were physically separated from the source of their moral and physical support.[2]

Above all, the war in Vietnam is *not* a spontaneous and local rebellion against the established government.

There are elements in the Communist program of conquest directed against South Vietnam common to each of the previous areas of aggression and subversion. But there is one fundamental difference. In Vietnam a Communist government has set out deliberately to conquer a sovereign people in a neighboring state. And to achieve its end, it has used every resource of its own government to carry out its carefully planned program of concealed aggression. North Vietnam's commitment to seize control of the South is no less total than was the commitment of the regime in North Korea in 1950. But knowing the consequences of the latter's undisguised attack, the planners in Hanoi have tried desperately to conceal their hand. They have failed and their aggression is as real as that of an invading army.

This report is a summary of the massive evidence of North Vietnamese aggression obtained by the Government of South Vietnam. This evidence has been jointly analyzed by South Vietnamese and American experts.

The evidence shows that the hard core of the Communist forces attacking South Vietnam were trained in the North and ordered into the South by Hanoi. It shows that the key leadership of the Vietcong (VC), the officers and much of the cadre, many of the technicians, political organizers, and propagandists have come from the North and operate under Hanoi's direction. It shows that the training of essential military personnel and their infiltration into the South is directed by the Military High Command in Hanoi.

The evidence shows that many of the weapons and much of the ammunition and other supplies used by the Vietcong have been sent into South Vietnam from Hanoi. In recent months new types of weapons have been introduced in the VC army, for which all ammunition must come from outside sources. Communist China and other Communist states have been the prime suppliers of these weapons and ammunition, and they have been channeled primarily through North Vietnam.[3]

---

2. Compare the 1961 "White Paper": "The basic pattern of Vietcong activity is not new, of course. It operated with minor variations in China, and Mao Tse-Tung's theories on the conduct of guerrilla warfare are known to every Vietcong agent and cadre. Most of the same methods were used in Malaya, in Greece, in the Philippines, in Cuba, and in Laos." *A Threat to the Peace: North Vietnam's Effort to Conquer South Vietnam* [US Department of State Publication 308; Far Eastern Series 110] (Washington, D.C., [December] 1961), p. 1—eds.

3. Compare with the 1961 "White Paper": "By hitting such targets [police stations, army outposts, etc.] suddenly and in superior force, the VC are able to assure themselves a supply of arms and ammunition. This reduces their dependence on the long supply line from the North. The weapons of the VC are largely French- or US-made, or handmade on primitive forges in the jungles." *A Threat to Peace*, p. 9—eds.

The directing force behind the effort to conquer South Vietnam is the Communist Party in the North, the Lao Dong (Workers) Party. As in every Communist state, the party is an integral part of the regime itself. North Vietnamese officials have expressed their firm determination to absorb South Vietnam into the Communist world. . . .

I. Hanoi Supplies the Key Personnel for the Armed Aggression Against South Vietnam

The hard core of the Communist forces attacking South Vietnam are men trained in North Vietnam. They are ordered into the South and remain under the military discipline of the Military High Command in Hanoi. Special training camps operated by the North Vietnamese army give political and military training to the infiltrators. Increasingly the forces sent into the South are native North Vietnamese who have never seen South Vietnam. A special infiltration unit, the 70th Transportation Group, is responsible for moving men from North Vietnam into the South via infiltration trails through Laos. Another special unit, the maritime infiltration group, sends weapons and supplies and agents by sea into the South.

The infiltration rate has been increasing. From 1959 to 1960, when Hanoi was establishing its infiltration pipeline, at least 1,800 men, and possibly 2,700 more, moved into South Vietnam from the North. The flow increased to a minimum of 3,700 in 1961 and at least 5,400 in 1962. There was a modest decrease in 1963 to 4,200 confirmed infiltrators, though later evidence is likely to raise this figure.

For 1964 the evidence is still incomplete. However, it already shows that a minimum of 4,400 infiltrators entered the South, and it is estimated more than 3,000 others were sent in.

There is usually a time lag between the entry of infiltrating troops and the discovery of clear evidence they have entered. This fact, plus collateral evidence of increased use of the infiltration routes, suggests strongly that 1964 was probably the year of greatest infiltration so far.

Thus, since 1959, nearly 20,000 VC officers, soldiers, and technicians are known to have entered South Vietnam under orders from Hanoi. Additional information indicates that an estimated 17,000 more infiltrators were dispatched to the South by the regime in Hanoi during the past six years. It can reasonably be assumed that still other infiltration groups have entered the South for which there is no evidence yet available.

To some the level of infiltration from the North may seem modest in comparison with the total size of the armed forces of the Republic of Vietnam. But one-for-one calculations are totally misleading in the kind of warfare going on in Vietnam. First, a high proportion of infiltrators from the North are well-trained officers, cadres, and specialists. Second, it has long been realized that in guerrilla combat the burdens of defense are vastly heavier than those of attack. In Malaya, the Philippines, and elsewhere a ratio of at least 10-to-1 in favor of the forces of order was required to meet successfully the threat of the guerrillas' hit-and-run tactics.

In the calculus of guerrilla warfare the scale of North Vietnamese infiltration into the South takes on a very different meaning. For the infiltration of 5,000 guerrilla fighters in a given year is the equivalent of marching perhaps 50,000 regular troops across the border, in terms of the burden placed on the defenders.

Above all, the number of proved and probable infiltrators from the North should be seen in relation to the size of the VC forces. It is now estimated that the Vietcong number approximately 35,000 so-called hard-core forces, and another 60,000–80,000 local forces. It is thus apparent that infiltrators from the North—allowing for casualties—makes up the majority of the so-called hard-core Vietcong. Personnel from the North, in short, are now and have always been the backbone of the entire VC operation.

It is true that many of the lower level elements of the VC forces are recruited within South Vietnam.[4] However, the thousands of reported cases of VC kidnapings and terrorism make it abundantly clear that threats and other pressures by the Vietcong play a major part in such recruitment.

A. The Infiltration Process

The infiltration routes supply hard-core units with most of their officers and non-commissioned personnel. This source helps fill the gaps left by battle casualties, illness, and defection and insures continued control by Hanoi. Also, as the nature of the conflict has changed, North Vietnam has supplied the Vietcong with technical specialists via the infiltration routes. These have included men trained in armor and ordnance, antiaircraft, and communications as well as medical corpsmen and transport experts.

There is no single infiltration route from the North to South Vietnam. But by far the biggest percentage of infiltrators follow the same general course. The principal training center for North Vietnamese army men assigned to join the Vietcong has been at Xuan Mai near Hanoi. Recently captured Vietcong have also reported an infiltration training camp at Thanh Hoa. After completion of their training course—which involves political and propaganda work as well as military subjects—infiltrating units are moved to Vinh on the east coast. Many have made stopovers at a staging area in Dong Hoi where additional training is conducted. From there they go by truck to the Laos border.

Then usually after several days' rest, infiltrators move southward through Laos. Generally they move along the Laos-South Vietnam border. Responsibility for infiltration from North Vietnam through Laos belongs to the 70th Transportation Group of the North Vietnamese army. After a time the infiltration groups turn

---

4. Compare the 1961 "White Paper": "During the months after the Geneva Agreements went into effect, most of the military units loyal to Ho Chi Minh were transferred to North Vietnam; but some of the best-trained guerrilla units moved to remote and inaccessible regions in the South . . . [that is, they remained]. Individual agents and many members of Communist cells were told to stay in place, to lead normal lives, and to wait until they received orders to carry out Party assignments." These assignments were mainly to prepare for the nationwide elections that the Geneva Agreements provided for in 1956. *A Threat to The Peace*, p. 3—eds.

eastward, entering South Vietnam in Quang Nam, Quang Tri, Thua Thien, Kontum, or another of the border provinces.

The Communists have established regular lanes for infiltration with way-stations established about one day's march apart. The way-stations are equipped to quarter and feed the Vietcong passing through. Infiltrators who suffer from malaria or other illnesses stay at the stations until they recover sufficiently to join another passing group moving South. . . .

Local guides lead the infiltration groups along the secret trails. Generally they direct their infiltrators from halfway between two stations, through their own base station, and on halfway to the next supply base. Thus the guides are kept in ignorance of all but their own way-stations. Only group leaders are permitted to talk with the guides in order to preserve maximum security. The men are discouraged from asking where they are or where they are going.

The same system of trails and guides used along the Laos infiltration routes is used within South Vietnam itself. Vietcong infiltrators may report directly to a reassignment center in the highlands as soon as they enter South Vietnam. But in the past year or more some groups have moved down trails in South Vietnam to provinces along the Cambodian border and near Saigon before receiving their unit assignment. Within South Vietnam infiltration and supplies are handled by VC units such as the Nam Son Transportation Group.

At the Laos border-crossing point infiltrators are re-equipped. Their North Vietnamese army uniforms must be turned in. They must give up all personal papers, letters, notebooks, and photographs that might be incriminating. Document control over the infiltrators has been tightened considerably over the past two years. A number of Vietnamese infiltrators have told of being fitted out with Lao "neutralist" uniforms for their passage through Laos.

Infiltration groups are usually issued a set of black civilian pajama-like clothes, two unmarked uniforms, rubber sandals, a sweater, a hammock, mosquito netting, and water-proof sheeting. They carry a 3–5 day supply of food. A packet of medicines and bandages is usually provided. . . .

II. Hanoi Supplies Weapons, Ammunition, and Other War Material to Its Forces in the South

When Hanoi launched the VC campaign of terror, violence, and subversion in earnest in 1959, the Communist forces relied mainly on stocks of weapons and ammunition left over from the war against the French. Supplies sent in from North Vietnam came largely from the same source. As the military campaign progressed, the Vietcong depended heavily on weapons captured from the Armed Forces in South Vietnam. This remains an important source of weapons and ammunition for the Vietcong. But as the pace of the war has quickened, requirements for up-to-date arms and special types of weapons have risen to a point where the Vietcong cannot rely on captured stocks. Hanoi has undertaken a program to reequip its forces in the South with Communist-produced weapons.

Large and increasing quantities of military supplies are entering South Vietnam from outside the country. The principal supply point is North Vietnam, which provides a convenient channel for material that originates in Communist China and other Communist countries.

An increasing number of weapons from external Communist sources have been seized in the South. These include such weapons as 57-mm. and 75-mm. recoilless rifles, dual-purpose machine guns, rocket launchers, large mortars, and antitank mines.

A new group of Chinese Communist-manufactured weapons has recently appeared in VC hands. These include the 7.62 semiautomatic carbine, 7.62 light machine gun, and the 7.62 assault rifle. These weapons and ammunition for them, manufactured in Communist China in 1962, were first captured in December 1964 in Chuong Thien Province. Similar weapons have since been seized in each of the four Corps areas of South Vietnam. Also captured have been Chinese Communist antitank grenade launchers and ammunition made in China in 1963.

One captured Vietcong told his captors that his entire company had been supplied recently with modern Chinese weapons. The reequipping of VC units with a type of weapons that require ammunition and parts from outside South Vietnam indicates the growing confidence of the authorities in Hanoi in the effectiveness of their supply lines into the South.

Incontrovertible evidence of Hanoi's elaborate program to supply its forces in the South with weapons, ammunition, and other supplies has accumulated over the years. Dramatic new proof was exposed just as this report was being completed.

On February 16. 1965, an American helicopter pilot flying along the South Vietnamese coast sighted a suspicious vessel. It was a cargo ship of an estimated 100-ton capacity, carefully camouflaged and moored just offshore along the coast of Phu Yen Province. Fighter planes that approached the vessel met machine gun fire from the guns on the deck of the ship and from the shore as well. A Vietnamese Air Force strike was launched against the vessel, and Vietnamese Government troops moved into the area. They seized the ship after a bitter fight with the Vietcong.

The ship, which had been sunk in shallow water, had discharged a huge cargo of arms, ammunition, and other supplies. Documents found on the ship and on the bodies of several Vietcong aboard identified the vessel as having come from North Vietnam. A newspaper in the cabin was from Haiphong and was dated January 23, 1965. The supplies delivered by the ship—thousands of weapons and more than a million rounds of ammunition—were almost all of Communist origin, largely from Communist China and Czechoslovakia, as well as North Vietnam. At least 100 tons of military supplies were discovered near the ship.

A preliminary survey of the cache near the sunken vessel from Hanoi listed the following supplies and weapons:

approximately 1 million rounds of small-arms ammunition;
more than 1,000 stick grenades;

500 pounds of TNT in prepared charges;
2,000 rounds of 82-mm mortar ammunition;
500 antitank grenades;
500 rounds of 57-mm. recoilless rifle ammunition;
more than 1,000 rounds of 75-mm. recoilless rifle ammunition;
1 57-mm. recoilless rifle;
2 heavy machine guns;
2,000 7.92 Mauser rifles;
more than 100 7.62 carbines;
1,000 submachine guns;
15 light machine guns;
500 rifles;
500 pounds of medical supplies (with labels from North Vietnam, Communist China, Czechoslovakia, East Germany, Soviet Union, and other sources). . . .

III. North Vietnam: Base for Conquest of the South[5]

The Third Lao Dong Party Congress in Hanoi in September 1960 set forth two tasks for its members: "to carry out the socialist revolution in North Vietnam" and "to liberate South Vietnam."

The resolutions of the congress described the effort to destroy the legal Government in South Vietnam as follows: "The revolution in the South is a protracted, hard, and complex process of struggle, combining many forms of struggle of great activity and flexibility, ranging from lower to higher, and taking as its basis the building, consolidation, and development of the revolutionary power of the masses."

At the September meeting the Communist leaders in the North called for formation of "a broad national united front." Three months later Hanoi announced creation of the "Front for Liberation of the South." This is the organization that Communist propaganda now credits with guiding the forces of subversion in the South; it is pictured as an organization established and run by the people in the South themselves. At the 1960 Lao Dong Party Congress the tone was different. Then, even before the front existed, the Communist leaders were issuing orders for the group that was being organized behind the scenes in Hanoi. "This front must rally . . ."; "The aims of its struggle are . . ."; "The front must carry out . . ."—this is the way Hanoi and the Communist Party addressed the "Liberation Front" even before its founding.

The Liberation Front is Hanoi's creation; it is neither independent nor Southern, and what it seeks is not liberation but subjugation of the South. . . .

---

5. Much of the material in this section is identical to that in the 1961 "White Paper." See *A Threat to the Peace*, especially pp. 14–25.—eds.

IV. Organization, Direction, Command, and Control of the Attack on South Vietnam Are Centered in Hanoi

The VC military and political apparatus in South Vietnam is an extension of an elaborate military and political structure in North Vietnam which directs and supplies it with the tools for conquest. The Ho Chi Minh regime has shown that it is ready to allocate every resource that can be spared—whether it be personnel, funds, or equipment—to the cause of overthrowing the legitimate Government in South Vietnam and of bringing all Vietnam under Communist rule.

A. Political Organization

Political direction and control of the Vietcong is supplied by the Lao Dong Party, i.e. the Communist Party, led by Ho Chi Minh. Party agents are responsible for indoctrination, recruitment, political training, propaganda, anti-Government demonstrations, and other activities of a political nature. The considerable intelligence-gathering facilities of the party are also at the disposal of the Vietcong.

Overall direction of the VC movement is the responsibility of the Central Committee of the Lao Dong Party. Within the Central Committee a special Reunification Department has been established. This has replaced the "Committee for Supervision of the South" mentioned in intelligence reports two years ago. It lays down broad strategy for the movement to conquer South Vietnam. . . .

The "Liberation Front." The National Front for the Liberation of South Vietnam is the screen behind which the Communists carry out their program of conquest. It is the creature of the Communist Government in Hanoi. As noted above, the Communist Party in the North demanded establishment of such a "front" three months before its formation was actually announced in December 1960. It was designed to create the illusion that the Vietcong campaign of subversion was truly indigenous to South Vietnam rather than an externally directed Communist plan.

The front has won support primarily from the Communist world. Its radio faithfully repeats the propaganda themes of Hanoi and Peking. When its representatives travel abroad, they do so with North Vietnamese passports and sponsorship.[6] The front's program copies that of the Lao Dong Party in North Vietnam.

B. Military Organization

Military affairs of the Vietcong are the responsibility of High Command of the People's Army of North Vietnam and the Ministry of Defense, under close supervision from the Lao Dong Party. These responsibilities include operational plans, assignments of individuals and regular units, training programs, infiltration of military personnel and supplies, and the like. The six military regions are the same as those of the VC political organization.

The military structure of the Vietcong is an integral part of the political ma-

---

6. Pictures of North Vietnamese passports and other travel documents used by officials of the National Liberation Front are included in appendix F of this "White Paper," not reproduced here. One doubts that NLF members would have found it easy to get passports from Saigon authorities.—eds.

chinery that controls every facet of VC activity in South Vietnam under Hanoi's overall direction. Each political headquarters from the Central Office down to the village has a military component which controls day-to-day military operations. Similarly, each military headquarters has a political element, an individual or a small staff. This meshing of political and military activity is designed to insure the closest cooperation in support of the total Communist mission. It also gives assurance of political control over the military. . . .

The size of the Vietcong regular forces has grown steadily in recent years. For example, the Vietcong have five regimental headquarters compared with two in 1961. And the main VC force is composed of 50 battalions, 50 per cent more than before. There are an estimated 139 VC companies. Hard-core VC strength now is estimated at about 35,000, whereas it was less than 20,000 in 1961. . . .

Supporting the main force units of the Vietcong are an estimated 60,000–80,000 part-time guerrillas. They are generally organized at the district level where there are likely to be several companies of fifty or more men each. These troops receive only half pay, which means they must work at least part of the time to eke out a living.

Below the irregular guerrilla forces of the district are the part-time, village-based guerrillas. They are available for assignment by higher headquarters and are used for harassment and sabotage. They are expected to warn nearby VC units of the approach of any force of the legal government. They provide a pool for recruitment into the VC district forces.

The record shows that many of the village guerrillas are dragooned into service with the Vietcong. Some are kidnaped; others are threatened; still others join to prevent their families from being harmed. Once in the Vietcong net, many are reluctant to leave for fear of punishment by the authorities or reprisal by the Communists. . . .

Officials and wealthy people have been kidnaped for ransom. The VC have often stopped buses and taken the money and valuables of all on board. For the most part, the VC have concentrated their attention on individuals, isolated or poorly defended outposts, and small centers of population. They have mercilessly killed or kidnaped thousands of village chiefs and other local officials. But over the past year the VC have moved into larger unit operations. Their ability to operate on a battalion level or larger has substantially increased.

C. Intelligence Organization

A key element in the Vietcong effort is an elaborate organization in Hanoi called the Central Research Agency (C.R.A.) (Cuc Nghien-Cuu Trung-Uong). Though it handles Hanoi's intelligence effort on a worldwide scale, the main focus of its operation is on South Vietnam. This agency is able to draw on the intelligence capabilities of both the Lao Dong Party and the North Vietnamese armed forces for information, personnel and facilities. . . .

Taken as a whole, the North Vietnamese intelligence operation in support of the Vietcong is one of the most extensive of its kind in the world.

V. A Brief History of Hanoi's Campaign of Aggression Against South Vietnam

While negotiating an end to the Indochina War in Geneva in 1954, the Communists were making plans to take over all former French territory in Southeast Asia. When Vietnam was partitioned, thousands of carefully selected party members were ordered to remain in place in the South and keep their secret apparatus intact to help promote Hanoi's cause. Arms and ammunition were stored away for future use. Guerrilla fighters rejoined their families to await the party's call. Others withdrew to remote jungle and mountain hideouts. The majority—an estimated 90,000—were moved to North Vietnam.

Hanoi's original calculation was that all of Vietnam would fall under its control without resort to force.[7] For this purpose, Communist cadres were ordered to penetrate official and non-official agencies, to propagandize and sow confusion, and generally to use all means short of open violence to aggravate war-torn conditions and to weaken South Vietnam's Government and social fabric.

South Vietnam's refusal to fall in with Hanoi's scheme for peaceful takeover came as a heavy blow to the Communists. Meantime, the Government had stepped up efforts to blunt Vietcong subversion and to expose Communist agents. Morale in the Communist organization in the South dropped sharply. Defections were numerous.

Among South Vietnamese, hope rose that their nation could have a peaceful and independent future, free of Communist domination. The country went to work. The years after 1955 were a period of steady progress and growing prosperity.

Food production levels of the prewar years were reached and surpassed. While per capita food output was dropping 10 per cent in the North from 1956 to 1960, it rose 20 per cent in the South. By 1963, it had risen 30 per cent—despite the disruption in the countryside caused by intensified Vietcong military attacks and terrorism. The authorities in the North admitted openly to continuing annual failures to achieve food production goals.

Production of textiles increased in the South more than 20 per cent in one year (1958). In the same year, South Vietnam's sugar crop increased more than 100 per cent. Despite North Vietnam's vastly larger industrial complex, South Vietnam's per capita gross national product in 1960 was estimated at $110 a person while it was only $70 in the North.

More than 900,000 refugees who had fled from Communist rule in the North were successfully settled in South Vietnam. An agrarian reform program was instituted. The elementary school population nearly quadrupled between 1956 and 1960. And so it went—a record of steady improvement in the lives of the people. It was intolerable for the rulers in Hanoi; under peaceful conditions, the South was

---

7. At this point in the historical section of the 1961 "White Paper" there is a discreet reference to the "nationwide elections" which the Viet Minh hoped to win. As I. F. Stone points out, there is no such reference in this "White Paper" (see Reading 38).—eds.

outstripping the North. They were losing the battle of peaceful competition and decided to use violence and terror to gain their ends.

After 1956, Hanoi rebuilt, reorganized, and expanded its covert political and military machinery in the South. Defectors were replaced by trained personnel from party ranks in the North. Military units and political cells were enlarged and were given new leaders, equipment, and intensified training. Recruitment was pushed. In short, Hanoi and its forces in the South prepared to take by force and violence what they had failed to achieve by other means.

By 1958 the use of terror by the Vietcong increased appreciably. It was used both to win prestige and to back up demands for support from the people, support that political and propaganda appeals had failed to produce. It was also designed to embarrass the Government in Saigon and raise doubts about its ability to maintain internal order and to assure the personal security of its people. From 1959 through 1961, the pace of Vietcong terrorism and armed attacks accelerated substantially.

The situation at the end of 1961 was so grave that the Government of the Republic of Vietnam asked the United States for increased military assistance. That request was met. Meantime, the program of strategic hamlets, designed to improve the peasant's livelihood and give him some protection against Vietcong harassment and pressure, was pushed energetically.

But the Vietcong did not stand still. To meet the changing situation, they tightened their organization and adopted new tactics, with increasing emphasis on terrorism, sabotage, and armed attacks by small groups. They also introduced from the North technicians in fields such as armor and antiaircraft. Heavier weapons were sent in to the regular guerrilla forces.

The military and insurgency situation was complicated by a quite separate internal political struggle in South Vietnam, which led in November 1963 to the removal of the Diem government and its replacement with a new one. Effective power was placed in the hands of a Military Revolutionary Council. There have been a number of changes in the leadership and composition of the Government in Saigon in the ensuing period.

These internal developments and distractions gave the Vietcong an invaluable opportunity, and they took advantage of it. Vietcong agents did what they could to encourage disaffection and to exploit demonstrations in Saigon and elsewhere. In the countryside the Communists consolidated their hold over some areas and enlarged their military and political apparatus by increased infiltration. Increasingly they struck at remote outposts and the most vulnerable of the new strategic hamlets and expanded their campaign of aggressive attacks, sabotage, and terror.

Any official, worker, or establishment that represents a service to the people by the Government in Saigon is fair game for the Vietcong. Schools have been among their favorite targets. Through harassment, the murder of teachers, and sabotage of buildings, the Vietcong succeeded in closing hundreds of schools and interrupting the education of tens of thousands of youngsters.

Hospitals and medical clinics have often been attacked as part of the anti-

Government campaign and also because such attacks provide the Vietcong with needed medical supplies. The Communists have encouraged people in rural areas to oppose the Government's antimalaria teams, and some of the workers have been killed. Village and town officers, police stations, and agricultural research stations are high on the list of preferred targets for the Vietcong.

In 1964, 436 South Vietnamese hamlet chiefs and other Government officials were killed outright by the Vietcong and 1,131 were kidnaped. More than 1,350 civilians were killed in bombings and other acts of sabotage. And at least 8,400 civilians were kidnaped by the Vietcong.

Today the war in Vietnam has reached new levels in intensity. The elaborate effort by the Communist regime in North Vietnam to conquer the South has grown, not diminished. Military men, technicians, political organizers, propagandists, and secret agents have been infiltrating into the Republic of Vietnam from the North in growing numbers. The flow of Communist-supplied weapons, particularly those of large caliber, has increased. Communications links with Hanoi are extensive. Despite the heavy casualties of three years of fighting, the hard-core VC force is considerably larger now than it was at the end of 1961.

The Government in Saigon has undertaken vigorous action to meet the new threat. The United States and other free countries have increased their assistance to the Vietnamese Government and people. Secretary of State Dean Rusk visited Vietnam in 1964, and he promised the Vietnamese: "We shall remain at your side until the aggression from the North has been defeated, until it has been completely rooted out and this land enjoys the peace which it deserves."

President Johnson has repeatedly stressed that the United States' goal is to see peace secured in Southeast Asia. But he has noted that "that will come only when aggressors leave their neighbors in peace."

Though it has been apparent for years that the regime in Hanoi was conducting a campaign of conquest against South Vietnam, the Government in Saigon and the Government of the United States both hoped that the danger could be met within South Vietnam itself. The hope that any widening of the conflict might be avoided was stated frequently.

The leaders in Hanoi chose to respond with greater violence. They apparently interpreted restraint as indicating lack of will. Their efforts were pressed with greater vigor and armed attacks and incidents of terror multiplied.

Clearly the restraint of the past was not providing adequately for the defense of South Vietnam against Hanoi's open aggression. It was mutually agreed between the Governments of the Republic of Vietnam and the United States that further means for providing for South Vietnam's defense were required. Therefore, air strikes have been made against some of the military assembly points and supply bases from which North Vietnam is conducting its aggression against the South. These strikes constitute a limited response fitted to the aggression that produced them.

Until the regime in Hanoi decides to halt its intervention in the South, or until effective steps are taken to maintain peace and security in the area, the Governments of South Vietnam and the United States will continue necessary measures of defense against the Communist armed aggression coming from North Vietnam.

VI. Conclusion

The evidence presented in this report could be multiplied many times with similar examples of the drive of the Hanoi regime to extend its rule over South Vietnam.

The record is conclusive. It establishes beyond question that North Vietnam is carrying out a carefully conceived plan of aggression against the South. It shows that North Vietnam has intensified its efforts in the years since it was condemned by the International Control Commission. It proves that Hanoi continues to press its systematic program of armed aggression into South Vietnam. This aggression violates the United Nations charter. It is directly contrary to the Geneva Accords of 1954 and of 1962 to which North Vietnam is a party. It shatters the peace of Southeast Asia. It is a fundamental threat to the freedom and security of South Vietnam.

The people of South Vietnam have chosen to resist this threat. At their request, the United States has taken its place beside them in their defensive struggle.

The United States seeks no territory, no military bases, no favored position. But we have learned the meaning of aggression elsewhere in the post-war world, and we have met it.

If peace can be restored in South Vietnam, the United States will be ready at once to reduce its military involvement. But it will not abandon friends who want to remain free. It will do what must be done to help them. The choice now between peace and continued and increasingly destructive conflict is one for the authorities in Hanoi to make.

38. Refutation of the "White Paper"*

By I. F. Stone

Considered a classic of American investigative journalism, this piece has been reprinted in a number of anthologies. Reporter for the New York Post, *as well as the* New York Star, PM, *and* New York Daily Compass, *I.F. Stone was associate editor of* The Nation, *and editor and publisher of* I. F. Stone's Weekly *(sometimes,* Bi-Weekly*) from 1953 to 1971. He is the author of several books, including* The Hidden History of the Korean War, The Truman Era, The Killings at Kent State, *and* Polemics and Prophecies.

I. F. Stone's Weekly [Washington, D.C.], XIII (March 8, 1965), pp. 1–4.

That North Vietnam supports the guerrillas in South Vietnam is no more a secret than that the United States supports the South Vietnamese government against them. The striking thing about the State Department's new White Paper is how little support it can prove. "Incontrovertible evidence of Hanoi's elaborate program to supply its forces in the South with weapons, ammunition, and other supplies," the White Paper says, "has accumulated over the years." A detailed presentation of this evidence is in Appendix D; unfortunately few will see the appendices since even *The New York Times* did not reprint them, though these are more revealing than the report.[1] Appendix D provides a list of weapons, ammunition, and other supplies of Chinese Communist, Soviet, Czech, and North Vietnamese manufacture, with the dates and place of capture from the Vietcong guerrillas, over the 18-month period from June 1962, to January 29 last year, when it was presented to the International Control Commission. The Commission was set up by the Geneva Agreements of 1954. This list provides a good point at which to begin an analysis of the White Paper.

The Pentagon's Figures

To put the figures in perspective, we called the Pentagon press office and obtained some figures the White Paper does not supply—the number of weapons captured from the guerrillas and the number lost to them in recent years.

	Captured from Guerrillas	*Lost to Them*
1962	4,800	5,200
1963	5,400	8,500
1964	4,900	13,700
3-Year-Total	15,100	27,400

In three years, the guerrillas captured from our side 12,300 more weapons than they lost to us.

What interests us at the moment is not this favorable balance but the number of guerrilla weapons our side captured during the past three years. The grand total was 15,100. If Hanoi has indeed engaged in an "elaborate program" to supply the Vietcong, one would expect a substantial number of enemy-produced weapons to turn up. Here is the sum total of enemy-produced weapons and supplies in that 18-month tally to the Control Commission—

72 rifles (46 Soviet, 26 Czech), 64 submachine guns (40 Czech, 24 French but "modified" in North Vietnam), 15 carbines (Soviet), 8 machine guns (6 Chinese, 2 North Vietnamese), 5 pistols (4 Soviet, 1 Czech), 4 mortars (Chinese), 3 recoilless 75-mm rifles (Chinese), 3 recoilless 57-mm guns (Chinese), 2 bazookas (1 Chinese, 1 Czech), 2 rocket launchers (Chinese), 1 grenade launcher (Czech). Total 179.

---

1. Space limitations unfortunately prevent us from reprinting Appendix D.—eds.

This is not a very impressive total. According to the Pentagon figures, we captured on the average of 7,500 weapons each 18 months in the past three years. If only 179 Communist-made weapons turned up in 18 months, that is less than 2½ per cent of the total. Judging by these White Paper figures, our military are wrong in estimating, as they have in recent months, that 80 per cent of the weapons used by guerrillas are captured from us. It looks as if the proportion is considerably higher. The material of North Vietnamese origin included only those 24 French submachine guns "modified" in North Vietnam, 2 machine guns made in North Vietnam, 16 helmets, a uniform, and an undisclosed number of mess kits, belts, sweaters, and socks. Judging by this tally, the main retaliatory blow should be at North Vietnam's clothing factories.

There is another way to judge this tally of captured Communist weapons. A Communist battalion has about 450 men. It needs 500 rifles, four 80-mm mortars, eight 60-mm mortars, and at least four recoilless rifles. The weapons of Communist origin captured in 18 months would not adequately outfit one battalion. The figures in the appendix on ammunition captured provide another index. We captured 183 (Chinese) shells for a 60-mm. mortar. This fires about 20 shells a minute, so that was hardly enough ammunition for 10 minutes of firing. There were 100,000 (Chinese) cartridges for 7.26-mm machine guns. That looks impressive until one discovers on checking with knowledgeable military sources that these machine guns fire 600 rounds a minute. A machine gun platoon normally has four machine guns. This was enough ammunition for about 40 minutes of firing by one platoon. Indeed, if the ratio of Communist-made weapons captured is the same for weapons used, then only 12½ days of those 18 months were fought by the guerrillas on the basis of Communist-made supplies.

If these figures were being presented in a court of law, they would run up against a further difficulty: one would have to prove the arms actually came from the Communist side. There is a world-wide market in second-hand weapons. One can buy Soviet, Czech, and Chinese Communist weapons of all kinds only two miles from the Pentagon through Interarmco, Ltd., 10 Prince Street, Alexandria, Va. Interarmco, one of the world's foremost dealers, can provide more Communist weapons than we picked up in 18 months on Vietnamese battlefields. The supply of East European Communist weapons comes in large part from the huge stocks of Soviet and Czech arms captured by the Israelis in the Suez campaign. Many Chinese Communist weapons were captured by our side in the Korean War. There is also, of course, a wide selection of our own military surplus. This has turned up in strange places.

For example, a book on the Algerian war, *Les Algériens en guerre*, by Dominique Darbois and Philippe Vingneau, was published in Milan in 1960 by Feltrinelli. It shows pictures of FLN (National Liberation Front) Algerian rebels wearing U.S. Marine Corps uniforms from which the "USM" and the eagle and globe insignia have not even been removed. It shows Algerians carrying U.S. 80-mm mortars and U.S. 50-caliber machine guns. Such photos could have been used by France to accuse the U.S. of supplying the Algerian rebels.

The State Department's White Paper says "dramatic new proof was exposed just as this report was being completed" in the discovery of a suspected Vietcong arms cargo ship on Feb. 16. *The New York Times* commented astringently on this in an editorial February 28:

Apparently, the major new evidence of a need for escalating the war, with all the hazards that this entails, was provided by the sinking in a South Vietnamese cove earlier this month of a 100-ton cargo ship loaded with Communist-made small arms and ammunition. A ship of that size is not much above the Oriental junk class. The standard Liberty or Victory ship of World War II had a capacity of 7,150 to 7,650 tons.

The affair of the cargo ship is curious. Until now there has been little evidence of arms coming in by ship. A huge fleet of small vessels patrols the coast and there have been glowing stories in the past of its efficiency. "About 12,000 vessels," the AP reported from Saigon (*The New York Times*, Feb. 22), "are searched each month by the South Vietnamese coastal junk patrol force but arrests are rare and no significant amounts of incriminating goods or weapons ever have been found." This lone case of a whole shipload of arms is puzzling.

Few Northern Infiltrees Cited

The White Paper's story on the influx of men from the North also deserves a closer analysis than the newspapers have given it. Appendix C provides an elaborate table from 1959–1960 to 1964 inclusive, showing the number of "confirmed" military infiltrees per year from the North. The total is given at 19,550. One way to measure this number is against that of the military we have assigned to South Vietnam in the same years. These now total 23,500, or 25 per cent more, and 1,000 are to be added in the near future. The number of North Vietnamese infiltrees is "based on information . . . from at least two independent sources." *Nowhere are we told how many men who infiltrated from the North have actually been captured.* There is reason to wonder whether the count of infiltrees may be as bloated as the count of Vietcong dead; in both cases the numbers used are estimates rather than actual bodies.

The White Paper claims "that as many as 75 per cent of the more than 7,000 Vietcong who are known to have entered the South in 1964 were natives of North Vietnam." But a careful reading of the text and the appendices turns up the names of only six North Vietnamese infiltrees. In Part I of the White Paper, Section B gives "individual case histories of North Vietnamese soldiers" sent South by Hanoi but all nine of these are of South Vietnamese origin. The next section, C, is headed "Infiltration of Native North Vietnamese." It names five infiltrees but one of these is also from the South. That leaves four North Vietnamese natives. Then, in Appendix C, we are given the case histories and photographs of nine other Vietcong sent South by Hanoi. The report does not explain which ones were originally from the South but it does give the names of the provinces in which they were born. When these are checked, it turns out that only two of the nine were born in North Vietnam. This gives us a total of six Northern infiltrees. It is strange that after five years of fighting, the White Paper can cite so few.

None of this is discussed frankly in the White Paper. To do so would be to bring the war into focus as a rebellion in the South, which may owe some men and materiel to the North but is largely dependent on popular indigenous support for its manpower, as it is on captured U.S. weapons for its supply. The White Paper withholds all evidence which points to a civil war. It also fails to tell the full story of the July 1962 Special Report by the International Control Commission. Appendix A quotes that portion in which the Commission 2-to-1 (Poland dissenting) declared that the North had in specific instances sent men and materiel south in violation of the Geneva accords. But nowhere does the State Department mention that the same report also condemned South Vietnam and the U.S., declaring that they had entered into a military alliance in violation of the Geneva Agreements. The U.S. was criticized because it then had about 5,000 military advisers in South Vietnam. The Geneva Accords limited the U.S. military mission to the 684 in Vietnam at the time of the 1954 cease-fire. The U.S. and South Vietnam were also criticized by the ICC for hamstringing the Commission's efforts to check on imports of arms in violation of the Geneva Accords.

The reader would never guess from the White Paper that the Geneva Accords promised that elections would be held in 1956 to reunify the country. The 1961 Blue Book[2] at least mentioned the elections, though somehow managing to make them seem a plot. "It was the Communists' calculation," the Blue Book put it, "that nationwide elections scheduled in the Accords for 1956 would turn all of South Vietnam over to them. . . . The authorities in South Vietnam refused to fall into this well-laid trap." The White Paper omits mention of the elections altogether and says, "South Vietnam's refusal to fall in with Hanoi's scheme for peaceful takeover came as a heavy blow to the Communists." This is not the most candid and objective presentation. From the Vietminh point of view, the failure to hold the elections promised them when they laid down their arms was the second broken promise of the West. The earlier one was in 1946 when they made an agreement to accept limited autonomy within the French union, and welcomed the returning French troops as comrades of the liberation. Most of the French military did not want to recognize even this limited form of independence, and chose instead the road which led after eight years of war to Dienbienphu.[3]

---

2. Stone is citing here *A Threat to the Peace* [p. 3], which we have called the "White Paper" of 1961. The State Department document of 1961 appears within blue covers; what Stone and we call the "White Paper" of 1965 has light brown covers.—eds.

3. See Jean Sainteny, *Histoire d'une paix manquée* (Paris, 1953); Ellen J. Hammer, *The Struggle for Indochina* (Stanford, Calif., 1954).

That Economic Miracle Again

The most disingenuous part of the White Paper is that in which it discusses the origins of the present war. It pictures the war as an attack from the North, launched in desperation because the "economic miracle" in the South under Diem had destroyed Communist hopes of a peaceful takeover from within. Even the strategic hamlets are described as "designed to improve the peasant's livelihood" and we are asked to believe that for the first time in history a guerrilla war spread not because the people were discontented but because their lot was improving!

The true story is a story of lost opportunities. The Communist countries acquiesced in the failure to hold elections. Diem had a chance to make his part of the country a democratic showcase. The year 1956 was a bad one in the North. There was a peasant uprising and widespread resentment among the intellectuals over the Communist Party's heavy-handed thought control. But Diem on the other side of the 17th Parallel was busy erecting a dictatorship of his own. In 1956 he abolished elections even for village councils. In 1957 his mobs smashed the press of the one legal opposition party, the Democratic Bloc, when it dared criticize the government. That was the beginning of a campaign to wipe out every form of opposition. It was this campaign and the oppressive exactions imposed on the peasantry, the fake land reform and the concentration camps Diem set up for political opponents of all kinds, which stirred even wider rebellion from 1958 onward in the grass roots *before* North Vietnam gave support.[4] It was this which drove oppositionists of all kinds into alliance with the Communists in the National Liberation Front.

Long before the North was accused of interference, its government was complaining to the Control Commission of "border and air-space violations by the South and infringements of the Geneva Agreements by the introduction of arms and U.S. servicemen."[5] For four years after Geneva, both North Vietnam and China followed the "peaceful coexistence" policy while the U.S. turned South Vietnam into a military base and a military dictatorship. It is in this story the White Paper does not tell, and the popular discontent it does not mention, that the rebellion and the aid from the North had their origins.

---

4. Philippe Devillers, "The Struggle for the Unification of Vietnam," *China Quarterly* (January–March, 1962).

5. *Survey of International Affairs 1956–1958*, by Geoffrey Barraclough, a publication of Britain's Royal Institute of International Affairs, p. 420.

39. "Defeat American Escalation": Report to the National Assembly of the Democratic Republic of Vietnam (1965)*

By Ho Chi Minh

Most Americans, in or out of the government, saw official DRV statements, reports, and speeches as propaganda. (Documents captured in the course of battle were an exception to this general rule.) Confident that American technology would carry the day, most US analysts simply dismissed reports such as the one reprinted below. And yet, Ho Chi Minh's words merit closer attention. He fully acknowledges the damage the US was inflicting on both North and South Vietnam, thanks China and the Soviet Union for their aid, and makes a distinction between the American people and their government. But above all else, his analysis of why the policy of escalating violence was bound to fail rested on the capacity of the people of Vietnam to resist and his conviction that increased "punishment" by the US would only reinforce that will. His conclusions echo those drawn by students of the effects of massive bombing on the German civilian population in World War II, where massive air attacks were shown to stiffen rather than weaken the determination of those under attack.

O ver the past ten years, the U.S. imperialists and their henchmen have carried out an extremely ruthless war and have caused much grief to our compatriots in South Vietnam. Over the past few months, they have frenziedly expanded the war to North Vietnam. In defiance of the 1954 Geneva Agreements and international law, they have sent hundreds of aircraft and dozens of warships to bomb and strafe North Vietnam repeatedly. Laying bare themselves their piratical face, the U.S. aggressors are blatantly encroaching upon our country. They hope that by resorting to the force of weapons they can compel our 30 million compatriots to become their slaves. But they are grossly mistaken. They will certainly meet with ignominious defeat.

Our Vietnamese people are a heroic people. Over the past ten years or more, our 14 million compatriots in the South have overcome all hardships, made every sacrifice and struggled very valiantly. Starting with their bare hands, they have seized guns from the enemy to fight against the enemy, have recorded victory after victory, and are launching a continual attack inflicting upon the U.S. aggressors and the traitors ever greater defeats and causing them to be bogged down more and more deeply. The greater their defeats, the more frantically they resort to the most cruel means, such as using napalm bombs and toxic gas to massacre our compa-

---

*Excerpted from Address to the National Assembly of the Democratic Republic of Vietnam, in *Vietnam Courier* [Hanoi], April 15, 1965.

triots in the South. It is because they are bogged down in South Vietnam that they have furiously attacked North Vietnam.

. . . The U.S. imperialists are precisely the saboteurs of the Geneva Agreements, yet they have brazenly declared that because they wished to "restore peace" and "defend the Geneva Agreements" they brought U.S. troops to our country to carry out massacres and destruction. . . .

U.S. President Johnson has . . . loudly threatened to resort to violence to subdue our people. This is a mere foolish illusion. Our people will definitely never be subjugated.

The Taylor plan has been frustrated. The McNamara plan has also gone bankrupt. The "escalation" plan which the U.S. imperialists are now endeavoring to carry out in North Vietnam will certainly fail, too. The U.S. imperialists may send in dozens of thousands more U.S. officers and men and make all-out efforts to drag more troops of their satellite countries into this criminal war, but our army and people are resolved to fight and defeat them. . . .

We love peace but we are not afraid of war. We are resolved to drive away the U.S. aggressors and to defend the freedom, independence, and territorial integrity of our Fatherland.

The people throughout our country are firmly confident that with their militant solidarity, valiant spirit, and creative wisdom, and with the sympathy and support of the world's peoples, they will certainly lead this great Resistance War to complete victory.

Our people are very grateful to and highly value the fraternal solidarity and devoted assistance of the socialist countries, especially the Soviet Union and China, of the people in all continents who are actively supporting us in our struggle against the U.S. imperialist aggressors, the most cruel enemy of mankind. . . .

The American people have been duped by the propaganda of their government, which has extorted from them billions of dollars to throw into the crater of war. Thousands of American youths—their sons and brothers—have met a tragic death or have been pitifully wounded on the Vietnamese battlefields thousands of miles from the United States. At present, many mass organizations of individuals in the United States are demanding that their government at once stop this unjust war and withdraw U.S. troops from South Vietnam. Our people are resolved to drive away the U.S. imperialists, our sworn enemy. But we always express our friendship with the progressive American people. . . .

Our people are living in an extremely glorious period of history. Our country has the great honor of being an outpost of the socialist camp and of the world's peoples who are struggling against imperialism, colonialism, and neocolonialism.

Our people have fought and made sacrifices not only for the sake of their own freedom and independence, but also for the common freedom and independence of the other peoples and for peace in the world.

On the battlefront against the U.S. aggressors, our people's task is very heavy but also very glorious. . . .

I call on our compatriots and fighters to constantly heighten their revolutionary heroism, vigilance, and fighting spirit—to promote the "everyone redoubles his efforts" emulation movement, resolutely overcome all difficulties, endeavor to build and defend socialist North Vietnam and wholeheartedly support the patriotic struggle of our compatriots in the South!

Let all of us single-mindedly unite as one man and be determined to defeat the U.S. aggressors!

For the future of our Fatherland, for the happiness of our people, let all compatriots and fighters throughout the country valiantly march forward!

40. Negotiations? Hanoi's Four Points (April 8, 1965) and Washington's Fourteen Points (January 7, 1966)*

Hanoi's four-point negotiating position was issued the day after President Johnson's "Johns Hopkins speech" of April 7, a "peace initiative" aimed more at placating growing domestic and international opposition to escalating US involvement in Vietnam than at negotiations. Growing numbers of Americans were perceiving the US war in Vietnam as immoral or impractical or both. For example, after Secretary of Defense McNamara announced on February 7 that the United States was bombing north of the 17th parallel, hundreds of women—many of them "housewives" and grandmothers taking such action for the first, but not the last, time—converged on Washington, going from one Congressional office to another begging to be heard, but were received, for the most part, as nuisances. At that point many, if not most, protesters thought that the new escalation was a "tragic mistake." Not until later was it learned that this Operation Flaming Dart was a prelude to Operation Rolling Thunder, the long-planned policy of gradually intensified bombing raids against the DRV. The "White Paper" issued later that month only increased anxiety (Reading 37). When combat troops were introduced in March with the reasoning that they were necessary to protect military installations, more people became concerned about the leapfrog nature of escalation. By the time Johnson spoke at Johns Hopkins, it was clear that the antiwar demonstration planned for April 17 was going to bring record numbers of protesters to the capital (see Introduction to Part VI). In this environment of teach-ins and demonstrations, the White House responded by sending spokesmen to the campuses and inviting campus leaders to Washington for discussions. President Johnson chose a university as the site for explaining why the United States was in Vietnam: "To

---

*A. Text as given by Hanoi Radio, April 13, 1965. B. From *State Department Bulletin*, LIII (February 14, 1966).

*help South Vietnam defend its independence" and "to strengthen world order."
While offering "unconditional discussions,"* [1] *Johnson also stated that "an independent South Vietnam" —that is, a South Vietnam separate from North Vietnam—
was essential to any final settlement. This was so diametrically opposed to the
aims of the DRV and the National Liberation Front (NLF) that it effectively pre-
cluded discussions or negotiations.* [2] *No sooner had Johnson spoken than Hanoi
announced its Four Points.*

*After eight more months of almost uninterrupted bombing of the DRV as well
as the everlasting bombing of the South and the commitment of tens of thousands
more US troops, the United States was no closer to winning the war; it was closer
to bringing that war home. Demonstrations, including the burning of draft cards,
and a campaign aimed specifically at the napalm being used against the peasants
of the South, were becoming the order of the day. At Christmas time, Johnson
suspended the bombing of the DRV, supposedly as an inducement to negotiations.
But Washington's Fourteen Points, issued two weeks later, disregarded the NLF
program (Reading 29) and even referred to the NLF as the "Vietcong." On January 31, 1966, the bombing of the DRV was resumed.*

A. Hanoi's Four Points, April 8, 1965

The unswerving policy of the DRV Government is to respect strictly the 1954
Geneva agreements on Vietnam and to implement correctly their basic provisions
as embodied in the following points:

1. Recognition of the basic national rights of the Vietnamese people—peace,
independence, sovereignty, unity, and territorial integrity. According to the Geneva
agreements, the U.S. Government must withdraw from South Vietnam U.S.
troops, military personnel, and weapons of all kinds, dismantle all U.S. military
bases there, and cancel its military alliance with South Vietnam. According to the
Geneva agreements, the U.S. Government must stop its acts of war against North
Vietnam and completely cease all encroachments on the territory and sovereignty
of the DRV.

2. Pending the peaceful reunification of Vietnam, while Vietnam is still temporarily divided into two zones the military provisions of the 1954 Geneva agreements on Vietnam must be strictly respected. The two zones must refrain from

---

1. In November 1965 Eric Sevareid, in a *Look* magazine article, disclosed that the United States
had rejected an offer made by the DRV in August 1964 to hold discussions aimed at ending hostilities.
Basing his report on a conversation with Adlai Stevenson August 12, 1965, two days before Stevenson, the US ambassador to the United Nations, died, Sevareid said the offer had been obtained privately by UN Secretary General U Thant. The United States postponed any decision until after the
presidential election. When U Thant pursued the matter after the election, the United States rejected
the offer. Robert J. McCloskey, State Department press officer, confirmed, after Sevareid's article
appeared, that such an offer had been rejected because "we did not believe at any time that North
Vietnam was prepared for serious peace talks." Such responses convinced the antiwar movement that
it was the DRV and not the United States that was open to negotiations.

2.See the first of the Four Points.

entering into any military alliance with foreign countries and there must be no foreign military bases, troops, or military personnel in their respective territory.

3. The internal affairs of South Vietnam must be settled by the South Vietnamese people themselves in accordance with the program of the National Liberation Front of South Vietnam without any foreign interference.

4. The peaceful reunification of Vietnam is to be settled by the Vietnamese people in both zones, without any foreign interference.

This stand of the DRV Government unquestionably enjoys the approval and support of all peace- and justice-loving governments and peoples in the world. The government of the DRV is of the view that the stand expounded here is the basis for the soundest political settlement of the Vietnam problem.

If this basis is recognized, favorable conditions will be created for the peaceful settlement of the Vietnam problem, and it will be possible to consider the reconvening of an international conference along the pattern of the 1954 Geneva conference on Vietnam.

The DRV Government declares that any approach contrary to the aforementioned stand is inappropriate; any approach tending to secure U.N. intervention in the Vietnam situation is also inappropriate. Such approaches are basically at variance with the 1954 Geneva agreements on Vietnam.

B. Washington's Fourteen Points, January 7, 1966

The following statements are on the public record about elements which the United States believes can go into peace in Southeast Asia:

1. The Geneva Agreements of 1954 and 1962 are an adequate basis for peace in Southeast Asia;

2. We would welcome a conference on Southeast Asia or on any part thereof;

3. We would welcome "negotiations without pre-conditions" as the 17 nations put it;

4. We would welcome unconditional discussions as President Johnson put it;

5. A cessation of hostilities could be the first order of business at a conference or could be the subject of preliminary discussions;

6. Hanoi's four points could be discussed along with other points which others might wish to propose;

7. We want no U.S. bases in Southeast Asia;

8. We do not desire to retain U.S. troops in South Vietnam after peace is assured;

9. We support free elections in South Vietnam to give the South Vietnamese a government of their own choice;

10. The question of reunification of Vietnam should be determined by the Vietnamese through their own free decision;

11. The countries of Southeast Asia can be nonaligned or neutral if that be their option;

12. We would much prefer to use our resources for the economic reconstruction of Southeast Asia than in war. If there is peace, North Vietnam could participate

in a regional effort to which we would be prepared to contribute at least one billion dollars;

13. The President has said, "The Vietcong would not have difficulty being represented and having their views represented if for a moment Hanoi decided she wanted to cease aggression. I don't think that would be an unsurmountable problem."

14. We have said publicly and privately that we could stop the bombing of North Vietnam as a step toward peace although there has not been the slightest hint or suggestion from the other side as to what they would do if the bombing stopped.

41. US Crisis Managers Choose from Among Diminishing Options (1965)*

By General William C. Westmoreland, George Ball, William P. Bundy, and Secretary of Defense Robert S. McNamara

By mid–1965 the Americans had tried every conceivable military strategy in Vietnam, except the use of atomic weapons (despite the attraction to some such as Barry Goldwater who wanted to "bomb it back to the stone age"). Counterinsurgency had been tried and found wanting; no Saigon regime supported by Washington seemed able to win the allegiance or trust of the peasantry; bombing of northern Vietnam seemed only to stiffen the will of the insurgents (Reading 39); no one was sure that introducing more American troops would turn the tide. Some US policymakers with long experience in foreign service, most notably Under Secretary of State George Ball,[1] began gingerly questioning the assumptions of US policy. But doubters like Ball were overruled by those who advocated further escalation, more bombing and more US troops.

General Westmoreland to CINCPAC, June 13, 1965

Subj: Concept of Operations—Force Requirements and Deployments, SVN. . . .

A. CINCPAC analysis of the situation and concept of operations is properly focused upon the population, that is, upon the people. There is no doubt whatsoever that the insurgency in South Vietnam must eventually be defeated among the

---

*From *The Pentagon Papers* (Gravel edition), vol. 4, pp. 606–624.

1. For analyses of the decision-making process in Washington, see Nina S. Adams, "The Last Line of Defense," in *The Pentagon Papers* (Gravel edition), vol. 5, pp. 143–158; Herbert Y. Schandler, *Lyndon Johnson and Vietnam: The Unmaking of a President* (Princeton, NJ: Princeton University Press, 1977), Chap. 2; Paul Joseph, *Cracks in the Empire: State Politics in the Vietnam War* (Boston: South End Press, 1981), Chap. III; Larry Berman, *Planning a Tragedy: The Americanization of the War in Vietnam* (New York: W.W. Norton, 1982), *passim*.

people in the hamlets and towns. However, in order to defeat the insurgency among the people, they must be provided security of two kinds:

(1) Security of the country as a whole from large well organized and equipped forces including those which may come from outside their country.

(2) Security from the guerrilla, the assassin, the terrorist and the informer.

B. MACV is convinced that US troops can contribute heavily in the first category of security as in paragraph (1) above, but that only the Vietnamese can make real progress and succeed in respect to the problem in paragraph (2) above. Unfortunately, the ARVN is being drawn away from the people and their security in order to meet the challenge of the main force VC/DRV offensive. The best illustration of this point is the fact that the II Corps Commander has removed most of the troops from the province of Binh Dinh with its nearly one million people in order to defend the relatively less important province capitals of Kontum and Pleiku. Therefore, the MACV concept is basically to employ US forces together with Vietnamese airborne and marine battalions of the General Reserve against the hard core DRV/VC forces in reaction and search and destroy operations, and thus permit the concentration of Vietnamese troops in the heavily populated areas along the coast, around Saigon and in the Delta. . . .

B. The VC are now maneuvering large forces up to reinforce regiments equipped with heavy weapons. Thus, we are approaching the kind of warfare faced by the French in the latter stages of their efforts here. It is entirely possible that the DRV can and will deploy three or more divisions into South Vietnam by infiltration. It is highly likely that one is already here. Therefore, it will be necessary to react to the introduction of DRV forces and to the shift and tactical play of the VC. Thus, tactical dispositions will change and only the major bases will be fixed. In short, we will be conducting mobile warfare from fixed and defended bases. Some of these bases will be major logistic centers at ports and airfields such as Chu Lai and Cam Ranh. Others will be tactical bases such as An Khe or Pleiku. The tactical bases will move as necessary and that may be with some frequency as the battle develops. . . .

The VC are destroying battalions faster than they can be reconstituted and faster than they were planned to be organized under the buildup program. The RVNAF commanders do not believe that they can survive without the active commitment of US ground combat forces. The only possible US response is the aggressive employment of US regular together with Vietnamese General Reserve Forces to react against strong VC/DRV attacks. To meet this challenge successfully, troops must be maneuvered freely, deployed and redeployed if necessary. . . .

Memo from George Ball to Dean Rusk, Robert McNamara, McGeorge Bundy, William Bundy, John McNaughton, and Leonard Unger, June 29, 1965

1. Plan for Cutting Our Losses

In essence, what we should seek to achieve is a posture *vis-à-vis* the various leaders in Saigon that will appear to the world as reasonable and lacking any suggestion of arbitrariness. What I have proposed is that we make it a condition of continued assistance that the various elements in Saigon put aside their petty differences and organize themselves to fight the war. The only argument against the reasonableness of this proposition is that we have not insisted on such performance in the past. This is not persuasive. From the point of view of legitimacy, effective representation of the major elements of opinion, and social and economic progressiveness, the present government seems even worse than its predecessors.

2. *The Task of Re-education*

It should by now be apparent that we have to a large extent created our own predicament. In our determination to rally support, we have tended to give the South Vietnamese struggle an exaggerated and symbolic significance (Mea culpa, since I personally participated in this effort).

The problem for us now—if we determine not to broaden and deepen our commitments—is to re-educate the American people and our friends and allies that:

(a) The phasing out of American power in South Vietnam should not be regarded as a major defeat—either military or political—but a tactical redeployment to more favorable terrain in the overall cold war struggle;

(b) The loss of South Vietnam does not mean the loss of all of Southeast Asia to the Communist power. Admittedly, Thailand is a special problem that will be dealt with later in this memo;

(c) We have more than met our commitments to the South Vietnamese people. We have poured men and equipment into the area, and run risks and taken casualties, and have been prepared to continue the struggle provided the South Vietnamese leaders met even the most rudimentary standards of political performance;

(d) The Viet Cong—while supported and guided from the North—is largely an indigenous movement. Although we have emphasized its cold war aspects, the conflict in South Vietnam is essentially a civil war within that country;

(e) Our commitment to the South Vietnamese people is of a wholly different order from our major commitments elsewhere—to Berlin, to NATO, to South Korea, etc. We ourselves have insisted the curtailment of our activities in South Vietnam would cast doubt on our fidelity to the other commitments. Now we must begin a process of differentiation being founded on fact and law. We have *never* had a treaty commitment obligating us to the South Vietnamese people or to a South Vietnamese government. Our only treaty commitment in that area is to our SEATO partners, and they have—without exception—viewed the situation in South Vietnam as not calling a treaty into play. To be sure, we *did* make a promise to the South Vietnamese people. But that promise is conditioned on their own performance, and they have not performed.

Memo from George Ball to President Johnson, July 1, 1965

A Compromise Solution in South Vietnam

(1) *A Losing War:* The South Vietnamese are losing the war to the Viet Cong. No one can assure you that we can beat the Viet Cong or even force them to the

conference table on our terms, no matter how many hundred thousand *white, foreign* (U.S.) troops we deploy.

No one has demonstrated that a white ground force of whatever size can win a guerrilla war—which is at the same time a civil war between Asians—in jungle terrain in the midst of a population that refuses cooperation to the white forces (and the South Vietnamese) and thus provides a great intelligence advantage to the other side. Three recent incidents vividly illustrate this point: (a) the sneak attack on the Da Nang Air Base which involved penetration of a defense parameter guarded by 9,000 Marines. This raid was possible only because of the cooperation of the local inhabitants; (b) the B–52 raid that failed to hit the Viet Cong who had obviously been tipped off; (c) the search and destroy mission of the 173rd Air Borne Brigade which spent three days looking for the Viet Cong, suffered 23 casualties, and never made contact with the enemy who had obviously gotten advance word of their assignment.

(2) The Question to Decide: Should we limit our liabilities in South Vietnam and try to find a way out with minimal long-term costs?

The alternative—no matter what we may wish it to be—is almost certainly a protracted war involving an open-ended commitment of U.S. forces, mounting U.S. casualties, no assurance of a satisfactory solution, and a serious danger of escalation at the end of the road.

(3) Need for a Decision Now: So long as our forces are restricted to advising and assisting the South Vietnamese, the struggle will remain a civil war between Asian peoples. Once we deploy substantial numbers of troops in combat it will become a war between the U.S. and a large part of the population of South Vietnam, organized and directed from North Vietnam and backed by the resources of both Moscow and Peiping.

The decision you face now, therefore, is crucial. Once large numbers of U.S. troops are committed to direct combat, they will begin to take heavy casualties in a war they are ill-equipped to fight in a non-cooperative if not downright hostile countryside.

Once we suffer large casualties, we will have started a well-nigh irreversible process. Our involvement will be so great that we cannot—without national humiliation—stop short of achieving our complete objectives. *Of the two possibilities I think humiliation would be more likely than the achievement of our objectives— even after we have paid terrible costs.*

(4) Compromise Solution: Should we commit U.S. manpower and prestige to a terrain so unfavorable as to give a very large advantage to the enemy—or should we seek a compromise settlement which achieves less than our stated objectives and thus cut our losses while we still have the freedom of maneuver to do so.

(5) Costs of a Compromise Solution: The answer involves a judgment as to the cost to the U.S. of such a compromise settlement in terms of our relations with the countries in the area of South Vietnam, the credibility of our commitments, and our prestige around the world. In my judgment, if we act before we commit a substantial U.S. truce [sic] to combat in South Vietnam we can, by accepting some short-term costs, avoid what may well be a long-term catastrophe. . . .

[For space reasons we omit Ball's detailed projections for troop deployments,

bombing targets, political initiatives, etc., under his plan for a "Compromise solution." In any case, his recommendations were rejected.—eds.]

Memo from William Bundy: "Holding on in South Vietnam," June 30, 1965

. . . The argument for "holding on"—the middle way—starts with the rejection of the other two possibilities [withdrawal or rapid escalation] for the following
reasons:

(a) Ultimatum/withdrawal would be an abandonment of the South Vietnamese
at a time when the fight is not, and certainly does not appear to the world and to
Asian countries to be, going all that badly. Such an abandonment would leave us
almost no leverage as to South Vietnam, and would create an immediate and maximum shock wave for Thailand and the rest of Asia. The rationale that it was all
the fault of the South Vietnamese, *in these circumstances*, where we ourselves had
pulled the plug, would have almost no offsetting effect. The American public
would not understand such a quick reversal of our position, and the political effects
at home would be most serious. There might also be serious adverse effects on our
whole leadership position. In short, while there may come a time when the South
Vietnamese really have shown they have abandoned the struggle, that time is by
no means here now.

(b) Major further deployments and pressures on the DRV. There is a case for
increased pressures on the DRV including selective bombings in the Hanoi area at
the proper time—when Hanoi is beginning to find the going hard in the South. But
again, that time is not yet. As long as Hanoi thinks it is winning in the South, such
pressures will not affect their determination, or in any significant way, their capacity. They will lose us a lot of support in the world, including such important elements as the backing of the British government. These are risks we may have to
take at some point, but not when the gains are just not there. As for major additional ground deployments, the first argument is simply whether they would be
militarily effective. As the Ball papers point out, Hanoi is by no means committed
to a really conventional type of war, and they could easily go on making significant
gains while giving us precious few opportunities to hit them. We just do not know
at this point how effective our forces will be in the reserve role. More basically,
none of us can now judge the extent to which major U.S. combat forces would
cause the Vietnamese government and army to think we were going to do the job
for them. Nor can we judge the extent to which the people in the countryside, who
have been exposed constantly to VC propaganda, the fight is against the American
successors to the French, would start really to buy this time when they saw U.S.
forces engaged in the countryside, and hence flock to the VC banner.

. . . In short, we have to make our own judgment based on the present reading
of popular feeling in South Vietnam, and based above all on the French experience.

From these factors, I would judge there is a point of sharply diminishing returns and adverse consequences that may lie somewhere between 70,000 and
100,000 U.S. forces in total, and a fairly limited number of combat battalions that

will actually get into the countryside to fight in case of need. If the Saigon government and its army perform better, U.S. forces fighting alongside a strong Vietnamese army might have little if any of these adverse effects. Until we have tested the water much further than at present, the odds favor a considerably more negative view of the actual effectiveness over any extended period of major added U.S. forces. In short, whatever we think the chances are now of making the effort in the South really costly to Hanoi, the present deployment of major added U.S. forces gives no real promise of helping the chances for this kind of success. If the South Vietnamese government and army perform well, the role and need of U.S. forces will become clear, and political liabilities may be less than we anticipate in the future. If the South Vietnamese government and army encounter a series of reverses in the next two months, the odds will rise that our own intervention would appear to be turning the conflict into a white man's war with the U.S. in the shoes of the French. In the first case, we can afford to wait at least in degree. In the second case, the added chances of success seem very small.

There is one further factor relating to the consequences of defeat, if we had made major U.S. deployments and have still been unable to turn the tide, largely because the South Vietnamese army ceases to perform well and the people turn against it. This would not be much worse in other forms of defeat in some Asian quarters, but it would be substantially worse in the impact on Japan, on Korea if Korea had likewise become involved on a major scale, and on our major allies in Europe. It will appear a significantly worse outcome on the American people.

(c) "The middle way" course of action.

1) We should have enough ground combat forces to give the reserve/reaction concept a fair test, but at the same time not to exceed significantly whatever the current Plimsoll line may be. This would appear to mean carrying through present decisions up to about 75,000 in total and possibly the early additional Marine deployments of an additional 8,000–10,000. We would then hold the air-mobile division for decision during the summer, realizing it would take roughly four weeks to deploy after a decision.

2) Our air actions against the South should be carried on a maximum effective rate. This could include substantial use of B–52s against VC havens, recognizing that we look silly and arouse criticism if these do not show significant results.

Possible Deployments Under the Proposed Course of Action:

A. We believe there is a fair chance that the Viet Cong tide could be stemmed by this course of action, and that over a period of 4–6 months we might confront Hanoi with a situation of military stalemate, where the costs of the effort would cause some decline in Viet Cong morale and lead Hanoi itself to consider political settlements that would still be very risky, but there would involve at least delay in any Communist takeover of South Vietnam, and some real chance that a new type of non-Communists in South Vietnam would emerge.

B. There is the possibility that neither Hanoi nor Saigon would weaken, and we would be carrying on an inclusive fight for a period of many months or even far longer.

C. The chances are greater that the Viet Cong tide would not be stemmed, that

Hanoi would not come to terms, and that at some time—on the order of two–four months—Saigon would in effect throw in the sponge and make a deal with the liberation front, and Hanoi.

This favorable turn of events would still require a carefully developed political plan that would present Hanoi with what it would regard as an acceptable alternative to continue the war. And it would, at the same time, offer a good chance of bringing about a non-Communist South Vietnam with a real chance to hold on for some time. Such a political plan should also be designed to appeal to the large number of individuals in the Viet Cong who have strong, southern, regional sentiments and can be lured away from the present high degree of Communist control of the Viet Cong.

The essentials of such a political plan have been developed by a State Department working group in the last two months. The plan calls for the Vietnamese government taking the lead and laying out a major program to extend government administration, with reform measures, with progressive local elections, and with an amnesty to members of the Viet Cong who do not resist the extension of government authority province by province. . . . Such a political program would fall short of our present objectives of getting Hanoi formerly [sic] to desist from all aid to the South. It would not call for the turning in of Viet Cong arms as an absolute condition, although much might be accomplished by the appeal of the program itself. It would leave the Hanoi dominated, political apparatus in existence on a covert basis, and thus a major long-term problem for South Vietnam to handle. We believe these concessions are essential if Viet Cong members are to be attracted into the program and if Hanoi itself is to accept it in practice and not continue the fight to the finish. It should be emphasized that such a program would have to be timed very carefully. It must come when the government is really starting to make progress, or at least if the situation leveled out somewhat, so that the offering of the program does not appear as some kind of weakness. That is [it] must come just as soon as the trend has been established, so that Hanoi is deflected from massive reinforcements on its own side.

In short, such a program would have tremendous problems. It appears to us the only avenue which offers real promise of obtaining an ultimate, non-Communist South Vietnam, without Hanoi feeling it must go all out in a military context. . . .

Conclusion: Despite its obvious difficulty and the uncertainty of success in South Vietnam under this or any other program, this middle way program seems to us to avoid the clear pitfalls of either of the major alternatives. It may not give us quite as much chance of a successful outcome as the major military actions proposed in the McNamara memorandum, but it avoids to a major extent the very serious risks involved in this program in any case, and the far more disastrous outcome that would eventuate if we acted along the lines of the McNamara memorandum and still lost in South Vietnam.

Above all, we must think of our South Vietnamese effort as giving us the best chance we can *reasonably* have of bringing Hanoi to terms, but also as an essential effort sustained to sustain the credibility of U.S. action in Asia and world wide—

and right alongside this, an effort to play for time and to give us the chance to line up a different kind of non-Communist structure in Southeast Asia if the worst should happen in South Vietnam. . . .

Notes for a Memorandum from McNamara to Johnson, July 20, 1965

Recommendations of additional deployments to VN:

1. Our object in VN is to create conditions for a favorable outcome by demonstrating to the VC/DRV that the odds are against their winning. We want to create these conditions, if possible, without causing the war to expand into one with China or the Soviet Union and in a way which preserves support of the American people and, hopefully, of our allies and friends.

2. In my view a "favorable outcome" has nine fundamental elements:
a. VC stop attacks and drastically reduce incidents of terror and sabotage.
b. DRV reduces infiltration to a trickle, with some reasonably reliable method of our obtaining confirmation of this fact.
c. US/GVN stop bombing of NVN.
d. GVN stays independent (hopefully pro-US, but possibly genuinely neutral).
e. GVN exercises governmental functions over substantially all of SVN.
f. Communists remain quiescent in Laos and Thailand.
g. DRV withdraws PAVN forces and other NVNese infiltrators (not regroupees) from SVN.
h. VC/NLF transform from a military to a purely political organization.
i. US combat forces (not advisors or AID) withdraw.

. . . more likely to evolve without an express agreement than with one.

3. Estimate: The situation in SVN is worse than a year ago (when it was worse than a year before that). After a few months of stalemate, the tempo of the war has quickened. . . . The central highlands could well be lost to the NLF during this monsoon season. Since June 1, the GVN has been forced to abandon six district capitals; only one has been retaken. US combat troop deployments and US/VNAF strikes against the North have put to rest most SVNese fears that the US will forsake them, and US/VNAF air strikes in-country have probably shaken VC morale somewhat. Yet the government is able to provide security to fewer and fewer people in less and less territory as terrorism increases.

. . . The odds are less than even that the Ky government will last out the year. Ky is "executive agent" for a directorate of generals.

. . . The Govt-to-VC ratio overall is now only a little better than 3-to-1, and in combat battalions little better than 1.5-to-1.

. . . Nor have our air attacks in NVN produced tangible evidence of willingness on the part of Hanoi to come to the conference table in a reasonable mood. The DRV/VC seem to believe that SVN is on the run and near collapse; they show no signs of settling for less than complete takeover.

4. Options open to us:

a. Cut our losses and withdraw under the best conditions that can be arranged—almost certainly conditions humiliating the US and very damaging to our future effectiveness on the world scene.

b. Continue at about the present level, with the US forces limited to say, 75,000, holding on and playing for the breaks—a course of action which, because our position would grow weaker, almost certainly would confront us later with a choice between withdrawal and an emergency expansion of forces, perhaps too late to do any good.

c. Expand promptly and substantially the US military pressure against the VC in the South and maintain the military pressure against the NVNese in the North while launching a vigorous effort on the political side to lay the groundwork for a favorable outcome by clarifying our objectives and establishing channels of communication. (Amb. Lodge states "any further initiative by us now—before we are strong—would simply harden the Communist resolve not to stop fighting." Ambs. Taylor and Johnson would maintain discreet contacts with the Soviets, but otherwise agree with Amb. Lodge.) This alternative would stave off defeat in the short run and offer a good chance of producing a favorable settlement in the longer run; at the same time, it would imply a commitment to see a fighting war clear through at considerable cost in casualties and materiel and would make any later decision to withdraw even more difficult and even more costly than would be the case today.

My recommendations in par. 5 below are based on the choice of the third alternative as the course of action involving the best odds of the best outcome with the most acceptable cost to the US.

5. There are now 15 US (and 1 Australian) combat battalions in VN; they together with other combat and non-combat personnel, bring the total US personnel in VN to approx. 15,000.

a. Increase by October to 34 maneuver battalions; plus other reinforcements, up to approx. 175,000. . . . It should be understood that the deployment of more men (perhaps 100,000) may be necessary in early 1966, and that the deployment of additional forces therefore is possible but will depend on developments. (Ask Congress to authorize call up of 235,000 men in Reserve and National Guard; increase regular forces by 375,000 men. By mid–66 US would have 600,000 additional men as protection against contingencies.)

((VNese have asked for forces: for 53 bns.))

. . . The DRV, on the other hand, may well send up to several divisions of regular forces in SVN to assist the VC if they see the tide turning and victory, once so near, being snatched away. This possible DRV action is the most ominous one, since it would lead to increased pressures on us to "counter-invade" NVN and to extend air strikes to population targets in the North; acceding to these pressures could bring the Sovs and the Chinese in.

. . . The success of the program from the military point of view turns on whether the VNese hold their own in terms of numbers and fighting spirit, and on whether the US forces can be effective in a quick-reaction reverse role, a role in which they are only now being tested. The number of US troops is too small to make a significant difference in the traditional 10-to-1 government-guerrilla formula, but it is not too small to make a significant difference in the kind of war which seems to be evolving in Vietnam—a "Third Stage" or conventional war in which it is easier to identify, locate and attack the enemy.

. . . The SVNese under one government or another will probably see the thing through (Amb Lodge points out that we may face a neutralist government at some time in the future and that in those circumstances the US should be prepared to carry on alone) and the US public will support the course of action because it is a sensible and courageous military-political program designed and likely to bring about a success in Vietnam.

It should be recognized, however, that success against the larger, more conventional, VC/PAVN forces could merely drive the VC back into the trees and back to their 1960–64 pattern—a pattern against which US troops and aircraft would be of limited value but with which the GVN, with our help, could cope. The questions here would be whether the VC could maintain morale after such a setback, and whether the SVNese would have the will to hang on through another cycle. It should be recognized also that even in "success" it is not obvious how we will be able to disengage our forces from Vietnam. It is unlikely that a formal agreement good enough for the purpose could possibly be negotiated—because the arrangement can reflect little more than the power situation. A fairly large number of US (or perhaps international) forces may be required to stay in Vietnam.

The overall evaluation is that the course of action recommended in this memo . . . stands a good chance of achieving an acceptable outcome within a reasonable time in Vietnam.

Report by McNamara After November 28–29 Visit to Vietnam, November 30, 1965

. . . the Ky "government of generals" is surviving, but not acquiring wide support or generating actions; pacification is thoroughly stalled, with no guarantee that security anywhere is permanent and no indications that able and willing leadership will emerge in the absence of that permanent security. (Prime Minister Ky estimates that his government controls only 25% of the population today and reports that his pacification chief hopes to increase that to 50% two years from now.)

The dramatic recent changes in the situation are on the military side. They are the increased infiltration from the North and the increased willingness of the Communist forces to stand and fight, even in large-scale engagements. The Ia Drang River Campaign of early November is an example. The Communists appear to have decided to increase their forces in SVN both by heavy recruitment in the South (especially in the Delta) and by infiltration of regular NVN forces from the

North. . . . the enemy can be expected to enlarge his present strength of 110 battalion equivalents to more than 150 battalion equivalents by the end of calendar 1966, when hopefully his losses can be made to equal his input.

As for the Communist ability to supply this force, it is estimated that, even taking account of interdiction of routes by air and sea, more than 200 tons of supplies a day can be infiltrated—more than enough, allowing for the extent to which the enemy lives off the land, to support the likely PAVN/VC force at the likely level of operations.

To meet this possible—and in my view likely—Communist buildup, the presently contemplated Phase I forces will not be enough (approx 220,000 Americans, almost all in place by end of 1965). Bearing in mind the nature of the war, the expected weighted combat force ratio of less than 2-to-1 will not be good enough. Nor will the originally contemplated Phase II addition of 28 more US battalions (112,000 men) be enough; the combat force ratio, even with 32 new SVNese battalions, would still be little better than 2-to-1 at the end of 1966. The initiative which we have held since August would pass to the enemy; we would fall far short of what we expected to achieve in terms of population control and disruption of enemy bases and lines of communications. Indeed, it is estimated that with the contemplated Phase II addition of 28 US battalions, we would be able only to hold our present geographical positions.

2. We have but two options, it seems to me. One is to go now for a compromise solution . . . and hold further deployments to a minimum. The other is to stick with our stated objectives and with the war, and provide what it takes in men and materiel. If it is decided not to move now toward a compromise, I recommend that the US both send a substantial number of additional troops and very gradually intensify the bombing of NVN. Amb. Lodge, Wheeler, Sharp and Westmoreland concur in this prolonged course of action, although Wheeler and Sharp would intensify the bombing of the North more quickly.

(recommend up to 74 battalions by end–66: total to approx 400,000 by end–66. And it should be understood that further deployments (perhaps exceeding 200,000) may be needed in 1967.)

3. Bombing of NVN. . . . over a period of the next six months we gradually enlarge the target system in the northeast (Hanoi-Haiphong) quadrant until, at the end of the period, it includes "controlled" reconnaissance of lines of communication throughout the area, bombing of petroleum storage facilities and power plants, and mining of the harbors. (Left unstruck would be population targets, industrial plants, locks and dams.)

4. Pause in bombing NVN. It is my belief that there should be a three- or four-week pause in the program of bombing the North before we either greatly increase our troop deployments to VN or intensify our strikes against the North. (My recommendation for a "pause" is not concurred in by Lodge, Wheeler, or Sharp.) The reasons for this belief are, first, that we must lay a foundation in the mind of the American public and in world opinion for such an enlarged phase of the war and, second, we should give NVN a face-saving chance to stop the aggression. I am

not seriously concerned about the risk of alienating the SVNese, misleading Hanoi, or being "trapped" in a pause; if we take reasonable precautions, we can avoid these pitfalls. I am seriously concerned about embarking on a markedly higher level of war in VN without having tried, through a pause, to end the war or at least having made it clear to our people that we did our best to end it.

5. Evaluation. We should be aware that deployments of the kind I have recommended will not guarantee success. US killed-in-action can be expected to reach 1000 a month, and the odds are even that we will be faced in early 1967 with a "no-decision" at an even higher level. My overall evaluation, nevertheless, is that the best chance of achieving our stated objectives lies in a pause followed, if it fails, by the deployments mentioned above.

Position Paper (Probably by McNamara), December 7, 1965

Military and Political Actions Recommended for SVN:

We believe that, whether or not major new diplomatic initiative[s] are made, the US must send a substantial number of additional forces to VN if we are to avoid being defeated there.

(30 Nov program; concurred in by JCS.)

Prognosis Assuming the Recommended Deployments:

Deployments of the kind we have recommended will not guarantee success. Our intelligence estimate is that the present Communist policy is to continue to prosecute the war vigorously in the South. They continue to believe that the war will be a long one, that time is their ally, and that their own staying power is superior to ours. They recognize that the US reinforcements of 1965 signify a determination to avoid defeat, and that more US troops can be expected. Even though the Communists will continue to suffer heavily from GVN and US ground and air action, we expect them, upon learning of any US intentions to augment its forces, to boost their own commitment and to test US capabilities and will to persevere at higher level of conflict and casualties (US KIA with the recommended deployments can be expected to reach 1000 a month).

If the US were willing to commit enough forces—perhaps 600,000 men or more—we could ultimately prevent the DRV/VC from sustaining the conflict at a significant level. When this point was reached, however, the question of Chinese intervention would become critical. (We are generally agreed that the Chinese Communists will intervene with combat forces to prevent destruction of the Communist regime in the DRV. It is less clear whether they would intervene to prevent a DRV/VC defeat in the South.) The intelligence estimate is that the chances are a little better than even that, at this stage, Hanoi and Peiping would choose to reduce the effort in the South and try to salvage their resources for another day; but there is an almost equal chance that they would enlarge the war and bring in large numbers of Chinese forces (they have made certain preparations which could point in this direction).

It follows, therefore, that the odds are about even that, even with the recommended deployments, we will be faced in early 1967 with a military standoff at a much higher level, with pacification still stalled, and with any prospect of military success marred by the chances of an active Chinese intervention.

[Despite this prediction of only a fifty-fifty chance for the success of these escalation plans of 1965, they were adopted and put into effect the following year by President Johnson. Some internal critics of escalation, such as George Ball, resigned from the government.—eds.]

Part VI

THE MOVEMENT AGAINST THE WAR

Editors' Introduction

The movement of American people against the US government's actions in Indochina forms one of the most complex and controversial elements of the Vietnam War. Was it a futile, ineffective gesture, or did it actually prevent a US military victory? Was it the outburst of a vocal minority, or did it express the deepest convictions of a majority of Americans? Was it mainly an activity of affluent youths on college campuses, or did it appear in its most militant forms among poor and working-class people in urban slums and within the army itself? Was the protest tantamount to treason, or did it represent the noblest traditions of American history? Did it divert from or reinforce the movement of black and other non-white people for equality? Did the revitalization of the movement for women's equality grow from the antiwar movement or develop as a reaction against male domination within it? Was the movement's cultural thrust coopted, nullified, even reversed by diffusion into designer jeans, disco, and cocaine, or did it profoundly advance the values of post–Vietnam War America? Did the movement disappear with the war, or did it continue to develop into other forms of activism in the late 1970s and the 1980s?

Obviously, there is not space here to explore these questions deeply. But neither the political nor the military history of the war can be understood without some comprehension of the character and role of the antiwar movement.

When did Americans begin to oppose the war? We can find a handful not only denouncing US policies, but accurately prophesying their effects even before the close of the 1954 Geneva Conference. For example, in "What Every American Should Know about Indo-China" (*Monthly Review*, June 1954), Leo Huberman and Paul Sweezy argued that "the American people, by and large, are against colonialism and aggression," but "if we send American forces into Indo-China, as Dulles and other high government spokesmen have repeatedly threatened to do in the last two months, we shall be guilty of aggression ourselves":

Are we going to take the position that anti-Communism justifies anything, including colonialism, interference in the affairs of other countries, and aggression? That way, let us be perfectly clear about it, lies war and more war leading ultimately to full-scale national disaster.

This June 1954 call for action concluded with these prophetic words:

There never has been and never will be a clearer test case than Indo-China. The time for decision is now. Let everyone who cares about the future of our country stand up and speak out today. Tomorrow may be too late.

These were the very feelings of ever-growing numbers of Americans in the next two decades. And for most of this period, the main form of antiwar action was to "speak out." Letters to editors and Congress, articles and books, petitions and advertisements, sermons and teach-ins, banners and picket signs, leaflets and graffiti, resolutions and demands, referenda and slogans, testimony before war crimes hearings and Congressional investigations, even phone calls explaining the significance of bombs planted in buildings—what were all these but words, a torrent of speech flowing against the acts of war. But the bombs obviously went beyond words. They represented the increasingly desperate urge to find actions to deter the men in power, who used their own words to hide and falsify deeds in Vietnam.

Although there was some organized opposition to the war in the late 1950s and early 1960s, the first large-scale national action against American participation in the Vietnam war was the electoral activity in 1964 on behalf of the first presidential peace candidate—Lyndon B. Johnson, who campaigned on the promise not to send American troops to Vietnam.

When the bombing of North Vietnam began in February 1965, less than three weeks after President Johnson's inauguration, and when the first acknowledged American combat troops went ashore in March, the antiwar movement appeared for the first time as a national phenomenon distinct from electoral politics. This was the period when government policies seemed to be based on ignorance and "mistakes," when the antiwar movement was mainly trying to *educate* Washington and the nation. The first teach-ins began in late March, women's organizations sent delegations to explain the situation to members of Congress, and there appeared articles (such as Reading 38) and books (such as the foundation of this present volume, the 1965 Gettleman documentary history of Vietnam discussed in the General Introduction).

Responding, in part, to this movement to educate the public about the war, President Johnson went on April 7 to Johns Hopkins University, where he announced that he was now ready for "unconditional negotiations"—but not with the NLF, and only to negotiate "an independent South Viet-Nam, securely guaranteed." If the speech had any effect on the antiwar movement, it was to increase anger at the President's duplicity and to galvanize more people into action.

Back in December 1964 an obscure little organization called Students for a Democratic Society (SDS) had issued a call for people to go to Washington on April 17, 1965, to march against the war. Only a few thousand were expected. But when the march took place, ten days after the President's Johns Hopkins speech, it turned out to be the largest antiwar demonstration in Washington's history— 25,000 people, most neatly dressed in jackets, ties, and skirts.

What seemed at the time very large demonstrations continued throughout 1965, with 15,000 marching in Berkeley on October 15, 20,000 marching in Manhattan the same day, and 25,000 marching again in Washington on November 27. These early demonstrations would not look so huge in 1967, when 300,000 to 500,000 joined a march in New York, or on November 15, 1969, when a million people marched against the war. On October 15, 1969, millions of Americans participated in the antiwar Moratorium. That April 1965 demonstration would have been imperceptible in May of 1971 among the estimated half–million who converged on Washington.

Demonstrations were one form of the attempt to go beyond mere words and research and reason, to put direct pressure on those who were conducting policy in apparent disdain for the will expressed by the voters in 1964. Other forms appeared in 1965. Many of the activists were veterans of the civil rights movement, who now began to apply its use of civil disobedience as a form of moral witness. On several days in August, the Vietnam Day Committee in northern California attempted to block troop trains by lying on the tracks. On August 6, 350 were arrested for civil disobedience in Washington. In midsummer came the first burnings of draft cards. Moral witness was taken to its ultimate by Norman Morrison, a thirty-two-year-old Quaker who drenched himself with gasoline and set himself on fire outside the Pentagon, with Secretary of Defense McNamara watching. A week later, pacifist Roger La Porte immolated himself at the United Nations; in Detroit, eighty-two-year-old Alice Herz burned herself to death in protest against the Vietnam War. By 1971 civil disobedience was so widespread that the number arrested in that May demonstration in Washington—14,000—would have been considered a good-sized march in 1965.

Whether the majority of Americans at any point supported the government's policies in Vietnam (or even knew what they were) is a matter of debate. Those who contend that they did cite some polls. But answering a question on a poll does not indicate the quality of either support or opposition. Whatever polls did or did not say, the American people never supported the war strongly enough to agree to pay for it with taxes, or even to demonstrate for it in significant numbers, much less to go fight in it willingly. Nor were they ever willing to vote for any national candidate who pledged the nation to fight until "victory." In fact, from 1964 through the end of the war, every nominee for president of both major parties, except Barry Goldwater in 1964, ran as some kind of self-professed peace candidate. It was the opponents of the war, not its supporters, who showed their resolve by expending time and money, risking arrest and loss of jobs, and making existential commitments with their lives.

Who were the people opposed to the war? Contrary to the impression systematically promulgated by its detractors ever since the antiwar movement began, opposition to the war was not concentrated among relatively affluent college students. In fact, every scientific poll and study has demonstrated that throughout the entire history of America's involvement in Vietnam, opposition to the war was *inversely* proportional to both wealth and education. The lower the income, the greater the opposition to the war; the lower the level of education, the greater the opposition to the war. Blue-collar workers generally considered themselves "doves" and tended to favor withdrawal from Vietnam, while those who considered themselves "hawks" and supported participation in the war were concentrated among the college-educated, high-income strata, including professionals.[1] This is not surprising if one considers which people were forced to do the fighting and to make the economic sacrifices. The results of lower-class opposition to the war showed up on what were ultimately to be the most decisive fronts: the cities and the army.

Opposition was especially intense among non-white people, though they tended not to participate heavily in the large demonstrations called by student, pacifist, and liberal organizations. One reason for their caution was that non-whites often had to pay a heavy price for protesting the war. When newly elected black legislator Julian Bond in 1966 spoke out against drafting black men to fight in Vietnam, the Georgia legislature illegally refused him his seat. When world heavyweight boxing champion Muhammad Ali declared himself against the war and claimed draft exemption as a minister of the Nation of Islam, he was stripped of his boxing title. When 25,000 Mexican-Americans staged the Chicano Moratorium, the largest antiwar demonstration held in Los Angeles, the police attacked not just with clubs but with guns, killing three, including popular television news director and *Los Angeles Times* reporter Ruben Salazar.

This is by no means to dismiss the campus movement, whose spectacular nature has in fact led to some of the misunderstanding of the class character of opposition to the war. The teach-ins of the spring of 1965 alone swept scores of campuses and involved probably hundreds of thousands of students. By the late 1960s, millions of students were intermittently involved in antiwar activities ranging all the way from petitions and candlelight marches to burning down ROTC buildings and going to prison for draft resistance. In May 1970, the invasion of Cambodia was met by the largest student protest movement in American history, a strike that led to the shutdown of hundreds of campuses across the nation, as well as the killing of students by national guardsmen at Kent State and by police and national guardsmen at Jackson State.

Several misconceptions about this college and university movement need to be addressed. First, it was not motivated primarily by the students' selfish desires to

---

1. Harlan Hahn, "Dove Sentiments Among Blue-Collar Workers," *Dissent*, 17 (May–June, 1970), pp. 202–205, and Richard F. Hamilton, "A Research Note on the Mass Support for 'Tough' Military Initiatives," *American Sociological Review*, 33 (June 1968), pp. 439–445.

avoid the draft, which was relatively easy for them. In fact, one of its earliest militant activities was disruption of the campus draft-deferment tests, during which the demonstrators attacked their own privileged exemptions as unfair to those young men not in college. Secondly, one should note that in late twentieth-century America, the majority of college students are not affluent. Though students at such elite universities as Harvard, Columbia, and Stanford certainly contributed much to the antiwar movement—and a good percentage of even these students were on financial aid—their militance was matched by students at the public colleges and universities such as Michigan, Maryland, Wisconsin, San Francisco State, and at other institutions none could label sanctuaries of the rich, such as, for example, Kent State and Jackson State. And though the waves of campus antiwar activism, seeming to crest higher each spring, certainly did hamper those in Washington who wished to conduct the war without hindrance, the most decisive opposition to the war was ultimately to come from poor and working people.

To understand the antiwar movement, one must perceive its relations with the other powerful mass movement that was hamstringing the Pentagon—the upsurge among black people. The civil rights movement of the late 1950s and early 1960s had not brought economic progress to the majority of blacks, whose conditions were made even worse as the war brought conscription and inflation into the ghettos. In the summer of 1964, rebellions broke out in several urban ghettos in different parts of the nation. Organizations such as the Nation of Islam stressed the identity of Afro-Americans as a colonized people, and revolutionary voices, such as that of Malcolm X, assassinated in 1965, linked their struggles to the national liberation movements in the Third World. Rioting spread in the summer of 1965, and by 1966 the pattern of "long, hot summers" seemed to be intensifying each year. In 1967, the uprisings reached new heights, especially in such blue-collar cities as Newark and Detroit. As Part VII shows, these urban insurrections played a pivotal role in President Johnson's March 1968 decision to move toward de-escalation and de-Americanization (or Vietnamization) of the war. Then in April, in the week after the assassination of Martin Luther King, rebellions broke out simultaneously in 125 US cities and towns.

During the critical years of the war, the black movement and the antiwar movement were converging, as Pentagon strategists so anxiously realized (Reading 50). In fact, many black civil rights activists first voiced the anti-imperialist consciousness toward which many antiwar activists would inevitably move. For example, in July 1965, the Mississippi Freedom Democratic Party issued a leaflet against black participation in the Vietnam War, arguing that: "No one has a right to ask us to risk our lives and kill other Colored People in Santo Domingo and Vietnam, so that the White American can get richer. We will be looked upon as traitors by all the Colored People of the world if the Negro people continue to fight and die without a cause."[2] In January 1966, the Student Nonviolent Coordinating Committee (SNCC) formally adopted a position against the Vietnam War, declaring:

---

2. "The War on Vietnam" in *Black Protest*, ed. Joanne Grant (New York: Fawcett 1979), p. 416.

We believe the United States government has been deceptive in claims of concern for the freedom of the Vietnamese people, just as the government has been deceptive in claiming concern for the freedom of the colored people in such other countries as the Dominican Republic, the Congo, South Africa, Rhodesia and in the United States itself.[3]

When Martin Luther King, representing what was generally considered the moderate spectrum of the civil rights movement, threw himself fully into the antiwar movement in April 1967 (Reading 48), some Pentagon analysts (Reading 50) saw the repercussions as potentially catastrophic. Most dangerous about the convergence of the black and antiwar movements was the situation inside the armed forces (Reading 51).

As supporters of the war found themselves in an ever more unpopular and dwindling minority, they were driven increasingly to rely on equating their position with "support for our boys in Vietnam." But even this tactic backfired as many GIs began openly to reject such support. As a public letter from twenty-five soldiers in Vietnam put it: "We do not want that kind of support. It is the kind of support that brought us here, keeps us here and which will bring our younger brothers or sons here or elsewhere" (*The New York Times*, November 26, 1969). These GIs identified their true supporters as those demonstrating to get them out of Vietnam: "We support the Moratorium participants who definitely do not support the reason for our being here."

The antiwar movement spread among the combat troops in Vietnam, who began to wear peace symbols and flash peace signs and movement salutes. Some units even organized their own demonstrations to link up with the movement at home. For example, to join the November 1969 antiwar Mobilization, a unit stationed at Pleiku fasted against the war, boycotting that year's Thanksgiving Day dinner—of the 141 soldiers below the rank of Spec 5, only 8 showed up for the traditional meal (*The New York Times*, November 28, 1969). When Bob Hope introduced General Creighton Abrams, commander of all US forces in Vietnam, to the 30,000 troops assembled for a Christmas show at the sprawling Long Binh base, the entire throng leaped to their feet and held their hands high in the salute of the peace movement (two fingers forming a "V"). The General, along with Ambassador Ellsworth Bunker, mistaking the symbol for its World War II meaning of "victory," returned the salute, bringing a tremendous roar from the soldiers (*San Francisco Chronicle*, December 23, 1968).

One problem of the antiwar movement at home was the difficulty of finding ways to move beyond protest and symbolic acts to deeds that would actually impede the war. Unlike college students and other civilians, the troops in Vietnam had no such problem. Individual acts of rebellion, ranging from desertion to killing officers who ordered search-and-destroy missions, merged into sporadic mutinies and large-scale resistance (see headnote to Reading 49). By June 1971, the *Armed Forces Journal* ran an article accurately entitled "The Collapse of the Armed Forces" (Reading 51).

---

3. "Statement on Vietnam" in Grant, p. 416.

Those who think the United States could have won a military victory in Vietnam, or those who think that the antiwar movement betrayed "our fighting men in Vietnam," ignore one crucial fact in the history of the war: by the early 1970s, large numbers of US combat troops in Vietnam had become the leading edge of the antiwar movement, which some hoped and others feared was on the verge of becoming a revolutionary movement.

42. "We Won't Go"*

By the May 2nd Movement

One of the earliest forms of resisting the war, instead of just protesting against it, was organized and open refusal to comply with the draft. Young men publicly proclaimed their defiance of the law, and many were imprisoned. Ultimately this antidraft resistance was to become a powerful social force that produced one of the clearest achievements of the antiwar movement: the abolition of the draft.

To comprehend the significance of this victory, one must remember that the draft had been reinstated in the "peacetime" year of 1948 and then continued without interruption until its abolition in January 1973. After the war, this anti-draft force continued to flow subterraneanly in American society. When President Carter in February 1980 reestablished not the draft itself but just registration for it, there were large nationwide protests, including a hastily called demonstration in Washington of 30,000 to 50,000 people.

The beginnings of the Vietnam War anti-draft movement seem tiny in comparison. On April 25, 1964, the following pledge, probably the first of many such statements, was published in the National Guardian *by the May 2nd Movement, a radical group that was organizing a march in New York. The march on May 2 was attended by about 600 to 800 people, mostly students. When the statement appeared again as an advertisement in the* New York Herald Tribune *of May 28, it had 149 signatures.*

W E THE UNDERSIGNED,
ARE YOUNG AMERICANS OF DRAFT AGE. We understand our obligations to defend our country and to serve in the armed forces but we object to being asked to support the war in South Vietnam.

Believing that United States' participation in the war is for the suppression of the Vietnamese struggle for national independence, we see no justification for our involvement. We agree with Senator Wayne Morse, who said on the floor of the Senate on March 4, 1964, regarding South Vietnam, that "We should never have gone in. We should never have stayed in. We should get out."

BELIEVING THAT WE SHOULD NOT BE ASKED TO FIGHT AGAINST THE PEOPLE OF VIETNAM, WE HEREWITH STATE OUR REFUSAL TO DO SO.

---

*From *We Won't Go*, ed. Alice Lynd (Boston: Beacon Press, 1968), p. 203.

43. *"Freedom Draft Card"**

This document, a "replacement" draft card, shows some of the connections between the civil rights and antiwar movements.

FREEDOM DRAFT CARD

I want to advance social and economic progress. I do not believe this can be achieved through military terror and indiscriminate killing.

I refuse to destroy a country by fighting for a government with no claim to represent its people. I believe that the U.S. must support movements abroad for revolutionary social change, and I am fully against their suppression by military force.

I oppose the draft because it is undemocratic and because it serves only those who wish to destroy.

I declare myself ready to use my abilities and knowledge for the development of truly democratic and progressive societies. I am prepared to risk my life in such projects as many have already done in the South.

name _____ address _____

    I want to work on such projects as these:
Rebuilding a democratic and progressive Vietnam . . . .
Social construction and economic development in
        Africa . . . . Asia . . . . South America . . . .
International non-violent peace keeping . . . .
Southern freedom schools . . . .
Voter registration . . . .
Community projects in slums, ghettos, and underdeveloped areas
    of the United States . . . .
Free Universities . . . .
Other . . . .

Personal Statement _____
_____
_____
_____

---

*Collected by the editors in 1965.

44. Two Poems:
"Afterthoughts on a Napalm-Drop on Jungle Villages near Haiphong" and "Truth Blazes Even in Little Children's Hearts"*

By Barbara Beidler and Huy Can

In 1965, twelve-year-old Barbara Beidler of Vero Beach, Florida, wrote a poem about the Vietnam War. When her poem was printed in the Presbyterian magazine Venture, *the Defense Department immediately dropped* Venture *from its list of recommended publications. This brought the poem to the attention of the media. Huy Can, one of the most famous poets in Vietnam, answered Barbara's poem. Read at many programs about the war during the next few years, this pair of poems came to symbolize a bond between the Vietnamese being attacked by the US government and the Americans opposed to the war.*

Afterthoughts on a Napalm-Drop on Jungle Villages near Haiphong

by Barbara Beidler

All was still.
The sun rose through silver pine boughs,
Over sleeping green-straw huts,
Over cool rice ponds,
Through the emerald jungles.
Into the sky.

The men rose and went out to the fields and ponds.
The women set pots on the fire, boiling rice and jungle berries,
                    and some with baskets went for fish.
The children played in the streams and danced through the weeds.

Then there was the flash—silver and gold
Silver and gold,
Silver birds flying,
Golden water raining.
The rice ponds blazed with the new water.
The jungles burst into gold and sent up little birds of fire.
Little animals with fur of flame.

---

*Both poems reprinted from a leaflet distributed by Paris American Committee to Stop War (PACS) at a joint United States-Vietnam July 4 celebration in 1967.

Then the children flamed.
Running—their clothes flying like fiery kites.
Screaming—their screams dying as their faces seared.
The women's baskets burned on their heads.
The men's blazed on the rice waters.
Then the rains came.

A rag, fire black, fluttered.
A curl of smoke rose from a lone rice stem.
The forest lay singed, seared.
A hut crumbled.

And all was still.
   Listen, Americans,
   Listen, clear and long.
   The children are screaming
   In the jungles of Haiphong.

Truth Blazes Even in Little Children's Hearts

by Huy Can (translated from the Vietnamese)

Little Barbara
Separated from us by the ocean
And by the color of your skin
You have heard and understood.

You have heard the screams
Of the children near Haiphong
Whose clothing turns to flame
From American napalm.

You are twelve years old
And your heart speaks
For the conscience of mankind
Tormented by each rain of bombs.

America, America!
Don't you hear the screams
Of those thousands of children
Consumed by the golden fire?

Golden fire of napalm
Golden fire of dollars
Which eats the flesh
Like a cancer.

A filthy cancer
Devouring the bones
The blood and the soul
Of the United States.

America, don't you feel
The fire burning your flesh
And your conscience
Killed by your bombs?

Little Barbara,
The fire of your poem
Scorches the demons
And drives them wild.

They would ban poetry
But how can they ban
The truth that blazes
Even in little children's hearts!

45. "Declaration of Conscience Against the War in Vietnam" (1965)*

The courage of the young men defying the draft inspired attempts by women and older men to find means of resistance that would place them also in jeopardy. One of the earliest was the following document, drafted in late 1964 and delivered to the White House in August 1965 with over 4,000 signatures, including those of many prominent Americans.

Because the use of the military resources of the United States in Vietnam and elsewhere suppresses the aspirations of the people for political independence and economic freedom;

Because inhuman torture and senseless killing are being carried out by forces armed, uniformed, trained and financed by the United States;

Because we believe that all peoples of the earth, including both Americans and non-Americans, have an inalienable right to life, liberty, and the peaceful pursuit of happiness in their own way; and

---

*Published jointly by the Catholic Worker, Committee for Nonviolent Action, Student Peace Union, and the War Resisters League (New York, 1965).

Because we think that positive steps must be taken to put an end to the threat of nuclear catastrophe and death by chemical or biological warfare, whether these result from accident or escalation—

We hereby declare our conscientious refusal to cooperate with the United States government in the prosecution of the war in Vietnam.

We encourage those who can conscientiously do so to refuse to serve in the armed forces and to ask for discharge if they are already in.

Those of us who are subject to the draft ourselves declare our own intention to refuse to serve.

We urge others to refuse and refuse ourselves to take part in the manufacture or transportation of military equipment, or to work in the fields of military research and weapons development.

We shall encourage the development of other nonviolent acts, including acts which involve civil disobedience, in order to stop the flow of American soldiers and munitions to Vietnam.

NOTE: *Signing or distributing this Declaration of Conscience might be construed as a violation of the Universal Military Training and Service Act, which prohibits advising persons facing the draft to refuse service. Penalties of up to 5 years imprisonment, and/or a fine of $5,000 are provided. While prosecutions under this provision of the law almost never occur, persons signing or distributing this declaration should face the possibility of serious consequences.*

46. *"We Refuse—October 16" (1967)**

Anti-draft resistance became a significant national movement in 1967. On April 15, 150 young men burned their draft cards at a rally in New York. The same day in San Francisco a new organization called the Resistance announced in "We Refuse" a national draft card turn-in to be held in October.

The October turn-in merged with other landmark events. On October 20, a group of distinguished citizens marched into the Justice Department and turned in a briefcase filled with over a thousand draft cards. Five of these delegates were later arrested and tried for this crime (Reading 47). The following day, after 100,000 people rallied in Washington, came the "siege" of the Pentagon. That night a spontaneous mass burning of draft cards swept through the thousands of protesters camped outside the Pentagon, who were soon physically attacked by military police and federal marshals leading US troops.

The October 16 turn-in of draft cards in San Francisco was followed by the concerted week-long attempt, sometimes successful, to shut down physically the

---

*From Michael Ferber and Staughton Lynd, *The Resistance* (Boston: Beacon Press, 1971), p. 90.

Oakland Induction Center, which processed the inductees from Oregon, northern California, and half of Nevada. Beginning with a nonviolent mass sit-in on Monday the 16th, the resistance escalated to Friday's five-hour battle between 2,000 police and 10,000 demonstrators, who used "mobile tactics" to gain control over most of the streets in downtown Oakland, thus showing that guerrilla tactics could be used in the movement at home.

When the buses heading for the Induction Center were blocked in the barricaded streets, many of the inductees on board exchanged "V" signs with the demonstrators, giving rise to the legend that this was the origin of the peace salute, and encouraging the movement to reach out to those in the armed forces.

The Resistance is a group of men who are bound together by one single and clear commitment: on October 16 we will hand in our draft cards and refuse any further cooperation with the Selective Service System. By doing so we will actively challenge the government's right to draft American men for its criminal war against the people of Vietnam. We of the Resistance feel that we can no longer passively acquiesce to the Selective Service System by accepting its deferments. The American military system depends upon students, those opposed to war, and those with anti-Vietnam war politics wrangling for the respective deferments. Those opposed to the war are dealt with quietly, individually and on the government's terms. If they do not get the deferments, they must individually find some extra-legal alternative. A popular last resort is Canada, and those who go to Canada must be politically silent in order to stay there. Legal draft alternatives are kept within reach of elite groups—good students, those who are able to express objection to all war on religious grounds, and those with the money to hire good lawyers. For the majority of American guys the only alternatives are jail or the army. While those who are most opposed to the war have been silenced, the system that provides the personnel for war crimes continues to function smoothly.

Many who wish to avoid the draft will, of course, choose to accept deferments; many, however, wish to do more than avoid the draft. Resistance means that if the government is to continue its crimes against humanity, it must first deal with our opposition. We do not seek jail, but we do this because as individuals we know of no justifiable alternative and we believe that in time many other American men will also choose to resist the crimes done in their names.

47. "A Call to Resist Illegitimate Authority" (1967)*

This document, published widely in the fall of 1967, became the main basis for the federal government's criminal prosecution of five of the signers: Dr. Benjamin Spock, Marcus Raskin, Mitchell Goodman, Michael Ferber, and the Reverend William Sloane Coffin. These men also turned in to the Justice Department a briefcase filled with draft cards (see headnote to Reading 46).

To the young men of America, to the whole of the American people, and to all men of goodwill everywhere:

1. An ever growing number of young American men are finding that the American war in Vietnam so outrages their deepest moral and religious sense that they cannot contribute to it in any way. We share their moral outrage.

2. We further believe that the war is unconstitutional and illegal. Congress has not declared a war as required by the Constitution. Moreover, under the Constitution, treaties signed by the President and ratified by the Senate have the same force as the Constitution itself. The Charter of the United Nations is such a treaty. The Charter specifically obligates the United States to refrain from force or the threat of force in international relations. It requires member states to exhaust every peaceful means of settling disputes and to submit disputes which cannot be settled peacefully to the Security Council. The United States has systematically violated all of these Charter provisions for thirteen years.

3. Moreover, this war violates international agreements, treaties and principles of law which the United States Government has solemnly endorsed. The combat role of the United States troops in Vietnam violates the Geneva Accords of 1954 which our government pledged to support but has since subverted. The destruction of rice, crops and livestock; the burning and bulldozing of entire villages consisting exclusively of civilian structures; the interning of civilian non-combatants in concentration camps; the summary executions of civilians in captured villages who could not produce satisfactory evidence of their loyalties or did not wish to be removed to concentration camps; the slaughter of peasants who dared to stand up in their fields and shake their fists at American helicopters;—these are all actions of the kind which the United States and the other victorious powers of World War II declared to be crimes against humanity for which individuals were to be held

---

*From *Resist*, 1967.

personally responsible even when acting under the orders of their governments and for which Germans were sentenced at Nuremberg to long prison terms and death. The prohibition of such acts as war crimes was incorporated in treaty law by the Geneva Conventions of 1949, ratified by the United States. These are commitments to other countries and to Mankind, and they would claim our allegiance even if Congress should declare war.

4. We also believe it is an unconstitutional denial of religious liberty and equal protection of the laws to withhold draft exemption from men whose religious or profound philosophical beliefs are opposed to what in the Western religious tradition have been long known as unjust wars.

5. Therefore, we believe on all these grounds that every free man has a legal right and a moral duty to exert every effort to end this war, to avoid collusion with it, and to encourage others to do the same. Young men in the armed forces or threatened with the draft face the most excruciating choices. For them various forms of resistance risk separation from their families and their country, destruction of their careers, loss of their freedom and loss of their lives. Each must choose the course of resistance dictated by his conscience and circumstances. Among those already in the armed forces some are refusing to obey specific illegal and immoral orders, some are attempting to educate their fellow servicemen on the murderous and barbarous nature of the war, some are absenting themselves without official leave. Among those not in the armed forces some are applying for status as conscientious objectors to American aggression in Vietnam, some are refusing to be inducted. Among both groups some are resisting openly and paying a heavy penalty, some are organizing more resistance within the United States and some have sought sanctuary in other countries.

6. We believe that each of these forms of resistance against illegitimate authority is courageous and justified. Many of us believe that open resistance to the war and the draft is the course of action most likely to strengthen the moral resolve with which all of us can oppose the war and most likely to bring an end to the war.

7. We will continue to lend our support to those who undertake resistance to this war. We will raise funds to organize draft resistance unions, to supply legal defense and bail, to support families and otherwise aid resistance to the war in whatever ways may seem appropriate.

8. We firmly believe that our statement is the sort of speech that under the First Amendment must be free, and that the actions we will undertake are as legal as is the war resistance of the young men themselves. But we recognize that the courts may find otherwise, and that if so we might all be liable to prosecution and severe punishment. In any case, we feel that we cannot shrink from fulfilling our responsibilities to the youth whom many of us teach, to the country whose freedom we cherish, and to the ancient traditions of religion and philosophy which we strive to preserve in this generation.

9. We call upon all men of good will to join us in this confrontation with immoral authority. Especially we call upon the universities to fulfill their mission of enlightenment and religious organizations to honor their heritage of brotherhood. Now is the time to resist.

48. "Declaration of Independence from the War in Vietnam" (April 1967)*

By the Reverend Martin Luther King, Jr.

In the two years after he received the Nobel Prize for Peace in 1964, the Reverend Martin Luther King made occasional public statements about his growing concern over the Vietnam War. But until early 1967, Dr. King maintained a moderate position on the issue, as he attempted to stay in the middle of the surging forces of the black movement. On one side, militant groups such as the Student Nonviolent Coordinating Committee (SNCC) and the Black Panther Party, as well as various nationalist organizations, were denouncing the war as an imperialist attack on another non-white people. On the other, such conservative older groups as the NAACP and the Urban League were attempting to fence off what they still called the "civil rights movement" both from the spontaneous urban rebellions and from the politically conscious younger activists who saw the war as a principal cause of the increasing desperation that was fueling these rebellions.

On April 4, 1967, Dr. King implemented a fateful decision when he went to the pulpit of Manhattan's Riverside Church to deliver the sermon here reprinted. The three thousand people who packed the church rose in a tumultuous ovation at the end of what they may have sensed to be one of the most profound statements of this historical period.

The significance of this "Declaration of Independence from the War in Vietnam" was obvious at once to all the contending forces. Dr. King was denounced by The New York Times, *black syndicated columnist Carl Rowan, many leaders of the black establishment, and of course by voices from the right shouting such epithets as "traitor" and "treason." The antiwar movement enthusiastically welcomed this powerful new recruit to its ranks. On April 15, in New York, Dr. King made a similar address to the hundreds of thousands who marched against the war from Central Park to the United Nations.*

Martin Luther King's "Declaration" had a profound influence, strengthening antiwar consciousness and activity everywhere from churches and colleges to the streets of the ghettos and the ranks of GIs in Vietnam (see Reading 50 for its influence within the military).

OVER THE PAST TWO YEARS, as I have moved to break the betrayal of my own silences and to speak from the burnings of my own heart, as I have called for radical departures from the destruction of Vietnam, many persons have questioned me about the wisdom of my path. At the heart of their concerns this query has often loomed large and loud: Why are *you* speaking about the war, Dr. King? Why

---

*From *Ramparts* (May 1967), pp. 33–37. This is the authorized form of the original address, slightly condensed for publication by Dr. King.

are *you* joining the voices of dissent? Peace and civil rights don't mix, they say. Aren't you hurting the cause of your people, they ask. And when I hear them, though I often understand the source of their concern, I am nevertheless greatly saddened, for such questions mean that the inquirers have not really known me, my commitment or my calling. Indeed, their questions suggest that they do not know the world in which they live.

In the light of such tragic misunderstanding, I deem it of signal importance to try to state clearly why I believe that the path from Dexter Avenue Baptist Church—the church in Montgomery, Alabama, where I began my pastorage—leads clearly to this sanctuary tonight.

I come to this platform to make a passionate plea to my beloved nation. This speech is not addressed to Hanoi or to the National Liberation Front. It is not addressed to China or to Russia.

Nor is it an attempt to overlook the ambiguity of the total situation and the need for a collective solution to the tragedy of Vietnam. Neither is it an attempt to make North Vietnam or the National Liberation Front paragons of virtue, nor to overlook the role they can play in a successful resolution of the problem. While they both may have justifiable reasons to be suspicious of the good faith of the United States, life and history give eloquent testimony to the fact that conflicts are never resolved without trustful give and take on both sides.

Tonight, however, I wish not to speak with Hanoi and the NLF, but rather to my fellow Americans who, with me, bear the greatest responsibility in ending a conflict that has exacted a heavy price on both continents.

Since I am a preacher by trade, I suppose it is not surprising that I have seven major reasons for bringing Vietnam into the field of my moral vision. There is at the outset a very obvious and almost facile connection between the war in Vietnam and the struggle I, and others, have been waging in America. A few years ago there was a shining moment in that struggle. It seemed as if there was a real promise of hope for the poor—both black and white—through the Poverty Program. Then came the build-up in Vietnam, and I watched the program broken and eviscerated as if it were some idle political plaything of a society gone mad on war, and I knew that America would never invest the necessary funds or energies in rehabilitation of its poor so long as Vietnam continued to draw men and skills and money like some demonic, destructive suction tube. So I was increasingly compelled to see the war as an enemy of the poor and to attack it as such.

Perhaps the more tragic recognition of reality took place when it became clear to me that the war was doing far more than devastating the hopes of the poor at home. It was sending their sons and their brothers and their husbands to fight and to die in extraordinarily high proportions relative to the rest of the population. We were taking the young black men who had been crippled by our society and sending them 8000 miles away to guarantee liberties in Southeast Asia which they had not found in Southwest Georgia and East Harlem. So we have been repeatedly faced with the cruel irony of watching Negro and white boys on TV screens as they kill and die together for a nation that has been unable to seat them together in the same schools. So we watch them in brutal solidarity burning the huts of a poor village, but we realize that they would never live on the same block in Detroit. I could not be silent in the face of such cruel manipulation of the poor.

My third reason grows out of my experience in the ghettos of the North over the last three years—especially the last three summers. As I have walked among the desperate, rejected and angry young men, I have told them that Molotov cocktails and rifles would not solve their problems. I have tried to offer them my deepest compassion while maintaining my conviction that social change comes most meaningfully through non-violent action. But, they asked, what about Vietnam? They asked if our own nation wasn't using massive doses of violence to solve its problems, to bring about the changes it wanted. Their questions hit home, and I knew that I could never again raise my voice against the violence of the oppressed in the ghettos without having first spoken clearly to the greatest purveyor of violence in the world today—my own government.

For those who ask the question, "Aren't you a Civil Rights leader?" and thereby mean to exclude me from the movement for peace, I have this further answer. In 1957 when a group of us formed the Southern Christian Leadership Conference, we chose as our motto: "To save the soul of America." We were convinced that we could not limit our vision to certain rights for black people, but instead affirmed the conviction that America would never be free or saved from itself unless the descendants of its slaves were loosed from the shackles they still wear.

Now, it should be incandescently clear that no one who has any concern for the integrity and life of America today can ignore the present war. If America's soul becomes totally poisoned, part of the autopsy must read "Vietnam." It can never be saved so long as it destroys the deepest hopes of men the world over.

As if the weight of such a commitment to the life and health of America were not enough, another burden of responsibility was placed upon me in 1964; and I cannot forget that the Nobel Prize for Peace was also a commission—a commission to work harder than I had ever worked before for the "brotherhood of man." This is a calling that takes me beyond national allegiances, but even if it were not present I would yet have to live with the meaning of my commitment to the ministry of Jesus Christ. To me the relationship of this ministry to the making of peace is so obvious that I sometimes marvel at those who ask me why I am speaking against the war. Could it be that they do not know that the good news was meant for all men—for communist and capitalist, for their children and ours, for black and white, for revolutionary and conservative? Have they forgotten that my ministry is in obedience to the One who loved His enemies so fully that He died for them? What then can I say to the Viet Cong or to Castro or to Mao as a faithful minister of this One? Can I threaten them with death, or must I not share with them my life?

And as I ponder the madness of Vietnam, my mind goes constantly to the people of that peninsula. I speak now not of the soldiers of each side, not of the junta in Saigon, but simply of the people who have been living under the curse of war for almost three continuous decades. I think of them, too, because it is clear to me that there will be no meaningful solution there until some attempt is made to know them and their broken cries.

They must see Americans as strange liberators. The Vietnamese proclaimed their own independence in 1945 after a combined French and Japanese occupation and before the communist revolution in China. Even though they quoted the American Declaration of Independence in their own document of freedom, we refused to recognize them. Instead, we decided to support France in its re-conquest of her former colony.

Our government felt then that the Vietnamese people were not "ready" for independence, and we again fell victim to the deadly Western arrogance that has poisoned the international atmosphere for so long. With that tragic decision, we rejected a revolutionary government seeking self-determination, and a government that had been established not by China (for whom the Vietnamese have no great love) but by clearly indigenous forces that included some communists. For the peasants, this new government meant real land reform, one of the most important needs in their lives.

For nine years following 1945 we denied the people of Vietnam the right of independence. For nine years we vigorously supported the French in their abortive effort to re-colonize Vietnam.

Before the end of the war we were meeting 80 per cent of the French war costs. Even before the French were defeated at Dien Bien Phu, they began to despair of their reckless action, but we did not. We encouraged them with our huge financial and military supplies to continue the war even after they had lost the will to do so.

After the French were defeated it looked as if independence and land reform would come again through the Geneva agreements. But instead there came the United States, determined that Ho should not unify the temporarily divided nation, and the peasants watched again as we supported one of the most vicious modern dictators—our chosen man, Premier Diem. The peasants watched and cringed as Diem ruthlessly routed out all opposition, supported their extortionist landlords and refused even to discuss reunification with the North. The peasants watched as all this was presided over by U.S. influence and then by increasing numbers of U.S. troops who came to help quell the insurgency that Diem's methods had aroused. When Diem was overthrown they may have been happy, but the long line of military dictatorships seemed to offer no real change—especially in terms of their need for land and peace.

The only change came from America as we increased our troop commitments in support of governments which were singularly corrupt, inept and without popular support. All the while, the people read our leaflets and received regular promises of peace and democracy—and land reform. Now they languish under our bombs and consider us—not their fellow Vietnamese—the real enemy. They move sadly and apathetically as we herd them off the land of their fathers into concentration camps where minimal social needs are rarely met. They know they must move or be destroyed by our bombs. So they go.

They watch as we poison their water, as we kill a million acres of their crops. They must weep as the bulldozers destroy their precious trees. They wander into the hospitals, with at least 20 casualties from American firepower for each Viet Cong-inflicted injury. So far we may have killed a million of them—mostly children.

What do the peasants think as we ally ourselves with the landlords and as we refuse to put any action into our many words concerning land reform? What do they think as we test out our latest weapons on them, just as the Germans tested out new medicine and new tortures in the concentration camps of Europe? Where are the roots of the independent Vietnam we claim to be building?

Now there is little left to build on—save bitterness. Soon the only solid physical foundations remaining will be found at our military bases and in the concrete of the concentration camps we call "fortified hamlets." The peasants may well wonder if we plan to build our new Vietnam on such grounds as these. Could we blame them for such thoughts? We must speak for them and raise the questions they cannot raise. These too are our brothers.

Perhaps the more difficult but no less necessary task is to speak for those who have been designated as our enemies. What of the NLF—that strangely anonymous group we call VC or communists? What must they think of us in America when they realize that we permitted the repression and cruelty of Diem which helped to bring them into being as a resistance group in the South? How can they believe in our integrity when now we speak of "aggression from the North" as if there were nothing more essential to the war? How can they trust us when now we charge *them* with violence after the murderous reign of Diem, and charge *them* with violence while we pour new weapons of death into their land?

How do they judge us when our officials know that their membership is less than 25 per cent communist and yet insist on giving them the blanket name? What must they be thinking when they know that we are aware of their control of major sections of Vietnam and yet we appear ready to allow national elections in which this highly organized political parallel government will have no part? They ask how we can speak of free elections when the Saigon press is censored and controlled by the military junta. And they are surely right to wonder what kind of new government we plan to help form without them—the only party in real touch with the peasants. They question our political goals and they deny the reality of a peace settlement from which they will be excluded. Their questions are frighteningly relevant.

Here is the true meaning and value of compassion and non-violence—when it helps us to see the enemy's point of view, to hear his questions, to know of his assessment of ourselves. For from his view we may indeed see the basic weaknesses of our own condition, and if we are mature, we may learn and grow and profit from the wisdom of the brothers who are called the opposition.

So, too, with Hanoi. In the North, where our bombs now pummel the land, and our mines endanger the waterways, we are met by a deep but understandable mistrust. In Hanoi are the men who led the nation to independence against the

Japanese and the French, the men who sought membership in the French common-wealth and were betrayed by the weakness of Paris and the willfulness of the colonial armies. It was they who led a second struggle against French domination at tremendous costs, and then were persuaded at Geneva to give up, as a temporary measure, the land they controlled between the 13th and 17th parallels. After 1954 they watched us conspire with Diem to prevent elections which would have surely brought Ho Chi Minh to power over a united Vietnam, and they realized they had been betrayed again.

When we ask why they do not leap to negotiate, these things must be remembered. Also, it must be clear that the leaders of Hanoi considered the presence of American troops in support of the Diem regime to have been the initial military breach of the Geneva Agreements concerning foreign troops, and they remind us that they did not begin to send in any large number of supplies or men until American forces had moved into the tens of thousands.

Hanoi remembers how our leaders refused to tell us the truth about the earlier North Vietnamese overtures for peace, how the President claimed that none existed when they had clearly been made. Ho Chi Minh has watched as America has spoken of peace and built up its forces, and now he has surely heard the increasing international rumors of American plans for an invasion of the North. Perhaps only his sense of humor and irony can save him when he hears the most powerful nation of the world speaking of aggression as it drops thousands of bombs on a poor, weak nation more than 8000 miles from its shores.

At this point, I should make it clear that while I have tried here to give a voice to the voiceless of Vietnam and to understand the arguments of those who are called enemy, I am as deeply concerned about our own troops there as anything else. For it occurs to me that what we are submitting them to in Vietnam is not simply the brutalizing process that goes on in any war where armies face each other and seek to destroy. We are adding cynicism to the process of death, for our troops must know after a short period there that none of the things we claim to be fighting for are really involved. Before long they must know that their government has sent them into a struggle among Vietnamese, and the more sophisticated surely realize that we are on the side of the wealthy and the secure while we create a hell for the poor.

Somehow this madness must cease. I speak as a child of God and brother to the suffering poor of Vietnam and the poor of America who are paying the double price of smashed hopes at home and death and corruption in Vietnam. I speak as a citizen of the world, for the world as it stands aghast at the path we have taken. I speak as an American to the leaders of my own nation. The great initiative in this war is ours. The initiative to stop must be ours.

This is the message of the great Buddhist leaders of Vietnam. Recently, one of them wrote these words: "Each day the war goes on the hatred increases in the hearts of the Vietnamese and in the hearts of those of humanitarian instinct. The Americans are forcing even their friends into becoming their enemies. It is curious that the Americans, who calculate so carefully on the possibilities of military victory, do not realize that in the process they are incurring deep psychological and political defeat. The image of America will never again be the image of revolution, freedom and democracy, but the image of violence and militarism."

If we continue, there will be no doubt in my mind and in the mind of the world that we have no honorable intentions in Vietnam. It will become clear that our minimal expectation is to occupy it as an American colony, and men will not refrain from thinking that our maximum hope is to goad China into a war so that we may bomb her nuclear installations.

The world now demands a maturity of America that we may not be able to achieve. It demands that we admit that we have been wrong from the beginning of our adventure in Vietnam, that we have been detrimental to the life of her people.

In order to atone for our sins and errors in Vietnam, we should take the initiative in bringing the war to a halt. I would like to suggest five concrete things that our government should do immediately to begin the long and difficult process of extricating ourselves from this nightmare:

1. End all bombing in North and South Vietnam.

2. Declare a unilateral cease-fire in the hope that such action will create the atmosphere for negotiation.

3. Take immediate steps to prevent other battlegrounds in Southeast Asia by curtailing our military build-up in Thailand and our interference in Laos.

4. Realistically accept the fact that the National Liberation Front has substantial support in South Vietnam and must thereby play a role in any meaningful negotiations and in any future Vietnam government.

5. Set a date on which we will remove all foreign troops from Vietnam in accordance with the 1954 Geneva Agreement.

Part of our ongoing commitment might well express itself in an offer to grant asylum to any Vietnamese who fears for his life under a new regime which included the NLF. Then we must make what reparations we can for the damage we have done. We must provide the medical aid that is badly needed, in this country if necessary.

Meanwhile, we in the churches and synagogues have a continuing task while we urge our government to disengage itself from a disgraceful commitment. We must be prepared to match actions with words by seeking out every creative means of protest possible.

As we counsel young men concerning military service we must clarify for them our nation's role in Vietnam and challenge them with the alternative of conscientious objection. I am pleased to say that this is the path now being chosen by more than 70 students at my own Alma Mater, Morehouse College, and I recommend it to all who find the American course in Vietnam a dishonorable and unjust one. Moreover, I would encourage all ministers of draft age to give up their ministerial exemptions and seek status as conscientious objectors. Every man of humane convictions must decide on the protest that best suits his convictions, but we must *all* protest.

There is something seductively tempting about stopping there and sending us all off on what in some circles has become a popular crusade against the war in Vietnam. I say we must enter that struggle, but I wish to go on now to say something even more disturbing. The war in Vietnam is but a symptom of a far deeper malady within the American spirit, and if we ignore this sobering reality we will find ourselves organizing clergy- and laymen-concerned committees for the next generation. We will be marching and attending rallies without end unless there is a significant and profound change in American life and policy.

In 1957 a sensitive American official overseas said that it seemed to him that our nation was on the wrong side of a world revolution. During the past ten years we have seen emerge a pattern of suppression which now has justified the presence of U.S. military "advisors" in Venezuela. The need to maintain social stability for our investments accounts for the counterrevolutionary action of American forces in Guatemala. It tells why American helicopters are being used against guerrillas in Colombia and why American napalm and green beret forces have already been active against rebels in Peru. With such activity in mind, the words of John F. Kennedy come back to haunt us. Five years ago he said, "Those who make peaceful revolution impossible will make violent revolution inevitable."

Increasingly, by choice or by accident, this is the role our nation has taken— by refusing to give up the privileges and the pleasures that come from the immense profits of overseas investment.

I am convinced that if we are to get on the right side of the world revolution, we as a nation must undergo a radical revolution of values. When machines and computers, profit and property rights are considered more important than people, the giant triplets of racism, materialism, and militarism are incapable of being conquered.

A true revolution of values will soon cause us to question the fairness and justice of many of our past and present policies. True compassion is more than flinging a coin to a beggar; it is not haphazard and superficial. It comes to see that an edifice which produces beggars needs re-structuring. A true revolution of values will soon look easily on the glaring contrast of poverty and wealth. With righteous indignation, it will look across the seas and see individual capitalists of the West investing huge sums of money in Asia, Africa and South America, only to take the profits out with no concern for the social betterment of the countries, and say: "This is not just." It will look at our alliance with the landed gentry of Latin America and say: "This is not just." The Western arrogance of feeling that it has everything to teach others and nothing to learn from them is not just. A true revolution of values will lay hands on the world order and say of war: "This way of settling differences is not just." This business of burning human beings with napalm, of filling our nation's homes with orphans and widows, of injecting poisonous drugs of hate into the veins of peoples normally humane, of sending men home from dark and bloody battlefields physically handicapped and psychologically deranged, cannot be reconciled with wisdom, justice, and love. A nation that continues year after year to spend more money on military defense than on programs of social uplift is approaching spiritual death.

America, the richest and most powerful nation in the world, can well lead the way in this revolution of values. There is nothing, except a tragic death wish, to prevent us from re-ordering our priorities, so that the pursuit of peace will take precedence over the pursuit of war. There is nothing to keep us from molding a recalcitrant status quo until we have fashioned it into a brotherhood.

This kind of positive revolution of values is our best defense against communism. War is not the answer. Communism will never be defeated by the use of atomic bombs or nuclear weapons. Let us not join those who shout war and through their misguided passions urge the United States to relinquish its participation in the United Nations. These are the days which demand wise restraint and calm reasonableness. We must not call everyone a communist or an appeaser who advocates the seating of Red China in the United Nations and who recognizes that hate and hysteria are not the final answers to the problem of these turbulent days. We must not engage in a negative anti-communism, but rather in a positive thrust for democracy, realizing that our greatest defense against communism is to take offensive action in behalf of justice. We must with positive action seek to remove those conditions of poverty, insecurity and injustice which are the fertile soil in which the seed of communism grows and develops.

These are revolutionary times. All over the globe men are revolting against old systems of exploitation and oppression, and out of the wombs of a frail world, new systems of justice and equality are being born. The shirtless and barefoot people of the land are rising up as never before. "The people who sat in darkness have seen a great light." We in the West must support these revolutions. It is a sad fact that, because of comfort, complacency, a morbid fear of communism, and our proneness to adjust to injustice, the Western nations that initiated so much of the revolutionary spirit of the modern world have now become the arch anti-revolutionaries. This has driven many to feel that only Marxism has the revolutionary spirit. Therefore, communism is a judgment against our failure to make democracy real and follow through on the revolutions that we initiated. Our only hope today lies in our ability to recapture the revolutionary spirit and go out into a sometimes hostile world declaring eternal hostility to poverty, racism, and militarism.

We must move past indecision to action. We must find new ways to speak for peace in Vietnam and justice throughout the developing world—a world that borders on our doors. If we do not act we shall surely be dragged down the long, dark and shameful corridors of time reserved for those who possess power without compassion, might without morality, and strength without sight.

Now let us begin. Now let us re-dedicate ourselves to the long and bitter—but beautiful—struggle for a new world. This is the calling of the sons of God, and our brothers wait eagerly for our response. Shall we say the odds are too great? Shall we tell them the struggle is too hard? Will our message be that the forces of American life militate against their arrival as full men, and we send our deepest regrets? Or will there be another message, of longing, of hope, of solidarity with their yearnings, of commitment to their cause, whatever the cost? The choice is ours, and though we might prefer it otherwise we *must* choose in this crucial moment of human history.

49. "Deserters' Manifesto" (1968)*

Although resistance to the draft posed problems for the government, far more serious trouble came from another form of resistance: desertion. The number of draft evaders and resisters was only a small fraction of the number of deserters from the armed forces. Many of the deserters embarrassed the government further by becoming politically active in such places as France, Germany, Sweden, Canada, the Netherlands, and England.

Some startling figures came to light as President Ford was pondering the amnesty he declared in September 1974 (the same day that he also issued the pardon of ex-President Nixon for all the federal crimes he may have committed while in office). According to the Department of Defense, there were 503,926 "incidents of desertion" between July 1, 1966, and December 31, 1973.[1] From 1963 through 1973 (a period almost half again as long), there were, according to the Justice Department, only 191,840 cases of men failing to respond to draft board directives, and of these, 80 per cent responded to second or third notices.[2] Only 9,118 were prosecuted during this period, and another 4,400 were "at large" the month before the amnesty was announced. The admitted total of deserters still "at large" at the time was 28,661—six and a half times the number of draft evaders and resisters.[3] Since the overwhelming majority of the armed forces were drawn from the working class, these statistics offer powerful evidence that resistance to the war was stronger among young working-class men than among more affluent draft-age men.

Some might dismiss this desertion as apolitical, reflecting merely a low level of motivation to fight. But this low level of motivation itself evinces the lack of support for the war. It is difficult to draw a clear line between this "apolitical" desertion and the kind of political consciousness expressed in the popular movement slogan, "Make Love, Not War." Moreover, significant numbers of deserters participated in organizing themselves, as well as active-duty GIs, against the war. For example, by early 1967, a network of deserters had helped build an underground organization in western Europe whose activities included leafleting US military bases and establishing sanctuaries.[4]

The following "Deserters' Manifesto" exemplifies the political consciousness of another group, in Canada.

---

*From *The Movement*, March, 1969.

1. *The New York Times*, August 20, 1974.

2. Ibid.

3. Ibid. These figures are probably all quite understated. As this article notes: ". . . during the Vietnam War officials tended to minimize the numbers in an effort to show that the war was not unpopular. Estimates of fugitives by pro-amnesty groups have run as high as 100,000. Some say that there are as many as 50,000 deserters and war-resisters in Canada alone."

4. "Déserteurs américains en France," *L'événement* (March, 1967), pp. 13–14; "The Resister/ Deserter Underground," *The Nation* (November, 1967), pp. 487–91; Bruce Franklin, *From the Movement: Toward Revolution* (New York: Van Nostrand Reinhold, 1971), p. 66.

We, American Deserters living in Montreal, in opposition to the U.S. imperialist aggression in Vietnam, have banded together to form the American Deserters Committee.

We Deserters and associates view ourselves as an integral part of the worldwide movement for fundamental social change. We express support and solidarity with the National Liberation Front of South Vietnam and the black liberation struggle at home. We are prepared to fight side by side with anyone who wants to bring fundamental social change to the U.S.

Our aim is to help U.S. Deserters and draft resisters gain a more political outlook toward their own actions—to show them that desertion and draft resistance are in fact political moves. Forced to live our lives as political exiles, we view ourselves as victims of the same oppression as the Vietnamese and the American people, not only the minority groups, but also the broad masses of American people who are becoming more aware of the need for change.

We will work to develop the political consciousness of American Deserters and to form a well-educated and determined group which will have a clear understanding of U.S. internal and international policies, especially those which affect Canada and Quebec.

We express solidarity with our fellow servicemen who are still in the military, and as yet are unable to resist actively. We will do all in our power to help all those who resist in the same way—DESERT.

We recognize U.S. imperialism as the greatest threat to the progress of freedom and self-determination for all people, and view desertion as the most effective way to resist.

American Deserters Committee
c/o P.O.B. 611
Station H
Montreal 25, Quebec
Canada
December 15, 1968

50. "Constraints of the Negro Civil Rights Movement on American Military Effectiveness" (1970)*

By Commander George L. Jackson

Writing in the Naval War College Review *of January 1970, Commander George L. Jackson of the School of Naval Command and Staff elucidated some of the black movement's influence on grave problems emerging within the armed forces. Commander Jackson notes the special significance of Martin Luther King's April 1967 declaration (Reading 48) and stresses the complex repercussions of the urban rebellions.*

While progress toward greater Negro civil rights was considerable during the two decades prior to 1960, many contended that the pace of change was too slow and advocated a departure from legal procedures. Negro civil rights activity became increasingly marked by illegitimate measures that challenged the legitimacy of established authority and instilled fear within the general population. When a significant segment of the society regarded civil rights activity as dangerous and reacted with suppressive measures, the civil rights movement took on the trappings of a revolution.

The Negro civil rights movement will continue to exert significant influence upon every aspect of American society in the immediate future. The nation's military establishment has been affected by the movement in much the same manner as principal social institutions. The morality of the movement notwithstanding, the Negro civil rights action has introduced definite constraints on the military capability of the United States.

The most important of these constraints is that produced by the coalition of civil rights organizations and the antiwar organizations. This coalition has spearheaded the shift of public opinion away from support of the Vietnam conflict. On the surface it would appear that the two do not possess sufficient common goals to justify such an alliance, but the concern of the civil rights leaders over the priority accorded Vietnam vice [*sic*] domestic reform programs has caused them to align themselves with the antiwar group.

The identification of the civil rights movement with the antiwar enthusiasts was given its greatest impetus in April of 1967, when the late Reverend Dr. Martin Luther King took a strong public stand on the issue. Labeling the American Government as "the greatest purveyor of violence in the world," Dr. King called for a halt in the bombing of North and South Vietnam, a unilateral cease-fire, the with-

---

*From *Naval War College Review* (January 1970), pp. 100–107.

drawal of American troops, and negotiation with the National Liberation Front. He urged all blacks and "white people of goodwill" to boycott the draft by seeking conscientious objector status until his program was achieved. Dr. King indicated that there were three primary reasons which compelled him to take a stand against the Vietnam war: first, an awareness that the war was "playing havoc with domestic destinies" and making it more difficult to implement programs to deal with the economic and social problems of the Negro and poor people generally; second, a fear that constant escalation of the war could lead to a grand war with China and another world war; and third, the extension to international affairs of his personal philosophy of nonviolence.[1]

While Dr. King did not gain the immediate adherence of other civil rights leaders to his position on the Vietnam war, he was a man of international stature and the acknowledged leader of the American Negro civil rights movement. His influence among Negroes was great, and his association with the antiwar groups was of profound significance on the national scene.

The growing public disillusionment with the Vietnam war, of which Dr. King's declaration was an essential part, made it more difficult for the military to conclude the war in Vietnam by reducing its ability to generate effective military-political pressure. . . .

Just as the civil rights movement has served as a restraint upon the ability of American forces in Vietnam to complete their mission, so it has altered and restricted the use of military resources. . . .

The most apparent effect that the civil rights movement has had upon military force employment has been the necessity of using troops to quell civil disturbances. The National Guard has traditionally been used for this purpose. During the fiscal year 1968, 104,665 National Guardsmen were called to quell civil disturbances, many of which were precipitated by the assassination of Dr. Martin Luther King. National Guard units were alerted for possible commitment in civil disturbances 77 times in 29 states and the District of Columbia. About one-fourth of those units alerted were used to quell disturbances in Detroit, Washington, and Chicago. The Detroit disturbance alone required 10,399 active duty Guardsmen and 5,547 active Army personnel to restore order.[2] In February of 1969 the Guard was also called to the campus of the University of Wisconsin to quell student disorders stemming from demands to establish a Negro curriculum and increase numbers of Negro students and faculty members. This was the first case in which Guardsmen were used to restore order on campus.[3]

The riots of 1968 produced changes in the organizational structure of the National Guard. A Department of Defense executive agency for civil disturbance matters was created within the Department of the Army, and emphasis was placed

---

1. "Dr. King to Weigh Civil Disobedience if War Intensifies," *The New York Times*, 2 April 1967, p.1:4, 76:1.

2. U.S. National Guard Bureau, *Annual Report, Fiscal Year 1968* (Washington: 1968), p. 13, 15.

3. "Troops Sent to U. of Wisconsin," *The New York Times*, 2 February 1967, p. 2:4.

on the Guard's training for handling such matters. In addition, authority was granted for assembling and training Guard units on short notice when intelligence reports indicated a high probability that forces would be required to quell civil disorder. The need for a Directorate for Civil Disturbance Planning and Operations with a permanent command center to handle concurrent civil disorder emergencies was also demonstrated.[4]

The direct influence of the civil rights movement on a specific military operation and underlying policy was witnessed in February 1967 when the U.S. Navy aircraft carrier U.S.S. *Franklin D. Roosevelt* made an operational visit to Capetown, Republic of South Africa. On 1 February, Negro leaders attending the third annual meeting of the American Negro Leadership Conference urged President Johnson to cancel the carrier's scheduled visit to Capetown and characterized the call as "an insult to American Negroes, to the black people of Africa, and to democratic men throughout the world." The African nation's apartheid policy was cited as the basis for the objection to the visit.[5]

The following day U.S. Navy sources indicated that the visit could not be canceled, despite opposition from civil rights leaders and Congressmen, because of the needs for fuel and shore liberty incident to the ship's 13,400-mile voyage from Southeast Asia to Mayport, Fla. The alternative to the visit would be to dispatch a fleet oiler on a 45-day voyage costing at least $250,000 to provide the fuel required for the carrier if the visit were canceled.[6]

Subsequent reports revealed that while *Roosevelt* called at Capetown on 4 February—based on a decision made at "the highest level in Washington"—the 3,400-man crew remained aboard during the port visit. Since the *Roosevelt* visit, U.S. Navy ships have been denied permission to call at ports in the Republic of South Africa.[7]

The American Negro civil rights movement has also tended to constrain military capability by competing with the Defense establishment for available Federal funds. Advocates of greater Federal aid to programs designed to improve the general situation of the Nation's minority groups, particularly in urban areas, recognize that substantial reductions in defense appropriations might free funds which might be channeled into domestic areas. One such advocate of greater emphasis on domestic social problems, Senator Eugene McCarthy, criticized policies which placed military action in Vietnam before domestic problems:

The most important struggle for the future welfare of America is not in the jungles of Vietnam; it is in the streets and schools and tenements of our cities. Yet the commitment

---

4. U.S. National Guard Bureau, p. 16.

5. Thomas A. Johnson, "Call at Capetown by Ship Opposed," *The New York Times*, 2 February 1967, p. 2:4.

6. Benjamin Welles, "Navy Stands Fast on Capetown Visit," *The New York Times*, 3 February 1967, p. 10:2.

7. "Apartheid Keeps Crew on U.S. Ship," *The New York Times*, 5 February 1967, p. 1:4, 26:1.

of resources and moral energy to the problems of our cities has been but a fraction of the amount committed to the Saigon regime.[8]

Professor Alfred G. Buehler, Director of the Public Finance Center at the University of Pennsylvania, considers that the 1967–68 struggle between Congress and the administration illustrates the severity of contemporary problems related to the formulation, control, and financing of Federal programs. While aspects of this struggle have been present in the past, he considers that the racial disturbances, riots, urban unrest, and other recent disorders associated with the Negro movement have suddenly thrust the problem of Federal financing to the fore.[9] Although the underlying pressures of poverty, unequal income distribution, and politics have long existed, black action has placed the matter squarely before the Nation. The influence that this pressure can have on Federal budgeting could have a serious and damaging effect on the Nation's military capability should it be decided to increase Federal support to domestic problems at the expense of military force levels.

There are also demographic factors related to the Nation's military force levels which have been influenced by the civil rights movement. Sharp criticism surfaced in the spring of 1967 when reports indicated that Negroes comprised 11 percent of the total enlisted strength in Vietnam but accounted for 14.5 percent of Army combat forces and 22.5 percent of all Army troops killed in action. In response to this criticism the Department of Defense took steps to readjust force levels in order to achieve an equitable proportion and employment of Negroes in Vietnam.[10] This has wider implications in future conflicts. The military planner could conceivably be required, by the adverse publicity, to consider assignment of personnel to combat units on an accepted racial proportion rather than on combat qualifications.

Leading advocates of the civil rights movement have also been critical of the fact that 30.2 percent of qualified Negroes are drafted, while only 18.8 percent of qualified whites are inducted because of educational and other deferments. Their criticism has led to various proposals for draft reform such as the lottery system and the volunteer army, both of which would have a great effect upon the composition and hence the capability of our military forces.

Further criticisms have been leveled at the various services on account of the percentage of Negro officers and enlisted men in each. Negroes at present compromise 13 percent of the Army, 10 percent of the Air Force, 8 percent of the Marine Corps, 5.6 percent of the Navy, and 1.26 percent of the National Guard. Because of educational differences, the proportion of Negro officers to white officers is consistently less than that of Negro enlisted men to white enlisted men. Efforts to bring these ratios into line with the ratio of whites to Negroes in the general population would have a marked effect on the military. Such efforts have already been

8. Eugene McCarthy, *First Things First: New Priorities for Americans* (New York: New American Library, 1968), p. 20.

9. Alfred G. Buehler, "The Cost of Democracy," *The Annals*, September 1968, p. 11.

10. Ulysses Lee, "The Draft and the Negro," *Current History*, July 1968, p. 47.

initiated by the Defense Department in relation to the National Guard.[11] In an effort to implement the recommendations of the National Advisory Commission on Civil Disorders, the Defense Department is expected to attempt to raise Negro membership to approximately the proportion of Negroes in the general population.

Military capability cannot be evaluated only in terms of force levels or employment. The factor of morale is extremely important, and a low morale on the part of Negro personnel lessens their effectiveness and that of the forces to which they are assigned.

Negro military personnel are exposed to a variety of conditions and influences which would tend to reduce their loyalty to the United States and its military forces. The most important of these is, perhaps, hostility among their fellow servicemen. The likely effect of racial dissention [*sic*] upon military effectiveness has been recognized by the Department of Defense. Reacting to an increasing number of reports of growing tensions between whites and Negroes in military organizations, Secretary of Defense Melvin R. Laird called upon military commanders to ensure that racial differences were removed.[12]

The Negro serviceman also faces discriminatory practices in his dealings with civilians, the Civil Rights Act of 1964 notwithstanding. While the Federal Government has undertaken to eliminate such discriminatory practices, it is still obvious to many Negro servicemen that they are not welcome in the housing, schools, and churches of some of the Nation's communities, and this does not fail to affect their morale.

Another extremely important factor in this situation is the appeal of Negro militants and civil rights leaders. The late Dr. Martin Luther King struck directly at the motivation of Negro military personnel when he asserted that the Vietnam war was an instrument of "Negro genocide" forged by America's "white masters."[13] Other Negroes have sought to enlist American servicemen in militant civil rights organizations, and radical student groups have urged election of officers, unionization of enlisted personnel, and the abolition of the salute and privileges of rank. It would be naive to think that such statements and appeals have no effect on the motivation and loyalty of Negro servicemen. Negro servicemen are, in fact, torn between appeals to their racial pride by civil rights organizations and the demands of military service.

Certain aspects of the antimilitary phase of the civil rights movement have been discussed previously. Aside from his basic objection to war, Dr. King based his objection to the Vietnam war on its effects on the civil rights effort, and the disproportionate burden on Negro military personnel. He considered the war was rooted in the militaristic nature of American society, and he observed: ". . . you can't

11. "Negro Membership in Guard Declines," *The Providence Journal*, 24 March 1969, p. 1:2, 8:3.

12. "Laird Warns of Growing Race Tensions in Services," *Navy Times*, 28 May 1969, p. 33:2.

13. *The United States in World Affairs 1967* (New York: 1968), p. 5.

really have freedom without justice, you can't have peace without justice, and you can't have justice without peace, so it is more of a realization of the interrelatedness of racism and militarism and the need to attack both problems rather than leaving one."[14] . . .

Accepting his party's nomination as a presidential candidate in the 1968 presidential campaign, Richard M. Nixon expressed the implications of the civil rights movement for the Nation's world military role: "A nation that can't keep the peace at home won't be trusted to keep the peace abroad."[15] . . .

51. "The Collapse of the Armed Forces" (1971)*

By Colonel Robert D. Heinl, Jr.

When Colonel Robert Heinl published this article in the Armed Forces Journal *in June 1971, it drew national attention. Hints of near-mutinous conditions among US combat forces in Vietnam and on the fleet off its coast had occasionally surfaced in the press. There had also been some coverage of the week-long April encampment in Washington of a thousand Vietnam veterans, who had chanted pro-NLF slogans outside the White House and hurled their hundreds of Purple Hearts and combat medals at the Capitol. But relatively few Americans were aware that by this time the antiwar movements at home and within the armed forces were often working in coordination, nor did many think of the US military as close to "collapse."*

It was hard to dismiss the views of Colonel Heinl, a combat veteran with twenty-seven years' experience in the Marines, former director of the Marine Corps historical program, distinguished military analyst, and author of five books, including The Marine Officer's Guide *and* Soldiers of the Sea, *the definitive history of the Marine Corps. His article was certainly controversial, but it was criticized as much for understating as for overstating the potentially insurrectionary situation within the armed forces.[1]*

---

14. "Dr. King to Weigh Civil Disobedience if War Intensifies," *The New York Times*, 2 April 1967, p. 76:1.

15. Richard M. Nixon, "Acceptance Speech," *Vital Speeches*, 1 September 1968, p. 676.

*From *Armed Forces Journal* (June 7, 1971), pp. 30–37.

1. For accounts of the organized movement in the military that go beyond Colonel Heinl's, see: Larry G. Waterhouse and Mariann G. Wizard, *Turning the Guns Around: Notes on the GI Movement* (New York: Delta Books, 1971); Richard Boyle, *Flower of the Dragon: The Breakdown of the U.S. Army in Vietnam* (San Francisco: Ramparts Press, 1973); Matthew Rinaldi, "The Olive-Drab Rebels: Military Organizing During the Vietnam Era," *Radical America*, 8 (1974), #3, pp. 17–52; H. Bruce Franklin, *Back Where You Came From* (New York: Harper's Magazine Press, 1975); David Cortright, *Soldiers in Revolt: The American Military Today* (Garden City, NY: Doubleday, 1975).

The morale, discipline and battleworthiness of the U.S. Armed Forces are, with a few salient exceptions, lower and worse than at any time in this century and possibly in the history of the United States.

By every conceivable indicator, our army that now remains in Vietnam is in a state approaching collapse, with individual units avoiding or having refused combat, murdering their officers and noncommissioned officers, drug-ridden, and dispirited where not near-mutinous.

Elsewhere than Vietnam, the situation is nearly as serious.

Intolerably clobbered and buffeted from without and within by social turbulence, pandemic drug addiction, race war, sedition, civilian scapegoatise, draftee recalcitrance and malevolence, barracks theft and common crime, unsupported in their travail by the general government, in Congress as well as the executive branch, distrusted, disliked, and often reviled by the public, the uniformed services today are places of agony for the loyal, silent professionals who doggedly hang on and try to keep the ship afloat.

The responses of the services to these unheard-of conditions, forces and new public attitudes, are confused, resentful, occasionally pollyanna-ish, and in some cases even calculated to worsen the malaise that is wracking them.

While no senior officer (especially one on active duty) can openly voice any such assessment, the foregoing conclusions find virtually unanimous support in numerous non-attributable interviews with responsible senior and midlevel officers, as well as career noncommissioned officers and petty officers in all services.

Historical precedents do exist for some of the services' problems, such as desertion, mutiny, unpopularity, seditious attacks, and racial troubles. Others, such as drugs, pose difficulties that are wholly new. Nowhere, however, in the history of the Armed Forces have comparable past troubles presented themselves in such general magnitude, acuteness, or concentrated focus as today.

By several orders of magnitude, the Army seems to be in worst trouble. But the Navy has serious and unprecedented problems, while the Air Force, on the surface at least still clear of the quicksands in which the Army is sinking, is itself facing disquieting difficulties.

Only the Marines—who have made the news this year by their hard line against indiscipline and general permissiveness—seem, with their expected staunchness and tough tradition, to be weathering the storm.

Back to Campus

To understand the military consequences of what is happening to the U.S. Armed Forces, Vietnam is a good place to start. It is in Vietnam that the rearguard of a 500,000-man army, in its day (and in the observation of the writer) the best army the United States ever put into the field, is numbly extricating itself from a nightmare war the Armed Forces feel they had foisted on them by bright civilians who are now back on campus writing books about the folly of it all.

"They have set up separate companies," writes an American soldier from Cu Chi, quoted in the *New York Times*, "for men who refuse to go out into the field.

It is no big thing to refuse to go. If a man is ordered to go to such and such a place he no longer goes through the hassle of refusing; he just packs his shirt and goes to visit some buddies at another base camp. Operations have become incredibly ragtag. Many guys don't even put on their uniforms any more . . . The American garrisons on the larger bases are virtually disarmed. The lifers have taken our weapons from us and put them under lock and key . . . There have also been quite a few frag incidents in the battalion."

Can all this really be typical or even truthful?

Unfortunately the answer is yes.

"Frag incidents" or just "fragging" is current soldier slang in Vietnam for the murder or attempted murder of strict, unpopular, or just aggressive officers and NCOs. With extreme reluctance (after a young West Pointer from Senator Mike Mansfield's Montana was fragged in his sleep) the Pentagon has now disclosed that fraggings in 1970 (209) have more than doubled those of the previous year (96).

Word of the deaths of officers will bring cheers at troop movies or in bivouacs of certain units.

In one such division—the morale-plagued Americal—fraggings during 1971 have been authoritatively estimated to be running about one a week.

Yet fraggings, though hard to document, form part of the ugly lore of every war. The first such verified incident known to have taken place occurred 190 years ago when Pennsylvania soldiers in the Continental Army killed one of their captains during the night of 1 January 1781.

Bounties and Evasions

Bounties, raised by common subscription in amounts running anywhere from $50 to $1,000, have been widely reported put on the heads of leaders whom the privates and Sp4s want to rub out.

Shortly after the costly assault on Hamburger Hill in mid-1969, the GI underground newspaper in Vietnam, "GI Says," publicly offered a $10,000 bounty on LCol Weldon Honeycutt, the officer who ordered (and led) the attack. Despite several attempts, however, Honeycutt managed to live out his tour and return Stateside.

"Another Hamburger Hill" (i.e., toughly contested assault), conceded a veteran major, "is definitely out."

The issue of "combat refusal," an official euphemism for disobedience of orders to fight—the soldier's gravest crime—has only recently been again precipitated on the frontier of Laos by Troop B, 1st Cavalry's mass refusal to recapture their captain's command vehicle containing communication gear, codes and other secret operation orders.

As early as mid-1969, however, an entire company of the 196th Light Infantry Brigade publicly sat down on the battlefield. Later that year, another rifle company, from the famed 1st Air Cavalry Division, flatly refused—on CBS-TV—to advance down a dangerous trail. . . .

While denying further unit refusals, the Air Cav has admitted some 35 individual refusals in 1970 alone. By comparison, only two years earlier in 1968, the entire number of officially recorded refusals for our whole army in Vietnam—from over seven divisions—was 68.

"Search and evade" (meaning tacit avoidance of combat by units in the field) is now virtually a principle of war, vividly expressed by the GI phrase, "CYA (cover your ass) and get home!"

That "search-and-evade" has not gone unnoticed by the enemy is underscored by the Viet Cong delegation's recent statement at the Paris Peace Talks that communist units in Indochina have been ordered not to engage American units which do not molest them. The same statement boasted—not without foundation in fact—that American defectors are in the VC ranks.

Symbolic anti-war fasts (such as the one at Pleiku where an entire medical unit, led by its officers, refused Thanksgiving turkey), peace symbols, "V"-signs not for victory but for peace, booing and cursing of officers and even of hapless entertainers such as Bob Hope, are unhappily commonplace.

As for drugs and race, Vietnam's problems today not only reflect but reinforce those of the Armed Forces as a whole. In April, for example, members of a Congressional investigating subcommittee reported that 10 to 15% of our troops in Vietnam are now using high-grade heroin, and that drug addiction there is "of epidemic proportions."

Only last year an Air Force major and command pilot for Ambassador Bunker was apprehended at Tan Son Nhut air base outside Saigon with $8-million worth of heroin in his aircraft. This major is now in Leavenworth.

Early this year, an Air Force regular colonel was court-martialed and cashiered for leading his squadron in pot parties, while, at Cam Ranh Air Force Base, 43 members of the base security police squadron were recently swept up in dragnet narcotics raids.

All the foregoing facts—and many more dire indicators of the worst kind of military trouble—point to widespread conditions among American forces in Vietnam that have only been exceeded in this century by the French Army's Nivelle mutinies of 1917 and the collapse of the Tsarist armies in 1916 and 1917.

Society Notes

It is a truism that national armies closely reflect societies from which they have been raised. It would be strange indeed if the Armed Forces did not today mirror the agonizing divisions and social traumas of American society, and of course they do.

For this very reason, our Armed Forces outside Vietnam not only reflect these conditions but disclose the depths of their troubles in an awful litany of sedition, disaffection, desertion, race, drugs, breakdowns of authority, abandonment of discipline, and, as a cumulative result, the lowest state of military morale in the history of the country.

Sedition—coupled with disaffection within the ranks, and externally fomented with an audacity and intensity previously inconceivable—infests the Armed Services:

•At best count, there appear to be some 144 underground newspapers published on or aimed at U.S. military bases in this country and overseas. Since 1970 the number of such sheets has increased 40% (up from 103 last fall). These journals are not mere gripe-sheets that poke soldier fun in the "Beetle Bailey" tradition, at the brass and the sergeants. "In Vietnam," writes the Ft Lewis-McChord Free Press, "the Lifers, the Brass, are the true Enemy, not the enemy." Another West Coast sheet advises readers: "Don't desert. Go to Vietnam and kill your commanding officer."

•At least 14 GI dissent organizations (including two made up exclusively of officers) now operate more or less openly. Ancillary to these are at least six antiwar veterans' groups which strive to influence GIs.

•Three well-established lawyer groups specialize in support of GI dissent. Two (GI Civil Liberties Defense Committee and New York Draft and Military Law Panel) operate in the open. A third is a semi-underground network of lawyers who can only be contacted through the GI Alliance, a Washington, D.C., group which tries to coordinate seditious antimilitary activities throughout the country.

One antimilitary legal effort operates right in the theater of war. A three-man law office, backed by the Lawyers' Military Defense Committee, of Cambridge, Mass., was set up last fall in Saigon to provide free civilian legal services for dissident soldiers being court-martialed in Vietnam.

Besides these lawyers' fronts, the Pacific Counseling Service (an umbrella organization with Unitarian backing for a prolifery [sic] of antimilitary activities) provides legal help and incitement to dissident GIs through not one but seven branches (Tacoma, Oakland, Los Angeles, San Diego, Monterey, Tokyo, and Okinawa).

Another of Pacific Counseling's activities is to air-drop planeloads of seditious literature into Oakland's sprawling Army Base, our major West Coast staging point for Vietnam.

•On the religious front, a community of turbulent priests and clergymen, some unfrocked, calls itself the Order of Maximilian. Maximilian is a saint said to have been martyred by the Romans for refusing military service as un-Christian. Maximilian's present-day followers visit military posts, infiltrate brigs and stockades in the guise of spiritual counseling, work to recruit military chaplains, and hold services of "consecrations" of post chapels in the name of their saintly draft-dodger.

•By present count at least 11 (some go as high as 26) off-base antiwar "coffee houses" ply GIs with rock music, lukewarm coffee, antiwar literature, how-to-do-it tips on desertion, and similar disruptive counsels. Among the best-known coffee houses are: The Shelter Half (Ft Lewis, Wash.); The Home Front (Ft Carson, Colo.); and The Oleo Strut (Ft Hood, Tex.).

•The nation-wide campus-radical offensive against ROTC and college officer-training is well known. Events last year at Stanford University, however, demonstrate the extremes to which this campaign (which peaked after Cambodia) has gone. After the Stanford faculty voted to accept a modified, specially restructured ROTC program, the university was subjected to a cyclone of continuing violence which included at least $200,000 in ultimate damage to buildings (highlighted by systematic destruction of 40 twenty-foot stained glass windows in the library). In the end, led by university president Richard W. Lyman, the faculty reversed itself. Lyman was quoted at the time that "ROTC is costing Stanford too much.". . .

One militant West Coast Group, Movement for a Democratic Military (MDM), has specialized in weapons theft from military bases in California. During 1970, large armory thefts were successfully perpetrated against Oakland Army Base, Fts Cronkhite and Ord, and even the Marine Corps Base at Camp Pendleton, where a team wearing marine uniforms got away with nine M–16 rifles and an M–79 grenade launcher.

Operating in the Middle West, three soldiers from Ft Carson, Colo., home of the Army's permissive experimental unit, the 4th Mechanized Division, were recently indicted by federal grand jury for dynamiting the telephone exchange, power plant and water works of another Army installation, Camp McCoy, Wis., on 26 July 1970.

The Navy, particularly on the West Coast, has also experienced disturbing cases of sabotage in the past two years, mainly directed at ships' engineering and electrical machinery.

It will be surprising, according to informed officers, if further such tangible evidence of disaffection within the ranks does not continue to come to light. Their view is that the situation could become considerably worse before it gets better. . . .

One area of the U.S. Government in which the Armed Forces are encountering noticeable lack of support is the federal judiciary. . . .

Part of the defense establishment's problem with the judiciary is the now widely pursued practice of taking commanding officers into civil courts by dissident soldiers either to harass or annul normal discipline or administrative procedures of the services.

Only a short time ago, for example, a dissident group of active-duty officers, members of the Concerned Officers' Movement (COM), filed a sweeping lawsuit against Defense Secretary Laird himself, as well as all three service secretaries, demanding official recognition of their "right" to oppose the Vietnam war, accusing the secretaries of "harassing" them, and calling for court injunction to ban disciplinary "retaliation" against COM members. . . .

Racial Incidents

Sedition and subversion, and legal harassment, rank near the top of what might be called the unprecedented external problems that elements in American society are inflicting on the Armed Forces.

Internally speaking, racial conflicts and drugs—also previously insignificant—are tearing the services apart today. . . .

Racial conflicts (most but not all sparked by young black enlisted men) are erupting murderously in all services.

At a recent high commanders' conference, General Westmoreland and other senior generals heard the report from Germany that in many units white soldiers are now afraid to enter barracks alone at night for fear of "head-hunting" ambushes by blacks.

In the quoted words of one soldier on duty in West Germany, "I'm much more afraid of getting mugged on the post than I am of getting attacked by the Russians."

Other reports tell of jail-delivery attacks on Army stockades and military police to release black prisoners, and of officers being struck in public by black soldiers. Augsburg, Krailsheim, and Hohenfels are said to be rife with racial trouble. Hohenfels was the scene of a racial fragging last year—one of the few so far recorded outside Vietnam.

In Ulm, last fall, a white noncommissioned officer killed a black soldier who was holding a loaded .45 on two unarmed white officers.

Elsewhere, according to *Fortune* magazine, junior officers are now being attacked at night when inspecting barracks containing numbers of black soldiers.

Kelley Hill, a Ft Benning, Ga., barracks area, has been the scene of repeated nighttime assaults on white soldiers. One such soldier bitterly remarked, "Kelley Hill may belong to the commander in the daytime but it belongs to the blacks after dark.". . .

But the Army has no monopoly on racial troubles.

As early as July 1969 the Marines (who had previously enjoyed a highly praised record on race) made headlines at Camp Lejeune, N.C., when a mass affray launched by 30–50 black Marines ended fatally with a white corporal's skull smashed in and 15 other white Marines in the sick bay.

That same year, at Newport, R.I., naval station, blacks killed a white petty officer, while in March 1971 the National Naval Medical Center in Bethesda, Md., outside Washington, was beset by racial fighting so severe that the base enlisted men's club had to be closed.

All services are today striving energetically to cool and control this ugly violence which in the words of one noncommissioned officer, has made his once taut unit divide up "like two street gangs.". . .

Drugs and the Military

The drug problem—like the civilian situation from which it directly derives—is running away with the services. In March, Navy Secretary John H. Chafee, speaking for the two sea services, said bluntly that drug abuse in both Navy and Marines is out of control.

In 1966, the Navy discharged 170 drug offenders. Three years later (1969), 3,800 were discharged. Last year in 1970, the total jumped to over 5,000.

Drug abuse in the Pacific Fleet—with Asia on one side, and kinky California on the other—gives the Navy its worst headaches. To cite one example, a destroyer due to sail from the West Coast last year for the Far East nearly had to postpone deployment when, five days before departure, a ring of some 30 drug users (over 10 percent of the crew) was uncovered.

Only last week, eight midshipmen were dismissed from the Naval Academy following disclosure of an alleged drug ring. While the Navy emphatically denies allegations in a copyrighted article by the *Annapolis Capitol* that up to 1,000 midshipmen now use marijuana, midshipman sources confirm that pot is anything but unknown at Annapolis.

Yet the Navy is somewhat ahead in the drug game because of the difficulty in concealing addiction at close quarters aboard ship, and because fixes are unobtainable during long deployments at sea.

The Air Force, despite 2,715 drug investigations in 1970, is in even better shape: its rate of 3 cases per thousand airmen is the lowest in the services.

By contrast, the Army had 17,742 drug investigations the same year. According to Col Thomas B. Hauschild, of the Medical Command of our Army forces in Europe, some 46 percent of the roughly 200,000 soldiers there had used illegal drugs at least once. In one battalion surveyed in West Germany, over 50 percent of the men smoked marijuana regularly (some on duty), while roughly half of those were using hard drugs of some type.

What those statistics say is that the Armed Forces (like their parent society) are in the grip of a drug pandemic—a conclusion underscored by the one fact that, just since 1968, the total number of verified drug addiction cases throughout the Armed Forces has nearly doubled. One other yardstick: according to military medical sources, needle hepatitis now poses as great a problem among young soldiers as VD.

At Ft Bragg, the Army's third largest post, adjacent to Fayetteville, N.C. (a garrison town whose conditions one official likened to New York's "East Village" and San Francisco's "Haight-Ashbury") a recent survey disclosed that 4% (or over 1,400) of the 36,000 soldiers there are hard-drug (mainly heroin and LSD) addicts. In the 82nd Airborne Division, the strategic-reserve unit that boasts its title of "America's Honor Guard," approximately 450 soldier drug abusers were being treated when this reporter visited the post in April. About a hundred were under intensive treatment in special drug wards. . . .

Desertions and Disasters

With conditions what they are in the Armed Forces, and with intense efforts on the part of elements in our society to disrupt discipline and destroy morale the consequences can be clearly measured in two ultimate indicators: manpower retention (reenlistments and their antithesis, desertions); and the state of discipline.

In both respects the picture is anything but encouraging. . . .

Desertion rates are going straight up in Army, Marines, and Air Force. Curiously, however, during the period since 1968 when desertion has nearly doubled for all three other services, the Navy's rate has risen by less than 20 percent.

In 1970, the Army had 65,643 deserters, or roughly the equivalent of four infantry divisions. This desertion rate (52.3 soldiers per thousand) is well over twice the peak rate for Korea (22.5 per thousand). It is more than quadruple the 1966 desertion-rate (14.7 per thousand) of the then well-trained, high-spirited professional Army.

If desertions continue to rise (as they are still doing this year), they will attain or surpass the WWII peak of 63 per thousand, which, incidentally, occurred in the same year (1945) when more soldiers were actually being discharged from the Army for psychoneurosis than were drafted.

The Air Force—relatively uninvolved in the Vietnam war, all-volunteer, management-oriented rather than disciplinary and hierarchic—enjoys a numerical rate of less than one deserter per thousand men, but even this is double what it was three years ago.

The Marines in 1970 had the highest desertion index in the modern history of the Corps and, for that year at least, slightly higher than the Army's. As the Marines now phase out of Vietnam (and haven't taken a draftee in nearly two years), their desertions are expected to decrease sharply. Meanwhile, grimly remarked one officer, "Let the bastards go. We're all the better without them."

Letting the bastards go is something the Marines can probably afford. "The Marine Corps Isn't Looking for a Lot of Recruits," reads a current recruiting poster, "We Just Need a Few Good Men." This is the happy situation of a Corps slimming down to an elite force again composed of true volunteers who want to be professionals.

But letting the bastards go doesn't work at all for the Army and the Navy, who do need a lot of recruits and whose reenlistment problems are dire.

Admiral Elmo R. Zumwalt, Jr, Chief of Naval Operations, minces no words. "We have a personnel crisis," he recently said, "that borders on disaster."

The Navy's crisis, as Zumwalt accurately describes it, is that of a highly technical, material oriented service that finds itself unable to retain the expensively-trained technicians needed to operate warships, which are the largest, most complex items of machinery that man makes and uses.

Non-Volunteer Force?

If 45% of his sailors shipped over after their first enlistment, Admiral Zumwalt would be all smiles. With only 13% doing so, he is growing sideburns to enhance the Navy's appeal to youth.

Among the Army's volunteer (non-draftee) soldiers on their first hitch, the figures are much the same: less than 14% re-up.

The Air Force is slightly, but not much, better off: 16% of its first-termers stay on.

Moreover—and this is the heart of the Army's dilemma—only 4% of the voluntary enlistees now choose service in combat arms (infantry, armor, artillery) and of those only 2.5% opt for infantry. Today's soldiers, it seems, volunteer readily enough for the tail of the Army, but not for its teeth.

For all services, the combined retention rate this past year is about half what it was in 1966, and the lowest since the bad times of similar low morale and national disenchantment after Korea.

Both Army and Navy are responding to their manpower problems in measures intended to seduce recruits and reenlistees: disciplinary permissiveness, abolition of reveille and KP, fewer inspections, longer haircuts—essentially cosmetic changes aimed at softening (and blurring) traditional military and naval images. . . .

The trouble of the services—produced by and also in turn producing the dismaying conditions described in this article—is above all a crisis of soul and backbone. It entails—the word is not too strong—something very near a collapse of the command authority and leadership George Washington saw as the soul of military forces. This collapse results, at least in part, from a concurrent collapse of public confidence in the military establishment.

General Matthew B. Ridgway, one of the Army's finest leaders in this century (who revitalized the shaken Eighth Army in Korea after its headlong rout by the Chinese in 1950) recently said, "Not before in my lifetime . . . has the Army's public image fallen to such low esteem. . . ."

But the fall in public esteem of all three major services—not just the Army—is exceeded by the fall or at least the enfeeblement of the hierarchic and disciplinary system by which they exist and, when ordered to do so, fight and sometimes die.

Part VII

THE DECISIVE YEAR: 1968

Editors' Introduction

In late January 1968, General Westmoreland gave a glowingly optimistic assessment of the US situation in Vietnam:

> During 1967, the enemy lost control of large sectors of the population. . . . In many areas the enemy has been driven away from the population centers; in others he has been compelled to disperse and evade contact, thus nullifying much of his potential. . . .
> The friendly picture gives rise to optimism for increased successes in 1968.[1]

Within less than five months, most of the countryside had been lost to the NLF, the pacification program had been devastated, the 1.4 million American, Vietnamese, Korean, Thai, Australian, and other troops under the US command were locked into a defense posture around their own bases and the cities and towns of the south. General Westmoreland had been dismissed from his command; the President of the United States had been forced to withdraw from the election campaign, and antiwar forces had overwhelmingly swept every Democratic primary. Rebellions had erupted in 125 US cities within a single week and police had battled demonstrators on college campuses across the country. The international finance system was reeling from blows to the US economy and its credibility, and the US administration had been forced into negotiations—the main immediate goal until then of the US antiwar movement.

The military situation had deteriorated so abruptly that both President Johnson and General Westmoreland characterized as a major "military victory" the ability of their forces to drive NLF combat units out of Saigon and to reoccupy the city of Hue, after twenty-five days of heavy fighting. Never again did the US military command regain the strategic offensive, and the negotiations that began in Paris in early May focused ever more clearly, during the ensuing five years, merely on

---

1. *The Pentagon Papers* (Gravel ed.), vol. 4, pp. 538–39.

establishing the precise terms for the complete withdrawal of US military forces from the entire country of Vietnam. Thus, 1968 may accurately be seen as the year that sealed the defeat of the United States in Vietnam.

The central event in this context, influencing other events as apparently disparate as presidential primaries, rebellions in the ghettos, and a crisis in the world monetary system, was the four-week Tet Offensive that began on January 30. Every history of America's war in Indochina must come to some interpretation of the Tet Offensive, for it is the key to the military history and outcome of that war. Was it the military victory for the United States claimed by President Johnson and General Westmoreland? Or was it—as it seemed at the time to most Americans and Vietnamese—a staggering military as well as political defeat for the United States?

This section includes major documents presenting each of these contradictory answers, as well as an account from *The Pentagon Papers* of the effects inside the US government, and President Johnson's historic speech signaling the beginning of the final stage of the Vietnam War.

To place these documents in context, one must recall or imagine the condition of America during and after the Tet Offensive.

After dispatching federal troops to quell the massive rebellion in Detroit in July 1967, President Johnson had established a National Advisory Commission on Civil Disorders. Just as the Tet Offensive was winding down, the Commission issued a major report with one central theme: "This is our basic conclusion: Our nation is moving toward two societies, one black, one white—separate and unequal." Even while this report was being prepared, police and national guardsmen in early February 1968 were carrying out the "Orangeburg Massacre," shooting thirty and killing three unarmed students at the black campus of South Carolina State College at Orangeburg (an event largely unnoticed in the white media, just as two years later the media ignored police shooting to death black students in their dormitory at Jackson State College, a few days after white students were gunned down at Kent State). On April 4, Martin Luther King, Jr. was assassinated in Memphis.

The nationwide reaction to the murder of Dr. King in some ways rivaled the Tet Offensive, to which it bore similarities by no means purely coincidental. Between April 4 and April 11, 1968, rebellions broke out in 125 US cities and towns.

A month prior to the uprisings, worried decision-makers in the Pentagon and the White House had contemplated the possible effects of their giving in to Westmoreland's demand for 206,000 additional troops: "We will have to mobilize reserves, increase our budget by billions. . . . Our balance of payments will be worsened considerably, and we will need a larger tax increase. . . ." They saw the consequent "growing unrest in the cities" posing "great risks of provoking a domestic crisis of unprecedented proportions." (*The Pentagon Papers*, Gravel edition, vol. 4, p. 564.) They expressed their anxiety about retaining both the financial and military "resources for the ghetto fight." (Ibid., p. 583.)

The uprisings of early April realized their worst fears. In that cataclysmic week, 55,000 troops had to be mobilized alongside tens of thousands of police.

Television viewers around the world saw Washington itself defended by federal combat troops, while columns of smoke from burning buildings towered above the Capitol. On April 11 came the biggest call-up of the reserves during the Vietnam War.

No sooner had the black rebellions been put down than the campuses erupted. Between April 23 and May 6, militant protest demonstrations swept public and private universities and colleges across the country. Large numbers of police battled students even at such elite universities as Stanford and Columbia, while campus activists increasingly linked the antiwar movement to the struggles of black people, GIs, and those parts of the working class suffering the gravest economic consequences of the war.

The increasingly ominous economic effects of the war, noted anxiously by the Pentagon strategists, not only exacerbated domestic turmoil but also began to threaten the entire system of international capitalist finance, which faced what President Johnson on March 31 labeled the most severe "threat in the postwar era." Unable to raise taxes to finance a war not supported by the American people, the administration was forced to rely more and more heavily on deficit financing, with its attendant domestic inflation and international shock waves. The 1968 budget included the largest post-World War II deficit—the astronomical (for that period) sum of $25.2 billion, more than the deficits of the previous five years combined.

The internationally fixed gold price of $35 per ounce, which had held since 1934, now hung tenuously on the world's confidence in the US dollar. This confidence was devastated by the Tet Offensive, which undermined, among other things, the myth of US invincibility. On March 1, a panicky gold-buying frenzy swept the world's markets. In a two-day emergency meeting March 9 and 10, the United States and its six European partners in the London Gold Pool pledged their commitment to sell gold to all comers at $35 an ounce. But by March 15, the fever had driven the spot price of gold to its then all-time high of $44.36 per ounce. The seven governments, with their own supplies nearing exhaustion, abandoned their commitment, deciding to sell $35 gold only to each other. This forced creation of a two-price market was quickly perceived by many economists as merely a bandage covering a cancer that threatened the entire capitalist world's monetary system. (See Reading 55 for President Johnson's analysis of the relations between the Vietnam War and the international financial and monetary crisis.) Those events precipitated the continuing and still-deepening worldwide crisis of escalating deficits, inflation, and monetary instability.

On March 12, Eugene McCarthy, running as a dark-horse antiwar candidate, came within a relative handful of votes of defeating the incumbent President, from his own Democratic party, in the New Hampshire primary. On March 16, Robert Kennedy entered the race for the Democratic nomination, also as an avowed antiwar candidate. On March 22, President Johnson announced that General Westmoreland was being relieved of his command. And on March 31, Lyndon Baines Johnson startled the nation by withdrawing from the presidential race, as a footnote to halting most of the air and naval bombardment of North Vietnam.

Vice President Hubert Humphrey, closely identified with previous administration Vietnam policy, announced his candidacy on April 27. Although too late to enter many primaries, in those where he did compete against the two antiwar candidates he was soundly trounced. Thus McCarthy and Kennedy swept the primaries (winning votes between them of 83 per cent in Pennsylvania, 63 per cent in Wisconsin, 78 per cent in Massachusetts, 63 per cent in the District of Columbia, 69 per cent in Indiana, 83 per cent in Nebraska, 82 per cent in Oregon, 67 per cent in New Jersey, 70 per cent in South Dakota, 72 per cent in Illinois, and 88 per cent in California). Altogether the two antiwar candidates polled 69 per cent of the total popular vote in the Democratic primaries, while Vice President Humphrey, who had been represented by various slates of electors in several states, garnered a mere 2.2 per cent.

But on June 4, Robert Kennedy was assassinated. Then, somehow, by the time the Democratic convention opened in Chicago at the end of August, Humphrey had gathered a majority of the delegates. The stage was set for the battles that raged outside the convention, pitting the police of Mayor Richard Daley, a machine boss who had helped engineer Humphrey's nomination, against the thousands of antiwar activists and Eugene McCarthy supporters who had come to protest what seemed a flagrant disregard of the will of the people. When the elite 82nd Airborne Division was ordered to Chicago for potential action, a dozen black paratroopers were court-martialed for refusing to oppose the demonstrators.

Accounts of this period tend to focus on the highly publicized confrontation in Chicago, with its television footage of police terror, while ignoring the even more volatile scene that menaced the Republican convention meeting in Miami Beach in early August. A line of tanks sealed Miami Beach off from Miami, where police and national guard units fought with rebelling blacks in what a Miami police spokesman (quoted in *The New York Times* of August 9) called "firefights like in Vietnam." Meanwhile, the convention was nominating Richard M. Nixon to be President of the United States. In his acceptance speech, after noting that "As we look at America, we see cities enveloped in smoke and flame," Nixon made these promises:

And I pledge to you tonight that the first priority foreign policy objective of our next Administration will be to bring an honorable end to the war in Vietnam.

We shall not stop there. We need a policy to prevent more Vietnams.

52. "The Year of Decision—1968"*

By General William C. Westmoreland

More than any other single figure, General William C. Westmoreland presided over the Americanization of the Vietnam War.

In June 1964, General Westmoreland was given command of the US military forces in Vietnam. Since these 16,000 soldiers were then officially just "advisers," this command was designated COMUSMACV (Commander, US Military Assistance Command, Vietnam). In early 1965, seeing that the Saigon army and government were nearing defeat, Westmoreland asked for and received tens of thousands of US marines and other combat units. By the end of 1967, as COMUSMACV he now commanded directly an army of well over half a million Americans and indirectly almost a million other soldiers—Vietnamese, Korean, Thai, Australian, and miscellaneous mercenaries—armed and paid for by the US.

The March 1968 announcement that he was being relieved of his command signaled the beginning of the end of the strategy of Americanization. As one immediate consequence of this strategic turnaround, Westmoreland's latest request for reinforcements—another 206,000 American soldiers—was denied. The subsequent strategy of "Vietnamization" was an attempt to restore the political-military relations between Saigon and Washington that had prevailed before General Westmoreland had taken over.

The following Reading, entitled by General Westmoreland "The Year of Decision—1968," is the final chapter, slightly abridged, of the unclassified version of his final official report. It is perhaps the single best document for assessing what has remained a most controversial issue: the accuracy, indeed the honesty, of General Westmoreland's reports, both those made to the public and those submitted to the Pentagon and the President. (Specific questions having to do with the issue of his accuracy and honesty are suggested in the footnotes accompanying the Reading.)

This issue surfaced dramatically in the 1982 CBS television documentary "The Uncounted Enemy: A Vietnamese Deception" and General Westmoreland's counterattack in the form of a $120 million libel suit against CBS and three individuals, including former CIA analyst Samuel Adams, a consultant for the documentary (see footnote 24 below). Just before the trial opened in October 1984, Westmoreland's attorneys made the startling announcement that they "didn't plan to contest in court the documentary's assertions that Gen. Westmoreland had engaged in a conspiracy to deceive the press, the public and Congress about the strength of the enemy in Vietnam to make it appear that the U.S. was winning the war" (Wall

---

*From *Report on the War in Vietnam (As of 30 June 1968)*, Section II: *Report on Operations in South Vietnam, January 1964–June 1968* by General W. C. Westmoreland, Commander, U.S. Military Assistance Command, Vietnam (Washington: US Government Printing Office, 1968).

Street Journal, *October 8, 1984). Instead the General was merely contesting the allegations that he had concealed information from "his superiors and from the president" (Ibid). Then, after more than four months of trial, and only a week before the case was to go to the jury, General Westmoreland dropped the suit.*

In 1968 the war in Vietnam reached the decisive stage. In my Overview for 1967, I described the dilemma facing the enemy and the decision taken by Hanoi because of that dilemma. During early 1968 the enemy made a determined effort to execute the plans which flowed from this decision.

As the new year opened, I had planned to continue pursuing the enemy throughout the Republic, thereby improving conditions for the pacification program to proceed at an ever-increasing pace. I had also intended clearing remaining enemy base areas in zones of the I and III Corps and deploying the rest of the U.S. 9th Infantry Division and an air cavalry squadron to the Delta to reinforce the Mobile Riverine Force. I had prepared plans to shift the 1st Cavalry Division to the III Corps for operations along the Cambodian border during the dry season in that area (December to April) and to move the division north to the I Corps for operations, including a foray into the A Shau Valley, during the dry season in the northern provinces (May to September). The operations by the 1st Cavalry Division were to be in conjunction with planned operations by other U.S. and ARVN troops in the areas.

In December of 1967 information of massive enemy troop movements had prompted me to cancel these plans. As 1968 began events verified this intelligence, as the enemy continued the forward movement of his main forces toward Saigon, Da Nang, Hue, Khe Sanh, the DMZ, and a number of provincial and district capitals. Incidents rose sharply, as did enemy casualties. By January the enemy was well into the winter-spring campaign which he had started in October. During January we began to receive numerous reports about a major offensive to be undertaken just before or immediately after *Tet*. These reports came from agents and prisoners with increasing frequency and credibility.

Based on these reports, in January I modified previous plans to conduct major offensive operations into the enemy's well-established base areas in War Zones C and D and the enemy's huge Military Region 10 (MR 10) and directed Lt. Gen. Frederick C. Weyand, II Field Force commander, to strengthen U.S. forces in the area around Saigon by redeploying forces which had been targeted on the bases of the Viet Cong main forces and the North Vietnamese Army. Likewise, I discussed the situation with my counterpart, General Vien, Chief of the Joint General Staff, who directed troop readjustments in coordination with our actions. In response to this changed enemy situation, just before *Tet*, well over half of the maneuver battalions plus most of the Regional and Popular Forces in the III Corps were either defending the immediate approaches to Saigon, inderdicting the corridors which lead to Saigon from War Zones C and D and the Plain of Reeds, or defending villages and hamlets.[1] Even though by mid-January we were certain that a major offensive action was planned by the enemy at *Tet*, we did not surmise the true nature or the scope of the countrywide attack. Because of this uncertainty, a number of battalions were designated as emergency reserves for any contingency. It did not occur to us that the enemy would undertake suicidal attacks in the face of our power. But he did just that.

For the celebration of the lunar new year—*Tet*—the Republic of Vietnam had, after discussions between President Thieu, Ambassador Bunker, and myself, declared a 36-hour cease-fire to be effective from the evening of 29 January through the early morning of 31 January. Upon my advice an exception was made during the last week in the I Corps, the Demilitarized Zone, and nearby infiltration routes north of the DMZ, since the enemy activity seriously imperiled our positions in those regions. The Viet Cong announced a seven-day *Tet* truce to last from 27 January until the early morning of 3 February. Under cover of this premeditated subterfuge, the enemy launched attacks of unprecedented scope.

Several days before *Tet* U.S. troops were placed on full alert. Owing to an apparent mixup in coordination, the enemy attack was launched in I and II Corps 24 hours ahead of the attack in the remainder of the country. This gave us additional warning, but still did not reveal the nature of his plans in the Saigon area. The enemy main attack was launched late on the 30th and in early morning of the 31st of January, employing about 84,000[2] Viet Cong and North Vietnamese troops. In addition to Saigon, initial assaults were mounted against 36 of the 4 provincial capitals [sic], 5 of the 6 autonomous cities, 64 of 242 district capitals, and 50 hamlets.

In preparation for the attacks, the enemy went to unprecedented lengths to assemble supplies and weapons and to infiltrate troops into the cities. After loss of his major base areas near Saigon in 1967, he made extensive use of Cambodia to establish secret bases and accumulate great quantities of arms, supplies, and troops. Along the Cambodian border north of Saigon he established Military Region 10 to coordinate the creation of a major logistics base. In the Plain of Reeds

---

1. This is a rather misleading account of the deployment of forces. Actually Westmoreland, under the impression that the NLF offensive would be aimed at turning the remote fire base at Khe Sanh into an American Dien Bien Phu, had rapidly moved US forces *away* from the cities and bases that were to be the targets of the Tet Offensive. From November 1967 on, under the code name "Checkers" he had pulled crack brigades and divisions from Saigon and the central highlands and jumped them north into I Corps, the northernmost military region in South Vietnam. By the opening of the Tet Offensive, he had a quarter of a million troops massed in this region, including the marines of the elite South Korean "Blue Dragon" brigade, two of the best ARVN divisions, and half of all the US ground troops in Vietnam (among them such vital units as the 1st Air Cavalry Division, 5,000 paratroopers of the 101st Airborne Division, and the Marines based in or near Khe Sanh itself).—eds.

2. This estimate is probably inflated. Other analysts have estimated that about 67,000 troops were committed to the Tet Offensive. By any count, this could hardly be construed as an all-out offensive against Westmoreland's 1.4 million troops.—eds.

and in the "Eagle's Beak" section of Cambodia that projects southeastward to within 30 miles of the South Vietnamese capital, he established clandestine sanctuaries and undertook a long-range program to stockpile supplies for support of operations in the zone of the III and IV Corps. In preparation for the *Tet* offensive against Saigon and the larger cities of the Delta, the enemy smuggled munitions and weapons to forward sites hidden in isolated areas or to underground installations. He also returned temporarily to his earlier practice of drawing reinforcements from the Delta to support operations in the vicinity of Saigon.

Over a long period of time and especially before *Tet*, enemy troops in civilian dress, assisted by well-organized agents, slipped into the cities, particularly Hue and Saigon, among crowds of holiday travelers on public conveyances, on produce trucks, and in private vehicles. In Saigon they used funeral processions to smuggle weapons and ammunition. Other quantities of supplies arrived in market baskets and vegetable trucks, under lumber, or in false-bottom sampans. The Vietnamese National Police were ineffective in stopping or detecting the magnitude of the enemy's effort. The minds of the Vietnamese in Saigon and the other cities were preoccupied with the approaching *Tet* holiday, and our efforts to change this state of mind were only partially effective.[3]

The enemy used primarily local forces rather than main force units to infiltrate the cities and conduct the first attacks. He held the larger main force units in reserve to exploit the anticipated popular uprisings. Some units had even planned victory parades in the cities.

In the areas around Saigon the terrain facilitated infiltration by large enemy units. Except for the few radial roads emanating from Saigon, the city is bounded to the north, west, and east by a combination of paddies, jungles, and swamps.

Notwithstanding efforts to increase the state of alert, large numbers of Vietnamese soldiers were on leave for *Tet* and their units were, in most cases, about half strength. The enemy penetrated in strength into Saigon, Quang Tri, Hue, Da Nang, Nha Trang, Qui Nhon, Kontum City, Ban Me Thout, My Tho, Can Tho, and Ben Tre. In most cities, Regional and Popular Forces and the South Vietnamese Army threw back the enemy attacks within two to three days—in some cases, within hours. However, very heavy fighting continued for some time in Kontum City, Ban Me Thout, Can Tho, and Ben Tre, and in Saigon and Hue the battle was protracted.

The Regional and Popular Forces demonstrated their growing tactical proficiency throughout this period. By their presence in the villages and hamlets they made it more difficult for the enemy to terrorize the people. Their contributions made it possible for U.S. and other allied forces to conduct mobile security operations rather than to be tied to static duties. This was particularly apparent in Quang Tri Province.

---

3. The minds of the Vietnamese were so "preoccupied" that they failed to notice three NLF divisions in and around Saigon, even though they brought with them big wheeled anti-aircraft batteries that had been towed hundreds of miles to be parked at the gates of Tan Son Nhut Airbase.—eds.

The enemy's attack in Saigon began with a sapper assault on the American Embassy, a move of dubious military value but psychologically important.[4] Although the Viet Cong succeeded in blowing a hole in the Embassy wall, aggressive reaction by U.S. military police and Marine guards prevented the enemy from entering the Embassy building and by midmorning security was established in the area. The Viet Cong coordinated this abortive attack with assaults on the Tan Son Nhut Airbase complex, the Presidential Palace, the Vietnamese Joint General Staff compound, and other installations in Saigon. Nearby Bien Hoa Airbase also came under attack. In some instances the VC dressed in ARVN uniforms to gain initial entry into South Vietnamese bases—a tactic they had used earlier and have also employed since *Tet*.

Throughout Saigon the National Police, who in most cases absorbed the brunt of the attack, fought well. They successfully blocked enemy assaults on such important installations as the radio station and Presidential Palace. Both Vietnamese and U.S. troops reacted quickly. Within hours the quick deployment of Vietnamese Ranger, airborne, Marine, and Regional Force battalions had thrown the Viet Cong on the defensive. Reluctantly, I was forced by the urgency of the situation to put U.S. combat troops into the Vietnamese capital city, Saigon, for the first time. For political and psychological reasons I had hoped that the Vietnamese could defend their own cities and carry the heavy fighting in the populated areas as in the past. In view of the enemy's major effort, the risk involved in pursuing this policy became unacceptable, and I unhesitatingly set aside such a policy then and for the future. Therefore, American forces moved in behind the Vietnamese, the first units arriving at 6 A.M. By the end of the day, five U.S. battalions were in and about the city and two more moved in the next day. Many more U.S. battalions occupied positions along roads leading to the city in order to block enemy reinforcements which, according to our intelligence, were to exploit the success of the shock troops.

The enemy forces, consisting of elements of 11 local force battalions, failed to take any of their objectives except the undefended Phu Tho Race Track, which they briefly used as a base area. Except for breaching the wall and entering the grounds of the U.S. Embassy, the only successes against a government target were brief incursions into the rear of the Vietnamese Joint General Staff compound and into two remote areas of Tan Son Nhut Airbase.[5]

At Hue the enemy had ready access to the city from his logistical base in the A Shau Valley, where we had no covering outpost like that at Khe Sanh. Under the concealment of low fog, enemy regular units consisting of eight battalions (made

---

4. Such dubious distinctions between military and psychological importance, at odds even with US military theory, have served as the basis for dismissing the Tet Offensive as a "military defeat" but "psychological victory" for the revolutionaries.—eds.

5. Actually insurgent units fought within Saigon itself until February 7, and when they withdrew they left behind several zones of the city that stayed under the control of the NLF infrastructure. See Reading 53.—eds.

up of both Viet Cong and North Vietnamese) were able to infiltrate Hue with the help of accomplices inside the city. These troops quickly captured most of that portion of the city on the south bank of the Perfume River. They later seized the bulk of the northern half, including the Imperial Citadel. U.S. Marines drove them from most of the south bank in the first few days, but the battle was fierce for the Imperial Citadel. Aided by very bad weather, the enemy was able to bring reinforcements from the Viet Cong 416th Battalion, NVA 5th Division, and NVA 324B Division, and to hold on until 25 February. Before the battle was over, some 16 North Vietnamese battalions had been identified in and around Hue.[6]

The recapture of Hue was a bitter fight directly involving three U.S. Marine Corps and 11 Vietnamese battalions. The struggle at first involved house-to-house fighting and then a long arduous process of routing the enemy from the heavily walled ancient fortress of the Imperial City. This urban warfare against fortified positions was not unlike that in European cities during World War II.

Heavy damage to the city and to the Citadel inevitably resulted, and some 116,000 civilians were made homeless. It was a costly battle in human lives as well: the enemy lost over 5,000 killed in the city and an additional 3,000 to its immediate north—at least the equivalent of a full division—while U.S. and South Vietnamese units lost just over 500 men killed. During the time the enemy controlled the city he singled out and executed over 1,000 government officials, school teachers, and others of known government loyalty.[7] This was a terrifying indication of what well might occur should the Communists succeed in gaining control of South Vietnam[8]. . . .

Destruction from the countrywide attack was widespread, creating hundreds of thousands of refugees. When Vietnamese forces moved to the defense of province and district capitals, the enemy was able to move with great freedom in the rural areas and in the regions immediately surrounding the defended towns.[9] Most of the battalions of the Vietnamese Army which had been providing security for the pacification effort also withdrew to the defense of government installations. They were often accompanied by the pacification cadre and in some cases by both Regional and Popular Forces, which withdrew from exposed outposts.

The *Tet* offensive was exceedingly costly to the enemy throughout the country. Between 29 January and 11 February the Communists lost some 32,000 men killed and 5,800 detained, out of an estimated force of 84,000 committed to the offensive. They also lost over 7,000 individual and almost 1,300 crew-served weapons

---

6. The force that seized Hue without being detected was about 3,000 strong. Several of the units reported to be involved in the fighting at Hue, such as the 24th and 29th Regiments, were also reported to be maintaining the siege at Khe Sanh.—eds.

7. This widely diffused allegation, later multiplied by three to five, was exposed as a fabrication by Gareth Porter in "The 1968 'Hue Massacre,'" *Indochina Chronicle*, 33 (June 24, 1974).—eds.

8. This exemplifies the myth of the "bloodbath," which proved false.—eds.

9. Most of the countryside was never regained. See Readings 53 and 54 for analyses of the almost total victory won by the insurgent forces in the rural areas.—eds.

(machine guns, mortars, etc.). Allied losses were 1,001 U.S. and 2,082 Vietnamese and Free World personnel. By the end of February the number of enemy killed had risen to more than 45,000.[10] In the same period the enemy lost over 12,500 weapons.

This was only the initial price he paid for his new strategy and his efforts to foreshorten the war. The enemy told his troops and his political cadre that the time had come for the general offensive and a general uprising. It is not entirely clear whether the enemy expected to succeed with one mighty blow or whether *Tet* was simply the most dramatic episode of his 1968 offensive.

There is much evidence to support the first interpretation. In Hue, Kontum City, Ban Me Thuot, Qui Nhon, and Nha Trang, for example, the local VC political and administrative organization accompanied the assault troops and planned to occupy these provincial capitals and thereafter to operate from them as the Liberation or Revolutionary Government. In Hue, the enemy announced the formation of a Revolutionary Government and the New Alliance for National Democratic and Peace Forces designed to attract the participation of anti-government, but non-Communist elements. In each of these areas, the clandestine shadow government came out into the open and was largely destroyed.

It is difficult to believe that the enemy would have sacrificed these experienced and hard-core cadres if he had not expected to succeed. There is also some evidence, which has more recently become available, that the enemy tried seriously to seize the border areas and particularly the northern two provinces with the massive forces of about six divisions which he committed there. Another strong indication that he entertained high hopes for a decisive victory is the fact that throughout the country, and particularly in the Delta, he impressed into his military units very large numbers of untrained, local Vietnamese, many of whom were very young and others very old. This move had all the signs of a one-shot, go-for-broke attempt.

On the other side of the argument, however, is the fact that large North Vietnamese formations were not used initially in the attack in the III Corps area, particularly the North Vietnamese 7th Division, which was held out of the early decision stage of the battle. These may have been exploitation forces which were not committed because of the failure of the initial assaults. Indeed, in Hue the enemy reinforced his initial success. In Saigon and elsewhere there was really inadequate success to reinforce.

---

10. The US military normally estimated that for each enemy soldier killed in Vietnam, another 3.5 were wounded. Therefore, according to Westmoreland's figure of 45,000 killed, the attacking force must have suffered 172,500 casualties—out of an attacking force he estimated to consist of 84,000. The enormous body count apparently resulted from the savage reprisals carried out by US troops against the civilian population, including such notorious incidents as the destruction of the town of Ben Tre, where the US officer in charge was widely quoted as saying "We had to destroy the town in order to save it," and the extermination of the villagers of My Lai 4 (Reading 56), each of whom, including small infants, was counted in the total of "enemy" killed.—eds.

The government of Vietnam did not collapse under this blow. To the contrary, it rallied in the face of the threat with a unity and purpose greater than that which had ever been displayed up to that time. Perhaps the greatest blow to the enemy's hopes and plans was the fact that there was no evidence of significant participation by the population in support of the enemy. In other words, the general uprising simply did not occur.

To the contrary, following the *Tet* offensive, the Government showed a willingness to place arms for self-defense in the hands of civilian inhabitants of cities, towns and hamlets—a willingness it had never previously exhibited in my experience. Although the fight was touch-and-go in many places at the outset, no South Vietnamese military units were destroyed and their casualties were relatively low considering the heavy engagements they fought.

After a second flurry of attacks on 18 February, enemy activity fell off sharply, although enemy forces remained in forward deployments around the major cities and towns.[11] These exposed forces continued to suffer heavy casualties. VC units had suffered the bulk of the casualties and this hastened the process of turning the war into more of a North Vietnamese affair. In October 1965 the North Vietnamese Army units had comprised about 25 percent of the combat maneuver forces in the south; but after the *Tet* and subsequent May offensive, that proportion increased to over 55 percent. Including North Vietnamese troops in Viet Cong units, the total percentage of North Vietnamese in combat maneuver forces had reached approximately 70 percent by June 1968.

Following the abortion of his February attacks, the enemy attempted to resupply some of his forces by landing along the coast four trawlers loaded with supplies, arms, and ammunition. The attempt was a disaster. U.S. and Vietnamese naval forces sank three of the trawlers. The fourth ship turned back before it entered South Vietnam's contiguous waters. In view of our well-organized coastal surveillance operations, this attempt to supply by sea was obviously a desperate measure.

Having sustained severe losses under the new tactics of a mobile war of decision,[12] the Communists found themselves with a significant replacement problem.

---

11. From this point on in the war, the major cities of South Vietnam were under intermittent attack until they were finally occupied by the insurgent forces. During the next wave of the offensive, over a hundred cities and towns were attacked in May, just prior to the opening of the Paris negotiations, and street fighting raged inside Saigon from May 5 well into June. One year after Tet, in February 1969, the insurgents launched another general offensive, this time striking against 105 cities and towns. An even larger offensive began in May 1969, when US troop strength reached its maximum of over 542,000. At this point, President Nixon finally began the withdrawal of US ground forces.—eds.

12. This passage seems to be based on a misunderstanding of Vo Nguyen Giap's theory of "People's War," a misunderstanding expanded in Westmoreland's 1976 *A Soldier Reports* (Garden City, NY: Doubleday), pp. 404–406. In Giap's theory, People's War moves from the first stage, dominated by guerrilla warfare, to the second stage, characterized by the development of large units and dominated by mobile warfare, when the balance of forces has shifted enough so that the people can go on the offensive against the imperialist army. That is precisely the point defined by the Tet Offensive. For a fuller exposition, see Readings 15 and 30.—eds.

Even more than in the preceding year, they had to turn in 1968 to North Vietnam for manpower to fill their ranks—and the reservoir of trained manpower in North Vietnam was fast being depleted. The number of replacements infiltrated from North Vietnam rose from fewer than 4,000 in December 1967[13] to approximately 23,000 in January 1968, followed by some 19,000 a month until May when the number rose to approximately 30,000. The average monthly infiltration for the first half of 1968 was above 22,000. Most of these were raw draftees who had received only rudimentary training; many had not fired a weapon before being recklessly thrown into combat.

For example, in October of 1967, 82 percent of captured enemy prisoners revealed that they had served for more than six months; but by May of 1968 only 40 percent had been in the North Vietnamese Army for that long and 50 percent had less than three months total service, including the time consumed in southward infiltration. By May in the III Corps area the Communists were resorting to committing raw replacements into combat as a group, controlled and led by the escort detachment that had guided them south. Not only did enemy losses soar in this pathetic situation, but the enemy began more and more to leave his dead and weapons on the battlefield, a sure sign of plummeting combat effectiveness.

The degradation in the quality of enemy troops was also reflected in the ratio of the enemy's battlefield losses to those of the South Vietnamese, U.S., and Free World forces. In 1966 the ratio of killed in action was 3.3 Communists to 1 of our side; in 1967 it was 3.9 to 1; during the first half of 1968 it rose to almost 6 to 1.

While attention was centered on Saigon and Hue, the enemy increased his pressure on the Marine base at Khe Sanh.[14] Located astride an east-west highway—Route 9—the Khe Sanh plateau commands the approaches from the west to Dong Ha and Quang Tri City and to the coastal corridor leading to Hue. Were we to relinquish the Khe Sanh area, the North Vietnamese would have had an unobstructed invasion route into the two northernmost provinces from which they might outflank our positions south of the Demilitarized Zone—positions which were blocking North Vietnamese attacks from the north.

Had we possessed greater strength, the Khe Sanh Airfield and nearby security base would have been less critical. We would have preferred to operate in this area with mobile forces, as we had done at Dak To and elsewhere; but at the time we had neither adequate troop resources in the north nor the logistical capacity to support them. In addition, another critical factor had to be considered—the weather. Poor visibility during the northeast monsoon in January, February, and March, because of low clouds and persistent ground fog, made helicopter movement hazardous if not impossible much of the time.

---

13. In the 1982 CBS documentary, "The Uncounted Enemy: A Vietnam Deception" (see note 24), Westmoreland asserted that the North Vietnamese infiltration rate of 20,000 per month began in the fall of 1967 and "continued."—eds.

14. The definitive study of Khe Sanh notes, on the contrary: "Just about the only place in South Vietnam of any significance that had not been attacked in the Tet Offensive was Khe Sanh." (Robert Pisor, *The End of the Line: The Siege of Khe Sanh* [New York: Ballantine, 1983], p. 151).—eds.

Lacking sufficient forces to counteract the enemy buildup with ground attacks, we had only two practical choices in regard to the Khe Sanh outpost: to withdraw or to reinforce. Despite the importance of the outpost, there were strong arguments for withdrawal. We were in the midst of the northeast monsoon with no prospect of relief from bad weather until the end of March. This posed major problems for close air support and supply by air. Because Route 9 was closed from a combination of enemy sabotage and heavy rains, Khe Sanh would have to be maintained entirely by aircraft until the weather improved and we could open the highway. The enemy had the advantage of a short line of communications from a big logistical base he had built a few miles away across the border in Laos. Judging from the size of his buildup, and from his own statements, he was hoping to achieve a military-political victory similar to the one 14 years earlier at Dien Bien Phu.[15]

On the other hand, adding to the importance of the Khe Sanh area from our viewpoint was the enemy's apparent determination to take it, which meant that by holding it we might tie down large North Vietnamese forces that otherwise would move against the populated areas. Furthermore, with the availability of artillery support—which was not hindered by weather—and our extensive capability for radar-controlled bombing, we were assured of a high level of fire support.

The question was whether we could afford the troops to reinforce, keep them supplied by air, and defeat an enemy far superior in numbers as we waited for the weather to clear, built forward bases, and made other preparations for an overland relief expedition. I believed we could do all of those things. With the concurrence of the III Marine Amphibious Force Commander, Lt. Gen. Robert E. Cushman, Jr., I made the decision to reinforce and hold the area while destroying the enemy with our massive firepower and to prepare for offensive operations when the weather became favorable. Because of our prior planning, we were able to solve the logistical problems in the north even during the height of the northeast monsoon. Ports, ramps, airfields, and roads were opened and put into use in record time.

In early January we had begun Operation NIAGARA I, an extensive reconnaissance program to obtain as much information as possible about the enemy. I reinforced the 3d Marine Division with special reconnaissance teams. Valuable intelligence was provided by a highly trained reconnaissance force of CIDG troops led by Vietnamese and U.S. Special Forces officers and men. Therefore, in mid-January we were prepared to initiate the firepower phase, NIAGARA II, which

---

15. Westmoreland here defends what many consider one of the most colossal blunders in military history. The siege of Khe Sanh by a relatively small insurgent force led Westmoreland to divert his major ground forces and air attacks to the area most remote from the Tet Offensive. In the very midst of the battle raging in and around Saigon, Westmoreland went on record before the 7½ million viewers of the January 31, 1968, CBS Special News Report with the opinion that the Tet Offensive was merely "diversionary," and that the main attack would soon "take place in Quang Tri Province, from Laos, toward Khe Sanh and across the Demilitarized Zone." This view was echoed by President Johnson in his February 2nd news conference, when he claimed that there was about to be "a major offensive in the area of Khe Sanh."—eds.

was to continue until late March. I instructed the Marines to dig in and to confine their patrols to those required for local security. Restricted ground maneuver would permit us the free use of massive supporting firepower without jeopardy to our troops and avoid risking the defeat of small elements by the larger enemy forces in the area. The supporting bombardment—placed in close proximity to our troops—was delivered by Marine artillery on the Khe Sanh plateau by 16 U.S. Army 175-mm guns that were positioned so as to be in range, and by Marine, Air Force, and Navy tactical fighters. Farther from our defensive perimeter, we used the B–52's. However, on several occasions we put the big bombs from these planes within a thousand meters of Marine positions. The bombardment continued day and night. During this battle, I slept in my headquarters next to the combat operations center and personally decided where the B–52's would strike.[16] To assist me in making these decisions, I met at least twice daily with my intelligence and operations officers.

At the beginning of the battle, two battalions of the U.S. 26th Marine Regiment held the position at Khe Sanh, located by an airfield just outside the village. The Marines flew in a third battalion from that regiment on 16 January from Phu Bai. Five days later the enemy attacked and overran the village of Khe Sanh, prompting our troops there and the villagers to withdraw to our defensive base near the airfield. The same day, the base itself and our outpost to the northwest on Hill 861 came under attack. From that time, this hill outpost and three others on Hills 558, 881 South, and 950 were resupplied, when possible, exclusively by helicopter.

On the 22d the base was further reinforced with the 1st Battalion, 9th Marine Regiment, from Gio Linh and four days later I persuaded the Vietnamese to reinforce with a Ranger battalion (the 37th) and to prepare to reinforce later with a second Ranger battalion if required. The 37th Ranger Battalion was deployed from the vicinity of Phu Loc. All together we had near the airstrip three Marine battalions, an ARVN Ranger battalion, and a U.S. Army Special Forces detachment together with a Civilian Irregular Defense Group company, and the vital aircraft-control radar detachments of the U.S. Air Force. Since the airstrip with its ground control devices was our lifeline, it had to be secured. A battalion and a reinforced company of Marines occupied the hilltop outposts. These allied forces faced an estimated two North Vietnamese Army divisions, some 15,000 to 20,000 strong, and one more enemy division within striking distance of our positions.

On 6 February concentrated artillery fire struck both the base at Khe Sanh and the Lang Vei Special Forces camp, a few miles to the southwest. During the night elements of the North Vietnamese 66th Regiment, 304th Division, attacked Lang Vei, employing heavy artillery, flamethrowers, mortars, and 9 Soviet PT–76 tanks (the Communists' first use of tanks in South Vietnam). In the face of overwhelming odds, most of the Special Forces and CIDG troops manning the camp fell back on the base at Khe Sanh. A few who held were soon trapped. The next day I

---

16. Westmoreland also set up a secret group, under his personal command, to plan for the use of tactical nuclear weapons in the defense of Khe Sanh.—eds.

directed a raid to retrieve the surrounded men. Under cover of artillery and air strikes, a rescue force of 10 U.S. Special Forces soldiers and 40 CIDG troops landed by Marine helicopter within a thousand yards of the camp and launched a ground attack to relieve the remaining defenders. When the rescuers were within 200 yards of the camp, the defenders broke out and joined the attackers. Helicopters evacuated the entire group.[17]

During an 11-week period of heavy enemy bombardment, the Marine garrison at Khe Sanh, together with the Vietnamese Ranger battalion, resisted and threw back all attacks. On 23 February alone the base received 1,307 rounds of mortar, rocket, and artillery fire; but the enemy never penetrated beyond the barbed wire at the base's outer perimeter.[18]

As the northeast monsoon waned, on 1 April we launched Operation PEGASUS-LAM SON 207 to reestablish land contact with Khe Sanh. Employing airmobile tactics, elements of the 1st Cavalry Division and three ARVN airborne battalions seized commanding positions to the east and south of Khe Sanh while U.S. Marines drove west from a base at Ca Lu along Route 9, clearing and repairing the road as they went. As the Marines neared the Khe Sanh base, the 26th Marines attacked from the base and linked up with the cavalrymen. None of our troops met much resistance, but they found ample evidence of the destruction our firepower had wrought, including over a thousand enemy dead and large quantities of abandoned supplies and equipment.[19]

As the battle raged in February and early March emergency reinforcement plans for Vietnam were developed by the MACV staff in close coordination with the CINCPAC staff and the joint staff of the Joint Chiefs of Staff. As a matter of military prudence in the face of uncertainties regarding North Vietnamese intentions and capabilities in the northern area and the ability of the South Vietnamese

---

17. The true story of the devastating defeat at Lang Vei is quite different. (See, for example, Pisor, pp. 165–175.) Of the nearly 500 CIDG soldiers at the camp, 316 were killed or missing, while of 24 Americans, 10 were killed and 11 wounded. Many hundreds, perhaps thousands, of associated irregular troops were also lost in this battle. Despite urgent pleas from the base commander and the acting commander of Special Forces in I Corps, the Marine command refused to carry out the prearranged emergency relief plan. The handful of survivors escaped to the old town of Lang Vei almost two miles north of the camp, where some but not all were picked up in the morning by the helicopter rescue team.—eds.

18. Actually the long-awaited attack on Khe Sanh never came. The NLF merely maintained its deadly daily bombardment while conducting occasional probes on the perimeter. For example, on February 8th, the outlying position on Hill 64 was overrun, with losses later described by the Khe Sanh base commander as "light" (in fact, there were 21 Marines killed, 26 badly wounded, 4 missing in action, while only one escaped unwounded).—eds.

19. The official body count for the entire battle of Khe Sanh was 1,602 enemy dead. But when Marine Commanding General Tompkins heard that only 117 rifles and 39 crew-served weapons had been captured, he dismissed even this official body count as "a bunch of poop" (Pisor, p. 237). The dead on the US side, officially listed as 205, were probably closer to 8,000, including the crews of downed planes and helicopters, the forces lost at Lang Vei and in the town of Khe Sanh, relief forces, and the thousands of irregulars killed in the fighting around the base. See Pisor, pp. 233–236 for an analysis of the concealed losses.—eds.

to regain the initiative, I asked that additional forces be prepared for deployment. However, by the end of March, the uncertainty surrounding the *Tet* offensive had abated. The enemy had committed a major share of his forces and had been severely defeated, the government of Vietnam had held firm, South Vietnamese troops in general had fought well, and there had been no public uprising. Further, the government of Vietnam had issued a national mobilization decree on 24 October 1967 which, although delayed in implementation, was to have become effective on 1 January 1968. On 9 February 1968 the Vietnamese general assembly gave approval to the government's accelerated mobilization plan based on this decree. Thus, greatly increased military and pacification forces seemed in prospect.

Therefore, major additional U.S. forces were not required,[20] but a decision was made to deploy 13,500 troops to provide necessary combat support and combat service support for the newly arrived 27th Marine Regimental Landing Team and 3d Brigade of the 82d Airborne Division that I had requested and received in February. The approval of this deployment raised our manpower authorization to 549,500. In addition, I received authority to hire 13,035 additional local civilians to augment selective logistic and construction units and thereby offset the need for additional U.S. military manpower. When it became known that the 27th Regimental Landing Team had to return to the United States, I requested as a replacement a brigade of the 5th Mechanized Division, consisting of one infantry battalion, one mechanized battalion, and one armored battalion. I asked for this highly mobile unit to operate in the coastal areas of Quang Tri and Thua Thien Provinces and in the area south of the Demilitarized Zone. . . .

After the linkup at Khe Sanh, I asked that the Provisional Corps—which I had introduced to assist in controlling the increased strength in the I Corps—make a study of possible redistribution of troops during the good weather of the next several months with emphasis on the Khe Sanh area and the DMZ. Lt. Gen. William B. Rosson, who commanded the corps, and General Cushman, Commanding General, III Marine Amphibious Force, subsequently recommended that the Khe Sanh base and airfield be abandoned and destroyed but that the Khe Sanh plateau, because of its tactical importance, be defended by airmobile troops supported from the new airfield and logistic base constructed by the 1st Cavalry Division at Ca Lu during Operation PEGASUS.[21]

We now had greater flexibility because of the forward base at nearby Ca Lu, improved logistics in the northern area of the I Corps (and particularly just below the Demilitarized Zone), additional troops in the northern part of the I Corps, and greater availability of helicopters in the north. Of particular importance, we now had weather that would permit routine use of helicopters for supply, as opposed to fixed wing aircraft dependent upon larger airfields. I approved the plan advanced

---

20. In fact, it was Westmoreland's desperate request for 206,000 more US troops that triggered the Administration's major reexamination of the war, leading to the fateful decisions of late March. See Reading 54.—eds.

21. On July 5, the last US troops, under fire until the very end, abandoned Khe Sanh.—eds.

by Generals Rosson and Cushman in principle but deferred placing it into effect until the A Shau operation was completed and additional troops could again be deployed to the Khe Sanh plateau where they could consume the supplies stockpiled near the airfield. Furthermore, since I was scheduled to depart in a matter of weeks, I deferred the final decision to my successor. . . .

Beginning in April U.S., Free World, and South Vietnamese forces everywhere moved to the offensive. Having met the challenge of the *Tet* offensive and the siege of Khe Sanh, we were prepared to exploit fully the dominant military position and high level of experience we had built up over the preceding three years. The operations ranged from the reconnaissance in force into the A Shau Valley to further forays by the Mobile Riverine Force in the Delta. In the III Corps, on 8 April, we launched a combined U.S.-ARVN campaign (TOAN THANG, or Complete Victory) employing 79 maneuver battalions, 42 U.S., and 47 Vietnamese. It was a highly decentralized operation since it consisted primarily of small search operations during the day and many ambushes at night, a continuation of our persistent security operations aimed at local forces, guerrillas, and infrastructure. When the operation came to a close on 31 May, the count of enemy killed had reached 7,600. Even more important, the operation had gone a long way toward disrupting Communist plans for a second-wave attack on Saigon.

In March and April the enemy replaced the bulk of his losses with North Vietnamese fillers and in May mounted the second major offensive of the year timed to coincide with the opening of negotiations in Paris. This second offensive was to have been a slightly scaled down model of the *Tet* attack. However, it aborted badly in two important areas.[22] The force which intended to attack Hue and nearby I Corps cities simply never got underway. North of Hai Van pass the U.S. Army's 1st Cavalry and 101st Airborne Divisions had joined the 3d Marine Division in the Provisional Corps. These very aggressive forces anticipated the attack and spoiled the enemy's plans.

The North Vietnamese had also planned to mount a major offensive in the Pleiku and Kontum area with forces of their so-called B–3 Front, which maintained its headquarters in adjacent Cambodia. The actions of the 4th Infantry Division and reinforcements from the 173d Airborne Brigade, plus the massive use of B–52 strikes, caused the enemy to abandon his plans in this area and to withdraw into Cambodia.

However, the main attack occurred again in the Saigon area. In an effort to achieve better coordination than he had managed in the *Tet* offensive, the enemy relaxed the tight security measures he had employed in January and disseminated widely his May attack plans. Some of these plans fell into our hands and aided us in disposing our forces to meet the attacks. Our troops around Saigon were particularly well situated for blocking the enemy's approach. Aggressive patrols and ambushes intercepted and disrupted many of his units. By moving at night and approaching through jungles and swamps, the enemy was nevertheless able to bring units close to the capital before being detected.

---

22. Weekly US casualties all during this offensive were higher than during Tet.—eds.

Of the large force intended to attack Tan Son Nhut Airbase, less than one battalion reached the defensive perimeter. South Vietnamese units quickly drove off this force and then destroyed it in the nearby French cemetery. Otherwise, only small units survived to reach Saigon, principally from the west, and most of those were destroyed as they approached the outskirts. . . .

After a brief lull, the Communists launched another strike at Saigon on 7 May. This time the attack had no apparent military objective but was instead mounted strictly for political and psychological gain. For the most part, the Communists infiltrated small guerrilla bands and dispersed them over a wide area, primarily in the Cholon sector. Groups of four or five men holed up in buildings and fought suicidally against Vietnamese police and soldiers, who gradually rooted them out position by position. A few platoon-sized elements launched small but violent attacks, employing large volumes of random small arms fire. In a number of places the enemy deliberately set fires. The objective clearly was to try to establish an impression of "Saigon under siege," create terror, destruction, and refugees to overburden and embarrass the government, and achieve propaganda and psychological gain to influence discussions between the U.S. and North Vietnam that had begun in Paris.

In only one instance, in the vicinity of the "Y" Bridge over the Kinh Doi Canal along the southern edge of the city, did a force of any appreciable size manage to get into the outskirts of the city. The eventual outcome of the fighting was as inevitable there as elsewhere, but the Communists with their usual tenacity forced a fight continuing for several days before the last elements were eliminated. By 13 May all attempts to infiltrate the city had ceased. Although the fighting soon flickered out, enemy troops continued for several weeks to emerge from hiding and surrender. Most of these were North Vietnamese.

Earlier, on 10 May, a North Vietnamese battalion struck far to the north in the western portion of Quang Tin Province at a CIDG base serving as an outpost for a Special Forces camp at Kham Duc. Badly outnumbered, the CIDG tribesmen, reinforced by a U.S. Marine artillery battery, withdrew after almost 12 hours of heavy fighting. Since the Special Forces camp itself was apparently destined for attack, General Cushman of the III Marine Amphibious Force strengthened the defenders with a reinforced battalion of the Americal Division. One infantry company moved by helicopter from a position near Chu Lai and a battalion of the 196th Light Infantry Brigade with a battery of artillery moved by C–130 aircraft from Quang Tri airfield.

Before daylight on 12 May the North Vietnamese struck in regimental strength supported by rockets and mortars. The enemy overran our outposts on the surrounding high ground, thereby gaining commanding positions. General Cushman, with my approval, decided to evacuate the remote border post.[23] During that afternoon planes and helicopters successfully evacuated our troops and Vietnamese

---

23. Nearly 800 US and ARVN troops were lost in this defeat. Reported enemy losses were 345.—eds.

dependents, but one C–130 aircraft was shot down with 150 Vietnamese passengers aboard, mostly civilian dependents of the Vietnamese garrison.

Enemy pressure and the speed of evacuation made it necessary to abandon and destroy large quantities of the unit's equipment and facilities of the camp. Over a period of several days—before, during, and after the evacuation—our total B–52 capability pounded enemy-held areas and suspected enemy locations, but marginal weather prevented assessment of the effectiveness of these massive strikes.

Also in May, after digesting the experiences of *Tet*, the enemy issued COSVN Resolution #6. The enemy's own statement of his strategic goals is interesting:

The Army and people as a whole must resolutely march forward and engage in a spontaneous uprising to drive out the Americans, overthrow the puppet regime, and turn over the reins of the Government to the people.

Create conditions for Pacifist movements in the U.S.A. to expand, and the doves to assail the hawks, thus forcing the U.S.A. to radically change its VN policy.

In their concerted drive to achieve these goals, the Communists had lost an estimated 120,000 men during the first six months of 1968. These losses were over one-half of their strength at the beginning of the year[24]. . . .

As I left Vietnam in June the enemy was preparing for another attack. This attack, which occurred in mid-August when General Abrams was in command, was even less productive than previous efforts. The enemy achieved none of his offensive goals in Vietnam. Indiscriminate mortar and rocket attacks on populated centers and costly attacks on remote outposts were all he could show for his highly propagandized military efforts. The *Tet* offensive had the effect of a "Pearl Harbor";

---

24. Prior to the Tet Offensive, Westmoreland had estimated the total enemy strength as 292,000. In the months after Tet, the official estimate was raised to over half a million. On January 23, 1982, CBS television broadcast a documentary, "The Uncounted Enemy: A Vietnamese Deception," which charged that Westmoreland had set an arbitrary ceiling of 300,000 for estimates of enemy strength and then had deliberately falsified reports to discount the estimates of well over half a million that were being submitted by the CIA and some of his own intelligence officers. The purpose of this deception, according to the documentary, was to create the illusion that military and pacification operations were being successful. Among the witnesses was retired Major General Joseph Mc-Christian, General Westmoreland's intelligence officer in 1966 and part of 1967, who alleged that this had been a "dishonorable" "falsification of the facts." Westmoreland later sued CBS, but dropped his suit just before it was to go to the jury, after CBS had produced numerous high-placed witnesses who swore that the General had consciously conspired to create fraudulently low estimates of NLF strength before Tet. What substantially reduced the pre-Tet estimates was Westmoreland's decision to delete NLF political cadre and local militia forces from the official "order of battle." These were the very groups that were then supposedly decimated during Tet, greatly swelling the body count. Indeed, one startling admission came out in court when Brigadier General George A. Godding, a witness for General Westmoreland, acknowledged in cross-examination that the NLF self-defense forces were in 1968 no longer counted as part of the enemy "when they were alive," though when dead they often became part of the body count, which was then subtracted from the official count of the living enemy (*New York Times*, October 30, 1984).—eds.

the South Vietnamese government was intact and stronger; the armed forces were larger, more effective, and more confident; the people had rejected the idea of a general uprising; and enemy forces, particularly those of the Viet Cong, were much weaker.

53. "Remembering the Tet Offensive"*

By David Hunt

Historian David Hunt here gives an interpretation of the Tet Offensive quite contradictory to that supplied by General Westmoreland. Hunt, an associate professor of history at the University of Massachusetts, Boston, is also the author of the widely respected Parents and Children in History: The Psychology of Family Life in Early Modern France *(New York: Basic Books, 1970).*

Ten years ago this month, the NLF, the National Liberation Front of South Vietnam, launched its Tet Offensive. The Offensive was a momentous event in modern history, comparable in importance to the storming of the Bastille at the beginning of the French Revolution in 1789, or to the Long March which saved the Chinese Communist Party in 1935 and set it on the road to eventual victory fourteen years later. Tet was decisive within Vietnam, where it marked the turning point in the struggle which had been inaugurated when the Vietnamese declared their independence from France in 1945 and which ended with the liberation of Saigon in April 1975. It also inspired the left in many countries, including the United States, and constituted a major step forward for socialism the world over.

Background to the Offensive

To recapture the full impact of the Tet Offensive, we need to think back to the 1965–1967 period when U.S. forces and Vietnamese guerrillas exchanged blow for blow and the outcome of the war seemed very much in doubt. On the one side, from its formation in 1960, the NLF had flourished in the countryside of Vietnam. The Front had promised to overthrow the landlords and to make the peasant ma-

*From *Radical America*, Vols. 11–12 (November, 1977–February 1978), pp. 79–96.

I would like to thank the following friends who helped me to put the Tet Offensive in historical perspective, and who happily reminisced with me about an important event in all of our lives: Feroz Ahmad, Margery Davies, Ann Froines, Milt Kotelchuck, Jack Spence, and Peter Weiler. [Note by David Hunt.—eds.]

jority "masters of the countryside."[1] Its policies of educational and medical reform, village democracy and economic equality by way of land reform, as well as its insistence on national independence, had won strong backing from the rural population. Over the years, the Front had organized a formidable military presence which had successfully contended with the U.S.-supported "Government of Vietnam" (GVN) and its puppet "Army of the Republic of Vietnam" (ARVN). By 1965, the NLF had liberated almost the entire countryside by expelling GVN authority from most villages and was on the verge of toppling the U.S. allies altogether. In desperation, President Johnson escalated the war, pouring in ground forces (535,000 by early 1968) and drastically increasing expenditures for equipment and technical assistance to be used against the insurgents.

Grasping the central reality of the war, which was that the NLF had sunk its roots deep into the rural social structure, and hoping to isolate and thus cripple the guerrillas, Pentagon strategists set out in 1965 to tear this society apart. U.S. and ARVN troops engaged in daily "search and destroy" missions, rounding up "suspects," burning villages and driving people into concentration camps called "strategic hamlets." Areas governed by the Front were declared "free fire zones," artillery shells rained down day and night, B–52's bombed densely populated villages, and helicopter gunships strafed "suspicious" individuals unlucky enough to be caught out in the open. U.S. planes blanketed crops with poison sprays while bulldozers tore up paddies, orchards and homes. Aiming to provide heavy rainfall and destructive flooding, U.S. scientists seeded the clouds; to strip the guerrillas of ground cover, they endeavored to set fire to the forests of the Highlands; they experimented with ever more fiendish varieties of napalm and anti-personnel bombs. In an effort to escape from this refined and murderous assault, many peasants spent days on end huddled in bunkers. Others moved out of the center of their villages into makeshift huts constructed to seek shelter under the walls of the nearest GVN military post, in a district or province capital city, or in Saigon. By sustaining this policy of "generating refugees," which its apologists glorified as the U.S.-sponsored "forced-draft urbanization and modernization of Vietnam," the Pentagon hoped to "drain the sea," leaving the "fish"—the guerrilla activists— with no "water," that is no rural society, in which to live.[2]

The NLF response to this aggression was total warfare, requiring the participation of the whole society. Picture a densely populated, flat terrain, generally devoid of ground cover (Vietnam's population and NLF strength was concentrated in the level, open areas of the Mekong Delta and the Central Lowlands, rather than in the "jungle" of the Highlands which was often stressed in U.S. media coverage

---

1. David Hunt, "Villagers at War: The National Liberation Front in My Tho Province, 1965– 1967," *Radical America* (Vol. 8, #1–2, January–April 1974), 124. This essay spells out in more detail my sense of NLF politics and U.S. escalation in the 1965–1967 period.

2. See the celebrated defense of U.S. policy by Samuel Huntington, "The Bases of Accommodation," *Foreign Affairs* (July 1968). Noam Chomsky's devastating critique of these apologetics is still to the point. See his *American Power and the New Mandarins* (New York, 1969).

of the war). In this confined space, the two sides jockeyed for position, striving to find and wipe out each other's military forces and to acquire tax payments and recruits from the local population. Here, the NLF organized its regular or "main force" units of full-time, highly-trained and heavily-armed soldiers. Staying together at battalion strength (500 or more troops), these units bivouacked in prepared camps located in different villages, whose residents provided food, shelter, intelligence concerning the other side, and moral support. Main force battalions never lingered long in one place. Trying to survive in the midst of a pre-industrial, subsistence economy where many villages had trouble simply supplying food for their own inhabitants, they could not overstrain the limited resources of the different communities. In any case, too long a stay might attract the attention of GVN observers who—in physical terms—were never too far away. Moving at night to avoid detection, the troops would head for the next village where an equally well-prepared camp had been arranged to shelter them for another brief period.

Wherever they went, NLF main force units acted in liaison with local paramilitary guerrillas who guarded their campsites and helped them slip across particularly dangerous terrain, a well-traveled highway, for example. Even more fundamentally, in every village, the battalions relied on an intricate and sophisticated "civilian" support network which provided the vast logistical base they needed to keep on fighting. Villagers all across the countryside stockpiled food and maintained fortified camp sites, trenches and underground shelters, along with medical stations, arsenals and storage areas for heavy equipment. And finally village cadres recruited volunteers into the local and regular forces and collected the taxes which financed this whole military effort.

Picking their spots with care, main force units only occasionally launched an operation. Attacks were organized in minute detail, with soldiers rehearsing their tactics in life-size models of the target area, built according to specifications supplied by undercover agents working within the GVN camp. Retreat routes, with fortified positions, food, ammunition and medical services, were set up so that NLF troops would not be caught off guard when the enemy rushed in reinforcements. Teams of villagers stood by to carry away captured equipment as well as the wounded and the dead. After the battle, units took refuge in a safe area, replaced their losses and critically reviewed every detail of the action.

To gauge the success of such tactics, the observer had to recognize that guerrilla war unfolds *over time*, and that morale and political strength, rather than territory occupied, are the keys to victory. In the wake of one of these local NLF attacks, GVN and U.S. units were rocked back on their heels and retreated behind the walls of their outposts, so that low-level harassment from local paramilitary guerrilla forces usually sufficed to keep them on the defensive. The terrain was thus left free for NLF political work to go on unhindered (even in the best of times, no GVN political cadres traveled without military escort), and for regular forces to catch their breath and heal their wounds. But as time passed and these main force units remained out of sight, the Americans and their allies took heart. Sorties began again, troops regained some of their former fighting spirit, search and de-

stroy missions ranged more widely. Under such conditions, the GVN was somewhat freer to contend with the NLF in the countryside, extorting taxes (and rents)
from the peasants and kidnapping conscripts for the ARVN. Growing more confident with each passing day, U.S. generals and advisers in the region would begin
to hope that the insurgents' main force units had disintegrated (we must remember
that throughout this time planes and artillery were hammering at areas in which
NLF battalions were circulating). But then, just when the end seemed to be in
sight, long-hidden regular units struck again, hurling their adversaries back into
outposts and cities and freeing the countryside once more from GVN interference.[3]

Lacking adequate sources of information, and misled by politicians and the
media, the American people could see in the fighting little beyond a welter of small
battles in provinces with strange names scattered all over the country. The overall
trend of events was lost amidst the numerous unsynchronized local and regional
struggles, each with its own particular timetable of lulls and sudden attacks. In the
absence of any compelling opposition analysis of events, the official explanation
of the situation gained a certain credence. According to this view, the U.S. military
was in a strong position. To be sure, casualties were high, and the expense of the
war was staggering (upward of $30 billion in 1967). But vast firepower and over a
million troops (counting ARVN soldiers and South Korean mercenaries) were
clearly doing a great deal of damage to the other side. In November 1967, U.S.
officials affirmed that 67% of the countryside was "secure" or "relatively secure"[4]
(at the end of the dry season, many NLF regular units had been inactive for several
weeks or even months), while in cities like Saigon, according to *New York Times*
military correspondent Hanson Baldwin (in an article published January 19, 1967),
the once formidable NLF underground network had supposedly been badly crippled. The domestic strains of a long inconclusive war were there for all to see, but
surely, U.S. authorities argued, the enemy had to be hurting even more.

Few Americans disagreed with this assessment. Critics of government policy
based their position on moral grounds, decrying the destruction being inflicted on
the defenseless Vietnamese, or arguing that, since no fundamental strategic interests were at stake in Vietnam, the war was not worth the effort and cost necessary
for victory. But, with a few exceptions, even the most militant anti-war activists
continued to assume that the Pentagon could win the war if it chose to keep up its
military pressure on the enemy. By and large, for the anti-war movement, the
people of Vietnam were victims, and the proper position for our government was
to "get out," leaving the Vietnamese to their own quarrels, which ultimately had
little bearing on our lives. Among opponents of government policy, there was little
understanding of NLF sources of strength and a minimal identification with its
vision of the future.

---

3. Wilfred Burchett's accounts of NLF military and political organization are basic. See *Vietnam:
Inside Story of the Guerrilla War* (New York, 1968) and *Vietnam Will Win!* (New York, 1970). The
latter volume, for example, has a wonderful description of an NLF unit "rehearsing" a battle plan
(pages 35 ff.).

4. *Le Monde*, February 1, 1968.

Straining to respond to U.S. escalation, the NLF was indeed shaken to its foundations. Casualties were high and morale among villagers faltered as they doggedly persisted with an endless round of tasks: maintaining underground tunnel systems, carrying ammunition, tending the wounded, cultivating their crops, paying taxes and contributing food to the troops—while bombs and shells rained down and enemy patrols periodically swept through. But Front organizations withstood this shock, cadres with "high morale and an everlasting endurance of hardship" refused to grow discouraged,[5] and enough villagers clung to their homes and to their roles within the resistance to keep the whole operation intact. The essential political strength of the guerrilla movement carried it through. Even in its brightest moments, the GVN had no real ties to the rural population (its landlord supporters had long ago fled to the cities) and survived only on the basis of U.S. money and military support. By contrast, even in the most trying times, the NLF was sustained by the reality, evident to most, that it alone had a program which made sense to the Vietnamese people.

On the other side, the morale of U.S.-GVN forces was deteriorating in a much more telling fashion. As the war dragged on, the resilience of the insurgents, who again and again demonstrated "the recuperative powers of the phoenix," demoralized soldiers who had no compelling reason of their own to keep on fighting.[6]

Even the leaders of the counter-insurgency effort began to falter, and their confident assertions in the quiet periods between battles took on an increasingly hollow ring. The NLF could sense this gradual loss of will. American troops had boldly sought out NLF regular forces in the winter-spring campaign of 1965–1966, and during the next year as well, although less aggressive, they had still been able to launch powerful thrusts into guerrilla base areas like "War Zone C," northwest of Saigon.[7] With the coming of a new dry season in late 1967, as the NLF in many regions lay low, the old optimistic note was again sounded by U.S. generals and politicians, though now colored by an unmistakable uneasiness. And indeed, another turnabout on the battlefield was in the offing. But this reversal was to differ from its predecessors, in that it was not to be confined to this local battlefield or that one. Instead, from one end of the country to the other, *all* of the NLF main force units *simultaneously* swung into action to build up momentum for the mighty blow which was to be the Tet Offensive.

Story of the Offensive

The Tet Offensive was a remarkable achievement, involving the simultaneous, coordinated activity of a great many small units spread over the whole terrain of

---

5. The phrase comes from a peasant of My Tho, quoted in Hunt, "Villagers at War," 106.

6. "Not only do the Viet Cong units have the recuperative powers of the phoenix, but they have an amazing ability to maintain morale," notes U.S. General Maxwell Taylor, in November 1964; quoted in *Pentagon Papers* (Boston, 1971), III, 668.

7. See the historical overview in Nguyen Khac Vien, *Histoire du Vietnam* (Paris, 1974), 246 ff. On the "pacification" of War Zone C, see the classic account of Jonathan Schell, *The Village of Ben Suc* (New York, 1967).

South Vietnam and often in the middle of areas ostensibly controlled by the other side. In the course of a generation of fighting, there had been many military campaigns launched by the revolutionary movement, but none, not even the legendary siege of Dienbienphu, had been conceived on such a grand scale, and none had drawn so generously on the heroism and ingenuity of the Vietnamese people. Having set the stage, we should now turn to the Offensive itself.

Right from the beginning of the dry season campaign of 1967–1968, the NLF seized the initiative. Its forces struck hard at U.S.-GVN positions in the northern provinces close to the DMZ and in the Central Highlands and Lowlands, they shelled installations within twenty miles of Saigon and assumed an increasingly menacing posture in the Mekong Delta. By mid-January, the French newspaper *Le Monde* was speaking of a "sustained and general offensive" which had the Americans pinned back in defensive positions. There was no longer any question of mounting punitive operations similar to those undertaken by U.S. forces during the previous two years. Nervous, yet reluctant to abandon their optimistic reading of the situation, U.S. leaders asserted that the attacks were a "desperation tactic," a final death throe before guerrilla resistance collapsed once and for all.[8]

These engagements, ominous as they were, did not significantly depart from the previously established character of the fighting. The real surprise was yet to come, for the NLF—and here lies the drama and originality of the Tet Offensive—was planning to bring the war into the cities. Surrounded by barren terrain and with rings of military bases nearby, the urban centers of GVN power had enjoyed a privileged, peaceful status throughout the war and seemed impregnable to direct assault. The unexpected way NLF strategists resolved this problem required a vast deployment of all the resources at its command. To bring about the needed mobilization, the Front instituted universal conscription in the areas it governed (astonishingly, from an American, not to speak of a GVN, point of view, the guerrilla forces relied entirely on volunteers during the harrowing 1966–1967 period).[9] In the weeks before the attack, the NLF secretly prepared forward positions in the suburbs, while main force troops disbursed, dressed in civilian clothes and set out in ones and twos to enter the cities. U.S. strategy, which had dislodged hundreds of thousands of peasants and sent them on the roads, facilitated this infiltration, while the travels habitually associated with the Tet holidays, a time for visiting and reunions, further covered NLF preparations. Once in the cities, as an American journalist noted, "the Viet Cong were absorbed into the population by the urban underground like out of town relatives attending a family reunion." Meanwhile, weapons were coming in too, hidden in peddlers' carts, amidst vegetables bound for market, in people's luggage. In turn, "the underground had . . . stockpiled arms, explosives and munitions, in dozens of innocent-looking places throughout the city," in private homes, in flower pots, even in coffins ceremoniously buried in cemeteries.[10]

---

8. *Le Monde*, January 11, 1968; *New York Times*, January 21, 1968.

9. Hunt, "Villagers at War," 98–99.

10. *New York Times*, February 4, 1977.

On January 20, liberation forces surrounded the U.S. Marine base at Khe Sanh high up in the mountainous jungle terrain close to the Laotian border in northwest South Vietnam. General Westmoreland, commander of U.S. forces in Vietnam, immediately assumed that the other side planned a re-run of their famous Dienbienphu campaign of fourteen years earlier. The guerrillas, he reasoned, were pouring all their resources into an effort to take the fortress, in the hope that this feat would demoralize the administration and lead to a negotiated settlement, just as the fall of Dienbienphu in 1954 had broken the resolve of the French and opened the way to the signing of the Geneva Accords. Forty-thousand troops were readied to come to the aid of the garrison, and an uneasy President Johnson forced a number of his top generals to endorse a statement, "signed in blood," as he put it, that they could hold Khe Sanh no matter what.

But of course the liberation forces were not planning to attack Khe Sanh, and their feint was brilliantly designed to take advantage of the incapacities of the U.S. high command. Thinking defensively and anxious above all to avoid a humiliating setback, the Pentagon strategists were bound to reflect first on ways of avoiding the kind of defeat suffered by their French predecessors. At the same time, a conventional "siege," with clear battle lines and objectives, and without the exasperating "political" distractions which resulted when fighting took place amidst densely populated villages, was bound to appeal to men who had never been able to pry the guerrillas loose from their base among the people. Unfortunately for the American public, the U.S. media fell into the same trap, and misleadingly emphasized the siege of Khe Sanh throughout the Offensive. In any case, Westmoreland stubbornly kept his attention focused on the fortress in subsequent weeks and refused to believe that the decisive battles might be going on elsewhere. Finally, when the damage had been done, the Vietnamese lifted their siege in early April, and in turn the Marines evacuated the base, which had no real strategic value, on June 28.[11]

The major part of the Offensive began on the night of January 29–30 in the Central Highlands and Lowlands, the next night in Saigon, Hue and the Mekong Delta. Guerrilla forces assembled, at times wearing insignias on their shirts to facilitate mutual recognition. In certain cities, they broke into laundries and stole ARVN uniforms which were worn during the attack, thus throwing even greater confusion into enemy ranks. Guns were removed from their hiding places and test-fired amidst the convenient explosion of holiday fireworks.[12] And then the NLF struck, hitting 34 of 44 province capitals, 64 district capitals, and numerous military installations, all in all over one hundred major targets from one end of the country to the other. The Front broke into prisons and freed thousands of political

---

11. On the siege of Khe Sanh, see *New York Times*, January 26, 1968; Frances Fitzgerald, *Fire in the Lake: The Vietnamese and the Americans in Vietnam* (New York, 1973), 543; Dan Oberdorfer, *Tet!* (New York, 1971), 189, 203; *Le Monde*, June 28, 1968. [By far the best source now is Robert Pisor, *The End of the Line: The Siege of Khe Sanh* (New York: W. W. Norton, 1982; New York: Ballantine Books, 1983).—eds.]

12. *New York Times*, February 4, 7, 1968.

prisoners, it occupied or burned down many GVN province headquarters and other government buildings, it overran bases, capturing or destroying millions of dollars worth of equipment, it inflicted telling losses on disoriented, often panic stricken U.S.-GVN forces hastily mobilized to repel the assault. The Americans had grown accustomed to an enemy which generally made it a principle to avoid frontal engagements. Now with shocking power, assaults by large bodies of regular forces came crushing into the middle of areas once judged absolutely "secure."

Let's review some of the particulars of the Offensive. In Hue on January 30, as the university was closing for the holidays, one of the teachers commented enigmatically to his class: "Soon you will witness the return of the conquerors of Dienbienphu." Later he was seen working with the NLF. Sure enough, as one resident remembered it, on January 31,

> at 3:00 in the morning . . . the Viet Cong came shouting into the city. They crossed the bridge on the run. They passed under my window running and yelling all the time. There were hundreds of them. I saw some young women who ran with them.

NLF occupation of Hue was swift and peaceful. GVN authorities put up no significant resistance, and in fact a number of local officials immediately switched sides and began working with the liberation forces. The Prison was opened and two to three thousand prisoners went free. In a dispatch dated February 2, Agence-France-Presse correspondent Francois Mazure noted:

> At dawn, the new masters of the city went through the streets in groups of ten. In each group, there was a leader who spoke to the people through a bullhorn. . . . The other members of the team . . . knocked on doors and passed out pamphlets and leaflets. Joking and laughing, the soldiers walk in the streets and gardens without showing any fear. . . . They give an impression of discipline and good training. . . . Numerous civilians brought them great quantities of food. It didn't seem that these residents were being coerced in any way.

A few days later, the Saigon government expelled Mazure from South Vietnam for spreading pro-communist propaganda.[13] For almost a month, the NLF flag flew over the city which many Vietnamese regarded as the traditional, authentic capital of their country.

First attempts by U.S. Marines and ARVN forces to retake Hue were unsuccessful. As one U.S. official stated:

> By resisting, the North Vietnamese force us to destroy Hue in order to retake the city. They know that they cannot hold it indefinitely. But they dig in, retreating only one step at a time, putting up the most stubborn resistance I have ever seen.[14]

---

13. The quotes in the paragraph and other information on events in Hue are found in *Le Monde*, February 6, 10, 17. 1968.

14. Quoted in *Le Monde*, February 9, 1968.

On February 14, the U.S. high command decided to use air power against the defenders, and by February 24, when liberation troops finally slipped away, Hue, historic capital of Vietnam and site of many old and distinguished monuments, had been almost completely levelled. For many a Vietnam veteran, memories of the battle in Hue are among the bitterest of the whole war. U.S. marines fought for days on end with no relief, largely because General Westmoreland was anxious to retake the city as soon as possible so that his troops would be ready for what he thought would be the real showdown—at Khe Sanh.[15] NLF guerrilla units surrounded Hue so that the Americans, who were attempting to encircle the enemy in the center of the city, were themselves being encircled and had to rely on air transport for food and supplies. The usual unfriendly relations between U.S. and ARVN troops deteriorated still further as the ARVN soldiers hung back from fighting and attempted to steal supplies which were being air-dropped to the marines. Seeing their neighborhoods destroyed and antagonized by incidents of looting and brutality on the part of U.S. troops, Hue residents viewed the Americans with undisguised hatred. "If looks could kill, very few marines would still be alive," remarked one young American officer.[16]

Although less prolonged, the battles in other provincial centers followed essentially these same lines. In one locale after another, NLF forces peacefully assumed control, then were driven out by U.S. bombing and shelling, with the occupation lasting anywhere from 24 hours to more than a week (Dalat, for example, was held for eight days).[17] "The Viet Cong had the Government by the throat in those provincial towns," explained one U.S. military adviser. "Ordinary methods would never have got them out, and the Government did not have enough troops to do the job, so firepower was substituted."[18] In My Tho, bombing and shelling reduced half of the city to rubble, according to the *New York Times*, or completely destroyed the city, if we are to accept the *Le Monde* account of February 6. "The looks the people of My Tho gave the Americans today appeared to be angry," the *Times* correspondent noted. But the most famous case of this strategy in action was Ben Tre in Kien Hoa Province. Here is an excerpt from the February 8 *New York Times*:

"The Viet Cong had people all over this town," said Maj. Philip Canella. . . . "Christ, they were everywhere. . . . They had apparently infiltrated into most of the town; they were probably living with the people. It was Tet and there were plenty of strangers in town."

Ben Tre was pulverized by U.S. firepower. "It became necessary to destroy the town to save it," an unidentified U.S. Major explained, thus coining one of the

---

15. *Le Monde*, February 25, 1968.
16. Quoted in *Le Monde*, February 21, 1968.
17. *Le Monde*, February 10, 1968.
18. Quoted in *New York Times*, February 11, 1968.

most notorious phrases of the war and a fitting motto for the U.S. counterattack against the Tet Offensive.[19]

Saigon itself was occupied by the revolutionaries. Packed with 4,000,000 people (more than 20% of the entire South Vietnamese population), many of whom were refugees from the countryside, the capital city witnessed two kinds of attack.[20] First, and most spectacular, were the assaults on highly visible targets right in the middle of town: the U.S. Embassy, the Presidential Palace, the Government radio station. Two employees in the Embassy helped an NLF attack team break in and hold the building for several hours.[21] All of these places were retaken within twenty-four hours, but as a *Le Monde* correspondent pointed out, the point of the actions in the heart of the most prosperous residential area of Saigon was not to seize and hold terrain, nor to liquidate political enemies, but rather to "shake up the bourgeoisie."[22] In pursuit of this aim, liberation troops moved freely, often making a point of knocking on doors with small requests—for example, a drink of water—content to make their presence known among the local notables who provided the main social base for the GVN regime.

Meanwhile, in many of Saigon's poorer neighborhoods, overflowing with refugees, the NLF took a different approach. Here, the troops, working in close coordination with the local underground, settled down to stay in the midst of the population, which had fed and housed them in the days before the attack and hidden their weapons. In effect, these quarters had become liberated territories. "I have always thought of this whole area as a Vietcong combat hamlet," said one military policeman of Cholon, one such Saigon neighborhood.[23] These occupations were still in force several weeks later when a French correspondent noted that in Cholon the visitor:

knows immediately that he is in a zone controlled by the NLF. The signs of this are scarcely perceptible. The expressions on the people's faces are closed, hostility is evident, manifested by the whole community: mocking dignity of the children, pretended indifference of the adults—that is of the women, since men are rare and are never less than fifty years old. One also notices the absence of urban misery and of begging. And especially conspicuous—the decisive proof of NLF control—is the total absence of the governmental army. The ARVN troops are content to block the streets leading into the neighborhood. The visitor quickly understands that he is not welcome, and the children, faithful guards, make him understand this very clearly as he leaves with some stones which whistle past his ears.[24]

---

19. These citations and other information on U.S. bombing and shelling are found in *New York Times*, February 6, 1968. According to the *Times*, there were at least 750 civilian casualties in My Tho, 350 in Can Tho, 2,500 in Ben Tre.

20. My account of events in Saigon is based on Jean-Claude Pomonti, "Les Saigonnais dans la guerre," *Le Monde*, February 7, 1968.

21. *New York Times*, February 5, 1968.

22. *Le Monde*, February 7, 1968.

23. Quoted in *New York Times*, February 11, 1968.

24. *Le Monde*, May 4; see also *New York Times*, February 8, 1968.

Here too the Americans were reduced to bombing and shelling, and by February 6 the *New York Times* stated that "in some places in the city and suburbs the destruction is almost total."

The Meaning of the Offensive

By permanently modifying the political and military balance of forces in South Vietnam, the Tet Offensive constituted a decisive moment in the history of the war. American politicians and journalists were quick to voice the opinion that the NLF had "lost militarily," because it had been forced to evacuate the cities, but somehow, as if by accident, had won a "psychological" victory during Tet. But from the NLF point of view, military methods were always conceived as a means of affecting the political—or "psychological"—situation. All tactical operations, even one as ambitious as the Tet Offensive, were designed not to seize and control some piece of territory, but to bring pressure to bear on enemy forces and to undermine their resolve to continue the war. Approached from this perspective, the Offensive amounted to a crushing defeat for the United States.

Even if we are content to view events from a narrowly military perspective, the Pentagon had little grounds for satisfaction. During the fighting ARVN forces were "cut to pieces" with some of the elite units "disintegrated to the highest degree." U.S. casualties were also substantial: 3895 dead between January 30 and March 31.[25] In their routine planning for the war, American strategists took for granted outlays for equipment which would seem staggering for any other nation, but even so the material losses suffered during the Tet Offensive gave pause. For example, the NLF claimed to have wrecked 1,800 aircraft during the fighting. Replacing the planes, trucks, radar and communications equipment, guns and ammunition lost during the Offensive was possible, of course, but such expenditures also increased the burden of the war on the already over-extended American economy. These losses also had repercussions on the battlefield where, as an NLF spokesperson explained,

The result in lowered U.S. military efficiency was immediately noticeable . . . in lack of coordination between American and Saigon forces; lack of coordination between their own ground units and between ground units and air support; and frequently a total absence of support for platoon and company-sized units caught in our ambushes.[26]

In February, the American situation was desperate, not only in Vietnam, but on a global scale as well. The military had no idea what to expect next. Another

---

25. *New York Times*, February 2, 1968; Oberdorfer, *Tet!*, "dedication."

26. See the analysis offered by an NLF spokesperson in Burchett, *Vietnam Will Win!*, 193 ff. According to this commentator, 200,000 Saigon troops, one third of the entire ARVN force, deserted in the first week of the Offensive. [According to the secret report of the US Joint Chiefs of Staff, the "average present for duty strength" of ARVN combat units dropped to 43–50 percent. See Reading 54.—eds.]

attack on Hue? Saigon? Khe Sanh? As *New York Times* pundit James Reston put it, Washington was "trying to anticipate the oriental mind, and . . . having a very hard time indeed."[27] U.S. Strategic reserves were exhausted, and the Pentagon realized that, in the event of a crisis elsewhere in the world (the Middle East, for example), its options would be limited. The Pueblo incident of January 23, 1968 (when the North Koreans captured a U.S. ship which had violated their territorial waters) had already made clear a vulnerability which Tet had succeeded in dangerously aggravating.[28]

For three years, U.S. forces had been endeavoring to push back the insurgents who in 1965 controlled almost the entire countryside and had the cities virtually surrounded. By 1968, and at a huge cost, some progress had been made in gaining a bit of breathing room. But in the course of the Offensive, the guerrillas once more tightened their lines around the urban areas, establishing a stranglehold on towns they had decided to evacuate to escape U.S. bombing and shelling. A State Department working paper dated March 3 analyzed the situation in these terms:

> We know that despite a massive influx of 500,000 U.S. troops, 1.2 million tons of bombs a year, 400,000 attack sorties per year, 200,000 enemy KIA in three years, 20,000 US KIA, etc., our control of the countryside and the defense of the urban levels is now essentially at pre-August 1965 levels. We have achieved stalemate at a high commitment.[29]

Of course the NLF had suffered losses of its own in reestablishing this commanding position. The Americans claimed that enemy casualties had been prohibitive, as many as 60,000 dead—which would have amounted to virtually the entire strike force employed in the Offensive. A *Le Monde* estimate suggested that all but 10–15% of these dead were residents of cities and towns who had been killed largely as a result of U.S. bombing and shelling,[30] but we can be sure that losses in NLF military units were substantial. At the same time, they had not fundamentally diminished the capabilities of the insurgents. From their advanced positions, they launched major attacks on February 18–19, March 4–5 and May 5, not on the scale of the original assaults, but still punishing. And of course shelling and harassment actions were constant throughout this period. In May, U.S. ground forces lost 2,215 dead (500 a week), compared to 2,043 in February at the apparent height of the offensive.[31]

The political ramifications of the Offensive were profound. As the attacks unfolded, GVN pacification cadres fled from the rural areas, and its troops were either shifted into the beleaguered cities or walled up in strongholds close to district

27. *New York Times*, February 4, 1968.
28. Burchett, *Vietnam Will Win!*, 187 ff.
29. *Pentagon Papers*, [Gravel edition], IV, 558. This U.S. view corresponds closely to the NLF analysis quoted in Burchett, *Vietnam Will Win!*, 193.
30. *Le Monde*, February 22, 1968.
31. *Le Monde*, June 7, 1968.

and province capitals. By early March, the pacification program in the Mekong Delta had been "entirely destroyed," and even on the most important highway, route 4, the NLF was collecting tolls and blocking enemy transport. The situation between Saigon and Danang was hardly better. In Thua Thien Province, while the battle in Hue got most of the attention within the U.S., guerrilla units were taking control of the rural terrain. In the other northern provinces, the Marines gave up pacification efforts and drew back into their bases.[32] Citing a report prepared in late February by General Wheeler, the authors of the Pentagon Papers noted that "the most important VC goal in the winter-spring offensive was the takeover of the countryside." According to Wheeler, this goal had been largely achieved.

The "main event" thus is still to come, not in a one-night offensive but in a week-by-week expulsion of GVN presence and influence from the rural areas, showing up on the pacification maps as a "red tide" flowing up to the edges of the province and district towns, and over some of them.

Once again "controlling" the countryside (to use the Pentagon's term), the NLF was free to carry on its political work, recruiting, collecting taxes, strengthening the logistical base for further military activities. As Wheeler put it, "the enemy is operating with relative freedom in the countryside. . . . His recovery [from the losses of the Tet Offensive] is likely to be rapid."[33]

In a more general sense, as always, the way the two sides fought conveyed a sense of who they were and what they stood for, and these lessons emerged all the more clearly because of the scope and drama of the Tet Offensive. NLF strategy involved a marked degree of decentralization and local initiative. Many main force troops had been given civilian clothes, spending money and identification papers, and then had been dispersed one by one or in small groups with orders to reassemble at a later date in the cities of South Vietnam. The readiness to give such orders (such a plan would have been inconceivable for ARVN or U.S. commanders) and the fact that the soldiers successfully regrouped at their assigned times and places spoke volumes about the state of mind of the guerrillas. Even the seemingly petty details which emerged from newspaper accounts of the fighting were full of import. Reflect, for example, on the fact that in some cities, the NLF attackers disguised themselves as ARVN forces, a ploy which sowed much confusion among Saigon and American personnel, but seemingly did not disrupt unit coordination among the guerrillas. Only troops who had been minutely prepared and who completely trusted each other and their leadership would have dared to employ such a device.

Every aspect of the campaign also clearly depended on civilian cooperation. Tens of thousands of people must have directly aided the revolutionary forces,

---

32. *Le Monde*, February 23, March 9, 13, 26, 1968; *Economist*, March 9, 1968; Burchett, *Vietnam Will Win!*, 198.

33. These two citations are from *Pentagon Papers* [Gravel edition], IV, 561, 547.

helping them to smuggle their weapons into cities, providing food and shelter once they had arrived, enabling them to blend into the urban neighborhoods from which they later launched their attacks. As in other aspects of guerrilla warfare, the fighting itself required civilian logistical support: maintenance of bunkers and other defensive positions, assistance in dealing with killed and wounded, transport and storage of supplies, information on the activity of enemy units. The failure of U.S. intelligence to anticipate the attack was also politically significant. Many Vietnamese had known what was coming, yet had failed to betray the secrecy of NLF preparations. As a *Le Monde* correspondent affirmed, the way the Offensive unfolded "implied the participation and the complicity of a significant part of the population."[34]

U.S. response to the Tet Offensive was also characteristic. After the NLF had for the most part peacefully occupied the cities, U.S.-GVN authorities were reduced to demolishing areas they stood no chance of regaining by other means. Their victory communiques could not hide, in the words of *Le Monde*, "the horrible massacre of a population, often complicit, but unarmed." By February 22, the French newspaper stated, literally "hundreds" of communities had suffered a substantial number of civilian casualties. The massive firepower which had been wrecking the liberated areas of the countryside for two years and driving refugees into the cities was now turned against these same cities, forcing the guerrillas and the inhabitants, many of them already uprooted, to flee. Not all the massacres resulted from the bombardment of heavily populated urban areas. In the countryside, U.S. troops were slaughtering villagers who seemed to side with the NLF, as in My Lai on March 16. On the ropes, without any political toe-hold, the Pentagon was compelled to drop all pretense and to commit its forces to the outright extermination of the rural population. Army morale, which had never been high, began to give way as this ruthless strategy emerged more clearly. The fact that word of the My Lai massacre was leaked by U.S. army personnel was a sign of what later was to grow into a substantial anti-war resistance among the GIs.[35]

The situation in the cities was more complex than in the countryside, but there too the Tet Offensive modified the balance of forces, shaking loose many students, Buddhists, and moderate politicians—the individuals and groups who later would constitute the "Third Force"—from their allegiance to the GVN. By showing their presence in the heart of cities many had believed to be entirely "secure," the insurgents had indeed "shaken up" the urban bourgeoisie. "The Front let them off this time," *Le Monde* explained, "did not ask them too choose. Too skillful, the NLF leaves them some time to reflect."[36] As a *New York Times* correspondent observed on February 4,

34. *Le Monde*, February 9, 1968.

35. On My Lai, see Seymour Hersh, *Cover-Up* (New York, 1972). When this story began to emerge in the autumn of 1969, U.S. authorities responded with counter-charges according to which the other side had also conducted massacres during the Tet Offensive, especially at Hue. The allegations were later exposed as fabrications by Gareth Porter, in "The 1968 'Hue Massacre,'" *Indochina Chronicle* (#33, June 24, 1974). [See Reading 56 for excerpts from *My Lai 4*, also by Hersh.—eds.]

36. *Le Monde*, February 7, 1968.

The complacent and prosperous dwellers in the big cities had, over several years of peace and a semblance of security, come to think of the Vietcong as a specter that haunted the fields and hamlets in the dark of night. Now, for the first time, they found the VC in the streets, shouting their slogans and fighting with nerve-shattering fury against the hastily gathered American and Vietnamese units sent to oppose them. It is unlikely that the well-to-do will ever feel quite the same confidence in the central Government.

In the following months, this erosion in Government support continued as various moderates came to realize that the NLF was there to stay and that the Americans would stop at nothing, not even the destruction of Vietnam, in order to "save" it from communism.[37] In April 1969, this political shift served as the basis for creation of the Provisional Revolutionary Government (PRG), a broad coalition which included the NLF and which from then on, in opposition to the claims of GVN authorities, asserted its right to speak for the Vietnamese people in Vietnam and in the world as well.

The Tet Offensive was the critical battle of the Vietnam war, an assertion we can make even while recognizing that there have been many "turning points" in the Vietnam struggle for national liberation: the Declaration of Independence from the French in 1945; Dienbienphu and the Geneva Accords in 1954; the founding of the NLF in 1960; the 1964 General Offensive which prompted U.S. escalation in the following year; the 1972 Spring Offensive and the Paris Peace Agreements of January 1973; the definitive liberation of the whole country in April 1975. Tet 1968 was only one phase in this sequence; in the words of North Vietnamese officials, it was not "final victory, the seizure of central power." But nonetheless, even then (in March 1968), they recognized it as "a decisive step in an unfolding process."[38] The revolutionary leaders had always been confident, and, on the other hand, they knew the suffering and destruction of the war were far from over. But after the spring of 1968 they were certain of final victory.

In the first place, the Offensive transformed the situation within South Vietnam. After 1968, there remained Catholics, political moderates, sectors of the bourgeoisie, not to speak of a hard core of drug dealers, profiteers and traitors, who continued to hold the Front at arms length and who lent a measure of support, however grudging it was in certain cases, to the Saigon regime. And so long as this regime remained in place, the U.S. would have a base for continuing the fighting. Still, a threshold had been crossed, and the insurgency was now broad enough to present itself to the country and to the world as a *government*, sure of its ultimate right to speak for the nation. In short, formation of the PRG was one of the enduring legacies of Tet.

The Offensive also permanently tipped the international balance of forces in

---

37. This process was carefully documented in a series of *Le Monde* dispatches; see, for example, the analysis in the May 4, 1968 edition. *Le Monde*'s coverage of the Tet Offensive was consistently excellent, and even today, ten years later, its dispatches are substantial, useful contemporary history. By contrast, the U.S. coverage makes painful reading today, reminding us of how inadequately the American people were served by papers like the *New York Times*, throughout the war.

38. Quoted in the dispatch filed by Jacques Decornoy in *Le Monde*, March 1, 1968.

favor of the Vietnamese and against their imperialist enemies. From the point of view of the Pentagon, the fight against the NLF was much more than a "police action," which could be carried off with limited means. On the contrary, it was a major war. Realizing that some measure of active participation of the "home front" would be necessary to offset the total effort which the guerrillas were able to command from their own mass base, they hoped to pit the American people against Vietnam's revolutionary movement. But this commitment was never forthcoming, and the attempts to make a political case for the war failed badly ("roughly half of those interviewed by the Gallup poll in June of 1967 said they had no clear idea of what the war was all about").[39] As a result, the government had to fall back on what was by definition an inadequate position: that the war could somehow be fought and won without seriously impinging on the lives of the American people, that we were capable of producing both "guns and butter." Finally, as the fighting persisted and losses mounted, U.S. leaders were left only with the cynical assertion that, right or wrong, escalation was winning and that, however people might feel about the conflict, it would soon be over with the Pentagon on top.

The Tet Offensive completely exploded this illusion and left Washington without any way of persuasively inviting mass participation in the war effort, and as a consequence without any prospect of winning the war. Indeed, Nixon and Kissinger were required to withdraw U.S. forces and bring down military spending on Indochina, in other words, to present Vietnam as a project which would cost the American people almost nothing. At the time, anti-war activists accorded to the Nixon strategy of "Vietnamization," and the technological destruction of the countryside, more military significance than it in fact deserved. Massive technological means of destruction had been employed with great ruthlessness from 1965 on. There was no doubt that such tactics caused great suffering across the countryside, but such means alone, even with refinements like computerized B–52 runs controlled from Thailand and "people sniffers" scattered along the Ho Chi Minh trail, could hardly accomplish what had not been achieved in conjunction with half a million troops. Human factors were what counted—on *both* sides. By undermining the morale of the U.S. expeditionary force and driving it out of the war, and by destroying public confidence in the war effort within the U.S., the Tet Offensive buried once and for all any realistic Pentagon hope for military victory.

Within the United States, changes wrought by the Tet Offensive, though not "decisive" in the sense just discussed, were nonetheless profound. President Johnson had crushed Barry Goldwater and the Republicans in 1964, winning one of the most one-sided elections in American history. But the NLF brought him down, enmeshing him in a tissue of lies and boastful predictions, then sending his whole administration foundering with their Offensive. This demonstration of the vulnerability of U.S. leadership was not lost on many sectors of the ruling class (Clark Clifford, the *New York Times*, etc.) who now began to argue openly that the government had made a mistake and that policy in Vietnam and elsewhere had to be

---

39. Oberdorfer, *Tet!*, 100.

rebuilt around a recognition of the limitations of U.S. power. Never again would any administration be able to unite the entire ruling class behind a strategy of U.S. aggressive military victory in Vietnam. More broadly, the realization that U.S. troops could not be committed to Third World battlefields without grave risk substantially reined in a foreign policy which for a generation had been both highly aggressive and firmly supported by the entire ruling class.

The NLF also singularly changed the relationship between the government and the American people. Tet made "the light at the end of the tunnel" into a widely recognized, derisive one-liner. Even today, it is not entirely clear how much administration propaganda grew out of an attempt to deliberately falsify what was happening in Vietnam and how much needs to be explained in terms of the ideological shortsightedness of U.S. leaders. Symbol at the same time of duplicity and contemptible self-deception, President Johnson was both the perpetrator and the victim of the war. But however we wish to read his motives, the Tet Offensive highlighted the gigantic incompetence and bad faith of U.S. leadership, and cruelly brought into the open the futility of the sacrifices which they had imposed on the American (and the Vietnamese) people. Perhaps more than any batch of Watergate tapes, it undermined the trust which many had once readily accorded national leaders.

Finally, Tet left its mark on the U.S. left. Over the years, we had argued against the Harvard-trained experts, with their seemingly scientific analysis of "modernization," "wars of national liberation," "counter insurgency." But even as we grew to despise the Bundy's, the Rostow's, and the others who defended the war, we were not sure we had the means or the knowledge to articulate a distinctive counter-explanation of events. The Tet Offensive indicated that they had been wrong and we had been right, more right even than we had dared to imagine. It showed that there was a reality which corresponded to the critical bent we were struggling to develop and encouraged us to probe more deeply into the intricacies of a world which U.S. power and its apologists previously seemed to own.

The demystifying character of the Tet Offensive was evident in countless incidents, large and small. Let us take, as an example, one among the many which might serve our purposes, President Johnson's press conference of February 2. According to the *New York Times'* account, Johnson

acknowledged that the Vietcong's simultaneous attacks on cities throughout South Vietnam had disrupted life in many communities and inflicted casualties on civilians. But "a few bandits can do that in any city," he remarked, pointing to the disruptions caused by riots in Detroit and other American communities.

The president himself thus confirmed something we were already beginning to suspect: that there were many similarities between Blacks in U.S. cities and Vietnamese peasants, and we could not help reflecting on his characterization of both these groups as "bandits." We were then also discovering that police violence was largely responsible for the deaths and destruction when people "rioted" in Detroit and Newark, just as U.S. bombs and shells caused most of the damage in Vietnamese cities "attacked" by the NLF. In both cases, revolt was greeted with a savagery designed to "save" a terrain U.S. leaders were unable to control by conventional means. The Tet Offensive was full of such moments of insight, when seemingly scattered events all over the world began to fit into an overall pattern of struggle between U.S. imperialism and its enemies.

More generally, the Tet Offensive made a powerful contribution to the rebuilding of some sort of socialist presence in the United States. For a whole generation of young people, socialism seemed to be the preserve of an isolated, defeated handful. The Cubans had given new life to socialist ideas, and the Cultural Revolution was beginning to bring the Chinese more into focus. Some of us, through family or friends, had been in touch with a more vital and persuasive vision of socialism all along, while others discovered this route in the civil rights movement or other struggles. But by and large leftist politics in 1968 were still moralistic, isolated from working people.

The Vietnamese helped to change all of that, and never more tellingly than with the Tet Offensive. As the insurgents burst into view, "shouting their slogans and fighting with nerve-shattering fury," we realized that they were not just noble victims, but that they were going to win the war. Trying to make sense of the details of the Offensive, we were bowled over by the sheer ingenuity of it, the thrilling spectacle of people performing miraculous feats. Tet brought into focus with blinding clarity just how much human beings are capable of accomplishing. Carried along by the momentum of their endeavor, we wanted to be associated with the Vietnamese revolutionaries (Tet made the NLF flag an emblem) and to figure out how our newly discovered vision of "power to the people" might be realized here in the United States. There was more than a little naivete in these sentiments, but a process had been set in motion, or, where already in motion, greatly speeded along. The Offensive demonstrated that socialism was not just a moral stance or an academic persuasion, but a real possibility embodied in the collective action of real people. On the other side, the capitalist-imperialist power of the United States was not as impregnable as it had seemed, there was hope that we too might discover how to exploit its contradictions and check its aggressions. In a context where it was almost impossible to feel confident about being a revolutionary, the Vietnamese endowed socialism with an aura of heroism and glory. The Tet Offensive made us proud to be socialists, for many, it enabled us truly to be socialists for the first time.

54. The Aftermath of Tet*

From *The Pentagon Papers*

The voluminous Defense Department study known as The Pentagon Papers *ends with analyses of how the Tet Offensive led to the administration's decision not to continue its policy of continuous escalation, but to take some first small steps toward de-escalation and possible negotiations.*

The Offensive seemed to indicate the failure of past and present strategy, a conclusion reinforced by General Westmoreland's request for another 206,000 troops, and the Joint Chiefs of Staff request for a massive escalation of the bombing of North Vietnam. So incoming Secretary of Defense Clark Clifford, replacing the abruptly dismissed McNamara, was charged with preparing an "A to Z Policy Review."

Staggered by the Joint Chiefs of Staff report that "to a large extent the VC now control the countryside" and its own analysts' conclusion that "the enemy's current offensive appears to have killed the [pacification] program once and for all," the Clifford policy study group thrashed around among the "very bleak alternatives for US policy-makers." They recognized that "VC penetration in the cities," as well as in the countryside, "has now gone or will soon go too far for real noncommunist political mobilization to develop." Meanwhile, the international financial crisis developing from the war, together with the insurrections in the cities of a deeply divided nation, meant that the new escalations proposed by the military would run "great risks of provoking a domestic crisis of unprecedented proportions."

Their memorandum, submitted to the President on March 4, 1968, merely recommended a deployment of 22,000 more troops, a Reserve call-up, more studies, and a "reexamination on a week-by-week basis" of more deployments. They also suggested "replacing the Prime Minister" of South Vietnam, a rather blatant statement of the puppet status of the Saigon regime.

Then in mid-March, after Eugene McCarthy's antiwar challenge came close to winning the New Hampshire primary, and with polls showing him a certain winner over President Johnson in the Wisconsin primary, Johnson met with a group of leading designers of the Cold War strategy of global confrontation with communism, some of whom had been key figures in planning and sustaining America's intervention in Vietnam. The so-called "wise men," actually representatives of the financial, industrial, and military circles in whose interests these policies had been arranged, decided almost unanimously "not to expand the war but to attempt a de-escalation." On March 31, President Johnson announced that decision in a nationwide television address, and then added that he would not seek, nor accept, his party's presidential nomination.

---

*From *The Pentagon Papers* (Gravel edition), vol. 4.

This history is covered in two quite separate narratives in volume 4 (Gravel edition) of The Pentagon Papers. *The first narrative comes from that group of the Pentagon historians assigned the task of tracing the history of the air war against Vietnam, the second from the group giving the history of the ground war. Each group attempted to evaluate simultaneously both the history of relevant policy and its success. Each interpolated many documents into its commentaries. Consequently, each narrative is difficult to follow, and trying to derive a coherent history from the two is a truly formidable task. Since both accounts cover the same events leading to those crucial early 1968 decisions, and since both arrive at similar conclusions (that both the air and ground wars had failed), we have decided to intercut sections of both versions to form a single coherent narrative. Page numbers in parentheses refer to volume 4 (Gravel Edition); ellipses (. . . .) indicate omitted material; asterisks (* * *) indicate a transition from one narrative to the other.*

The Corner Is Turned—January–March 1968

The Johnson Administration began 1968 in a mood of cautious hope about the course of the war. Within a month those hopes had been completely dashed. In late January and early February, the Viet Cong and their North Vietnamese supporters launched the massive Tet assault on the cities and towns of South Vietnam and put the Johnson Administration and the American public through a profound political catharsis on the wisdom and purpose of the U.S. involvement in Vietnam and the soundness of our policies for the conduct of the war. The crisis engendered the most soul-searching debate within the Administration about what course to take next in the whole history of the war. In the emotion laden atmosphere of those dark days, there were cries for large-scale escalation on the one side and for significant retrenchment on the other. In the end an equally difficult decision—to stabilize the effort in the South and de-escalate in the North—was made. One of the inescapable conclusions of the Tet experience that helped to shape that decision was that as an interdiction measure against the infiltration of men and supplies, the bombing had been a near total failure. Moreover, it had not succeeded in breaking Hanoi's will to continue the fight. The only other major justification for continuing the bombing was its punitive value, and that began to pale in comparison with the potential (newly perceived by many) of its suspension for producing negotiations with the DRV, or failing that a large propaganda windfall for the U.S. negotiating position. The President's dramatic decision at the end of March capped a long month of debate. Adding force to the President's announcement of the partial bombing halt was his own personal decision not to seek re-election. (P. 232)

*   *   *

The enemy's Tet offensive, which began with the attack on the U.S. Embassy in Saigon on 31 January 1968, although it had been predicted, took the U.S. command and the U.S. public by surprise, and its strength, length, and intensity prolonged this shock. As the attacks continued, the Secretary of Defense, on 9 February, requested the Joint Chiefs of Staff to furnish plans which would provide for emergency reinforcement of COMUSMACV.

After extensive backchannel communication with General Westmoreland, the JCS forwarded these plans on 12 February. The Joint Chiefs' assessment of the current Vietnam situation differed markedly from COMUSMACV's year-end assessment submitted only 17 days earlier:

a. The VC/NVA forces have launched large-scale offensive operations throughout South Vietnam.

b. As of 11 February 1968, Headquarters, MACV, reports that attacks have taken place on 34 provincial towns, 64 district towns, and all of the autonomous cities.

c. The enemy has expressed his intention to continue offensive operations and to destroy the Government of Vietnam and its Armed Forces.

d. The first phase of his offensive has failed in that he does not have adequate control over any population center to install his Revolutionary Committees which he hoped to form into a coalition with the NLF. . . .

i. South Vietnamese forces have suffered nearly two thousand killed, over seven thousand wounded, and an unknown number of absences. MACV suspects the desertion rate may be high. The average present for duty strength of RVN infantry battalions is 50 percent and Ranger Battalions, 43 percent. Five of nine airborne battalions are judged by MACV to be combat ineffective at this time. . . .

In examining the capacity to meet the possibility of widespread civil disorder in the United States, the Joint Chiefs of Staff concluded that, whether or not deployments under any of the plans were directed, it appeared that sufficient forces would still be available for civil disorder control. . . .

. . . the Joint Chiefs emphasized [that] our posture of readily available combat forces was seriously strained. Any decision to deploy emergency augmentation forces should be accompanied by the recall of at least an equivalent number, or more prudently, additional Reserve component forces and an extension of terms of service for active duty personnel. . . .

Thus, for perhaps the first time in the history of American involvement in Vietnam, the Joint Chiefs of Staff recommended against deploying the additional forces requested by the field commander, in the absence of other steps to reconstitute the strategic reserve. At long last, the resources were beginning to be drawn too thin, the assets became unavailable, the support base too small. (Pp. 539–542)

*   *   *

The primary focus of the U.S. reaction to the Tet offensive was . . . another reexamination of force requirements for avoiding defeat or disaster in the South. On February 9, McNamara asked the Chiefs to provide him with their views on what forces General Westmoreland would require for emergency augmentation and where they should come from. The Chiefs replied on February 12 to the startling effect that while the needs in South Vietnam were pressing, indeed perhaps urgent, any further reduction in the strategic reserve in the U.S. would seriously compromise the U.S. force posture worldwide and could not be afforded. They reluctantly recommended deferring the requests of General Westmoreland for an emergency augmentation. Rather, they proposed a callup of reserves to meet both the requirements of Vietnam augmentation in the intermediate future and to bring drawndown forces in the strategic reserve up to strength. The tactic the Chiefs were using was clear: by refusing to scrape the bottom of the barrel any further for Vietnam they hoped to force the President to "bite the bullet" on the callup of the reserves— a step they had long thought essential, and that they were determined would not now be avoided. Their views notwithstanding, the Secretary the next day ordered an emergency force of 10,500 to Vietnam immediately to reconstitute COMUS-MACV's strategic reserve and put out the fire.

With the decision to dispatch, among others, the remainder of the 82nd Airborne Division as an emergency augmentation and its public announcement, the policy process slowed down appreciably for the following ten days. The troops were loaded aboard the aircraft for the flight to Vietnam on February 14 and the President flew to Ft. Bragg to personally say farewell to them. The experience proved for him to be one of the most profoundly moving and troubling of the entire Vietnam war. The men, many of whom had only recently returned from Vietnam, were grim. They were not young men going off to adventure but seasoned veterans returning to an ugly conflict from which they knew some would not return. The film clips of the President shaking hands with the solemn but determined paratroopers on the ramps of their aircraft revealed a deeply troubled leader. He was confronting the men he was asking to make the sacrifice and they displayed no enthusiasm. It may well be that the dramatic decisions of the succeeding month and a half that reversed the direction of American policy in the war had their genesis in those troubled handshakes.

The Reassessment Begins

For roughly ten days, things were quiet in Washington. In Vietnam, the battle for the recapture of the Citadel in Hue raged on until the 24th of February before the last North Vietnamese defenders were overrun. As conditions in South Vietnam sorted themselves out and some semblance of normality returned to the command organizations, MACV began a comprehensive reassessment of his requirements. Aware that this review was going on and that it would result in requests for further troop augmentation, the President sent General Wheeler, the chairman of the JCS to Saigon on February 23 to consult with General Westmoreland and report back on the new situation and its implication for further forces. Wheeler returned from Vietnam on the 25th and filed his report on the 27th. The substance of his and General Westmoreland's recommendations had preceded him to Washington, however, and greatly troubled the President. The military were requesting a major reinforcement of more than 3 divisions and supporting forces totalling in excess of

200,000 men, and were asking for a callup of some 280,000 reservists to fill these requirements and flesh out the strategic reserve and training base at home. The issue was thus squarely joined. To accept the military recommendations would entail not only a full-scale callup of reserves, but also putting the country economically on a semi-war footing, all at a time of great domestic dissent, dissatisfaction, and disillusionment about both the purposes and the conduct of the war. The President was understandably reluctant to take such action, the more so in an election year.

The assessments of North Vietnamese intention, moreover, were not reassuring. The CIA, evaluating a captured document, circulated a report on the same day as General Wheeler's report that stated:

Hanoi's confident assessment of the strength of its position clearly is central to its strategic thinking. Just as it provided the rationale for the Communists' "winter-spring campaign," it probably will also govern the North Vietnamese response to the present tactical situation. If Hanoi believes it is operating from a position of strength, as this analysis suggests, it can be expected to press its military offensive—even at the cost of serious setbacks. Given their view of the strategic balance, it seems doubtful that the Communists would be inclined to settle for limited military gains intended merely to improve their bargaining position for negotiations. (Pp. 238–239)

*   *   *

The Troop Request

In his report, General Wheeler summarized the situation in Vietnam as follows:

—The enemy failed to achieve his initial objective but is continuing his effort. Although many of his units were badly hurt, the judgment is that he has the will and the capability to continue.

—Enemy losses have been heavy; he has failed to achieve his prime objectives of mass uprisings and capture of a large number of the capital cities and towns. Morale in enemy units which were badly mauled or where the men were oversold the idea of a decisive victory at TET probably has suffered severely. However, with replacements, his indoctrination system would seem capable of maintaining morale at a generally adequate level. His determination appears to be unshaken.

—The enemy is operating with relative freedom in the countryside, probably recruiting heavily and no doubt infiltrating NVA units and personnel. His recovery is likely to be rapid; his supplies are adequate; and he is trying to maintain the momentum of his winter-spring offensive.

—The structure of the GVN held up but its effectiveness has suffered.

—The RVNAF held up against the initial assault with gratifying, and in a way, surprising strength and fortitude. However, ARVN is now in a defensive posture around towns and cities and there is concern about how well they will bear up under sustained pressure.

—The initial attack nearly succeeded in a dozen places, and defeat in those places was only averted by the timely reaction of US forces. In short, it was a very near thing.

—There is no doubt that the RD Program has suffered a severe set back.

—RVNAF was not badly hurt physically—they should recover strength and equipment rather quickly (equipment in 2–3 months—strength in 3–6 months). Their problems are more psychological than physical.

—US forces have lost none of their pre-TET capability.

—MACV has three principal problems. First, logistic support north of Danang is marginal owing to weather, enemy interdiction and harassment and the massive deployment of US forces into the DMZ/Hue area. Opening Route 1 will alleviate this problem but takes a substantial troop commitment. Second, the defensive posture of ARVN is permitting the VC to make rapid inroads in the formerly pacified countryside. ARVN, in its own words, is in a dilemma as it cannot afford another enemy thrust into the cities and towns and yet if it remains in a defensive posture against this contingency, the countryside goes by default. MACV is forced to devote much of its troop strength to this problem. Third, MACV has been forced to deploy 50% of all US maneuver battalions into I Corps, to meet the threat there, while enemy synchronizes an attack against Khe Sanh/Hue-Quang Tri with an offensive in the Highlands and around Saigon while keeping the pressure on throughout the remainder of the country. MACV will be hard pressed to meet adequately all threats. Under these circumstances, we must be prepared to accept some reverses.

As to the future, General Wheeler saw the enemy pursuing a strategy of a reinforced offensive in order to enlarge his control throughout the countryside and keep pressure on the government and the allies. The enemy is likely, the Chairman indicated:

To maintain strong threats in the DMZ area, at Khe Sanh, in the highlands, and at Saigon, and to attack in force when conditions seem favorable. He is likely to try to gain control of the country's northern provinces. He will continue efforts to encircle cities and province capitals to isolate and disrupt normal activities, and infiltrate them to create chaos. He will seek maximum attrition of RVNAF elements. Against US forces, he will emphasize attacks by fire on airfields and installations, using assaults and ambushes selectively. His central objective continues to be the destruction of the Government of SVN and its armed forces. As a minimum he hopes to seize sufficient territory and gain control of enough people to support establishment of the groups and committees he proposes for participation in an NLF dominated government. . . .

. . . General Wheeler indicated the following tasks:

(1) *Security of Cities and Government*. MACV recognizes that US forces will be required to reinforce and support RVNAF in the security of cities, towns and government structure. At this time, 10 US battalions are operating in the environs of Saigon. It is clear that this task will absorb a substantial portion of US forces.

(2) *Security in the Countryside*. To a large extent the VC now control the countryside.

Most of the 54 battalions formerly providing security for pacification are now defending district or province towns. MACV estimates that US forces will be required in a number of places to assist and encourage the Vietnamese Army to leave the cities and towns and reenter the country. This is especially true in the Delta.

(3) *Defense of the borders, the DMZ and the northern provinces.* MACV considers that it must meet the enemy threat in I Corps Tactical Zone and has already deployed there slightly over 50% of all US maneuver battalions. US forces have been thinned out in the highlands, notwithstanding an expected enemy offensive in the early future.

(4) *Offensive Operations.* Coupling the increased requirement for the defense of the cities and subsequent reentry into the rural areas, and the heavy requirement for defense of the I Corps Zone, MACV does not have adequate forces at this time to resume the offensive in the remainder of the country, nor does it have adequate reserves against the contingency of simultaneous large-scale enemy offensive action throughout the country.

The conclusion was obvious:

Forces currently assigned to MACV, plus the residual Program Five forces yet to be delivered, are inadequate in numbers and balance to carry out the strategy and to accomplish the tasks described above in the proper priority.

However, it was the extent and magnitude of General Wheeler's request that stimulated the initiation of a thorough review of the direction of U.S. policy in SVN. To contend with, and defeat, the new enemy threat, MACV indicated a total requirement of 206,756 spaces over the 525,000 ceiling imposed by Program Five, or a new proposed ceiling of 731,756. All of these forces, which included three Division equivalents, 15 tactical fighter squadrons, and augmentation for current Navy programs, were to be deployed into country by the end of CY 68. . . . (Pp. 546–548)

*　　　*　　　*

The alternatives for the President, therefore, did not seem very attractive. With such a major decision to make he asked his incoming Secretary of Defense, Clark Clifford, to convene a senior group of advisors from State, Defense, CIA, and the White House and to conduct a complete review of our involvement, reevaluating both the range of aims and the spectrum of means to achieve them. The review was soon tagged the "A to Z Policy Review" or the "Clifford Group Review." (P. 239)

*　　　*　　　*

A fork in the road had been reached. Now the alternatives stood out in stark reality. To accept and meet General Wheeler's request for troops would mean a total U.S. military commitment to SVN—an Americanization of the war, a callup of reserve forces, vastly increased expenditures. To deny the request for troops, or to attempt to again cut it to a size which could be sustained by the thinly stretched active forces, would just as surely signify that an upper limit to the U.S. military commitment in SVN had been reached.

"A to Z" Reassessment

These thoughts were very much on Secretary Clifford's mind during his first meeting on 29 February with the people who were to conduct the reassessment of U.S. strategy. Present, in addition to Clifford, were McNamara, General Taylor, Nitze, [Treasury Secretary Henry] Fowler, Katzenbach, Rostow, Helms, Bundy, [Assistant Secretary of Defense Paul] Warnke, and Habib.[1] Mr. Clifford outlined the task as he had received it from the President. He indicated to the group that he felt that the real problem to be addressed was not whether we should send 200,000 additional troops to Vietnam. The real questions were: Should we follow the present course in SVN; could it ever prove successful even if vastly more than 200,000 troops were sent? The answers to these questions, the formulation of alternative courses open to the U.S., was to be the initial focus of the review. To that end, general assignments were made concerning papers to be written. . . . (P. 549)

[Following are summaries by the Pentagon historians of some of the papers presented for review by the Clifford Group, together with some excerpts from these papers.—eds.]

These CIA assessments, then, painted very bleak alternatives for U.S. policy-makers. If U.S. policy and force levels did not change, there was a high risk that ARVN and the GVN would be seriously weakened, perhaps decisively so. The US would assume the major burden of the war, and the situation would be no better than a standoff. If U.S. forces were increased by as much as 100,000, the Communists would probably be able to introduce sufficient new units in the South to offset this increase. If the U.S. changed its strategy toward greater control over population centers, with or without increased forces, the Communists would adjust their strategy so as to preclude the achievement of U.S. aims. . . . (Pp. 552–553)

Papers were also furnished concerning pacification, costs and probable results of alternative U.S. strategies in South Vietnam, the status of RVNAF, problems of inflation, and data for analysis of strategies. The main thrust of most of these papers was that "more of the same" in South Vietnam would not achieve decisive results and, indeed, would not be satisfactory. The paper on pacification indicated that:

Hamlet Evaluation Systems (HES) reports for CY 1967 indicate that pacification progressed slowly during the first half of 1967, and lost ground in the second half. Most (60%) of the 1967 gain results from accounting type changes to the HES system, not from pacification progress; hamlet additions and deletions, and revised population estimates accounted for half of the January–June increase and all of the June–December increase. In the area that really counts—VC-D-E hamlets rising to A-B-C ratings—we actually suffered a net loss of 10,100 people between June and December 1967.

---

1. The positions of the other men in this list appear later in this Reading.—eds.

Based on General Wheeler's statement in his report to the President, that "to a large extent the VC now control the countryside," the paper concluded that "the enemy's current offensive appears to have killed the program once and for all."

In analyzing the status of RVNAF, the Systems Analysis paper concluded:

Highest priority must be given to getting RVNAF moving. In the short run re-equipping the Vietnamese and helping them regain their combat power insures that we can prevent unnecessary loss should the enemy attack the cities or put pressure there while hitting Khe Sanh. Further, present US force commitments mean that only a recuperated RVNAF will permit release of US units for other missions and accomplish any objectives in pacification. Finally, restoration of security in the cities in conjunction with the National Police is a major new mission for RVNAF which requires forces.

What can we do? There are many indications that the manpower situation is worse than reported. Every effort must be made to determine how many deserters there are and to approach them. Rounding up trained manpower delinquent in returning from Tet will help. . . .

The paper entitled "Alternate Strategies" painted a bleak picture of American failure in Vietnam:

We lost our offensive stance because we never achieved the momentum essential for military victory. Search and Destroy operations can't build this kind of momentum and the RVNAF was not pushed hard enough. We became mesmerized by statistics of known doubtful validity, choosing to place our faith only in the ones that showed progress. We judged the enemy's intentions rather than his capabilities because we trusted captured documents too much. We were not alert to the perils of time lag and spoofing. In short, our setbacks were due to wishful thinking compounded by a massive intelligence collection and/or evaluation failure.

Indeed, in examining U.S. objectives in SVN, the picture of failure was manifest:

Since the original commitment of large US forces in 1965, our stated objectives have been to:

(1) Make it as difficult and costly as possible for NVN to continue effective support of the VC and cause NVN to cease its direction of the VC insurgency.

(While we have raised the price to NVN of aggression and support of the VC, it shows no lack of capability or will to match each new US escalation. Our strategy of attrition has not worked. Adding 206,000 more US men to a force of 525,000, gaining only 27 additional maneuver battalions and 270 tactical fighters at an added cost to the US of $10 billion per year raises the question of who is making it costly from whom.)

(2) Extend GVN dominion, direction and control over SVN.

(This objective can only be achieved by the GVN through its political and economic processes and with the indispensable support of an effective RVNAF. The TET offensive demonstrated not only that the US had not provided an effective shield, it also demonstrated that the GVN and RVNAF had not made real progress in pacification—the essential first step along the road of extending GVN dominion, direction and control.)

(3) Defeat the VC and NVA forces in SVN and force their withdrawal. (The TET offensive proves we were further from this goal than we thought. How much further remains to be seen.)

(4) Deter the Chinese Communists from direct intervention in SEA. (This we have done successfully so far; however, greatly increased U.S. forces may become counterproductive.)

We know that despite a massive influx of 500,000 US troops, 1.2 million tons of bombs a year, 400,000 attack sorties per year, 200,000 enemy KIA in three years, 20,000 US KIA, etc., our control of the countryside and the defense of the urban areas is now essentially at pre-August 1965 levels. We have achieved stalemate at a high commitment. A new strategy must be sought. . . . (Pp. 556–558)

[The next section describes the drafting of the Memorandum forwarded to the President on March 4, including the struggles within the Department of Defense that led to a compromise version. Excerpts from this section follow.—eds.]

This paper began with an assessment of the current situation in South Viet Nam and a discussion of the prospects over the next 10 months. Quoting General Wheeler's report, the draft memorandum indicated that the most important VC goal in the winter-spring offensive was the takeover of the countryside. In many parts of the country, it was stated, they may have already succeeded in achieving this goal.

The "main event" thus is still to come, not in a one-night offensive but in a week-by-week expulsion of GVN presence and influence from the rural areas, showing up on the pacification maps as a "red tide" flowing up to the edges of the province and district towns, and over some of them. . . .

In the new, more dangerous environment to come about in the countryside, and as currently led, motivated, and influenced at the top, ARVN is even *less* likely than before to buckle down to the crucial offensive job of chasing district companies and (with U.S. help) provincial battalions. In that environment, informers will clam up, or be killed; the VC will get more information and cooperation, the GVN less; officials and police will be much less willing to act on information or VC suspects and activities.

The memorandum was even more pessimistic concerning the future direction and abilities of the South Vietnamese Government, and read more into the TET offensive than had been noted there by other observers.

It is unlikely that the GVN will rise to the challenge. It will not move toward a Government of National Union. Current arrests of oppositionists further isolate and discredit it, and possibly foreshadow the emasculation of the Assembly and the undoing of all promising political developments of the past year. Furthermore, it is possible that the recent offensive was facilitated by a newly friendly or apathetic urban environment, and a broad low-level cooperative organization that had not existed on the same scale before. If, in fact, the attacks reflect new VC opportunities and capability in the cities, then the impact of the attacks themselves, the overall military response, and the ineffective GVN political response may still further improve the VC cause in the cities, as well as in the countryside. Even if the political makeup of the GVN should change for the better, it may well be that VC penetration in the cities has now gone or will soon go too far for real non-communist political mobilization to develop. . . .

The current strategy thus can promise no early end to the conflict, nor any success in attriting the enemy or eroding Hanoi's will to fight. Moreover, it would entail substantial costs in South Viet Nam, in the United States, and in the rest of the world.

These substantial costs, the paper indicated, would indeed preclude the attainment of U.S. objectives. In South Vietnam,

. . . the presence of more than 700,000 U.S. military can mean nothing but the total Americanization of the war. There is no sign that ARVN effectiveness will increase, and there will be no pressure from the U.S. or the GVN for ARVN to shape up if the U.S. appears willing to increase its force levels as necessary to maintain a stalemate in the country.

The effect on the GVN would be even more unfortunate. The Saigon leadership shows no signs of a willingness—let alone an ability—to attract the necessary loyalty or support of the people. It is true that the GVN did not totally collapse during TET, but there is not yet anything like an urgent sense of national unity and purpose. A large influx of additional U.S. forces will intensify the belief of the ruling elite that the U.S. will continue to fight its war while it engages in backroom politics and permits widespread corruption. The proposed actions will also generate increased inflation, thereby reducing the effectiveness of the GVN and making corruption harder to control. Reform of the GVN will come only when and if they come to believe that our continued presence in South Viet Nam depends on what the GVN does. Certainly, a U.S. commitment to a substantial troop increase before the GVN commits itself to reform and action can only be counterproductive. Whatever our success on the battlefield, our chances of leaving behind an effective functioning national government when we at last withdraw will be sharply diminished.

In the United States, the effects would be equally unfortunate.

We will have to mobilize reserves, increase our budget by billions, and see U.S. casualties climb to 1,300–1,400 per month. Our balance of payments will be worsened considerably, and we will need a larger tax increase—justified as a war tax, or wage and price controls. . . .

It will be difficult to convince critics that we are not simply destroying South Viet Nam in order to "save" it and that we genuinely want peace talks. This growing disaffection accompanied, as it certainly will be, by increased defiance of the draft and growing unrest in the cities because of the belief that we are neglecting domestic problems, runs great risks of provoking a domestic crisis of unprecedented proportions. . . . (Pp. 561–564)

Recommendation to the President

The Secretary of Defense [in the Memorandum forwarded to the President on March 4] recommended:

1. An immediate decision to deploy to Vietnam an estimated total of 22,000 additional personnel (approximately 60% of which would be combat). An immediate decision to deploy the three tactical fighter squadrons deferred from Program 5 (about 1,000 men). This would be over and above the four battalions (about 3700 men) already planned for deployment in April which in themselves would bring us slightly above the 525,000 authorized level. . . .

2. Either through Ambassador Bunker or through an early visit by Secretary Clifford, a highly forceful approach to the GVN (Thieu and Ky) to get certain key commitments for improvement, tied to our own increased effort and to increased US support for the ARVN. . . .

3. Early approval of a Reserve call-up and an increased end strength adequate to meet the balance of the Westmoreland request and to restore a strategic reserve in the United States, adequate for possible contingencies world-wide. . . .

4. Reservation of the decision to meet the Westmoreland request in full. While we would be putting ourselves in a position to make these additional deployments, the future decision to do so would be contingent upon:

a. Reexamination on a week-by-week basis of the desirability of further deployments as the situation develops;

b. Improved political performance by the GVN and increased contribution in effective military action by the ARVN;

c. The results of a study in depth, to be initiated immediately, of possible new political and strategic guidance for the conduct of US operations in South Vietnam, and of our Vietnamese policy in the context of our world-wide politico-military strategy. . . .

5. No new peace initiative on Vietnam. Re-statement of our terms for peace and certain limited diplomatic actions to dramatize Laos and to focus attention on the total threat to Southeast Asia. . . .

6. A general decision on bombing policy, not excluding future change, but adequate to form a basis for discussion with the Congress on this key aspect. Here your advisers are divided:

a. General Wheeler and others would advocate a substantial extension of targets and authority in and near Hanoi and Haiphong, mining of Haiphong, and naval gunfire up to a Chinese Buffer Zone;

b. Others would advocate a seasonal step-up through the spring, but without these added elements.

In proposing this course of action, the Secretary of Defense indicated that he recognized that there were many negative factors and certain difficulties. Nevertheless, he indicated the belief that this course of action, at least in its essential outline, was urgently required to meet the immediate situation in Vietnam, as well as wider possible contingencies there and elsewhere. . .

Among those things considered essential and feasible, the following actions were listed:

Getting the Government Back into the Countryside—We must win the race to the countryside, go on the offensive, re-establish security in the rural areas, and restore the government's presence in the villages. The ARVN and other security forces must deploy aggressively, the RD cadre must return to their tasks and governmental services reach out from the province capitals. . . .

The Prime Minister—We should solicit Ambassador Bunker's views on the desirability of replacing the Prime Minister. If he is to be replaced we should agree on his successor beforehand, in consultation with Thieu and Ky. . . .

There were many other reasons for conducting a study of our Vietnamese policy in the context of the U.S. worldwide political/military strategy. No matter what the result in Vietnam itself, we will have failed in our purpose, the memorandum stated, if:

a. The war in Vietnam spreads to the point where it is a major conflict leading to direct military confrontation with the USSR and/or China;

b. The war in Vietnam spreads to the point where we are so committed in resources that our other world-wide commitments—especially NATO—are no longer credible;

c. The attitudes of the American people towards "more Vietnams" are such that our other commitments are brought into question as a matter of US will;

d. Other countries no longer wish the US commitment for fear of the consequences to themselves as a battlefield between the East and the West.

In addition, any intensive review should focus on the ability of the GVN and the ARVN to demonstrate significant improvement, both in their ability to win popular support and their willingness to fight aggressively for their own security.

Finally, the memorandum stated:

. . . the striking change in the enemy's tactics, his willingness to commit at least two additional divisions to the fighting in the South over the past few weeks and the obvious and not wholly anticipated strength of the Viet Cong infrastructure, shows that there can be no prospect of a quick military solution to the aggression in South Vietnam. Under these circumstances, we should give intensive study to the development of new strategic guidance to General Westmoreland. This study may show that he should not be expected either to destroy the enemy forces or to rout them completely from South Vietnam. The kind of American commitment that might be required to achieve these military objectives cannot even be estimated. There is no reason to believe that it could be done by an additional 200,000 American troops or double or triple that quantity. . . .

The exact nature of the strategic guidance which should be adopted cannot now be predicted. It should be the subject of a detailed interagency study over the next several weeks. During the progress of the study, discussions of the appropriate strategic guidance and its nature and implications for the extent of our military commitment in South Vietnam should be undertaken with both General Westmoreland and Ambassador Bunker.

Thus, the "A to Z reassessment" of U.S. strategy requested by the President was relegated by the Working Group to a future date. . . .

Tabs G and H, the final Tabs, considered the public affairs problems in dealing with increased U.S. troop commitments to SVN and to the calling up of reserve forces. In dealing with public opinion and with Congress, these Appendices concluded that from a public affairs viewpoint:

Beyond the basic points of establishing that the war is in the national interest, that there is a plan to end it satisfactorily and that we can identify the resources needed to carry out that plan, we must prove:

1. That General Westmoreland needs the additional troops being sent him.
2. That he does not need further additional troops at this time.
3. That the Strategic Reserve does need reconstitution at this time.
4. That the possible need of General Westmoreland for possible future reinforcement is sufficiently important to merit the callup.
5. That there is not a bottomless pit.
6. That the nation still has the resources for the ghetto fight.

Thus, the memorandum forwarded to the President by the Secretary of Defense in response to the Presidential request for an "A to Z reassessment" of our Vietnam policy again represented a compromise. In this case, it was a compromise brought about by differences between the Assistant Secretary of Defense for International Security Affairs and his staff, and the Chairman of the Joint Chiefs of Staff and his officers. Initially, ISA had prepared a draft Presidential memorandum which had indeed reassessed U.S. strategy in SVN, found it faulty, and recommended a new strategy of protecting the "demographic frontier" with basically the U.S. forces presently in-country. The Chairman of the Joint Chiefs of Staff found "fatal flaws" in this strategy, could not accept the implied criticism of past strategy in the ISA proposal, did not think that the Defense Department civilians should be involved in issuing specific guidance to the military field commander, and supported this field commander in his request for the forces required to allow him to "regain the initiative." The compromise reached, of course, was that a decision on new strategic guidance should be deferred pending a complete political/military reassessment of the U.S. strategy and objectives in Vietnam in the context of our worldwide commitments.

The recommendation for additional forces was also a compromise and was based, as had past decisions of this nature, on what could be done by the forces in-being without disrupting the nation. However, there were additional reasons adduced for not meeting all of COMUSMACV's requirements for forces. The situation in SVN was not clear. The ability of the Government and of the Army of South Vietnam to survive and to improve were in serious question. The ability of the U.S. to attain its objectives in SVN by military force of whatever size was not clear. Weighing heavily upon the minds of the senior officials who prepared and approved the 4 March memorandum to the President was, indeed, what difference in the war, what progress toward victory such a buildup as requested by MACV would make. These leaders were, finally, prepared to go a long way down the road in meeting COMUSMACV's request. They recommended to the President that the first increment of this request be met. They also recommended a partial mobilization so as to be prepared to meet additional requirements if and when it was demonstrated that these forces were necessary and would make a strategic difference. More importantly, however, these officials finally came to the realization that no military strategy could be successful unless a South Vietnamese political and military entity was capable of winning the support of its people. Thus, for the first time, U.S. efforts were to be made contingent upon specific reform measures undertaken by the GVN, and U.S. leverage was to be used to elicit these reforms. South Vietnam was to be put on notice that the limit of U.S. patience and commitment had been approached.

Concerning negotiations and the bombing of the North, the Memorandum for the President was conventional. No changes in our negotiating position were recommended and no really new diplomatic initiatives were suggested. Concerning the bombing of the North, the only issue indicated concerned the degree of intensification. There was no mention made of partial reduction or cessation.

Thus, faced with a fork in the road of our Vietnam policy, the Working Group failed to seize the opportunity to change directions. Indeed, they seemed to recommend that we continue rather haltingly down the same road, meanwhile consulting the map more frequently and in greater detail to insure that we were still on the right road. . . .

From the 4th of March until the final Presidential decision was announced to the country, the written record becomes sparse. The debate within the Administration was argued and carried forward on a personal basis by the officials involved, primarily, the Secretary of Defense and the Secretary of State. . . .

. . . many political events in the first few weeks of March 1968 gave strong indications that the country was becoming increasingly divided over and disenchanted with the current Vietnam strategy, and would no longer settle for "more of the same" with no indication of an eventual end to the conflict. That the President was aware of these external political pressures and that they influenced his decision is evident.

Focus to this political debate and sense of dissatisfaction was given by a startlingly accurate account, published in *The New York Times* on 10 March, of General Westmoreland's request and of the strategic reassessment which was being conducted within the executive branch of the government. It also indicated the growing doubt and unease in the nation concerning this policy review. (Pp. 575–585)

*   *   *

The New Hampshire Primary

In the days immediately following the early March deliberations, the President, toiling over the most difficult decision of his career, was faced with another problem of great magnitude—how to handle the public reaction to Tet and the dwindling public support for his war policies. From this point of view probably the most difficult week of the Johnson Presidency began on March 10 when *The New York Times* broke the story of General Westmoreland's 206,000 man troop request in banner headlines. The story was a collaborative effort by four reporters of national reputation and had the kind of detail to give it the ring of authenticity to the reading public. In fact, it was very close to the truth in its account of the proposal from MACV and the debate going on within the Administration. The story was promptly picked up by other newspapers and by day's end had reached from one end of the country to the other. The President was reportedly furious at this leak which amounted to a flagrant and dangerous compromise of security. Later in the month an investigation was conducted to cut down on the possibility of such leaks in the future.

The following day, March 11, Secretary Rusk went before Fulbright's Senate Foreign Relations Committee for the first time in two years for nationally televised hearings on U.S. war policy. In sessions that lasted late that Monday and continued on Tuesday, the Secretary was subjected to sharp questioning by virtually every member. While he confirmed the fact of an "A to Z" policy review within the Administration, he found himself repeatedly forced to answer questions obliquely or not at all to avoid compromising the President. These trying two days of testimony by Secretary Rusk were completed only hours before the results from the New Hampshire primary began to come in. To the shock and consternation of official Washington, the President had defeated his upstart challenger, Eugene McCarthy, who had based his campaign on a halt in the bombing and an end to the war, by only the slenderest of margins. (In fact when the write-in vote was finally tabulated later that week, McCarthy had actually obtained a slight plurality over the President in the popular vote.) The reaction across the country was electric. It was clear that Lyndon Johnson, the master politician, had been successfully challenged, not by an attractive and appealing alternate vote-getter, but by a candidate who had been able to mobilize and focus all the discontent and disillusionment about the war. National politics in the election year 1968 would not be the same thereafter.

Critics of the President's policies in Vietnam in both parties were buoyed by the New Hampshire results. But for Senator Robert Kennedy they posed a particularly acute dilemma. With the President's vulnerability on Vietnam now demonstrated, should Kennedy, his premier political opponent on this and other issues, now throw his hat in the ring? After four days of huddling with his advisers, and first informing both the President and Senator McCarthy, Kennedy announced his candidacy on March 16. For President Johnson, the threat was now real. McCarthy, even in the flush of a New Hampshire victory, could not reasonably expect to unseat the incumbent President. But Kennedy was another matter. The President now faced the prospect of a long and divisive battle for renomination within his own party against a very strong contender, with the albatross of an unpopular war hanging around his neck.

For the moment at least, the President appeared determined. On March 17, he spoke to the National Farmers' Union and said that the trials of American responsibility in Vietnam would demand a period of domestic "austerity" and a "total national effort." Further leaks, however, were undercutting his efforts to picture the Administration as firm and resolute about doing whatever was necessary. On March 17, *The New York Times* had again run a story on the debate within the Administration. This time the story stated that the 206,000 figure would not be approved but that something between 35,000 and 50,000 more troops would be sent to Vietnam, necessitating some selective call-up of reserves. Again the reporters were disturbingly accurate in their coverage. Criticism of the President continued to mount. Spurred by the New Hampshire indications of massive public disaffection with the President's policy, 139 members of the House of Representatives co-authored a resolution calling for a complete reappraisal of U.S. Vietnam policy including a Congressional review. . . .

The "Senior Informal Advisory Group"

At this juncture in mid-March, with the President vacillating as to a course of action, probably the most important influence on his thinking and ultimate decision was exercised by a small group of prominent men outside the Government, known in official Washington as the "Senior Informal Advisory Group." All had at one time or another over the last twenty years served as Presidential advisers. They gathered in Washington at the request of the President on March 18 to be briefed on the latest developments in the war and to offer Mr. Johnson the benefit of their experience in making a tough decision. Stuart Loory of the *Los Angeles Times* in an article in May reported what has been generally considered to be a reliable account of what took place during and after their visit to Washington and what advice they gave the President. The story as Loory reported it is included here in its entirety.

Hawks' Shift Precipitated Bombing Halt

Eight prominent hawks and a dove—all from outside the government—gathered in the White House for a night and day last March to judge the progress of the Vietnam war for President Johnson.

Their deliberations produced this verdict for the chief executive:

Continued escalation of the war—intensified bombing of North Vietnam and increased American troop strength in the South—would do no good. Forget about seeking a battlefield solution to the problem and instead intensify efforts to seek a political solution at the negotiating table.

The manner in which Mr. Johnson sought the advice of the nine men before arriving at the conclusion to de-escalate the war announced in his now famous March 31 speech, has been pieced together from conversations with reliable sources who asked to remain anonymous.

The nine men, Republicans and Democrats with extensive experience in formulating foreign policy, were among those frequently consulted by Mr. Johnson from time to time during the war. At each consultation prior to March they had been overwhelmingly in favor of prosecuting the war vigorously with more men and material, with intensified bombing of North Vietnam, with increased efforts to create a viable government in the South.

As recently as last December they had expressed this view to the President. The only dissenter among them—one who had been a dissenter from the beginning—was former Undersecretary of State George Ball.

March 18th Meeting

The men who have come to be known to a small circle in the government as the President's "senior informal advisory group" convened in the White House early on the evening of March 18th.

Present in addition to Ball were: Arthur Dean, a Republican New York lawyer who was a Korean War negotiator during the Eisenhower administration; Dean Acheson, former President Truman's Secretary of State; Gen. Matthew B. Ridgeway, the retired commander of United Nations troops in Korea; Gen. Maxwell Taylor, former Chairman of the Joint Chiefs of Staff; Cyrus Vance, former Deputy Defense Secretary and a key troubleshooter for the Johnson Administration; McGeorge Bundy, Ford Foundation President who had been special assistant for National security affairs to Mr. Johnson and former President Kennedy; former Treasury Secretary C. Douglas Dillon and Gen. Omar Bradley, a leading supporter of the President's war policies.

First the group met over dinner with Secretary of State Dean Rusk; Defense Secretary Clark M. Clifford; Ambassador W. Averell Harriman; Walt W. Rostow, the President's special assistant for National security affairs; Gen. Earle G. Wheeler, Chairman of the Joint Chiefs of Staff; Richard Helms, Director of the Central Intelligence Agency; Paul Nitze, Deputy Defense Secretary; Nicholas Katzenbach, Undersecretary of State; and William P. Bundy, Assistant Secretary of State for East Asian and Pacific Affairs.

The outsiders questioned the government officials carefully on the war, the pacification program and the condition of the South Vietnamese government after the Tet offensive. They included in their deliberations the effect of the war on the United States.

Three Briefings

After dinner the government officials left and the group received three briefings.

Philip C. Habib, a deputy to William Bundy and now a member of the American negotiating team in Paris, delivered an unusually frank briefing on the conditions in Vietnam after the Tet offensive. He covered such matters as corruption in South Vietnam and the growing refugee problem.

Habib, according to reliable sources, told the group that the Saigon government was generally weaker than had been realized as a result of the Tet offensive. He related the situation, some said, with greater frankness than the group had previously heard.

In addition to Habib, Maj. Gen. William E. DePuy, special assistant to the Joint Chiefs for counterinsurgency and special activities, briefed the group on the military situation, and George Carver, a CIA analyst, gave his agency's estimates of conditions in the war zone.

The briefings by DePuy and Carver reflected what many understood as a dispute over enemy strength between the Defense Department and the CIA which has been previously reported. Discrepancies in the figures resulted from the fact that DePuy's estimates of enemy strength covered only identifiable military units, while Carver's included all known military, paramilitary and parttime enemy strength available.

Striking Turnabout

The morning of March 19, the advisory group assembled in the White House to discuss what they had heard the previous evening and arrived at their verdict. It was a striking turnabout in attitude for all but Ball.

After their meeting, the group met the President for lunch. It was a social affair. No business was transacted. The meal finished, the advisers delivered their verdict to the President.

He was reportedly greatly surprised at their conclusions. When he asked them where they had obtained the facts on which the conclusions were based, the group told him of the briefings by Habib, DePuy and Carver.

Mr. Johnson knew that the three men had also briefed his governmental advisers, but he had not received the same picture of the war as Rostow presented the reports to him.

As a result of the discrepancy, the President ordered his own direct briefings. At least Habib and DePuy—and almost certainly Carver—had evening sessions with the President.

Habib was reportedly as frank with the President as he had been with the advisory group. The President asked tough questions. "Habib stuck to his guns," one source reported.

On top of all this, Clifford, since he had become Defense Secretary, came to the same conclusions Robert S. McNamara had reached—that the bombing of North Vietnam was not achieving its objectives.

The impact of this group's recommendation coupled with the new briefings the President received about conditions and prospects in the war zone were major factors in cementing the decision not to expand the war but to attempt a de-escalation. . . .

March 31—"I Shall Not Seek . . . Another Term as Your President."

No exact date on which the President made the decision to curtail the bombing can be identified with certainty. It is reasonably clear that the decisions on the ground war were made on or before March 22. On that date, the President announced that General William Westmoreland would be replaced as COMUS-MACV during the coming summer. He was to return to Washington to become Chief of Staff of the Army. The decision was clearly related to the force deployment decisions explicitly taken and the new strategy they implied. Three days after this announcement, that had been greeted in the press as a harbinger, General Creighton Abrams, Deputy COMUSMACV, arrived in Washington without prior announcement for conferences with the President. Speculation was rife that he was to be named Westmoreland's successor. On the 26th he and the President huddled and Mr. Johnson probably informed him of his intentions, both with respect to force augmentations and the bombing restraint, and his intention to designate Abrams the new COMUSMACV. In the days that followed, the speech drafters took over, writing and rewriting the President's momentous address. Finally, it was decided that the announcement speech would be made on nation-wide television from the White House on the evening of March 31. . . .

The speech had an electric effect on the U.S. and the whole world. It completely upset the American political situation, spurred world-wide hopes that peace might be imminent and roused fear and concern in South Vietnam about the depth and reliability of the American commitment. As already noted, no one in the Administration had seriously expected a positive reaction from Hanoi, and when the North Vietnamese indicated three days later that they would open direct contacts with the U.S. looking toward discussions and eventual negotiation of a peaceful settlement of the conflict, the whole complexion and context of the war was changed. To be sure, there was the unfortunate and embarrassing wrangle about exactly where the northern limit of the U.S. bombing would be fixed, with CINC-PAC having sent extremely heavy sorties to the very limits of the 20th parallel on the day after the announcement only to be subsequently ordered to restrict his attacks below 19° on April 3. And there was the exasperatingly long public struggle between the U.S. and the DRV about where their representatives would meet and what title the contacts would be given, not finally resolved until May. But it was unmistakably clear throughout all this time that a major corner in the war and in American policy had been turned and that there was no going back. The President's decision was enormously well received at home and greeted with enthusiasm abroad where it appeared at long last there was a possibility of removing this annoyingly persistent little war in Asia as a roadblock to progress on other matters of worldwide importance involving East and West.

The President's speech at the end of March was, of course, not the end of the bombing much less the war, and a further history of the role of the limited air strikes could and should be undertaken. But the decision to cut back the bombing, the decision that turned American policy toward a peaceful settlement of the war, is a logical and fitting place to terminate this particular inquiry into the policy process that surrounded the air war. Henceforth, the decisions about the bombing would be made primarily in the Pacific by the field commanders since no vitally sensitive targets requiring continuing Washington level political review were within the reduced attack zone. A very significant chapter in the history of U.S. involvement in the Vietnam war had come to a close.[2] (Pp. 262–275)

*   *   *

In March of 1968, the choice had become clear-cut. The price for military victory had increased vastly, and there was no assurance that it would not grow again in the future. There were also strong indications that large and growing elements of the American public had begun to believe the cost had already reached unacceptable levels and would strongly protest a large increase in that cost.

The political reality which faced President Johnson was that "more of the same" in South Vietnam, with an increased commitment of American lives and money and its consequent impact on the country, accompanied by no guarantee of

---

2. In fact, the air war reached unprecedented extremes after this optimistic conclusion was written and published. See Part Eight.—eds.

military victory in the near future, had become unacceptable to these elements of the American public. The optimistic military reports of progress in the war no longer rang true after the shock of the TET offensive.

Thus, the President's decision to seek a new strategy and a new road to peace was based upon two major considerations:

(1) The convictions of his principal civilian advisers, particularly Secretary of Defense Clifford, that the troops requested by General Westmoreland would not make a military victory any more likely; and

(2) A deeply-felt conviction of the need to restore unity to the American nation.

For a policy from which so little was expected, a great deal was initiated. The North Vietnamese and the Americans sat down at the conference table in Paris to begin to travel the long road to peace; the issue of Vietnam largely was removed from American political discord; a limit to the commitment of U.S. forces was established; and the South Vietnamese were put on notice that, with our help, they would be expected to do more in their own defense.

The "A to Z" reassessment of U.S. strategy in South Vietnam in the wake of the TET offensive did not result in the announcement of a new ground strategy for South Vietnam. But in placing General Westmoreland's request for forces squarely in the context of the achievement of U.S. political-military objectives in South Vietnam, the limited political nature of those objectives was for the first time affirmed. A new ground strategy, based on these limited objectives and upon the ceiling on U.S. troops became a corollary for the new U.S. commander.

American forces initially were deployed to Vietnam in order to prevent the South Vietnamese from losing the war, to insure that aggression from the north would not succeed. Having deployed enough troops to insure that NVN aggression would not succeed, it had been almost a reflex action to start planning on how much it would take to "win" the war. Lip service was given to the need for developing South Vietnamese political institutions, but no one at high levels seemed to question the assumption that U.S. political objectives in South Vietnam could be attained through military victory.

However, it was quickly apparent that there was an embarrassing lack of knowledge as to how much it would take to win the war. This stemmed from uncertainty in two areas: (1) how much effort the North Vietnamese were willing to expend in terms of men and materiel; and (2) how effective the South Vietnamese armed forces would be in establishing security in the countryside. As the war progressed, it appeared that our estimates of the former were too low and of the latter too high. However, committed to a military victory and having little information as to what was needed militarily, the civilian decision makers seemed willing to accept the field commander's estimate of what was needed. Steady progress was promised and was apparently being accomplished, although the commitment of forces steadily increased.

The TET offensive showed that this progress in many ways had been illusory. The possibility of military victory had seemingly become remote and the cost had become too high both in political and economic terms. Only then were our ultimate objectives brought out and re-examined. Only then was it realized that a clear-cut military victory was probably not possible or necessary, and that the road to peace would be at least as dependent upon South Vietnamese political development as it would be on American arms. This realization, then, made it possible to limit the American military commitment to South Vietnam to achieve the objectives for which this force had originally been deployed. American forces would remain in South Vietnam to prevent defeat of the Government by Communist forces and to provide a shield behind which that Government could rally, become effective, and win the support of its people.[3] (pp. 603–604)

55. "Peace in Vietnam and Southeast Asia": Address to the Nation (March 31, 1968)*

By President Lyndon Baines Johnson

This speech, in which President Johnson announced the curtailment of the bombing of North Vietnam and his decision not to seek reelection, is often considered the beginning of the end of America's war in Vietnam. For the background, see the previous Readings in this section.

Good evening, my fellow Americans:

Tonight I want to speak to you of peace in Vietnam and Southeast Asia.

No other question so preoccupies our people. No other dream so absorbs the 250 million human beings who live in that part of the world. No other goal motivates American policy in Southeast Asia.

For years, representatives of our Government and others have traveled the world—seeking to find a basis for peace talks.

Since last September, they have carried the offer that I made public at San Antonio.

That offer was:

That the United States would stop its bombardment of North Vietnam when that would lead promptly to productive discussions—and that we would assume that North Vietnam would not take military advantage of our restraint.

Hanoi denounced this offer, both privately and publicly. Even while the search

---

3. In the light of subsequent events, this conclusion, along with the assertion above that "the issue of Vietnam largely was removed from American political discord," reads like wishful thinking. See Part Eight for the history of what actually happened in the ensuing seven years.—eds.

*From *Public Papers of the Presidents of the United States, 1968–1969* (Washington: U.S. Government Printing Office, 1970), pp. 468–476.

for peace was going on, North Vietnam rushed their preparations for a savage assault on the people, the government, and the allies of South Vietnam.

Their attack—during the Tet holidays—failed to achieve its principal objectives.

It did not collapse the elected government of South Vietnam or shatter its army—as the Communists had hoped.

It did not produce a "general uprising" among the people of the cities as they had predicted.

The Communists were unable to maintain control of any of the more than 30 cities that they attacked. And they took very heavy casualties.

But they did compel the South Vietnamese and their allies to move certain forces from the countryside into the cities.

They caused widespread disruption and suffering. Their attacks, and the battles that followed, made refugees of half a million human beings.

The Communists may renew their attack any day.

They are, it appears, trying to make 1968 the year of decision in South Vietnam—the year that brings, if not final victory or defeat, at least a turning point in the struggle.

This much is clear:

If they do mount another round of heavy attacks, they will not succeed in destroying the fighting power of South Vietnam and its allies.

But tragically, this is also clear: Many men—on both sides of the struggle—will be lost. A nation that has already suffered 20 years of warfare will suffer once again. Armies on both sides will take new casualties. And the war will go on.

There is no need for this to be so.

There is no need to delay the talks that could bring an end to this long and this bloody war.

Tonight, I renew the offer I made last August—to stop the bombardment of North Vietnam. We ask that talks begin promptly, that they be serious talks on the substance of peace. We assume that during those talks Hanoi will not take advantage of our restraint.

We are prepared to move immediately toward peace through negotiations.[1]

So, tonight, in the hope that this action will lead to early talks, I am taking the first step to deescalate the conflict. We are reducing—substantially reducing—the present level of hostilities.

And we are doing so unilaterally, and at once.

Tonight, I have ordered our aircraft and our naval vessels to make no attacks on North Vietnam, except in the area north of the demilitarized zone where the continuing enemy buildup directly threatens allied forward positions and where the movements of their troops and supplies are clearly related to that threat.

---

1. The DRV surprised the United States by accepting this proposal for negotiations. Formal talks between the DRV and the United States opened in Paris on May 13, 1968.—eds.

The area in which we are stopping our attacks includes almost 90 percent of North Vietnam's population, and most of its territory. Thus there will be no attacks around the principal populated areas or in the food-producing areas of North Vietnam.

Even this very limited bombing of the North could come to an early end—if our restraint is matched by restraint in Hanoi. But I cannot in good conscience stop all bombing so long as to do so would immediately and directly endanger the lives of our men and our allies. Whether a complete bombing halt becomes possible in the future will be determined by events.[2]

Our purpose in this action is to bring about a reduction in the level of violence that now exists.

It is to save the lives of brave men—and to save the lives of innocent women and children. It is to permit the contending forces to move closer to a political settlement.

And tonight, I call upon the United Kingdom and I call upon the Soviet Union—as cochairmen of the Geneva Conferences, and as permanent members of the United Nations Security Council—to do all they can to move from the unilateral act of deescalation that I have just announced toward genuine peace in Southeast Asia.

Now, as in the past, the United States is ready to send its representatives to any forum, at any time, to discuss the means of bringing this ugly war to an end.

I am designating one of our most distinguished Americans, Ambassador Averell Harriman, as my personal representative for such talks. In addition, I have asked Ambassador Llewellyn Thompson, who returned from Moscow for consultation, to be available to join Ambassador Harriman at Geneva or any other suitable place—just as soon as Hanoi agrees to a conference.

I call upon President Ho Chi Minh to respond positively, and favorably, to this new step toward peace.

But if peace does not come now through negotiations, it will come when Hanoi understands that our common resolve is unshakable, and our common strength is invincible.

Tonight, we and the other allied nations are contributing 600,000 fighting men to assist 700,000 South Vietnamese troops in defending their little country.

Our presence there has always rested on this basic belief: The main burden of preserving their freedom must be carried out by them—by the South Vietnamese themselves.

We and our allies can only help to provide a shield behind which the people of South Vietnam can survive and can grow and develop. On their efforts—on their determination and resourcefulness—the outcome will ultimately depend.

That small, beleaguered nation has suffered terrible punishment for more than 20 years.

---

2. On October 31, 1968, a few days before the US presidential election, Johnson announced that the United States would halt all air, naval, and artillery bombardment of North Vietnam. The bombing, however, was not completely stopped (see Reading 58, fn. 10).—eds.

I pay tribute once again tonight to the great courage and endurance of its people. South Vietnam supports armed forces tonight of almost 700,000 men—I call your attention to the fact that this is the equivalent of more than 10 million in our own population. Its people maintain their firm determination to be free of domination by the North.

There has been substantial progress, I think, in building a durable government during these last 3 years. The South Vietnam of 1965 could not have survived the enemy's Tet offensive of 1968. The elected government of South Vietnam survived that attack—and is rapidly repairing the devastation that it wrought.

The South Vietnamese know that further efforts are going to be required:

—to expand their own armed forces,

—to move back into the countryside as quickly as possible,

—to increase their taxes,

—to select the very best men that they have for civil and military responsibility,

—to achieve a new unity within their constitutional government, and

—to include in the national effort all those groups who wish to preserve South Vietnam's control over its own destiny.

Last week President Thieu ordered the mobilization of 135,000 additional South Vietnamese. He plans to reach—as soon as possible—a total military strength of more than 800,000 men.

To achieve this, the Government of South Vietnam started the drafting of 19-year-olds on March 1st. On May 1st, the Government will begin the drafting of 18-year-olds.

Last month, 10,000 men volunteered for military service—that was two and a half times the number of volunteers during the same month last year. Since the middle of January, more than 48,000 South Vietnamese have joined the armed forces—and nearly half of them volunteered to do so.

All men in the South Vietnamese armed forces have had their tours of duty extended for the duration of the war, and reserves are now being called up for immediate active duty.

President Thieu told his people last week:

"We must make greater efforts and accept more sacrifices because, as I have said many times, this is our country. The existence of our nation is at stake, and this is mainly a Vietnamese responsibility."

He warned his people that a major national effort is required to root out corruption and incompetence at all levels of government.

We applaud this evidence of determination on the part of South Vietnam. Our first priority will be to support their effort.

We shall accelerate the reequipment of South Vietnam's armed forces—in order to meet the enemy's increased firepower. This will enable them progressively to undertake a larger share of combat operations against the Communist invaders.

On many occasions I have told the American people that we would send to Vietnam those forces that are required to accomplish our mission there. So, with that as our guide, we have previously authorized a force level of approximately 525,000.

Some weeks ago—to help meet the enemy's new offensive—we sent to Vietnam about 11,000 additional Marine and airborne troops. They were deployed by air in 48 hours, on an emergency basis. But the artillery, tank, aircraft, medical, and other units that were needed to work with and to support these infantry troops in combat could not then accompany them by air on that short notice.

In order that these forces may reach maximum combat effectiveness, the Joint Chiefs of Staff have recommended to me that we should prepare to send—during the next 5 months—support troops totaling approximately 13,500 men.

A portion of these men will be made available from our active forces. The balance will come from reserve component units which will be called up for service.

The actions that we have taken since the beginning of the year

—to reequip the South Vietnamese forces,

—to meet our responsibilities in Korea, as well as our responsibilities in Vietnam,

—to meet price increases and the cost of activating and deploying reserve forces,

—to replace helicopters and provide the other military supplies we need, all of these actions are going to require additional expenditures.

The tentative estimate of those additional expenditures is $2.5 billion in this fiscal year, and $2.6 billion in the next fiscal year.

These projected increases in expenditures for our national security will bring into sharper focus the Nation's need for immediate action: action to protect the prosperity of the American people and to protect the strength and the stability of our American dollar.

On many occasions I have pointed out that, without a tax bill or decreased expenditures, next year's deficit would again be around $20 billion. I have emphasized the need to set strict priorities in our spending. I have stressed that failure to act and to act promptly and decisively would raise very strong doubts throughout the world about America's willingness to keep its financial house in order.

Yet Congress has not acted. And tonight we face the sharpest financial threat in the postwar era—a threat to the dollar's role as the keystone of international trade and finance in the world.

Last week, at the monetary conference in Stockholm, the major industrial countries decided to take a big step toward creating a new international monetary asset that will strengthen the international monetary system. I am very proud of the very able work done by Secretary Fowler and Chairman Martin of the Federal Reserve Board.

But to make this system work the United States just must bring its balance of payments to—or very close to—equilibrium. We must have a responsible fiscal policy in this country. The passage of a tax bill now, together with expenditure control that the Congress may desire and dictate, is absolutely necessary to protect this Nation's security, to continue our prosperity, and to meet the needs of our people.

What is at stake is 7 years of unparalleled prosperity. In those 7 years, the real income of the average American, after taxes, rose by almost 30 percent—a gain as large as that of the entire preceding 19 years.

So the steps that we must take to convince the world are exactly the steps we must take to sustain our own economic strength here at home. In the past 8 months, prices and interest rates have risen because of our inaction.

We must, therefore, now do everything we can to move from debate to action—from talking to voting. There is, I believe—I hope there is—in both Houses of the Congress—a growing sense of urgency that this situation just must be acted upon and must be corrected.

My budget in January was, we thought, a tight one. It fully reflected our evaluation of most of the demanding needs of this Nation.

But in these budgetary matters, the President does not decide alone. The Congress has the power and the duty to determine appropriations and taxes.

The Congress is now considering our proposals and they are considering reductions in the budget that we submitted.

As part of a program of fiscal restraint that includes the tax surcharge, I shall approve appropriate reductions in the January budget when and if Congress so decides that that should be done.

One thing is unmistakably clear, however: Our deficit just must be reduced. Failure to act could bring on conditions that would strike hardest at those people that all of us are trying so hard to help.

These times call for prudence in this land of plenty. I believe that we have the character to provide it, and tonight I plead with the Congress and with the people to act promptly to serve the national interest, and thereby serve all of our people.

Now let me give you my estimate of the chances for peace:

—the peace that will one day stop the bloodshed in South Vietnam,

—that will permit all the Vietnamese people to rebuild and develop their land,

—that will permit us to turn more fully to our own tasks here at home.

I cannot promise that the initiative that I have announced tonight will be completely successful in achieving peace any more than the 30 others that we have undertaken and agreed to in recent years.

But it is our fervent hope that North Vietnam, after years of fighting that have left the issue unresolved, will now cease its efforts to achieve a military victory and will join with us in moving toward the peace table.

And there may come a time when South Vietnamese—on both sides—are able to work out a way to settle their own differences by free political choice rather than by war.

As Hanoi considers its course, it should be in no doubt of our intentions. It must not miscalculate the pressures within our democracy in this election year.

We have no intention of widening this war.

But the United States will never accept a fake solution to this long and arduous struggle and call it peace.

No one can foretell the precise terms of an eventual settlement.

Our objective in South Vietnam has never been the annihilation of the enemy. It has been to bring about a recognition in Hanoi that its objective—taking over the South by force—could not be achieved.

We think that peace can be based on the Geneva Accords of 1954—under political conditions that permit the South Vietnamese—all the South Vietnamese—to chart their course free of any outside domination or interference, from us or from anyone else.

So tonight I reaffirm the pledge that we made at Manila—that we are prepared to withdraw our forces from South Vietnam as the other side withdraws its forces to the north, stops the infiltration, and the level of violence thus subsides.

Our goal of peace and self-determination in Vietnam is directly related to the future of all of Southeast Asia—where much has happened to inspire confidence during the past 10 years. We have done all that we knew how to do to contribute and to help build that confidence.

A number of its nations have shown what can be accomplished under conditions of security. Since 1966, Indonesia, the fifth largest nation in all the world, with a population of more than 100 million people, has had a government that is dedicated to peace with its neighbors and improved conditions for its own people. Political and economic cooperation between nations has grown rapidly.

I think every American can take a great deal of pride in the role that we have played in bringing this about in Southeast Asia. We can rightly judge—as responsible Southeast Asians themselves do—that the progress of the past 3 years would have been far less likely—if not completely impossible—if America's sons and others had not made their stand in Vietnam.

At Johns Hopkins University, about 3 years ago, I announced that the United States would take part in the great work of developing Southeast Asia, including the Mekong Valley, for all the people of that region. Our determination to help build a better land—a better land for men on both sides of the present conflict—has not diminished in the least. Indeed, the ravages of war, I think, have made it more urgent than ever.

So, I repeat on behalf of the United States again tonight what I said at Johns Hopkins—that North Vietnam could take its place in this common effort just as soon as peace comes.

Over time, a wider framework of peace and security in Southeast Asia may become possible. The new cooperation of the nations of the area could be a foundation-stone. Certainly friendship with the nations of such a Southeast Asia is what the United States seeks—and that is all that the United States seeks.

One day, my fellow citizens, there will be peace in Southeast Asia.

It will come because the people of Southeast Asia want it—those whose armies are at war tonight, and those who, though threatened, have thus far been spared.

Peace will come because Asians were willing to work for it—and to sacrifice for it—and to die by the thousands for it.

But let it never be forgotten: Peace will come also because America sent her sons to help secure it.

It has not been easy—far from it. During the past 4½ years, it has been my fate and my responsibility to be Commander in Chief. I have lived—daily and nightly—with the cost of this war. I know the pain that it has inflicted. I know, perhaps better than anyone, the misgivings that it has aroused.

Throughout this entire, long period, I have been sustained by a single principle: that what we are doing now, in Vietnam, is vital not only to the security of Southeast Asia, but it is vital to the security of every American.

Surely we have treaties which we must respect. Surely we have commitments that we are going to keep. Resolutions of the Congress testify to the need to resist aggression in the world and in Southeast Asia.

But the heart of our involvement in South Vietnam—under three different Presidents, three separate administrations—has always been America's own security.

And the larger purpose of our involvement has always been to help the nations of Southeast Asia become independent and stand alone, self-sustaining, as members of a great world community—at peace with themselves, and at peace with all others.

With such an Asia, our country—and the world—will be far more secure than it is tonight.

I believe that a peaceful Asia is far nearer to reality because of what America has done in Vietnam. I believe that the men who endure the dangers of battle—fighting there for us tonight—are helping the entire world avoid far greater conflicts, far wider wars, far more destruction, than this one.

The peace that will bring them home someday will come. Tonight I have offered the first in what I hope will be a series of mutual moves toward peace.

I pray that it will not be rejected by the leaders of North Vietnam. I pray that they will accept it as a means by which the sacrifices of their own people may be ended. And I ask your help and your support, my fellow citizens, for this effort to reach across the battlefield toward an early peace.

Finally, my fellow Americans, let me say this:

Of those to whom much is given, much is asked. I cannot say and no man could say that no more will be asked of us.

Yet, I believe that now, no less than when the decade began, this generation of Americans is willing to "pay any price, bear any burden, meet any hardship, support any friend, oppose any foe to assure the survival and the success of liberty."

Since those words were spoken by John F. Kennedy, the people of America have kept that compact with mankind's noblest cause.

And we shall continue to keep it.

Yet, I believe that we must always be mindful of this one thing, whatever the trials and the tests ahead. The ultimate strength of our country and our cause will lie not in powerful weapons or infinite resources or boundless wealth, but will lie in the unity of our people.

This I believe very deeply.

Throughout my entire public career I have followed the personal philosophy that I am a free man, an American, a public servant, and a member of my party, in that order always and only.

For 37 years in the service of our Nation, first as a Congressman, as a Senator, and as Vice President, and now as your President, I have put the unity of the people first. I have put it ahead of any divisive partisanship.

And in these times as in times before, it is true that a house divided against itself by the spirit of faction, of party, of region, of religion, of race, is a house that cannot stand.

There is division in the American house now. There is divisiveness among us all tonight. And holding the trust that is mine, as President of all the people, I cannot disregard the peril to the progress of the American people and the hope and the prospect of peace for all peoples.

So, I would ask all Americans, whatever their personal interests or concern, to guard against divisiveness and all its ugly consequences.

Fifty-two months and 10 days ago, in a moment of tragedy and trauma, the duties of this office fell upon me. I asked then for your help and God's, that we might continue America on its course, binding up our wounds, healing our history, moving forward in new unity, to clear the American agenda and to keep the American commitment for all of our people.

United we have kept that commitment. United we have enlarged that commitment.

Through all time to come, I think America will be a stronger nation, a more just society, and a land of greater opportunity and fulfillment because of what we have all done together in these years of unparalleled achievement.

Our reward will come in the life of freedom, peace, and hope that our children will enjoy through ages ahead.

What we won when all of our people united just must not now be lost in suspicion, distrust, selfishness, and politics among any of our people.

Believing this as I do, I have concluded that I should not permit the Presidency to become involved in the partisan divisions that are developing in this political year.

With America's sons in the fields far away, with America's future under challenge right here at home, with our hopes and the world's hopes for peace in the balance every day, I do not believe that I should devote an hour or a day of my time to any personal partisan causes or to any duties other than the awesome duties of this office—the Presidency of your country.

Accordingly, I shall not seek, and I will not accept, the nomination of my party for another term as your President.

But let men everywhere know, however, that a strong, a confident, and a vigilant America stands ready tonight to seek an honorable peace—and stands ready tonight to defend an honored cause—whatever the price, whatever the burden, whatever the sacrifice that duty may require.

Thank you for listening.

Good night and God bless all of you.

56. What Happened at My Lai?*

By Seymour M. Hersh

How many NLF combatants and cadre were killed during and after the Tet Offensive? How many of those corpses in the "body count" were actually "enemy" dead? Since the NLF was so integral to the population, how could one distinguish between combatants and civilians, living or dead? Who, after all, was the "enemy"?

These questions, so agonizing for many US servicemen, are still at the heart of critical controversies about the war. For example, arguments that the United States "won" the Tet campaign depend heavily on the "kill ratio" and the belief that the NLF suffered heavy percentage losses. An opposing view holds that killing tens of thousands of civilians hardly constitutes a military "victory."

Estimates of "enemy" dead fluctuated wildly in 1968. As Newsweek *put it on February 26, 1968:*

The Pentagon is now giving out a figure of more than 30,000 killed during the first-wave Tet offensive in Vietnam. But the actual number of Viet Cong and North Vietnamese regulars killed has been scaled down drastically to about 7,000. Reasons for the inflated figure: first, many of the bodies were counted more than once; second, the original body count included such paramilitary types as ammunition bearers, political workers, part-time guerrillas—and Vietnamese civilians.

As The Pentagon Papers *note (Reading 54), the Tet Offensive destroyed the Pacification program and left most of the countryside under NLF control. The United States counterattack in the countryside was a systematic campaign of mass killing aimed at large segments of the rural population. It took three main forms: (1) massive assaults from the air, including saturation bombing by B–52s and concentrated napalm strikes by fighter bombers; (2) systematic destruction of villages by ground troops; (3) the Phoenix program of mass arrests, torture, and assassination coordinated by the CIA.*

President Johnson's halt of bombing over most of North Vietnam was important to the first mode; the full fury of Air Force and Navy air power, from Guam to Thailand, from South Vietnam to the carriers in the Gulf of Tonkin, could concentrate on the rural areas of South Vietnam.

The Phoenix program alone added many thousands to the "enemy" dead. In a speech broadcast over Saigon Radio on December 31, 1968, President Thieu boasted that the Phoenix program, which had just begun in the middle of that year, had already killed 18,393 Communist cadre.[1] When a US congressional committee

---

*From Seymour M. Hersh, *My Lai 4: A Report on the Massacre and Its Aftermath* (New York: Random House, 1970), pp. 48–75.
   1. George Kahin and John W. Lewis, *The United States in Vietnam*, Rev. Ed. (New York: Delta Books, 1969), p. 392n.

called witnesses in 1971, they heard blood-curdling testimony of almost random kidnapping, torture, and murder from former American intelligence operatives in the program. One of those testified:

I will say this: individually I never knew an individual to be detained as a VC suspect who ever lived through an interrogation in a year and a half, and that included quite a number of individuals. . . . They all died. There was never any reasonable establishment of the fact that any one of those individuals was, in fact, cooperating with the Vietcong, but they all died and the majority were either tortured to death or things like thrown from helicopters.[2]

Intelligence gathered during interrogation was often used to direct "search and destroy" missions aimed at wiping out whole villages, or groups of villages. In some areas where the population was believed to support the NLF strongly, entire provinces were subjected to campaigns of destruction and mass killing. Thus by late 1967, even before the Tet Offensive, 70 percent of the villages in Quang Ngai province had already been destroyed.[3]

In response to Tet, this slaughter was intensified literally with a vengeance. In mid-March of 1968, Quang Ngai province was the scene of what was to become one of the most notorious examples: the massacre of the villagers in My Lai 4. There the killing of hundreds of unarmed civilians, almost all women, children, and old men, so successfully swelled the body count that General Westmoreland sent a personal message of "Congratulations to officers and men of Charlie Company, 1st Battalion, 20th Infantry for outstanding action" that "dealt enemy heavy blow."[4]

When the carnage finally came to light, evidence poured in showing that this massacre was not an aberration but just an especially appalling instance of a systematic strategy. In fact, when the news finally hit the media in November 1969, a lieutenant then commanding a platoon near My Lai described to the press how his men, organized in the usual "Zippo squads," had burned down thirteen villages in the same area in the last week of October 1969.[5]

The day the news broke, a directive went out from the Army ordering an inquiry into My Lai, also known as Son My, to be conducted by three-star General William Peers, former OSS and CIA officer, later a division commander in Vietnam. General Peers's official report, based on over three months of investigation, concluded that many "war crimes" had been committed, including "individual and group acts of murder, rape, sodomy, maiming, and assault on noncombatants," and that "At every command level within the Americal Division, actions

---

2. "U.S. Assistance Programs in Vietnam," Hearings before a Subcommittee of the Committee on Government Operations, House of Representatives, 92nd Congress, First Session, pp. 321, 357.

3. This is described in detail in Jonathan Schell, *The Military Half: An Account of Destruction in Quang Ngai and Quang Tin* (New York: Alfred A. Knopf, 1968).

4. Hersh, *My Lai 4*, p. 80.

5. *New York Times*, November 26, 1969.

were taken, both wittingly and unwittingly, which effectively suppressed informa-
tion concerning war crimes committed at Son My Village." 6 General Peers rec-
ommended action by courts-martial against over two dozen officers, including the
commanding and assistant commanding generals of the American Division.
Charges against almost all were dismissed. Only one man, Lieutenant William
Calley, was ever tried and convicted.

General Peers's inquiry revealed an elaborate cover-up of the massacre. Then
his report, too, was covered up. To this day, the Army refuses to release most of it
to the public.

Seymour Hersh is the person most responsible for bringing the facts surround-
ing My Lai to the public. His thoroughly researched stories broke in the press in
November 1969. Using in-depth interviews with the participants, he pieced to-
gether an overwhelming narrative, later developed into his landmark book, My
Lai 4, *from which the excerpt below describing the day's actions is taken.*

Although Hersh won the Pulitzer Prize and many other top journalism awards
for his reporting of My Lai, the Army continued trying to suppress the evidence
about the massacre and its much larger context. In 1972, Hersh published Cover-
Up, *which described another massacre on the same day, the role of the CIA in*
arranging these actions, and the conspiracy at the highest levels to conceal the
truth.

The first two platoons of Charlie Company, still unfired upon, entered the hamlet. Behind them, still in the rice paddy, were the third platoon and Captain
[Ernest] Medina's command post. [Lt. William] Calley and some of his men
walked into the plaza area in the southern part of the hamlet. None of the people
was running away; they knew that U.S. soldiers would assume that anyone running
was a Viet Cong and would shoot to kill. There was no immediate sense of panic.
The time was about 8 A.M. Grzesik and his fire team were a few meters north of
Calley; they couldn't see each other because of the dense vegetation. Grzesik and
his men began their usual job of pulling people from their homes, interrogating
them, and searching for Viet Cong. The villagers were gathered up, and Grzesik
sent Meadlo, who was in his unit, to take them to Calley for further questioning.
Grzesik didn't see Meadlo again for more than an hour.

Some of Calley's men thought it was breakfast time as they walked in; a few
families were gathered in front of their homes cooking rice over a small fire. Without a direct order, the first platoon also began rounding up the villagers. There was
still no sniper fire, no sign of a large enemy unit. Sledge re⸱ ⸱embered thinking that
"if there were VC around, they had plenty of time to leave before we came in. We
didn't tiptoe in there."

The killings began without warning. Harry Stanley told the C.I.D. that one
young member of Calley's platoon took a civilian into custody and then "pushed

---

6. *Report of Department of Army Review of Preliminary Investigations into My Lai Incident*
(Washington, D.C.: U.S. Government Printing Office, 1976), pp. 12–1 through 12–5.

the man up to where we were standing and then stabbed the man in the back with his bayonet. . . . The man fell to the ground and was gasping for breath." The GI then "killed him with another bayonet thrust or by shooting him with a rifle. . . . There was so many people killed that day it is hard for me to recall exactly how some of the people died." The youth next "turned to where some soldiers were holding another forty- or fifty-year-old man in custody." He "picked this man up and threw him down a well. Then [he] pulled the pin from a M26 grenade and threw it in after the man." Moments later Stanley saw "some old women and some little children—fifteen or twenty of them—in a group around a temple where some incense was burning. They were kneeling and crying and praying, and various soldiers . . . walked by and executed these women and children by shooting them in the head with their rifles. The soldiers killed all fifteen or twenty of them. . . ."

There were few physical protests from the people; about eighty of them were taken quietly from their homes and herded together in the plaza area. A few hollered out, "No VC. No VC." But that was hardly unexpected. Calley left Meadlo, Boyce and a few others with the responsibility of guarding the group. "You know what I want you to do with them," he told Meadlo. Ten minutes later—about 8:15 A.M.—he returned and asked, "Haven't you got rid of them yet? I want them dead." Radioman Sledge, who was trailing Calley, heard the officer tell Meadlo to "waste them." Meadlo followed orders: "We stood about ten to fifteen feet away from them and then he [Calley] started shooting them. Then he told me to start shooting them. I started to shoot them. So we went ahead and killed them. I used more than a whole clip—used four or five clips." There are seventeen M16 bullets in each clip. Boyce slipped away, to the northern side of the hamlet, glad he hadn't been asked to shoot. Women were huddled against children, vainly trying to save them. Some continued to chant, "No VC." Others simply said, "No. No. No."

Do Chuc is a gnarled forty-eight-year-old Vietnamese peasant whose two daughters and an aunt were killed by the GIs in My Lai 4 that day. He and his family were eating breakfast when the GIs entered the hamlet and ordered them out of their homes. Together with other villagers they were marched a few hundred meters into the plaza, where they were told to squat. "Still we had no reason to be afraid," Chuc recalled. "Everyone was calm." He watched as the GIs set up a machine gun. The calm ended. The people began crying and begging. One monk showed his identification papers to a soldier, but the American simply said, "Sorry." Then the shooting started. Chuc was wounded in the leg, but he was covered by dead bodies and thus spared. After waiting an hour, he fled the hamlet. . . .

The few Viet Cong who had stayed near the hamlet were safely hidden. Nguyen Ngo, a former deputy commander of a Viet Cong guerrilla platoon operating in the My Lai area, ran to his hiding place 300 meters away when the GIs came in shooting, but he could see that "they shot everything in sight." His mother and sister hid in ditches and survived because bodies fell on top of them. Pham Lai, a former hamlet security guard, climbed into a bunker with a bamboo top and heard but did not see the shootings. His wife, hidden under a body, survived the massacre.

By this time, there was shooting everywhere. Dennis I. Conti, a GI from Providence, Rhode Island, later explained to C.I.D. investigators what he thought had happened: "We were all psyched up, and as a result, when we got there the shooting started, almost as a chain reaction. The majority of us had expected to meet VC combat troops, but this did not turn out to be so. First we saw a few men running . . . and the next thing I knew we were shooting at everything. Everybody was just firing. After they got in the village, I guess you could say that the men were out of control."

Brooks and his men in the second platoon to the north had begun to systematically ransack the hamlet and slaughter the people, kill the livestock and destroy the crops. Men poured rifle and machine-gun fire into huts without knowing—or seemingly caring—who was inside.

Roy Wood, one of Calley's men who was working next to Brooks' platoon, stormed into a hut, saw an elderly man hiding inside along with his wife and two young daughters: "I hit him with my rifle and pushed him out." A GI from Brooks' platoon, standing by with an M79 grenade launcher, asked to borrow his gun. Wood refused, and the soldier asked another platoon mate. He got the weapon, said, "Don't let none of them live," and shot the Vietnamese in the head. "These mothers are crazy," Wood remembered thinking. "Stand right in front of us and blow a man's brains out." Later he vomited when he saw more of the dead residents of My Lai 4.

The second platoon went into My Lai 4 with guns blazing. Gary Crossley said that some GIs, after seeing nothing but women and children in the hamlet, hesitated: "We phoned Medina and told him what the circumstances were, and he said just keep going. It wasn't anything we wanted to do. You can only kill so many women and children. The fact was that you can't go through and wipe out all of South Vietnam."

Once the first two platoons had disappeared into the hamlet, Medina ordered the third platoon to start moving. He and his men followed. Gary Garfolo was caught up in the confusion: "I could hear heavy shooting all the time. Medina was running back and forth everywhere. This wasn't no organized deal." So Garfolo did what most GIs did when they could get away with it. "I took off on my own." He ran south; others joined him. Terrified villagers, many carrying personal belongings in wicker baskets, were running everywhere to avoid the carnage. In most cases it didn't help. The helicopter gunships circling above cut them down, or else an unfortunate group ran into the third platoon. Charles West sighted and shot six Vietnamese, some with baskets, on the edge of My Lai 4: "These people were running into us, away from us, running every which way. It's hard to distinguish a mama-san from a papa-san when everybody has on black pajamas."

West and his men may have thought that these Vietnamese were Viet Cong.

Later they knew better. West's first impression upon reaching My Lai 4: "There were no people in the first part. . . . I seen bodies everywhere. I knew that everyone was being killed." His group quickly joined in.

Medina—as any combat officer would do during his unit's first major engagement—decided to move his CP from the rice paddy. John Paul, one of Medina's radiomen, figured that the time was about 8:15 A.M.. West remembered that "Medina was right behind us" as his platoon moved inside the hamlet. There are serious contradictions about what happened next. Medina later said that he did not enter the hamlet proper until well after 10 A.M. and did not see anyone kill a civilian. John Paul didn't think that Medina ever entered the hamlet. But Herbert Carter told the C.I.D. that Medina did some of the shooting of civilians as he moved into My Lai 4.

Carter testified that soon after the third platoon moved in, a woman was sighted. Somebody knocked her down, and then, Carter said, "Medina shot her with his M16 rifle. I was fifty or sixty feet away and saw this. There was no reason to shoot this girl." The men continued on, making sure no one was escaping. "We came to where the soldiers had collected fifteen or more Vietnamese men, women and children in a group. Medina said, 'Kill every one. Leave no one standing.'" A machine gunner began firing into the group. Moments later one of Medina's radio operators slowly "passed among them and finished them off." Medina did not personally shoot any of them, according to Carter, but moments later the captain "stopped a seventeen- or eighteen-year-old man with a water buffalo. Medina told the boy to make a run for it," Carter told the C.I.D. "He tried to get him to run but the boy wouldn't run, so Medina shot him with his M16 rifle and killed him. . . . I was seventy-five or eighty meters away at the time and I saw it plainly." At this point in Carter's interrogation, the investigator warned him that he was making very serious charges against his commanding officer. "What I'm telling is the truth," Carter replied, "and I'll face Medina in court and swear to it."

If Carter was correct, Medina walked first into the north side of My Lai 4, then moved south with the CP to the hamlet plaza and arrived there at about the time Paul Meadlo and Lieutenant Calley were executing the first group of villagers. Meadlo still wonders why Medina didn't stop the shooting, "if it was wrong." Medina and Calley "passed each other quite a few times that morning, but didn't say anything. I don't know if the CO gave the order to kill or not, but he was right there when it happened. . . . Medina just kept marching around."

Roberts and Haeberle also moved in just behind the third platoon. Haeberle watched a group of ten to fifteen GIs methodically pump bullets into a cow until it keeled over. A woman then poked her head out from behind some brush; she may have been hiding in a bunker. The GIs turned their fire from the cow to the woman. "They just kept shooting at her. You could see the bones flying in the air chip by chip." No one had attempted to question her; GIs inside the hamlet also were asking no questions. Before moving on, the photographer took a picture of the dead woman. Haeberle took many more pictures that day; he saw about thirty GIs kill at least a hundred Vietnamese civilians.

When the two correspondents entered My Lai 4, they saw dead animals, dead people, burning huts and houses. A few GIs were going through victims' clothing, looking for piasters. Another GI was chasing a duck with a knife; others stood around watching a GI slaughter a cow with a bayonet.

Haeberle noticed a man and two small children walking toward a group of GIs: "They just kept walking toward us . . . you could hear the little girl saying, 'No, no. . . .' All of a sudden the GIs opened up and cut them down." Later he watched a machine gunner suddenly open fire on a group of civilians—women, children and babies—who had been collected in a big circle: "They were trying to run. I don't know how many got out." He saw a GI with an M16 rifle fire at two young boys walking along a road. The older of the two—about seven or eight years old— fell over the first to protect him. The GI kept on firing until both were dead.

As Haeberle and Roberts walked further into the hamlet, Medina came up to them. Eighty-five Viet Cong had been killed in action thus far, the captain told them, and twenty suspects had been captured. Roberts carefully jotted down the captain's statistics in his notepad.

The company's other Vietnamese interpreter, Sergeant Duong Minh, saw Medina for the first time about then. Minh had arrived on a later helicopter assault, along with Lieutenant Dennis H. Johnson, Charlie Company's intelligence officer. When he saw the bodies of civilians, he asked Medina what happened. Medina, obviously angry at Minh for asking the question, stalked away.

Now it was nearly nine o'clock and all of Charlie Company was in My Lai 4. Most families were being shot inside their homes, or just outside the doorways. Those who had tried to flee were crammed by GIs into the many bunkers built throughout the hamlet for protection—once the bunkers became filled, hand grenades were lobbed in. Everything became a target. Gary Garfolo borrowed someone's M79 grenade launcher and fired it point-blank at a water buffalo: "I hit that sucker right in the head; went down like a shot. You don't get to shoot water buffalo with an M79 every day." Others fired the weapon into the bunkers full of people.

Jay Roberts insisted that he saw Medina in My Lai 4 most of the morning: "He was directing the operations in the village. He was in the village the whole time I was—from nine o'clock to eleven o'clock."

Carter recalled that some GIs were shouting and yelling during the massacre: "The boys enjoyed it. When someone laughs and jokes about what they're doing, they have to be enjoying it." A GI said, "Hey, I got me another one." Another said, "Chalk up one for me." Even Captain Medina was having a good time, Carter thought: "You can tell when someone enjoys their work." Few members of Charlie Company protested that day. For the most part, those who didn't like what was going on kept their thoughts to themselves.

Herbert Carter also remembered seeing Medina inside the hamlet well after the third platoon began its advance: "I saw all those dead people laying there. Medina came right up behind me." At one point in the morning one of the members of Medina's CP joined in the shooting. "A woman came out of a hut with a baby in her arms and she was crying," Carter told the C.I.D. "She was crying because her little boy had been in front of their hut and . . . someone had killed the child by shooting it." When the mother came into view, one of Medina's men "shot her with an M16 and she fell. When she fell, she dropped the baby." The GI next "opened up on the baby with his M16." The infant was also killed. Carter also saw an officer grab a woman by the hair and shoot her with a .45-caliber pistol: "He held her by the hair for a minute and then let go and she fell to the ground. Some enlisted man standing there said, 'Well, she'll be in the big rice paddy in the sky.'". . .

Grzesik and his men, meanwhile, had been slowly working their way through the hamlet. The young GI was having problems controlling his men; he was anxious to move on to the rice paddy in the east. About three quarters of the way through, he suddenly saw Meadlo again. The time was now after nine. Meadlo was crouched, head in his hands, sobbing like a bewildered child. "I sat down and asked him what happened." Grzesik felt responsible; after all, he was supposed to be a team leader. Meadlo told him Calley had made him shoot people. "I tried to calm him down," Grzesik said, but the fire-team leader couldn't stay long. His men still hadn't completed their sweep of My Lai 4.

Those Vietnamese who were not killed on the spot were being shepherded by the first platoon to a large drainage ditch at the eastern end of the hamlet. After Grzesik left, Meadlo and a few others gathered seven or eight villagers in one hut and were preparing to toss in a hand grenade when an order came to take them to the ditch. There he found Calley, along with a dozen other first platoon members, and perhaps seventy-five Vietnamese, mostly women, old men and children.

Not far away, invisible in the brush and trees, the second and third platoons were continuing their search-and-destroy operations in the northern half of My Lai 4. Ron Grzesik and his fire team had completed a swing through the hamlet and were getting ready to turn around and walk back to see what was going on. And just south of the plaza, Michael Bernhardt had attached himself to Medina and his command post. Shots were still being fired, the helicopters were still whirring overhead, and the enemy was still nowhere in sight.

One of the helicopters was piloted by Chief Warrant Officer Hugh C. Thompson of Decatur, Georgia. For him, the mission had begun routinely enough. He and his two-man crew, in a small observation helicopter from the 123rd Aviation Battalion, had arrived at the area around 9 A.M. and immediately reported what appeared to be a Viet Cong soldier armed with a weapon and heading south. Although his mission was simply reconnaissance, Thompson directed his men to fire at and attempt to kill the Viet Cong as he wheeled the helicopter after him. They missed. Thompson flew back to My Lai 4, and it was then, as he told the Army Inspector General's office in June, 1969, that he began seeing wounded and dead Vietnamese civilians all over the hamlet, with no sign of an enemy force.

The pilot thought that the best thing he could do would be to mark the location of wounded civilians with smoke so that the GIs on the ground could move over and begin treating some of them. "The first one that I marked was a girl that was wounded," Thompson testified, "and they came over and walked up to her, put their weapon on automatic and let her have it." The man who did the shooting was a captain, Thompson said. Later he identified the officer as Ernest Medina.

Flying with Thompson that day was Lawrence M. Colburn, of Mount Vernon, Washington, who remembered that the girl was about twenty years old and was lying on the edge of a dyke outside the hamlet with part of her body in a rice paddy. "She had been wounded in the stomach, I think, or the chest," Colburn told the Inspector General (IG). "This captain was coming down the dyke and he had men behind him. They were sweeping through and we were hovering a matter of feet away from them. I could see this clearly, and he emptied a clip into her."

Medina and his men immediately began moving south toward the Viet Cong sighted by Thompson. En route they saw the young girl in the rice paddy who had been marked by the smoke. Bernhardt had a ground view of what happened next: "He [Medina] was just going alone . . . he shot the woman. She seemed to be busy picking rice, but rice was out of season. What she really was doing was trying to pretend that she was picking rice. She was a hundred meters away with a basket . . . if she had a hand grenade, she would have to have a better arm than me to get us. . . . Medina lifted the rifle to his shoulder, looked down the barrel and pulled the trigger. I saw the woman drop. He just took a potshot . . . he wasn't a bad shot. Then he walked up. He got up real close, about three or six feet, and shot at her a couple times and finished her off. She was a real clean corpse . . . she wasn't all over the place, and I could see her clothing move when the bullets hit. . . . I could see her twitch, but I couldn't see any holes . . . he didn't shoot her in the head." A second later, Bernhardt remembered, the captain "gave me a look, a dumb shit-eating grin."

By now it was past 9:30 A.M. and the men of Charlie Company had been at work for more than two hours. A few of them flung off their helmets, stripped off their heavy gear, flopped down and took a smoke break. . . .

Hugh Thompson's nightmare had only begun with the shooting of the girl. He flew north back over the hamlet and saw a small boy bleeding along a trench. Again he marked the spot so that the GIs below could provide some medical aid. Instead, he saw a lieutenant casually walk up and empty a clip into the child. He saw yet another wounded youngster; again he marked it, and this time it was a sergeant who came up and fired his M16 at the child.

Larry Colburn, who was just eighteen years old at the time, noticed that "the infantrymen were killing everything in the village. The people didn't really know what was happening. Some of them began walking out of there and the GIs just started going up to them and shooting them all in the back of the head." He added, "We saw this one woman hiding there. She was alive and squatting; she looked up when we flew over. We dropped a smoke marker. When we came back she was in the same position—only she was dead. The back of her head was blown off. It had to be point-blank."

Thompson was furious. He tried unsuccessfully to radio the troops on the ground to find out what was going on. He then reported the wild firings and un-necessary shootings to brigade headquarters. All the command helicopters flying overhead had multi-channel radios and could monitor most conversations. Lieuten-ant Colonel Barker apparently intercepted the message and called down to Medina at the CP just south of the plaza. John Kinch of the mortar platoon heard Medina answer that he "had a body count of 310." The captain added, "I don't know what they're doing. The first platoon's in the lead. I am trying to stop it.". . .

Harry Stanley was standing a few feet away from Calley near some huts at the drainage ditch when the call came from Medina. . . . Calley said "he got some VC, or some people that needed to be checked out." At this point Medina cau-tioned Calley to tell his men to save their ammunition because the operation still had a few more days to run.

It is not clear how soon or to whom Medina's order was given, but Stanley told the C.I.D. what Calley did next: "There was an old lady in a bed and I believe there was a priest in white praying over her. . . . Calley told me to ask about the VC and NVA and where the weapons were. The priest denied being a VC or NVA." Charles Sledge watched with horror as Calley pulled the old man outside: "He said a few more words to the monk. It looked like the monk was pleading for his life. Lieutenant Calley then took his rifle and pushed the monk into a rice paddy and shot him point-blank."

Calley then turned his attention back to the crowd of Vietnamese and issued an order: "Push all those people in the ditch." Three or four GIs complied. Calley struck a woman with a rifle as he pushed her down. Stanley remembered that some of the civilians "kept trying to get out. Some made it to the top. . . ." Calley began the shooting and ordered Meadlo to join in. Meadlo told about it later: "So we pushed our seven to eight people in with the big bunch of them. And so I began shooting them all. So did Mitchell, Calley. . . . I guess I shot maybe twenty-five or twenty people in the ditch . . . men, women and children. And babies." Some of the GIs switched from automatic fire to single-shot to conserve ammunition. Herbert Carter watched the mothers "grabbing their kids and the kids grabbing their mothers. I didn't know what to do."

Calley then turned again to Meadlo and said, "Meadlo, we've got another job to do." Meadlo didn't want any more jobs. He began to argue with Calley. Sledge watched Meadlo once more start to sob. Calley turned next to Robert Maples and said, "Maples, load your machine gun and shoot these people." Maples replied, as he told the C.I.D., "I'm not going to do that." He remembered that "the people firing into the ditch kept reloading magazines into their rifles and kept firing into the ditch and then killed or at least shot everyone in the ditch." William C. Lloyd of Tampa, Florida, told the C.I.D. that some grenades were also thrown into the ditch. Dennis Conti noticed that "a lot of women had thrown themselves on top of the children to protect them, and the children were alive at first. Then the children who were old enough to walk got up and Calley began to shoot the children."

One further incident stood out in many GIs' minds: seconds after the shooting stopped, a bloodied but unhurt two-year-old boy miraculously crawled out of the ditch, crying. He began running toward the hamlet. Someone hollered, "There's a kid." There was a long pause. Then Calley ran back, grabbed the child, threw him back in the ditch and shot him.

Moments later Thompson, still in his helicopter, flew by. He told the IG what happened next: "I kept flying around and across a ditch . . . and it . . . had a bunch of bodies in it and I don't know how they got in the ditch. But I saw some of them were still alive." Captain Brian W. Livingston was piloting a large helicopter gunship a few hundred feet above. He had been monitoring Thompson's agonized complaints and went down to take a look for himself. He told a military hearing: "There were bodies lying in the trenches. . . . I remember that we remarked at the time about the old Biblical story of Jesus turning water into wine. The trench had a grey color to it, with the red blood of the individuals lying in it."

By now Thompson was almost frantic. He landed his small helicopter near the ditch, and asked a soldier there if he could help the people out: "He said the only way he could help them was to help them out of their misery." Thompson took off again and noticed a group of mostly women and children huddled together in a bunker near the drainage ditch. He landed a second time. . . . He then saw Calley and the first platoon, the same group that had shot the wounded civilians he had earlier marked with smoke. "I asked him if he could get the women and kids out of there before they tore it [the bunker] up, and he said the only way he could get them out was to use hand grenades. 'You just hold your men right here,'" the angry Thompson told the equally angry Calley, "'and I will get the women and kids out.'"

Before climbing out of his aircraft, Thompson ordered Colburn and his crew chief to stay alert. "He told us that if any of the Americans opened up on the Vietnamese, we should open up on the Americans," Colburn said. Thompson walked back to the ship and called in two helicopter gunships to rescue the civilians. While waiting for them to land, Colburn said, "he stood between our troops and the bunker. He was shielding the people with his body. He just wanted to get those people out of there.". . .

The helicopters landed, with Thompson still standing between the GIs and the Vietnamese, and quickly rescued nine persons—two old men, two women and five children. One of the children later died en route to the hospital. . . .

Gregory Olsen, who had watched the encounter from his machine-gun position a few dozen meters away, said that "the next thing I knew Mitchell was just shooting into the ditch." At this point Grzesik and his fire team came strolling into the area; they had gone completely through the hamlet, had a break, and were now returning. It was about ten o'clock. Grzesik saw bodies all over the northeastern quarter of My Lai 4. He glanced at the ditch. Suddenly Mitchell yelled, "Grzesik, come here." He walked over. Calley then ordered him to go to the ditch and "finish off the people." Grzesik had seen the helicopter carrying some wounded Vietnamese take off from the area a moment earlier; much later he concluded that Calley—furious with Thompson's intervention—wanted to make sure there were no more survivors in the ditch. Calley told Grzesik to gather his team to do the job. "I really believe he expected me to do it," Grzesik said later, with some amazement. Calley asked him again, and Grzesik again refused. The lieutenant then angrily ordered him to take his team and help burn the hootches. Grzesik headed for the hamlet plaza.

Thompson continued to fly over the ditch and noticed that some of the children's bodies had no heads. He landed a third time after his crew chief told him that he had seen some movement in the mass of bodies and blood below. The crew chief and Colburn began walking toward the ditch. "Nobody said anything," Colburn said. "We just got out." They found a young child still alive. No GIs were in the immediate area, but Colburn was carrying a rifle. The crew chief climbed into the ditch. "He was knee-deep in people and blood," Colburn recalled. The child was quiet, buried under many bodies. "He was still holding onto his mother. But she was dead." The boy, clinging desperately, was pried loose. He still did not cry. Thompson later told the IG, "I don't think this child was even wounded at all, just down there among all the other bodies, and he was terrified." Thompson and his men flew the baby to safety.

In other parts of My Lai 4, GIs were taking a break, or loafing. Others were systematically burning those remaining houses and huts and destroying food. Some villagers—still alive—were able to leave their hiding places and walk away. Charles West recalled that one member of his squad who simply wasn't able to slaughter a group of children asked for and received permission from an officer to let them go.

West's third platoon went ahead, nonetheless, with the killing. They gathered a group of about ten women and children, who huddled together in fear a few feet from the plaza, where dozens of villagers already had been slain. West and the squad had finished their mission in the north and west of the hamlet, and were looking for new targets. They drifted south toward the CP. Jay Roberts and Ron Haeberle, who had spent the past hour watching the slaughter in other parts of the hamlet, stood by—pencil and cameras at the ready. A few men now singled out a slender Vietnamese girl of about fifteen. They tore her from the group and started to pull at her blouse. They attempted to fondle her breasts. The old women and children were screaming and crying. One GI yelled, "Let's see what she's made of." Another said, "VC Boom, Boom," meaning she was a Viet Cong whore. Jay Roberts thought that the girl was good-looking. An old lady began fighting with fanatical fury, trying to protect the girl. Roberts said, "She was fighting off two or three guys at once. She was fantastic. Usually they're pretty passive. . . . They hadn't even gotten that chick's blouse off when Haeberle came along." One of the GIs finally smacked the old woman with his rifle butt; another booted her in the rear.

Grzesik and his fire team watched the fight develop as they walked down from the ditch to the hamlet center. Grzesik was surprised: "I thought the village was cleared. . . . I didn't know there were that many people left." He knew trouble was brewing, and his main thought was to keep his team out of it. He helped break up the fight. Some of the children were desperately hanging onto the old lady as she struggled. Grzesik was worried about the cameraman. He may have yelled, "Hey, there's a photographer." He remembered thinking, "Here's a guy standing there with a camera that you've never seen before." Then somebody said, "What do we do with them?" The answer was, "Waste them." Suddenly there was a burst of automatic fire from many guns. Only a small child survived. Somebody then carefully shot him, too. A photograph of the woman and child, with the young Vietnamese girl tucking in her blouse, was later published in *Life* magazine. Roberts tried to explain later: "It's just that they didn't know what they were supposed to do; killing them seemed like a good idea, so they did it. The old lady who fought so hard was probably a VC." He thought a moment and added, "Maybe it was just her daughter."

West was annoyed at the photographer: "I thought it was wrong for him to stand up and take pictures of this thing. Even though we had to do it, I thought, we didn't have to take pictures of it.". . .

By now it was nearly 10:30 A.M. and most of the company began drifting aimlessly toward the plaza and the command post a few yards to the south. Their work was largely over; a good part of the hamlet was in flames. The villagers "were laying around like ants," William Wyatt remembered. "It was just like somebody had poisoned the water and everybody took a drink and started falling out."

Herb Carter and Harry Stanley had shed their gear and were taking a short break at the CP. Near them was a young Vietnamese boy, crying, with a bullet wound in his stomach. Stanley watched one of Captain Medina's three radio operators walk along a trail toward them; he was without his radio gear. As Stanley told the C.I.D., the radio operator went up to Carter and said, "Let me see your pistol." Carter gave it to him. The radio operator "then stepped within two feet of the boy and shot him in the neck with a pistol. Blood gushed from the child's neck. He then tried to walk off, but he could only take two or three steps. Then he fell onto the ground. He lay there and took four or five deep breaths and then he stopped breathing." The radio operator turned to Stanley and said, "Did you see how I shot that son of a bitch?" Stanley told him, "I don't see how anyone could just kill a kid." Carter got his pistol back; he told Stanley, "I can't take this no more. . . ." Moments later Stanley heard a gun go off and Carter yell. "I went to Carter and saw he had shot himself in the foot. I think Carter shot himself on purpose."

Other children were also last-minute targets. After the scene with the women and children, West noticed a small boy, about seven years old, staring dazedly beside a footpath. He had been shot in the leg. "He was just standing there staring; I don't think he was crying. Somebody asked, 'What do we do with him?'" At this point West had remembered there had been an order from Captain Medina to stop the shooting. "I just shrugged my shoulders," West recalled, "and said, 'I don't know,' and just kept walking." Seconds later he heard some shots, turned around and saw the boy no longer standing on the trail.

Haeberle and Roberts were walking together on the edge of the hamlet when they also noticed the wounded child with the vacant stare. In seconds, Roberts said, "Haeberle, envisioning the war-torn-wounded-waif picture of the year, got within five feet of the kid for a close-up. He was focusing when some guy, just walking along, leveled his rifle, fired three times and walked away." Haeberle saw the shooting through the lens of his camera. "He looked up in shock," Roberts added. "He just turned around and stared. I think that was the thing that stayed in our mind. It was so close, so real, we just saw some kid blown away.". . .

Sergeant Mitchell . . . saw both Calley and Medina interrogating an old man; Mitchell thought he was a monk. "Four or five of us weren't far away. We were watching. The old monk mumbled something and Medina walked off. I looked away for a second, and when I looked back the old man had been shot and Calley was standing over him."

Richard Pendleton remembered Medina himself shooting a civilian that day. Pendleton was standing about fifty feet away from the captain sometime that morning—Pendleton isn't sure exactly when. Pendleton hadn't seen the captain earlier and he wondered what Medina thought about what was going on. "Medina was standing there with the rest of the CP. It was right there in the open. I was watching." There was a small Vietnamese child, "the only one alive among a lot of dead people." He said he watched Medina carefully aim his M16 rifle at the child. "He shot him in the head, and he went down."

Pendleton may have been mistaken. There was a child shot near the command post that day, after Carter shot himself. Charles Gruver of Tulsa, Oklahoma, remembered vividly how it happened: he saw a small boy, about three or four years old, standing by a trail with a wound in his arm. "He just stood there with big eyes staring like he didn't believe what was happening. Then the captain's RTO [radio operator] put a burst of 16 [M16 rifle fire] into him." Ronald Grzesik also saw it. He was just watching the child when he heard a rifle shot; he looked back and saw that the radio operator was still in braced firing position. But Medina, Grzesik recalled, "was around the corner" in the command post at the time. Roberts also witnessed the shooting; he thought the toddler was searching through the pile of dead bodies for his mother or father, or a sister. He was wearing only a shirt. The impact of the M16 flung the small body backward onto the pile. . . .

There were some small acts of mercy. A GI placed a blanket over the body of a mutilated child. An elderly woman was spared when some GIs hollered at a soldier just as he was about to shoot her. Grzesik remembered watching a GI seem to wrestle with his conscience while holding a bayonet over a wounded old man. "He wants to stab somebody with a bayonet," Grzesik thought. The GI hesitated . . . and finally passed on, leaving the old man to die.

Some GIs, however, didn't hesitate to use their bayonets. Nineteen-year-old Nguyen Thi Ngoc Tuyet watched a baby trying to open her slain mother's blouse to nurse. A soldier shot the infant while it was struggling with the blouse, and then slashed at it with his bayonet. Tuyet also said she saw another baby hacked to death by GIs wielding their bayonets.

Le Tong, a twenty-eight-year-old rice farmer, reported seeing one woman raped after GIs killed her children. Nguyen Khoa, a thirty-seven-year-old peasant, told of a thirteen-year-old girl who was raped before being killed. GIs then attacked Khoa's wife, tearing off her clothes. Before they could rape her, however, Khoa said, their six-year-old son, riddled with bullets, fell and saturated her with blood. The GIs left her alone. . . .

In the early afternoon the men of Charlie Company mopped up to make sure all the houses and goods in My Lai 4 were destroyed. Medina ordered the underground tunnels in the hamlet blown up; most of them already had been blocked. Within another hour My Lai 4 was no more: its red-brick buildings demolished by explosives, its huts burned to the ground, its people dead or dying.

Michael Bernhardt later summarized the day: "We met no resistance and I only saw three captured weapons. We had no casualties. It was just like any other Vietnamese village—old papa-sans, women and kids. As a matter of fact, I don't remember seeing one military-age male in the entire place, dead or alive. The only prisoner I saw was in his fifties."

The platoons pulled out shortly after noon, rendezvousing in the rice paddies east of My Lai 4. Lieutenant Brooks' platoon had about eighty-five villagers in tow; it kept those of military age with them and told the rest to begin moving south. Following orders, Medina then marched the GIs northeast through the nearly deserted hamlets of My Lai 5 and My Lai 6, ransacking and burning as they went. In one of the hamlets, Medina ordered the residents gathered, and then told Sergeant Phu, the regular company interpreter, to tell them, as Phu later recalled, that "they were to go away or something will happen to them—just like what happened at My Lai 4."

By nightfall the Viet Cong were back in My Lai 4, helping the survivors bury the dead. It took five days. Most of the funeral speeches were made by the Communist guerrillas. Nguyen Bat was not a Communist at the time of the massacre, but the incident changed his mind. "After the shooting," he said, "all the villagers became Communists."

When Army investigators reached the barren area in November, 1969, in connection with the My Lai probe in the United States, they found mass graves at three sites, as well as a ditch full of bodies. It was estimated that between 450 and 500 people—most of them women, children and old men—had been slain and buried there.

Part VIII

VIETNAMIZATION, 1969–1975

Editors' Introduction

In November 1969, when President Richard Nixon presented his plan for "Viet-namization" of the war (Reading 58), he was taking quite a different position from the one he took in April 1954 (Reading 14). Then he had said that "the Vietnamese lack the ability to conduct a war by themselves or govern themselves" and that, if necessary, the United States "must face up to the situation and dispatch forces." Fourteen years later the United States had experienced the devastating results of dispatching forces to Vietnam. By the time of his March 31, 1968 speech (Reading 55), President Lyndon Johnson had decided that "the main burden of preserving their freedom must be carried out by them—by the South Vietnamese themselves."

Formal peace negotiations began May 13, 1968, after the Democratic Republic of Vietnam (DRV) surprised the United States by accepting Johnson's March 31 proposal for negotiations. At first the talks in Paris included only the DRV and the United States but they expanded in January 1969 to include both the Government of South Vietnam (GVN) and the National Liberation Front (NLF), which was replaced in June by the Provisional Revolutionary Government (PRG) of South Vietnam. (Recognized immediately by several countries after its formation in June, the PRG enabled the southern opposition to negotiate as a parallel government.)

During his presidential campaign Nixon said that the war must be ended, but ended "honorably." US officials were still hoping to "win" South Vietnam. "Viet-namization" was an attempt to turn the actual fighting over to ARVN troops while destroying or at least punishing all resistance with massive firepower in an effort to break the will of the opposition. As president, Nixon's policy was to escalate militarily while continuing the process of negotiations, which took place off and on, sometimes openly and sometimes secretly (Henry Kissinger, then head of the National Security Agency, began secret meetings with Xuan Thuy of the DRV in August 1969 and with Le Duc Tho in February 1970).

However, there were limits on precisely how the President could escalate: with US ground forces disintegrating (Reading 51) and the antiwar movement intensifying, he was forced to begin the withdrawal of troops. The number of US troops in Vietnam increased after Nixon was inaugurated to around 543,000. In June he announced the first withdrawal, numbering only 25,000. The reductions were so gradual that almost as many Americans were killed during Nixon's presidency as in all the previous years, finally amounting, to over 58,000 dead.

⨉ During his 1968 campaign for American votes, Nixon promised to give the American people the truth. Yet, once in office, Nixon began weaving circles of deceit so intricate that he ended up trapping himself. When he was inaugurated, the United States had been waging "secret" air and ground war in Laos for years. Within two months Nixon added the "secret" air war in Cambodia. *The New York Times* of May 9, 1969 reported the bombing of Cambodia as well as the bombing of North Vietnam, in violation of Johnson's publicly announced bombing halt (Reading 55). This "leak" enraged Nixon and Kissinger, resulting in the kind of wiretapping campaign that escalated finally into the Watergate scandal.[1]

Nixon, who had pointed the finger at Johnson for not being able to go anywhere in the country without being met by protesters, was now met wherever he went by protests even larger than those against Johnson. His response was the Counter-Intelligence Program (COINTELPRO) aimed at "neutralizing" opposition ranging from the Black Panther Party to the women's liberation movement. Exposure of the methods used by the FBI and the CIA both at home and abroad led, years later, to congressional investigations of those agencies, resulting in some minor and ineffective congressional restraints.

Congress, in fact, was at most a reluctant brake on the powers of the executive branch throughout the war. Its strongest legislation—the law that ended all US combat activity in Indochina (Reading 61) and the War Powers Resolution (Reading 67)—was passed *after* the Paris Peace Accords of January 1973. Yet several members of Congress kept the Vietnam issue constantly on the agenda and, with popular support, forced congressional hearings that did provide the public with crucial facts. It was congressional hearings about the "secret" war in Laos that compelled the President to issue a "Statement on the Situation in Laos" (Reading

---

1. In response to the unauthorized release of *The Pentagon Papers* by Daniel Ellsberg and Anthony Russo in 1971, the Nixon administration sought a court injunction to block its publication. Although the Federal Court of Appeals upheld the Government's argument that "national security" was at stake, the US Supreme Court found the Government's attempt a violation of free speech (*United States Government* v. *New York Times and Washington Post*, 403 U.S. 713 [1971]). Then, in one of the most bizarre episodes to come to light in modern US political history, Nixon's staff attempted to get material damaging to Ellsberg from his psychiatrist, Dr. Lewis Fielding. When Fielding refused to discuss the matter with FBI officials, an informal group of White House agents (the "Plumbers") broke into Fielding's Beverly Hills, California, office in search of Ellsberg's psychiatric records. The "Plumbers" also carried out the burglary of the Democratic National Committee headquarters in the "Watergate" office-residential complex on the Potomac River. This led to the Watergate scandal, which drove Richard Nixon in disgrace from the White House in August 1974. For basic documentation on all aspects of Watergate, see *The Watergate Hearings: Break-in and Cover-up* (New York: Viking Press, 1973); *The Presidential Transcripts* (New York: Dell Publishing Co., 1974); Carl Bernstein and Bob Woodward, *All the President's Men* (New York: Simon and Schuster, 1974).

60), which was aimed at explaining what the US government was doing there. These government explanations, like the "White Paper" of 1965 (Reading 37), replete with misinformation, only increased skepticism and fueled the opposition. Despite this, Nixon continued to escalate the war, and on April 30, 1970 announced the invasion of Cambodia (Reading 61). At that point, withdrawal of US troops came to a halt; instead an increase of 3,250 was instituted between April and May.

Ten months later came the invasion of Laos, called a "test" of "Vietnamization," a perplexing one in that it involved a test not of whether ARVN troops could defend the Thieu regime in South Vietnam, but of whether they could successfully invade another country. The invasion was carried out by ARVN troops with US equipment, but allegedly without US troops. Within five weeks it was all over. With 9,000 dead or wounded, ARVN troops were routed and forced to retreat. Several hundred Americans were also killed or wounded, despite their mere "support" role.

A few weeks later, in April 1971, Vietnam Veterans Against the War (VVAW) held a week-long protest in Washington, demanding immediate withdrawal of US troops. John Kerry, speaking for VVAW, pointed out to the Senate Foreign Relations Committee and a national television audience that soldiers in Vietnam would not agree with Vice-President Spiro Agnew's characterization of protesters as "criminal misfits," and that, to the contrary, "so many who have died would have returned to this country to join the misfits in their efforts to ask for an immediate withdrawal" (Reading 62).[2]

Despite the obvious failure of "Vietnamization" during the invasion of Laos, the United States continued to back the Thieu regime (Reading 63). US policy remained what it was back in 1964 when President Johnson cabled Ambassador Henry Cabot Lodge about the purpose of his mission in Saigon: "knocking down the idea of neutralization wherever it rears its ugly head" (Reading 35). With that clearly understood, DRV-PRG forces prepared their spring offensive of 1972. Nixon responded with intensive bombing of the North, along with a naval blockade and the mining of Haiphong Harbor—essentially implementing proposals made by the Joint Chiefs of Staff in early 1968 (Reading 54). Washington was trying everything, but at this point everything had been tried before.

The devastation that resulted from this bombing of the North and from the Christmas bombing raids later in 1972 was of course intended to put pressure on the Vietnamese at the bargaining table; but the damage was also aimed at leaving North Vietnam with the costly task of rebuilding while still fighting the Thieu regime even after US troop withdrawal in early 1973. The destruction of Indochina also served as a "lesson" to other countries of how much ecological damage Washington could inflict (Reading 64).

Yet when the Peace Accords (Reading 65) were signed on January 27, 1973,

---

2. Vice President Agnew was forced to resign from office because of financial scandals in 1973. He later pled no contest to felony charges.

Communist forces in the small country of Vietnam had defeated the mightiest military power ever employed against another country. The DRV-PRG achieved their most fundamental demand: the withdrawal of all US troops and those of its foreign allies such as Australia, New Zealand, the Philippines, South Korea, and Thailand. The United States, on the contrary, had, despite the objections of the Thieu regime, given up the demand that all "non-South Vietnamese forces"—i.e., the DRV—withdraw from the South. The most significant concession of the DRV-PRG forces was dropping their demand for the formation of a coalition government prior to elections; the cease-fire instead left the PRG and the GVN co-existing in the South. After over four additional years of war, the United States agreed to a settlement substantially the same as it could have negotiated when peace talks began (Reading 57).

After the last US troops withdrew in March 1973, the United States continued to support Thieu militarily and economically. But, in the absence of reintervention by the United States, the widespread support of the population became the critical factor. Popular support was precisely what the Thieu regime had never possessed.

When the Ho Chi Minh Campaign, the final campaign of the war, was victorious on April 30, 1975 (Reading 68), the struggle was not entirely over. Decades of war left Vietnam—and the entire region—with severe problems. The United States would continue its efforts, by various means, to "win" in Vietnam. But "Vietnamization," the perpetuation of a US client regime, had proved impossible. North and South were reunited in a real "Vietnamization."

57. Negotiating Positions of 1969: The NLF's Ten Points (May 8) and Nixon's Eight Points (May 14)*

In January 1969, the Government of South Vietnam (GVN), headed by Nguyen Van Thieu, and the National Liberation Front (NLF) joined the Democratic Republic of [North] Vietnam (DRV) and the United States at the Paris negotiations. The GVN based its claim to legitimacy on a 1967 election in which all the candidates had to be approved by the regime then in power, which was headed by Premier Nguyen Cao Ky. The election results were predictable: Thieu became president and Ky became vice president. The symbol of their campaign was a map of Vietnam—not just the South but the whole country, clear recognition of the fact that

---

*A. From *South Vietnam in Struggle*, Special Issue of the South Vietnam National Front for Liberation Information Commission [1969]. B. *Public Papers of the Presidents of the United States: Richard Nixon, 1969* (Washington: US Government Printing Office, 1971), p. 373.

there were not two Vietnams. Yet on April 7, 1969, President Thieu said that the first step toward peace must be an end to North Vietnam's "aggression" and withdrawal of all its forces. Then he would "urge" the United States and the other "Allied nations" to withdraw. He said the NLF could participate in South Vietnam's politics if they first surrendered their arms and agreed to obey the constitution. This constitution, drawn up with US approval, became effective May 1, 1967, and outlawed all "communist" and "neutralist" activity.

Faced with this concept of "free elections" (as President Nixon referred to Thieu's offer in his May 14 speech), the NLF put forward the following ten-point "overall solution to the South Vietnam problem," which was presented at the Paris negotiations on May 8, 1969.

In a nationwide speech on May 14, Nixon presented the eight-point proposal reprinted below,[1] prefaced by this warning: "If we are to move successfully from an era of confrontation to an era of negotiation, then we have to demonstrate . . . that confrontation with the United States is costly and unrewarding."

The two proposals demonstrated key differences that would continue to be major until the final Peace Accords (see Editors' Introduction, Part VIII), including differences over which troops would be withdrawn and whether a coalition government would be established before general elections in the South. As its program stated, the NLF wanted the coalition government formed before elections that DRV-PRG forces believed could not be "free" under Thieu (Reading 63). A month after presenting this program, the NLF joined with other opposition groups in the South to form the Provisional Revolutionary Government (PRG) of South Vietnam, which negotiated in Paris on the basis of these ten points.

A. The NLF's Ten-Point Program

The South Vietnam National Front for Liberation sets forth the principles and main content of an overall solution to the South Vietnam problem to help restore peace in Vietnam as follows:

1. To respect the Vietnamese people's fundamental national rights, i.e., independence, sovereignty, unity and territorial integrity, as recognized by the 1954 Geneva Agreements on Vietnam.

---

1. Henry Kissinger, who wrote the May 14 speech, presented an even harder-line position at the negotiations. For informative accounts of the peace negotiations, see especially Hal Dareff, *From Vietnam to Cambodia* (New York: Parents Magazine Press, 1971); George C. Herring, *America's Longest War: The United States and Vietnam, 1950–1975* (New York: John Wiley & Sons, 1979); Seymour M. Hersh, *The Price of Power: Kissinger in the Nixon White House* (New York: Summit Books, 1983); Gareth Porter, *A Peace Denied: The United States, Vietnam and the Paris Agreement* (Bloomington: Indiana University Press, 1975); Gareth Porter, ed., *Vietnam: A History in Documents* (New York: New American Library, 1979); Richard Nixon, *RN: The Memoirs of Richard Nixon* (New York: Grosset & Dunlap, 1978); Henry Kissinger, *White House Years* (Boston: Little, Brown and Co., 1979) and *Years of Upheaval* (Boston: Little, Brown and Co., 1982).

2. The U.S. Government must withdraw from South Vietnam all U.S. troops, military personnel, arms and war matériel, and all troops, military personnel, arms and war matériel of the other foreign countries of the U.S. camp without posing any condition whatsoever; liquidate all U.S. military bases in South Vietnam; renounce all encroachments on the sovereignty, territory and security of South Vietnam and the Democratic Republic of Vietnam.

3. The Vietnamese people's right to fight for the defense of their Fatherland is the sacred, inalienable right to self-defense of all peoples. The question of the Vietnamese armed forces in South Vietnam shall be resolved by the Vietnamese parties among themselves.

4. The people of South Vietnam settle themselves their own affairs without foreign interference. They decide themselves the political regime of South Vietnam through free and democratic general elections. Through free and democratic general elections, a Constituent Assembly will be set up, a Constitution worked out, and a coalition Government of South Vietnam installed, reflecting national concord and the broad union of all social strata.

5. During the period intervening between the restoration of peace and the holding of general elections, neither party shall impose its political regime on the people of South Vietnam.

The political forces representing the various social strata and political tendencies in South Vietnam, that stand for peace, independence and neutrality, including those persons who, for political reasons, have to live abroad, will enter into talks to set up a provisional coalition government based on the principle of equality, democracy and mutual respect with a view to achieving a peaceful, independent, democratic and neutral South Vietnam.

The provisional coalition government is to have the following tasks:

(a) To implement the agreements to be concluded on the withdrawal of the troops of the United States and the other foreign countries of the American camp, etc.

(b) To achieve national concord, and a broad union of all social strata, political forces, nationalities, religious communities, and all persons, no matter what their political beliefs and their past may be, provided they stand for peace, independence and neutrality.

(c) To achieve broad democratic freedoms—freedom of speech, freedom of the press, freedom of gathering, freedom of belief, freedom to form political parties and organizations, freedom to demonstrate, etc.; to set free those persons jailed on political grounds; to prohibit all acts of terror, reprisal and discrimination against people having collaborated with either side, and who are now in the country or abroad, as provided for in the 1954 Geneva Agreements on Vietnam.

(d) To heal the war wounds, to restore and develop the economy, to restore the normal life of the people, and to improve the living conditions of the laboring people.

(e) To hold free and democratic general elections in the whole of South Vietnam with a view to achieving the South Vietnam people's right to self-determination, in accordance with the content of point 4 mentioned above.

6. South Vietnam will carry out a foreign policy of peace and neutrality:

To carry out a policy of good neighborly relations with the Kingdom of Cambodia on the basis of respect for her independence, sovereignty, neutrality and territorial integrity within her present borders; to carry out a policy of good neighborly relations with the Kingdom of Laos on the basis of respect for the 1962 Geneva Agreements on Laos.

To establish diplomatic, economic and cultural relations with all countries, irrespective of political and social regime, including the United States, in accordance with the five principles of peaceful coexistence: mutual respect for the independence, sovereignty and territorial integrity, non-aggression, non-interference in the internal affairs, equality and mutual benefit, peaceful coexistence; to accept economic and technical aid with no political conditions attached from any country.

7. The reunification of Vietnam will be achieved step by step, by peaceful means, through discussions and agreement between the two zones, without foreign interference.

Pending the peaceful reunification of Vietnam, the two zones reestablish normal relations in all fields on the basis of mutual respect.

The military demarcation line between the two zones at the 17th parallel, as provided for by the 1954 Geneva Agreements, is only of a provisional character and does not constitute in any way a political or territorial boundary. The two zones reach agreement on the statute of the Demilitarized Zone, and work out modalities for movements across the provisional military demarcation line.

8. As provided for in the 1954 Geneva Agreements on Vietnam, pending the peaceful reunification of Vietnam, the two zones North and South of Vietnam undertake to refrain from joining any military alliance with foreign countries, not to allow any foreign country to maintain military bases, troops and military personnel on their respective soil, and not to recognize the protection of any country or military alliance or bloc.

9. To resolve the aftermath of the war:

(a) The parties will negotiate the release of the armymen captured in war.

(b) The U.S. Government must bear full responsibility for the losses and devastations it has caused to the Vietnamese people in both zones.

10. The parties shall reach agreement on an international supervision about the withdrawal from South Vietnam of the troops, military personnel, arms and war matériel of the United States and the other foreign countries of the American camp.

The principles and content of the overall solution expounded above form an integrated whole. On the basis of these principles and content, the parties shall reach understanding to the effect of concluding agreements on the above-mentioned questions with a view to ending the war in South Vietnam, and contributing to restore peace in Vietnam.

B. The United States' Eight Points

—As soon as agreement can be reached, all non-South Vietnamese forces would begin withdrawals from South Vietnam.

—Over a period of 12 months, by agreed-upon stages, the major portions of all U.S., allied, and other non-South Vietnamese forces would be withdrawn. At the end of this 12-month period, the remaining U.S., allied, and other non-South Vietnamese forces would move into designated base areas and would not engage in combat operations.

—The remaining U.S. and allied forces would complete their withdrawals as the remaining North Vietnamese forces were withdrawn and returned to North Vietnam.

—An international supervisory body, acceptable to both sides, would be created for the purpose of verifying withdrawals, and for any other purposes agreed upon between the two sides.

—This international body would begin operating in accordance with an agreed timetable and would participate in arranging supervised cease-fires in Vietnam.

—As soon as possible after the international body was functioning, elections would be held under agreed procedures and under the supervision of the international body.

—Arrangements would be made for the release of prisoners of war on both sides at the earliest possible time.

—All parties would agree to observe the Geneva Accords of 1954 regarding South Vietnam and Cambodia, and the Laos Accords of 1962.[2]

58. *"Vietnamization" (November 3, 1969)**

By President Richard M. Nixon

Given the deteriorating battlefield situation and the massive participation by Americans in the 1969 October Moratorium against the war,[1] many people expected President Nixon's speech, announced for November 3, to spell out a plan for ending the war. Instead, it showed that Nixon was still searching for "peace with honor," a way to get out of Vietnam without "losing." Having "American-

---

2. For the accords regarding Cambodia in the 1954 Geneva Accords and the Laos Accords of 1962, see Marvin and Susan Gettleman, Lawrence and Carol Kaplan, eds., *Conflict in Indochina: A Reader on the Widening War in Laos and Cambodia* (New York: Vintage Books, 1970), Readings 8, 13, 14.—eds.

**Public Papers of the Presidents of the United States: Richard Nixon, 1969* (Washington: US Government Printing Office, 1971), pp. 901–909.

1. There was no way to count the participants in this nationwide protest with events ranging from door-to-door leafleting to prayer vigils and marches. It's safe to say that a million would be an underestimate. The country's two largest unions, the Teamsters and the Auto Workers, joined with the Chemical Workers to support the Moratorium. In Vietnam many GIs wore black armbands to demonstrate support for "bringing the boys home now." Veterans of Vietnam joined the protests at home.

ized" the war, the United States would now "Vietnamize" it in line with the Nixon Doctrine described in the speech reprinted below.

On July 15, Nixon had sent a letter to Ho Chi Minh saying that Nixon's May 14 proposals (Reading 57) were "fair to all parties" but that he was also willing to "discuss" other proposals as well, specifically the NLF's ten points (Reading 57). Ho Chi Minh, in his letter of August 25 (only nine days before he died), responded that the United States was intensifying military operations and that the B-52 bombings and use of chemical warfare "multiply the crimes against the Vietnamese people." He reiterated the DRV position that the ten points of the NLF and the PRG provided a "logical and reasonable basis" for settlement. By referring to the Provisional Revolutionary Government (PRG), as Nixon had not, he reminded the President that the status of the opposition in South Vietnam was now that of a recognized government. Again he demanded that the United States "cease its war of aggression and withdraw" from the South, respecting the right of the Vietnamese to handle their own affairs. This, he wrote, would be the way to get out of Vietnam "with honor."[2]

In this speech, Nixon told his national radio and TV audience that Ho Chi Minh's letter "flatly rejected" his "initiative." Yet in his memoirs, Nixon indicated that the secret meetings which began August 4 between Henry Kissinger and Xuan Thuy of the DRV were in fact a response. We still do not know the whole story of what transpired. Nixon's memoirs say that when the French intermediary picked up the letter for Ho Chi Minh, Nixon sent an oral message as well: an ultimatum that unless there was some serious breakthrough by November 1 (anniversary of Johnson's halt in bombing North Vietnam[3]*), Nixon would have no choice but to resort "to measures of great consequence and force."*[4] *Kissinger's memoirs*[5] *say he relayed the threat at his first meeting with Xuan Thuy. On the other hand, Seymour Hersh reported that in interviews which took place in 1979 North Vietnamese officials said no direct threats were relayed to them.*[6]

The layers of misinformation and disinformation made it impossible for the American public to have the facts. In this speech Nixon told the public that he was seeking the "goal of a just and lasting peace" without disclosing that he was at that very moment waging covert wars in Cambodia and Laos. He called upon "the great silent majority" to stand behind him in his "plan of action." The White House claimed that most of the 80,000 letters and telegrams in response supported

---

2. Both letters were printed in *The New York Times*, November 4, 1969, the day after Nixon released them to the press.

3. See footnote 10 below.

4. Message quoted by Nixon in *RN: The Memoirs of Richard Nixon* (New York: Grosset & Dunlap, 1978), pp. 393–394.

5. Henry Kissinger's two-volume memoirs, *White House Years* (Boston: Little, Brown and Co., 1979) and *Years of Upheaval* (Boston: Little, Brown and Co., 1982), sometimes agree and sometimes conflict with Richard Nixon's.

6. Seymour M. Hersh's *The Price of Power: Kissinger in the Nixon White House* (New York: Summit Books, 1983) provides an illuminating account of this period.

the President. But twelve days later at least half a million people participated in the largest antiwar demonstration ever in the capital, part of the nationwide November Mobilization to end the war.

Good evening, my fellow Americans:
Tonight I want to talk to you on a subject of deep concern to all Americans and to many people in all parts of the world—the war in Vietnam.

I believe that one of the reasons for the deep division about Vietnam is that many Americans have lost confidence in what their Government has told them about our policy. The American people cannot and should not be asked to support a policy which involves the overriding issues of war and peace unless they know the truth about that policy.

Tonight, therefore, I would like to answer some of the questions that I know are on the minds of many of you listening to me.

How and why did America get involved in Vietnam in the first place?

How has this administration changed the policy of the previous administration?

What has really happened in the negotiations in Paris and on the battlefront in Vietnam?

What choices do we have if we are to end the war?

What are the prospects for peace?

Now, let me begin by describing the situation I found when I was inaugurated on January 20.

—The war had been going on for 4 years.

—31,000 Americans had been killed in action.[7]

—The training program for the South Vietnamese was behind schedule.

—540,000 Americans were in Vietnam with no plans to reduce the number.

—No progress had been made at the negotiations in Paris and the United States had not put forth a comprehensive peace proposal.

—The war was causing deep division at home and criticism from many of our friends as well as our enemies abroad.

In view of these circumstances there were some who urged that I end the war at once by ordering the immediate withdrawal of all American forces.

From a political standpoint this would have been a popular and easy course to follow. After all, we became involved in the war while my predecessor was in office. I could blame the defeat which would be the result of my action on him and come out as the peacemaker. Some put it to me quite bluntly: This was the only way to avoid allowing Johnson's war to become Nixon's war.

But I had a greater obligation than to think only of the years of my administra-

---

7. By the time the war ended this figure rose to over 58,000; the number of Vietnamese killed could never be counted but is thought to be over four million (Stanley Karnow, *Vietnam: A History* [New York: Viking Press, 1983], p. 11). These numbers do not include the Laotians, Cambodians, and citizens of other countries killed in the war.—eds.

tion and of the next election. I had to think of the effect of my decision on the next generation and on the future of peace and freedom in America and in the world.

Let us all understand that the question before us is not whether some Americans are for peace and some Americans are against peace. The question at issue is not whether Johnson's war becomes Nixon's war.

The great question is: How can we win America's peace?

Well, let us turn now to the fundamental issue. Why and how did the United States become involved in Vietnam in the first place?

Fifteen years ago North Vietnam, with the logistical support of Communist China and the Soviet Union, launched a campaign to impose a Communist government on South Vietnam by instigating and supporting a revolution.

In response to the request of the Government of South Vietnam, President Eisenhower sent economic aid and military equipment to assist the people of South Vietnam in their efforts to prevent a Communist takeover. Seven years ago, President Kennedy sent 16,000 military personnel to Vietnam as combat advisers. Four years ago, President Johnson sent American combat forces to South Vietnam.

Now, many believe that President Johnson's decision to send American combat forces to South Vietnam was wrong. And many others—I among them—have been strongly critical of the way the war has been conducted.

But the question facing us today is: Now that we are in the war, what is the best way to end it?

In January I could only conclude that the precipitate withdrawal of American forces from Vietnam would be a disaster not only for South Vietnam but for the United States and for the cause of peace.

For the South Vietnamese, our precipitate withdrawal would inevitably allow the Communists to repeat the massacres which followed their takeover in the North 15 years before.

—They then murdered more than 50,000 people and hundreds of thousands more died in slave labor camps.

—We saw a prelude of what would happen in South Vietnam when the Communists entered the city of Hue last year. During their brief rule there, there was a bloody reign of terror in which 3,000 civilians were clubbed, shot to death, and buried in mass graves.[8]

—With the sudden collapse of our support, these atrocities of Hue would become the nightmare of the entire nation—and particularly for the million and a half Catholic refugees who fled to South Vietnam when the Communists took over in the North.

For the United States, this first defeat in our Nation's history would result in a collapse of confidence in American leadership, not only in Asia but throughout the world.

---

8. This is a variation of an allegation exposed as a fabrication by Gareth Porter in "The 1968 'Hue Massacre,'" *Indochina Chronicle*, 33 (June 24, 1974). See Reading 52 for Westmoreland's use of it.—eds.

Three American Presidents have recognized the great stakes involved in Vietnam and understood what had to be done.

In 1963, President Kennedy, with his characteristic eloquence and clarity, said: ". . . we want to see a stable government there, carrying on a struggle to maintain its national independence.

"We believe strongly in that. We are not going to withdraw from that effort. In my opinion, for us to withdraw from that effort would mean a collapse not only of South Viet-Nam, but Southeast Asia. So we are going to stay there."

President Eisenhower and President Johnson expressed the same conclusion during their terms of office.

For the future of peace, precipitate withdrawal would thus be a disaster of immense magnitude.

—A nation cannot remain great if it betrays its allies and lets down its friends.

—Our defeat and humiliation in South Vietnam without question would promote recklessness in the councils of those great powers who have not yet abandoned their goals of world conquest.

—This would spark violence wherever our commitments help maintain the peace—in the Middle East, in Berlin, eventually even in the Western Hemisphere.

Ultimately, this would cost more lives.

It would not bring peace; it would bring more war.

For these reasons, I rejected the recommendation that I should end the war by immediately withdrawing all of our forces. I chose instead to change American policy on both the negotiating front and battlefront.

In order to end a war fought on many fronts, I initiated a pursuit for peace on many fronts.

In a television speech on May 14, in a speech before the United Nations, and on a number of other occasions I set forth our peace proposals in great detail.

—We have offered a complete withdrawal of all outside forces within 1 year.

—We have proposed a cease-fire under international supervision.

—We have offered free elections under international supervision with the Communists participating in the organization and conduct of the elections as an organized political force. [See Reading 57.—eds.] And the Saigon Government has pledged to accept the result of the elections.

We have not put forth our proposals on a take-it-or-leave-it basis. We have indicated that we are willing to discuss the proposals that have been put forth by the other side. We have declared that anything is negotiable except the right of the people of South Vietnam to determine their own future. At the Paris peace conference, Ambassador Lodge has demonstrated our flexibility and good faith in 40 public meetings.

Hanoi has refused even to discuss our proposals. They demand our unconditional acceptance of their terms, which are that we withdraw all American forces immediately and unconditionally and that we overthrow the Government of South Vietnam as we leave.

We have not limited our peace initiatives to public forums and public statements. I recognized, in January, that a long and bitter war like this usually cannot be settled in a public forum. That is why in addition to the public statements and negotiations I have explored every possible private avenue that might lead to a settlement.

Tonight I am taking the unprecedented step of disclosing to you some of our other initiatives for peace—initiatives we undertook privately and secretly because we thought we thereby might open a door which publicly would be closed.

I did not wait for my inauguration to begin my quest for peace.

—Soon after my election, through an individual who is directly in contact on a personal basis with the leaders of North Vietnam, I made two private offers for a rapid, comprehensive settlement. Hanoi's replies called in effect for our surrender before negotiations.

—Since the Soviet Union furnishes most of the military equipment for North Vietnam, Secretary of State Rogers, my Assistant for National Security Affairs, Dr. Kissinger, Ambassador Lodge, and I, personally, have met on a number of occasions with representatives of the Soviet Government to enlist their assistance in getting meaningful negotiations started. In addition, we have had extended discussions directed toward that same end with representatives of other governments which have diplomatic relations with North Vietnam. None of these initiatives have to date produced results.

—In mid-July, I became convinced that it was necessary to make a major move to break the deadlock in the Paris talks. I spoke directly in this office, where I am now sitting, with an individual who had known Ho Chi Minh [President, Democratic Republic of Vietnam] on a personal basis for 25 years. Through him I sent a letter to Ho Chi Minh.

I did this outside of the usual diplomatic channels with the hope that with the necessity of making statements for propaganda removed, there might be constructive progress toward bringing the war to an end. Let me read from that letter to you now.

"Dear Mr. President:

"I realize that it is difficult to communicate meaningfully across the gulf of four years of war. But precisely because of this gulf, I wanted to take this opportunity to reaffirm in all solemnity my desire to work for a just peace. I deeply believe that the war in Vietnam has gone on too long and delay in bringing it to an end can benefit no one—least of all the people of Vietnam. . . .[9]

"The time has come to move forward at the conference table toward an early resolution of this tragic war. You will find us forthcoming and open-minded in a common effort to bring the blessings of peace to the brave people of Vietnam. Let history record that at this critical juncture, both sides turned their face toward peace rather than toward conflict and war."

I received Ho Chi Minh's reply on August 30, 3 days before his death. It simply

---

9. Nixon omitted the portion of his letter mentioned in the headnote above.—eds.

reiterated the public position North Vietnam had taken at Paris and flatly rejected my initiative.

The full text of both letters is being released to the press.

—In addition to the public meetings that I have referred to, Ambassador Lodge has met with Vietnam's chief negotiator in Paris in 11 private sessions.

—We have taken other significant initiatives which must remain secret to keep open some channels of communication which may still prove to be productive.

But the effect of all the public, private, and secret negotiations which have been undertaken since the bombing halt a year ago and since this administration came into office on January 20, can be summed up in one sentence: No progress whatever has been made except agreement on the shape of the bargaining table.

Well now, who is at fault?

It has become clear that the obstacle in negotiating an end to the war is not the President of the United States. It is not the South Vietnamese Government.

The obstacle is the other side's absolute refusal to show the least willingness to join us in seeking a just peace. And it will not do so while it is convinced that all it has to do is to wait for our next concession, and our next concession after that one, until it gets everything it wants.

There can now be no longer any question that progress in negotiation depends only on Hanoi's deciding to negotiate, to negotiate seriously.

I realize that this report on our efforts on the diplomatic front is discouraging to the American people, but the American people are entitled to know the truth—the bad news as well as the good news—where the lives of our young men are involved.

Now let me turn, however, to a more encouraging report on another front.

At the time we launched our search for peace I recognized we might not succeed in bringing an end to the war through negotiation. I, therefore, put into effect another plan to bring peace—a plan which will bring the war to an end regardless of what happens on the negotiating front.

It is in line with a major shift in U.S. foreign policy which I described in my press conference at Guam on July 25. Let me briefly explain what has been described as the Nixon Doctrine—a policy which not only will help end the war in Vietnam, but which is an essential element of our program to prevent future Vietnams.

We Americans are a do-it-yourself people. We are an impatient people. Instead of teaching someone else to do a job, we like to do it ourselves. And this trait has been carried over into our foreign policy.

In Korea and again in Vietnam, the United States furnished most of the money, most of the arms, and most of the men to help the people of those countries defend their freedom against Communist aggression.

Before any American troops were committed to Vietnam, a leader of another Asian country expressed this opinion to me when I was traveling in Asia as a private citizen. He said: "When you are trying to assist another nation defend its freedom, U.S. policy should be to help them fight the war but not to fight the war for them."

Well, in accordance with this wise counsel, I laid down in Guam three principles as guidelines for future American policy toward Asia:

—First, the United States will keep all of its treaty commitments.

—Second, we shall provide a shield if a nuclear power threatens the freedom of a nation allied with us or of a nation whose survival we consider vital to our security.

—Third, in cases involving other types of aggression, we shall furnish military and economic assistance when requested in accordance with our treaty commitments. But we shall look to the nation directly threatened to assume the primary responsibility of providing the manpower for its defense.

After I announced this policy, I found that the leaders of the Philippines, Thailand, Vietnam, South Korea, and other nations which might be threatened by Communist aggression, welcomed this new direction in American foreign policy.

The defense of freedom is everybody's business—not just America's business. And it is particularly the responsibility of the people whose freedom is threatened. In the previous administration, we Americanized the war in Vietnam. In this administration, we are Vietnamizing the search for peace.

The policy of the previous administration not only resulted in our assuming the primary responsibility for fighting the war, but even more significantly did not adequately stress the goal of strengthening the South Vietnamese so that they could defend themselves when we left.

The Vietnamization plan was launched following Secretary Laird's visit to Vietnam in March. Under the plan, I ordered first a substantial increase in the training and equipment of South Vietnamese forces.

In July, on my visit to Vietnam, I changed General Abrams' orders so that they were consistent with the objectives of our new policies. Under the new orders, the primary mission of our troops is to enable the South Vietnamese forces to assume the full responsibility for the security of South Vietnam.

Our air operations have been reduced by over 20 percent.[10]

And now we have begun to see the results of this long overdue change in American policy in Vietnam.

---

10. Apparently Nixon was not counting the raids in the "secret" bombing of Cambodia which had begun in March and was continuing intensively as he spoke. Nor was he probably counting the 1969 eight-month bombing campaign against the Plain of Jars in north-central Laos; some of those sorties were being reported as bombings of southern Laos while others were being reported as bombings of South Vietnam. Perhaps Nixon was counting the latter. The bookkeeping gets very difficult. As William Shawcross points out in *Sideshow: Kissinger, Nixon and the Destruction of Cambodia* (New York: Pocket Books, 1979), p. 93: "When Lyndon Johnson decided to cut back the bombing of North Vietnam in November 1968, the Joint Chiefs of Staff reluctantly agreed after Secretary of Defense Clark Clifford assured them that the strikes could be redirected against Laos. The statistics help tell the story. In 1968, 172,000 sorties were flown against North Vietnam and 136,000 against Laos. In 1969 the bombing halt reduced sorties against the North to 37,000—the attacks in Laos rose to 242,000." Note that during the supposed "halt" in bombing the North during 1969, Shawcross reports 37,000 sorties.—eds.

—After 5 years of Americans going into Vietnam, we are finally bringing men home. By December 15, over 60,000 men will have been withdrawn from South Vietnam—including 20 percent of all of our combat forces.

—The South Vietnamese have continued to gain in strength. As a result they have been able to take over combat responsibilities from our American troops.

Two other significant developments have occurred since this administration took office.

—Enemy infiltration, infiltration which is essential if they are to launch a major attack, over the last 3 months is less than 20 percent of what it was over the same period last year.

—Most important—United States casualties have declined during the last 2 months to the lowest point in 3 years.

Let me now turn to our program for the future.

We have adopted a plan which we have worked out in cooperation with the South Vietnamese for the complete withdrawal of all U.S. combat ground forces, and their replacement by South Vietnamese forces on an orderly scheduled timetable. This withdrawal will be made from strength and not from weakness. As South Vietnamese forces become stronger, the rate of American withdrawal can become greater.

I have not and do not intend to announce the timetable for our program. And there are obvious reasons for this decision which I am sure you will understand. As I have indicated on several occasions, the rate of withdrawal will depend on developments on three fronts.

One of these is the progress which can be or might be made in the Paris talks. An announcement of a fixed timetable for our withdrawal would completely remove any incentive for the enemy to negotiate an agreement. They would simply wait until our forces had withdrawn and then move in.

The other two factors on which we will base our withdrawal decisions are the level of enemy activity and the progress of the training programs of the South Vietnamese forces. And I am glad to be able to report tonight progress on both of these fronts has been greater than we anticipated when we started the program in June for withdrawal. As a result, our timetable for withdrawal is more optimistic now than when we made our first estimates in June. Now, this clearly demonstrates why it is not wise to be frozen in on a fixed timetable.

We must retain the flexibility to base each withdrawal decision on the situation as it is at the time rather than on estimates that are no longer valid.

Along with this optimistic estimate, I must—in all candor—leave one note of caution.

If the level of enemy activity significantly increases we might have to adjust our timetable accordingly.

However, I want the record to be completely clear on one point.

At the time of the bombing halt just a year ago, there was some confusion as to whether there was an understanding on the part of the enemy that if we stopped the bombing of North Vietnam they would stop the shelling of cities in South

Vietnam. I want to be sure that there is no misunderstanding on the part of the enemy with regard to our withdrawal program.

We have noted the reduced level of infiltration, the reduction of our casualties, and are basing our withdrawal decisions partially on those factors.

If the level of infiltration or our casualties increase while we are trying to scale down the fighting, it will be the result of a conscious decision by the enemy.

Hanoi could make no greater mistake than to assume that an increase in violence will be to its advantage. If I conclude that increased enemy action jeopardizes our remaining forces in Vietnam, I shall not hesitate to take strong and effective measures to deal with that situation.

This is not a threat. This is a statement of policy, which, as Commander in Chief of our Armed Forces, I am making in meeting my responsibility for the protection of American fighting men wherever they may be.

My fellow Americans, I am sure you can recognize from what I have said that we really only have two choices open to us if we want to end this war.

—I can order an immediate, precipitate withdrawal of all Americans from Vietnam without regard to the effects of that action.

—Or we can persist in our search for a just peace through a negotiated settlement if possible, or through continued implementation of our plan for Vietnamization if necessary—a plan in which we will withdraw all our forces from Vietnam on a schedule in accordance with our program, as the South Vietnamese become strong enough to defend their own freedom.

I have chosen this second course.

It is not the easy way.

It is the right way.

It is a plan which will end the war and serve the cause of peace—not just in Vietnam but in the Pacific and in the world.

In speaking of the consequences of a precipitate withdrawal, I mentioned that our allies would lose confidence in America.

Far more dangerous, we would lose confidence in ourselves. Oh, the immediate reaction would be a sense of relief that our men were coming home. But as we saw the consequences of what we had done, inevitable remorse and divisive recrimination would scar our spirit as a people.

We have faced other crises in our history and have become stronger by rejecting the easy way out and taking the right way in meeting our challenges. Our greatness as a nation has been our capacity to do what had to be done when we knew our course was right.

I recognize that some of my fellow citizens disagree with the plan for peace I have chosen. Honest and patriotic Americans have reached different conclusions as to how peace should be achieved.

In San Francisco a few weeks ago, I saw demonstrators carrying signs reading: "Lose in Vietnam, bring the boys home."

Well, one of the strengths of our free society is that any American has a right to reach that conclusion and to advocate that point of view. But as President of the

United States, I would be untrue to my oath of office if I allowed the policy of this Nation to be dictated by the minority who hold that point of view and who try to impose it on the Nation by mounting demonstrations in the street.

For almost 200 years, the policy of this Nation has been made under our Constitution by those leaders in the Congress and the White House elected by all of the people. If a vocal minority, however fervent its cause, prevails over reason and the will of the majority, this Nation has no future as a free society.

And now I would like to address a word, if I may, to the young people of this Nation who are particularly concerned, and I understand why they are concerned, about this war.

I respect your idealism.

I share your concern for peace.

I want peace as much as you do.

There are powerful personal reasons I want to end this war. This week I will have to sign 83 letters to mothers, fathers, wives, and loved ones of men who have given their lives for America in Vietnam. It is very little satisfaction to me that this is only one-third as many letters as I signed the first week in office. There is nothing I want more than to see the day come when I do not have to write any of those letters.

—I want to end the war to save the lives of those brave young men in Vietnam.

—But I want to end it in a way which will increase the chance that their younger brothers and their sons will not have to fight in some future Vietnam someplace in the world.

—And I want to end the war for another reason. I want to end it so that the energy and dedication of you, our young people, now too often directed into bitter hatred against those responsible for the war, can be turned to the great challenges of peace, a better life for all Americans, a better life for all people on this earth.

I have chosen a plan for peace. I believe it will succeed.

If it does succeed, what the critics say now won't matter. If it does not succeed, anything I say then won't matter.

I know it may not be fashionable to speak of patriotism or national destiny these days. But I feel it is appropriate to do so on this occasion.

Two hundred years ago this Nation was weak and poor. But even then, America was the hope of millions in the world. Today we have become the strongest and richest nation in the world. And the wheel of destiny has turned so that any hope the world has for the survival of peace and freedom will be determined by whether the American people have the moral stamina and the courage to meet the challenge of free world leadership.

Let historians not record that when America was the most powerful nation in the world we passed on the other side of the road and allowed the last hopes for peace and freedom of millions of people to be suffocated by the forces of totalitarianism.

And so tonight—to you, the great silent majority of my fellow Americans—I ask for your support.

I pledged in my campaign for the Presidency to end the war in a way that we could win the peace. I have initiated a plan of action which will enable me to keep that pledge.

The more support I can have from the American people, the sooner that pledge can be redeemed; for the more divided we are at home, the less likely the enemy is to negotiate at Paris.

Let us be united for peace. Let us also be united against defeat. Because let us understand: North Vietnam cannot defeat or humiliate the United States. Only Americans can do that.

Fifty years ago, in this room and at this very desk, President Woodrow Wilson spoke words which caught the imagination of a war-weary world. He said: "This is the war to end war." His dream for peace after World War I was shattered on the hard realities of great power politics and Woodrow Wilson died a broken man.

Tonight I do not tell you that the war in Vietnam is the war to end wars. But I do say this: I have initiated a plan which will end this war in a way that will bring us closer to that great goal to which Woodrow Wilson and every American President in our history has been dedicated—the goal of a just and lasting peace.

As President I hold the responsibility for choosing the best path to that goal and then leading the Nation along it.

I pledge to you tonight that I shall meet this responsibility with all of the strength and wisdom I can command in accordance with your hopes, mindful of your concerns, sustained by your prayers.

Thank you and goodnight.

59. *"Our People's Struggle": A Last Testament (May 1969)**

By Ho Chi Minh

On May 10, 1969, Ho Chi Minh prepared his last testament. He was about to be 79 years old on May 19, and his health was failing. He died on September 3.

He had devoted his life to the independence of his country. Although he did not live to see the end of the war, the final campaign to take Saigon was named in his memory—the Ho Chi Minh Campaign—and Saigon was renamed Ho Chi Minh City. His last testament was part of preparations for a smooth transition in the event of his death. When the transition did take place, the collective leadership exhibited no signs of any turmoil or difficulty—except for mourning. Le Duan, the First Secretary of the Lao Dong (Communist) Party, read from this testament at the funeral service on September 9.

*From *Guardian: A Radical Newsweekly* [New York], March 21, 1970.

Our people's struggle against U.S. aggression, for national salvation, may have to go through even more difficulties and sacrifices, but we are bound to win total victory.

This is a certainty.

I intend, when that comes, to tour both North and South to congratulate our heroic compatriots, cadres and combatants, and visit old people and our beloved youth and children.

Then, on behalf of our people, I will go to the fraternal countries of the socialist camp and friendly countries in the world, and thank them for their wholehearted support and assistance to our people's patriotic struggle against U.S. aggression.

Tu Fu, the well-known Chinese poet of the T'ang period, wrote: "Few have ever reached the age of seventy."

This year, being seventy-nine, I count among those "few"; still, my mind has remained very lucid, though my health has somewhat declined in comparison with previous years. When one is on the wrong side of seventy, health deteriorates with age. This is no wonder.

But who can say how much longer I shall be able to serve the revolution, the Fatherland and the people?

I therefore leave these few lines in anticipation of the day when I shall go and join Karl Marx, V. I. Lenin and other elder revolutionaries; this way, our people throughout the country, our comrades in the Party, and our friends in the world will not be taken by surprise.

First about the Party: Thanks to its close unity and total dedication to the working class, the people and the Fatherland, our Party has been able, since its founding, to unite, organize and lead our people from success to success in a resolute struggle.

Unity is an extremely precious tradition of our Party and people. All comrades, from the Central Committee down to the cell, must preserve the unity and oneness of mind in the Party as the apple of their eye.

Within the Party, to achieve broad democracy and to practice self-criticism and criticism regularly and seriously is the best way to consolidate and further solidarity and unity. Comradely affection should prevail.

Ours is a Party in power. Each Party member, each cadre, must be deeply imbued with revolutionary morality, and show industry, thrift, integrity, uprightness, total dedication to public interests and complete selflessness. Our Party should preserve absolute purity and prove worthy of its role as leader and very loyal servant of the people.

About the working youth and union members and our young people: On the whole they are excellent; they are always ready to come forward, fearless of difficulties and eager for progress. The Party must foster their revolutionary virtues and train them as our successors, both "red" and "expert," in the building of socialism.

Training and educating future revolutionary generations is of great importance and necessity.

About our laboring peoples: In the plains as in the mountain areas, they have for ages endured hardships, feudal and colonial oppression and exploitation; they have moreover experienced many years of war.

Yet, our people have shown great heroism, courage, enthusiasm and industriousness. They have always followed the Party since it came into being, with unqualified loyalty.

The Party must work out a very effective plan for economic and cultural development constantly to raise the living standard of the people.

About the resistance war against U.S. aggression: It may drag on. Our compatriots may have to face new sacrifices in property and life. Whatever may happen, we must keep firm our resolve to fight the U.S. aggressors till total victory.

Our rivers, our mountains, our people will always be;

The American aggressors defeated, we will build a country ten times more beautiful.

Whatever difficulties and hardships may be ahead, our people are sure of total triumph. The U.S. imperialists shall have to quit. Our Fatherland shall be reunified. Our compatriots in the North and in the South shall be reunited under the same roof. We, a small nation, will have earned the unique honor of defeating, through a heroic struggle, two big imperialisms—the French and the American—and making a worthy contribution to the national liberation movement.

About the world communist movement: Having devoted my whole life to the revolution, I am proud of the growth of the international communist and workers' movement as well as grieved at the dissensions now dividing the fraternal parties.

I hope that our Party will do its best to contribute effectively to the restoration of unity among the fraternal parties on the basis of Marxism-Leninism and proletarian internationalism, in a way which conforms to both reason and sentiment.

I am sure that the fraternal parties and countries will have to unite again.

About personal matters: All my life, I have served the Fatherland, the revolution and the people with all my heart and strength. If I should now depart from this world, I would regret nothing, except not being able to serve longer and more.

When I am gone, grand funerals should be avoided so as not to waste the people's time and money.

Finally, to the whole people, the whole Party, the whole army, to my nephews and nieces, the youth and children, I leave my boundless love.

I also convey my cordial greetings to our comrades and friends, to the youth and children of the world.

My ultimate wish is that our whole Party and people, closely joining their efforts, build a peaceful, unified, independent, democratic and prosperous Vietnam, and make a worthy contribution to the world revolution.

60. Explaining the "Secret War" in Laos (March 6, 1970)*

By President Richard M. Nixon

The Geneva Accords of 1962 (signed for the United States by Dean Rusk and Averell Harriman) declared that Laos would be a neutral country.[1] Involved militarily in Laos since the 1950s, the United States agreed, under the Geneva Accords, to remove all military personnel, including the CIA. Instead, the CIA turned the "civilian" Agency for International Development (AID) mission into its cover[2] for training an anti-Communist army of Meo (Hmong) tribesmen which numbered 44,330[3] by 1973. The commander of this army was General Vang Pao,[4] a key figure also in the CIA's support of the opium and heroin business in the Golden Triangle area of Laos, Burma and Thailand.[5]

CIA activities in Laos and the fact that Thai troops and US Special Forces were operating in Laos were no secret to the Royal Lao Government, supported by the United States, nor to the Pathet Lao guerrillas and peasants being attacked. These operations and the bombing that began in 1964 were supposed to be a secret from the American people as well as a "diplomatic" secret (acknowledgment would make the US warfare an "official" act). Yet by 1967 this "secret" war was being reported not only by the press outside the United States but even by US press agencies. UPI, for example, reported from Saigon on August 13, 1967 an official confirmation by the US Air Force that it had been bombing neutral Laos on a daily

---

Public Papers of the Presidents of the United States: Richard Nixon, 1970 (Washington: US Government Printing Office, 1971), pp. 244–249.

1. For historical background and analysis of the Laotian situation, see Marvin and Susan Gettleman, Lawrence and Carol Kaplan, eds., *Conflict in Indochina: A Reader on the Widening War in Laos and Cambodia* (New York: Vintage Books, 1970) and Nina S. Adams and Alfred W. McCoy, eds., *Laos: War and Revolution* (New York: Harper Colophon Books, 1970).

2. John Hannah, AID administrator in Laos, admitted on June 7, 1970, that the CIA used AID as a cover, a decision made in 1962 (*San Francisco Chronicle*, June 8, 1970). In May 1971 Hannah reported that by the beginning of fiscal year 1972, AID financing for CIA work would be terminated. However, in March 1972 Senator Edward Kennedy, chairman of the Judiciary Subcommittee on Refugees, revealed that the Government Accounting Office had found that more than half the AID funds earmarked for civilian victims of the war in Laos were being used to finance the CIA's continuing "secret" army (*San Francisco Chronicle*, March 26, 1972).

3. *San Francisco Chronicle*, June 18, 1973. This article concerned the first confirmed US POW in Laos since the cease-fire of February 1973. Emmet Kay was a pilot for Continental Air Services, Inc., one of the three CIA airlines in Laos (according to congressional investigators); the others were Air America and Lao Air Development.

4. After the war Vang Pao settled on his own ranch in Montana. Many other Meo (Hmong) CIA army members also came to the United States.

5. *The Politics of Heroin in Southeast Asia* by Alfred W. McCoy (New York: Harper & Row, 1972), with Cathleen B. Read and Leonard P. Adams II, is a carefully researched account of CIA involvement in the drug trade. See Reading 20.

basis for over three years. The Air Force maintained that its primary target was the "Ho Chi Minh trail" (southeastern Laos) used for "infiltration" by North Vietnamese into the South. Actually, by this time dozens of villages in north central Laos had been flattened and the peasants had been forced to live underground or flee. Within a short time, one-third of the population was forcibly turned into refugees, part of the US policy (as in Cambodia and South Vietnam) of trying to separate the people from the guerrillas, the "sea" from the "fish."

The public outcry against all the "secret" bombing and "incursions" finally led, in October 1969, to a congressional hearing behind the closed doors of the Senate Foreign Relations Committee's Subcommittee on United States Security Agreements and Commitments Abroad.[6] Chairman Stuart Symington, previously Secretary of the Air Force, called it a "travesty" to deny fighting in Laos "when not only the enemy but also the American participants including those who are casualties and some of their families know the truth."[7]

The White House opposed releasing the results of the 1969 congressional investigation to the public. When it became clear that most of the information would be released, the President issued a statement attempting to explain the situation in Laos.[8] Excerpts from that explanation are reprinted below. On April 19, 1970, portions of the congressional investigation were made public; ten percent remained classified.

Less than a year later, on February 8, 1971, the United States backed an invasion of Laos by ARVN troops (see footnote 13), resulting in a debacle when ARVN troops started retreating within three weeks.

In 1973 a Peace Accord was signed and in 1974 a coalition government was formed. With the Pathet Lao having secured the position as the major force in the new coalition Laotian government, Secretary of State Kissinger announced in May 1975 a "substantial reduction" in the 1,000-strong, 24-year-old AID mission in Laos. At the time of the announcement, an AID installation in Vientiane was being occupied by a student sit-in and other AID offices throughout the country were wrecked and empty.[9]

In light of the increasingly massive presence of North Vietnamese troops and their recent offensives in Laos, I have written letters today to British Prime Minister Wilson and Soviet Premier Kosygin asking their help in restoring the 1962 Geneva agreements for that country.

---

6. This was not the first hearing on the matter, but previously, according to Senator William Fulbright, the senators "did not ask the right questions."

7. *San Francisco Chronicle*, October 20, 1969.

8. Many parts of President Nixon's statement have been challenged. An article by Peter Dale Scott (*New York Review of Books*, XIV [April 9, 1970], reprinted in Gettleman and Kaplan, *Conflict in Indochina*, Reading 21) persuasively counters the President's view of the history of early U.S. involvement.

9. *Hartford Courant* (Conn.), May 23, 1975.

As Cochairmen of that conference, the United Kingdom and the Soviet Union have particular responsibilities for seeing that its provisions are honored. My letters note the persistent North Vietnamese violations of the accords and their current offensives; support the Laotian Prime Minister's own current appeal to the Cochairmen for consultations; urge the Cochairmen to work with other signatories of the Geneva accords; and pledge full United States cooperation.

Hanoi's most recent military build-up in Laos has been particularly escalatory. . . .

North Vietnam's military escalation in Laos has intensified public discussion in this country. The purpose of this statement is to set forth the record of what we found in January 1969 and the policy of this administration since that time. . . .

By early 1963 the North Vietnamese and Pathet Lao had openly breached the 1962 agreements by attacking the neutralist government forces in north Laos and by occupying and fortifying the area in southeast Laos along what came to be known as the Ho Chi Minh Trail. In these circumstances, the Laotian Prime Minister [Souvanna Phouma][10] requested American aid in the form of supplies and munitions. The Kennedy administration provided this assistance in line with the Laotian Government's right under the Geneva Accords to seek help in its self-defense.

In mid-May 1964 the Pathet Lao supported by the North Vietnamese attacked Prime Minister Souvanna Phouma's neutralist military forces on the Plain of Jars.[11] North Vietnam also began to increase its use of the Ho Chi Minh Trail to further its aggression against South Vietnam. The Johnson administration responded to Royal Laotian Government requests to meet this escalation by increasing our training and logistic support to the Royal Lao Government. In May 1964, as North Vietnamese presence increased, the United States, at Royal Lao Government request, began flying certain interdictory missions against invaders who were violating Lao neutrality. . . .

Since this administration has been in office, North Vietnamese pressure has continued. Last spring, the North Vietnamese mounted a campaign which threatened the royal capital and moved beyond the areas previously occupied by Communists. A counterattack by the Lao Government forces, intended to relieve this military pressure and cut off supply lines, caught the enemy by surprise and succeeded beyond expectations in pushing them off the strategic central plain in north Laos known as the Plain of Jars.[12]

The North Vietnamese left behind huge stores of arms, ammunition, and other supplies cached on the Plain. During their operations in the Plain of Jars last summer and fall, Lao Government forces captured almost 8,000 tons of Communist

---

10. After the war, when his brother, Pathet Lao leader Souphanouvong, became president of the People's Democratic Republic of Laos, Souvanna Phouma stayed in Laos as an "adviser" to the government until he died January 11, 1984.—eds.

11. The main CIA base in Laos was in Long Cheng (or Long Tieng) on the southern edge of the Plain of Jars.—eds.

12. This was the period when the United States was engaged in a particularly intensive bombing campaign on the Plain of Jars for eight months.—eds.

equipment, supplies and weapons, including tanks, armored cars, artillery pieces, machine guns, and thousands of individual weapons including about 4,000 tons of ammunition. The size and nature of these supply caches the Communists had emplaced on the Plain by the summer of 1969 show clearly that many months ago the North Vietnamese were preparing for major offensive actions on Laotian territory against the Royal Lao Government.

During the final months of 1969 and January 1970, Hanoi sent over 13,000 additional troops into Laos and rebuilt their stocks and supply lines. They also introduced tanks and long-range artillery.

During January and February, Prime Minister Souvanna Phouma proposed to the other side that the Plain of Jars be neutralized. The Communists' response was to launch their current offensive which has recaptured the Plain of Jars and is threatening to go beyond the furthest line of past Communist advances.

The Prime Minister is now once again trying to obtain consultations among all the parties to the Geneva accords, envisaged under Article IV when there is a violation of Lao sovereignty, independence, neutrality, or territorial integrity.

In this situation, our purposes remain straightforward.

We are trying above all to save American and allied lives in South Vietnam which are threatened by the continual infiltration of North Vietnamese troops and supplies along the Ho Chi Minh Trail. Hanoi has infiltrated over 100,000 men through Laos since this administration took office and over 500,000 altogether. Our airstrikes have destroyed weapons and supplies over the past 4 years which would have taken thousands of American lives.

We are also supporting the independence and neutrality of Laos as set forth in the 1962 Geneva agreements. . . .

In recent days . . . there has been intense public speculation to the effect that the United States involvement in Laos has substantially increased in violation of the Geneva accords, that American ground forces are engaged in combat in Laos, and that our air activity has had the effect of escalating the conflict.

Because these reports are grossly inaccurate, I have concluded that our national interest will be served by putting the subject into perspective through a precise description of our current activities in Laos.

These are the facts:

—There are no American ground combat troops in Laos.[13]

—We have no plans for introducing ground combat forces into Laos.

—The total number of Americans directly employed by the U.S. Government

---

13. On December 29, 1969, the Cooper-Church Amendment became law; attached to the 1970 Defense Department Appropriations Act was the stipulation that "none of the funds appropriated by this Act shall be used to finance the introduction of American ground combat troops into Laos or Thailand." The ban was extended to Cambodia a year later. But on March 27, 1974, Senator Harold Hughes told the Senate that several witnesses had testified to the Senate Armed Services Committee that US combat troops entered Laos and Cambodia after they were forbidden to do so. Quoting a Defense Department white paper, Hughes said there were 16 platoon-sized operations in Laos in 1970 and 13 more between January 1971 and April 1972—plus 3 multiplatoon operations in Laos in 1970; in Cambodia there were 22 platoon-sized operations after January 1, 1971, plus 9 multiplatoon missions (*San Francisco Chronicle*, March 28, 1974).—eds.

in Laos is 616. In addition, there are 424 Americans employed on contract to the Government or to Government contractors. Of these 1040 Americans, the total number, military and civilian, engaged in a military advisory or military training capacity numbers 320. Logistics personnel number 323.[14]

—No American stationed in Laos has ever been killed in ground combat operations.[15]

—U.S. personnel in Laos during the past year has not increased while during the past few months, North Vietnam has sent over 13,000 additional combat ground troops into Laos.

—When requested by the Royal Laotian Government, we have continued to provide military assistance to regular and irregular Laotian forces in the form of equipment, training and logistics. The levels of our assistance have risen in response to the growth of North Vietnamese combat activities.

—We have continued to conduct air operations. Our first priority for such operations is to interdict the continued flow of troops and supplies across Laotian territory on the Ho Chi Minh Trail. As Commander in Chief of our Armed Forces, I consider it my responsibility to use our air power to interdict this flow of supplies and men into South Vietnam and thereby avoid a heavy toll of American and allied lives.

—In addition to these air operations on the Ho Chi Minh Trail, we have continued to carry out reconnaissance flights in Northern Laos and to fly combat support missions for Laotian forces when requested to do so by the Royal Laotian Government.

—In every instance our combat air operations have taken place only over those parts of Laos occupied and contested by North Vietnamese and other Communist forces. They have been flown only when requested by the Laotian Government. The level of our air operations has been increased only as the number of North Vietnamese in Laos and the level of their aggression has increased. . . .

I hope that a genuine quest for peace in Indochina can now begin. For Laos, this will require the efforts of the Geneva conference cochairmen and the signatory countries.

But most of all it will require realism and reasonableness from Hanoi. For it is the North Vietnamese, not we, who have escalated the fighting. Today there are 67,000 North Vietnamese troops in this small country.[16] There are no American

---

14. When the declassified portion of the Senate hearing on Laos was released April 19, a few weeks after this statement, it made clear, as subcommittee sources said, that "tens of thousands" of Americans were involved in the Laotian war, operating from Thailand, South Vietnam, and aircraft carriers, not to mention Laos itself (*San Francisco Chronicle*, April 20, 1970).—eds.

15. In his memoirs Kissinger calls this the "one inaccuracy" in an otherwise "full and candid account" (*White House Years*, p. 455).—eds.

16. Seymour Hersh (*The Price of Power*, p. 171) reports that Kissinger took charge of drafting this statement, but Kissinger's memoirs blame it on his new assistant, Winston Lord (*White House Years*, pp. 455–456). Whoever it was did not clear it with the "experts." Hersh relates how Jerome H. Doolittle, then press attaché in Laos, had told a press briefing in Vientiane only the night before (March 5) that there were 40,000 North Vietnamese troops in Laos.—eds.

troops there. Hanoi is not threatened by Laos; it runs risks only when it moves its forces across borders.

We desire nothing more in Laos than to see a return to the Geneva agreements and the withdrawal of North Vietnamese troops, leaving the Lao people to settle their own differences in a peaceful manner. . . .

61. Rationale for the Invasion of Cambodia (April 30, 1970)*

By President Richard M. Nixon

On March 18, 1970, while Prince Norodom Sihanouk was out of the country, General Lon Nol and other anti-communist officials staged a coup which placed Lon Nol at the head of the Cambodian government, as he announced on March 20.[1] Sihanouk had attempted to walk the thin line of neutrality, which was erased when the Lon Nol military government launched an all-out campaign to destroy any opposition. When Cambodian rebel forces retaliated with ambushes of troops and support for Sihanouk, government forces massacred thousands of ethnic Vietnamese citizens of Cambodia. With the battle between the Lon Nol government and communist forces intensifying, President Nixon, in the April 30 speech excerpted below, announced the invasion of Cambodia.

The United States was already attacking Cambodia by air, but this remained unacknowledged in this speech. The Nixon administration had launched an intensive "secret" bombing campaign, Operation Menu, against Cambodia in March 1969,[2] and there had been some bombing even earlier. On August 2, 1966, while six Americans were in Cambodia to verify reports of previous US bombing raids, they witnessed another attack on a village by US F–105 fighter-bombers.[3]

Although the "secret" bombing was not officially exposed until 1973, it was nevertheless covered in sporadic reports. On May 9, 1969, a "leak" in The New

---

*Public Papers of the Presidents of the United States: Richard Nixon, 1970 (Washington: US Government Printing Office, 1971), pp. 405–410.

1. For historical background and analysis, see Marvin and Susan Gettleman, Lawrence and Carol Kaplan, eds., *Conflict in Indochina: A Reader on the Widening War in Laos and Cambodia* (New York: Vintage Books, 1970).

2. For an informative view of the war in Cambodia from that time until the end, see William Shawcross, *Sideshow: Kissinger, Nixon and the Destruction of Cambodia* (New York: Pocket Books, 1979).

3. *San Francisco Chronicle*, August 4, 1966. The Americans were part of "Americans Want to Know" and included author Kay Boyle and Floyd McKissick of the Congress of Racial Equality (CORE). Throughout the war in Indochina, US private citizens went to the front lines and brought back firsthand information.

York Times *"enraged" Nixon and Kissinger.*[4] The London Times *also blew the whistle after a reporter saw B–52 craters while on a commercial flight. The Pentagon confirmed on June 22, 1970, that US raids were going deep into Cambodia, but Pentagon spokesman Jerry Friedheim*[5] *said they had begun a week earlier. Other reports said they started April 30 at the time of the invasion.*[6] *The Cooper-Church Amendment, which on December 29, 1969, had banned ground troops in Laos and Thailand, was extended a year later to include Cambodia, but did not cover air attacks.*

The extent of opposition to the invasion had an immediate effect. On May 8, the day before a huge antiwar demonstration in Washington and four days after the Kent State killings, Nixon announced that most US troops would be pulled out of Cambodia by mid-June, and that all would be out by July 1. On June 3, 1970, he said the "only remaining American activity in Cambodia after July 1 will be air missions to interdict the movement of enemy troops and materiel where I find it is necessary to protect the lives and security of our men in South Vietnam." But clandestine ground troop operations continued (Reading 60, footnote 13) and, after all US troops had been brought home from Vietnam (March 1973), Cambodia was bombed with an intensity it had not experienced before. The San Francisco Sunday Examiner and Chronicle *reported on April 8, 1973, that attacks by US jet fighter-bombers based in Thailand averaged at least 120 strikes a day, and attacks by B–52s (which can carry up to 60,000 pounds of bombs) totaled about fifty a day. On one day of that week, 120 B–52 sorties were flown. The amount of damage inflicted can be measured by what happened on August 6, 1973, when either a single B-52 (according to the Pentagon) or about four B-52s (according to the villagers) "mistakenly" bombed Neak Luong, a "friendly" (rather than an "enemy") village, killing and wounding hundreds of people in a pre-dawn raid.*[7]

On July 1, 1973, Congress passed a law forbidding the use of any funds for combat in, over, or off the shores of Cambodia, Laos, North Vietnam, and South Vietnam as of August 15, 1973. The bombing continued right up to the deadline. Less than two years later, on April 16, 1975, the Khmer Rouge rebels took Phnom Penh.

---

4. Richard Nixon, *RN: The Memoirs of Richard Nixon* (New York: Grosset & Dunlap, 1978), p. 388.

5. *San Francisco Chronicle*, June 23, 1970. Friedheim continued to provide this kind of double and sometimes triple cover-up story for years. On July 19, 1973, for example, he acknowledged providing the Senate Armed Services Committee with a false report the previous month that covered up the "secret" bombing of Cambodia; "I knew at the time it was wrong and I'm sorry," he said. But five hours later a "clarification" was issued which said that he had not realized the report was "incomplete" until it had been distributed to the committee (*San Francisco Chronicle*, July 20, 1973). *The New York Times*, February 7, 1984, mentioned Jerry Friedheim in his current position: executive vice president of the American Society of Newspaper Publishers.

6. *San Francisco Chronicle*, June 22, 1970.

7. *San Francisco Chronicle*, August 7, 1973. Such "mistakes" were not uncommon in the air war. Sometimes US troops were the victims. In this particular bombing about half the people killed were government soldiers, US allies.

Good evening my fellow Americans:
   Ten days ago, in my report to the Nation on Vietnam, I announced a decision
to withdraw an additional 150,000 Americans from Vietnam over the next year. I
said then that I was making that decision despite our concern over increased enemy
activity in Laos, in Cambodia, and in South Vietnam.

   At that time, I warned that if I concluded that increased enemy activity in any
of these areas endangered the lives of Americans remaining in Vietnam, I would
not hesitate to take strong and effective measures to deal with that situation.

   Despite that warning, North Vietnam has increased its military aggression in
all these areas, and particularly in Cambodia.

   After full consultation with the National Security Council, Ambassador
Bunker, General Abrams, and my other advisers, I have concluded that the actions
of the enemy in the last 10 days clearly endanger the lives of Americans who are
in Vietnam now and would constitute an unacceptable risk to those who will be
there after withdrawal of another 150,000.

   To protect our men who are in Vietnam and to guarantee the continued success
of our withdrawal and Vietnamization programs, I have concluded that the time
has come for action.

   Tonight, I shall describe the actions of the enemy, the actions I have ordered to
deal with that situation, and the reasons for my decision.

   Cambodia, a small country of 7 million people, has been a neutral nation since
the Geneva agreement of 1954—an agreement, incidentally, which was signed by
the Government of North Vietnam.

   American policy since then has been to scrupulously respect the neutrality of
the Cambodian people. We have maintained a skeleton diplomatic mission of
fewer than 15 in Cambodia's capital, and that only since last August. For the
previous 4 years, from 1965 to 1969, we did not have any diplomatic mission
whatever in Cambodia. And for the past 5 years, we have provided no military
assistance whatever and no economic assistance to Cambodia.

   North Vietnam, however, has not respected that neutrality.

   For the past 5 years—as indicated on this map that you see here—North Vietnam has occupied military sanctuaries all along the Cambodian frontier with South
Vietnam. Some of these extend up to 20 miles into Cambodia. . . .

   For 5 years, neither the United States nor South Vietnam has moved against
these enemy sanctuaries because we did not wish to violate the territory of a neutral nation. Even after the Vietnamese Communists began to expand these sanctuaries 4 weeks ago, we counseled patience to our South Vietnamese allies and
imposed restraints on our own commanders. . . .

   North Vietnam in the last 2 weeks has stripped away all pretense of respecting
the sovereignty or the neutrality of Cambodia. Thousands of their soldiers are
invading the country from the sanctuaries; they are encircling the capital of Phnom
Penh. Coming from these sanctuaries, as you see here, they have moved into
Cambodia and are encircling the capital. . . .

   In cooperation with the armed forces of South Vietnam, attacks are being launched this week to clean out major enemy sanctuaries on the Cambodian-Vietnam border.

A major responsibility for the ground operations is being assumed by South Vietnamese forces. . . .

There is one area, however, immediately above Parrot's Beak, where I have concluded that a combined American and South Vietnamese operation is necessary.

Tonight, American and South Vietnamese units will attack the headquarters for the entire Communist military operation in South Vietnam. This key control center has been occupied by the North Vietnamese and Vietcong for 5 years in blatant violation of Cambodia's neutrality.[8]

This is not an invasion of Cambodia. The areas in which these attacks will be launched are completely occupied and controlled by North Vietnamese forces.[9] Our purpose is not to occupy the areas. Once enemy forces are driven out of these sanctuaries and once their military supplies are destroyed, we will withdraw. . . .

We take this action not for the purpose of expanding the war into Cambodia but for the purpose of ending the war in Vietnam and winning the just peace we all desire. We have made—we will continue to make every possible effort to end this war through negotiation at the conference table rather than through more fighting on the battlefield.

Let us look again at the record. We have stopped the bombing of North Vietnam. We have cut air operations by over 20 percent. We have announced withdrawal of over 250,000 of our men. We have offered to withdraw all of our men if they will withdraw theirs. We have offered to negotiate all issues with only one condition—and that is that the future of South Vietnam be determined not by North Vietnam, and not by the United States, but by the people of South Vietnam themselves. . . .

The action that I have announced tonight puts the leaders of North Vietnam on notice that we will be patient in working for peace; we will be conciliatory at the conference table, but we will not be humiliated. We will not be defeated. We will not allow American men by the thousands to be killed by an enemy from privileged sanctuaries.

The time came long ago to end this war through peaceful negotiations. We stand ready for those negotiations. . . .

---

8. The Central Office for South Vietnam (COSVN), headquarters for the guerrilla war in South Vietnam, was never found, not in Cambodia or anywhere else. It was also used as a reason for bombing Cambodia. Many lives were lost in the search for COSVN. Particularly interesting is Seymour Hersh's account of a Green Beret mission sent to capture COSVN. When they were ordered to try a second time after what happened the first time, they refused to go (*The Price of Power: Kissinger in the Nixon White House* [New York: Summit Books, 1983], pp. 63–64).—eds.

9. In fact the American troops encountered and destroyed Cambodian villages. William Shawcross (*Sideshow*, pp. 150–151) describes this destruction, including the killing of civilians. When the officer in charge was asked why he had to destroy a village, he replied, "We had no choice. We had to take it . This was a hub of North Vietnamese activity."—eds.

But if the enemy response to our most conciliatory offers for peaceful negotiation continues to be to increase its attacks and humiliate and defeat us, we shall react accordingly.

My fellow Americans, we live in an age of anarchy, both abroad and at home. We see mindless attacks on all the great institutions which have been created by free civilizations in the last 500 years. Even here in the United States, great universities are being systematically destroyed. . . .

If, when the chips are down, the world's most powerful nation, the United States of America, acts like a pitiful, helpless giant, the forces of totalitarianism and anarchy will threaten free nations and free institutions throughout the world.

It is not our power but our will and character that is being tested tonight. . . .

I have rejected all political considerations in making this decision.

Whether my party gains in November is nothing compared to the lives of 400,000 brave Americans fighting for our country and for the cause of peace and freedom in Vietnam. Whether I may be a one-term President is insignificant compared to whether by our failure to act in this crisis the United States proves itself to be unworthy to lead the forces of freedom in this critical period in world history. I would rather be a one-term President and do what I believe is right than to be a two-term President at the cost of seeing America become a second-rate power and to see this Nation accept the first defeat in its proud 190-year history. . . .

It is customary to conclude a speech from the White House by asking support for the President of the United States. Tonight, I depart from that precedent. What I ask is far more important. I ask for your support for our brave men fighting tonight halfway around the world—not for territory—not for glory—but so that their younger brothers and their sons and your sons can have a chance to grow up in a world of peace and freedom and justice.

Thank you and good night.

62. Vietnam Veterans Against the War: Testimony to the US Senate Foreign Relations Committee (April 22, 1971)*

By John Kerry

US troops were told during training that they were being sent to "save" the South Vietnamese from communists. As soon as they got involved in South Vietnam, many began to question what they were doing. A widely published report (Associated

---

*From the *Congressional Record*, May 3, 1971. The statement was made April 22, 1971, during the week of antiwar protests by Vietnam Veterans Against the War.

Press) on September 30, 1965, quoted a letter from a Wichita, Kansas, soldier: "There are so many Cong here that in three days we captured 12 VC and killed 33. Mom, I had to kill a woman and a baby. . . . I swear to God this place is worse than hell. Why must I kill women and kids? Who knows who's right?" As these soldiers became veterans, they brought the war's experience home with them. In 1967 Vietnam Veterans Against the War (VVAW) was formed.

In February 1971, about 150 veterans convened "The Winter Soldier Investigation" in Detroit to hold hearings on the violence they had committed or witnessed in Vietnam. They took the name from Thomas Paine's words of 1776: "The summer soldier and the sunshine patriot will, in this crisis, shrink from the service of his country." The media paid little attention. There was some attempt to discredit the hearings by suggesting that the veterans were fakes. But on April 6, 1971, Republican Senator Mark Hatfield of Oregon introduced the entire testimony into the Congressional Record.

VVAW carried out Operation Dewey Canyon III, "a limited incursion[1] into the country of Congress," during the week of April 19–23, 1971. (Dewey Canyon I was a covert invasion of Laos in 1969; Dewey Canyon II was the first week of the invasion of Laos that had just taken place in February.) Along with Gold Star Mothers (mothers whose sons were killed in Vietnam), they spoke to tourists and passersby, dramatizing their message with "guerrilla war" skits. Over a thousand veterans took part, some in wheelchairs and others on crutches. They camped on the Capitol mall, defying a Supreme Court injunction. Some of them tried to turn themselves in as war criminals at the Pentagon.

The most dramatic event of Dewey Canyon III came on the final day of the protest. About 800 veterans lined up at the barricade built that week to keep demonstrators off the Capitol steps. One by one they stepped up to the microphones and made a statement. Then they tossed their Bronze Stars, Silver Stars, Purple Hearts, and campaign ribbons over the barricade. Millions of Americans watched on TV as veterans voiced their feelings: "Here's my merit badges for murder . . . from the country I betrayed by enlisting in the US Army." "I'd like to say just one thing for the people of Vietnam. I'm sorry. I hope that someday I can return to Vietnam and help rebuild that country we tore apart."[2]

A day earlier, John Kerry, representing VVAW, made the statement reprinted below before the Senate Foreign Relations Committee. Kerry had been awarded the Silver Star, the Bronze Star with oak leaf cluster, and three Purple Hearts. In 1982 he was elected lieutenant governor of Massachusetts, and in 1984 he was elected to the US Senate.

---

1. President Nixon preferred the word "incursion" to "invasion."

2. John Kerry and Vietnam Veterans Against the War, *The New Soldier*, David Thorne and George Butler, eds. (New York: Collier Books, 1971), p. 134. *The New Soldier* is an illustrated record of Dewey Canyon III and also contains testimony from the Winter Soldier Investigation.

Thank you very much, Senator Fulbright, Senator Javits, Senator Symington, Senator Pell. I would like to say for the record, and also for the men behind me who are also wearing the uniform and their medals, that my sitting here is really symbolic. I am not here as John Kerry. I am here as one member of the group of 1,000 which is a small representation of a very much larger group of veterans in this country, and were it possible for all of them to sit at this table they would be here and have the same kind of testimony.

I would simply like to speak in very general terms. I apologize if my statement is general because I received notification yesterday you would hear me and I am afraid that because of the court injunction I was up most of the night and haven't had a great deal of time to prepare for this hearing.[3]

I would like to talk on behalf of all those veterans and say that several months ago in Detroit we had an investigation at which over 150 honorably discharged, and many very highly decorated, veterans testified to war crimes committed in Southeast Asia. These were not isolated incidents but crimes committed on a day to day basis with the full awareness of officers at all levels of command.

It is impossible to describe to you exactly what did happen in Detroit—the emotions in the room and the feelings of the men who were reliving their experiences in Vietnam. They relived the absolute horror of what this country, in a sense, made them do.

They told stories that at times they had personally raped, cut off ears, cut off heads, taped wires from portable telephones to human genitals and turned up the power, cut off limbs, blown up bodies, randomly shot at civilians, razed villages in fashion reminiscent of Genghis Khan, shot cattle and dogs for fun, poisoned food stocks, and generally ravaged the countryside of South Vietnam in addition to the normal ravage of war and the normal and very particular ravaging which is done by the applied bombing power of this country.

We call this investigation the Winter Soldier Investigation. The term Winter Soldier is a play on words of Thomas Paine's in 1776 when he spoke of the Sunshine Patriots and summer time soldiers who deserted at Valley Forge because the going was rough.

We who have come here to Washington have come here because we feel we have to be winter soldiers now. We could come back to this country, we could be quiet, we could hold our silence, we could not tell what went on in Vietnam, but we feel because of what threatens this country, not the reds, but the crimes which we are committing that threaten it, that we have to speak out.

I would like to talk to you a little bit about what the result is of the feelings

---

3. The Supreme Court injunction forbade sleeping on the mall. The evening before Kerry made this statement, there was a long meeting with a vote on whether or not to stay in the mall overnight. The vote was 480 to 400 to stay. See Art Goldberg, "Vietnam Vets: The Anti-War Army," *Ramparts*, July 1971, reprinted in Judith Carnoy and Marc Weiss, eds., *A House Divided: Radical Perspectives on Social Problems* (Boston: Little, Brown and Co., 1973).—eds.

these men carry with them after coming back from Vietnam. The country doesn't know it yet but it has created a monster, a monster in the form of millions of men who have been taught to deal and to trade in violence and who are given the chance to die for the biggest nothing in history; men who have returned with a sense of anger and a sense of betrayal which no one has yet grasped.

As a veteran and one who feels this anger I would like to talk about it. We are angry because we feel we have been used in the worst fashion by the administration of this country.

In 1970 at West Point Vice President Agnew said "some glamorize the criminal misfits of society while our best men die in Asian rice paddies to preserve the freedom which most of those misfits abuse," and this was used as a rallying point for our effort in Vietnam.

But for us, as boys in Asia whom the country was supposed to support, his statement is a terrible distortion from which we can only draw a very deep sense of revulsion, and hence the anger of some of the men who are here in Washington today. It is a distortion because we in no way consider ourselves the best men of this country; because those he calls misfits were standing up for us in a way that nobody else in this country dared to; because so many who have died would have returned to this country to join the misfits in their efforts to ask for an immediate withdrawal from South Vietnam; because so many of those best men have returned as quadriplegics and amputees—and they lie forgotten in Veterans Administration Hospitals in this country which fly the flag which so many have chosen as their own personal symbol—and we cannot consider ourselves America's best men when we are ashamed of and hated for what we were called on to do in Southeast Asia.

In our opinion, and from our experience, there is nothing in South Vietnam which could happen that realistically threatens the United States of America. And to attempt to justify the loss of one American life in Vietnam, Cambodia or Laos by linking such loss to the preservation of freedom, which those misfits supposedly abuse, is to us the height of criminal hypocrisy, and it is that kind of hypocrisy which we feel has torn this country apart.

We are probably much more angry than that, but I don't want to go into the foreign policy aspects because I am outclassed here. I know that all of you talk about every possible alternative for getting out of Vietnam. We understand that. We know you have considered the seriousness of the aspects to the utmost level and I am not going to try to dwell on that. But I want to relate to you the feeling that many of the men who have returned to this country express because we are probably angriest about all that we were told about Vietnam and about the mystical war against communism.

We found that not only was it a civil war, an effort by a people who had for years been seeking their liberation from any colonial influence whatsoever, but also we found that the Vietnamese whom we had enthusiastically molded after our own image were hard put to take up the fight against the threat we were supposedly saving them from.

We found most people didn't even know the difference between communism and democracy. They only wanted to work in rice paddies without helicopters strafing them and bombs with napalm burning their villages and tearing their country apart. They wanted everything to do with the war, particularly with this foreign presence of the United States of America, to leave them alone in peace, and they practiced the art of survival by siding with whichever military force was present at a particular time, be it Viet Cong, North Vietnamese or American.

We found also that all too often American men were dying in those rice paddies for want of support from their allies. We saw first hand how monies from American taxes were used for a corrupt dictatorial regime. We saw that many people in this country had a one-sided idea of who was kept free by our flag, and blacks provided the highest percentage of casualties. We saw Vietnam ravaged equally by American bombs and search and destroy missions, as well as by Viet Cong terrorism, and yet we listened while this country tried to blame all of the havoc on the Viet Cong.

We rationalized destroying villages in order to save them. We saw America lose her sense of morality as she accepted very coolly a My Lai and refused to give up the image of American soldiers who hand out chocolate bars and chewing gum.

We learned the meaning of free fire zones, shooting anything that moves, and we watched while America placed a cheapness on the lives of orientals.

We watched the United States falsification of body counts, in fact the glorification of body counts. We listened while month after month we were told the back of the enemy was about to break. We fought using weapons against "oriental human beings." We fought using weapons against those people which I do not believe this country would dream of using were we fighting in the European theater. We watched while men charged up hills because a general said that hill has to be taken, and after losing one platoon or two platoons they marched away to leave the hill for reoccupation by the North Vietnamese. We watched pride allow the most unimportant battles to be blown into extravaganzas, because we couldn't lose, and we couldn't retreat, and because it didn't matter how many American bodies were lost to prove that point, and so there were Hamburger Hills and Khe Sanhs and Hill 81s and Fire Base 6s, and so many others.

Now we are told that the men who fought there must watch quietly while American lives are lost so that we can exercise the incredible arrogance of Vietnamizing the Vietnamese.

Each day to facilitate the process by which the United States washes her hands of Vietnam someone has to give up his life so that the United States doesn't have to admit something that the entire world already knows, so that we can't say that we have made a mistake. Someone has to die so that President Nixon won't be, and these are his words, "the first President to lose a war."

We are asking Americans to think about that because how do you ask a man to be the last man to die in Vietnam? How do you ask a man to be the last man to die for a mistake? But we are trying to do that, and we are doing it with thousands of rationalizations, and if you read carefully the President's last speech to the people of this country, you can see that he says, and says clearly, "but the issue, gentlemen, is communism, and the question is whether or not we will leave that country to the communists or whether or not we will try to give it hope to be a free people." But the point is they are not a free people now under us. They are not a free people, and we cannot fight communism all over the world. I think we should have learned that lesson by now.

But the problem of veterans goes beyond this personal problem, because you think about a poster in this country with a picture of Uncle Sam and the picture says "I want you." And a young man comes out of high school and says, "that is fine, I am going to serve my country," and he goes to Vietnam and he shoots and he kills and he does his job. Or maybe he doesn't kill. Maybe he just goes and he comes back, and when he gets back to this country he finds that he isn't really wanted, because the largest corps of unemployed in the country—it varies depending on who you get it from, the Veterans Administration says 15 percent and various other sources 22 percent—but the largest corps of unemployed in this country are veterans of this war, and of those veterans 33 percent of the unemployed are black. That means one out of every ten of the nation's unemployed is a veteran of Vietnam.

The hospitals across the country won't, or can't meet their demands. It is not a question of not trying; they haven't got the appropriations. A man recently died after he had a tracheotomy in California, not because of the operation but because there weren't enough personnel to clean the mucus out of his tube and he suffocated to death.

Another young man just died in a New York VA hospital the other day. A friend of mine was lying in a bed two beds away and tried to help him but he couldn't. He rang a bell and there was nobody there to service that man and so he died of convulsions.

I understand 57 percent of all those entering the VA hospitals talk about suicide. Some 27 percent have tried, and they try because they come back to this country and they have to face what they did in Vietnam, and then they come back and find the indifference of a country that doesn't really care.

Suddenly we are faced with a very sickening situation in this country, because there is no moral indignation and, if there is, it comes from people who are almost exhausted by their past indignations, and I know that many of them are sitting in front of me. The country seems to have lain down and shrugged off something as serious as Laos, just as we calmly shrugged off the loss of 700,000 lives in Pakistan, the so-called greatest disaster of all times [the November 13, 1970, cyclone in what is now Bangladesh—eds.].

But we are here as veterans to say we think we are in the midst of the greatest disaster of all times now because they are still dying over there—not just Americans, but Vietnamese—and we are rationalizing leaving that country so that those people can go on killing each other for years to come.

Americans seem to have accepted the idea that the war is winding down, at least for Americans, and they have also allowed the bodies which were once used by a President for statistics to prove that we were winning that war, to be used as evidence against a man who followed orders and who interpreted those orders no differently than hundreds of other men in Vietnam.[4]

We veterans can only look with amazement on the fact that this country has been unable to see there is absolutely no difference between ground troops and a helicopter crew, and yet people have accepted a differentiation fed them by the administration.

No ground troops are in Laos so it is all right to kill Laotians by remote control. But believe me the helicopter crews fill the same body bags and they wreak the same kind of damage on the Vietnamese and Laotian countryside as anybody else, and the President is talking about allowing that to go on for many years to come. One can only ask if we will really be satisfied only when the troops march into Hanoi.

We are asking here in Washington for some action; action from the Congress of the United States of America which has the power to raise and maintain armies, and which by the Constitution also has the power to declare war.

We have come here, not to the President, because we believe that this body can be responsive to the will of the people, and we believe that the will of the people says that we should be out of Vietnam now.

We are here in Washington also to say that the problem of this war is not just a question of war and diplomacy. It is part and parcel of everything that we are trying as human beings to communicate to people in this country—the question of racism which is rampant in the military, and so many other questions such as the use of weapons; the hypocrisy in our taking umbrage at the Geneva Conventions and using that as justification for a continuation of this war when we are more guilty than any other body of violations of those Geneva Conventions; in the use of free fire zones, harassment interdiction fire, search and destroy missions, the bombings, the torture of prisoners, the killing of prisoners, all accepted policy by many units in South Vietnam. That is what we are trying to say. It is part and parcel of everything.

An American Indian friend of mine who lives in the Indian Nation of Alcatraz put it to me very succinctly. He told me how as a boy on an Indian reservation he had watched television and he used to cheer the cowboys when they came in and shot the Indians, and then suddenly one day he stopped in Vietnam and he said "my God, I am doing to these people the very same thing that was done to my people," and he stopped. And that is what we are trying to say, that we think this thing has to end.

We are also here to ask, and we are here to ask vehemently, where are the leaders of our country? Where is the leadership? We are here to ask where are McNamara, Rostow, Bundy, Gilpatric and so many others? Where are they now that we, the men whom they sent off to war, have returned? These are commanders

---

4. On March 29, 1971, a court-martial jury convicted Lt. William Calley Jr. of the premeditated murder of 22 South Vietnamese at My Lai, March 16, 1968.—eds.

who have deserted their troops, and there is no more serious crime in the laws of war. The Army says they never leave their wounded. The Marines say they never leave even their dead. These men have left all the casualties and retreated behind a pious shield of public rectitude. They have left the real stuff of their reputations bleaching behind them in the sun in this country.

Finally, this administration has done us the ultimate dishonor. They have attempted to disown us and the sacrifices we made for this country. In their blindness and fear they have tried to deny that we are veterans or that we served in Nam. We do not need their testimony. Our own scars and stumps of limbs are witness enough for others and for ourselves.

We wish that a merciful God could wipe away our own memories of that service as easily as this administration has wiped away their memories of us. But all that they have done and all that they can do by this denial is to make more clear than ever our own determination to undertake one last mission—to search out and destroy the last vestige of this barbaric war, to pacify our own hearts, to conquer the hate and the fear that have driven this country these last ten years and more, so when 30 years from now our brothers go down the street without a leg, without an arm, or a face, and small boys ask why, we will be able to say "Vietnam" and not mean a desert, not a filthy obscene memory, but mean instead the place where America finally turned and where soldiers like us helped it in the turning.

Thank you.

63. *"Nonelection" in South Vietnam (1971)**

By Congressman Abner Mikva

Throughout 1971 Washington demonstrated that it was still determined to "win" in South Vietnam. The October 1971 election was further proof, that, no matter how corrupt the Saigon regime, US policy continued to depend on Thieu as an anti-communist bulwark.

At his secret negotiations with Le Duc Tho, Henry Kissinger presented a plan (May 31) that, for the first time, did not demand withdrawal of DRV troops from the South. But the plan required all parties to accept the Thieu regime as sovereign during a cease-fire, at which time the United States was to negotiate a date for US troop withdrawal. Point five of the NLF's ten points (Reading 57) proposed that between cease-fire and elections "neither party shall impose its political regime" on the South. US officials referred to that as a demand for the "overthrow" of Thieu; the PRG saw it as an end to US imposition of Thieu. As the election approached, various South Vietnamese constituencies, including Buddhist groups,

*From the *Congressional Record*, September 28, 1971.

were coalescing around the presidential candidacy of retired general and former Chief of State Duong Van Minh. Minh also had the support of many Americans, including a group of former AID personnel in Saigon; the DRV and PRG had also indicated that he was a candidate with whom they could work.

Hoping that the United States would take advantage of this chance to move toward a coalition government, Le Duc Tho presented a proposal from the DRV (June 26) which asked that the United States stop supporting the Thieu regime "to allow the formation in Saigon of a new administration standing for peace, independence, neutrality and democracy."[1] The PRG followed (July 1) with a plan calling for the United States to "respect the South Viet Nam people's right to self-determination" and "stop all maneuvers, including tricks on elections" aimed at maintaining Thieu as president.

It soon became clear that "tricks on elections" were indeed taking place.[2] Minh requested that the United States put pressure on Thieu to allow a free election,[3] but such pressure was not applied. Vice President Nguyen Cao Ky was forced out of the presidential race on August 6 after Thieu got a special law passed that disqualified him. That maneuver left Minh as the only opposition candidate. On August 12 Minh turned over to the US Embassy in Saigon the "Election Campaign Strategy" of the Thieu regime. Marked "top secret," it detailed plans for intimidating voters and rigging the election. This led to an uproar in both Vietnam and the United States. Congress received mail from citizens angry that the ideal of free election was being flagrantly violated by the regime for which the United States was fighting. Senator Henry Jackson, hardly a "dove," introduced the "Election Campaign Strategy" text into the Congressional Record *(September 10) and called for US pressure for a fair election.*

Despite the $3 million bribe offered by US Ambassador Ellsworth Bunker[4] to Minh if he would remain in the race, Minh withdrew on August 20, calling the election a farce. Bunker then went to Ky and told him the South Vietnamese Supreme Court would reinstate him on the ballot, which it did at noon August 21. But Ky refused to run as a candidate doomed to lose.[5]

Asked about the election at a September 16 press conference, President Nixon

---

1. For the text of both the DRV and PRG proposals, see Gareth Porter, ed., *Vietnam: A History in Documents* (New York: New American Library, 1979). The US proposal made by Henry Kissinger was not made public.

2. In *The Price of Power* (New York: Summit Books, 1983), Seymour Hersh reports that the CIA Station in Saigon had been preparing for over a year for Thieu's reelection.

3. *Congressional Record*, July 29, 1971.

4. After over six years of official denials, a CIA memo, inadvertently disclosed in May 1978, revealed that Bunker did indeed offer such a bribe to Minh, as had been charged at the time and later in accounts such as Frank Snepp's *Decent Interval: An Insider's Account of Saigon's Indecent End Told by the CIA's Chief Strategy Analyst in Vietnam* (New York: Vintage Books, 1978). The memo came to light during a deposition proceeding in the US government's civil suit against Snepp over evasion of CIA censorship in the publication of *Decent Interval*. (Eventually the courts ruled that royalties from the book must go to the CIA.)

5. *Congressional Record*, September 9, 1971.

explained, "We would have preferred to have had a contested election in South Vietnam. We, however, cannot get people to run when they do not want to run." Then on September 21, US bombers flew 200 sorties against North Vietnam.

It was in this context that on September 28, 1971, Congressman Abner Mikva, Democrat of Illinois, made the statement reprinted here. As expected, Thieu won the election October 3. The DRV and PRG had by this time realized that a coalition government was not in Washington's plans and began to prepare their 1972 spring offensive.

M r. Speaker, there had been an election scheduled for this Sunday [October 3] in South Vietnam. However, for all practical purposes, that election has been called off because there is but one candidate for the presidency, the incumbent. The best description for this forthcoming nonevent would be to call it a "nonelection."

The incumbent has eliminated his two potential opponents, but has agreed to resign if he does not get 50 percent of the vote only after severe pressure from the United States and his own legislature. That concession is just a facade, as one of the eliminated opponents, Gen. Duong Van Minh, pointed out:

President Thieu has written the electoral law. Now he will organize the election. He prints the voting cards and the ballots. He has the keys to the ballot boxes. He will count the votes. He will draw up the returns. He will proclaim the results. He can decide beforehand how many per cent of the votes he wishes to have, and he can rectify the figures to match 50 per cent or any other percentages he wishes to have. That is a joke, a very big joke.[6]

The U.S. Government has taken a rather curious position throughout all of this. We have always proclaimed our concern that the people should have the opportunity to determine who will govern them. That opportunity has been sabotaged—not by the Vietcong—but by the President of South Vietnam.

In the face of this impending political hoax, the administration has heroically defended its attitude of "neutrality" in the election. Unfortunately, "neutrality" in this case has amounted to a tacit approval of the corruption and the heavy-handed rule of the Thieu government in Saigon. South Vietnam somehow has strayed far from the principles of democracy that the American presence there was supposed to guarantee.

At the very least, this country should force the government in South Vietnam to postpone the election. The National Assembly in Saigon already has recommended that, even though President Thieu has said he is determined to hold the "election." The nonelection episode is but another piece of evidence that this country's involvement in Southeast Asia has been a failure, a very disastrous failure.

---

6. Thieu got over 80 percent of the vote.—eds.

The United States should admit that and set a date for withdrawal so that this dismal chapter in American history might be ended without more lives being lost.

There should be no doubt by now that the great majority of people in this country favor a speedy withdrawal. Any number of national polls have indicated so, not to mention the volume of antiwar mail that my colleagues and I receive each day. . . .

64. The Ecological Impact of the Air War*

By Paul Feeny with Jim Allaway

During all of World War II, the United States dropped about 2,000,000 tons of bombs in all theaters, including the strategic bombing of Europe and Japan, and the tactical bombing in all campaigns throughout the Pacific and European theaters. By the end of 1971, the United States had dropped 6,300,000 tons of bombs on Indochina.[1] In just two years, 1968–1969, the United States dropped over one-and-a-half times more tonnage on South Vietnam alone than all the Allies dropped on Germany throughout World War II.[2] By 1969, North Vietnam was being hit each month with the explosive force of two atomic bombs. The 1972 Christmas bombing alone ravaged Hanoi and Haiphong with more tonnage than Germany dropped on Great Britain from 1940 through 1945. The total firepower used by the United States on Vietnam probably exceeded the amount used in all previous wars combined. Bombs dropped on Vietnam between 1965 and 1969 equaled "500 pounds . . . for every man, woman, and child in Vietnam."[3] Even these statistics do not convey the vast ecological disaster caused by just the immediate after-effects of the high explosives, such as the 21 million bomb craters created in South Vietnam alone, not to mention the prolonged effects of chemical warfare.[4]

The US air war in Indochina employed unprecedented technological sophistication. The incendiary bombs of World War II and Korea were refined into new napalm and phosphorus bombs with the capacity for creating far greater areas of burning, more intense heat, and improved ability to stick to human skin. The gargantuan "Daisy Cutter," weighing 7.5 tons, was dropped by parachute and detonated above the ground, flattening all trees and human structures in an area with a diameter equal to ten football fields. "Smart bombs" were guided by laser. The major university laboratories worked to perfect a whole arsenal of fragmentation bombs, including cluster bombs carried in a "mother bomb" and "flechette bombs" designed to maximize internal body wounds. When Vietnamese surgeons became adept at removing the metal flechettes imbedded deeply in the victims'

*From *The Air War in Indochina*, Raphael Littauer and Norman Uphoff, editors (Boston: Beacon Press, 1972).

bodies, *US scientists redesigned the bombs to use plastic flechettes that could not be detected by X-rays.*

The essence of air war is terror: planes appear suddenly, and nobody in their path knows their intended target. In the South, this terror was aimed at the rural population, seeking to drive them into government-controlled areas, punishing them for supporting the guerrillas, and trying to isolate the guerrilla army from its base among the people. This strategic theory tends to ignore the possibility that the terror may translate into anger and hatred. Indeed, many analysts have concluded that the terror bombing of the countryside in Vietnam probably created more opponents than it destroyed.

Against the North, the terror was first called "retaliatory" and a means to "punish" those supporting the insurrection in the South. But even before the admitted bombing began, another possible aim of the air war had been suggested by CIA analyst William Kaye: "Unless major military operations sap a substantial proportion of North Viet Nam's national effort, a degree of industrial progress is likely to be achieved that may well become a more effective means of political penetration in neighboring countries than direct military intervention."[5] When the "retaliatory" raids commenced, their very first targets—announced as military bases—were North Vietnam's most advanced industrial centers. For example, the air raids in "retaliation" for the Gulf of Tonkin incidents (Reading 36) were officially described as PT bases. But, as journalist Bernard Fall pointed out in the Washington Post, *"none of the targets attacked was previously known as a regular port or base area. Hon-gay, for example, was one of the largest open-pit mining operations in Asia, if not the world."[6] By 1967, the secret study conducted by the Jason Division of the Institute for Defense Analysis reached this conclusion:*

The bombing of North Vietnam has inflicted heavy costs not so much to North Vietnam's military capability or its infiltration system as to the North Vietnam economy as a whole. . . . Virtually all of the military and economic targets in North Vietnam that can be considered even remotely significant have been struck, except for a few targets in Hanoi and Haiphong. Almost all modern industrial output has been halted. . . .[7]

---

1. *The Air War in Indochina*, p. 9. This volume, prepared by the Air War Study Group of Cornell University, is the essential text on the air war through mid–1971, giving rich bibliographic material and statistics.

2. Ibid, pp. 10 and 203.

3. Noam Chomsky, *At War with Asia* (New York: Pantheon Books, 1970), pp. 290–291.

4. "The Legacy of the Vietnam War," *Indochina Newsletter*, No. 18 (November–December, 1982), p. 12.

5. In *China Quarterly*, January–February, 1962, as quoted in Carol Brightman's invaluable article, "The Discriminating Air War: The Real Targets in North Vietnam," *Viet Report*, 3 (April–May, 1967), p. 21.

6. *Washington Post*, August 9, 1964.

7. As quoted in *Air War in Indochina*, p. 47.

During the first year of the bombing of the North, the destruction of hospitals, schools, and churches seemed to be too systematic to be explained as accidental. Between August 5, 1964 and July 11, 1965 nearly thirty medical establishments of the DRV, including internationally acclaimed hospitals, were destroyed. The bombing of the Quynh Lap leper sanatorium seemed particularly difficult to accept as an "accident"—the explanation offered by US Ambassador to Japan Edwin O. Reischauer after footage of the actual raids taken by Japanese journalists was played on Japanese television. This was the world's most famous facility for the treatment of leprosy; it was located on an isolated coastal spot far removed from other habitations; its 160 buildings displayed prominent Red Crosses on the roofs. After the first attack on June 12, 1965, by several waves of US planes, the Japanese journalists witnessed and photographed thirteen more low-level strafing and bombing attacks in the next ten days. After the Peace Accords, the Senate Armed Services Committee heard testimony about this kind of raid. For example, Alan Stevenson, by then a stockbroker, testified that, as an Army intelligence specialist, he had routinely listed hospitals among targets: "The bigger the hospital the better it was."[8] In fact, the classified US Air Force bombing manual (in Chapter 6) defined hospitals, schools, and churches as "psycho-social targets," useful for the destruction of civilian order and morale.

This Reading focuses on yet another form of the air war: chemical warfare. In 1961 President Kennedy authorized a massive campaign of chemical warfare, Operation Hades, later renamed Operation Ranch Hand.[9] This poisoning and defoliation of Vietnamese cropland and forests lasted for at least ten years, from 1961 to 1971.[10] At first it was secret; the spray crews were listed as members of the US Embassy in Saigon.[11] Of course, it was no secret to those being sprayed:

. . . At first they felt sick and had some diarrhea, then they began to feel it hard to breathe and they had low blood pressure; some serious cases had trouble with their optic

---

8. *San Francisco Chronicle*, August 9, 1973.

9. For the official report, see Major William A. Buckingham, Jr., *Operation Ranch Hand: The Air Force and Herbicides in Southeast Asia, 1961–1971* (Office of Air Force History, U.S. Air Force, Washington, D.C., 1982). A pioneering source of information about chemical and biological warfare in Southeast Asia was *Viet Report*, particularly the issue of June–July 1966, with data about bacteriological weapons and official Cambodian charges that the United States was spraying a "deadly yellow powder" within its border. Other excellent sources include: Thomas Whiteside, *The Withering Rain: America's Herbicidal Folly* (New York: Dutton, 1971); J.B. Neilands, Gordon H. Orians, E.W. Pfeiffer, Alje Vennema, Arthur H. Westing, eds., *Harvest of Death: Chemical Warfare in Vietnam and Cambodia* (New York: Free Press, 1972); John Lewallen, *Ecology of Devastation: Indochina* (Baltimore: Penguin, 1971); E.W. Pfeiffer, "Operation Ranch Hand: the U.S. Herbicide Program," *Bulletin of the Atomic Scientists*, May, 1982, pp. 20–24.

10. Defoliation was also employed in Laos (1965–1969) and Cambodia (1969).

11. Michael Uhl and Tod Ensign, *GI Guinea Pigs: How the Pentagon Exposed Our Troops to Dangers More Deadly Than War—Agent Orange and Atomic Radiation* (New York: Playboy Press, 1980), p. 117.

nerves and were blind. Pregnant women gave birth to stillborn or premature children. Most of the affected cattle died from serious diarrhea, and the river fish floated on the surface of the water belly up, soon after the chemicals were spread.[12]

In South Vietnam alone, US planes sprayed eighteen million gallons of poisonous chemicals.[13]

One of the defoliants, Agent Orange, contained TCDD-dioxin, the most toxic known substance,[14] which is also "100,000 times more potent than thalidomide as a cause of birth defects in some species."[15] The Indochinese were not the only peoples who came into contact with dioxin; so did Americans involved in Operation Ranch Hand and GIs on the ground. Some of these veterans now have many of the same symptoms, including children with birth defects, as the Vietnamese. After over a decade of protest and litigation, the House of Representatives approved legislation in January 1984, providing benefits to veterans suffering health problems as a result of exposure to Agent Orange. Then in May 1984, seven chemical companies agreed to pay $180 million to settle a class action suit brought on behalf of tens of thousands of Vietnam veterans, many of whom denounced this settlement as a sell-out designed to prevent full disclosure of the health disorders caused by this particular form of chemical warfare.

ONLY WE CAN PREVENT FORESTS

—Motto over the door to headquarters,
Operation Ranch Hand, Saigon

A. Defoliants and Herbicides

Use of defoliants in South Vietnam began on an experimental basis in 1961 and became fully operational the following year.[16] This program had two major objectives. The first was *defoliation* (operation RANCH HAND), in which forests, roadsides, base perimeters, etc., were sprayed in order to remove the foliage cover which had afforded concealment to the enemy. At low concentrations these chemicals do indeed act merely as defoliants; at the concentrations used in Vietnam, however, they normally act also as herbicides, killing a significant fraction of the

---

12. Report of Cao Van Nguyen, M.D., after chemical attack near Saigon, October 3, 1964, as quoted in Committee of Concerned Asian Scholars, *The Indochina Story: A Fully Documented Account* (New York: Bantam, 1970).

13. "The Legacy of the Vietnam War," p. 12.

14. *New York Times*, February 1, 1984.

15. Dr. Jacqueline Verrett of the Food and Drug Administration, as quoted in Fred A. Wilcox, *Waiting for an Army to Die: The Tragedy of Agent Orange* (New York: Vintage Books, 1983), p. xi.

16. Herbicide Assessment Commission for the American Association for the Advancement of Science, *Background Material Relevant to the Presentations at the 1970 Annual Meeting of the AAAS*, Chicago, Ill., December 29, 1970, p. 14.

plants in addition to defoliating them. The second major objective was the *destruction of crops*, mostly rice, carried out in the hope of denying food to the enemy.[17] Crop destruction was largely confined to the mountainous areas of northern and western South Vietnam, where the impact was felt most severely by the small population of about one million, mostly Montagnards. Crop destruction may also have had the objective of driving South Vietnamese civilians into the "strategic hamlets" set up for them by the South Vietnamese Government.[18]

Though some spraying in Vietnam has been done with helicopters or ground equipment, the principal means of application has been the twin-engine C–123 cargo plane. In the years 1962 through 1968 these aircraft made more than 19,000 individual spray flights. Each plane is fitted with a 950-gallon tank from which the herbicide is pumped to spray booms under each wing and at the tail. When the herbicide hits the airstream it is dispersed into fine droplets. One aircraft flying at about 150 feet above the tree tops produces a swath of affected vegetation about 300 feet wide and ten miles long.[19] Precautions must be taken that the sprayed chemical does not drift into adjacent, non-target areas. Occasional incidents occur in which an aircraft is forced to dump its herbicide quickly; it can pump out the entire 950 gallons in about 30 seconds.[20]

Three formulations account for almost all the herbicides used in Indochina: agents Orange, White, and Blue. The composition and mode of action of these agents are discussed in greater detail in Appendix E [not reprinted here—eds.], which also contains a listing of appropriate references; a summary of the main facts is given below.

Orange: Composition, 2,4-D and 2,4,5-T; an oily liquid insoluble in water. Mainly used against broad-leaved and woody vegetation. One application defoliates hardwoods and kills some canopy trees; two applications produce a heavy kill of all woody vegetation; the resulting invasion by bamboo and grasses may arrest forest regeneration indefinitely. On mangrove forests Orange kills almost all trees in a single application; mangrove areas sprayed in 1961 have still shown no significant signs of regeneration. The chemical itself persists for only a few weeks, except in stagnant water or poorly aerated ground, where high concentrations could conceivably accumulate. 2,4,5-T or an associated impurity

---

17. Stanford Biology Study Group, 1971, "The Destruction of Indochina," *Bulletin of the Atomic Scientists*, 27 (1971), pp. 36–40; A. H. Westing, "Agent Blue in Vietnam," *New York Times*, July 12, 1971.

18. Ngo Vinh Long, "Leaf Abscission?," *Bulletin of Concerned Asian Scholars* (October 1969), p. 54.

19. The C–123 cruises at 230 miles per hour; at this low speed and at minimal altitude, it becomes vulnerable to ground fire from any weapons, even small-caliber. Hence in all areas where hostile elements may be present, even if they have no conventional anti-aircraft capability, the spraying missions are preceded by fighter-bomber sweeps providing maximum-intensity ground-fire suppression. The effects of this support activity must be reckoned as a contingent cost of the herbicide program.

20. Orians and Pfeiffer, "Ecological Effects of the War in Vietnam," *Science*, 168 (1970), pp. 544–554.

(dioxin) is thought to be a teratogen (causing serious birth deformities, like thalidomide); its use in the U.S. has been restricted since late 1969. Orange accounts for about 60 percent of the herbicide used in Vietnam; it was being sprayed at least until August 1970.

White: Composition, butyl esters of 2,4-D and picloram; a solution in water. Used much like Orange, but less volatile and therefore less subject to wind drift; it is preferred near populated areas. Picloram is one of the most potent herbicides known; it is remarkably persistent, like the insecticide DDT; its use on agricultural land in the U.S. is prohibited. since White is water soluble, it can easily be washed by rainfall into adjacent areas.

Blue: Composition, organic arsenates including cacodylic acid; a solution in water. Its prime use is for crop destruction, especially rice. It is more effective against grasses than are Orange or White, and acts more rapidly (within a few days).

Herbicides are sprayed at a rate of about three gallons per acre, the stock solution of each agent being formulated to obtain the desired coverage. In the case of Orange, the rate of application is about 26 pounds per acre, almost ten times the rate recommended for use in the U.S.[21] It is estimated that more than 100 million pounds of herbicides have by now been sprayed on Vietnam, covering a total of almost six million acres;[22]. . .

The greatest impact has been on tropical hardwood forests. About 35 percent of South Vietnam's 14 million acres of dense forest have been sprayed one or more times, resulting in the destruction of enough merchantable timber (six billion board feet) to supply the country's domestic needs for about 30 years; this also represents a loss of about $500 million in taxes that would otherwise have accrued to the South Vietnamese Government. Of the three-quarter million acres of coastal mangrove forests, mostly in the Delta area, about one-half have been totally destroyed.

B. Bombing and Spraying: The Potential Consequences

Forests are first to go. Then the animals—some, like the elephant, are killed deliberately since they could be used to transport supplies; others just happen to be in the wrong place at the wrong time. Finally, the land itself is destroyed: farms, rice paddies, and village sites in many regions are bomb-pocked and barren.

In the brief discussion that follows, only the most obvious environmental effects of the air war will be mentioned, but even such a superficial enumeration conveys an idea of the pervasiveness of the damage. The very fact that data on the present extent of this damage are scant, combined with the virtual impossibility of

---

21. Statement of A. W. Galston before the Subcommittee on National Security Policy and Scientific Developments, U.S. House of Representatives, December 1969; reprinted in T. Whiteside, *Defoliation* (New York: Ballantine, 1970), p. 107.

22. "Impact of the Vietnam War," a report prepared for the Committee on Foreign Relations, U.S. Senate, by the Congressional Research Service of the Library of Congress, June 30, 1971 (USGPO, 1971). The figures which follow are abstracted from the excellent summary presented in this report, pp. 10 ff.

predicting future consequences, is in itself one of the most ominous signs of danger.

The air war has been a severe shock to all the natural ecosystems of Indochina. Such damage would be of concern wherever it occurred since it affects an intricate web of relationships; but Indochina is especially sensitive because tropical ecosystems are thought to be less resilient than those of temperate regions. Tropical systems are characterized by many more species per unit area; each is finely adapted and food webs are complex and intricate. In a northern forest a major calamity has relatively short-term consequences, since most of the species are already adapted to surviving frosts and unseasonal floods. The rates of reproduction and recolonization are usually high. In tropical regions, where the climatic conditions are much more predictable and favorable, species tend to be less well adapted to rapid change.

Flora. The direct attack on the flora by defoliation and the use of herbicides has been described above. In addition to the very extensive damage done by this chemical warfare, fires—many undoubtedly caused by bombing and napalm—have consumed or defoliated large areas of forest. Revegetation of soils in severely defoliated forests may be retarded by rapid loss of plant nutrients following defoliation and by invasion of bamboo and other grasses. Tropical forests carry most of their nutrients in the vegetation itself, rather than in the soil; hence, following decomposition of the plants, most of the nutrients are lost directly, with the remainder being subject to leaching from the soils.[23]

Mangrove forests have suffered particularly severe damage from defoliation—about half have been totally destroyed in South Vietnam—and so far there is no evidence of regeneration. These forests play an important part in the natural process of delta formation, and stabilize the coastline and river banks. They also provide essential cover and food during the life cycles of many fish and other animals.

Fauna. The weapons of air warfare affect animals directly by killing them, and indirectly by changing their environment, with the result that populations are changed and the diversity of species is reduced. Natural checks and balances to pests and disease vectors may be upset, particularly as predatory fauna are killed. The invasion of destroyed areas by other plant groups may result in larger populations of undesired animals favoring this new habitat—rats, for example, often thrive in bamboo, which is a predominant regrowth species in defoliated forest areas. The population of the tiger has apparently increased as its natural food supply has been augmented by battlefield casualties.

There are contradictory claims about the toxicity of herbicides to animals. Though some authorities claim there is little danger, evidence indicates that 2,4-D

---

23. In temperate zones, by contrast, most of the nutrients reside in the soil rather than in the flora of the forest. L. E. Rodin and N. I. Bazilevich, *Production and Mineral Cycling in Terrestrial Vegetation* (Edinburgh and London: Oliver & Boyd, 1967), p. 246. (Translated from Russian edition, 1965.)

in moderate doses may be toxic to some fish, that plants treated with 2,4-D may accumulate toxic quantities of nitrates (which could affect domestic stock as well as wild fauna), and that dioxin, a contaminant of some 2,4,5-T solutions used, is toxic and concentrates in the food chain since it does not break down with time. Finally, domestic livestock are affected by herbicides, both directly and indirectly, as they eat plants that have been contaminated.

Agriculture. Agriculture, and land utilization in general, are affected not only by chemical warfare but also directly by bombing. One may estimate that at least 12,000,000 craters have been produced in the Indochina air war so far, covering an area of at least 200,000 acres and excavating about 1.5 billion cubic yards of soil.[24] (Roughly two-thirds of the bomb tonnage was deployed within South Vietnam, whose total area is 42 million acres.) Some areas in Indochina have been likened to moonscapes. The long-term effects of this cratering are hard to assess, but the fact that craters do not naturally fill in is evidenced by craters from World War II which are still found in the jungles of New Guinea. A bomb crater destroys the surface organic layer and throws up subsoil; it creates severe local relief and erosion in the soil and may disrupt drainage patterns. Usually it fills with water and becomes very difficult to drain, making heavily bombed areas virtually unsuitable for cultivation.

Flooding. The control of water flow is a vital problem in many areas of Indochina. Defoliation and laterization lead to more rapid runoff of rain water; the destruction of many man-made control structures compounds the problem. The destructiveness of the floods in central South Vietnam in November 1970 was blamed in part on defoliation and bomb damage. People were driven by the floods out of refugee camps to which they had come, in the first place, because of crop destruction or bombing in their native highlands.

Malnutrition. It is generally recognized that crop destruction has had its chief impact on the civilian population rather than on enemy soldiers, who are in the best position to obtain food in times of scarcity. The Herbicides Assessment Commission has concluded that the food destroyed would have been enough to feed 600,000 persons for a year, and that nearly all of it would have been consumed by civilians. Although the amount destroyed is less than two percent of the national crop of South Vietnam in any one year, the most extensive crop destruction has been carried out in the central highlands, a food-scarce area with a population of about one million, mainly Montagnards. It is among these people that problems of malnutrition and starvation are most severe.

Birth abnormalities. According to a report released by the National Institutes of Health in the fall of 1969, 2,4,5-T (or an associated impurity, dioxin) was shown

---

24. Total expenditure of aerial munitions through 1971 is about 6,300,000 tons. If half of this is crater-producing, in the form of 500-pound bombs, there will be about 12,000,000 craters. Taking each to be 30 feet in diameter, conical in shape and with a maximum depth of 15 feet, the quoted figures for area and volume can be derived. [We are indebted to Professor A. H. Westing for discussion of this point. . . .]

to produce significant increases in the incidence of fetus malformation in animals as early as 1965. Moreover, the Herbicide Assessment Commission team in Vietnam has found a suggestive correlation between years of peak defoliation in Tay Ninh province and an increase in stillbirths and birth deformities.

Malaria. Of the endemic diseases in Indochina, malaria is probably the most widespread; in the past it has been far more common in the upland regions than in the lowlands. Now, large numbers of bomb craters have filled with water. This stagnant water, present throughout Vietnam and parts of Laos and Cambodia, is an ideal breeding habitat for various species of mosquito, including those which are malaria vectors. . . .

Americans have begun to become aware of the vast complexity of their environment, and of the unpredictable consequences that go with disturbing it. In Indochina, the environment has not merely been disturbed—there has been a deliberate and unprecedented onslaught on it, with chemicals, with explosives, and with fire. The short listing just given, incomplete and inconclusive as it is, by its very open-endedness points up the ominous results which may have been, and which may continue to be, provoked in Indochina.

65. Ending the War and Restoring Peace in Vietnam: The Paris Peace Accords (January 27, 1973)*

In 1972, the United States continued to try to bomb the Vietnamese into submission. In May, Nixon announced Operation Linebacker, which combined mining Haiphong Harbor with a naval blockade and increased bombing of the North. But the policy of "Vietnamization" meanwhile continued to fail. ARVN forces, when confronted with DRV-PRG forces, suffered high casualty and desertion rates. Corruption and inflation in the South also increased. The US antiwar movement intensified its protests.

On October 8, there was a breakthrough in the negotiations in Paris.[1] Le Duc Tho proposed a cease-fire in place; the United States would withdraw all its troops; between the cease-fire and the installation of a new government "after free and democratic general elections," the "two present administrations in South Viet-

United States Treaties and Other International Agreements, compiled and edited under the direction of the U.S. Secretary of State (1U.S.C.112A), Vol. 24, Part 1, 1973 (Washington, D.C.: U.S. Government Printing Office, 1974), pp. 1–224, *passim*.

1. The Paris talks were no longer secret; Nixon announced them in January 1972. For background of these negotiations, see Readings 39, 40, 53, 54, 55, 57 and 63, in particular.

nam will remain in existence." There was no longer the demand for a coalition government before elections. Kissinger and Le Duc Tho reached an accord which Nixon approved. But Thieu demanded sixty-nine changes; he particularly objected to the agreement's failure to require the withdrawal of DRV forces from the South. Nevertheless, on October 26, a few days before Nixon faced another election, Kissinger told reporters that "peace is at hand."

Although the United States did not sign on the agreed-upon date of October 31, negotiations resumed after Nixon's reelection, with Kissinger demanding all sixty-nine changes. On December 18, the United States launched Operation Linebacker II—intensive bombing of Hanoi and Haiphong. For twelve days, US bombers blasted the two cities, but the Vietnamese had long expected that the United States would try to break their will by destroying Hanoi and Haiphong.[2] The B–52 bombers suffered devastating damage: many US airmen were killed or captured. On December 30, Nixon called a halt to the bombing.

In early January, Nixon sent General Alexander Haig to Saigon to tell Thieu that the US government planned to proceed with the agreement with or without Thieu's consent, which was then tacitly obtained. When the agreement was reached, it was almost identical to the October agreement. Despite the Christmas bombing, only foreign troops were forced to leave, while DRV troops were allowed to remain below the 17th parallel.

The 1973 accords (presented here with certain technical portions omitted) invite comparison with the Peace Accords of 1954 (Reading 16). Much of the 1954 agreement is incorporated in the 1973 accords (1973 Chapter V, Article 15, for example). Yet, between the two, Vietnam had to endure over eighteen years of continued war, including some of the most destructive attacks of any war. Even after the signatures were affixed, there would be another two years of fighting before the war was finally ended with what some called the fall, and others the liberation, of Saigon, April 30, 1975.

Although the cease-fire did not last, the war was clearly on its way to a conclusion. With US troops withdrawn, the "protection" of their lives could no longer be used as a bargaining chip for obtaining military aid for the Thieu regime. As long as the actual fighting was only among the Vietnamese, there was little doubt about who would win, but there was a great doubt about whether the United States would ever honor its commitment (Chapter VIII, Article 21) to contribute to postwar reconstruction in the DRV and throughout Indochina (Reading 66).

Ending the War and Restoring Peace in Viet-Nam

Multilateral

Agreement and protocols signed on behalf of the United States of America, the Republic of Viet-Nam, the Democratic Republic of Viet-Nam, and the Provisional Revolutionary Government of South Viet-Nam at Paris, January 27, 1973;

Entered into force January 27, 1973.

---

2. See Gareth Porter, *A Peace Denied; The United States, Vietnam, and the Paris Agreement* (Bloomington: Indiana University Press, 1975), pp. 160 ff.

Bilateral

Agreement and protocols signed on behalf of the United States of America and the Democratic Republic of Viet-Nam at Paris, January 27, 1973;
Entered into force January 27, 1973.

[Multilateral Agreement]

AGREEMENT ON ENDING THE WAR
AND
RESTORING PEACE IN VIET-NAM

The Parties participating in the Paris Conference on Viet-Nam,

With a view to ending the war and restoring peace in Viet-Nam on the basis of respect for the Vietnamese people's fundamental national rights and the South Vietnamese people's right to self-determination, and to contributing to the consolidation of peace in Asia and the world,

Have agreed on the following provisions and undertake to respect and to implement them:

Chapter I

THE VIETNAMESE PEOPLE'S
FUNDAMENTAL NATIONAL RIGHTS

Article 1

The United States and all other countries respect the independence, sovereignty, unity, and territorial integrity of Viet-Nam as recognized by the 1954 Geneva Agreements on Viet-Nam.

Chapter II

CESSATION OF HOSTILITIES—WITHDRAWAL OF TROOPS

Article 2

A cease-fire shall be observed throughout South Viet-Nam as of 2400 hours G.M.T., on January 27, 1973.

At the same hour, the United States will stop all its military activities against the territory of the Democratic Republic of Viet-Nam by ground, air and naval forces, wherever they may be based, and end the mining of the territorial waters, ports, harbors, and waterways of the Democratic Republic of Viet-Nam. The United States will remove, permanently deactivate or destroy all the mines in the territorial waters, ports, harbors, and waterways of North Viet-Nam as soon as this Agreement goes into effect.

The complete cessation of hostilities mentioned in this Article shall be durable and without limit of time.

Article 3

The parties undertake to maintain the cease-fire and to ensure a lasting and stable peace.

As soon as the cease-fire goes into effect:

(a) The United States forces and those of the other foreign countries allied with the United States and the Republic of Viet-Nam shall remain in-place pending the implementation of the plan of troop withdrawal. The Four-Party Joint Military Commission described in Article 16 shall determine the modalities.

(b) The armed forces of the two South Vietnamese parties shall remain in-place. The Two-Party Joint Military Commission described in Article 17 shall determine the areas controlled by each party and the modalities of stationing.

(c) The regular forces of all services and arms and the irregular forces of the parties in South Viet-Nam shall stop all offensive activities against each other and shall strictly abide by the following stipulations:

—All acts of force on the ground, in the air, and on the sea shall be prohibited;

—All hostile acts, terrorism and reprisals by both sides will be banned.

Article 4

The United States will not continue its military involvement or intervene in the internal affairs of South Viet-Nam.

Article 5

Within sixty days of the signing of this Agreement, there will be a total withdrawal from South Viet-Nam of troops, military advisers, and military personnel, including technical military personnel and military personnel associated with the pacification program, armaments, munitions, and war material of the United States and those of the other foreign countries mentioned in Article 3 (a). Advisers from the above-mentioned countries to all paramilitary organizations and the police force will also be withdrawn within the same period of time.

Article 6

The dismantlement of all military bases in South Viet-Nam of the United States and of the other foreign countries mentioned in Article 3 (a) shall be completed within sixty days of the signing of this Agreement.

Article 7

From the enforcement of the cease-fire to the formation of the government provided for in Article 9 (b) and 14 of this Agreement, the two South Vietnamese parties shall not accept the introduction of troops, military advisers, and military personnel including technical military personnel, armaments, munitions, and war material into South Viet-Nam.

The two South Vietnamese parties shall be permitted to make periodic replacement of armaments, munitions and war material which have been destroyed, damaged, worn out or used up after the cease-fire, on the basis of piece-for-piece, of the same characteristics and properties, under the supervision of the Joint Military Commission of the two South Vietnamese parties and of the International Commission of Control and Supervision.

Chapter III

THE RETURN OF CAPTURED MILITARY PERSONNEL
AND FOREIGN CIVILIANS, AND CAPTURED
AND DETAINED VIETNAMESE CIVILIAN PERSONNEL

Article 8

(a) The return of captured military personnel and foreign civilians of the parties shall be carried out simultaneously with and completed not later than the same day as the troop withdrawal mentioned in Article 5. The parties shall exchange complete lists of the above-mentioned captured military personnel and foreign civilians on the day of the signing of this Agreement.

(b) The Parties shall help each other to get information about those military personnel and foreign civilians of the parties missing in action, to determine the location and take care of the graves of the dead so as to facilitate the exhumation and repatriation of the remains, and to take any such other measures as may be required to get information about those still considered missing in action.

(c) The question of the return of Vietnamese civilian personnel captured and detained in South Viet-Nam will be resolved by the two South Vietnamese parties on the basis of the principles of Article 21 (b) of the Agreement on the Cessation of Hostilities in Viet-Nam of July 20, 1954. The two South Vietnamese parties will do so in a spirit of national reconciliation and concord, with a view to ending hatred and enmity, in order to ease suffering and to reunite families. The two South Vietnamese parties will do their utmost to resolve this question within ninety days after the cease-fire comes into effect.

Chapter IV

THE EXERCISE OF THE SOUTH VIETNAMESE PEOPLE'S
RIGHT TO SELF-DETERMINATION

Article 9

The Government of the United States of America and the Government of the Democratic Republic of Viet-Nam undertake to respect the following principles for the exercise of the South Vietnamese people's right to self-determination:

(a) The South Vietnamese people's right to self-determination is sacred, inalienable, and shall be respected by all countries.

(b) The South Vietnamese people shall decide themselves the political future of South Viet-Nam through genuinely free and democratic general elections under international supervision.

(c) Foreign countries shall not impose any political tendency or personality on the South Vietnamese people.

Article 10

The two South Vietnamese parties undertake to respect the cease-fire and maintain peace in South Viet-Nam, settle all matters of contention through negotiations, and avoid all armed conflict.

Article 11

Immediately after the cease-fire, the two South Vietnamese parties will:
—achieve national reconciliation and concord, end hatred and enmity, prohibit all acts of reprisal and discrimination against individuals or organizations that have collaborated with one side or the other;
—ensure the democratic liberties of the people: personal freedom, freedom of speech, freedom of the press, freedom of meeting, freedom of organization, freedom of political activities, freedom of belief, freedom of movement, freedom of residence, freedom of work, right to property ownership, and right to free enterprise.

Article 12

(a) Immediately after the cease-fire, the two South Vietnamese parties shall hold consultations in a spirit of national reconciliation and concord, mutual respect, and mutual non-elimination to set up a National Council of National Reconciliation and Concord of three equal segments. The Council shall operate on the principle of unanimity. After the National Council of National Reconciliation and Concord has assumed its functions, the two South Vietnamese parties will consult about the formation of councils at lower levels. The two South Vietnamese parties shall sign an agreement on the internal matters of South Viet-Nam as soon as possible and do their utmost to accomplish this within ninety days after the cease-fire comes into effect, in keeping with the South Vietnamese people's aspirations for peace, independence and democracy.

(b) The National Council of National Reconciliation and Concord shall have the task of promoting the two South Vietnamese parties' implementation of this Agreement, achievement of national reconciliation and concord and ensurance of democratic liberties. The National Council of National Reconciliation and Concord will organize the free and democratic general elections provided for in Article 9 (b) and decide the procedures and modalities of these general elections. The institutions for which the general elections are to be held will be agreed upon through consultations between the two South Vietnamese parties. The National Council of National Reconciliation and Concord will also decide the procedures and modalities of such local elections as the two South Vietnamese parties agree upon.

Article 13

The question of Vietnamese armed forces in South Viet-Nam shall be settled by the two South Vietnamese parties in a spirit of national reconciliation and concord, equality and mutual respect, without foreign interference, in accordance with the postwar situation. Among the questions to be discussed by the two South Vietnamese parties are steps to reduce their military effectives and to demobilize the troops being reduced. The two South Vietnamese parties will accomplish this as soon as possible.

Article 14

South Viet-Nam will pursue a foreign policy of peace and independence. It will be prepared to establish relations with all countries irrespective of their political and social systems on the basis of mutual respect for independence and sovereignty and accept economic and technical aid from any country with no political conditions attached. The acceptance of military aid by South Viet-Nam in the future shall come under the authority of the government set up after the general elections in South Viet-Nam provided for in Article 9 (b).

Chapter V

THE REUNIFICATION OF VIET-NAM AND THE
RELATIONSHIP BETWEEN NORTH AND SOUTH VIET-NAM

Article 15

The reunification of Viet-Nam shall be carried out step by step through peaceful means on the basis of discussions and agreements between North and South Viet-Nam, without coercion or annexation by either party, and without foreign interference. The time for reunification will be agreed upon by North and South Viet-Nam.

Pending reunification:

(a) The military demarcation line between the two zones at the 17th parallel is only provisional and not a political or territorial boundary, as provided for in paragraph 6 of the Final Declaration of the 1954 Geneva Conference.

(b) North and South Viet-Nam shall respect the Demilitarized Zone on either side of the Provisional Military Demarcation Line.

(c) North and South Viet-Nam shall promptly start negotiations with a view to reestablishing normal relations in various fields. Among the questions to be negotiated are the modalities of civilian movement across the Provisional Military Demarcation Line.

(d) North and South Viet-Nam shall not join any military alliance or military bloc and shall not allow foreign powers to maintain military bases, troops, military advisers, and military personnel on their respective territories, as stipulated in the 1954 Geneva Agreements on Viet-Nam.

Chapter VI

THE JOINT MILITARY COMMISSIONS,
THE INTERNATIONAL COMMISSION
OF CONTROL AND SUPERVISION,
THE INTERNATIONAL CONFERENCE

Article 16

(a) The Parties participating in the Paris Conference on Viet-Nam shall immediately designate representatives to form a Four-Party Joint Military Commission with the task of ensuring joint action by the parties in implementing the following provisions of this Agreement:

[We omit references to sections of Articles 2, 3, 5, 6 and 8.—eds.]

(b) The Four-Party Joint Military Commission shall operate in accordance with the principle of consultations and unanimity. Disagreements shall be referred to the International Commission of Control and Supervision.

(c) The Four-Party Joint Military Commission shall begin operating immediately after the signing of this Agreement and end its activities in sixty days, after the completion of the withdrawal of U.S. troops and those of the other foreign countries mentioned in Article 3 (a) and the completion of the return of captured military personnel and foreign civilians of the parties.

(d) The four parties shall agree immediately on the organization, the working procedure, means of activity, and expenditures of the Four-Party Joint Military Commission.

Article 17

(a) The two South Vietnamese parties shall immediately designate representatives to form a Two-Party Joint Military Commission with the task of ensuring joint action by the two South Vietnamese parties in implementing the following provisions of this Agreement:

[We omit references to sections of Articles 2, 3, 7, 8 and 13.—eds.]

(b) Disagreements shall be referred to the International Commission of Control and Supervision.

(c) After the signing of this Agreement, the Two-Party Joint Military Commission shall agree immediately on the measures and organization aimed at enforcing the cease-fire and preserving peace in South Viet-Nam.

Article 18

(a) After the signing of this Agreement, an International Commission of Control and Supervision shall be established immediately.

(b) Until the International Conference provided for in Article 19 makes definitive arrangements, the International Commission of Control and Supervision will report to the four parties on matters concerning the control and supervision of the implementation of the following provisions of this Agreement:

[We omit references to sections of Articles 2, 3, 5, 6 and 8.—eds.]

The International Commission of Control and Supervision shall form control teams for carrying out its tasks. The four parties shall agree immediately on the location and operation of these teams. The parties will facilitate their operation.

(c) Until the International Conference makes definitive arrangements, the International Commission of Control and Supervision will report to the two South Vietnamese parties on matters concerning the control and supervision of the implementation of the following provisions of this Agreement:

[We omit further operational details of the International Commission of Control and Supervision in Articles 18 and 19 and the agreement regarding Laos and Cambodia in Article 20.—eds.]

Chapter VIII

THE RELATIONSHIP BETWEEN
THE UNITED STATES AND
THE DEMOCRATIC REPUBLIC OF VIET-NAM

Article 21

The United States anticipates that this Agreement will usher in an era of reconciliation with the Democratic Republic of Viet-Nam as with all the peoples of Indochina. In pursuance of its traditional policy, the United States will contribute to healing the wounds of war and to postwar reconstruction of the Democratic Republic of Viet-Nam and throughout Indochina.

Article 22

The ending of the war, the restoration of peace in Viet-Nam, and the strict implementation of this Agreement will create conditions for establishing a new, equal and mutually beneficial relationship between the United States and the Democratic Republic of Viet-Nam on the basis of respect for each other's independence and sovereignty, and non-interference in each other's internal affairs. At the same time this will ensure stable peace in Viet-Nam and contribute to the preservation of lasting peace in Indochina and Southeast Asia.

Chapter IX

OTHER PROVISIONS

Article 23

This Agreement shall enter into force upon signature by plenipotentiary representatives of the parties participating in the Paris Conference on Viet-Nam. All the parties concerned shall strictly implement this Agreement and its Protocols.

Done in Paris this twenty-seventh day of January, one thousand nine hundred and seventy-three, in English and Vietnamese. The English and Vietnamese texts are official and equally authentic.

FOR THE GOVERNMENT OF THE
UNITED STATES OF AMERICA

William P. Rogers
Secretary of State

FOR THE GOVERNMENT OF THE
DEMOCRATIC REPUBLIC OF
VIET-NAM

Nguyen Duy Trinh
Minister for Foreign Affairs

FOR THE GOVERNMENT OF THE
REPUBLIC OF VIET-NAM:

Tran Van Lam
Minister for Foreign Affairs

FOR THE PROVISIONAL
REVOLUTIONARY GOVERNMENT OF THE
REPUBLIC OF SOUTH VIET-NAM

Nguyen Thi Binh
Minister for Foreign Affairs

PROTOCOL
TO THE AGREEMENT ON ENDING THE WAR
AND RESTORING PEACE IN VIET-NAM
CONCERNING
THE RETURN OF CAPTURED MILITARY PERSONNEL
AND FOREIGN CIVILIANS AND CAPTURED AND DETAINED
VIETNAMESE CIVILIAN PERSONNEL

The Parties participating in the Paris Conference on Viet-Nam,

In implementation of Article 8 of the Agreement on Ending the War and Restoring Peace in Viet-Nam signed on this date providing for the return of captured military personnel and foreign civilians, and captured and detained Vietnamese civilian personnel,

Have agreed as follows:

THE RETURN OF CAPTURED MILITARY PERSONNEL
AND FOREIGN CIVILIANS

Article 1

The parties signatory to the Agreement shall return the captured military personnel of the parties mentioned in Article 8 (a) of the Agreement as follows:

—all captured military personnel of the United States and those of the other foreign countries mentioned in Article 3 (a) of the Agreement shall be returned to United States authorities;

—all captured Vietnamese military personnel, whether belonging to regular or irregular armed forces, shall be returned to the two South Vietnamese parties; they shall be returned to that South Vietnamese party under whose command they served.

Article 2

All captured civilians who are nationals of the United States or of any other foreign countries mentioned in Article 3 (a) of the Agreement shall be returned to United States authorities. All other captured foreign civilians shall be returned to the authorities of their country of nationality by any one of the parties willing and able to do so.

Article 3

The parties shall today exchange complete lists of captured persons mentioned in Articles 1 and 2 of this Protocol.

Article 4

(a) The return of all captured persons mentioned in Articles 1 and 2 of this Protocol shall be completed within sixty days of the signing of the Agreement at a rate no slower than the rate of withdrawal from South Viet-Nam of United States forces and those of the other foreign countries mentioned in Article 5 of the Agreement.

(b) Persons who are seriously ill, wounded or maimed, old persons and women shall be returned first. The remainder shall be returned either by returning all from one detention place after another or in order of their dates of capture, beginning with those who have been held the longest.

Article 5

The return and reception of the persons mentioned in Articles 1 and 2 of this Protocol shall be carried out at places convenient to the concerned parties. Places of return shall be agreed upon by the Four-Party Joint Military Commission. The parties shall ensure the safety of personnel engaged in the return and reception of those persons.

Article 6

Each party shall return all captured persons mentioned in Articles 1 and 2 of this Protocol without delay and shall facilitate their return and reception. The detaining parties shall not deny or delay their return for any reason, including the fact that captured persons may, on any grounds, have been prosecuted or sentenced.

THE RETURN OF CAPTURED AND
DETAINED VIETNAMESE CIVILIAN PERSONNEL

Article 7

(a) The question of the return of Vietnamese civilian personnel captured and detained in South Viet-Nam will be resolved by the two South Vietnamese parties on the basis of the principles of Article 21 (b) of the Agreement on the Cessation of Hostilities in Viet-Nam of July 20, 1954, which reads as follows:

"The term 'civilian internees' is understood to mean all persons who, having in any way contributed to the political and armed struggle between the two parties, have been arrested for that reason and have been kept in detention by either party during the period of hostilities."

(b) The two South Vietnamese parties will do so in a spirit of national reconciliation and concord with a view to ending hatred and enmity in order to ease suffering and to reunite families. The two South Vietnamese parties will do their utmost to resolve this question within ninety days after the cease-fire comes into effect.

(c) Within fifteen days after the cease-fire comes into effect, the two South Vietnamese parties shall exchange lists of the Vietnamese civilian personnel captured and detained by each party and lists of the places at which they are held.

TREATMENT OF CAPTURED PERSONS DURING DETENTION

Article 8

(a) All captured military personnel of the parties and captured foreign civilians of the parties shall be treated humanely at all times, and in accordance with international practice.

They shall be protected against all violence to life and person, in particular against murder in any form, mutilation, torture and cruel treatment, and outrages upon personal dignity. These persons shall not be forced to join the armed forces of the detaining party.

They shall be given adequate food, clothing, shelter, and the medical attention required for their state of health. They shall be allowed to exchange post cards and letters with their families and receive parcels.

(b) All Vietnamese civilian personnel captured and detained in South Viet-Nam shall be treated humanely at all times, and in accordance with international practice.

They shall be protected against all violence to life and person, in particular against murder in any form, mutilation, torture and cruel treatment, and outrages against personal dignity. The detaining parties shall not deny or delay their return for any reason, including the fact that captured persons may, on any grounds, have been prosecuted or sentenced. These persons shall not be forced to join the armed forces of the detaining party.

They shall be given adequate food, clothing, shelter and the medical attention required for their state of health. They shall be allowed to exchange post cards and letters with their families and receive parcels.

Article 9

(a) To contribute to improving the living conditions of the captured military personnel of the parties and foreign civilians of the parties, the parties shall, within fifteen days after the cease-fire comes into effect, agree upon the designation of two or more national Red Cross societies to visit all places where captured military personnel and foreign civilians are held.

(b) To contribute to improving the living conditions of the captured and detained Vietnamese civilian personnel, the two South Vietnamese parties shall, within fifteen days after the cease-fire comes into effect, agree upon the designation of two or more national Red Cross societies to visit all places where the captured and detained Vietnamese civilian personnel are held.

WITH REGARD TO DEAD AND MISSING PERSONS

Article 10

(a) The Four-Party Joint Military Commission shall ensure joint action by the parties in implementing Article 8 (b) of the Agreement. When the Four-Party Joint Military Commission has ended its activities, a Four-Party Joint Military team shall be maintained to carry on this task.

(b) With regard to Vietnamese civilian personnel dead or missing in South Viet-Nam, the two South Vietnamese parties shall help each other to obtain information about missing persons, determine the location and take care of the graves of the dead, in a spirit of national reconciliation and concord, in keeping with the people's aspirations.

OTHER PROVISIONS

Article 11

(a) The Four-Party and Two-Party Joint Military Commissions will have the responsibility of determining immediately the modalities of implementing the provisions of this Protocol consistent with their respective responsibilities under Articles 16 (a) and 17 (a) of the Agreement. In case the Joint Military Commissions, when carrying out their tasks, cannot reach agreement on a matter pertaining to the return of captured personnel they shall refer to the International Commission for its assistance.

(b) The Four-Party Joint Military Commission shall form, in addition to the teams established by the Protocol concerning the cease-fire in South Viet-Nam and the Joint Military Commissions, a sub-commission on captured persons and, as required, joint military teams on captured persons to assist the Commission in its tasks.

(c) From the time the cease-fire comes into force to the time when the Two-Party Joint Military Commission becomes operational, the two South Vietnamese parties' delegations to the Four-Party Joint Military Commission shall form a provisional sub-commission and provisional joint military teams to carry out its tasks concerning captured and detained Vietnamese civilian personnel.

(d) The Four-Party Joint Military Commission shall send joint military teams to observe the return of the persons mentioned in Articles 1 and 2 of this Protocol at each place in Viet-Nam where such persons are being returned, and at the last detention places from which these persons will be taken to the places of return. The Two-Party Joint Military Commission shall send joint military teams to observe the return of Vietnamese civilian personnel captured and detained at each place in South Viet-Nam where such persons are being returned, and at the last detention places from which these persons will be taken to the places of return.

Article 12

In implementation of Articles 18 (b) and 18 (c) of the Agreement, the International Commission of Control and Supervision shall have the responsibility to control and supervise the observance of Articles 1 through 7 of this Protocol through observation of the return of captured military personnel, foreign civilians and captured and detained Vietnamese civilian personnel at each place in Viet-Nam where these persons are being returned, and at the last detention places from which these persons will be taken to the places of return, the examination of lists, and the investigation of violations of the provisions of the above-mentioned Articles.

Article 13

Within five days after signature of this Protocol, each party shall publish the text of the Protocol and communicate it to all the captured persons covered by the Protocol and being detained by that party.

Article 14

This Protocol shall come into force upon signature by plenipotentiary representatives of all the parties participating in the Paris Conference on Viet-Nam. It shall be strictly implemented by all the parties concerned.

Done in Paris this twenty-seventh day of January, one thousand nine hundred and seventy-three, in English and Vietnamese. The English and Vietnamese texts are official and equally authentic.

FOR THE GOVERNMENT OF THE
UNITED STATES OF AMERICA

William P. Rogers
Secretary of State

FOR THE GOVERNMENT OF THE
DEMOCRATIC REPUBLIC OF
VIET-NAM:

Nguyen Duy Trinh
Minister for Foreign Affairs

FOR THE GOVERNMENT OF THE
REPUBLIC OF VIET-NAM:

Tran Van Lam
Minister for Foreign Affairs

FOR THE PROVISIONAL
REVOLUTIONARY GOVERNMENT OF
THE REPUBLIC OF SOUTH VIET-NAM:

Nguyen Thi Binh
Minister for Foreign Affairs

PROTOCOL
TO THE AGREEMENT ON ENDING THE WAR
AND RESTORING PEACE IN VIET-NAM
CONCERNING
THE CEASE-FIRE IN SOUTH VIET-NAM
AND THE JOINT MILITARY COMMISSIONS

. . . Cease-fire in South Viet-Nam
Article 1

The High Commands of the parties in South Viet-Nam shall issue prompt and timely orders to all regular and irregular armed forces and the armed police under their command to completely end hostilities throughout South Viet-Nam. . . .

Article 2

(a) As soon as the cease-fire comes into force and until regulations are issued by the Joint Military Commissions, all ground, river, sea and air combat forces of the parties in South Viet-Nam shall remain in place; that is, in order to ensure a stable cease-fire, there shall be no major redeployments or movements that would extend each party's area of control or would result in contact between opposing armed forces and clashes which might take place.

(b) All regular and irregular armed forces and the armed police of the parties in South Viet-Nam shall observe the prohibition of the following acts:

(1) Armed patrols into areas controlled by opposing armed forces and flights by bomber and fighter aircraft of all types, except for unarmed flights for proficiency training and maintenance;

(2) Armed attacks against any person, either military or civilian, by any means whatsoever, including the use of small arms, mortars, artillery, bombing and strafing by airplanes and any other type of weapon or explosive device;

(3) All combat operations on the ground, on rivers, on the sea and in the air;

(4) All hostile acts, terrorism or reprisals; and

(5) All acts endangering lives or public or private property.

Article 3

The above-mentioned prohibitions shall not hamper or restrict:

(1) Civilian supply, freedom of movement, freedom to work, and freedom of the people to engage in trade, and civilian communication and transportation between and among all areas in South Viet-Nam;

(2) The use by each party in areas under its control of military support elements, such as engineer and transportation units, in repair and construction of public facilities and the transportation and supplying of the population. . . .

Article 4

In order to avert conflict and ensure normal conditions for those armed forces which are in direct contact, and pending regulation by the Joint Military Commissions, the commanders of the opposing armed forces at those places of direct contact shall meet as soon as the cease-fire comes into force with a view to reaching an agreement on temporary measures to avert conflict and to ensure supply and medical care for these armed forces.

Article 5

(a) Within fifteen days after the cease-fire comes into effect, each party shall do its utmost to complete the removal or deactivation of all demolition objects, mine-fields, traps, obstacles or other dangerous objects placed previously. . . .

Article 6

Civilian police and civilian security personnel of the parties in South Viet-Nam, who are responsible for the maintenance of law and order, shall strictly respect the prohibitions set forth in Article 2 of this Protocol. . . .

Article 7

(a) The entry into South Viet-Nam of replacement armaments, munitions, and war material permitted under Article 7 of the Agreement shall take place under the supervision and control of the Two-Party Joint Military Commission and of the International Commission of Control and Supervision and through such points of entry only as are designated by the two South Vietnamese parties. . . .

(b) Each of the designated points of entry shall be available only for that South Vietnamese party which is in control of that point. The two South Vietnamese parties shall have an equal number of points of entry.

Article 8

(a) In implementation of Article 5 of the Agreement, the United States and the other foreign countries referred to in Article 5 of the Agreement shall take with them all their armaments, munitions, and war material. . . .

Article 9

(a) In implementation of Article 6 of the Agreement, the United States and the other foreign countries referred to in that Article shall dismantle and remove from South Viet-Nam or destroy all military bases in South Viet-Nam of the United States and of the other foreign countries referred to in that Article, including weapons, mines, and other military equipment at these bases, for the purpose of making them unusable for military purposes. . . .

[We omit Article 10 concerning the operations of the Joint Military Commissions.—eds.]

Article 11

(g). . . With respect to Article 7 of the Agreement, the two South Vietnamese parties' delegations to the Four-Party Joint Military Commission shall establish joint military teams at the points of entry in South Viet-Nam used for replacement of armaments, munitions and war material which are designated in accordance with Article 7 of this Protocol. . . .

[We omit Articles 12 through 17 with further operational details of the Joint Military Commissions.—eds.]

Article 18

The common expenses of the Four-Party Joint Military Commission shall be borne equally by the four parties, and the common expenses of the Two-Party Joint Military Commission in South Viet-Nam shall be borne equally by these two parties.

Article 19

This Protocol shall enter into force upon signature by plenipotentiary representatives of all the parties participating in the Paris Conference on Viet-Nam. It shall be strictly implemented by all the parties concerned.

Done in Paris this twenty-seventh day of January, one thousand nine hundred and seventy-three, in English and Vietnamese. The English and Vietnamese texts are official and equally authentic.

FOR THE GOVERNMENT OF THE
UNITED STATES OF AMERICA

William P. Rogers
Secretary of State

FOR THE GOVERNMENT OF THE
DEMOCRATIC REPUBLIC OF
VIET-NAM:

Nguyen Duy Trinh
Minister for Foreign Affairs

FOR THE GOVERNMENT OF THE
REPUBLIC OF VIET-NAM:

Tran Van Lam
Minister for Foreign Affairs

FOR THE PROVISIONAL
REVOLUTIONARY GOVERNMENT OF THE
REPUBLIC OF SOUTH VIET-NAM:

Nguyen Thi Binh
Minister for Foreign Affairs

[We omit the largely procedural protocol concerning the International Commission of Control and Supervision, in implementation of Article 18.—eds.]

[Bilateral Agreement Between DRV and US]

[We omit the "Agreement on Ending the War and Restoring Peace in Viet-Nam" signed by the DRV and the United States because it is identical to the same agreement signed by all four parties. We are including here those sections of the bilateral Agreement which are not included in the multilateral Agreement, with one exception: the Protocol on the removal by the United States of the mines it placed in the waterways of the DRV in such operations as the mining of the Haiphong Harbor.—eds.]

PROTOCOL
TO THE AGREEMENT ON ENDING THE WAR
AND RESTORING PEACE IN VIET-NAM
CONCERNING
THE RETURN OF CAPTURED MILITARY PERSONNEL
AND FOREIGN CIVILIANS AND CAPTURED AND DETAINED
VIETNAMESE CIVILIAN PERSONNEL

The Government of the United States of America, with the concurrence of the Government of the Republic of Viet-Nam,

The Government of the Democratic Republic of Viet-Nam, with the concurrence of the Provisional Revolutionary Government of the Republic of South Viet-Nam,

In implementation of Article 8 of the Agreement on Ending the War and Restoring Peace in Viet-Nam signed on this date providing for the return of captured military personnel and foreign civilians, and captured and detained Vietnamese civilian personnel,

Have agreed as follows:

[Text of protocol Articles 1–13 same as multilateral protocol above.—eds.]

Article 14

The Protocol to the Paris Agreement on Ending the War and Restoring Peace in Viet-Nam concerning the Return of Captured Military Personnel and Foreign Civilians and Captured and Detained Vietnamese Civilian Personnel shall enter into force upon signature of this document by the Secretary of State of the Government of the United States of America and the Minister for Foreign Affairs of the Government of the Democratic Republic of Viet-Nam, and upon signature of a document in the same terms by the Secretary of State of the Government of the United States of America, the Minister for Foreign Affairs of the Government of the Republic of Viet-Nam, the Minister for Foreign Affairs of the Government of the Democratic Republic of Viet-Nam, and the Minister for Foreign Affairs of the Provisional Revolutionary Government of the Republic of South Viet-Nam. The Protocol shall be strictly implemented by all the parties concerned.

Done in Paris this twenty-seventh day of January, one thousand nine hundred and seventy-three, in English and Vietnamese. The English and Vietnamese texts are official and equally authentic.

FOR THE GOVERNMENT OF THE
UNITED STATES OF AMERICA

William P. Rogers
Secretary of State

FOR THE GOVERNMENT OF THE
DEMOCRATIC REPUBLIC OF VIET-NAM

Nguyen Duy Trinh
Minister for Foreign Affairs

PROTOCOL
TO THE AGREEMENT ON ENDING THE WAR
AND RESTORING PEACE IN VIET-NAM
CONCERNING
THE CEASE-FIRE IN SOUTH VIET-NAM
AND THE JOINT MILITARY COMMISSIONS

The Government of the United States of America, with the concurrence of the Government of the Republic of Viet-Nam,

The Government of the Democratic Republic of Viet-Nam, with the concurrence of the Provisional Revolutionary Government of the Republic of South Viet-Nam,

In implementation of the first paragraph of Article 2, Article 3, Article 5, Article 6, Article 16 and Article 17 of the Agreement on Ending the War and Restoring Peace in Viet-Nam signed on this date which provide for the cease-fire in South Viet-Nam and the establishment of a Four-Party Joint Military Commission and a Two-Party Joint Military Commission,

Have agreed as follows:

[Text of protocol Articles 1–18 same as multilateral protocol above.—eds.]

Article 19

The Protocol to the Paris Agreement on Ending the War and Restoring Peace in Vietnam concerning the Cease-fire in South Viet-Nam and the Joint Military Commissions shall enter into force upon signature of this document by the Secretary of State of the Government of the United States of America and the Minister for Foreign Affairs of the Government of the Democratic Republic of Viet-Nam, and upon signature of a document in the same terms by the Secretary of State of the Government of the United States of America, the Minister for Foreign Affairs of the Government of the Republic of Vietnam, the Minister for Foreign Affairs of the Government of the Democratic Republic of Viet-Nam, and the Minister for Foreign Affairs of the Provisional Revolutionary Government of the Republic of South Viet-Nam. The Protocol shall be strictly implemented by all the parties concerned.

Done in Paris this twenty-seventh day of January, one thousand nine hundred and seventy-three, in English and Vietnamese. The English and Vietnamese texts are official and equally authentic.

FOR THE GOVERNMENT OF THE
UNITED STATES OF AMERICA

FOR THE GOVERNMENT OF THE
DEMOCRATIC REPUBLIC OF VIET-NAM

William P. Rogers
Secretary of State

Nguyen Duy Trinh
Minister for Foreign Affairs

[We omit the largely procedural protocol concerning the International Commission of Control and Supervision, in implementation of Article 18.—eds.]

66. United States Promise of Postwar Reconstruction: Letter to DRV Prime Minister Pham Van Dong (February 1, 1973)*

By President Richard M. Nixon

Vietnamese officials repeatedly claimed that President Nixon pledged postwar aid amounting to over $4 billion to the DRV. US officials maintained that the only mention of aid was in Article 21 of the Peace Accords (Reading 65), which they

---

*From *The New York Times* of May 20, 1977, the day after the declassification of this document by the US State Department.

did not consider binding. Secretary of State Rogers testified before the House International Relations Committee on February 8, 1973: "We have not made any commitment for any reconstruction or rehabilitation effort" in North Vietnam.[1] Henry Kissinger testified to the same committee on March 29, 1973, but apparently no record was kept of what he said. The State Department steadily maintained it had no copy of a reported letter from President Nixon promising aid. But on May 19, 1977, over four years after it was written, the letter was declassified by the State Department and released to Congress and the media. The release of the letter came in response to a threat by Congressman Lester Wolff, Democrat of New York and chairman of the House International Relations Subcommittee on Asian and Pacific Affairs, to subpoena former President Nixon to testify about the Vietnamese claim that there was indeed a promise by the President. The text of the letter mentions a "range of $3.25 billion" over five years, and one of the two addenda mentions $1 billion to $1.5 billion in other forms of aid, amounting to well over $4 billion. Kissinger and Le Duc Tho had negotiated the terms of the letter during the peace ta!ks. It was addressed to Prime Minister Pham Van Dong of the DRV and signed by President Richard Nixon February 1, 1973.

The President wishes to inform the Democratic Republic of Vietnam of the principles which will govern United States participation in the postwar reconstruction of North Vietnam. As indicated in Article 21 of the Agreement on Ending the War and Restoring Peace in Vietnam signed in Paris on Jan. 27, 1973, the United States undertakes this participation in accordance with its traditional policies. These principles are as follows:

1. The Government of the United States of America will contribute to postwar reconstruction in North Vietnam without any political conditions.

2. Preliminary United States studies indicate that the appropriate programs for the United States contribution to postwar reconstruction will fall in the range of $3.25 billion of grant aid over five years. Other forms of aid will be agreed upon between the two parties. This estimate is subject to revision and to detailed discussion between the Government of the United States and the Government of the Democratic Republic [of] Vietnam.

3. The United States will propose to the Democratic Republic of Vietnam the establishment of a United States-North Vietnamese Joint Economic Commission within 30 days from the date of this message.

4. The function of the commission will be to develop programs for the United States contribution to reconstruction of North Vietnam. This United States contribution will be based upon such factors as:

(a) the needs of North Vietnam arising from the dislocation of war;

(b) The requirements for postwar reconstruction in the agricultural and industrial sectors of North Vietnam's economy.

5. The Joint Economic Commission will have an equal number of representa-

---

1. *New York Times*, May 20, 1977.

tives from each side. It will agree upon a mechanism to administer the program which will constitute the United States contribution to the reconstruction of North Vietnam. The commission will attempt to complete this agreement within 60 days after its establishment.

6. The two members of the commission will function on the principle of respect for each other's sovereignty, noninterference in each other's internal affairs, equality and mutual benefit. The offices of the commission will be located at a place to be agreed upon by the United States and the Democratic Republic of Vietnam.

7. The United States considers that the implementation of the foregoing principles will prompt economic, trade and other relations between the United States of America and the Democratic Republic of Vietnam and will contribute to insuring a stable and lasting peace in Indochina. These principles accord with the spirit of Chapter VIII of the Agreement on Ending the War and Restoring Peace in Vietnam which was signed in Paris on Jan. 27, 1973.

Addenda²

Understanding Regarding Economic Reconstruction Program

It is understood that the recommendations of the Joint Economic Commission mentioned in the President's note to the Prime Minister will be implemented by each member in accordance with its own constitutional provisions.

Note Regarding Other Forms of Aid

In regard to other forms of aid, United States studies indicate that the appropriate programs could fall in the range of $1 billion to $1.5 billion, depending on food and other commodity needs of the Democratic Republic of Vietnam.

67. *War Powers Resolution of 1973**

The United States Constitution provides that Congress "shall have the power . . . To declare war." Congress never declared war against Vietnam,[1] nor was it ever asked to do so. In fact, Congress has not been asked to declare war since World War II. Yet, that has not stopped presidents from sending US forces to fight in Greece, Korea, the Dominican Republic, Lebanon, and Grenada, to name just a few.

---

2. Undated.—eds.

*Text from the *United States Code*, 1976 edition, Vol. 11, Title 50, Ch. 33 (Washington: U.S. Government Printing Office, 1977), pp. 1926–1929.

1. See Reading 36 for how Congress, in passing the Gulf of Tonkin Resolution of August 1964, essentially abrogated its constitutional power to declare war.

During the long war in Vietnam, Congress never forced the issue of its constitutional authority over the making of war. In fact, year after year, Congress appropriated funds to pay for the war. But after the Paris Peace Accords of January 1973, Congress took two major steps. First, in July, it passed a law cutting off all funding for combat activities in Indochina effective August 15 (Reading 61). Then, over President Nixon's veto, it enacted the War Powers Resolution—an attempt to reassert its authority provided by Article I, Section 8 of the Constitution.

The War Powers Resolution became law on November 7, 1973. The executive branch has complained that it places excessive limits on presidential action. Yet its effectiveness in curtailing presidential war-making power is debatable, especially in the light of subsequent events.

During the war in Vietnam, Congressman Andrew Jacobs, Jr., Democrat of Indiana, repeatedly inserted a question into the Congressional Record, *asking if any congressmen were ready to sacrifice their lives in the war as they were asking others to do every day. In late 1983, with US "advisers" in El Salvador, US troops taking over Grenada and fighting in Lebanon, and the CIA waging a "secret" war in Nicaragua, Congressman Jacobs began inserting an 1848 letter from Abraham Lincoln, which includes this observation:*

The provision of the Constitution giving the war-making power to Congress was dictated, as I understand it, by the following reasons. Kings had always been involving and impoverishing their people in wars, pretending generally, if not always, that the good of the people was the object. This our Convention understood to be the most oppressive of all kingly oppressions: and they resolved to so frame the Constitution that no one man should hold the power of bringing this oppression upon us.[2]

War Powers Resolution

§ 1541. Purpose and policy

(a) Congressional declaration

It is the purpose of this chapter to fulfill the intent of the framers of the Constitution of the United States and insure that the collective judgment of both the Congress and the President will apply to the introduction of United States Armed Forces into hostilities, or into situations where imminent involvement in hostilities is clearly indicated by the circumstances, and to the continued use of such forces in hostilities or in such situations.

(b) Congressional legislative power under necessary and proper clause

Under article I, section 8, of the Constitution, it is specifically provided that the Congress shall have the power to make all laws necessary and proper for carrying into execution, not only its own powers but also all other powers vested by the Constitution in the Government of the United States, or in any department or officer hereof.

---

2. *The New York Times*, November 12, 1983.

(c) Presidential executive power as Commander-in-Chief; limitation

The constitutional powers of the President as Commander-in-Chief to introduce United States Armed Forces into hostilities, or into situations where imminent involvement in hostilities is clearly indicated by the circumstances, are exercised only pursuant to (1) a declaration of war, (2) specific statutory authorization, or (3) a national emergency created by attack upon the United States, its territories or possessions, or its armed forces.

EFFECTIVE DATE

Section 10 of Pub. L. 93–148 provided that: "This joint resolution [this chapter] shall take effect on the date of its enactment [Nov. 7, 1973]."

§ 1542. Consultation; initial and regular consultations

The President in every possible instance shall consult with Congress before introducing United States Armed Forces into hostilities or into situations where imminent involvement in hostilities is clearly indicated by the circumstances, and after every such introduction shall consult regularly with the Congress until United States Armed Forces are no longer engaged in hostilities or have been removed from such situations.

§ 1543. Reporting requirement

(a) Written report; time of submission; circumstances necessitating submission; information reported

In the absence of a declaration of war, in any case in which United States Armed Forces are introduced—

(1) into hostilities or into situations where imminent involvement in hostilities is clearly indicated by the circumstances;

(2) into the territory, airspace or waters of a foreign nation, while equipped for combat, except for deployments which relate solely to supply, replacement, repair or training of such forces; or

(3) in numbers which substantially enlarge United States Armed Forces equipped for combat already located in a foreign nation;

the President shall submit within 48 hours to the Speaker of the House of Representatives and to the President, pro tempore of the Senate a report, in writing, setting forth—

(A) the circumstances necessitating the introduction of United States Armed Forces;

(B) the constitutional and legislative authority under which such introduction took place; and

(C) the estimated scope and duration of the hostilities or involvement.

(b) Other information reported

The President shall provide such other information as the Congress may request in the fulfillment of its constitutional responsibilities with respect to committing the Nation to war and to the use of United States Armed Forces abroad.

(c) Periodic reports; semiannual requirement

Whenever United States Armed Forces are introduced into hostilities or into any situation described in subsection (a) of this section, the President shall, so long as such armed forces continue to be engaged in such hostilities or situation, report to the Congress periodically on the status of such hostilities or situation as well as on the scope and duration of such hostilities or situation, but in no event shall he report to the Congress less often than once every six months.

§ 1544. Congressional action

(a) Transmittal of report and referral to Congressional Committees; joint request for convening Congress

Each report submitted pursuant to section 1543(a)(1) of this title shall be transmitted to the Speaker of the House of Representatives and to the President pro tempore of the Senate on the same calendar day. Each report so transmitted shall be referred to the Committee on International Relations of the House of Representatives and to the Committee on Foreign Relations of the Senate for appropriate action. If, when the report is transmitted, the Congress has adjourned sine die or has adjourned for any period in excess of three calendar days, the Speaker of the House of Representatives and the President pro tempore of the Senate, if they deem it advisable (or if petitioned by at least 30 percent of the membership of their respective Houses) shall jointly request the President to convene Congress in order that it may consider the report and take appropriate action pursuant to this section.

(b) Termination of use of United States Armed Forces; exceptions; extension period

Within sixty calendar days after a report is submitted or is required to be submitted pursuant to section 1543(a)(1) of this title, whichever is earlier, the President shall terminate any use of United States Armed Forces with respect to which such report was submitted (or required to be submitted), unless the Congress (1) has declared war or has enacted a specific authorization for such use of United States Armed Forces, (2) has extended by law such sixty-day period, or (3) is physically unable to meet as a result of an armed attack upon the United States. Such sixty-day period shall be extended for not more than an additional thirty days if the President determines and certifies to the Congress in writing that unavoidable military necessity respecting the safety of United States Armed Forces requires the continued use of such armed forces in the course of bringing about a prompt removal of such forces.

(c) Concurrent resolution for removal by President of United States Armed Forces

Notwithstanding subsection (b) of this section, at any time that United States Armed Forces are engaged in hostilities outside the territory of the United States, its possessions and territories without a declaration of war or specific statutory authorization, such forces shall be removed by the President if the Congress so directs by concurrent resolution.

§ 1545. Congressional priority procedures for joint resolution or bill

(a) Time requirement; referral to Congressional committee; single report

Any joint resolution or bill introduced pursuant to section 1544(b) of this title at least thirty calendar days before the expiration of the sixty-day period specified in such section shall be referred to the Committee on International Relations of the House of Representatives or the Committee on Foreign Relations of the Senate, as the case may be, and such committee shall report one such joint resolution or bill, together with its recommendations, not later than twenty-four calendar days before the expiration of the sixty-day period specified in such section, unless such House shall otherwise determine by the yeas and nays.

(b) Pending business; vote

Any joint resolution or bill so reported shall become the pending business of the House in question (in the case of the Senate the time for debate shall be equally divided between the proponents and the opponents), and shall be voted on within three calendar days thereafter, unless such House shall otherwise determine by yeas and nays.

(c) Referral to other House committee

Such a joint resolution or bill passed by one House shall be referred to the committee of the other House named in subsection (a) of this section and shall be reported out not later than fourteen calendar days before the expiration of the sixty-day period specified in section 1544(b) of this title. The joint resolution or bill so reported shall become the pending business of the House in question and shall be voted on within three calendar days after it has been reported, unless such House shall otherwise determine by yeas and nays.

(d) Disagreement between Houses

In the case of any disagreement between the two Houses of Congress with respect to a joint resolution or bill passed by both Houses, conferees shall be promptly appointed and the committee of conference shall make and file a report with respect to such resolution or bill not later than four calendar days before the expiration of the sixty-day period specified in section 1544(b) of this title. In the event the conferees are unable to agree within 48 hours, they shall report back to their respective Houses in disagreement. Notwithstanding any rule in either House concerning the printing of conference reports in the Record or concerning any delay in the consideration of such reports, such report shall be acted on by both Houses not later than the expiration of such sixty-day period.

§ 1546. Congressional priority procedures for concurrent resolution

(a) Referral to Congressional committee; single report

Any concurrent resolution introduced pursuant to section 1544(c) of this title shall be referred to the Committee on International Relations of the House of Representatives or the Committee on Foreign Relations of the Senate, as the case may be, and one such concurrent resolution shall be reported out by such committee together with its recommendations within fifteen calendar days, unless such House shall otherwise determine by the yeas and nays.

(b) Pending business; vote

Any concurrent resolution so reported shall become the pending business of the House in question (in the case of the Senate the time for debate shall be equally divided between the proponents and the opponents) and shall be voted on within three calendar days thereafter, unless such House shall otherwise determine by yeas and nays.

(c) Referral to other House committee

Such a concurrent resolution passed by one House shall be referred to the committee of the other House named in subsection (a) of this section and shall be reported out by such committee together with its recommendations within fifteen calendar days and shall thereupon become the pending business of such House and shall be voted upon within three calendar days, unless such House shall otherwise determine by yeas and nays.

(d) Disagreement between Houses

In the case of any disagreement between the two Houses of Congress with respect to a concurrent resolution passed by both Houses, conferees shall be promptly appointed and the committee of conference shall make and file a report with respect to such concurrent resolution within six calendar days after the legislation is referred to the committee of conference. Notwithstanding any rule in either House concerning the printing of conference reports in the Record or concerning any delay in the consideration of such reports, such report shall be acted on by both Houses not later than six calendar days after the conference report is filed. In the event the conferees are unable to agree within 48 hours, they shall report back to their respective Houses in disagreement.

§ *1547. Interpretation of joint resolution*

(a) Inferences from any law or treaty

Authority to introduce United States Armed Forces into hostilities or into situations wherein involvement in hostilities is clearly indicated by the circumstances shall not be inferred—

(1) from any provision of law (whether or not in effect before November 7, 1973), including any provision contained in any appropriation Act, unless such provision specifically authorizes the introduction of United States Armed Forces into hostilities or into such situations and states that it is intended to constitute specific statutory authorization within the meaning of this chapter; or

(2) from any treaty heretofore or hereafter ratified unless such treaty is implemented by legislation specifically authorizing the introduction of United States Armed Forces into hostilities or into such situations and stating that it is intended to constitute specific statutory authorization within the meaning of this chapter.

(b) Joint headquarters operations of high-level military commands

Nothing in this chapter shall be construed to require any further specific statutory authorization to permit members of United States Armed Forces to participate jointly with members of the armed forces of one or more foreign countries in the headquarters operations of high-level military commands which were established prior to November 7, 1973, and pursuant to the United Nations Charter or any treaty ratified by the United States prior to such date.

(c) Introduction of United States Armed Forces

For purposes of this chapter, the term "introduction of United States Armed Forces" includes the assignment of members of such armed forces to command, coordinate, participate in the movement of, or accompany the regular or irregular military forces of any foreign country or government when such military forces are engaged, or there exists an imminent threat that such forces will become engaged, in hostilities.

(d) Constitutional authorities or existing treaties unaffected; construction against grant of Presidential authority respecting use of United States Armed Forces

Nothing in this chapter—

(1) is intended to alter the constitutional authority of the Congress or of the President, or the provisions of existing treaties; or

(2) shall be construed as granting any authority to the President with respect to the introduction of United States Armed Forces into hostilities or into situations wherein involvement in hostilities is clearly indicated by the circumstances which authority he would not have had in the absence of this chapter.

§ 1548. Separability of provisions

If any provision of this chapter or the application thereof to any person or circumstance is held invalid, the remainder of the chapter and the application of such provision to any other person or circumstance shall not be affected thereby.

68. The "Great Spring Victory: An Account of the Liberation of South Vietnam" (1975)*

By General Van Tien Dung

The last US troops were pulled out of Vietnam March 29, 1973, as North Vietnam released its last US prisoners of war. Thieu still hoped for US reintervention. In a news conference, March 15, Nixon threatened to take some action but, once the

---

*Selection from General Van Tien Dung, *Our Great Spring Victory: An Account of the Liberation of South Vietnam*, translated by John Spragens, Jr. (New York: Monthly Review Press, 1977).

Paris Peace Accords had been signed, the mood in Congress was to get out. On July 1, Congress passed a law prohibiting expending any funds for US combat activities "in or over or from off the shores of North Vietnam, South Vietnam, Laos or Cambodia" as of August 15, 1973. That law ended the bombing of Cambodia (Reading 61) and prevented Nixon and his successor, Gerald Ford, from reintroducing troops. It did not, however, end US military and economic aid to the Thieu regime, although the amounts approved by Congress were reduced. The bombing of the South continued with US-supplied equipment. In late 1973, Thieu declared the Third Indochina War and went on the offensive, only to be routed by the DRV-PRG counterattack. In the United States, media attention was focused primarily on the Watergate scandal as the nation watched Nixon avoid impeachment proceedings by resigning from office August 9, 1974.

General Van Tien Dung, General Vo Nguyen Giap's Chief of Staff at Dien Bien Phu, was the only military person besides Giap among the eleven-member Politburo after Ho Chi Minh's death. He had the responsibility of leading the final offensive in South Vietnam. Our Great Spring Victory, the book from which this reading is selected, is his account of that offensive. In the introduction, he says the army and the people of Vietnam were determined "to fulfill the testament of President Ho Chi Minh" (Reading 59) and won the final offensive in only fifty-five days, with three major campaigns: the campaign to liberate Tay Nguyen (the Central Highlands), which began with the attack on Ban Me Thuot; the campaign to liberate Hue and Danang and to drive ARVN troops out of the coastal areas of Central Vietnam; and the Ho Chi Minh Campaign to liberate Saigon and nearby provinces.

The final offensive was launched in March, 1975. On April 21, Thieu resigned, turning the presidency over to Vice President Tran Van Huong. In his book about the final offensive, Decent Interval, Frank Snepp, who was a CIA agent at the time, describes how he drove Thieu to the airport on the night of April 25 when Thieu left the country aboard a US Air Force plane. US Ambassador Graham Martin was waiting there to bid "farewell to the last vestige of three decades of bad policy."[1] On April 28, General Duong Van Minh (see Reading 63) replaced Huong as president.

On April 30, Communist forces reached the Presidential Palace. Minh surrendered. Denied peace in 1954 and 1973, Vietnam became one country again. Saigon was renamed Ho Chi Minh City. The following excerpts by General Van Tien Dung describe some of what happened on April 30 and May 1, 1975.

W hen it was almost light, the American news services reported that [U.S. Ambassador Graham] Martin had cleared out of Saigon in a helicopter. This viceregal mandarin, the final American plenipotentiary in South Vietnam, beat a

---

1. Frank Snepp, *Decent Interval: An Insider's Account of Saigon's Indecent End Told by the CIA's Chief Strategy Analyst in Vietnam* (New York: Vintage, 1978), p. 437. Although told from an opposite perspective, Snepp's book, which focuses on the debacle of United States withdrawal from Saigon, agrees in many respects with Dung's.

most hasty and pitiful retreat. As it happened, up until the day he left Saigon, Martin still felt certain that the quisling administration could be preserved, and that a ceasefire could be arranged, so he was halfhearted about the evacuation, waiting and watching. He went all the way out to Tan Son Nhat airfield to observe the situation. Our barrage of bombs and our fierce shelling had nearly paralyzed this vital airfield, and the fixed-wing aircraft they had intended to use for their evacuation could no longer operate. The encirclement of Saigon was growing tighter by the day. The Duong Van Minh card[2] which they had played far too late proved useless. When Martin reported this to Washington, President Ford issued orders to begin a helicopter evacuation. Coming in waves for eighteen hours straight, they carried more than 1,000 Americans and over 5,000 of their Vietnamese retainers, along with their families, out of the South. Ford also ordered Martin to evacuate immediately "without a minute's delay."

The American evacuation was carried out from the tops of thirteen tall buildings chosen as landing pads for their helicopters. The number of these landing pads shrank gradually as tongues of fire from our advancing troops came closer. At the American embassy, the boarding point for the evacuation copters was a scene of monumental confusion, with the Americans' flunkies fighting their way in, smashing doors, climbing walls, climbing each other's backs, tussling, brawling, and trampling each other as they sought to flee. It reached the point where Martin, who wanted to return to his own house for his suitcase before he fled, had to take a back street, using the rear gate of the embassy. When "Code 2," Martin's code name, and "Lady 09," the name of the helicopter carrying him, left the embassy for the East Sea, it signaled the shameful defeat of U.S. imperialism after thirty years of intervention and military adventures in Vietnam. At the height of their invasion of Vietnam, the U.S. had used 60 percent of their total infantry, 58 percent of their marines, 32 percent of their tactical air force, 50 percent of their strategic air force, fifteen of their eighteen aircraft carriers, 800,000 American troops (counting those stationed in satellite countries who were taking part in the Vietnam war), and more than 1 million Saigon troops. They mobilized as many as 6 million American soldiers in rotation, dropped over 10 million tons of bombs, and spent over $300 billion, but in the end the U.S. ambassador had to crawl up to the helicopter pad looking for a way to flee. Today, looking back on the gigantic force the enemy had mobilized, recalling the malicious designs they admitted, and thinking about the extreme difficulties and complexities which our revolutionary sampan had had to pass through, we were all the more aware how immeasurably great this campaign to liberate Saigon and liberate the South was. . . .

The most extraordinary thing about this historic campaign was what had sprouted in the souls of our cadres and fighters. Why were our soldiers so heroic and determined during this campaign? What had given all of them this clear understanding of the great resolution of the party and of the nation, this clear understanding of our immeasurably precious opportunity, and this clear understanding of our unprecedented manner of fighting? What had made them so extraordinarily

---

2. This refers to the final move of putting Minh in power.

courageous and intense, so outstanding in their political acumen in this final phase of the war?

The will and competence of our soldiers were not achieved in a day, but were the result of a continuous process of carrying out the party's ideological and organizational work in the armed forces. And throughout our thirty years of struggle, there had been no campaign in which Uncle Ho had not gone into the operation with our soldiers. Going out to battle this time, our whole army had been given singular, unprecedented strength because this strategically decisive battle bore his name: Ho Chi Minh, for every one of our cadres and fighters, was faith, strength, and life. Among the myriad troops in all the advancing wings, every one of our fighters carried toward Ho Chi Minh City the hopes of the nation and a love for our land. Today each fighter could see with his own eyes the resiliency which the Fatherland had built up during these many years, and given his own resiliency there was nothing, no enemy scheme that could stop him.

Our troops advanced rapidly to the five primary objectives, and then spread out from there. Wherever they went, a forest of revolutionary flags appeared, and people poured out to cheer them, turning the streets of Saigon into a giant festival. From the Binh Phoc bridge to Quan Tre, people carrying flags, beating drums and hollow wooden fish, and calling through megaphones, chased down the enemy, disarmed enemy soldiers, neutralized traitors and spies, and guided our soldiers. In Hoc Mon on Route 1, the people all came out into the road to greet the soldiers, guide them, and point out the hiding places of enemy thugs. Everywhere people used megaphones to call on Saigon soldiers to take off their uniforms and lay down their guns. The people of the city, especially the workers, protected factories and warehouses and turned them over to our soldiers. In all the districts bordering the city—Binh Hoa, Thanh My Tay, Phu Nhuan, Go Vap, and Thu Duc—members of the revolutionary infrastructure and other people distributed leaflets, raised flags, called on enemy soldiers to drop their guns, and supplied and guided our soldiers. Before this great army entered the city, the great cause of our nation and the policies of our revolution had entered the hearts of the people.

We were very pleased to hear that the people of the city rose up when the military attacks, going one step ahead, had given them the leverage. The masses had entered this decisive battle at just the right time, not too early, but not too late. The patriotic actions of the people created a revolutionary atmosphere of vast strength on all the city's streets. This was the most precious aspect of the mass movement in Saigon-Gia Dinh, the result of many years of propaganda, education, organizing, and training by the municipal party branch. When the opportune moment arrived, those political troops had risen up with a vanguard spirit, and advanced in giant strides along with our powerful main-force divisions, resolutely, intelligently, and courageously. The people of the city not only carried flags and food and drink for the troops, but helped disperse large numbers of enemy soldiers, forced many to surrender, chased and captured many of those who were hiding out, and preserved order and security in the streets. And we will never forget the widespread and moving images of thousands, of tens of thousands of people enthusiastically giving directions to our soldiers and guiding them as they entered the city, and helping all the wings of troops strike quickly and unexpectedly at enemy positions. Those nameless heroes of Saigon-Gia Dinh brought into the general offensive the fresh and beautiful features of people's war.

As we looked at the combat operations map, the five wings of our troops seemed like five lotuses blossoming out from our five major objectives. The First Army Corps had captured Saigon's General Staff headquarters and the command compounds of all the enemy armed services. When the Third Army Corps captured Tan Son Nhat they met one wing of troops already encamped there—our military delegation at Camp Davis; it was an amazing and moving meeting. The Fourth Army Corps captured Saigon's Ministry of Defense, the Bach Dang port, and the radio station. The 232nd force took the Special Capital Zone headquarters and the Directorate-General of Police. The Second Army Corps seized "Independence Palace," the place where the quisling leaders, those hirelings of the United States, had sold our independence, traded in human blood, and carried on their smuggling. Our soldiers immediately rushed upstairs to the place where the quisling cabinet was meeting, and arrested the whole central leadership of the Saigon administration, including their president, right on the spot. Our soldiers' vigorous actions and firm declarations revealed the spirit of a victorious army. By 11:30 A.M. on April 30 the revolutionary flag flew from "Independence Palace"; this became the meeting point for all the wings of liberating troops.

At the front headquarters, we turned on our radios to listen. The voice of the quisling president called on his troops to put down their weapons and surrender unconditionally to our troops. Saigon was completely liberated! Total victory! We were completely victorious! All of us at headquarters jumped up and shouted, embraced and carried each other around on our shoulders. The sound of applause, laughter, and happy, noisy, chattering speech was as festive as if spring had just burst upon us. It was an indescribably joyous scene. Le Duc Tho and Pham Hung embraced me and all the cadres and fighters present. We were all so happy we were choked with emotion. I lit a cigarette and smoked. Dinh Duc Thien, his eyes somewhat red, said, "Now if these eyes close, my heart will be at rest." This historic and sacred, intoxicating and completely satisfying moment was one that comes once in a generation, once in many generations. Our generation had known many victorious mornings, but there had been no morning so fresh and beautiful, so radiant, so clear and cool, so sweet-scented as this morning of total victory, a morning which made babes older than their years and made old men young again. . . .

Le Duc Tho, Pham Hung, and I leaned on our chairs looking at the map of Ho Chi Minh City spread out on the table. We thought of the welter of jobs ahead. Were the electricity and water still working? Saigon's army of nearly 1 million had disbanded on the spot. How should we deal with them? What could we do to help the hungry and find ways for the millions of unemployed to make a living? Should we ask the center to send in supplies right away to keep the factories in Saigon alive? How could we quickly build up a revolutionary administration at the grassroots level? What policy should we take toward the bourgeoisie? And how could we carry the South on to socialism along with the whole country? The conclusion of this struggle was the opening of another, no less complex and filled with hardship. The difficulties would be many, but the advantages were not few. Saigon and the South, which had gone out first and returned last, deserved a life of peace, plenty, and happiness. . . .

On May 1. . .

We took a car to Saigon, past areas and positions so vital for the liberation of the city, like Trang Bang and Cu Chi, and past areas which had been revolutionary bases for many years, since the founding of the party, like Hoc Mon and Ba Diem. Along the highway, in the villages, and in the city streets there was no sea of blood, only a sea of people in high spirits, waving their hands and waving flags to welcome peace and the revolution. That sea of people, mingling endlessly with the long lines of our soldiers' trucks, tanks, and cars, in itself proclaimed our total victory. The sides of the road were still clogged with uniforms, rank insignia, guns and ammunition, boots, helmets, vehicles, and artillery the puppet army had abandoned in defeat. Spread out around us were not only the relics of a military force that had been smashed, but the relics of a reactionary political doctrine that had unraveled, the doctrine of a crew of imperialists so arrogant about their wealth and so worshipful of possessions that it blinded them. It was ironic that at every enemy base and barracks a sign had been erected, painted in large letters with the words, "Honor—Responsibility—Fatherland." What the enemy did not have, they had to shout about loudest. The main road to Saigon was very good, built by the enemy in the past to serve their operations. All of the enemy bases and storage depots were vast. The banks, the American billets, the hotels, many stories tall, were imposing advertisements for neocolonialism, implying that it would stand firm here, that it would stand for time without end. In 1968 Westmoreland boasted, "We will always be in Vietnam. Our bombs and bullets will prove it." But in fact the proof was exactly the opposite. We went into the headquarters of Saigon's General Staff. Here, as at the enemy Directorate-General of Police, the files of the enemy commanders' top secret documents remained. Their modern computer with its famous memory containing bio-data on each officer and soldier in their million-plus army was still running. American computers had not won in this war. The intelligence and will of our nation had won completely.

Editors' Epilogue

Our purpose has been to provide a documented history of the war between the United States and Vietnam. We have not attempted to deal with the regional and global effects of the war, whose sequels include upheaval and conflicts within Indochina, an attempt by China to invade Vietnam, severe internal problems of postwar reconstruction within Vietnam, deep contradictions in economic, political, social, and cultural life in the United States, intensified national liberation struggles of other Third World peoples, and perhaps significant shifts in global alliances and the balance of forces in the world.

By ending our book with the Vietnamese victory of 1975, we by no means wish to imply that this is the final event of the struggle. For, in fact, the war is still with us and, in some senses, still goes on.

For a brief period after 1975, it seemed possible that there would be a normalization of relations between Vietnam and the United States, and that the US government would abide by its pledge to aid Vietnam's recovery from the most colossal destruction one nation ever inflicted upon another. But then the Carter administration, which assumed office in 1977, reaffirmed earlier policy decisions which favored strategic cooperation with China. Vietnam was reconfirmed as the official "enemy."

Meanwhile, efforts continue to rewrite the history of the war, to produce new fantasies to substitute for its reality, or to leach its meaning, sanitize it, bury it, and forget it—to make us forsake the national consensus of "No More Vietnams." On the other hand, millions of Americans now seem determined to confront the true history of the war, as evidenced by the popular success of educational endeavors on television, in books, and in college courses. Unlike the government, many citizens have also shown an eagerness to help victims of the war, at least in America if not in Vietnam.

Instead of dealing with the problems of Vietnam's veterans, the government cuts GI benefits and attempts to cover up the psychological and physiological damage inflicted by the war on those for whom Vietnam remains the central and most disturbing event of their lives. Although only 1,830 Americans are still listed as missing in action in Vietnam, plus 560 in Laos and 100 in Cambodia—a far smaller percentage than after the Civil War, World War I, or World War II—heavily financed campaigns, aided by the government, seek to exploit the emotions of their loved ones by promulgating the preposterous myth, contrary to all evidence and common sense, that the Vietnamese and Laotians are still holding many of these men as prisoners. This illusion is intensified in multimillion-dollar entertainment spectaculars such as the film *Uncommon Valor*, which fantasizes a military-style rescue of US POWs, with predictable effects on the public; in the words of a movie-goer explaining the "satisfaction of the bloody ending in which dozens of the enemy are mowed down by the Americans, 'We get to win the Vietnam War.'" (*New York Times*, February 13, 1984). Meanwhile, there are indeed many tens of thousands of imprisoned Vietnam veterans, but these are not the subject of popular entertainment and jingoist propaganda. In 1978, the Government Accounting Office estimated that there were then 125,000 Vietnam veterans (over twice the total of those reported killed) not in Laotian or Vietnamese but in American prisons.

The statistics of Vietnam continue to stagger. Thousands of children deaf as a result of the Christmas bombing; daily injuries from unexploded ordnance left behind like lethal garbage after US withdrawal; the genetic damage that threatens Americans and Vietnamese who were exposed to Agent Orange; the frequent suicides of veterans; the countless nightmares and ruined lives here and in Indochina. The effort of this book is to encourage precise remembering. Only in this way can the statistics and the history be made to yield sense and meaning and, perhaps, guidance.

Glossary

AA: Air America (one of the CIA airlines in Indochina)

AFB: Air Force Base

AID: (US) Agency for International Development, often used by CIA

ARVN: Army of the Republic of (South) Vietnam

ASAP: As soon as possible

Binh: A paramilitary group organized by SMM to pose as "patriotic Vietnamese" in order to infiltrate "enemy" forces

Black radio: In psychological warfare, broadcasts by one side that are disguised as broadcasts for the other side (compare white radio)

Bn: Battalion

B–52: US heavy bomber

Cao Dai: Vietnamese religious sect

CAP: Prefix designating White House cablegrams sent via CIA channel; also Country Assistance Program of AID; also combat air patrol

CAS: Covert Action branch, Saigon office of the CIA. Also applied to CIA in Laos

CAT: Civil Air Transport (one of the CIA airlines, based on Taiwan)

Chief of Staff: Joint Chiefs of Staff of US Armed Forces

Chinat: Chinese Nationalist

CHMAAG: Chief, Military Assistance Advisory Group

CI: Counterinsurgency

CIA: (US) Central Intelligence Agency

CIDG: Civilian Irregular Defense Group

CINCPAC: Commander in Chief, Pacific

CIO: Central Intelligence Organization of South Vietnam, organized at the behest of the United States as a condition for CIP implementation

CIP: Counterinsurgency Plan

Civic Action teams: Teams organized by CIA to promote Diem regime

CJCS: Chairman, Joint Chiefs of Staff

COMUS: US Commander

COMUSMACV: Commander, U.S. Military Assistance Command, Vietnam

Corps: Military regions

   I Corps: Military region comprising five northern provinces of South Vietnam

   II Corps: Military region comprising Central Highlands and Central Coastal area of South Vietnam

   III Corps: Military region comprising provinces surrounding Saigon

   IV Corps: Military region, comprising southern Vietnam

COS: Chief of Station, CIA country team

COSVN: Council of senior US officials in South Vietnam, including ambassador, commander of US forces, CIA chief, and others

Country team: Same as COSVN

CPSVN: Comprehensive Plan for South Vietnam

CY: Calendar year

C–123: US transport aircraft

DASD: Deputy Assistant Secretary of Defense

DCM: Deputy Chief of Mission

De Soto patrols: US destroyer patrols in Tonkin Gulf, specifically used for espionage

DIA: Defense Intelligence Agency

Disinformation: Information deliberately designed to distort or cover up facts or to make up misinformation for the purpose of misleading various groups of people

DMZ: Demilitarized zone

Doc: Document

DOD: Department of Defense

DRV: Democratic Republic of (North) Vietnam

E and E: Escape and Evasion

Eastern Construction Company: CIA front for UW and other activities (see Freedom Company)

FAL: *Forces Armées Laotiennes* (Lao Armed Forces)

FAR: *Forces Armées Royales* (Royal Armed Forces of Laos)

Farmgate: Clandestine USAF strike unit in Vietnam (1964)

FOA: Foreign Operations Administration

Fragging: Murder or attempted murder of US military officers by US troops

Freedom Company: CIA front for secretly recruiting and training anti-communists in the Philippines and elsewhere

Free World: Capitalist countries

FW: Free World

FWMA: Free World Military Assistance

FWMAF: Free World Military Assistance Forces

GNP: Gross National Product

GVN: Government of (South) Vietnam

G–3: US Army General Staff branch handling plans and operations

G–5: A group of Vietnamese military personnel trained for special operations by MAAG

Hao: A paramilitary group organized by SMM

HES: Hamlet Evaluation System

Hoa Hao: Vietnamese religious sect
Hop Tac plan: Operation planned to clear and hold Saigon and its surroundings, 1964
IAP: Immediate Action Program
ICA: International Cooperation Administration, sometimes used as a cover for CIA operations
ICC: International Control Commission for Vietnam, Laos
ICP: Indochinese Communist Party
ICSC: International Commission for Supervision and Control in Vietnam
IDA: Institute for Defense Analysis
INR: Bureau of Intelligence and Research in Department of State and CIA
ISA: International Security Agency; also Office of International Security Affairs in Department of Defense
JCS: Joint Chiefs of Staff
JCSM: JCS Memorandum
Joint Chiefs: Joint Chiefs of Staff of US Armed Forces
KIA: Killed in action
Lao Dong: Communist Party of Vietnam
Liberation Front: National Liberation Front of South Vietnam
MAAG: (US) Military Assistance Advisory Group
MAC: Military Assistance Command
MACV: Military Assistance Command, Vietnam
MAP: Military Assistance Program
Michigan State team: see MSU group
MPs: Military Police
MSS: Military Security Service, Saigon
MSU group or team or project: A group of Michigan State University professors who went to South Vietnam officially as part of ICA but actually as a CIA cover
NAACP: National Association for the Advancement of Colored People (US civil rights group)
NATO: North Atlantic Treaty Organization
NCO: Noncommissioned Officer (US Armed Forces)
NLF: National Liberation Front of South Vietnam
NSA: National Security Agency
NSAM: NSA Memorandum
NSC: National Security Council
NVA: North Vietnamese Army
NVN: Democratic People's Republic of (North) Vietnam
OB: Operation Brotherhood
OCO: Office of Civil Operations (pacification)
Operation Brotherhood: Front for CIA operations
Oplan: Operations plan
Ops: Operations
OSD: Office of the Secretary of Defense
Para: Paragraph

PARU: Police Aerial Resupply Unit

PAT: Political Action Team

PAV: People's Army of Vietnam

PAVN: People's Army of (North) Vietnam

PL: Pathet Lao (Laotian revolutionary forces)

"Plimsoll line": "Reserve mobilization line" or the complex factors which the US government has to take into account when considering a mobilization of the Reserves

POL: Petroleum, oil, lubricants

PRG: Provisional Revolutionary Government of South Vietnam

PRV: People's Republic of Vietnam

Psychological warfare: Tactics aimed at enemy morale through the use of disinformation, rumors, certain kinds of sabotage, etc.

Psyops: Psychological operations

Psywar: Psychological warfare

PT: Patrol boat

PTF: Fast patrol boat

RAND: Rand Corporation (US research organization)

RD: Rural development

Ref: Reference

RLG: Royal Laotian Government

ROTC: Reserve Officers Training Corps, military training program in US schools

RVN: Republic of (South) Vietnam

RVNAF: RVN Air or Armed Forces

SEA: Southeast Asia

SEATO: Southeast Asia Treaty Organization

SMM: Saigon Military Mission, one of the centers of CIA operations

SNCC: Student Non-Violent Coordinating Committee (US civil rights group)

Sovs: Soviets

Special Group: Created by NSAM 124 January 18, 1962, Special Group (Counterinsurgency) includes military representatives of the President, the Attorney General, Deputy Under Secretary of State for Political Affairs, Deputy Secretary of Defense, JCS Chairman, CIA Director, USIA Director for the purpose of promoting and overseeing counterinsurgency; an annex to NSAM 124 immediately assigned Laos, South Vietnam, and Thailand to the Group's "cognizance."

STC: Security Training Center, CIA-sponsored school for counterinsurgency training in the Philippines

SVN: South Vietnam

34A: 1964 Oplan covering covert actions against North Vietnam

Urban League: US civil rights group

USAF: US Air Force

USG: US Government

USIA: US Information Agency

USIS: US Information Service

USOM: US Operations Mission (US economic aid apparatus, including CIA activities, in Saigon)

UW: Unconventional warfare

U–2: US reconnaissance (spy) plane

VC: Viet Cong

Viet Cong: Pejorative term for Vietnamese Communists

VM: Viet Minh

VN: Vietnam

VNAF: (South) Vietnamese Air or Armed Forces

VNQDD: Vietnam Quoc Dan Dong (Vietnamese Nationalist Party)

VOA: Voice of America radio broadcasts

VPA: Vietnam People's Army

White radio: In psychological warfare, broadcasts admitted by the side transmitting them (compare black radio)

Select Bibliography

The literature on Vietnam and America is vast, and growing rapidly. A comprehensive bibliography would take at least a separate volume. We have attempted throughout the text to provide some bibliographic guidance to readers who wish to explore further. Here we should like just to suggest to readers how they can find resources to deepen their understanding.

First there are several useful bibliographic volumes: Roy Jumper, *Bibliography of the Political and Administrative History of Vietnam, 1802–1962* (n.p.: Michigan State University Advisory Group, 1962); Milton Leitenberg and Richard Dean Burns, *The Vietnam Conflict* (Santa Barbara, CA: ABC-CLIO Press, 1973); John Chen, *Vietnam: A Comprehensive Bibliography* (Metuchen, NJ: Scarecrow Press, 1973); Michael Cotter, *Vietnam: A Guide to Resources* (Boston: G. K. Hall, 1977); *Vietnam War Literature: An Annotated Bibliography of Imaginative Works about Americans Fighting in Vietnam* (Metuchen, NJ: Scarecrow Press, 1982) by John Newman, special collections librarian at Colorado State University in Fort Collins, where a definitive archive of Vietnam War literature is housed. See also Gordon O. Taylor, "American Personal Narrative of the War in Vietnam," *American Literature,* 52 (May 1980), pp. 294–308.

An indispensable source for serious inquiry into the American war against Vietnam is that unique body of materials known as the Pentagon Papers, which we have used extensively in this volume. There are three separate editions of the Pentagon Papers, each with variations surrounding a common core of documentation and analysis by Pentagon (Defense Department) historians. The best edition is based on the documents read into the Congressional Record by Senator Mike Gravel (Dem., Alaska); entitled *The Pentagon Papers*, and often referred to as the Gravel Edition, it was published in four volumes by Beacon Press (Boston) in 1971, with a fifth volume containing commentary, supplementary essays placing the documents in historical perspective, and two essential tools: a glossary and an index. The "official" U. S. Government edition, entitled *United States-Vietnam Relations, 1954–1967* (12 mimeographed volumes, Washington, D.C.: U. S. Government Printing Office, 1971), is barely legible, unindexed, and not continuously paginated. A third version, also entitled *The Pentagon Papers*, and usually referred to as The New York Times Edition, reproduces the documents and commentary originally published in *The New York Times*; published in mass-market paperback by Bantam Books (Toronto/New York/London, 1971), it is still widely available and is useful as a handy condensed version. The Pentagon Papers are by no means an uncontaminated source of pure truth; the Defense Department historians who compiled it had their own well-defined goals, values, and perspective. But these documents contain many extraordinary and priceless revelations.

Supplementing the main Pentagon Papers material is George C. Herring, ed., *The Secret Diplomacy of the Vietnam War: The PENTAGON PAPERS Negotiating Volumes* (Austin: University of Texas Press, 1983). Among the veritable library of books based on the Pentagon Papers we particularly note Herbert Y. Schandler, *Lyndon Johnson and Vietnam: The Unmaking of a President* (Princeton, NJ: Princeton University Press, 1977); Larry Berman, *Planning a Tragedy: The Americanization of the War in Vietnam* (New York: W. W. Norton, 1982) and, especially insightful, Paul Joseph, *Cracks in the Empire: State Politics in the Vietnam War* (Boston: South End Press, 1981).

Vietnamese sources in English are relatively sparse, but an important selection can be found in Gareth Porter, ed., *Vietnam: A History in Documents* (two volumes, Stanfordville, NY: Earl M. Coleman, 1979; one-volume abridged edition, New York: New American Library, 1981), which counterpoints Vietnamese documents with the unfolding story of American intervention as revealed in a variety of documents from U. S. government agencies and individuals. Materials from the southern provinces are presented in Don Luce and John Sommers, eds., *Vietnam: The Unheard Voices* (Ithaca: Cornell University Press, 1969). Nguyen Thi Dinh's memoir of her life in the southern resistance (a section of which appears here as Reading 28) is a gripping narrative rich in historical materials: *No Other Road to Take: Memoir of Mrs. Nguyen Thi Dinh*, translated by Mai Van Elliott (Ithaca, NY: Cornell University Southeast Asia Program, 1976). From the north, there is the invaluable series of monographs and collections published in Hanoi in English as several dozen separately numbered volumes of *Vietnam Studies*.

The war cannot be understood without making a serious effort to comprehend the people against whom it was waged. In this pursuit, the work of David Marr represents the best western scholarship, grounded in knowledge of the indigenous languages as well as first-hand experience in Vietnam. Marr's *Vietnamese Anticolonialism, 1885–1925* (Berkeley: University of California Press, 1971) and *Vietnamese Tradition on Trial, 1920–1945* (Berkeley: University of California Press, 1981) portray not only the development of Vietnamese resistance but also the ways in which Vietnam was transformed by French colonialism. Further explorations of that transformation are available in Martin Murray, *The Development of Capitalism in Colonial Indochina, 1870–1940* (Berkeley: University of California Press, 1980) and Ngo Vinh Long, *Before the Revolution: The Vietnamese Peasants*

Under the French (Cambridge: MIT Press, 1973). Nguyen Khac Vien's *Tradition and Revolution in Vietnam* (Berkeley: Indochina Resource Center, 1974) includes thoughtful essays on society and culture.

Much of the war was fought in, around, and by villages in the south. Five very different books provide a start on learning what happened at the village level. An early account, unfriendly to the insurgency but interesting for its details of rural life, is Gerald C. Hickey, *Village in Vietnam* (New Haven: Yale University Press, 1960). Jonathan Schell's *The Village of Ben Suc* (New York: Knopf, 1967) is a powerful description of the obliteration of a village by American forces. James W. Trullinger has put together from oral and written sources a history of one village from the turn of the century to 1975: *Village at War: An Account of Revolution in Vietnam* (New York: Longman, 1980). Jeffrey Race's *War Comes to Long An* (Berkeley: University of California Press, 1972) covers an entire province, dealing constantly with life and politics at the village level as well. In *Vietnam: Inside Story of the Guerrilla War* (New York: International Publishers, 1965), Wilfred Burchett provides a truly astonishing account of his eight-month journey with National Liberation Front guerrillas through southern Vietnam right up to the outskirts of Saigon.

More theoretical and historical accounts of Vietnamese tactics and strategy are available in several collections in English of Vo Nguyen Giap's writings; the most widely available of these is *People's War, People's Army* (New York: Praeger, 1962). General Van Tien Dung's *Our Great Spring Victory* (New York: Monthly Review Press, 1977) is an inside account of the final Vietnamese offensive by the commander of the Vietnam People's Army. An overview of the relations between military and political development in the two parts of the country is provided in Le Duan's 1970 report to the Vietnam Workers Party (the governing party of the DRV), published in English as *The Vietnamese Revolution* (New York: International Publishers, 1971).

A striking comparison to these Vietnamese analyses of the war is General William C. Westmoreland's *A Soldier Reports* (New York: Dell Publishing, 1980). Westmoreland's view is subjected to piercing analysis in Robert Pisor's *The End of the Line: The Siege of Khe Sanh* (New York: W. W. Norton, 1982), which uses an extraordinarily deep exploration of that battle to focus key questions of U. S. military theory and practice in the war.

No single volume adequately deals with the war from both the U. S. and Vietnamese sides. Three readable accounts are: George C. Herring, *America's Longest War: The U. S. and Vietnam, 1950 to 1975* (New York: John Wiley, 1979); Michael Maclear, *The Ten Thousand Day War; Vietnam: 1945–1975* (New York: St. Martin's Press, 1981); and James P. Harrison, *Fifty Years of Struggle in Vietnam* (New York: Free Press, 1982), which gives a somewhat fuller picture of the Vietnamese side. Probably the most readily available one-volume Vietnamese account is Nguyen Khac Vien, *The Long Resistance (1858–1975)* (Hanoi: Foreign Languages Publishing House, 1975).

Several books focus on an often neglected aspect of the war, the turmoil and transformations it induced within the American military forces. Especially noteworthy are Larry G. Waterhouse and Mariann G. Wizard, *Turning the Guns Around: Notes on the GI Movement* (New York: Delta Books, 1971); Richard Boyle, *Flower of the Dragon: The Breakdown of the U. S. Army in Vietnam* (San Francisco: Ramparts Press, 1972); and David Cortright, *Soldiers in Revolt: The American Military Today* (Garden City, NY: Doubleday, 1975).

Unfortunately, the Pentagon Papers serve to illuminate the U. S. side of the war only up to 1968. For the war under Richard Nixon, other sources must be consulted. One might start with the sometimes conflicting accounts provided by the memoirs of the two principal U. S. figures, President Nixon and Secretary of State Kissinger: Richard Nixon, *RN: The Memoirs of Richard Nixon* (New York: Grosset & Dunlap, 1978); Henry Kissinger, *White House Years* (Boston: Little, Brown and Co., 1979) and *Years of Upheaval* (Boston: Little, Brown and Co., 1982). One could then get quite different views of this period from two highly-regarded studies: Gareth Porter, *A Peace Denied: The United States, Vietnam and the Paris Agreement* (Bloomington: Indiana University Press, 1975), and Seymour Hersh, *The Price of Power: Kissinger in the Nixon White House* (New York: Summit Books, 1983). Also helpful are Frank Snepp's *A Decent Interval* (New York: Random House, 1977), the inside account by a CIA official of the fall of Saigon, and Arnold Isaac's *Neither Peace Nor Honor* (Baltimore: Johns Hopkins University Press, 1984), a reporter's understanding of the same period.

The aftermath of the war has as many aspects as the war itself. A few of them are explored in: Gloria Emerson, *Winners and Losers: Battles, Retreats, Gains, Losses and Ruins from a Long War* (New York: Random House, 1977); Fred A. Wilcox, *Waiting for an Army to Die: The Tragedy of Agent Orange* (New York: Vintage, 1983); Wilfred Burchett, *The China Cambodia Vietnam Triangle* (Chicago: Vanguard Books, 1981); and David W. P. Elliott, *The Third Indochina Conflict* (Boulder, Colo.: Westview Press, 1981).

Among periodicals with useful information about Vietnam and related matters are *Citizen Soldier* (175 Fifth Ave., New York, NY 10010), dealing with veterans' issues; *Indochina Issues* (Center for International Policy, 120 Maryland Ave., Washington, D. C. 20002); *Indochina Newsletter* (P. O. Box 129, Dorchester, Mass., 02122); *Southeast Asia Chronicle* (Southeast Asia Resource Center, Dept. J, P. O. Box 4000D, Berkeley, Cal., 94704); *Vietnam Courier* (Hanoi), monthly review in English; *Vietnam War Newsletter* (P. O. Box 122, Collinsville, CT 06022); *Intervention: A Political and Cultural Journal Exploring Issues of War & Peace and the Vietnam Experience* (545 W. 111 St., Suite 9M, New York, NY 10025). Invaluable information and analysis can still be gleaned from *Viet Report*, which appeared monthly and bi-monthly during most of the last decade of the war.

Of the many fine documentary films on Vietnam and the war, we list here only a handful: *Hearts and Minds* (1975—90 minutes; available through American Friends Service Committee, 2161 Massachusetts Ave., Cambridge, Mass. 02140);

Inside North Vietnam (1968—85 minutes; available through San Francisco Newsreel); *Vietnam: An American Journey* (1978—85 minutes; available from Films, Inc.); *Ecocide* (1981—23 minutes; available from Green Mountain Post Films, Box 229, Turners Falls, Mass., 01376); *Going Back: A Return to Vietnam* (1982— 67 minutes; available from Producer Services Group, Inc., 100 Winchester Street, Brookline, Mass., 02146).

VIETNAM AND AMERICA: INDEX

[For abbreviations, also consult the Glossary.]